A DELICATE BALANCE

An Essential Introduction to American Government

A DELICATE BALANCE

[An Essential
Introduction
to American
Government]

PAUL LIGHT

The Pew Charitable Trusts
University of Minnesota

St. Martin's Press
New York

Sponsoring editor: Beth A. Gillett
Manager, publishing services: Emily Berleth
Senior editor, publishing services: Douglas Bell
Project management: Omega Publishing Services, Inc.
Production supervisor: Joe Ford
Text and cover design: Patricia McFadden
Cover photo: Copyright © 1996 Eric Jacobson

Library of Congress Catalog Card Number: 95-73199

Manufactured in the United States of America.

1 0 9 8 7
f e d c b a

For information, write:
St. Martin's Press, Inc.
175 Fifth Avenue
New York, NY 10010

ISBN: 0-312-08969-4

Acknowledgments

Acknowledgments and copyrights appear at the back of the book on pages 1-1 and 1-2, which constitute an extension of the copyright page.

To Kate, Max, and Wheeler

BRIEF CONTENTS

Preface xvii

CONTENTS

PREFACE

A Delicate Balance: An Essential Introduction to American Government began as a simple hunch: a concise introductory American government book that could cover the basics, carry a central theme, and still be easy to read would be appreciated by students and professors alike. Such a book would be inviting in its language, current in its examples, appealing in its design, and slimmer than the usual books in length. This book would reach out to instructors and students who need a comprehensive introduction without the clutter of larger, aircraft-carrier textbooks that try to do too much. On the other hand, this text would offer instructors and students more than a cut down "nuts-and-bolts" approach of the brief texts. If done well, a text built on these premises could help faculty deliver a well evaluated American government course and might very well lead more students to think about majoring in political science.

HIGHLIGHTS

A Delicate Balance is grounded in real politics, yet it remains tightly anchored to the leading scholarship in political science. It has many distinguishing characteristics that make it a new kind of American government book.

- **Design and format.** Published in paperback and with a clean, straightforward design, *A Delicate Balance* has the look and feel of an easy-to-read, mass-market, trade paperback, rather than a bulky, hardcover textbook. Charts, boxes, and photographs are kept to a minimum so that students will not get lost in a maze of chopped up pages that distract them from the flow of the prose. Pedagogy is kept to one place in the chapter and tabbed in color so students can easily and quickly access information they need to study.

- **Consistent voice.** Written by a single author, *A Delicate Balance* carries a consistent voice throughout. The writing style is smooth and comfortable, leading students to stick with each chapter from beginning to end. Points are clearly made and stories well told. Chapter subtitles carry a punch. When taken all together, this text can claim what others cannot: the book is actually fun to read. Having begun his career as a newspaper reporter at the *Minneapolis Tribune,* Paul Light remembers what it takes to get a reader's interest and hold it.

- **A government that is just strong enough.** The book is built on the simple theme that in order for liberty to flourish, political change must be harnessed. In other words, the Founders intended government to be just strong enough to meet national and international threats without compromising liberty. In today's cynical environment, it is a theme that should help keep the day-to-day frustrations of American government in perspective. The book does not suggest American government can do no wrong, but neither does it assume that it can do no right.

- **Coverage of the essential elements of American government.** Careful measures have been taken to ensure that the essentials of American government are covered in the book. Students will be spurred on by good writing and cohesive, pithy narrative while getting the facts and process they need. In other words, *A Delicate Balance* reads great and is still filling.

- **Stimulating discussion puts issues "In a Different Light."** The book challenges students to think hard about current controversies through "In a Different Light" discussions in every chapter. By asking students to think about more nontraditional topics like gated communities, assisted suicide, and negative advertising, *A Delicate Balance* gets your students thinking critically about political issues without raising some of the more highly emotional topics such as abortion and gun control.

- **"Just the Facts."** Unlike other texts' review sections, "Just the Facts" not only summarizes the chapter's basic points, key terms, and discussion issues but it also challenges students to formulate a deeper analyisis of the information they have learned. In addition to substantial critical thinking apparatus, each "Just the Facts" section ends with one-line descriptions of the author's endnotes to offer students a bibliography of sources that would be most appropriate for further study. These sources are denoted by a color arrow before the entry. More in-depth than other texts while still being to the point, this section eliminates the expense of the conventional study guide while truly encouraging students to take another look at what they have read.

INSTRUCTIONAL PACKAGE

A Delicate Balance stands by the basic premise that students won't learn what students won't read. So, in addition to this highly readable text, it offers professors an instructional package to make the teaching of this text easier and more effective while continuing to stimulate students' reading of the text.

- *Instructor's Manual.* Written by Janet Martin of Bowdoin College, a veteran instructor of the American government course, this comprehensive *Instructor's Manual* includes chapter outlines, discussion questions, classroom activities, and a series of lectures to accompany each chapter. Experienced professors, adjunct faculty, and graduate assistants will appreciate the teaching suggestions found in this manual.

- *Test Item File.* Written by Sharon and Paul Light, this *Test Item File* offers close to 1,000 multiple-choice, short-answer, and essay questions. The computerized *Test*

Item File is available in three formats (DOS, Macintosh, or Windows) and has full authoring capabilities.

- **Student Survey of Political Attitudes.** Produced by Clyde Wilcox at Georgetown University, this questionnaire allows an instructor to administer, at the outset of the course, a survey of students' attitudes toward political issues. When results are sent to St. Martin's Press, they will be promptly tabulated and compared to national data. The survey will then be returned to the instructor in graph, table, or chart form for use throughout the course.

- **Web site.** *A Delicate Balance* can be found on-line. In addition to the table of contents and other basic information about the text, this Web page offers professors and students a plethora of activities and projects that tie both to the book and to various American government Web sites. Students also have access to **The St. Martin's Political Science Links Page;** one place they can go to access 1,000 sites in all of the major areas of political science. In addition, students can explore the national results of the **St. Martin's Student Survey of Political Attitudes** and compare their political opinions with those of American government students across the United States. Furthermore, the site offers students instant access to the pages of TIME magazine and TIME Internet resources. Finally, there is a bulletin board where professors can share syllabi and classroom experiences with the text.

- **Documents.** This collection of key primary source documents, compiled by Jacqueline Vaughn Switzer (Southern Oregon State College) are available on line. They include primary sources such as *The Articles of Confederation* and excerpts from *The Federalist Papers* as well as landmark Supreme Court decisions and memorable political speeches.

AUTHOR ACKNOWLEDGMENTS

This book could not have been written without the help of a small army of friends and colleagues. The project began in Minnesota where I received encouragement and support from the University of Minnesota's department of political science and Humphrey Institute of Public Affairs, both of which conveyed the sense that I just might be able to do this work. I also had the help of a small group of research assistants, ably led by Karen Doyle, as well as the patience of friends such as John Brandl, Larry Jacobs, James Jernberg, and Judy Leahy. I also had the strong support of Gerry McCauley, a tireless advocate on my behalf.

The project continued in Philadelphia where I continued to be blessed by strong support from The Pew Charitable Trusts. Rebecca Rimel, the president of the Trusts, and Nadya Shmavonian, had unyielding tolerance for this work, and pushed me to find the intersections between my writing and my responsibilities in developing a new funding program on strengthening civic engagement and improving government performance in America. I also had the strong encouragement of the public policy program staff: Caitlyn Frost, Elizabeth Hubbard, and Steve Del Rosso. They uttered not a word of complaint as I tried to juggle my duties as program director and textbook author. I have also been blessed through this period by a dedicated corps of supporters at St. Martin's Press, including Beth Gillett, Kimberly Wurtzel, Steven Debow, Rob Mejia, Barbara Heinssen, Chris Helms, Jayme Heffler, and Ed Stanford. Beth in particular saw the potential in this project, and inspired me to make this book as good as it could be. She and Barbara also recruited Joanne Tinsley as my development editor who was central in bringing the final draft of the book to fruition. She is the best I could have had. Finally, Rich Wright at Omega Publishing did a remarkable job managing the production of the book.

Ultimately, however, none of these contributions can compare to the energy supplied by my partner in life, Sharon Pamepinto Light. She was involved at every step of the project, from doing the basic research on what needed to be in the book to writing the *Test Item File,* from collating materials on a host of subjects to supplying much of the energy for "The Constitution" and "Civil Rights and Civil Liberties" chapters. She smoothed many rough edges in the text, and supplied far more than could have been expected by way of patient editing along the way, all the way while never wavering in her faith in me and the book.

Woe be to anyone who would blame any of these supporters for what ails the book, for the errors and misinterpretations are mine and mine alone.

I appreciate the efforts made by St. Martin's Press to enlist the following individuals to review the various drafts of the manuscript. The comments and suggestions made by these individuals were extremely helpful and appreciated.

David W. Ahern	University of Dayton
Timothy Amato	University of Iowa
Andrew Aoki	Augsburg College
Christine Arnold-Lourie	Charles County Community College
Michael Berheide	Berea College
Melanie J. Blumberg	Kent State University
Keith Boeckelman	Louisiana State University
William Borges	Southwest State University
Gary Bryner	Brigham Young University
John P. Burke	University of Vermont
Allan Cigler	University of Kansas
Stanley E. Clark	California State University–Bakersfield
John Coleman	University of Wisconsin–Madison
Gary Copeland	University of Oklahoma
Paige Cubbison	Miami Dade Community College
Grady S. Culpepper	Atlanta Metropolitan College
Richard Davis	Brigham Young University
Sue Davis	University of Delaware
Kathleen Dolan	University of Wisconsin–Oshkosh
Delmer D. Dunn	University of Georgia
Kathryn Dunn Tenpas	University of South Florida
Paul Goren	University of Pittsburgh
Kenneth Hayes	University of Maine

Meredith Heiser	Foothill College
James Henson	University of Texas–San Antonio
Michael Hoover	Seminole Community College
William E. Kelly	Auburn University
David C. Maas	University of Alaska–Anchorage
Thomas Marshall	University of Texas–Arlington
Janet M. Martin	Bowdoin College
Michael Martinez	University of Florida
Daniel S. Masters	University of Central Florida
Daniel McCool	University of Utah
Wayne V. McIntosh	University of Maryland
Lauri McNown	University of Colorado–Boulder
William Mishler	University of South Carolina
Bruce Odom	Trinity Valley Community College
Rex Peebles	Austin Community College
Mark Petracca	University of California–Irvine
James P. Pfiffner	George Mason University
David Porter	Youngstown State University
Sandra Powell	San Francisco State University
Timothy Prinz	University of Virginia
Russell D. Renka	Southeast Missouri State University
Leonard G. Ritt	Northern Arizona University
David Schwartz	Southern Illinois University at Edwardsville
Mark Silverstein	Boston University
Allan Spitz	University of Alabama at Huntsville
Paul Sracic	Youngstown State University
Sharon A. Sykora	Slippery Rock University
Roy E. Thoman	West Texas State University
Richard Timpone	SUNY Stony Brook
Joseph Unekis	Kansas State University
Thomas Walker	Emory University
Eric N. Waltenburg	Purdue University
Christopher Wlezien	University of Houston
Sandra L. Wood	University of North Texas

INTRODUCTION

CHAPTER

1

T his book is based on the simple notion that American government was never meant to be pretty or fast. The fifty-five delegates who gathered for the Constitutional Convention in the summer of 1787 wanted a government that would be strong enough to protect the young nation against its foreign and domestic threats, but never so strong as to become a threat to liberty itself. The Founders' new government had to protect America as a nation, even as it protected every American as an individual. Not too strong, not too weak, just strong enough.

This delicate balance is clear in the documents written by the Founders who led the fight for independence and drafted the new Constitution in Philadelphia. Under the Preamble to the Constitution, which can be read in Appendix B of this book, the new government was to create laws and courts ("establish Justice"), keep the peace ("insure domestic tranquility"), defend the nation against foreign threats ("provide for the common defence"), and assure that every American had a chance at a better future ("promote the general Welfare"). To protect the young nation, America would need a government strong enough to raise taxes, tough enough to enforce the laws, and powerful enough to win wars.

A Government Just Strong Enough

Yet, the Founders also wanted the new government to defend individual Americans from tyranny ("secure the Blessings of Liberty to ourselves and our Posterity"). To protect what Thomas Jefferson's Declaration of Independence had called the "unalienable Rights" of "Life, Liberty and the pursuit of Happiness," America could never have a government so strong that it could be captured by a majority to be used against a minority. After all, the war for independence had been fueled by resentment toward the British government, which had stripped its American colonists of these unalienable rights.

It is important to note that Americans had once been deeply loyal to the British. Americans had fought in British wars and celebrated British victories. But during the decade that preceded the Declaration of Independence, Americans came to believe that the British government had betrayed their loyalty. The Declaration of Independence, which was signed on July 4, 1776, lists more than twenty-five "injuries and usurpations" by an increasingly hostile British government, ranging from "imposing taxes on us without our consent" to having "plundered our seas, ravaged our coasts, burned our towns, and destroyed the lives of our people," and "transporting large armies of foreign mercenaries to complete the works of death, desolation and tyranny." The Declaration is a very tough document, indeed, and can be read in full in Appendix A at the back of this book.

The Founders clearly understood that government could be used to oppress the very citizens it was supposed to protect. They rightly worried about how to make sure their new government could never be captured by tyrants, as the British government had been captured by King George III, the British monarch who launched the "long train of injuries" listed in the Declaration of Independence. The Founders recognized that government is an instrument that can be used for good or bad.

To understand the Founders' intent one must recognize that American **government** is basically a set of institutions (Congress, the presidency, the executive branch, and the courts) for managing politics, and **politics** is basically how people decide who gets what, when, and how.[1] Politics is about how people govern themselves, and government is just one of many devices that people use for making political decisions. Government can be designed to make it easy or difficult for strong majorities to use politics to impose their will on the rest of a nation.

The challenge in designing a new government was that the Founders believed human beings were mostly incapable of governing themselves. "If men were angels, no government would be necessary," Virginia's James Madison wrote in advertising the Constitution to the public in *Federalist Paper No. 51,* which can be read in full in Appendix C.[2] As the intellectual leader of the Constitutional Convention, Madison believed human beings were far less than angels. He believed human beings will inevitably divide into factions, or groups, and fight to impose their will on others. (Madison made his argument about human nature in *Federalist Paper No. 10,* which can also be found in Appendix C.)

For Madison, there were two cures for what he called the "mischiefs of faction": either destroy liberty by creating an all-powerful government or give every citizen the very same opinions and interests. Since the first was a cure worse than the disease and the second was impossible in such a diverse nation as America, the best Madison and the other Founders could do was design a government that could never be used by the people against the people. In short, they designed government to make it difficult for strong majorities to assert their will. This is one reason why government can sometimes be so frustrating. It will always be much more difficult to pass a law than defeat one, even when huge numbers of Americans want action.

Curious as it might sound, the Founders worried about protecting the people against government because government was, in fact, the people. Americans were just as divided against each other in the 1780s as today. Indeed, it is something of a miracle that American democracy survived its first thirty years at all. The young nation came close to civil war twice and was plagued by deep social and economic divisions. Facing that uncertain future in 1787, the Founders created a government that would be extremely difficult for any one faction to control. Occasional stalemate in making the basic decisions about what government does was a small price to pay for liberty.

The tendency of Americans to divide against each other usually expresses itself in legal activities such as voting and peaceful protest, but can also express itself in extremist acts such as the bombing of the Murrah Federal Building in Oklahoma City on April 19, 1995.

The Founders did not want government to be incompetent, however. They knew the nation needed an effective army and navy to survive, and most certainly wanted the mail to run on time. They meant for **public policy,** which involves decisions about *what* government does, to be frustrating and difficult, but for **public administration,** which is *how* government implements and manages public policy once the decisions are made, to be as efficient as possible. Indeed, New York's Alexander Hamilton argued that a "government ill executed, whatever it may be in theory, must be in practice a bad government."[3] Occasional stalemate in fighting the wars and delivering the mail was anything but fine.

This chapter will take a much closer look at the different visions of democracy facing the Founders as they designed their new government. They had plenty of options from which to choose, running the gamut from giving Americans a direct say in every decision government would make to denying any say at all.

VISIONS OF DEMOCRACY

The "people" have always had a mixed role in American government. On the one hand, the Founders asked the people to give their consent to be governed, whether through approval of the Constitution itself in 1789, or through regular elections for president and members of Congress. "I know of no safe depository of the ultimate powers of society," wrote Thomas Jefferson late in his long and productive life, "but the people themselves."[4]

On the other hand, the Founders asked the people to give consent indirectly, through representatives of one kind or another. They never gave the people a chance to vote on any public policy issue directly. The Founders simply did not trust the people to govern themselves. In fact, they were so worried about the direct rule of the people that they never used the word "democracy" in the Constitution. And no wonder. The word is a combination of two ancient Greek words: *demos,* meaning the common people, and *kratos,* meaning rule. Put the two parts together and democracy becomes rule by the common people. Having government by the people can never work, Madison argued in *Federalist Paper No. 10,* because people are people. Give the people a direct role in the new government, he wrote, and America's future would be short and its death almost certainly violent.[5]

The problem with government by the people was sown in the nature of humankind itself. Bluntly put, the Founders were deeply concerned about what the people might do if ever given the power to govern themselves. They saw people as easily manipulated by great orators and clever advertisers alike.[6] Surely, such a public could not be allowed to govern directly. Subject to "every sudden breeze of passion, or to every transient impulse," as Alexander Hamilton argued in *Federalist Paper No. 71,* the public was likely to sway back and forth with the promises of skillful tyrants.[7] Convinced that human beings would fight about even the most trivial of issues, the Founders tried to insulate government against public opinion. The people would be asked for their consent to be governed, but only through a system that diffused that consent across the competing institutions of government.

The Founders did not believe all human beings were flawed, however. Even as Madison worried about the "degree of depravity in mankind," he celebrated the potential for virtue among America's future leaders. The mischiefs of faction could be solved in part, he wrote, by straining public opinion through the filter of "a chosen body of citizens" whose patriotism and love of justice would be so great that the new government could somehow rise above the petty conflicts of ordinary life.[8] That "chosen body" would be found in the Congress, the presidency, and the Supreme Court, all of which would be led by gifted patriots who would set aside their own interests for the greater good of the nation. The Founders simply believed the public would be better off giving their consent to be governed than governing themselves.

It was this rather gloomy view of ordinary people that led the founders to worry about the proper balance between majority rule and minority rights. American government is clearly run by **majority rule,** which simply means that those who have more than half of the vote have the greatest say over what government does. Majority rule clearly holds in Congress, where it always takes at least 50 percent of the Senate or House to pass a bill, and sometimes takes a "supermajority" of

60 percent and more. Majority rule usually holds for most elections, where the candidate who gets the greatest number of votes almost always wins. The sole exception is a presidential election, where the Founders created the very real possibility that a candidate could win a majority of popular votes but not the presidency itself. Finally, majority rule holds in the Supreme Court, where a majority of the nine justices determines the final opinion on most cases.

Yet, even though the majority has the greatest influence in making public policy and shaping government, the Constitution also creates **minority rights** to protect those who do not happen to have the most popular position or the most numerous supporters. The Constitution contains these rights in its first ten amendments, which are called the **Bill of Rights.** The Bill of Rights can be read in Appendix B at the end of the Constitution. Under the First Amendment in the Bill of Rights, for example, Congress is prohibited from making any laws either creating a national religion or interfering with the free exercise of religion, limiting freedom of speech or the press, or denying the right of individual citizens to gather together in peaceful assembly.

Democratic Options

The Founders clearly did not believe in government *by* the people. As much as they may have believed in a government *for* the people that would protect unalienable rights, and as much as they believed in a government *of* the people that would rely on elections as a basic device for selecting the government's leaders, the Founders simply did not consider the people learned enough to make decisions about the future of the nation, at least not directly.

The Founders created a government by representatives instead—that is, the president, members of the House and Senate, and justices of the Supreme Court. Because the Founders gave each set of representatives a different term of office (two years for House members, four years for presidents, six years for senators, and life for Supreme Court justices), and a different collection of voters (House members would be elected by districts, senators by individual state legislatures, presidents by all the states together, and Supreme Court justices by no voters at all), the Founders made certain that no single faction of the public could ever impose its will on the rest of the country by capturing one branch of government.

Given the prevailing image of the public as always prone to fighting, it is hardly surprising that the Founders insulated government from the governed. The people may get to elect at least some of their representatives every few years, but otherwise have to trust that their elected leaders will act in the nation's best interest. Given a choice between the turmoil of a **direct democracy,** in which every citizen has a say in every decision, and the virtue of a **representative democracy,** in which the people vote for elected leaders who make the decisions on their behalf, the Founders clearly preferred a representative system. The Founders defined government by the people as government by the people the people elect. The contrasts between direct and representative democracy are summarized in Box 1–1.

Much as Americans might long for democracy based on small town-hall meetings and face-to-face debates, representative democracy may be the only choice in a country as large and diverse as America. As political scientist E. E. Schattschneider wrote when America was just 230 million strong, "We ought to get rid of confusing language such as 'government by the people.'" The fact is that Americans are spread out across four million square miles of nation. Even if they could be brought together in one place, 270 million Americans would create a mosh pit covering 70 square miles, filling the entire District of Columbia.[9]

BOX
1-1

Who's in Charge?
A Comparison of Direct and
Representative Democracy

Direct Democracy	Representative Democracy
All eligible Americans have the opportunity to participate in every decision.	All eligible Americans have the opportunity to choose the representatives who will participate on their behalf in every decision.
Elections offer choices between candidates, as well as choices between different public policies.	Elections offer choices only between candidates.
The people have the opportunity to place public policies on the ballot.	The people have no opportunity to place public policies on the ballot.
Representatives of the people must always do exactly what the people want.	Representatives of the people are free to act according to their own views, which may or may not fit what the public wants them to do.
The agenda of government decisions about who gets what, when, and how is set by the people.	The agenda of government decisions about who gets what, when, and how is set by representatives according to their own views.
The majority rules in all decisions.	The will of the majority can be denied in order to protect the rights of minorities.

Under the Constitution, states are free to make their own decisions about how to run government, provided they do not violate the basic rights of individual citizens. The Founders did not want citizens to vote on public policy, but many states allow just that through the **referendum** and **initiative.** Under the referendum, state legislatures ask their citizens to vote on a specific proposal, leaving it up to a majority to decide what gets done—for example, whether to allow riverboat gambling. Under an initiative, the public is allowed to put a proposal on the state ballot by gathering some minimum number of signatures from individual voters. Once an initiative reaches the ballot, the majority rules on what gets done—for example, whether to keep taxes down, allow school prayer, or stop gay rights. Twenty-one, mostly western states currently allow both referendums and initiatives; five others allow one or the other.

Despite these occasional opportunities for direct input, America is primarily a representative democracy. The key question in such a system is who represents the people. One option is to let property owners speak for the people. As John Jay, one of the great champions of the Constitution in 1787, once said, "the people who own the country ought to govern it."[10] Although the Founders decided not to require property ownership as one of the qualifications to be president, that is precisely what has happened in fact (de facto). Under **elitism,** government by the people becomes government by the people with the resources and family ties to get to the top.

A second option is to let **organized interests** represent the people. Organized interests are collections of people who join together to make their views known to government. Students, the elderly, women, small businesses, hospital corporations, doctors, veterans of foreign wars, trial lawyers, even political scientists and college professors have their own organized interest groups that try to influence government decisions. So, too, do people who care about food safety, dolphins, old-growth forests, children, abortion, and equal rights for women.

Together, these organized interests constitute a vision of democracy that political scientists call **pluralism,** under which government by the people gets changed into government by the many (or plural) organized interests the people join. The American Association of Retired Persons (AARP), for example, has grown from just 400,000 members in 1960 to 33 million by 1993. Instead of consulting those 33 million members one by one, government often consults AARP and its handful of lobbyists instead. Unfortunately, not every American belongs to an interest group. Children do not join organized interests, and must rely on adults to make their case. Poor people rarely join either, and must hope that someone else speaks on their behalf.

A Government of Which People?

Questions of who has a voice in America's representative democracy are played out every day in Washington, whether in who testifies before Congress, who serves

The face of American government has changed dramatically since George Washington appointed all white males to his first Cabinet of department secretaries in 1789. Although Bill Clinton's first Cabinet appointees in 1993 were much more diverse in gender and race, they were also better educated and had higher incomes than Washington's appointees 200 years before, and, therefore, perhaps just as out of touch with the lives of ordinary Americans.

as presidential appointees in the executive branch, even who brings a case before the Supreme Court. Even today, America's government of the people is not always of *all* the people.

George Washington, for example, had little trouble appointing a government that looked like "the people" as defined by the Constitution in 1789. He simply appointed white, male property owners. This is not to argue that the nation was only composed of white male property owners. Of the nearly 4 million Americans counted in 1790 government census, one in six were slaves and slightly over half were women.

Rather, it is to note that white, male property owners were the only people recognized under the state laws then in effect. New York voters had to own roughly $40 dollars worth of property and voters in Massachusetts $120, a considerable amount of money at the time. Although the Constitution did not restrict the vote to property owners, it, too, defined the people as white males.

America had clearly changed by the bicentennial of the Constitution. States had lowered the barriers to voting, sometimes on their own, sometimes under orders from the Supreme Court, sometimes under constitutional amendments. The Fifteenth Amendment (1870) gave the vote to males of all races; the Nineteenth (1920) to women; the Twenty-Sixth (1971) to citizens over the age of eighteen.

Today, presidents are not only free to appoint women and minorities to their administrations, but would be criticized if they did not. The face of American government has changed dramatically as a result. Thus, the first wave of Clinton administration appointees in 1993 looked almost exactly like the rest of America: 13 percent were African American compared to 12 percent in the general public; 46 percent were women compared to 51 percent in the general public.

Nevertheless, America is still some distance from having government of all the people. Most presidential appointees, members of Congress, and federal judges are highly educated. Many enter public service after high-paying careers in business. President Bill Clinton's first department secretaries were no exception. Almost half had done their undergraduate work at Harvard, Yale, or Stanford, and almost all had graduate degrees: two-thirds were lawyers and one-fifth had doctorates.[11] As for income, almost all made $200,000 or more in the year before joining the administration. Clinton's secretary of labor made $540,000 and his secretary of education even more. Even Clinton's relatively young White House staff had substantial resources—thirty-something George Stephanopoulos bought an $835,000 Washington office building as an investment in 1994.[12]

As the Clinton appointments suggest, American government may look more like the rest of the country today, but may be just as unrepresentative of ordinary Americans as George Washington's administration 200 years ago.

ⓘⓃ A DIFFERENT LIGHT ━━━━━━━━━ ■ ■ ■

GATED COMMUNITIES

Every morning, tens of millions of schoolchildren start their day by reciting the Pledge of Allegiance: "I pledge allegiance to the flag of the United States of America, and to the republic for which it stands, one nation, under God, indivisible, with liberty and justice for all."

At the end of the day, however, increasing numbers of children go home to gated communities that are clearly divided from the rest of America. Gated communities, or residential community associations as they are sometimes called, are higher income, private housing developments that exercise tight control over their citizens. Residents of gated communities usually pay a fee for common services such as garbage pick-up, private police, and park maintenance.

Residents also agree to abide by the rules, or covenant, of the development, covering everything from who can drive on the streets, to whether they can build basketball hoops in their driveways, to what color of paint they can use on their shutters. Homeowners who break the rules can be fined by the development or forced to leave. People who live in these communities appear ready to surrender a great deal of their individual freedom in return for the safety and property value that come from building a wall around their communities.[13]

Gated communities have become particularly popular in large urban areas where crime and poor government services have led a growing number of Americans to leave their traditional neighborhoods. Roughly 28 million Americans now live in the 150,000 gated communities around the country, a number that is expected to grow to 50 million by the year 2000. As many as a third of all new developments in Southern California are gated. Some include private schools, grocery stores, and fitness centers, all of which are open only to homeowners in the development. Since the streets are all private, many gated communities are not even on the local road maps.

The rise of gated communities presents two challenges to the Founders' vision of democracy. First, residents are often separated from the rest of society, commuting into work in the morning, and returning safely home through the gates at night. Cut off from the real problems of the cities and ongoing contact with people not like themselves, residents can lose touch with the "commons," that is, the shared concerns that affect all Americans.

Second, the residents may be unwilling to pay taxes to support their local or state governments. Why should they pay for public services they do not consume? The problem is that residents of gated communities are usually very well off financially. To the extent they are allowed to opt out of paying local taxes, the rest of the city suffers. The result may be a growing gap between the streets, parks, and services inside the gated communities and the streets, parks, and services outside. And there is no wall high enough to keep out the resulting social unrest that might eventually arise.

Besides the security and higher property values, one of the advantages of living in a gated community is that residents are often very active in deciding who gets what, when, and how within the development. Residents tend to care deeply about maintaining a high quality of life within their

A gate guard checks all cars in and out of the Bear Creek gated community outside Seattle, Washington. Like most gated communities, the roads, sewer systems, parks, and playgrounds at Bear Creek are all private. House colors and shrubbery heights are tightly regulated by the Bear Creek resident association, which has the legal authority to enforce its rules.

gated communities, and are ready to give time, money, and energy to the effort. They are very good citizens, indeed. Yet, what makes politics inside gated communities different from the rest of America is that the citizens inside the gates are mostly the same. They may disagree about the shrubbery height and acceptable paint color, but are very much alike in their overall view of the world. By debating just among themselves, they learn little about the quality of life in the rest of their cities, also creating an ever-widening gap between life inside and outside the gates.

■ ■ ■

Parallels to Today

Whatever its flaws, the Founders' new government has been just strong enough to make American democracy a beacon for the world. The fact that the Founders' design has survived does not mean it has never been tested, however. Its survival was anything but guaranteed.

Nevertheless, America tends to look back on the founding through a gossamer lens. The nation celebrates Independence Day on the Fourth of July with fireworks, band concerts, picnics and sparklers, but fully a quarter of Americans do not know just what happened more than two hundred years ago to make the day special, and more than half see it more as an opportunity to be with friends and families or just another day off from work than as a day to honor the history and freedoms of the country.[14] (July 4th did not become a holiday until 1783, seven years after the Declaration of Independence was signed. Until then, the real independence day was celebrated on March 5th, marking the day in 1770 when British soldiers fired on unarmed protesters in the Boston Massacre, killing five.[15])

The fact that America survived its first thirty years is actually something of a miracle.[16] There were repeated threats to the new government: riots, a failed first constitution, highly unpopular government decisions, and at least two times when America came close to civil war, once surrounding preparations for a war with France, a second time over the deadlocked 1800 election.[17]

That American democracy has survived the past three decades might also be considered something of a miracle. The last thirty years have produced a remarkable amount of political and social crisis: three assassinations (President John F. Kennedy, civil rights leader Rev. Martin Luther King, Jr., and Bobby Kennedy, a senator and presidential candidate), an unpopular war in Vietnam, and racial unrest. Still, American democracy, and the liberty it both protects and reflects, endures at home and spreads throughout the rest of the world.

Indeed, the America of the late 1700s shows striking similarities to today. Colonial America was sharply divided on the issues of the day. The population was growing rapidly and was highly mobile. The "haves" tried to protect their interests as best they could; the "have-nots" wanted a piece of the growing economy. Civil unrest was frequent before and during the revolution—historian Richard Brown identified at least twenty-eight riots between 1760 and 1775.[18] The public was angry about government in general, and seemed willing to strike out against anyone in charge.

The social tensions continue to this day, and may even be growing as America becomes more diverse and the economy tightens. The result can be seen in the 1992 Los Angeles riots and the 1995 Oklahoma City bombing. America is hardly bracing for another revolution—indeed, much of the violence today appears random and senseless—but the divisions remain.

Alongside the anger, Americans have never seemed so distrusting of their government and each other. Just as the Founders felt the British government was unresponsive and oppressive, many Americans have come to believe that American government today creates far more problems than it solves. By 1996, for example, almost nine out of every ten Americans had come to believe that politicians will say and do anything to get elected, while seven in ten had concluded that government is run for the benefit of special interests. As for trusting each other, barely one in three Americans currently believes that most people can be trusted, while the rest say that "you can't be too careful in dealing with people."

Together, these parallels suggest that having a government just strong enough is as important to the present as it was to the past. America still has plenty of factions and relatively few angels. Indeed, it is precisely in moments of deep public unrest that the Founders' design seems so effective. Its greatest strength, perhaps, is in keeping strong majorities from imposing their will on weak minorities, even when that means government is slow.

CONCLUSION

It is no wonder that Americans are often frustrated by the stalemate and confusion in Washington. In their quest to create a government strong enough to protect a young nation, yet not so strong as to threaten liberty, the Founders created a very complicated government, indeed. It is a government that can work very well, as it did in the Gulf War of 1991, and as it does every day in working to assure that America's drinking water is safe, its air is clean, and the elderly's Social Security checks accurate and on time.

But it is also a government that can sometimes teeter on the edge of complete paralysis, as it did in the fall and winter of 1995, when federal agencies were closed on two separate occasions as Congress and the president battled over the federal budget. With the Washington Monument, the National Air and Space Museum, and the Yellowstone Park all closed for a lack of money, and federal employees in line for welfare, Americans had to wonder what kind of government they had. What kind of business would tolerate such behavior?

The answer is that Americans have a government that is just strong enough. It was designed to work very well both when the nation is threatened, and when Congress, the president, and the Supreme Court generally agree. Given a clear job to do, government can be very effective at public administration.

But when strong majorities come to threaten the rights of individual Americans, or when the public is sharply divided over politics and policy, American government can be very frustrating. A single committee of Congress, a strong-willed president, a single federal court, even a single U.S. senator can sometimes grind the entire system to a halt. And that is exactly what the Founders wanted. They designed a government that would be painfully easy to stalemate. It is helpful to remember that long train of injuries and usurpations in the Declaration of Independence the next time another stalemate hits Washington, as it most surely will. The Founders would not be troubled a bit, unless, of course, the stalemate threatens the safety of the nation as a whole.

The rest of this book will examine the Founders' design in more detail, asking how their "government just strong enough" works today. Chapter 2 opens the book by discussing the founding of the Constitution, asking what the Founders wanted as they gathered in Philadelphia in the summer of 1787.

The next four chapters then turn to the role of the people in government. Chapter 3 examines how public opinion gets formed, with particular attention to the role of the media in shaping what people think. Chapter 4 addresses the political parties and organized interests as key institutions that exist in between the public and government. Chapter 5 examines how citizens participate in democratic life, with a particular emphasis on the rules that affect who gets to vote, while Chapter 6 examines the role of campaigns in shaping how people make the choice among candidates.

The next five chapters examine the institutions of America's representative democracy, asking how the will of the people gets converted into specific decisions about who gets what, when, and how through the laws made by government. Chapter 7 starts with the first institution listed in the Constitution: the legislative branch, which is composed of two chambers, the House and the Senate, that make the laws. Chapter 8 examines the second institution listed: the executive branch, meaning the presidency, which has the power to execute the laws. Chapter 9 reviews the federal bureaucracy in more detail, noting that this "fourth branch" of government was left virtually undefined by the Founders. Chapter 10 addresses the third and final institution listed in the Constitution: the federal judiciary, specifically the Supreme Court, which has the power to interpret the laws.

The book then puts the people and their representative institutions together in two final chapters. Chapter 11 asks how the people are protected against their government and each other through civil liberties and civil rights, while Chapter 12 examines the making of public policy with a particular concern for the trends that are shaping America's future.

THE BASICS

■ The Founders who gathered in Philadelphia for the Constitutional Convention two hundred years ago wanted a government that would be strong enough to protect a young nation against foreign and domestic threats, but not so strong that it could ever be used to oppress the people.

■ The Founders could remember a time when the thirteen colonies had been deeply loyal to the British government, only to find that the British government could be used against them by a tyrant named King George III. These memories about how government can sometimes be used against the people led the Founders to design their government to be just strong enough.

KEY CONCEPTS

■ American government is a set of institutions (Congress, the presidency, the executive branch, and the courts) for managing politics, which is about how people decide who gets what, when, and how. Politics is not something that just happens in government, however. It occurs in every corner of life, even in debates about where to go to dinner and what kind of pizza to order. Government can be designed to make it easier or harder for strong majorities to use politics to impose their will on the rest of a nation.

■ The Founders decided to design government to make such control harder because they worried that Americans were basically incapable of governing themselves. The Founders had a very dim view of most human beings, believing it was natural for people to divide into factions, or groups, and fight about even the most trivial issue. They definitely did not believe people were angels.

■ Since there is no cure for being human, the Founders designed a government based on representative rather than direct democracy. Representative government is government by the representatives who the people elect, not by the people themselves. The people do not have a direct voice in making decisions about what government does, just about who makes the decisions.

IN A DIFFERENT LIGHT

■ The growing popularity of gated communities threatens the notion of "one nation . . . indivisible." Residents of gated communities pay fees for private roads, parks, and police, and often surrender significant freedom in return for safety and higher property values. Although residents of gated communities are often very active in their local politics, they tend to interact only with people very much like themselves. This means that gated communities are cut off from the ordinary lives of the cities to which they are only lightly attached. Whether gated communities can ignore the problems of those cities is in doubt.

OPEN QUESTIONS

■ At what point does the effort to balance majority rule with minority rights shift toward one side or the other? When might majority rule be most likely—that is, during wars, economic depressions, good times? When might minority rights get in the way of government solving pressing problems?

■ When does government become too strong or too weak? Just what constitutes a foreign or domestic threat anyway? Is global economic competition a threat worth suspending minority rights? Or must minority rights be protected even in wartime?

■ Who are the people? Does the fact that so many come into office with money matter? Are all the people represented in the Founders' government? And if not, does it matter?

...TERMS TO REMEMBER

government

politics

public policy

public administration

majority rule

minority rights

Bill of Rights

direct democracy

representative democracy

referendum

initiative

elitism

organized interests

pluralism

Endnotes to Chapter 1

1. Harold D. Lasswell, *Politics: Who Gets What, When, and How* (New York: McGraw-Hill, 1938).
2. In Roy P. Fairfield, ed., *The Federalist Papers* (Baltimore: Johns Hopkins University Press, 1981), p. 160.
▶ 3. Fairfield, ed., *The Federalist Papers,* p. 198.
4. Edward Dumbauld, ed., *The Political Writings of Thomas Jefferson: Representative Selections* (New York: Liberal Arts Press, 1955), p. 93.
5. Fairfield, ed., *The Federalist Papers,* p. 20.
6. For an alternative view, see Benjamin Page and Robert Shapiro, *The Rational Public: Fifty Years of Trends in Americans' Policy Preferences* (Chicago: University of Chicago Press, 1992).
▶ 7. Fairfield, ed., *The Federalist Papers,* p. 206.
8. Fairfield, ed., *The Federalist Papers,* p. 22.
9. E. E. Schattschneider, *Two Hundred Million Americans in Search of a Government* (New York: Holt, Rinehart and Winston, 1969), p. 63.
10. Catherine Drinker Bowen, *Miracle at Philadelphia: The Story of the Constitutional Convention, May to September 1787* (Boston: Little, Brown, 1966), p. 72.
▶ 11. These figures are drawn from Martha Farnsworth Riche, "An Administration that Mirrors America," *Washington Post National Weekly Edition,* January 31–February 6, 1994, p. 25
12. See Thomas Dye, "The Friends of Bill and Hillary," *PS: Political Science and Politics,* volume 26, number 4 (December 1993).
13. Timothy Egan, "The Serene Fortress: A Special Report: Many Seek Security in Private Communites," *New York Times,* September 3, 1995, p. A1.
14. The survey was conducted by the ABC News/*Washington Post* Poll on July 19, 1986.
15. Among the first to fall was a former slave named Crispus Attucks. For his story, see William C. Nell, *The Colored Patriots of the American Revolution* (New York: Arno Press and The New York Times, 1968, originally published in Boston, 1855).
16. See James Roger Sharp, *American Politics in the Early Republic: The New Nation in Crisis* (New Haven: Yale University Press, 1993).
17. See Sharp, *American Politics in the Early Republic,* Chapter One.
18. Richard Brown, "Violence and the American Revolution," in S. Kurtz and J. Hutson, eds., *Essays on the American Revolution* (Chapel Hill: University of North Carolina Press, 1973), p. 101 ff.

Note: The color arrow that precedes select endnote entries denotes sources that would be most appropriate for further study.

THE CONSTITUTION

CHAPTER

2

T he Founders came to Philadelphia with very strong opinions about a national government. They most certainly knew what they did not like. They could still remember how the British government had oppressed the colonies before the Revolutionary War, and believed that America's first national government had been much too weak.

The Founders also knew what they liked. Many had been involved in writing their state constitutions, and brought that experience to Philadelphia. Nine of the thirteen states had a single executive for implementing the laws, eleven had two-house legislatures for making the laws, and all had state courts both for protecting individual citizens and prosecuting criminals. Not surprisingly, the Founders favored a similar division of responsibility for their new national government.

The Founders did not copy every last detail from the states, however. The Founders decided not to make property ownership a condition for holding federal office, even though most states required just that of their governors and legislators. Members of the North Carolina legislature had to own at least 100 acres of land, for example, while the governor of South Carolina had to have an estate worth at least 10,000 British pounds, a huge sum of money at that time. The Founders also decided not to include a bill of rights in their final draft of the Con-

stitution, in part because most of the states already provided a mix of basic protections. Although only one state, Virginia, had a comprehensive Declaration of Rights, the Founders simply felt a national bill of rights was unnecessary. (As we will see later in this chapter, the Founders added a national bill of rights later.)

It is important to note that the Founders did not come to Philadelphia with the explicit purpose of writing a new constitution. Rather, they were appointed by their states after the Continental Congress called a convention "for the sole and express purpose of revising the Articles of Confederation." One historian argues that two-thirds of the Founders would have been scared off had they known they would end up writing a new constitution from scratch.[1] Once in Philadelphia, however, the fifty-five delegates soon concluded that the Articles could not be saved. They would have to start over from scratch.

Starting with their likes and dislikes, the Founders began a process of inventing a new government. Some argued for a three-headed presidency; others for a single house legislature; still others for the popular election of the president, a debate that was only settled after sixty ballots in the convention. The Founders generally agreed that they wanted some kind of **legislative branch,** composed of a body of elected representatives to make the laws, an **executive branch,** composed of one or more presidents to execute the laws, and a **judicial branch,** composed of a Supreme Court to interpret the laws and protect individual rights.

But beyond these three basic components, the details were in flux. With a full summer to work, the debate pitched back and forth over a host of proposals, most of which sought to balance the power of big states against the rights of the small.

As the convention dragged on through the long summer, the debate turned on one central question: how could the new government be strong enough to protect the young nation, yet not so strong as to threaten liberty itself? Although Americans frequently complain about how little gets done in Washington, the Founders arrived at an ingenious answer. Their new government would be able to act with surprising speed and strength in answering threats to its survival, but would otherwise be easy to stalemate. They created a government that would teeter precariously on the verge of complete frustration, but one that would be difficult to capture by strong-willed majorities intent on oppression. It would be just strong enough.

It is important to remember that the Constitutional Convention was not just some intellectual debate about designing a new government. The Founders came to Philadelphia convinced that the nation was on the verge of collapse. America was hardly a superpower just yet, and was saddled with a huge debt from fighting the war.

Because the constitution would have to be approved by a two-thirds majority of the state legislatures, the Founders had to design a government that the country would support, one not so strong as to frighten an anxious public, but not so weak as to fail in the future. This chapter will review the compromises leading up to the final design, as well as the design itself. It will also end by showing how the Constitution is a work in progress—that is, how the Founders always intended for American government to change with the times.

PRELUDE TO A CONSTITUTION

The fact that the Constitution was written after a war of independence reveals a great deal about why the Founders worried so about creating a government just strong enough. A government built to simultaneously protect the nation as a whole and its citizens as individuals is quite different from a government built solely to do either. Combining these two very different goals assured that American government would be relatively easy to stalemate.

The Revolutionary Mind

No single event provoked the American Revolution. Rather, the Revolution reflected what Thomas Jefferson called a "long train" of insults and injuries, many of which involved efforts by the British to raise money from the colonies, including the Tea Act of 1773, which raised the price of tea and prompted 150 colonists to disguise themselves as Mohawk Indians and dump three cargo holds of tea into Boston Harbor. (See Box 2–1 for a list of events leading to the Revolution.)

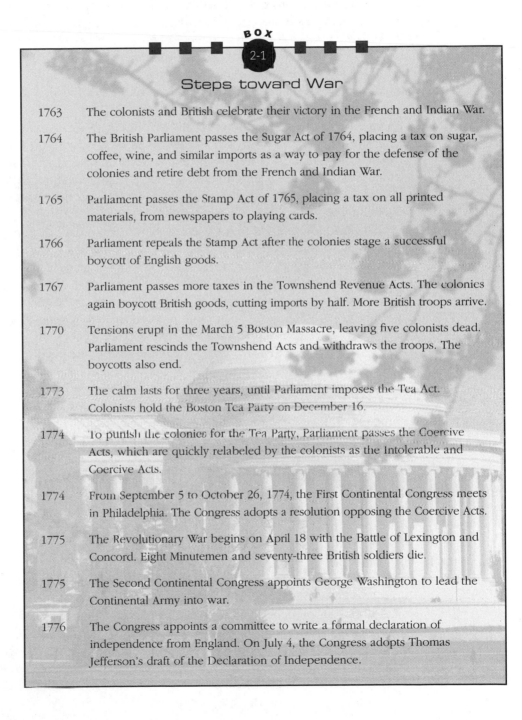

BOX
2-1

Steps toward War

1763	The colonists and British celebrate their victory in the French and Indian War.
1764	The British Parliament passes the Sugar Act of 1764, placing a tax on sugar, coffee, wine, and similar imports as a way to pay for the defense of the colonies and retire debt from the French and Indian War.
1765	Parliament passes the Stamp Act of 1765, placing a tax on all printed materials, from newspapers to playing cards.
1766	Parliament repeals the Stamp Act after the colonies stage a successful boycott of English goods.
1767	Parliament passes more taxes in the Townshend Revenue Acts. The colonies again boycott British goods, cutting imports by half. More British troops arrive.
1770	Tensions erupt in the March 5 Boston Massacre, leaving five colonists dead. Parliament rescinds the Townshend Acts and withdraws the troops. The boycotts also end.
1773	The calm lasts for three years, until Parliament imposes the Tea Act. Colonists hold the Boston Tea Party on December 16.
1774	To punish the colonies for the Tea Party, Parliament passes the Coercive Acts, which are quickly relabeled by the colonists as the Intolerable and Coercive Acts.
1774	From September 5 to October 26, 1774, the First Continental Congress meets in Philadelphia. The Congress adopts a resolution opposing the Coercive Acts.
1775	The Revolutionary War begins on April 18 with the Battle of Lexington and Concord. Eight Minutemen and seventy-three British soldiers die.
1775	The Second Continental Congress appoints George Washington to lead the Continental Army into war.
1776	The Congress appoints a committee to write a formal declaration of independence from England. On July 4, the Congress adopts Thomas Jefferson's draft of the Declaration of Independence.

Thus did the Revolution start, one small act leading to another, each one easy enough to resolve on its own, but together leading eventually to war. Although each small step is important for illuminating the spiral toward war, the true revolution occurred before the war in the minds of the people. "What do we mean by the American Revolution?" John Adams asked in 1818. "Do we mean the American war? The Revolution was effected before the war commenced. The Revolution was in the minds and hearts of the people; a change in their religious sentiments, of their duties and obligations. . . . This radical change in the principles, opinions, sentiments and affections of the people was the real American Revolution."[2]

No one was more important to this revolution of ideas than John Locke, an English political philosopher who wrote his *Second Treatise of Government* in the 1600s. Locke had argued that people enjoyed certain natural, or unalienable, rights, which included "life, health, liberty, and possessions."[3] The role of government is not to give people these natural rights, but to protect the rights that people already have.

Locke had also argued that government was merely a mechanism created by the people for the people. Government only retained its power if it did not violate the natural rights of the people. People do not give up their rights just because they vote for a president or a member of Congress. Rather, the people *consent* to be governed, and always retain their absolute right to change their minds. The people, not the government, are always the best judges of their best interests. Government should be limited to what the people want, enact only those laws that are necessary and good for the people, and never raise taxes without the consent of the people, whether given directly or through their elected representatives.[4]

The colonists blended Locke's thinking with their own experience to create an image of government in direct conflict with what was happening in the 1760s and 1770s. It is not that the colonists wanted to fight the British. They had fought side-by-side with the British in the 1763 French and Indian War, which had given the British complete ownership of everything east of the Mississippi River. Rather, the colonists simply believed they had the same unalienable rights to life, liberty, and the pursuit of happiness as all British citizens. As the British increased the troops and taxes, the colonists concluded that they would never be accepted as true citizens of England, but would always be subjects of an increasingly oppressive government.

Having decided that a separation from Britain was nearly inevitable, the Founders convened the **First Continental Congress** in September 1774 to consider options for independence. Drawing colonial delegates to Philadelphia from every colony but Georgia, the Congress provided little drama. It passed a resolution opposing the latest British tightening, supported another boycott of British products, passed a few other resolutions of minor note, and planned to meet again in May 1775. It was the fact that it met that mattered most. The colonies were starting to come together to determine their future; they were asserting their right to legislate for themselves and denying England's right to do it for them.

By the time the **Second Continental Congress** met in May the following year, a full-scale revolutionary war was on. In April 1775, British troops had marched from Boston to Concord in an effort to capture a stock of patriot rifles and ammunition. They were intercepted in Lexington by a loosely formed group of seventy soldiers called the Minutemen, who had been alerted by Paul Revere's famous ride. The British tried to march past, a single shot was fired (the shot heard 'round the world), the British fired back, eight Minutemen were killed on the village green. The colonists quickly regrouped and forced the British to retreat, killing seventy-three British soldiers on the road back to Boston.

There was no declaration of war at the time—it took weeks to travel from one end of the colonies to the other—but the Revolution was clearly on. Some colonies were writing their own constitutions and others were voting to support independence from Britain.

This Second Continental Congress produced the **Declaration of Independence,** which was signed on July 4, 1776. Written by Thomas Jefferson, the Declaration was clearly a political document, the centerpiece of an advertising campaign to convince the colonists of the need for war and to show Britain that the colonists were serious. At the same time, the Declaration made a series of promises that would be difficult to keep. Guaranteeing that "all men are created equal" may have made sense for rallying an angry nation to war, but would be anything but easy to deliver in a nation that had long benefited from the slave trade and saw women as anything but endowed with the same rights as men.

War and Peace

Launched with the call to liberty, the **Revolutionary War** eventually became one of America's longest and costliest wars, lasting eight years from 1775 to 1783, and creating a staggering debt for the new nation. (By comparison, the Civil War lasted five years, World War II less than four, Vietnam over ten, the 1990 Gulf War exactly 100 hours.) A quarter of a million colonists fought in the Revolutionary War, and casualties were often heavy. One-fourth of Washington's Continental Army froze to death at Valley Forge in the winter of 1778.

The war itself was an on-again/off-again event. There were years early on when the Continental Army was simply unable to fight. It was poorly equipped, poorly fed, and poorly paid. Many women followed their husbands, brothers, and fathers into the war. Some supported the troops by doing the laundry, cooking meals, and caring for the wounded. Others stood side-by-side with their husbands loading rifles and cannons. Still others fought in the war disguised as men. One woman, Deborah Sampson, eventually received a veterans pension from the State of Massachusetts for her service; her husband was the first American to receive a pension as a soldier's widower. There were no questions about women in combat in 1775. It was either pick up the rifle, reload the cannons of wounded or dead husbands, or perish.[5]

What is remarkable, of course, is that the Continental Army survived at all. The winter of 1778 was particularly brutal. Washington "wrote that the men starving at Valley Forge, leaving occasional bloody footprints in the snow for lack of shoes, would have been helpless against a British attack and unable to retreat for want of transport. The army was in even worse condition in 1780, when Washington wrote that the men had been 'five or six days together without meat; then as many without bread, and once or twice, two or three days without either. . . .'"[6]

The question, therefore, is how the Americans won the war. After all, the British had better training and weapons. They controlled the seas, and had more of just about everything a nation needs to win a war, including better uniforms. The one thing they did not have was leadership. They bungled nearly every engagement, while Washington seemed to make the most of what he had. Equally important, the British were absolutely unprepared for the American style of guerilla war. The British army was particularly skilled at fighting formal wars, forming ranks and firing in unison, while the colonists were gifted at hit-and-run tactics, moving quickly from skirmish to skirmish, rarely providing clean targets. As a result, the British were eventually worn down more by the nature of the conflict than by any stunning series of victories by the Continental Army.

Such long wars of attrition are rarely popular, however, if only because public enthusiasm is always highest before the first bodies fall. Had there been pollsters at the time, the lead story in the papers of the early 1780s might have been titled "Public Support for War Falling Fast; Majority No Longer Supports." As the war turned sour and prospects for a quick end faded, many Americans may have started questioning the true price of independence. Some historians argue that support for the war had fallen to roughly 40 percent of the American public by 1780, with the rest of the nation divided between outright opposition to continued fighting and simple neutrality.

Even as America celebrated its victory, social tensions remained high, culminating in a series of small "rebellions," including one in the summer of 1786, led by a former soldier named Daniel Shays who marched first on Springfield, Massachusetts, and then to Boston with nearly one thousand men to express a host of social and economic ills. The precise goals of the protest were unclear, yet four marchers died before it was over.

A Summer of Reform

Shays's Rebellion was hardly essential to the second Constitution America lives with today. It was but one event on the long list of unrest that had begun before the war and continued after. Indeed, Thomas Jefferson remarked that "A little rebellion now and then is a good thing. . . . God forbid that we should ever be twenty years without such a rebellion. . . . The tree of liberty must be refreshed from time to time with the blood of patriots and tyrants." It was easy for him to say, of course: he was in Paris at the time.

Shays's Rebellion convinced the Founders that America desperately needed a stronger national government than the one established under the **Articles of Confederation.** Adopted in 1777 in the midst of war and ratified by all the states by 1781, the Articles of Confederation can be called America's first constitution. Under the Articles, the national government consisted of a single-house legislature with no formal executive or judical branch. Most of the power remained in the thirteen states. Like the Declaration of Independence, the Articles were drafted in part to satisfy the public, which opposed any national government, and in part to satisfy the states. The result was a national government mostly incapable of protecting the nation from foreign or domestic threats.

It was to the task of building a stronger national government that the fifty-five delegates came to Philadelphia in the summer of 1787.[7] Writers have usually described the summer as blistering hot, presumably to make the Constitution seem an even more heroic act than it clearly was. In fact, the weather was actually rather cool as Philadelphia summers go.

Washington presides over the Constitutional Convention in a painting by Stearns. The Founders had substantial experience in politics before coming to Philadelphia and organized the convention as a legislature, complete with committees, floor rules, and formal votes.

Temperatures were anything but cool in Independence Hall, however, as the delegates struggled to draft a new constitution in just four short months, May to September. The disagreements were sharp, dividing delegates between big states and small over who would control the new legislature, and between southern states and northern on how much power the new government would have to raise taxes.

The first and most important debate centered on just how strong the new government should be. Virginia delegates offered the first answer, a vision of a strong national government that was sometimes sharp and other times fuzzy. Under what became known as the **Virginia Plan,** which was drafted by James Madison, the new government would have three branches: a legislative branch to make the laws would be composed of two houses, the first selected by the people and the second selected by the first; an executive branch to implement and enforce the laws would be led by one or more presidents appointed for a single term by the legislative branch; and a judicial branch to interpret the laws would be composed of a supreme court and lower courts of some number and size.

The national government would also have the power to reject, or **veto,** laws passed by the states, and a panel representing the executive and judicial branches would have the power to veto laws passed by the legislative branch, which would, in turn, have the power to overturn the veto **(veto override).** Although the convention would change many of the details, and add more specifics, the Virginia Plan defined the basic outlines for what was a much stronger new government.

An alternative vision was drafted by a single New Jersey delegate in response. Under the **New Jersey Plan,** the national government would be far less powerful, perhaps even less powerful than the government under the Articles of Confederation. Although the New Jersey Plan shared some similarities with the Virginia alternative, it represented a last gasp for weak national government and was easily defeated at the very beginning of the convention.

The New Jersey Plan did not disappear altogether, however. Unlike the Virginia Plan, which determined the number of seats in Congress by either the total population of or taxes paid by each state, the New Jersey Plan gave an equal number of slots to each state regardless of size. Small states were obviously drawn to the New Jersey view, while large states preferred the Virginia approach. The debate was finally resolved under the **Great Compromise** of early July when the convention agreed to a two-house, or bicameral legislature. Small states would be more heavily represented in the Senate (where each state would receive two seats regardless of size), large states more heavily represented in the House of Representatives (where seats would be apportioned, or granted, on the basis of population), and the power of taxation would be reserved for the House.

These compromises involved more than power politics between big states and small. In addition to their own experiences living under governments of one kind or another, the Founders read widely in the leading scholarship of their era. Benjamin Franklin was already an expert on the Iroquois Indian constitution, which had united the seven warring nations of the Iroquois; and James Madison quickly emerged as the convention's chief political philosopher. Before arriving in Philadelphia, he had asked Thomas Jefferson, who was serving in Paris as America's Ambassador to France, to send "whatever may throw light on the general constitution."[8]

The Founders had the personal resources to be curious, of course. They did not get to be Founders without belonging to a distinguished elite. Forty-two of the original delegates had been members of the Continental Congress, thirty-one had attended college—Princeton claimed ten delegates among the fifty-five, William and Mary four, Yale three, Harvard two, and Columbia two—and thirty-four were practicing law. Although twenty-one of the delegates were under the age of forty, with the youngest twenty-six years old, most had accumulated at least some property along the way, including fifteen who owned slaves. They were, as historian James MacGregor Burns called them, "the well-bred, the well-fed, the well-read, and well-wed."[9] Given their status and wealth, it is tempting to ascribe the origins of the Constitution in purely economic terms. Perhaps the Founders were concerned about protecting individual citizens because they worried about their own economic interests.

That is just how historian Charles Beard described the founding in his 1913 book, *An Economic Interpretation of the Constitution*. According to Beard, there was no doubt why the founders worked through that long summer in Philadelphia: money. The Articles of Confederation had threatened the rich by giving the states too much power. No wonder the new government made passing legislation so difficult, Beard argued: the Founders did not want a popularly elected Congress and president forcing the rich to pay higher taxes or redistribute the wealth to the common people. In short, the Constitution could best be viewed as an economic document "drawn with superb skill by men whose property interests were immediately at stake."[10]

The only problem with Beard's interpretation is that it does not fit the facts. The Founders were certainly wealthier than average Americans, and more likely to own both land and slaves. And they were most certainly among the colonial elite. Yet, there is little evidence that they schemed to protect their interests from an increasingly unhappy public. According to painstaking research by historian Forrest McDonald, the Founders did not act as a unified economic group, nor was ratification an expression of some great class struggle. Farmers, bankers, and merchants lined up on both sides of the ratification debate, rendering an economic interpretation virtually useless in explaining the actual decisions in Philadelphia.[11]

The better explanation for what the Founders did rests in their worries about the future of the nation. Although their self-interest was obviously at stake if the young nation failed, the Founders came to Philadelphia because they believed that the nation was in crisis. Recalling the oppression of British rule, and having concluded that the Articles of Confederation had failed, the Founders set out to build a government strong enough to meet domestic and foreign threats, but not so strong as to threaten basic **civil liberties,** which involve efforts to protect individuals from their government, and **civil rights,** which involve efforts to protect individuals from each other.

Ultimately, the Founders saw their new government as the foundation of a **republic,** which they defined as a society in which the people give their consent to be governed through the election of representatives. As opposed to rule by a single king or queen (monarchy), an elite group of citizens (aristocracy), the people themselves (direct democracy), or by no one at all (anarchy), the Founders were willing to try an entirely new form of government (representative democracy). Power in a republic would reside with the people, but would be exercised by their representatives.

The Founders went further, however, by narrowing the definition of people to include only white males like themselves. And even then, the Founders still did not trust the people to govern. As John Adams argued in 1787, "the proposition that [the people] are the best keeper of their liberties is not true. They are the worst conceivable; they are no keepers at all. They can neither act, judge, think, or will."[12] The Founders may have been ahead of their time in creating a new form of democratic government, but had done so by defining the majority of America as either ineligible for citizenship or unsuitable for governing. So much for John Locke. The creator apparently only shined on certain human beings.

The Basic Framework

Imagine designing a new government based on the notion that the people, however defined, could not be trusted. An all-powerful government would be just about the worst option possible. What if some faction of the public captured the government and inflicted their opinions on the minority? What if some president became so popular that he or she established a kind of elected monarchy? What if politicians became so addicted to their careers that they would do just about anything to get elected? The risk of tyranny would be too great.

A far better option would be a government with just enough power to act in crisis, but not so much power as to allow a majority to control the government during periods of calm. Such a government might divide power among several branches, giving each one a stake in every decision. It might create competition among the branches through different terms of offices and different constituencies. It might reserve many decisions for states and localities in an effort to diffuse power even further. And it might give each branch a way to slow, if not stop the other branches cold. Let the president cancel the Congress, let the Supreme Court cancel the president—give voters a bigger say in controlling some of the branches, but not all of them, and never, ever let any one person act alone. Such a government might occasionally drift into stalemate, but it would be far less of a threat to liberty.

That is just the kind of "limited" government the Founders wanted. Although they struggled over the details—should there be a single president or a council of three? should there be a single chamber of Congress or two?—the Founders were willing to accept occasional stalemate in making public policy to avoid the capture of government by strong-willed majorities, and they used four basic devices to raise the odds against oppression: separate powers, separate interest, separate layers, and checks and balances. (See Appendix B for the text of the Constitution.)

Separate Powers. The Founders clearly did not want any single branch to control all decisions about who gets what, when, and how from government. To ensure that this does not happen, they first created three separate branches, each with **separate powers** and enough authority to cancel a strong-willed majority in the other two. Article I created the Congress, Article II the presidency, and Article III the Supreme Court. Next, they divided the branch that they thought would be most powerful into two separate chambers, the House and the Senate, each again with enough authority to cancel a strong-willed majority in the other chamber. Finally, they told each branch what it could and could not do through **express powers**—for example, Congress was given the power to pass the laws, create inferior, or lower, courts, and declare war; the presidency was given the power to execute the laws, nominate judges and other executive officers, and grant pardons; and the judiciary was given the power to make sure that Congress and the president only exercise their respective powers.

Separate Interests. To assure that the three branches would remain independent of each other, the Founders gave the leaders of each branch and the two houses of Congress **separate interests**—different sets of voters and different terms of office from the other two.

In Congress, senators would represent entire states and representatives would represent districts within the states. There would be *two* senators for *every* state, which would favor voters in smaller states who get "more senator" per vote, but just *one* representative for what was every district containing roughly *30,000* voters, which would favor voters in larger states who get more representatives per state. Although the number of representatives per vote has changed over the past two hundred years as the population has grown—it was one representative per 570,000 voters in 1990—the basic principle has remained the same: small states have more power in the Senate, large states more power in the House. Some small states—Wyoming and Vermont—have two senators and only one representative, while large states have two senators and dozens of representatives—California now has fifty-two House members, Texas thirty, New York thirty-one.

The Founders diffused power even more by giving the two chambers different terms of office. Senators would serve six-year terms, and representatives two-year terms. Further, only one-third of the Senate would run for reelection in any one campaign, guaranteeing that no one election can sweep the Senate clean. Finally, until the 1900s, senators were selected by their state legislatures, further insulating the chamber from the public. Under the Seventeenth Amendment to the Constitution, which was ratified in 1913, senators were finally subject to direct election by popular vote.

Turn to the presidency second. Not surprisingly, given the Founders' effort to insulate the new government from the public, the president and vice president received an entirely different calendar. They would serve *four-year* terms, and campaign before the voters on a state-by-state basis. To this day, presidents are not technically elected by the voters at all. Voters actually vote for their state's delegation to the **electoral college**—the number of electors on the ballot equals the number of senators plus representatives in a given state. It is the electors who then cast the ballots for the president.

Until the Twelfth Amendment in 1804, presidential candidates did not run on a ticket together with their choice for vice president. The winner of the election was the president, while the second-place finisher became the vice president. Like the appointment of senators by state legislatures, the electoral college was designed to keep voters at a distance. Unlike the appointment of senators, the electoral college is still part of the process today.

Consider the federal courts last. Federal judges are appointed by the president with the consent of the Senate, not the House, and have no term at all. They can stay in office until they decide to retire on their own, as long as they do not break the law themselves. Voters have no direct say in judicial decisions, and can only influence the courts by electing the president (through the electoral college), whose enumerated powers include making judicial nominations, and by electing their senators, whose enumerated powers include confirming the president's appointees. The lack of a direct say creates enormous independence for the courts, giving them the freedom to reject even the most popular laws.

Separate Layers.   Beyond dividing control among the separate branches, the founders also divided power vertically, in **separate layers,** between the national and state levels of government, and assumed, in turn, that the states would continue to divide their power with local governments. These divisions create what is called a federalist system of government. As a result, the term "federal" can take on a very different meaning depending on how it is used in a sentence. When experts talk about **federalism** or the federalist system, the term "federal" refers to the American system of layers—that is, National, state, and local. But when they talk about the federal government, it is typically meant to refer to the national government located in Washington, D.C.

The Founders had no choice but to create a federal system, if only because the people would have a say on final approval through special state ratifying conventions. Facing strong opposition to the Constitution, the Founders eventually agreed to reserve all powers explicitly *not* given to the national government for the states. Under federalism, the Constitution created at least three kinds of enumerated powers: (1) **exclusive powers** given to the national government—for example, the power to declare war, make treaties with other governments, create money; (2) **reserved powers** given to the states—the power to regulate commerce within state borders, police the public, prosecute most crimes; and (3) **concurrent powers** shared by both—the power to raise taxes. The federal government has a very clear and short list of powers, while the states have everything else.[13]

Checks and Balances. Once the basic institutions of the new national government were established, the Founders decided to give each one a way to check, or stop, the others. Each institution would have its separate powers, but would also share power with the others, meaning no single institution could ever act alone. These **checks and balances** are part of what so many politicians now call gridlock, or stalemate between the branches, but they are essential for preventing any single branch or layer of government from ganging up on the rest. The Founders gave the president the power to veto legislation—the president can either sign an act of Congress into law, or reject it with a stroke of the pen. The Founders then gave the Congress the power to override the veto with a two-thirds vote. If the vote to override is successful, the bill becomes law without the president's signature. Otherwise, most legislation passes with a simple majority.

The Founders did not stop sharing powers with legislation, however. They gave the House the power to initiate the impeachment process to remove the president from office (by charging the president with "high crimes and misdemeanors"), but gave the Senate the power to convict. They gave the Senate the power to confirm presidential appointees to the court, but because they saw the House as more responsive to public passion, they gave the House authority to start all tax bills on the way to final passage.

A DIFFERENT LIGHT

THE ODDS AGAINST ACTION

Insulating the government against capture by a strong-willed majority intent on oppression clearly increases the odds against action. Even routine ideas may have trouble winning passage into law. The current Congress will consider nearly 8,000 proposals, or bills, for legislation. Of those, about 3,000 will be considered good enough to be placed on the calendar for actual votes. Of those, only 1,000 or so will be passed by either the House or the Senate. Of those, only 500 will be passed by both, printed on parchment paper and hand-carried to the president for signature into law. The odds that a bill will actually become law are only 1 in 15, odds that fall even farther if an idea is particularly controversial.

The odds against passage have increased in recent decades. During the first years of Congress, almost every bill introduced was passed into law. Although the number fell steadily over the 1800s, Congress was still passing roughly one in five bills as late as the 1940s.

The declining odds are definitely *not* because Congress is overwhelmed by the sheer number of bills introduced. Back in the 1960s, for example, Congress handled over twenty thousand bills a year. However, as the number of bills introduced has declined, the number of pages of each bill has climbed dramatically. Whereas the average law in the 1960s was only three pages long, the average law today will top fifteen pages. Bills seem to be more complex today, thereby requiring more time and energy to pass.

The odds against passage create both pros and cons for American government. On the one hand, the nation is spared rapid changes in who gets what, where, and how from government. Just because an idea is popular with the public or hot in one branch of government does not necessarily mean it is a good idea. The fact that major reforms are a long time coming also means that society has time to adjust to new ideas.

On the other hand, the odds against passage clearly protect the status quo. Although the Founders' government is very effective at meeting foreign threats such as the Gulf War of 1990, it may be less able to agree on just what constitutes a domestic threat. Problems such as racial inequality, ozone depletion, or the lack of health insurance may go unaddressed for decades as Americans debate whether a problem actually exists. This is one reason government can often be so frustrating to the public. The effort to protect the country from strong-willed majorities makes the odds against even the most compelling action painfully high.

Constitutional Advertising

The Founders clearly succeeded in designing a government that would be strong enough to protect a young republic, but not so strong that it would threaten liberty. They most certainly succeeded in creating a government that would be nearly impossible to capture by strong-willed majorities intent on oppressing the nation. The separate powers and checks and balances alone assured that government would always be perilously close to stalemate; the national government would be stronger than it was under the Articles of Confederation, but would never be a model for tyrants and dictators to admire.

Despite achieving their goals, the final signing of the Constitution by the Founders on September 17, 1787, was anything but a great celebration. "Even now, at the very end, a half dozen men were wrangling about minor details," writes one historian of the final days, "and three others flatly refused to sign the instrument. Another group was already worrying about and planning for the strenuous campaign for ratification which lay ahead. Mostly, however, the atmosphere pervading the room was one of exhaustion and a sense of relief that the four month ordeal was over."[14]

Perhaps the Founders also recognized that the nation had to be persuaded that a stronger government made sense. Americans were hardly enthusiastic about a new national government, and remained much more loyal to their state and local governments than to the broad promises of the more perfect union envisioned in the Constitution. Mostly, Americans wanted to be left alone, particularly if a new government wanted to impose new taxes to pay off the war debt. Put to a national referendum, the Constitution probably would have failed, which is one reason why, perhaps, the Founders did not permit referendum or initiative in their design.

This opposition would not have mattered but for another protection against tyranny: **ratification,** or approval, of the Constitution itself. In order to win ratification, the Constitution would need majority votes from nine state ratifying conventions, a number that constituted a three-fourths majority of the thirteen states. Part of the effort to win this "supermajority," as political scientists might call it today, was an advertising campaign built around eighty-four brief explanations of the Constitution written anonymously by New York's Alexander Hamilton and John Jay, and Virginia's James Madison. These documents eventually became known as *The Federalist Papers.* (*Federalist Paper No. 10* and *Federalist Paper No. 51* can be read in Appendix C.)

Despite the advertising, ratification remained very much in doubt. New York, Pennsylvania, and Virginia were sharply divided. The Founders would either have to go back to scratch and redraft the Constitution, or find some way to reassure the public.

Constitutional advertisers. Alexander Hamilton (left), John Jay (middle), and James Madison (right) wrote *The Federalist Papers* to advertise the Constitution as it moved through the states toward ratification.

Taking the latter course, the Founders promised the states that the very first item on the agenda of the new federal government would be a list, or bill, of amendments guaranteeing basic freedoms. Drawing from nearly two hundred proposals, the First Congress proposed ten amendments that became known as the Bill of Rights. The list was less an endorsement of new government powers and much more a statement of what the national government could not do. The amendments were passed in 1789 and ratified in 1791.

The First Amendment was designed to protect the most basic freedoms of all: worship, speech, the press, and peaceful assembly. There was to be no national religion, no limit on free speech, no government press, and no limit on peaceful protest.

The Second Amendment was to guarantee the right to keep and bear arms, a great concern to a public that had armed itself against the British. The Third Amendment was to protect citizens from being forced to house soldiers during peacetime, another reaction to British practice in the prewar period. The Fourth Amendment was to guard against unreasonable search and seizure, assuring the public's basic right to be safe from their own government.

The Fifth through the Eighth Amendments were created to protect people accused of crimes. Under the Fifth Amendment, government would be unable to force people to testify against themselves, nor could it try a person twice for the same crime or fine or put people in jail without "due process" of law—requiring, for example, that the accused be told of the charges and given a chance to cross-examine witnesses. Under the Sixth Amendment, the courts would have to provide speedy and public trials by jury in criminal matters. Under the Seventh Amendment, the accused would be guaranteed a trial by jury in certain civil matters. Under the Eighth Amendment, individuals would be protected against excessive bail, unreasonable fines, and cruel and unusual punishment.

Protecting the accused was essential to the rest of the freedoms guaranteed in the Constitution and Bill of Rights. It hardly made sense, for example, to guarantee free speech, then allow government to jail Americans for exercising that right. Providing due process, public trials, protection against being tried twice for the same crime, and so forth, made such political harassment much more difficult.

The Ninth and Tenth Amendments were written to cover the remaining bases. The Ninth Amendment would simply state that people do have rights other than those specifically listed in the Constitution. The Tenth Amendment would reserve all powers not given to the national government for the states.

As a political strategy, the promised Bill of Rights succeeded: the Constitution was ratified in 1788, the Bill of Rights in 1791. Yet, by agreeing to the guarantees, the Founders also set a precedent in favor of change. The Constitution would be an evolving document. Madison had said as much at the Constitutional Convention: "in framing a system which we wish to last for ages, we should not lose sight of the changes which ages will produce."

A FEDERAL RESULT

Just because the Constitution was ratified does not mean the battle for a stronger national government was over. Having lost their campaign against ratification, opponents of the Constitution formed their own quasi-political party and continued to fight for a smaller national government. The Anti-Federalists, as they were called, worked to limit the exercise of federal power at almost every turn in the first decade under the new Constitution, all the while arguing that states know best what their citizens need. Although the Anti-Federalist label had mostly disappeared by the 1820s, elements of the Anti-Federalist philosophy of government are still popular today.

Despite the Anti-Federalist worries, the Founders never doubted that states would continue to provide most of the basic services that shape daily life. What they wanted was a federal government to worry about the whole. Hence, the Constitution contains a mix of both guarantees and limitations on state power. On the one hand, all powers not given to the federal government are reserved for the states. On the other hand, all powers given to the federal government are denied to the states. As a result, states cannot enter into treaties, alliances, or confederations with other nations on their own.

This mix of constitutional guarantees and limitations was hardly the end of the debate over federalism. Over the past two hundred years, there have been at least three different eras in the ebb and flow of power between the three levels of government.

The first is often called the era of layer-cake, or **dual federalism.** The theory underpinning dual federalism is simple: each layer of cake has its own powers, duties, and loyalties, and never the twain shall meet. Like a layer cake, which separates its parts with a sugar frosting, dual federalism holds the nation together only through patriotism and worries about the future. The federal government does not give money to the state and local governments, and most certainly does not tell citizens who gets what, when, and how from their own state and local governments. The federal government is also the smallest of the layers, holding a mere fraction of the power of state and local government.

The layer-cake era began with ratification of the Constitution and continued off and on until the 1930s. States frequently asserted their rights to be left alone, claiming that the federal government could only exercise the enumerated powers of the Constitution. Central to dual federalism was **states' rights,** a rallying cry for those who believed that states should have the primary role in a federal system. With the Tenth Amendment as their rallying flag, advocates of states' rights often argued that the federal government had no right to interfere in most state activity. Under that amendment, all "powers not delegated to the United States by the Constitution, nor prohibited to the States, are reserved to the states respectively, or to the people." In strictest terms, states' rights advocates argued that the federal government could only exercise the specific powers listed in each section of the Constitution. Everything else was off-limits.

The states' rights movement experienced its greatest setback in the Civil War. Southern states claimed that the federal government had no business interfering in the practice of slavery, even arguing that states are free to ignore, or nullify, national laws that they felt violated the Tenth Amendment. The Civil War and the Thirteenth Amendment ultimately resolved the nullification debate once and for all. States would have to abide by federal law, particularly regarding the good of America as a whole and the protection of Americans (in this case, slaves) as individual citizens.

The debate over nullification may have been over with Robert E. Lee's surrender at Appomattox, but dual federalism continued for another eighty years. The federal government had more than enough to do at a national level managing westward expansion, the Spanish-American War, and World War I, let alone find the resources to meddle in state and local affairs. Even when it did try to regulate the states, as it did in the early 1900s when it passed laws to protect children from being forced to work, the Supreme Court used the Tenth Amendment to declare the laws unconstitutional. In one famous case, the Supreme Court even rewrote the Tenth Amendment to say "the powers not *expressly* delegated to the national government are reserved" to the states and the people.[15] In fact, the amendment never used the word "expressly" at all.

The second era of federalism is often called the era of marble-cake, or **cooperative federalism.** Instead of the sharp divisions of dual federalism, cooperative federalism imagines federal, state, and local governments working together to solve pressing problems: like a marble cake, in which the different flavors merge together, it is often impossible to tell where one ends and the other begins.

The era of marble-cake federalism began with the Great Depression in the 1930s and continued through the 1960s. As the Founders knew, some threats to the nation were just too big to be handled by state governments alone. The Great Depression was just such a problem. Started with a stock market crash in 1929, and driven forward by a worldwide economic collapse, the depression created wave upon wave of business failures, which, in turn, generated a vast population of unemployed, homeless Americans. Arguments about whether the federal government had the power to act under the Tenth Amendment hardly made sense when the entire nation was on the verge of economic and social collapse. Led by President Franklin D. Roosevelt's "New Deal," a package of federal spending programs, the three levels of government worked together to get the unemployed back to work, whether paving roads, painting murals, clearing forests, or sweeping floors. The federal government ran some of the programs itself, but it also gave states money to put Americans back to work. By the end of the 1930s, federal dollars accounted for one-tenth of all state spending.

This spirit of cooperation continued into the 1960s with President Lyndon Johnson's "Great Society" agenda, which was designed to end poverty and strengthen opportunities for America's racial and ethnic minorities. The three levels of government seemed quite able to cooperate as long as big federal grants to the states and localities were involved. Federal spending for education, interstate highways, and welfare all set new records in the 1960s, leading some politicians to wonder whether America had entered an era of upside-down cake federalism—that is, with the federal government and its "sugar" of grants completely covering the states and localities underneath. By the end of the 1960s, federal dollars accounted for one-fifth of all state spending.

The third era of federalism is often called the era of **new federalism,** a term President Richard Nixon used in the early 1970s for describing his plans to shift federal responsibilities and dollars back to the states and localities. Nixon knew the era of dual federalism was long over, but believed states and localities should have a greater say over how they use the federal dollars they get.

Many federal grants go down to the states with strings attached—that is, with rules for how the states and localities must behave if they want the money. If states want federal dollars for highway construction, for example, they must set the minimum drinking age at twenty-one. Nixon succeeded in loosening some of the strings, and also convinced Congress to create a program called **general revenue sharing.** Under the program, which began in 1972 and ended in 1986, states and localities received a total of over $6 billion a year to use as they wished with no strings attached.

Nixon's ideas for returning power to the states are still active today. They were adopted by the new Republican House majority in 1994, where they came to be known as the "New(t) federalism" in honor of Republican House Speaker Newt Gingrich, a contemporary advocate of states' rights.[16]

A DIFFERENT LIGHT

THE DEVOLUTION REVOLUTION

The reason Nixon's new federalism still lives is that Americans trust their state and local governments more than the federal government. They believe that state and local taxes are the fairer taxes, and also believe they get more for their money from state and local agencies. Half of Americans believe that local government spends their taxes the most wisely, compared to a quarter for state government, and just a tenth for the federal government.[17]

Despite their distrust, Americans still see a role for the federal government. They think the federal government should continue to provide funding for welfare, environmental protection, improving opportunities for minorities, and national defense. But when it comes time to make decisions about roads and highways, public education, employment and job training, and law enforcement, Americans increasingly think the federal government should leave the states and localities alone. Americans simply believe the federal government causes more problems than it solves.

The effort to shift power downward toward state and local government is often called the **devolution revolution**. Much of the revolution involves changes in the way the federal government gives its $250 billion or so a year to the states. Most federal money has traditionally gone to the states in **categorical grants,** which carry tight rules on how the money must be spent. Advocates of devolution prefer **block grants,** which are lump sums of money that can be used pretty much as states wish as long as they stay within broad policy areas. Whereas a categorical grant would tell a state exactly what kind of job training program it must provide, even down to the reading lists for the classes, a block grant would provide federal money for job training without any details on how it must be spent.

Americans clearly like the notion that states know best what their citizens need. By 1995, over half of the public had come to believe that states should be given block grants with no federal control. Another quarter said the federal government should go to block grants, but keep at least some minimum standards telling states where to put the dollars. Only a tenth believed the federal government should keeping giving money with strings attached.

Although the devolution revolution appeals to American loyalties toward state and local government, shifting control downward has at least two drawbacks. The first is that some states may take the federal money but ignore the responsibilities, using the block grants to cover other priorities.

The second drawback is that the federal government may devolve the responsibilities but not the money. Indeed, one of the reasons states have become so hungry for block grants is that the federal government had already ordered the states to do so much. With prison populations rising, health costs for the poor skyrocketing, and the education budget exploding, many states will enter the twenty-first century facing severe financial shortages. Given even more federal responsibilities without money, poor states will tend to cut programs to make ends meet, while rich states may be able to raise taxes. Once again, the result will be a growing inequality among the states.

The Founders would hardly be surprised to discover that some states are more generous toward libraries and schools, others more generous toward roads and health care, and still others unable to be generous at all. They did not intend, of course, that all states be perfectly equal. Nevertheless, they might ask whether the devolution revolution can go too far.

■ ■ ■

A WORK IN PROGRESS

The Constitution was far from finished when New Hampshire became the ninth state to ratify it in June 1788, nor when Virginia became the last state needed to ratify the Bill of Rights in December 1791. The fact is that the Founders had done the very best they could to create a new government but had left many unanswered questions. Some of the answers have come in formal amendments to the Constitution; others from the courts; still others from the testing that comes with time. We will examine each of these three tools of change below.

The Amending Process

At least one of the Founders' questions was answered almost two hundred years later by a college student at the University of Texas in Austin. The Bill of Rights had actually included twelve, not ten, amendments when first proposed. One of the two "lost" amendments was proposed by James Madison, and involved a ban against Congress raising its pay *before* an election; the other was a limit on the ultimate size of Congress.[18] Both failed to win ratification. The Madison pay amendment was approved by only six states between 1789 and 1791, but it was far from dead.

Except for ratification by the state of Ohio in 1873 and Wyoming in 1978, the amendment seemed dead, at least that is until a student named Gregory Watson found it while researching a paper for his American government course in 1982. Watson believed that the amendment was still alive—just because it never passed did not mean it was dead. He said just that in his paper, only to get a "C" from his disbelieving professor.

Gregory Watson, ten years after receiving a "C" for arguing that James Madison's proposed constitutional amendment limiting congressional pay was still alive. Watson led a successful campaign to ratify the Twenty-Seventh Amendment, which was added to the Constitution 203 years after it was first passed by Congress.

What happened next is nothing short of amazing: Watson mounted a one-person campaign over the next ten years to get state legislatures to ratify Madison's pay ban. He had plenty of supporters, of course, reflecting the growing public anger toward Congress. By 1990, for example, a Gallup Poll found that almost half of Americans felt their members of Congress were paid "a lot too much," while another quarter said "a little too much."[19]

Passing the amendment became plain good politics. Maine ratified in 1983, Colorado in 1984. Five states followed in 1985, another seventeen were added before 1990, and six more by 1992. Add up the numbers: six in the 1700s, plus one in the 1800s, thirty in the 1900s, and, by the time Michigan ratified the amendment in 1992, Watson had the thirty-eight required to reach the three-fourths needed to ratify. The amendment became part of the Constitution 203 years after it was proposed. It was a hard way to protest a grade, but Watson had his amendment.

The Founders would have been pleased. They never saw the Constitution as a perfect document and had provided a two-stage process for amendments. The first stage involves presenting a formal proposal, which can be made in two ways. One, which has been used on all twenty-seven amendments, is for Congress to pass a proposed amendment by a two-thirds vote in each house. The other, which has never been used, is for Congress to call a national convention at the request of two-thirds of the state legislatures. The risk of a national convention is that the entire Constitution would be open for review. Apparently, the fear of changing the document too much has been enough to prevent such a convention from ever being called.

The second stage of the process involves ratification. As with proposals for amendment, ratification can occur two ways. One, which has been used on twenty-six of the twenty-seven amendments, calls for a vote in three-fourths of the state legislatures. Because the constitution itself does not say just how the state legislatures are to vote, some states use a simple majority to approve amendments, while others use a supermajority of either two-thirds or three-quarters. The other ratification device, used but once, calls for majority votes in three-fourths of state ratifying conventions, which is how the states passed the Twenty-First Amendment repealing the Eighteen Amendment's prohibition on liquor.

Judicial Review

Under the new Constitution, Congress would make the laws, presidents would enforce them, and the federal courts would determine consistency with the Constitution. This power of **judicial review,** which gives the courts the power to overturn an act of Congress, was far from automatic, however. After all, the courts had absolutely no way to enforce their decisions—no army, no special police. They would have to rely on Congress, presidents, and the public to accept their decisions as fact.

For the first decade, there were no opportunities to assert that power of review. As political scientist David O'Brien writes, "the Supreme Court had little business, frequent turnover in personnel, no chambers or staff, no fixed customs, and no institutional identity."[20] At the time, of course, there were very few laws to review, and the lower courts that now act as a "feeder" or source of cases were just getting underway. It was not until 1803 that the Supreme Court had a case that would give it the chance to exercise judicial review to overturn an act of Congress. To this day, the courts can only decide the cases that are brought before them; they can give signals about what cases they might like to hear, but must wait until cases arrive before making the decision.

That case, *Marbury v. Madison,* was another product of the continuing conflict over states' rights. The case began with the bitterly contested presidential election of 1800, one of only two elections ever decided by the House of Representatives. Thomas Jefferson won the election on the thirty-sixth ballot in the House, defeating the incumbent president, John Adams. (We will look at the election process in more detail in Chapter 6).

The case turned on a simple problem of timing. In a last-minute effort to frustrate the incoming president, Adams and his Federalist Party supporters in Congress created a number of new judgeships, one of which was to be filled by a William Marbury. Unfortunately, Marbury was one of seventeen new judges who had not received their papers of appointment by the time Jefferson was inaugurated as president. The papers were stuck in Washington. Acting on his authority as the new president, Jefferson immediately ordered his secretary of state, James Madison, not to issue the papers.

Marbury sued, arguing that Jefferson had no authority to undo the legal actions of a previous Congress and president, and asking the Supreme Court to use its power to force the president to release his appointment papers. It was a power that the Congress had clearly given the Supreme Court under the 1789 Judiciary Act, which had also created the federal court system.

The case offered a first test of the Supreme Court's legitimacy. On the one hand, the Supreme Court could not let a clearly illegal action stand, lest future presidents refuse to execute faithfully laws they did not like. On the other hand, the Supreme Court had no real power to make the president release the appointment papers. It had no army, no police, no history of making presidents obey. What if the president said "Make me?" Could the Supreme Court do so?

The Supreme Court needed a way out of the dilemma. Chief Justice John Marshall soon found one. The Supreme Court would declare that Jefferson could not legally withhold the papers, but would simultaneously declare itself powerless to order the release. Writing for a unanimous 4–0 Supreme Court, Marshall first argued that Marbury deserved his appointment—Jefferson could not take advantage of administrative red tape to undo a legitimate act of Congress. However, Marshall also argued that Congress had violated the Constitution by expanding the Supreme Court's jurisdiction under a section of the 1789 Judiciary Act. Because

Congress could not give the Supreme Court a jurisdiction that the Constitution had clearly omitted, that section was unconstitutional. Lacking jurisdiction, the Supreme Court could not order the president to deliver Marbury's appointment.

The Supreme Court thereby declared one part of the 1789 act unconstitutional, trading a small congressionally derived power—the authority to order a specific member of the executive branch (in this case the secretary of state) to do something (in this case deliver a commission)—for the much larger constitutionally derived power of judicial review. In doing so, Marshall also avoided a confrontation with Jefferson, for it was almost certain that the new president would not have delivered the commission whatever the order.

There were other cases early on that helped define the Constitution in practical terms. If *Marbury v. Madison* defined the power of judicial review, then *McCulloch v. Maryland* in 1819 established the dominance of federal law over the states.

The facts of the case are simple. The state of Maryland decided to put a tax on a branch of the Bank of the United States. When the tax collectors called on James McCulloch, cashier of the Baltimore branch, he refused to pay. The federal courts faced two questions: (1) because creating banks was never listed as an enumerated power of Congress, was creating the Bank of the United States thereby unconstitutional, and (2) does a state have the power to tax the federal government? The answer to both questions was "no."

McCulloch was a much easier decision for the Marshall Court than *Marbury*. On the question of whether the federal government could create a national bank, the Supreme Court turned to Article I of the Constitution. Under the **necessary and proper clause,** Congress had the power "To make all Laws which shall be necessary and proper" for carrying out its duties. Creating a national bank may not have been the very best decision for the future of the nation (the bank was abolished in 1832), but it was certainly acceptable under the clause. Indeed, the clause is so broad that it is also known as the **elastic clause:** it will stretch to cover just about any exercise of power the Congress might imagine. Even though creating a national bank was never listed as an enumerated power of Congress, it could be considered one of the hidden, or **implied powers** granted to Congress in the Constitution.

On the question of whether a state can tax the federal government, the Supreme Court turned to Article VI of the Constitution. Under the **supremacy clause,** the Constitution and all laws made under its auspices and institutions were to be the supreme "Law of the Land." Allowing a state to tax the federal government would make that state's law supreme over every American regardless of where they lived, thereby violating the clause.

What makes *Marbury* and *McCulloch* important is that the judicial branch successfully exerted its power to interpret the Constitution. By declaring an act of Congress unconstitutional, the courts established themselves as the ultimate brake against Congress and the presidency. And by creating a list of implied powers, the courts invited both government and citizens alike to imagine rights and duties hiding between the written lines of the Constitution.

Testing the Constitution

The Constitution is a remarkably short document for the complex government it created. It says little about how the three branches should operate and left the structure of the congressional committee system, executive departments, and lower courts entirely to the future. Many of the details emerged as the first Congress, president, and Supreme Court set precedents that stand to this day.

The Constitution was also tested almost immediately when western Pennsylvania farmers protested the federal government's new tax on whiskey by burning down the house of the local tax inspector. The 1794 "Whiskey Rebellion" bluntly asked whether the Constitution applied all the way to what was then the farthest outpost of the young nation. The answer came fast and hard. President Washington ordered the states to assemble an army of twelve thousand men—many more than needed—to demonstrate the government's readiness to respond to any internal threat. The rebellion—if such a small collection of protestors can be called such—quickly evaporated.

Not all of the Constitution's questions were dealt with so easily. The question of whether the Constitution would ever protect those who were enslaved was not answered for seventy years. This is not to argue that slavery was ignored in Philadelphia. Slavery was central to determining the number of seats each state would get in the new House of Representatives. Recall that the number of seats was determined by population, the question being whether slaves counted in the calculation. If yes, the slave-holding states of the South were sure to benefit. The founders eventually agreed to the **three-fifths compromise,** which calculated each slave as three-fifths of a person toward the total population of a state.

Nor is it that opponents of slavery never rose to demand an end to the human bondage. Slavery was the subject of intense debate several times during the convention; the Constitution even prohibited Congress from taking any action to end the importation of slaves before 1808 (see Article I, Section 9, Subsection 1).

Rather, the Founders simply could not resolve the issue of slavery. There is some confusion, for example, in the records as to what the passage in Article I meant. Some Founders thought the ban was a first step toward outright abolition of slavery after 1808; others, most notably Charles Pinckney of South Carolina, swore that no such agreement had been made. In the end, the ban may have been the kind of political agreement that allows each side to claim victory without making a final commitment at all, the kind made to this day by artful politicians who are not quite sure what they can deliver. Thus, resolving the tension between a state's right to continue slavery and the national responsibility to honor the pledge of liberty for all Americans was left to a future battlefield. Had the Founders known that so many thousands would die resolving the question, perhaps they might have tried harder to strike a compromise. Then again, such a compromise might have doomed the Constitution to defeat.

IN A DIFFERENT LIGHT

MAKING TOUGH CHOICES

There is no more difficult task facing Congress and the presidency today than cutting popular programs. It has always been easier to give than to take away. The problem, therefore, is finding the political courage to act.

One answer is to exit the constitutional process for making the laws entirely. In 1983, for example, Congress and the presidency created a national commission to fix the Social Security system. Facing a crisis that would have delayed benefit checks to over 30 million elderly, the only ways to fix the system were to raise taxes or cut benefits, just the kind of taking away that presidents and members of Congress avoid. Operating behind closed doors, the commission provided a meeting place for a secret "gang" of nine negotiators who assembled a package of just such painful solutions.[21]

The Founders probably would not object to the Social Security Commission and its hidden gang. After all, the final product of the commission was introduced in Congress, passed by both chambers, and signed by the president into law, all steps in the ordinary process the Founders designed.

The Founders might be much more troubled by the device Congress and the president used to close obsolete military bases. Members of Congress have long liked nothing better than to create military bases in their home districts. A base is a boost to a local economy and provides an ongoing source of jobs and money for the district. With the collapse of the Soviet Union and the end of the Cold War in the late 1980s, however, Congress and the president admitted that America did not need as many bases. Unfortunately, neither branch could bring itself to make the needed cuts.

The best the two branches could do was establish a military base closing commission in 1990. Unlike the Social Security Commission, which only had authority to make recommendations, the military base closure commission was to hold hearings on possible closings (traditionally an exercise of legislative power), take advice from the secretary of defense (an executive power), and make a final list of cuts. The president would then have the option to accept or reject the entire list (a legislative power), and the Congress had forty-five days to veto the president's decision (an executive power).

It was a twist on the constitutional system. With its combined legislative and executive powers, the commission acted almost as a separate government.[22] By offering a "take it or leave it" list of closings to Congress and the president, it provided political protection from an angry public back home. "The commission made me do it," members and presidents could say. In all, the commission closed 243 bases and cut over 100,000 federal jobs before it went out of business in 1995.

Protesting the closing of an airbase. Facing enormous public resistance to closing obsolete military bases, Congress and the president created a military base closure commission, which acted with combined legislative and executive powers to close 243 bases and cut over 100,000 federal jobs.

Given the odds against action discussed earlier, the base closure commission may have been the only hope for doing what had to be done. Yet, the commission may have let Congress and the president off the political hook, sheltering the public from the truth about what government can and cannot afford. It might have been better for the two branches to help the public understand why so many bases had to be closed. In doing so, they might have created support for the kinds of tough choices needed to reach a budget agreement later in 1995. Lacking that support, Congress and the president were forced to close the government twice late in the year, sending nearly a million federal employees home when their funding ran out and closing national parks, museums, passport offices, and a host of other services in the process.

CONCLUSION

The Constitution has survived to the present because of its three basic features. First, the Constitution created a government that was just strong enough to protect the new nation, but not so strong as to threaten basic liberty. So noted, the protection did not always include all Americans. Slavery continued for another "four-score-and-seven years," as Abraham Lincoln put it in his Gettysburg Address, leading to the bloodiest war in American history. Women were denied the vote for another three score, or sixty, years. Native Americans are still struggling to regain a measure of economic security lost in the taking of their lands. It is safe to argue, however, that Americans today have never been better protected, whether from foreign threats or from domestic oppression. Separate powers, separate interests, separate layers, and checks and balances may be frustrating—particularly when some lone senator stops a hot idea with a deadly filibuster or when some district court voids a popular law—but that is the way it was meant to be.

Second, the Constitution is always evolving. It was never meant to be a finished product. Some of the changes have come from amendments, others from interpretation and legislation, still others from a combination of action. The Thirteenth, Fourteenth, and Fifteenth Amendments finally may have given African Americans equal treatment under the law, for example, but it was left to Congress, the president, and the civil rights movement of the 1950s and 1960s to assure that the equal treatment actually occurred.

Third, despite its checks and balances, the Constitution occasionally, and only occasionally, permits gifted leaders to move the nation forward. Such leaders are rare, indeed. A George Washington, a James Madison, a Thomas Jefferson, a John Marshall, an Abraham Lincoln, a Franklin or Theodore Roosevelt, may come along only once or twice in a political generation. Such leaders must have a clear vision of the future, a gift for engaging the public, and raw courage to face the inevitable opposition, qualities that seem in short supply today. But when such leaders arrive in office, American government often works better than the Founders could have hoped.

THE BASICS

■ No single event started the Revolutionary War. Rather, the fight for independence involved a "long train" of actions by the British. Over time, the colonies became convinced that the British would never treat them as true citizens of England, but always as mere subjects of an increasingly oppressive government.

■ The Founders were called to Philadelphia by the Continental Congress to revise the Articles of Confederation. Once assembled, however, they quickly concluded that the articles could not be saved. They wanted a government strong enough to protect the nation from foreign and domestic threats, but not so strong as to become a threat to liberty itself.

■ The greatest controversy of the Constitutional Convention centered on just how strong the new government should be. The Founders eventually adopted a structure based on the Virginia Plan, which created a strong national government around three branches: legislative (to make the laws), executive (to execute the laws), and judicial (to interpret the laws and protect individual rights). Under the "Great Compromise," the convention gave big states more power in the House of Representatives and small states more power in the Senate.

■ Once finished drafting the Constitution, the Founders began the campaign for ratification. Part of the campaign involved an advertising campaign, built around eighty-four brief explanations of the Constitution called *The Federalist Papers*, and part involved a promised list of rights that would be added to the Constitution by the First Congress. That list was composed of ten amendments and is known as the Bill of Rights.

KEY CONCEPTS

■ The Founders' view of government was deeply influenced by their views of human nature. Led by James Madison as their chief political philosopher, the Founders tried to balance the need for a stronger national government against their fears of government directly by the people. They protected the government against capture by majorities intent on oppression through four basic devices.

1. *Separate powers* meant giving each of the three branches enough authority to cancel a strong-willed majority in the other two. The Founders also separated what they thought would be the strongest branch, the legislature, into two chambers, each again with enough authority to cancel the other.

2. *Separate interests* meant giving the leaders of each of the branches and each of the chambers different terms of office and different sets of voters from the other two. Senators would serve for six years and be elected by the state legislatures (the Seventeenth Amendment changed the method of selection to direct election by popular vote), presidents would serve for four years and be elected by electors from every state, members of the House would serve for two-year terms and be elected by small districts of voters (numbering 30,000 in 1789 and 570,000 today), and federal judges would be given no terms at all, serving for good behavior until they decided to retire on their own.

3. *Separate layers* meant dividing power vertically between the national, state, and local levels of government, creating a federalist system. Over the years, the Founders' federalist system has evolved from dual federalism (meaning the layers of government were strictly separate and rarely worked together) to cooperative federalism (meaning the layers of government worked together) and the new federalism (meaning an effort to restore power to the states and localities).

4. *Checks and balances* meant giving each branch of national government the power to check, or stop, the other. The president has the power to veto, or reject, legislation passed by Congress, for example, while Congress has the power to override, or overturn, the veto by a two-thirds vote.

■ The Constitution is still evolving two hundred years after ratification. Some of the evolution comes from amendments, the most recent being an idea originally proposed by James Madison that was one of the two "lost" items on the Bill of Rights. Some of the evolution comes from the federal courts, which established the power of judicial review in *Marbury v. Madison*, and made clear that the federal constitution and laws were supreme under *McCulloch v. Maryland*.

IN A DIFFERENT LIGHT

■ The Founders' design increases the odds against action, which, in turn, protects the nation from rapid swings in who gets what, when, and how from government. The nation also has time to prepare for major reform. At the same time, however, the odds against action clearly protect the status quo. It can take decades for an idea whose time has come to actually pass through Congress. Along the way, serious domestic problems such as poverty and racial inequality, may remained unsolved.

■ Americans are particularly suspicious toward the federal level of government. They believe state and local governments are more trustworthy, and would like to see more power shifted, or devolved down to the states. This devolution revolution involves efforts to reduce the strings, or rules, attached to federal grants to the states. Although devolution shifts programs such as welfare, education, and roads closer to the people, it may increase the inequality between the states, thereby dividing America as a whole.

■ Faced with difficult policy decisions, Congress and the president have recently turned to national commissions to help create the political courage to act. A national commission on Social Security helped solve a major financial crisis with the program in the early 1980s, while a more powerful commission helped close hundreds of obsolete military bases in the early- to mid-1990s. Although these commissions help make tough choices, they tend to shelter the public from facing the truth about what government can and cannot do.

OPEN QUESTIONS

■ What kind of government would the Founders have designed if they thought human beings could be trusted? Would it have been faster, bigger, stronger? Or not even needed at all? What did they see in human nature that made them think they had to worry about oppression? Is there any evidence today that some Americans would use government to oppress minorities?

■ The Founders created a complicated government that is sometimes difficult to understand, particularly when a popular idea is defeated by some obscure check and balance. To what extent does that complexity reduce public confidence in government? Do most Americans understand why the government works the way it does? Instead of pointing fingers at each other when stalemate occurs, should the nation's leaders occasionally simply say that is the way it was meant to be?

■ Thinking back to the late 1700s, would the Founders be surprised by the changes in their government over the years? What would trouble them most in the news today? Where would they congratulate themselves? Where would they say they had made a mistake?

...TERMS TO REMEMBER

legislative branch
executive branch
judicial branch
First Continental Congress
Second Continental Congress
Declaration of Independence
Revolutionary War
Articles of Confederation
Virginia Plan
veto
veto override
New Jersey Plan
Great Compromise
civil liberties
civil rights
republic
separate powers
express powers
separate interests
electoral college
separate layers

federalism
exclusive powers
reserved powers
concurrent powers
checks and balances
ratification
dual federalism
states rights
cooperative federalism
new federalism
general revenue sharing
devolution revolution
categorical grants
block grants
judicial review
necessary and proper clause
elastic clause
implied powers
supremacy clause
three-fifths compromise

Endnotes to Chapter 2

1. Catherine Drinker Bowen, *Miracle at Philadelphia: The Story of the Constitutional Convention, May to September 1787* (Boston: Little, Brown, 1966), p. 4.

2. Bernard Bailyn, *The Ideological Origins of the American Revolution* (Cambridge, MA: Belknap Press of Harvard University Press, 1967), p. 160.

3. Quoted in Dante Germino, *Modern Western Political Thought: Machiavelli to Marx* (Chicago: Rand McNally and Co., 1972), p. 127.

4. See Dante Germino, *Modern Western Political Thought:* p. 127.

▶ 5. For more information about women in the revolutionary period, see Sara M. Evans, *Born for Liberty: A History of Women in America* (New York: Free Press, 1989).

▶ 6. E. James Ferguson, *The American Revolution: A General History, 1763–1790* (Homewood, IL: Dorsey Press, 1974), p. 139; for a discussion of the meaning of the revolution for social, political, and economic life, see Gordon S. Wood, *The Radicalism of the American Revolution* (New York: Vintage, 1991).

7. For an easily readable account of the Constitutional Convention, see Catherine Drinker Bowen, *Miracle at Philadelphia.* For more in-depth coverage, see Max Farrand, ed., *The Records of the Federal Convention of 1787* (New Haven, CT: Yale University Press, 1966).

▶ 8. See Catherine Drinker Bowen, *Miracle at Philadelphia.*

9. James MacGregor Burns, *The American Experiment: The Vineyard of Liberty* (Knopf, 1982), p. 37.

10. Charles Beard, *An Economic Interpretation of the Constitution* (New York: Macmillan, 1913), p. 324.

▶ 11. Forrest McDonald, *We the People: The Economic Origins of the Constitution* (New Brunswick, NJ: Transaction Publishers, 1992).

▶ 12. James A. Morone, *The Democratic Wish: Popular Participation and the Limits of American Government* (New York: Basic Books, 1990), p. 33.

13. The quote is from Madison's *Federalist Paper No. 45,* in Roy P. Fairfield, ed., *The Federalist Papers* (Baltimore: Johns Hopkins University Press, 1981), p. 137.

14. Forrest McDonald, *We the People,* p. 1.

15. The case was *Hammer v. Dagenhart, 247* U.S. 241 (1918).

16. See Richard Nathan, "Hard Road Ahead: Block Grants and the 'Devolution Revolution,'" Discussion Paper, Nelson Rockefeller Institute of Government, State University of New York, Albany.

17. These figures are drawn from a survey conducted on behalf of the Council for Excellence in Government in March 1995.

18. For a complete history of the Twenty-Seventh Amendment, see Richard Bernstein, "The Sleeper Wakes: The History and Legacy of the Twenty-Seventh Amendment," *Fordham Law Review,* volume 61, number 3 (December 1992), pp. 497–557.

19. *Gallup Poll Monthly,* December 1990.

▶ 20. David M. O'Brien, *Constitutional Law and Politics: Civil Rights and Civil Liberties* (New York: W. W. Norton, 1991), p. 29.

21. For the story of the commission and its gang, see Paul C. Light, *Still Artful Work: The Continuing Politics of Social Security Reform* (New York: McGraw-Hill, 1994).

22. Although some communities challenged the law establishing the commission as a violation of the *nondelegation doctrine,* which says simply that a power given to one or the other branch cannot be delegated to another through legislation, the Supreme Court has consistently denied such claims. As long as Congress sets strict limits on the delegation and reserves a final vote for itself, the Supreme Court does not say "no."

PUBLIC OPINION AND THE MEDIA

T he Founders hoped American government would not pay much attention to **public opinion,** the collected views of Americans on government, politics, and society. They wanted a government headed by virtuous, moral individuals who would worry more about protecting the nation as a whole than the passing concerns of the far less virtuous Americans they represented.

This does not mean the Founders had no interest in knowing what the people thought about the issues of the day. They were experienced politicians in their own right, who would marvel at today's sophisticated techniques for tracking voters late in an election campaign. Had they known how to conduct a scientific poll of public opinion, they probably would have done so to gauge the fight for ratification, perhaps even tailoring *The Federalist Papers* to answer public concerns about the new constitution. After all, they had already promised to add a Bill of Rights in an effort to calm public resistance. In short, the Founders would have viewed public opinion polls as a way to help leaders lead—that is, to help virtuous leaders explain the needs of the nation or the rights of individuals in such a way that the public would give its consent to be governed.

The Consent of the Governed

What would trouble the Founders is the use of public opinion polls to help leaders follow—that is, to determine the best course for the nation by asking the public what it wants. Indeed, it was their concern that government would follow, not lead, that convinced the Founders to insulate government against capture by strong-willed majorities. Hence, they created the system of separate powers, separate interests, separate layers, and checks and balances that would insulate each branch from the others. Even if a strong-willed majority somehow captured the House, for example, it would be buffered by the Senate, the presidency, and the judiciary.

Although most of the Founders' original buffers are still in place today (though senators are now elected directly by the voters, not indirectly through state legislatures), the Founders would still be troubled by the remarkable volume of public opinion that now flows through American government. Presidents, members of Congress, and the political parties have nearly instant access to every opinion poll conducted, and can easily commission their own polls if they want extra details. Presidents even have their own pollsters, who serve on the White House staff as constant barometers on what the people think. If a strong-willed majority exists out there on a public policy issue such as abortion, national health insurance, or Bosnia, America's leaders are going to know about it.

Because questions about the role of public opinion appear throughout this book, this chapter will provide a much deeper definition of just what public opinion is:

where it comes from, how it is measured, what Americans know about politics, how they divide, and where they unite. The chapter will also examine the role of the media in modern American politics. It is impossible to talk about public opinion without addressing the role of the media (newspapers, television, radio, magazines, even the Internet) in shaping both what the public thinks and what the public thinks about.

PUBLIC OPINION

American government is currently awash in public opinion. Starting in the 1930s when statisticians figured out how a few hundred randomly selected Americans could speak for a nation of millions, the polling business has never stopped growing. Hardly a day goes by without some new polling effort to find out what Americans think about politics and society. (**Polling** is a term that refers to the collection of public opinion by asking a small number of individuals the same set of questions about a given topic.)

Nevertheless, polling has been part of American politics for at least two hundred years. Newspapers have been conducting polls since the early 1800s when the *Harrisburg Pennsylvanian* and *Raleigh Star* began tracking public support for the presidential candidates. By the early 1900s, newspapers were routinely running "straw polls" of voters, an unscientific version of polling that asks people who happen to show up on a street corner what they think about a given issue. Like throwing a piece of straw into the air, such polls can only reveal the opinions of people who happen to pass by, and are notorious for their errors.

Although polling has become more scientific over time, its purpose has never changed: to find out what the American public thinks. It is important to note, however, that public *opinions* are different from public *beliefs*. Beliefs are the most basic, long-term commitments people have, and are often rooted in their religious and social backgrounds: a belief in God, in the importance of hard work, equal opportunity for all, government by the people. Opinions flow in part from these beliefs but are much more responsive to short-term events. Opinions are specific responses to immediate issues. Opinions change, beliefs are much more durable.

It is also important to note that polling is designed to measure more than just the simple number of people who favor one issue or another at a specific point in time. They also want to measure the *direction* of opinion—whether the public is moving one way or the other on some issue—and the *intensity* of opinion—how strongly people feel about their position. Not all opinions are held strongly. It is entirely possible, for example, that a small minority of Americans will have stronger feelings about abortion or gun control than the vast majority.

Where Opinions Come From

Public opinions are shaped by the public's underlying beliefs about politics and government, which are, in turn, learned in childhood and adolescence in a process called **political socialization.** Even preschoolers are likely to form general opinions about government as they encounter police officers and firefighters, and as they celebrate holidays such as the Fourth of July. Although such early experiences tend to build a core of often glossy patriotic beliefs about their country, children rarely develop specific opinions about who gets what, when, and how from government until they reach adolescence.

The Impact of Events. As children grow older, events become more important in shaping what they believe about government. And many events tend to take the shine off children's early patriotism. Just imagine the effect of the Rodney King beating and the resulting Los Angeles riots on children. Because they have yet to be "inoculated" by age and experience, and because events often come into the home live and unvarnished on television, children and adolescents can carry the effect of particularly dramatic events throughout their political lives.

Robert F. Kennedy, Edward Kennedy, and John F. Kennedy confer in 1959 (top left), Martin Luther King in 1967 (top right), and a scene from the Vietnam War in 1965 (bottom left). The assassinations of Robert Kennedy, John Kennedy, and Martin Luther King, and an unpopular war all contributed to declining trust in government during the 1960s. By the early 1970s, children had stopped thinking of their presidents as benevolent and began viewing them as malevolent.

There can be little doubt, for example, that the 1960s left such a mark on the children of the era. The war in Vietnam, the civil rights movement, the urban unrest of the mid-1960s, and the assassination of three popular leaders—John F. Kennedy, civil rights leader Martin Luther King, and Bobby Kennedy—changed how children viewed the president and politics.

By 1973, research showed that many grade-school children had come to view the president as "truly malevolent, undependable, untrustworthy, yet powerful and dangerous."[1] What a difference as decade had made. When Kennedy was president, roughly half of grade-school children said the president was their favorite politician of all. Ten years later, two-thirds of a new generation of young children said the president was not one of their favorites at all. In the wake of a turbulent decade, the president had gone from a *benevolent* leader in children's minds to a *malevolent* leader.

The Impact of Family, Teachers, and Peers.

Events are not the only way that children learn about government and politics. They also learn from agents of socialization: parents, teachers, friends, brothers, and sisters. As children get older, parents fade as agents, and teachers and friends take on a greater role.

Because parents are one of the few sources of information children have early in life, they play the key role in socializing children to the outside world. They introduce children to the basic concept of government through the rules they set, as well as to the familiar faces of government, mostly police officers and firefighters. They may also introduce children to some of the key policy issues of the day, particularly if they talk about politics around the dinner table and if they agree on most of the issues.[2] Many children can identify a parent's political views even without knowing the first thing about government and politics.

Regardless of who does the socializing, the more children learn about government and politics, the more distrusting they seem to become. As people get older, they tend to see politics and government in less and less trusting terms. Most come to experience government as both a source of help and a limit on individual freedom—it is easy to love government before the Internal Revenue Service takes a bite out of that first paycheck or before that first speeding ticket. Just as a vaccination inoculates children against disease, aging tends to inoculate adolescents and adults against rosy promises, and people come to learn that government is filled with human beings, not childhood heroes.

Socialization does not end with high school, however. People continue learning about politics from a number of agents: their co-workers, college classmates, bosses, churches, spouses, and, eventually, even their children. And they continue to respond to events. The 1960s were not just important for children, for example. Many adults changed how they thought about American government during the period, becoming much more distrusting toward the president. As we will see later, people also learn a great deal about politics from the media.

How Opinions Are Measured

Measuring public opinion has come a long way since one of America's most popular magazines, *Literary Digest,* used a straw poll to predict that Republican Alf Landon would win the 1936 election by a landslide. There was a landslide that year, but it was the Democratic candidate, Franklin Roosevelt, who won. *Literary Digest* went out of business as a result.

Polling today is a science that mixes mathematics, linguistics, and statistical analysis to predict everything from the next election to the sales potential for a new product. There are three parts to an accurate poll: a representative sample, a good question, and a fair interpretation. Each will be discussed briefly below.

The Sample. Most polls use a **random sample** of no more than 1,000 Americans to represent the entire population of 270 million. As pollster George Gallup once argued, an accurate blood test requires only a few drops of blood, not a gallon.

This is not the book to go into the statistical details of random sampling.[3] Suffice it to say that a random sample gives every American an equal and random chance to be interviewed. As long as everyone has this random chance, 1,000 Americans can, indeed, speak for the country—plus or minus three percentage points.[4]

Because samples are not perfect images of the entire public, all polls carry a **sampling error,** which is the degree to which the result could be wrong one way or the other. This error is the simple product of having such a small number of people represent such a large population. Most polls carry a sampling error of plus or minus 3 to 4 percent. This means that pollsters are 95 percent certain that any given question in a survey could be off by 3 to 4 percent in either direction—if one candidate is leading an election campaign by a 52 percent to 49 percent margin, for example, sampling error might mean that the candidate could actually be trailing by the same margin or even be ahead by 55 percent to 46 percent.

The Question. Drawing a random sample is only the first challenge in conducting an accurate poll. The pollster also has to write a good question. It is possible to write a polling question that will make Americans say just about anything.

It is also possible to write a question that generates little more than confusion. Consider the following Roper Poll question from 1992: "As you know, the term Holocaust usually refers to the killing of millions of Jews in Nazi death camps during World War II. Does it seem possible or does it seem impossible to you that the Nazi extermination of the Jews never happened?" The question produced a deeply troubling result: a third of Americans were not sure the Holocaust had occurred, of which 22 percent even said it was entirely "possible" that the Holocaust never occurred.

The problem was in the double negative: does it seem *impossible* that the extermination *never happened?* Many respondents who answered yes actually meant the exact opposite.[5] When the question was changed to whether it seems "possible to you that the Nazi extermination of the Jews never happened, or do you feel certain that it happened?", the number of doubters fell to just 1 percent, with another 8 percent unsure.

The Interpretation. Once the samples are drawn and the questions asked, the challenge is to make the right interpretation of the results. Unfortunately, many Americans read far too much into polls. They tend to believe polls are based on actual behavior, even though respondents sometimes tell a pollster what they think the pollster or society wants to hear.

Take church attendance as an example. Asking someone in a survey whether they went to church last week is quite different from actually watching them walk in the door. People like to express the socially desirable thing. In 1992, Gallup found that 45 percent of Protestants and 51 percent of Catholics said they go to church regularly. However, a study based on actual counts of people in the pews found the rate to be significantly lower: 20 percent of Protestants and 28 percent of Catholics attend church in any given week. Just because students tell their parents they study every night of the week and never party on Thursdays does not make it so.

What Americans Think

As the public opinion polls have piled up over the years, Americans have learned a great deal about themselves. Although the media often pays the greatest attention to divisions, Americans actually share a number of beliefs about government and politics.[6] Consider just a sampling of the agreements.[7]

Americans are *nationalistic*—that is, they take great pride in being Americans. They overwhelmingly describe themselves as patriotic. Nine out of ten feel it is their duty as citizens to vote, and seven out of ten say they feel guilty when they do not get a chance to vote.

Americans are *individualistic*. Nine out of ten Americans say society should do what is necessary to make sure that everyone has an equal chance to succeed, but then let individuals rise or fall on their own. The vast majority of Americans admire people who get rich by working hard, and believe that everyone has it in their own power to succeed. They also believe that the strength of the country is based on the success of American business and a healthy market economy.

Americans are deeply *religious*. Nine out of ten believe that God exists, while eight in ten believe that everyone will be called before God at Judgment Day to answer for their sins. Most Americans also believe in the power of prayer, and say that miracles are performed by the power of God. The vast majority of Americans say that religion, whether formal or informal, plays an important role in their daily lives.

Finally, Americans tend to want government to be *activist* in protecting the quality of their lives. Nine out of ten believe that the country should be active in foreign affairs (even though they also think the nation should pay less attention to problems overseas and concentrate more on problems at home). Similar numbers say the federal government should spend more money to provide education and job training for American workers whose jobs have been cut, and that there should be stricter laws to protect the environment.

All is not agreement, of course. Where Americans tend to divide is when the broad goals conflict—for example, when activism conflicts with religious beliefs on issues such as abortion, gay and lesbian rights, and pornography; when patriotism conflicts with individualism on issues such as flag burning, freedom of speech, and opposition to war; when activism conflicts with individualism on issues such as affirmative action for racial minorities or spending more money on the poor.

Before turning to the differences in opinion in more detail, however, it is first useful to ask how much Americans know about the issues they face. One of the first rules of public opinion polling is that respondents will give answers to questions even if they know absolutely nothing about the topic involved. The result is that at least some polling results are based more on ignorance than on an informed citizenry.

How Much Americans Know.   The Constitution does not require Americans to know anything about government. No one has to take a test to write a letter to Congress, cast a vote in an election, or answer a question in a poll. No one has to pass a course on being a citizen, calling a talk-radio show, or surfing the Internet. Perhaps the Founders knew that most Americans would never pass.

Take basic information about the American government as a first example. Most Americans simply do not know much about either how American government works or who is in charge at any given moment. Only a quarter of Americans know the names of their two U.S. senators, and well over half wrongly believe that foreign aid involves a greater share of the federal budget than health care for the elderly. In fact, Medicare for the elderly dwarfs foreign aid by a margin of well over $10 to $1. (See Box 3–1 for a political pop quiz.)

The lack of information about American government often affects other opinions. Asked in 1974, for example, whether President Nixon should be "impeached and compelled to leave the Presidency" for his role in covering up the Watergate burglary, most Americans said "no." But asked whether "there is enough evidence of possible wrongdoing in the case of President Nixon to bring him to trial before the Senate," which is the technical definition of impeachment, a majority in favor suddenly appeared. Apparently, voters either did not know what impeachment was (it is merely the indictment leading to Senate trial) or did know and felt Nixon should not be convicted without a trial.[8]

A Political Pop Quiz

Answer the following questions to the best of your ability. (The answers given by a national sample of Americans in early 1996 are shown for comparison.)

1. Can you tell me who was president when the Watergate scandal took place? (86 percent of Americans answered this one correctly)

2. As far as you know, is there a limit on the number of terms in office a president of the United States can serve, or not? (81 percent answered correctly)

3. Can you tell me which party—the Democrats or the Republicans—has the most members in the U.S. Senate? (62 percent answered correctly)

4. Can you tell me which party—the Democrats or the Republicans has the most members in the U.S. House of Representatives? (61 percent answered correctly)

5. Can you tell me the name of the current vice president of the United States? (60 percent answered correctly)

6. As far as you know, who has the final responsibility to decide if a law is constitutional or not? (54 percent answered correctly)

7. Can you tell me the name of the Speaker of the U.S. House of Representatives? (53 percent answered correctly)

8. Which party do you think is more conservative: the Republican Party or the Democratic Party? (52 percent answered correctly)

9. Can you tell me the name of the current majority leader of the U.S. Senate? (34 percent answered correctly)

10. How many years is a single term of office for a U.S. Senator? (26 percent answered correctly)

11. Can you tell me the name of the current Chief Justice of the U.S. Supreme Court? (6 percent answered correctly)

Source: The Washington Post, *January 29, 1996, p. A6.*

Pollsters call answers or opinions based on a lack of information **nonattitudes.** Such opinions are not real at all, just a passing response to a pollster's question. Public opinions on the 1975 Public Affairs Act are just one example. Asked in a 1995 survey whether the act should be repealed, 24 percent of Americans said yes, 19 percent said no, and the rest had no opinion. The only problem is that there was no such thing as the Public Affairs Act, meaning that 43 percent of Americans had invented opinions about something they could have known nothing about. The number of respondents ready to answer this false question went ten points higher when they were told that President Clinton and the Republicans in Congress favored repeal.[9]

The problem with such nonattitudes is not just in creating a flawed portrait of what Americans think, but in the very real possibility that government might actually make a hard choice based on artificial opinions. If Congress and the president ignore Medicare in the budget debate because the public thinks it is but a small program, or decide not to commit troops to Bosnia because less than one in ten Americans know where Bosnia is, they will be making decisions on misinformation. And those decisions may turn out to be bad for the nation as a whole or the rights of Americans as individuals.

How Americans Divide. As noted above, Americans may agree on a host of broad social goals, but are sharply divided on the basic role of government in American life. The differences come from two sources: (1) **demographics,** which involve unchangeable personal characteristics such as race, gender, and age, and life experiences such as education and income, and (2) **ideology,** which covers the underlying views of how much government should be involved in the day-to-day activities of American society. Each source of differences will be explored below.

Demographic Characteristics and Life Experiences. Characteristics such as race, gender, and age clearly affect how Americans think about issues, in part because demographic groups are socialized differently. Scholars know, for example, that girls and boys are given very different introductions to life, as are minority children. Scholars also know that people change as they age.

Demographic differences also have some impact on life experiences such as education and income, which translate into **socioeconomic status,** a measure of where individual Americans stand in society relative to everyone else. Socioeconomic status is a blend of education and income. Although not an absolute guarantee of future success, higher education underpins so much of an individual's later experience that it is often seen as the single most important predictor of how people think about politics.

Education and income are not the only personal experiences that matter to politics, however. Religion also plays an important role in an individual's view of politics. In recent years, for example, evangelical Christians have become much more active in election campaigns at all levels of government. Many evangelicals believe that government can play an important role in strengthening the moral fiber of the country.

Other experiences affect public opinion, as well. Where people live, what they do for a living, whether they belong to a labor union, whether they are veterans of war, even whether they are married, divorced, or remarried, all matter to what they think about who gets what, when, and how from government. And the impact of these and other experiences often vary depending on demographics.

Consider how gender, race, age, education, income, and religious preference affected views in 1996 about whether a balanced federal budget would help or hurt individual respondents versus approval of First Lady Hillary Clinton. (See Box 3–2 for a summary of what Americans thought about these two issues in early 1996.)

Women were slightly more likely to see a balanced budget as hurting themselves or their families, and much less likely than men to disapprove of Hillary Clinton. These differences between men and women illustrate the **gender gap,** which first emerged in the 1980s and continues to the present. The gender gap is rooted in the early socialization experiences of men and women, and also reflects the generally poorer economic performance of women.

Non-whites were also likely to see the personal impact of a balanced budget, and even more approving of Hillary Clinton, differences which again emerge from socialization and economic inequality between the races. As we will see, race is one of the most important predictors of how people vote, with African Americans giving the vast majority of their support to Democratic candidates.

Age did not matter much to approval of Hillary Clinton, but clearly shaped views of the balanced budget. Older Americans were the most likely to see a balanced budget as hurting them personally, in large measure because so much of the debate about spending involved Medicare. Young people were also more likely to conclude that a balanced budget hurts, perhaps because they believe their taxes might go up.

Finally, the two measures of socioeconomic status—education and income— made a difference in how Americans think. People who never completed high school were much more likely to see a balanced budget as hurting and somewhat more approving of the First Lady. They may not have completed high school, but these Americans certainly recognized that a smaller federal budget may mean lower funding for programs to help people with lower incomes and poorer job prospects. It is a point that is well supported by the figures on family income. People with lower incomes were more likely to see a balanced budget as hurting, and far less likely to see it as helping, than those with higher incomes.

Ideology. Alongside demographics and life experiences, Americans also divide by ideology—that is, their general view of how involved government should be in society.

Some Americans believe, for example, that government should play a strong role in solving social problems, intervening where necessary to create a better society. They believe it is the job of government to help create jobs, assure equal opportunity, clean up the environment, provide a base of support for poor people, and protect the rights of people accused of crimes. Such self-described **liberals,** as they are labeled, constitute roughly a quarter of all Americans, and just about a quarter of college students.

BOX 3-2

Attitudes by Group on a Balanced Budget and Hillary Clinton

	Impact of Balanced Budget		View of Hillary Clinton	
	Help	Hurt/Not Affect	Favorable	Unfavorable
Gender				
Male	45%	51%	36%	61%
Female	36	58	48	48
Race				
White	41%	53%	39%	58%
Nonwhite	34	61	63	32
Black	34	62	67	27
Age				
Under 30	41%	57%	45%	51%
30–49	45	50	42	56
50–64	45	50	38	57
65 and Older	24	67	43	51
Education				
Less than High School	33%	60%	46%	47%
High School Graduate	41	54	41	56
Some College	42	54	41	56
College Graduate	44	51	43	54
Yearly Family Income				
Less than $20,000	39%	54%	47%	48%
$20,000–$29,999	33	62	39	60
$30,000–$49,999	42	53	44	52
$50,000–$74,999	46	52	38	61
$75,000 and Over	51	47	36	62
Religious Preference				
White Protestant	41%	54%	36%	60%
White Protestant Evangelical	39	56	25	71
White Protestant Non-Evangelical	44	51	46	50
White Catholic	43	53	37	61

Source: "Balanced Budget a Public Priority, But Few See Personal Payoff," Pew Research Center for The People & The Press News Release, January 18, 1996, pp. 11-12, 16-17. The questions were: "What's your opinion ... if the federal budget is balanced in seven years, do you think it will help you and your family financially, hurt you and your family financially, or not affect you and your family financially?" and "Would you say your overall opinion of Hillary Clinton is very favorable, mostly favorable, or very unfavorable?"

Other Americans believe that government should play a much more limited role in solving the nation's problems, letting individuals rise and fall on their own without help one way or the other. They tend to argue that it is the job of the market economy to create jobs, hire good people, use the environment wisely, and support the less fortunate primarily through private charities. They generally take a harder line on crime, and believe that it is the job of government to protect citizens from crime, not criminals from prosecution. These self-described **conservatives** account for roughly a third of all Americans, but only a fifth of college students.

Still other Americans are caught in the middle. These **moderates** tend to see benefits of intervention on some issues and limited government on others. Moderates account for roughly a third of all Americans, but almost 50 percent of all college students.

Interestingly, the mix of self-reported liberals, conservatives, and moderates in America as a whole and on college campuses has remained relatively stable over time, with an ever-so-slight shift toward conservative in recent years. Americans seem rather content not to come to final closure on most issues, with a vast middle ground that sometimes gets forgotten in the heat of national debates over abortion, budget cuts, or presidential campaigns. (See Box 3–3 for the number of liberals, conservatives, and moderates over the past two decades.)

There is some debate about whether and how ideology shapes actual public opinions. Do most people say to themselves "I am a liberal; therefore, I support policy X idea?" Or do most people mix and match issues together and say to themselves "I support policy X and policy Y; therefore I am a liberal?"

Some political scientists argue that most Americans are not capable of using ideology to shape other decisions. It simply takes too much discipline. The authors of one of the most famous books on voting and elections, *The American Voter,* concluded that only 15 percent of 1950s-era voters were sophisticated enough to use ideology to package their views of candidates and political parties.[10] Things had changed so little by the end of the 1980s that political scientist Eric Smith decided to title his investigation of public ideology *The Unchanging American Voter.*[11]

A small but growing number of political scientists believe that the American public is quite right not to think ideologically. The world is hardly a simple liberal-conservative place. Moreover, just because some of the issue positions do not fit a particular definition of consistency or sophistication does not mean the public is incapable of thoughtful judgment.[12]

Most Americans turn out to be rather balanced on even the most divisive issues. They make tough choices about when abortion should be permitted and when it should not, when spotted owls should be protected, and when old-growth forests should be cut. Indeed, the American public may be far less volatile or unpredictable than the Founders once believed. There is ample evidence that they are quite predictable in their views. Although the public may be uninformed about

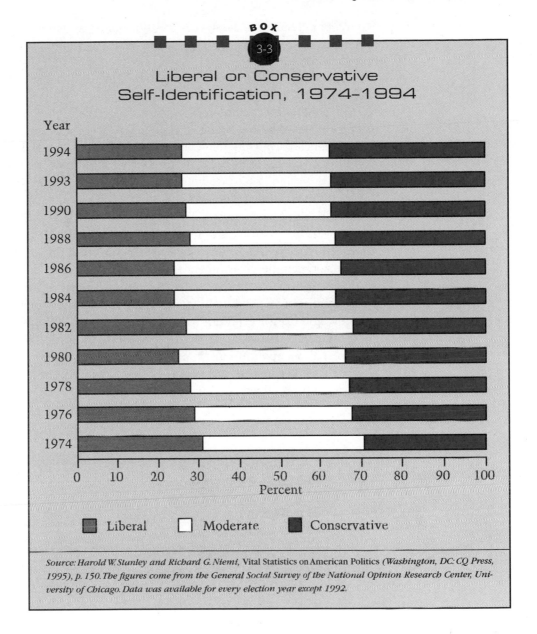

BOX 3-3

Liberal or Conservative Self-Identification, 1974–1994

Source: Harold W. Stanley and Richard G. Niemi, *Vital Statistics on American Politics (Washington, DC: CQ Press, 1995), p. 150. The figures come from the General Social Survey of the National Opinion Research Center, University of Chicago. Data was available for every election year except 1992.*

the details of many policy decisions, they have remarkable common sense when given the facts.

The Angry American. Although Americans disagree on many issues, they are almost uniformly angry toward government. By 1995, 93 percent of Americans said that government wastes too much of their money; 88 percent believed that leaders say what they think will get them elected, not what they are really thinking; 73 percent agreed politicians work for themselves and their own careers, not for the people they represent; and 70 percent said government is run for the benefit of special interests.

Pollsters seem unable to write a question that might prompt a favorable view of government and its leaders. As E. J. Dionne writes in his popular book, *Why Americans Hate Politics,* "At the very moment when democracy is blossoming in Eastern Europe, it is decaying in the United States. Over the last three decades, the faith of the American people in their Democratic institutions has declined, and Americans have begun to doubt their ability to improve the world through politics."[13]

Take trust in Washington to do what is right as one example. In 1958, 16 percent of the public said they could "always" trust Washington to do what was right, 57 percent said "most of the time," 23 percent said "only some of the time," and none said "never." By 1994, just 1 percent answered "always," 19 percent said "most of the time," and the majority of Americans, 74 percent, said "only some of the time." Five percent said that the government never can be trusted to do what is right.[14]

The trend is undeniable. In the 1950s, the vast majority of Americans said public officials cared about what they thought, believed that government did not waste much money, and felt government was run for the benefit of all the people.[15] By the 1990s, the numbers were exactly the opposite. Americans had come to believe the worst about government, in part because of the inability to win the Vietnam War, in part because of the Watergate scandal, in part because of poor economic performance over the decades.[16]

IN A DIFFERENT LIGHT

DELIBERATIVE POLLS

Given the low levels of information that Americans bring to politics, some political scientists have wondered what Americans might think if they actually had the facts. What would they think about Bosnia, for example, if they knew what the war is about? What would they think about welfare if they knew more about how today's global economy works?

It was precisely to get the answers to such questions that the University of Texas and the Public Broadcasting System (PBS) teamed up to conduct what they billed as the nation's first "deliberative poll." Unlike a traditional poll, which merely asks respondents for their opinions at a given point in time, a deliberative poll first gives respondents detailed information on the issues, and only then asks for their opinions. Toward that end, organizers of the deliberative poll invited 450 randomly selected Americans to Austin for three days in early 1996. By comparing interviews after the event with interviews taken before, organizers hoped to learn whether information changes public opinion.[17]

For its part, the poll would get everyone to Austin, Texas (airfare was donated by American Airlines), provide free meals and lodging, and give each respondent $325 for expenses. In return, the respondents would read some background materials on issues such as foreign aid and international trade, meet in small groups to debate their views, and listen to presentations by the Democratic and Republican presidential candidates. If everything worked, the deliberative poll would provide a snapshot of what a random sample of Americans would think about the issues if they actually had the facts.

The poll's organizers believe that is exactly what their poll did. The poll was able to convince 450 Americans to come to Austin on what was a very cold and dreary weekend. Of those who came, roughly a quarter had never flown in an airplane before, and several did not have the picture ID to get through the airport. (They were sent to get a Sam's Club card.) At the very least, the 450 respondents who gathered in the University of Texas auditorium gave the rest of the country a rare chance to see the remarkable diversity of America collected in one place: farmers, welfare mothers, corporate lawyers, schoolteachers, housewives, the unemployed, young and old, rich and poor.

Alongside small changes in their views of government and society, the 450 respondents also became more trusting toward their government. The number who strongly agreed that they had opinions about politics worth listening to jumped from 41 percent before the event to 68 percent at the end, while the number who said public officials care about what the people think increased from 41 percent to 51 percent. Those are big jumps given the long-term decline in public trust documented elsewhere in this chapter.

Although the event had its flaws as a polling technique, not the least of which was that it cost $4 million to conduct, it does show that knowledge does affect public opinions. As Thomas Jefferson once argued: "I know of no safe depository of the ultimate powers of the society but the people themselves. . . . If we think them not enlightened enough to exercise their control with a wholesome discretion, the remedy is not to take from them but to inform their discretion by education." The deliberative poll shows one way to do so.

THE MEDIA AND PUBLIC OPINION

The Founders saw the role of the media in government as uncomplicated: the three branches would make, execute, and interpret the laws, and the media would tell the people whatever the government wanted them to hear. As such, the media would be little more than a passive instrument for sending messages downward.

Over the years, of course, the role of the media has become anything but passive. To be sure, the media still send messages downward to the people on behalf of government, and are often manipulated to do so against their better judgment. Yet, the media also send messages back upward from the people, whether in publishing public opinion polls or in covering stories that government would rather ignore. And by picking and choosing among the many stories that they could cover, the media also shape what the public thinks is important. As one observer said, the media do not tell the people what to think, but most certainly tell the people what to think *about*.

A Brief History of the Media and Politics

People have always used the media to communicate. Whether prehistoric drawings on a cave wall or e-mail on the Internet, the role of media has remained the same over history: send messages across, up, and down society, recording history and public opinion along the way.

That was certainly the role of the media in 1787 when the Founders met to design their new government. Back then, the media consisted mostly of printed communication—newspapers, occasional magazines, and pamphlets of one kind or another. Although town criers did their share of communicating, too—a rather primitive version of the ten o'clock news—most information traveled on the printed page.

Benjamin Franklin, who would later be a delegate to the Philadelphia convention, was one of the first publishers in the colonies, launching his *Pennsylvania Gazette* in 1729. Having started out as a printer, Franklin had a remarkable influence on the newspaper profession, proving that newspapers could be both profitable and respectable at the same time. As America grew, so did the newspaper business. By 1750, six colonies had weekly papers; by the 1780s, the number was up to all thirteen. The first daily paper appeared in 1783, a faster form of communication that spread rapidly to other large cities.

Although the Founders protected freedom of the press in the very first amendment in the Bill of Rights, it is not clear just how they viewed the role of the press in their new government. On the one hand, they most certainly understood the need for protection. They did not talk much about freedom of the press in the convention largely because the press could remain free on its own. On the other hand, they certainly recognized the importance of the press in shaping public opinion. After all, *The Federalist Papers* appeared one by one in the semiweekly *New York Journal* from October 1787 to April 1788.

Yet, for most of America's first one hundred years, freedom of the press largely meant publishing what government wanted the people to read. Until the mid-1800s, for example, the House and Senate did not publish their own records. The majority party gave this lucrative business to newspapers that provided favorable coverage. Once Congress began publishing the *Congressional Record* on its own in 1860, newspapers had more freedom to print the news as they saw fit. For the most part, however, the news that they saw fit to print was the news the government saw fit to provide.

It was not until the late 1800s that the press took on a more adversarial role. With their government business cut off, publishers had no choice but to sell papers through the headlines. The drive for sensational stories led to the "yellow journalism" of the period—outrageous stories and inflated headlines that might even make the *National Enquirer* uncomfortable. It was yellow journalism, for example, that created the war hysteria that led in part to the Spanish-American War in 1898. "The Whole Country Thrills with War Fever" was the sensational headline in the *New York Journal* following the sinking of the U.S.S. Maine in Havana harbor.[18]

In the midst of all the excess, a special brand of reporter emerged called the "muckraker." Muckrakers saw their job as telling the truth about the world as they saw it—whether about meatpacking plants or child labor. Mostly publishing their work in magazines, muckrakers had a dramatic impact on public opinion. Upton Sinclair's famous novel *The Jungle,* about meatpacking plants, led directly to federal regulation of food safety. *Cosmopolitan,* which is now a glamour magazine, was once a popular vehicle for muckraking, running stories on the "Treason of the Senate" and the sordid careers of America's leading millionaires. It was a new role for the media. Instead of just printing what the government wanted to tell, newspapers and magazines began to show the world as it was.

New technologies could only enhance this new power to communicate. Starting in the 1920s, Americans could get their news on radio, giving information an intimacy that the printed media simply could not match. And starting in the 1950s with television, Americans no longer even needed a reporter to interpret the news: they could hear and watch the events unfolding live and in chilling detail. As Americans enter the twenty-first century, the media are about to make another leap forward, this time on the Internet. But whatever the technology, the role of the media will remain the same: communicate across, up, and down society.

The Four Roles of the Media Today

Whatever the technology, the media do not exist to provide a free service. They exist to make money. They cover government and politics in large part because there are viewers and readers to be found. The reason the media seem preoccupied with the unseemly side of politics—the scandals, the waste, the negative— is that controversy sells. However, even as they make money, the media play four key roles in mediating the dialogue between citizens and government: information source, opinion maker, agenda setter, and government instrument.

The Media as a Source of Information.   The news is more than raw controversy. It starts with information about events and people. The standard news story begins with six questions: who, what, when, where, why, and how?

The public clearly relies on the news for the basics of American politics. (See Box 3–4 for a list of sources Americans use for following politics.) Each source

BOX 3-4

Where Americans Get Political News

Percent of Americans who regularly or sometimes use the following sources of information on government and politics:

TV news magazines (*Sixty Minutes, 20/20,* etc.)	87%
TV evening news programs	81
Daily newspapers	74
Cable News Network (CNN)	69
TV "tabloid" shows (*Hard Copy, Inside Edition,* etc.)	64
Newsmagazines (*Time, Newsweek,* etc.)	59
Radio news	52
Talk radio shows	46
C-SPAN live coverage	35
MacNeil/Lehrer (Public Broadcasting's Evening News)	30
National Public Radio	27
Business Magazines (*Fortune, Business Week,* etc.)	26
Rush Limbaugh	26
MTV	25
Tabloid newspapers (*National Enquirer,* etc.)	18
Imus in the Morning (New York talk radio show)	8
Howard Stern (New York talk radio show)	7

Source: *Times Mirror Center for The People & The Press, "The People, the Press & Politics: The New Political Landscape," September 21, 1994, poll release, p. 110.*

provides somewhat different kinds of information. C-SPAN, the television network that provides live coverage of political events, is the purest source of information the public has. There are no interruptions of its live Senate and House coverage, no interviews on the floor of the conventions, no post-debate analysis, and, most importantly, no interpretation. People who watch C-SPAN have to form their own opinions.

MTV is one of the newest players in the news business. Although MTV and its anchor, Tabitha Soren, provide solid factual coverage of political events, they sometimes feature an unusual cast of correspondents. Megadeath's Dave Mustaine conducted floor interviews at the 1992 Democratic National Convention, while rapper M. C. Lyte added comments on the party's platform. Ted Nugent filled both jobs at the Republican National Convention the same year. As for setting the stage for traditional reports, MTV showed a clip of then-Vice President Dan Quayle delivering a campaign speech with R.E.M.'s "Shiny Happy People" as the background music, and introduced vice presidential candidate Al Gore with Arrested Development's "Tennessee" in honor of the candidate's home state.

MTV is not just interested in providing raw information, however. Its coverage is also designed in part to encourage the political participation of its viewers. For the 1992 election, MTV mounted a $1 million "Choose or Lose" campaign designed to educate its audience on the issues. The "Choose or Lose" spots were often paired back-to-back with "Rock the Vote" spots. Madonna regularly appeared on the announcements, even though she was not registered to vote herself.[19] The campaign seemed to work—MTV surveys found that 76 percent of its viewers were very likely or almost certain to vote. MTV polls also showed that its viewers preferred Bill Clinton to George Bush by 24 points.[20]

The Media as Opinion Maker. The media are rarely just a passive instrument for providing information. Reporters often put a "spin," or angle, on the news

Republican presidential candidate Bob Dole appears on MTV with news anchor Tabitha Soren. MTV entered the news business in the 1992 presidential campaign with its "Choose or Lose" campaign and continued the effort in 1996.

that helps Americans interpret what they are hearing. In turn, this spin affects how Americans think about politics and government.

Almost all reporters spin to one degree or the other, and there is little doubt that the spinning has gotten more negative in recent years. "The voters begin each campaign without a firm opinion of the candidates," writes media expert Thomas Patterson, "but after months of news that tells them over and over again that their choices are no good, they believe it."[21]

Patterson seems to have the numbers to prove it. Campaign coverage has gotten steadily more negative over the past thirty years. In 1960, for example, the number of "good news" stories about the candidates outnumbered the "bad news" stories by roughly four to one. The ratio of good to bad steadily dwindled during the Vietnam War, and continued downward during the 1970s and 1980s. By 1992, the number of bad news stories outweighed the good by a ratio of roughly 1.5 to 1.[22]

The Media as Agenda Setter.   Editing the news involves tough decisions about what to cover and what to ignore. After all, there are only so many pages in a paper (and only one front page) and so many minutes in a broadcast (and only one opening image). These choices have an important bearing on what the public comes to believe are the most important issues in the country. Today's headline might be the subject of tomorrow's legislative hearing or presidential press conference.

Once past events that cannot be ignored (elections, crises, and natural disasters), the media have significant discretion in setting the news agenda. In doing so, the media may create the impression that certain problems are more important than others. As such, the media have a profound impact on the *intensity* of public opinion. The more compelling the story, the more likely the public will say that a problem is very important. The media may not be able to tell Americans what to think, but they may be remarkably effective in telling them what to think about.[23] And, to the extent that agenda setting shows up in polls, the public will be telling politicians what to act upon.

Not all media have the same influence on public opinion, however. Under the old adage that "seeing is believing," a majority of Americans trust television news the most, with newspapers, radio, and magazines far behind.[24] Although television may not be able to create the depth of understanding that comes from the printed media, if only because most stories last but a minute or two, it is able to convey the kind of searing images that stay with viewers longer.

The Media as an Instrument of Government.   Much as reporters swear by their independence from governments they cover, they are sometimes used by government to send selective messages. Remember, the media exist as a business. Getting the edge on a story, even if it is planted by the government, might boost viewership, in turn, boosting advertising revenue.

There are a variety of ways that government tries to use the media to its advantage, not the least of which is shaping the news through press conferences and news releases. As the media have become accustomed to ignoring releases, government has become more skilled at manipulation. Presidents and members of Congress can always "leak," or secretly release, a piece of information, hoping that a newspaper or television network will jump on the news just because it is secret.

Presidents and members of Congress can also try to put their own interpretation on the news. Such efforts have grown so visible over the years that they are now known by a simple term: "spin control." The White House even has a special unit, the Office of Communications, completely dedicated to shaping what the media think about the news.[25] Its goal is simple: get the president on the evening news, where a picture is truly worth a thousand words.

A Declining Market

The public has few sources of absolutely pure information. Even the Internet, which is often characterized as an untamed frontier of information, is becoming populated by a growing amount of carefully crafted messages and advertising. Moreover, even the most neutral television or newspaper story almost always has a spin, whether given by reporters (who tend to be moderate to liberal), their publishers (who tend to be conservative), or the political leaders they talk to.

It should also be clear that there is no single source of information that might somehow tie citizens together—not unless the story involves catastrophe. Americans will tune in together to watch coverage of the space shuttle Challenger explosion in 1986, the Los Angeles riots in 1992, and the Oklahoma City bombing in 1995, but little else. Fox TV's *Living Single,* for example, was the number one rated show among African American viewers in 1995, but the number 110 show for whites; NBC's *Seinfeld* was the number one show among whites, but number 109 among African Americans.[26]

Over the past thirty years, loyalty to any single media source has declined. Americans may say they trust television for the bulk of their information, but which of the eighty-eight channels do they watch? Gone are the days when the big three networks (actually big two in the 1950s before the upstart ABC launched itself) could guarantee consistent audience share. Gone are the days when the *New York Times, Washington Post,* and the *Wall Street Journal,* along with a handful of other national papers, could set the newspaper agenda.

The trends are in the numbers. The number of Americans who read a newspaper, any newspaper, for any topic—comics, movie reviews, sports, or campaign coverage—fell by nearly 25 percent between 1970 and 1995, as did the combined audiences of the three networks. The networks held a 77 share of the TV audience in 1980—a share equaling 1 percent of all households watching television—

but only a 51 share by 1995.[27] One reason for the network decline: The percentage of homes with cable TV increased from 20 percent in 1980 to roughly 65 percent by 1995.

Newspapers have been the hardest hit by the declining attention. Circulation hit a high of 66 million in 1967, and has been falling ever since. Television first passed newspapers as the public's primary source of news in 1963 and has never looked back.[28]

If Americans are getting more and more of their political information from television—and polls say they are—it is not from the evening news. Many are turning instead to the Cable News Network (CNN), where more than one third of Americans tune in during any given week. Others are watching *Hard Copy* and calling it news. Still others watch *The 700 Club, Oprah Winfrey,* or *Larry King Live,* or hear Rush Limbaugh on the way to work. As the number of VCRs increased from just 1 percent of all households in 1980 to 72.5 percent in 1992, some are just tuning in a video instead.[29]

Part of the separation from the traditional media can be traced to the same public distrust that has plagued government. As one observer remarked in 1993, reporters used to be "of the people, not above the people." Indeed, they were portrayed in popular culture as ordinary people with family values. The image was not that far from reality. In real life, reporters were "typically underpaid, unsophisticated, chain-smoking, hard-drinking, blue-collar, salt-of-the-earth types" who "stood up for the 'little guy.'"[30]

Today, reporters often travel in the same social circles as the well-to-do officials they cover. According to Hodding Carter, former press secretary to Jimmy Carter and now a senior ABC analyst, "The top journalists move in packs with the affluent and powerful in Washington. They swarm with them in the summer to every agreeable spot on the Eastern Seaboard. When any three or four of them sit down together on a television talk show, it is not difficult to remember that the least well paid of these pontificators make at least six times more each year than the average American family."[31]

The public seems to agree. According to a 1993 *Los Angeles Times* poll, Americans faulted reporters on a number of levels. Nearly two in three felt that most reporters were just concerned with getting a good story and not worried about hurting people, rather than balancing their desire to get a good story with concern about hurting people. Roughly the same number believed that the press looks out mainly for powerful people, rather than looking out mainly for ordinary people. Almost nine in ten thought that the media should protect the interests of people like themselves, but only half actually felt that the media were doing so.[32]

In short, the public believes that the media have lost touch with ordinary America, rarely able to see beyond their own cynical view of the subject they cover. As *Atlantic Monthly* editor James Fallows writes, "a relentless emphasis on the cynical game of politics threatens public life itself, by implying day after day that the political sphere is nothing more than an arena in which ambitious politicians

Dole appears on the airport tarmac before the crucial South Carolina primary in late February 1996. Much of the media coverage focused on the horse race between Dole and his chief opponent Phil Gramm (right).

struggle for dominance, rather than a structure in which citizens can deal with worrisome collective problems."[33] At some point, the cynicism the media show toward those they cover has to rub off

IN A DIFFERENT LIGHT

CIVIC JOURNALISM

Americans view the media as both a friend and an enemy of democracy. On the one hand, Americans expect the media to tell it like it is. If there is corruption, nail it. If there is crime, show it. If the bad guys are in charge, report it. On the other hand, Americans have come to believe that the media are just as corrupt and unhelpful as the rest of politics.

Anger toward television news and newspapers has skyrocketed, catching up with anger toward government in record time. The number of Americans who have a great deal or some confidence in television and newspapers fell from roughly 50 percent in 1988 to just over 20 percent today. By 1994, 70 percent of Americans said the media had come to "stand in the way of America solving its problems."[34]

This plunge in public support has led some journalists to argue for a change in how the media work. Instead of concentrating just on the bad news, they believe the media should become a partner with citizens in improving communities, solving problems, even giving citizens a voice in saying which stories get covered. These advocates label their cause public or **civic journalism.** As one of the Founders of the movement defines the term: "It's a set of practices in which journalists attempt to reconnect with citizens, improve public discussion and generally try to make public life go well."[35]

As such, civic journalism involves everything from conducting a local deliberative poll to producing in-depth stories on what citizens say are the most important issues in their communities. The *Portland Press Herald* and *Minneapolis Star-Tribune* have sponsored neighborhood meetings in which citizens meet to discuss public issues. The *Daily Oklahoman* and *Boulder Daily Camera* have convened discussions among community leaders to create solutions to local problems. The *Wichita Eagle, Charlotte Observer,* and *Tallahassee Democrat* have all used deliberative polls of one kind or another to determine which issues they will cover in election campaigns. In all of these examples, citizens get a say in telling the media what to cover.

On the positive side, civic journalism invites citizens to participate in solving local problems and opens the press to hearing about problems from a different perspective. In 1994, for example, the *Boston Globe* launched its election coverage with a series of polls asking citizens what issues they wanted talked about in the campaign, and later matched candidate positions on those issues against citizen positions. The *Globe* also ran stories on how citizens could learn more about the issues, and even offered advice on how to get involved in the campaign.

On the negative side, some critics argue that civic journalism invites citizens too far into the newsroom. "Too much of what's called public journalism appears to be what our promotion department does," says *Washington Post* editor Leonard Downie, "only with a different kind of name and a fancy, evangelistic fervor."[36] At what point, for example, does an effort to convene community leaders to solve local problems compromise a paper's ability to cover those same leaders when they go wrong? At what point does letting citizens set the election news agenda compromise a television station's judgment about the stories people need to hear?

The answer to such questions is that reporters must always take care that they do not become cheerleaders for false hopes. At the same time, however, telling it like it is hardly matters if people get so disgusted with the negative spins that they no longer read the newspaper or watch the news. Giving the public a greater voice in setting the news agenda is more than just good for the news business, it also appears to be good for communities.

■ ■ ■

The Rise of the New Media

Declining trust in the networks and the national press may explain why citizens and candidates are spending more time with new media such as cable television, specialized magazines, talk radio, and the Internet, all of which give consumers far greater control over what they see and hear. Not only do the new media provide more places to obtain information, government and its leaders can use the new media to get to the voters with much greater ease.

Take television talk shows as an example. In 1992 the three presidential candidates appeared ninety-six times on talk shows: *Donahue* hosted four visits, including three by Bill Clinton; CNN's *Larry King Live* and ABC's *Good Morning America* each hosted thirteen; NBC's *Today Show* hosted ten; CBS's *This Morning* hosted twenty-one.[37] As the list suggests, the candidates preferred the cheerful settings of *Good Morning America* and the *Today Show* to the hard questioning of *Meet the Press, 20/20,* or *Sixty Minutes.*

Bill Clinton was by far the most active guest of the talk shows, accounting for forty-seven, or almost half of the ninety-six appearances. He had breakfast with the American people—or at least the ones watching morning news programs—forty times during the campaign. Not that Clinton slighted the late-night audience. He also showed up on Fox's *Arsenio Hall* to wear his shades and play his saxophone. Ross Perot was the second most active guest on the talk shows with thirty-three appearances over the campaign season. George Bush trailed both with seventeen appearances.

As for hard questioners, ABC's Sam Donaldson faced Bush and Clinton once, but never Perot; *ABC Nightline* anchor Ted Koppel and *CBS Evening News* anchor Dan Rather got no interviews at all.

What the New Media Provides. The most important feature of the new media is choice. Consumers have a much greater say in what they get and when they get it. There has been a significant increase in what might be called *raw* information—information that goes to citizens direct and untouched by the reporters they have grown to distrust.

The new media offer more than just a vast inventory of choices, however. They give individual Americans unparalled access to instant information and greater control over the messages they receive, even as they give government and its leaders a greater ability to target information to specific audiences and demographic groups.

For individual viewers, the new media provide much greater access to information when each viewer wants it. No longer must readers wait for the morning paper to find out what happened the night before—they can tune into CNN for an instant update, or get a quick update from the Internet. No longer must they wait until the end of the week for their favorite magazine—they can almost always find a cable channel that specializes in their favorite sport or hobby, and can find an electronic "home page" on just about any subject.

The new media give the viewer, not the editor or producer, the power to determine when the news comes in and what gets read and seen. The viewer, not the network, decides when the news is relevant, whether by setting the VCR to record a presidential debate, tuning in *CNN Headline News* at 2:00 A.M., or plugging in a ten-minute candidate "infomercial." In a sense, each viewer can become his or her own "network program executive," choosing what to watch and when to watch it, using a handheld remote to "zap" through programming with the flick of a finger.[38]

Even as the new media give the viewer more control over what gets watched, they give candidates much greater ability to target messages to specific audiences. Candidates can reach the elderly on the QVC shopping network in the morning, news junkies on *CNN Headline News* in the afternoon, trial lawyers on Court TV after dinner, and young Americans on MTV after everyone else goes to bed, and never the audiences shall meet. Such strategies reflect a change from **broadcasting,** in which messages go out to all viewers on a single network, to **narrowcasting,** which goes out to much smaller numbers of people on highly specialized channels.

This does not mean, however, that the new media are somehow more democratic. Many of the new media are controlled by a small number of very large corporations such as Time Warner, which owns TBS, *Time* magazine, and a large number of cable stations; Viacom, which owns Paramount Pictures, Blockbuster Video, Simon & Schuster, and MTV; and last but not least, the Walt Disney Corporation, which already owned Touchstone and Walt Disney Pictures, Hyperion Publishing, and The Mighty Ducks hockey team before paying $19 billion in 1995 for Capital Cities/ABC, which owns ABC television, EPSN and ESPN2, A&E and Lifetime Television, and *The Kansas City Star.*

The Newest of the New. No one knows just what the future of the media holds. New magazines will come and go; new technologies will rise and fall. For the time being, however, the two newest new media are talk radio and the Internet, both of which substantially increase interaction between those who talk and those who listen. Only time will tell whether either will survive.

Start with talk radio, one of the fastest growing media in recent history. Between 1982 and 1992, the number of radio stations devoted entirely to talk radio tripled from two hundred to six hundred, a number that does not include the stations that include talk radio somewhere in their daily programming.[39]

Like most new media, talk radio does not talk to everyone. It mainly reaches out to conservatives. It is a very narrow band, indeed. As Bill Clinton argued immediately after the Oklahoma City bombing, talk radio is too often used "to keep some people as paranoid as possible and the rest of us all torn up and upset with each other. They spread hate, they leave the impression, by their very words, that violence is acceptable. . . . It is time we all stood up and spoke against that kind of reckless speech and behavior." Some callers argued, for example, that the bombing was planned and executed by the government itself as a plot to generate public support for greater gun control.[40]

This suggests that talk radio does draw a somewhat narrow audience, although hardly one as extreme as Clinton described. Talk-radio regulars are twice as likely

Howard Stern (left) and Rush Limbaugh (right), two of America's leading talk show hosts. Although once considered more of a disk jockey than talk show host, Stern has become a best-selling author and controversial commentator on political and social issues.

to label themselves as Republicans and conservatives than as Democrats and liberals. They are also more likely to be men, over thirty years old, from the West, and slightly more wealthy and educated than the country as a whole. (One reason talk radio attracts such a conservative audience is that there are few successful liberal talk shows. Conservative Rush Limbaugh reaches 20 million listeners a week on over 600 stations; no liberal hits even a million.) About 30 percent of regulars tune in to keep up on current issues, 20 percent to learn how different people feel, roughly 10 percent each for entertainment and as a forum for public opinion, and just 1 percent because they like the host.[41]

Like talk radio, the Internet (and its associated on-line services) imposes very few barriers to participation. But unlike talk radio, which often binds its listeners to a specific broadcast time, the Internet is open twenty-four hours a day. All a user needs is a personal computer and a modem, and the opportunities for uninterrupted browsing are limitless.

Politicians have been quick to recognize the new audience. All of the 1996 presidential candidates had their own home pages, as do most departments and agencies of the federal government. Most members of Congress have e-mail addresses, as do the president and vice president of the United States. Want to send a message or mail to Bill Clinton? Address it to bclinton@whitehouse.gov. Would you like to receive a government owner's manual? Get on the world wide web and visit http://www.vote-smart.org. (See Box 3–5 for a list of other interesting web sites.)

BOX
3-5

Web Sites on Politics

Politics USA (http://politicsusa.com)
Posted by the National Journal and the American Political Network. Access to polling numbers on just about any topic. Great political games.

AllPolitics (http://allpolitics.com)
A joint venture of *Time* magazine and the Cable News Network (CNN). Up-to-date reporting on the campaigns. Solid background reports on politics in general.

ElectionLine (http://www.electionline.com)
Newsweek reporters contribute to the page. "Soap Box" allows browsers to post their own opinions on current issues. Good archive of old stories on politics from *Newsweek, Washington Post,* and ABC News.

Doonesbury Electronic Town Hall (http//www.doonesbury.com)
Get the latest news from Mike, Duke, Joanie, Zonker, and the crew, plus old comic strips on politics.

Project Vote Smart (http://www.vote-smart.org)
Everything you need to know about your politician—money raised, key votes, ratings by interest groups, a voter's guide to government. Good jokes.

Given the costs of buying a personal computer, it should hardly be a surprise that the most active Internet users are either college graduates with high incomes, or students still in college. And given the newness of the technology, it should not be surprising that young Americans are the most active users of all. While high socioeconomic status (present or future) is an entry price for buying the equipment, youth often seems a prerequisite for learning the ropes.

Internet users are also much more likely to identify themselves as political independents than nonusers, and to be sharply opposed to restrictions on freedom of information. Eighty percent of Internet users believe, for example, that public school libraries should be allowed to carry any books they want, compared to just 50 percent of nonusers; 70 percent of users oppose making it illegal for a computer network to carry pornographic or adult materials, compared to 40 percent of nonusers. Although most Internet users have little sympathy for the kinds of conservative views heard on talk radio, both audiences share a common concern about big government. Among Internet users who participate in on-line discussions of politics—as opposed to those who go on line for e-mail, chat groups, financial information, and games—one in five agreed that while there was no excuse for the Oklahoma City bombing, they could nevertheless understand "the frustrations and anger that may have led people to carry it out."[42]

CONCLUSION

Public opinion and the media are inextricably linked today. How the public thinks about issues clearly influences at least some media coverage, if only because most media must turn a profit to stay in business; how the media covers issues clearly influences what the public thinks, if only because so many Americans rely on the media for basic information about the issues of the day.

As newspaper readership declines and network loyalties evaporate, expect the media to become even more aggressive in courting, some might even say exploiting, the public's attention. If that means playing to the nation's worst fears and deepest divisions, the media seems to be saying "so be it." If that means constantly digging for more dirt on the nation's leaders and institutions, so be it, too.

The problem is that many Americans seem addicted to cynicism. As the cartoon character Pogo once said, "we have met the enemy and it is us." As long as the public pays attention to the latest scandal and freshest dirt, the media may have little choice but to put the stories on page one. "If it bleeds, it leads," or so the old newspaper maxim goes. The reason it leads is that the public reads.

There is hope for the future, however, in the nation's common sense.

In spite of the Founders' worries about human nature, Americans seem remarkably well centered. Staying firmly in the middle on ideology, they are deeply committed to their country, proud of their individualism, and profoundly religious. Ordinary Americans might not be able to pass a citizenship test, but they have a common sense that the Founders might well admire.

This is not to argue that the Founders would embrace direct democracy. Americans show a troublesome tendency to answer polling questions whether they know anything about the issue at hand or not, and seem easily led by the media. They also seem ready to "throw the bums out" at every election, blaming government for much that ails the country. And even though they avoid extremes on most issues, they are deeply divided by gender, race, education, and income.

As if to confirm the strength of the Founders' design, however, no strong-willed majority has yet been able to dominate the three branches at one time. Indeed, the rise of scientific polling actually appears to have created a stalemate of minorities, in which polls get used to justify just about any position an official wishes to defend, leading to a greater risk of complete stalemate. The more Congress and the president pay attention to the numbers, the less they seem ready to act. With so many different polls, and so many different answers, the rising tide of opinion seems to do more to confuse the policy process than drive it forward.

Ironically, as polls have strengthened the public's voice in democracy, the public's trust in democracy has gone down. Trust has gone down for many reasons, of course: wars, inflation, riots, and scandals. Yet, it may also be the case that the more government caters to the public *will* through public opinion polls, the less it responds to the public *need*. The Founders believed that government had to be insulated from the public in order to make virtuous decisions about the future of the nation. To them, giving the people a direct voice meant catering to division and self-interest. Two hundred years later, the division and self-interest have never been more visible, in part because pollsters may get the greatest media attention when they find conflict.

THE BASICS

■ The Founders hoped government would not pay much attention to public opinion in making decisions about who gets what, when, and how. Although leaders could use public opinion to help them explain issues to the public, the Founders would be deeply troubled by the use of polls to help make decisions. Much as they wanted a government that would have the consent of the governed, they did not want government to use public opinion in making decisions about what to do.

■ Although the media often pays its greatest attention to the divisions, Americans share many broad agreements. Americans take great pride in their country, believe that individuals should rise and fall on their own, have deep religious convictions, and want government to be active in protecting their quality of life. Where they often divide is when these agreements collide.

■ Public opinion polling has come a long way since the days straw polls measured views through biased samples of whomever showed up on the street corner. Modern polling is based on scientific samples that allow small numbers of Americans to speak for millions. All that is required for a scientific sample is that every American be given an equal and random chance of being asked. Such random samples are not perfect, however. They carry sampling errors that can move a given result several percentages one way or the other.

■ The media play an important role in shaping public opinion today. The media clearly influence what the people think. As the media have become more independent over the past one hundred years, they have adopted four key roles related to public opinion: (1) they act as a source of information, (2) they often "spin" the news as opinion maker, (3) they help set the agenda of what people think about, and (4) they act as instruments of the government directly or through leaks.

KEY CONCEPTS

■ Polls show that Americans do not know much about the issues of the day. They have very high levels of nonattitudes, which are opinions invented in response to polling questions, and are often confused about specific subjects. The Constitution does not require a test for citizenship, but if it did, many Americans would surely fail.

■ Americans share a number of beliefs about government and politics. They have great pride in their country, believe in individualism, are deeply religious, and want an activist government. Americans tend to divide against each other by demographic characteristics such as race, gender, and age; by life experiences such as education and income, which come together as socioeconomic status; and by their views of government's role in society, which is often labeled ideology.

■ Trust in government has fallen dramatically over the past three decades. In the 1950s, most Americans trusted government to do what was right, and believed that government officials cared about what ordinary people think. A popular book of the early 1990s was quite accurately titled *Why Americans Hate Politics*. Much of the decline in trust began with the Vietnam War and Watergate scandal, and continues with a long list of scandals to this day. Poor economic performance also plays a role in distrust.

■ Public confidence in the media has also fallen over the years, and as it has fallen, so has newspaper circulation and network viewership. As the traditional media have weakened, new media have arisen to take their place in shaping public opinion. Two of the newest of the new media are talk radio and the Internet, each of which has a rather separate audience from the other.

IN A DIFFERENT LIGHT

■ Deliberative polls are designed to measure what Americans might think about issues if they only had more facts. Unlike traditional polls, which merely ask for opinions at a given point in time, deliberative polls give respondents detailed information on the issues, and only then ask for opinions. A national deliberative poll conducted in January 1996 showed that getting more information helps poll respondents form different opinions.

■ Civic journalism reflects an effort to reverse public distrust toward both the media and government by giving citizens more of a say in what stories get covered. Newspapers have been experimenting with a number of ways of taking the lead in improving civic engagement, including convening deliberative polls, sponsoring neighborhood meetings, and encouraging greater citizen involvement in election coverage. Critics of civic journalism believe that the movement weakens the independence of the media.

OPEN QUESTIONS

■ How has socialization to politics changed over the past few decades? What changes in American society have had an impact on how children and young adults are socialized? Does the decline of the traditional two-parent family matter? What about high divorce rates, or changes in how schools operate? Does the Internet now socialize children? And if so, how?

■ Just how much information should citizens have to participate in government and politics? Should there be some minimum test to screen out people who know less? And how would such a test weaken the consent of the governed? (Such tests of knowledge, which were called "literacy tests," were used in the South before the 1960s to deny the vote to African Americans.)

■ To what extent is the media beginning to act as a passive instrument for whatever news the government wants the citizen to read and hear? With so much pure information now available, does the fact that Americans know so little about government and politics matter more?

■ Does the rise of the new media, with its narrowcasting potential, create greater opportunity for division in America? Does it matter if Americans get their news from so many different sources?

TERMS TO REMEMBER

public opinion

polling

political socialization

random sample

sampling error

nonattitudes

demographics

ideology

socioeconomic status

gender gap

liberals

conservatives

moderates

civic journalism

broadcasting

narrowcasting

Endnotes to Chapter 3

1. Christopher Arterton, "The Impact of Watergate on Children's Attitudes toward Political Authority," *Political Science Quarterly,* volume 89, number 2 (June 1974), p. 286.

2. See M. Kent Jennings and Richard Niemi, "Issues and Inheritance in the Formation of Party Identification," *American Journal of Political Science,* volume 35, number 3 (Fall 1991), pp. 970–88.

▶ 3. Those who want to learn more should read Herbert Asher's *Polling and the Public: What Every Citizen Should Know,* second edition (Washington, DC: CQ Press, 1992); see also Michael W. Traugott and Paul J. Lavrakas, *The Voter's Guide to Election Polls* (Chatham, N.J.: Chatham House, 1996).

4. Michael Kagay with Janet Elder, "Numbers Are No Problem for Pollsters. Words Are." *New York Times,* August 9, 1992, p. D4.

5. Quoted in Richard Morin, "From Confusing Questions, Confusing Answers," *Washington Post National Weekly Edition,* July 18–24, 1994, p. 37.

▶ 6. See Seymour Martin Lipset, *American Exceptionalism: A Double-Edged Sword* (New York: W.W. Norton & Company, 1996).

7. The numbers below are drawn from The Times Mirror Center for The People & The Press, *The People, the Press and Politics: The New Political Landscape,* September 21, 1994.

8. See Kagay with Elder, "Numbers Are No Problem for Pollsters," p. D5.

9. Richard Morin, "What Informed Public Opinion," *Washington Post National Weekly Edition,* April 10–16, 1995, p. 36.

10. Angus Campbell, Philip Converse, Warren Miller, and Donald Stokes, *The American Voter* (Chicago: University of Chicago Press, 1960), pp. 216–65.

▶ 11. Eric R. A. N. Smith, *The Unchanging American Voter* (Berkeley: University of California Press, 1989).

▶ 12. See Benjamin Page and Robert Shapiro, *The Rational Public: Fifty Years of Trends in Americans' Policy Preferences* (Chicago: University of Chicago Press, 1992).

13. E. J. Dionne, *Why Americans Hate Politics* (New York: Simon and Schuster/Touchstone, 1991), p. 9.

14. Trend summarized in *The Gallup Poll Monthly,* June 1992, p. 39.

15. Harold W. Stanley and Richard G. Niemi, *Vital Statistics on American Politics* (Washington, D.C.: CQ Press, 1995), p. 157.

▶ 16. For a broader discussion of trust in government, see Stephen C. Craig, *The Malevolent Leaders: Popular Discontent in America* (Boulder, CO: Westview Press, 1993).

17. For a description of the deliberative polling approach, see James S. Fishkin, *Democracy and Deliberation: New Directions for Democratic Reform* (New Haven, CT: Yale University Press, 1991).

▶ 18. See Edwin Emery and Michael Emery, *The Press and America: An Interpretive History of the Mass Media,* fifth edition (Englewood Cliffs, NJ: Prentice-Hall, 1984), pp. 281–98, for a history of the period.

19. Madonna's failure to register was noted in The Freedom Forum Media Studies Center, *The Homestretch: New Politics. New Media. New Voters?* (New York: Freedom Forum, October 1992), p. 24.

20. Judith Miller, "But Can You Dance to It? MTV Turns to News," *New York Times Magazine,* October 11, 1992, p. 32.

▶ 21. Thomas Patterson, *Out of Order* (New York: Knopf, 1993), p. 24.

22. Patterson, *Out of Order,* p. 20.

▶ 23. For thorough discussions of the impact of the media on public opinion, see Doris A. Graber, *Mass Media and American Politics* (Washington, DC: Congressional Quarterly, 1993) and

Shanto Iyengar and Donald R. Kinder, *News that Matters* (Chicago: University of Chicago Press, 1989).

24. Stanley and Niemi, *Vital Statistics,* p. 68.

▶ 25. John Maltese, *Spin Control: The White House Office of Communication and the Management of Presidential News,* revised edition (Chapel Hill, NC: University of North Carolina Press, 1994), pp. 238–39.

26. Noel Holston, "TV Viewing Habits Reveal a Contrast of Black and White," *Minneapolis Star Tribune,* May 3, 1995, p. 11E.

27. Lawrie Mifflin, "Trial Gives Cable Stations Inroads on Top Networks," *New York Times,* February 20, 1995, p. C1.

28. Stanley and Niemi, *Vital Statistics,* p. 68.

29. Stanley and Niemi, *Vital Statistics,* p. 47.

30. Quoted in David Shaw, "Distrustful Public Views Media as 'Them'—Not 'Us,'" *Los Angeles Times,* April 1, 1993, p. A19.

31. In Shaw, "Distrustful Public," p. A19.

32. Poll results in Shaw, "Distrustful Public," p. A19.

▶ 33. James Fallows, "Why Americans Hate the Media," *Atlantic Monthly,* February 1996, p. 55.

34. Times Mirror Center for the People and the Press, *The People, the Press and Politics,* p. 178.

35. The quote is from New York University journalism professor Jay Rosen, quoted in *APME Readership Committee,* August 1994, p. 4; the movement is supported in part by the Pew Center for Civic Journalism in Washington, DC.

36. Tony Case, "Public Journalism Denounced," *Editor & Publisher,* November 12, 1994, p. 14.

37. Dirk Smillie, "Breakfast with Bill, George, and Ross," in The Freedom Forum Media Studies Center, *The Finish Line: Covering the Campaign's Final Days,* January 1993, p. 124.

▶ 38. See Jeffrey Abramson, F. Christopher Arterton, and Gary Orren, *The Electronic Commonwealth: The Impact of New Media Technologies on Democratic Politics* (New York: Basic Books, 1988).

39. Thomas Rosenstiel, "The Talk is About New Media," *Los Angeles Times,* May 23, 1992, p. A20.

40. See Nell Henderson, "Real Right-Wing Radio," *Washington Post National Weekly Edition,* May 1–7, 1995, p. 8.

41. Times Mirror Center for The People & The Press, *The Vocal Minority in American Politics,* July 16, 1993.

42. Times Mirror Center for The People & The Press, *Americans Going Online. . . . Explosive Growth, Uncertain Destinations,* October 16, 1995.

POLITICAL PARTIES AND ORGANIZED INTERESTS

T he Founders designed their new government with two basic parts: the people and the institutions of government (the three branches, their leaders, state governments, etc.). The people would elect their representatives on the basis of a candidate's character, and their representatives would act on the people's behalf in protecting the nation as a whole, even as they protected every American as an individual. Government would be composed of institutions and people with nothing in between.

Over the decades, however, the space between government and the people has filled with a vast collection of individuals and organizations who try to shape what the people think and what the government does. Although never listed in the Constitution itself, these go-betweens play a key role in helping government work. Americans cannot hope to know each candidate well enough to make an informed choice on every race, nor can they hope to track the thousands of bills and other government decisions that might make a difference in their lives. There is just too much going on for any individual American to keep up. Even the institutions of government have trouble keeping up. They need help keeping track of decisions, too.

This is why political parties and organized interests have become so important to American government: they give individual Americans and their institu-

Go-Betweens in Government

tions shortcuts for understanding many of the key decisions they face, and often act on the people's behalf in influencing government. A **political party** is a broad membership organization designed to win elections and influence government, in part by helping citizens decide how to vote. An **organized interest,** on the other hand, is an organization that exists for the purpose of influencing government for the benefit of its member or members. As much as both organizations help Americans stay in touch with government, parties and organized interests ultimately exist to influence government.

The Founders would not be surprised to find parties and organized interests collected *around* government. They saw factions, or divisions, as both a natural product of freedom and its greatest threat. Give the people freedom, the Founders believed, and they will divide into groups competing for power over who gets what, when, and how; give them a government that caters to those divisions, and the people will not be free for long. Although the First Amendment clearly guarantees the right to petition, or lobby, government for a redress of grievances, much of the rest of the Constitution is designed to make such petitions difficult to win.

Thus, the Founders' great challenge was to design a new government that would both control the mischiefs of factions, while protecting basic liberties. The Founders settled upon an untested solution. As Madison explained the idea in *Federalist Paper No. 51,* "Ambition must be made to counteract ambition." (*Federalist*

Paper No. 51 can be read in Appendix C.) Creating separate powers, separate layers, and checks and balances, all led by leaders with separate interests, would assure that no single faction, be it a political party or an organized interest, could ever capture all three branches of government.

Rather, what might trouble the Founders is that political parties and organized interests are so often actually *part* of government. As we will see in the first half of this chapter, political parties play a central role in who gets what, when, and how from government, whether by recruiting candidates for office, running campaigns, organizing the institutions once their ballots are counted, or helping voters think through their choices on election day. As we will see in the second half of the chapter, organized interests spend enormous energy trying to influence government, whether by providing information to government officers, building public support for specific decisions, or trying to influence elections. Sometimes, organized interests get so close to government that it is hard to see where government ends and the organized interests begin.

PARTIES IN AMERICAN POLITICS

The Founders did not view political parties as essential to government. To the contrary, they saw political parties as a threat to democracy. George Washington warned that parties were likely "to become potent engines by which cunning, ambitious and unprincipled men will be able to subvert the power of the people and to usurp themselves the reins of government." John Adams expressed "dread" toward the notion that two "great parties" might emerge from the debate over ratification. And in 1789, Thomas Jefferson went so far as to say that if he "could not go to heaven but with a party," he would "not go at all."[1]

Despite their warnings, a version of the modern two-party system had emerged by the early 1790s built by the *Federalists,* who supported ratification of the Constitution, and the *Anti-Federalists,* who opposed it. Although the Founders expected these two early parties to disappear once the fate of the Constitution was resolved, other battles soon arose. As power ebbed and flowed between the two early parties, the public became increasingly comfortable with choosing between two alternatives. At the same time, the two parties quickly developed into efficient mechanisms for both recruiting candidates for office and giving voters an easy way to make decisions. Knowing that a candidate was a Federalist or a Democratic-Republican (as the Anti-Federalists came to call themselves) helped voters decide.

Before turning to the roles and history of the American political parties, it is useful to remember that American government has had just four major parties over its entire two hundred years. (See Box 4–1 for a list and description of the four.) The two major parties have been very effective at either defeating or absorbing the smaller minor, or third parties, that have arisen from time to time.

BOX 4-1

The Four Major American Political Parties

Party	Founded	Last Won Presidency	Comments
Federalists	1796	1796	Founded by Alexander Hamilton and other supporters of a strong central government; last president was John Adams.
Democrats	1800	1992	Founded by Thomas Jefferson as Republicans; became Democratic-Republicans in 1828 and Democrats in 1840.
Whigs	1834	1848	Last president was Zachary Taylor; broke apart over the issue of slavery.
Republicans	1856	1988	Founded largely by remnants of the Northern Whigs and antislavery Democrats; Abraham Lincoln was first Republican to be elected president.

Source: James M. Perry, "Win or Lose, Perot Proves One Can Run without Major Parties," Wall Street Journal, July 14, 1992, p. A11.

The Three Roles of Parties Today

Political parties exist to influence what government does. Just as individual citizens have ideologies, so, too, do parties have different views about how much government should be involved in the day-to-day activities of American society. They exist to translate those views into action, primarily through the exercise of three roles (1) contesting elections, (2) organizing government, and (3) helping citizens decide how to vote.

Contesting Elections. The first role of the parties is to nominate and elect candidates. They do their work primarily through national, state, and local organizations called **party committees.** The party committees and their staffs do much of the routine work involved in making democracy work. They recruit candidates for office, register citizens to vote, raise money, campaign for their slates of party candidates, and get out the vote on election day. Although most candidates today run their own campaigns independent of their party's effort, the party committees still host the conventions that endorse those candidates, write the **party**

platforms that tell the public what the party stands for, and generally keep the party alive when it is out of power.[2]

(At one time, the parties once even printed their own election ballots listing only their own candidates. Until the late 1800s, when the nation switched to secret ballots listing all the candidates, citizens had to give all their votes to one or the other party. And because the party ballots were often printed in bright colors, there was rarely any doubt about voters' party loyalty as they walked to the ballot box with their decisions in hand.)

Although the national, state, and local party committees still work closely together on national campaigns, they no longer act as a kind of political pyramid all the way from local voting precincts at the bottom to the national party committees in Washington. Rather, each tends to concentrate on its own level of government: the national committees focus on winning the presidency and Congress; the state parties, on the governorship and state legislature; the local parties, on county and city posts. It is best to think of today's party system as a federalist system—that is, it has multiple layers that often go their own ways.

The national party committees invariably receive the greatest media attention, especially during presidential election years. Headed by national party commit-

Presidential candidates Bob Dole (left) and Bill Clinton (right). Both candidates were nominated on the first ballot in their respective party conventions. Today's conventions serve more as opportunities to promote the presidential candidates than as events in which delegates actually make real choices.

tees with representatives from every state, these national party organizations are responsible for managing the **national party conventions** that take place every four years. The most important purpose of a national convention is to generate momentum behind the party's presidential candidate. Today's primary election process virtually guarantees that a single candidate will come to the convention with enough delegates to win the party's nomination on the first ballot and get quick approval of a vice presidential nominee. Although delegates to the national convention also ratify a platform summarizing the party's views on the issues of the day, national conventions have become carefully staged events designed to give the presidential and vice presidential candidates a surge of support that will carry into the fall general election campaign.

Running this process takes more than party volunteers, of course. Both national party committees have permanent staffs that have grown dramatically in recent years. In the early 1970s, the Democratic and Republican National Committees had fewer than thirty employees each. By 1988, the Democratic National Committee (DNC) staff had grown to 160, while the Republican National Committee (RNC) staff had increased to 435.[3] These staffs are responsible for everything from planning the conventions to raising money for voter education. Given the difference in staff size, it is no surprise that the RNC consistently raises more money, writes more letters, and runs more national advertisements than the DNC. In 1991–1992, for example, the RNC raised $273 million, while the DNC raised $164 million.

The national organizations may get the headlines, but it is the state and local party organizations that often make or break a campaign. Indeed, for much of the nation's history, big city **party machines** did the heavy lifting, even in presidential campaigns. A machine consisted of a party boss, thousands of party workers, and lots of cash to ensure that voters got to the polls and cast the "right" ballots.

Although the party machines are long gone, replaced by sophisticated campaign organizations, state and local parties are still essential for national success, in large part because they remain closest to the grass roots, or the actual voters. They recruit most of the candidates who run for office—Bill Clinton started his career as a candidate for Arkansas attorney general—and run the get-out-the-vote efforts that can spell victory or defeat in a close campaign.

The state parties also play a central role in the national party conventions. The national committees set the number of delegates each state may send to the national conventions based on the size of the state (California sent 383 delegates to the Democratic National Convention in 1996, Alaska just 20) and on how well the party's nominee did in the state in the previous presidential election, but each state party decides just how to select its delegates. Thirty-nine states now use some form of primary election to make the choice. (States where the party candidate for president did well in the most recent primary election are seated at the front of the convention floor.)

IN A DIFFERENT LIGHT

WHO SHOWS UP FOR THE PARTY?

Because the national party committees are built from the bottom up, starting with people involved in the local party, they tend to represent those who have the greatest commitment to serve. Because that commitment often comes from ideology, party activists who eventually make it to the national party conventions may be very different from both the party's regular voters and the general population as a whole.

The differences are clear in the ideological composition of the 1996 Democratic and Republican National Conventions. Delegates who made it to Chicago and San Diego were not only different from each other, but were arguably out of touch with the attitudes of ordinary Americans.[4] (See Box 4–2 for the comparisons of convention delegates, party regulars, and the general population.)

The differences start with basic demographics. Although Democratic convention delegates were much more likely to be women and minorities than Republican delegates, both party conventions had much higher proportions of college educated, financially secure elites than their party regulars or general population. The delegates are also older than the general population.

The differences are also clear in political ideology. Democratic convention goers were much more liberal than the rest of the population, while Republican convention goers were much more conservative. Most Americans were very much in the ideological middle.

Finally, the differences are clear on the issues of the day. Democratic convention goers were much more likely than Republicans to favor government intervention to solve the nation's problems, while Republican delegates were much more likely to favor government intervention in promoting family values. Similar differences showed up on other issues. Democratic convention delegates were much more likely than even their party regulars to favor abortion rights, a nationwide ban on assault weapons, affirmative action programs to help women and minorities, and to oppose organized prayer in public schools. With one-third of their 1996 delegates coming from labor unions, it is not surprising that Democratic convention goers also favored international trade restrictions to protect domestic industries.

In a similar vein, Republican convention delegates were much more likely than their party regulars to oppose abortion rights, an assult weapons ban, affirmative action, and to favor public school prayer.

These differences affect the national parties in several important ways. In order to win their party's nomination, for example, presidential candidates often have to take more extreme positions than they would otherwise favor. Republicans have to lean to the right, Democrats to the left. Ideological activists can also have a substantial role in writing the party's platform, again driving the parties toward the ideological extremes.

If a convention is visibly ideological, the party's candidate may be unable to move back toward the center during the general election campaign. Activists may determine the nomination,

BOX
4-2

A Comparison of Convention Delegates with the General Public, 1996

	Democratic Delegates	Democratic Party Regulars	General Public	Republican Party Regulars	Republican Delegates
Demographics					
Men	47%	37%	46%	53%	64%
Women	53	63	54	47	36
White	71	71	84	95	91
Black	17	20	11	2	3
Age					
18–29 years old	6	18	17	19	2
30–44 years old	27	29	32	33	26
45–64 years old	55	30	30	25	53
65 and older	11	23	21	22	17
Labor union member	34	13	11	7	4
College graduate	69	17	23	30	73
Family income					
under $50,000	29	78	71	60	23
$50,000–$75,000	22	10	14	19	18
over $75,000	46	8	11	17	47
Political Views					
Ideology					
very liberal	15	7	4	1	0
somewhat liberal	28	20	12	6	0
moderate	48	54	47	39	27
somewhat conservative	4	14	24	36	31
very conservative	1	3	8	17	35
Government should do more					
to solve the nation's problems	76	53	36	20	4
regulate the environment and safety practices of businesses	60	66	53	37	4
promote traditional values	27	41	42	44	56

Source: New York Times, *August 26, 1996, p. A12.*

but party regulars and independents determine the final victory. In 1992, for example, conservative delegates to the Republican National Convention in Houston forced the party so far right on issues such as school prayer and abortion that George Bush could not regain the center. Moderate women deserted the party, creating a large gender gap in favor of Bill Clinton. Although 1996 Republican convention goers were as ideological as their 1992 predecessors, presidential nominee Bob Dole succeeded in creating a convention that looked inclusive and open, while minimizing his commitment to the party's intensely ideological party platform. "I haven't read it yet," he said of the platform upon leaving San Diego.

The fact that party conventions tend to overrepresent ideological extremes may reduce the general public's party loyalty. To the extent that ordinary citizens see no place for themselves in the views of their party, they may end up voting for third-party candidates such as Ross Perot or simply staying home on election day.

Organizing Government. The second role of the parties is to help structure the government once the campaigns are over. Being in the majority clearly matters, especially on Capitol Hill. Both the Speaker of the House and the Majority Leader of the Senate, the two key positions on Capitol Hill, are chosen from the ranks of the majority party.

The same is true for determining who in Congress gets the committee chairs, the best offices, the largest staffs, the fastest service from the departments of government, the best seats for the president's State of the Union address, and even who gets quoted more frequently by the media.[5] And, of critical importance, members of the majority party also determine which bills get to the floor of Congress for final passage. In short, being in the majority determines who gets what, when, and how in government.

Party is not equally important to all three branches of government, however. There is no explicit role for the parties in the federal judiciary, although being involved in party politics sometimes helps in getting an appointment as a federal judge. Party is more important in the presidency, where the president is viewed as the party's most visible leader, and where being involved in party politics is often essential in getting an appointment as a presidential aide. The president also has a great say in who runs the national party committee.

Party is most important in organizing Congress, where the majority party rules. Congress relies on the majority party for everything from organizing the committees to hiring Capitol Hill police. Although the majority party determines how many members of each party get appointed to each committee, the two parties select their own leaders and make their own committee assignments.

As we will see in Chapter 7, in many ways there are four parties in Congress—the Senate majority and minority and the House majority and minority—each of which has slightly different rules. However, all of the parties behave the same at the beginning of each two-year congressional term. Meeting in secret party caucuses, party members first decide who will be their party leader. The majority party in the House appoints the Speaker, majority leader, and majority whip (who "whips" up party support on legislation), and a host of lesser posts; the minority party appoints the minority leader, minority whip, and so forth. Each party in each chamber also appoints its own **congressional campaign committee,** which raises money for its members and candidates.

All four parties share the same broad goal: to create party unity on legislation. It is a goal that is often measured by asking how often party members vote together on the same bill. In the early 1970s, for example, party unity in the House and Senate averaged 60 to 65 percent—that is, Democrats voted with Democrats and Republicans with Republicans about two-thirds of the time. By the 1990s, the unity scores had increased dramatically. House Democrats voted together 88 percent of the time in 1994; House Republicans 88 percent as well.[6] Party loyalty may be down among American voters, as we will see, but it appears to be up among their elected representatives in Washington.

Helping Voters Decide.　The third role of parties is to help voters decide. Parties exist as more than formal organizations with national, state, and local headquarters. Over the years, they have come to exist inside the voter's mind as a memory shortcut in making choices. Knowing that a candidate is a Democrat or Republican is often enough for most voters to act.

There was a time, as recently as the 1950s, when a voter's **party identification** was the single most important factor in voting. Not only was party identification a powerful predictor of how people would vote, being a Democrat or Republican shaped much of what voters cared about—which issues they believed were most important to the campaign and where they stood, how they felt about each candidate and who they liked, and most importantly, who would get their vote. Indeed, party identification served as a single lens through which voters viewed campaigns, casting the party's candidate in a positive light.

This is not to say that party identification is no longer a potent force in voting decisions. It is still a very strong predictor of how people will vote—90 percent of Democrats voted for Democrats in the 1994 congressional elections, 93 percent of Republicans voted for Republicans. However, it is no longer clear that party identification shapes what people think in quite the way it once did. As we will see, party identification may now be less a funnel for sorting views than just one of many factors voters consider when making a choice.

Political scientists break party identification into seven distinct categories from left to right: strong Democrats, weak Democrats, independents who lean toward the Democrats, pure independents, independents who lean toward the Republicans, weak Republicans, and strong Republicans. Strong and weak members of each party are often lumped together, as are leaners and independents.

Strong Democrats and strong Republicans are the most loyal to their parties. They tend to turn out for elections in higher numbers than any of the other identifiers, and vote much more consistently for party candidates. In 1952, 36 percent of the public were strong identifiers. By 1992, the number was down to 28 percent.[7] (See Box 4–3 for the overall trend in party competition between Democrats, Republicans, and independents.)

In contrast, pure **independents** are barely attached to the political process at all. They tend to follow elections less closely, and show up for elections less frequently. They are more likely than other voters to feel that politicians do not care much about their opinions. In 1952, only 6 percent of the public said they were independents. By 1992, the number had grown to 12 percent. Independents are the least likely to use issues as a basis for voting, seeming to rely on candidate advertisements and other imagery as their primary reasons for choosing one candidate over another.

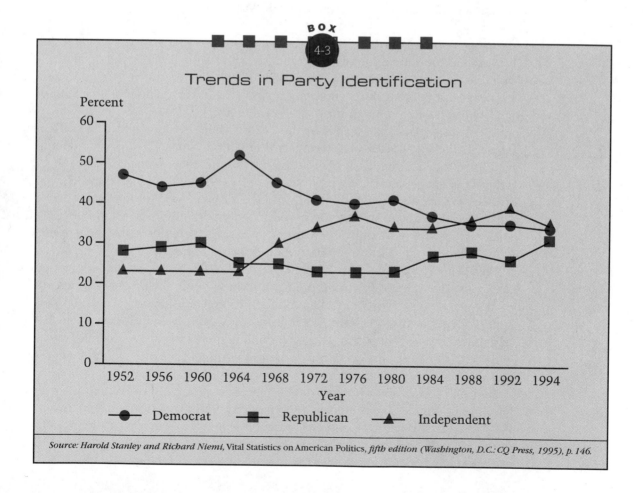

BOX 4-3

Trends in Party Identification

Percent

Year

● Democrat   ■ Republican   ▲ Independent

Source: Harold Stanley and Richard Niemi, Vital Statistics on American Politics, *fifth edition (Washington, D.C.: CQ Press, 1995), p. 146.*

In between strong identifiers and independents are two different groups: the weak identifiers and the independents who lean toward one or the other party. The number of weak identifiers dropped from 39 percent in 1952 to 33 percent in 1992, while the number of "leaners" grew from 17 percent all the way to 27 percent. Interestingly, leaners actually behave more like strong party loyalists than the weak party identifiers. They follow elections more closely and show up for elections more frequently. Political scientists believe they are actually party loyalists in disguise—that is, they like to call themselves independents, but are actually very loyal to their party.

Democrats were the big losers over the years, as their share of strong and weak loyalists fell from 47 percent in 1952 to just 34 percent in 1994; pure and leaning independents gained the most, rising 12 points over the period. Among the independents, Republican leaners and pure independents outgained Democratic leaners by a margin of three to one.

A DIFFERENT LIGHT

WHY THIRD PARTIES DO NOT WIN

It is nearly impossible to create a serious third party in national politics, even though a majority of Americans think having a third party is a good idea.[8] For starters, it is difficult, although not impossible, for a third party to get on the presidential ballot in most states.

Because the Constitution gives states authority to set the times, manner, and places for elections, a third-party campaign must get on the ballot state by state. In California, for example, that meant convincing 89,007 registered voters to sign a ballot petition a year in advance of the 1996 election. That means, in turn, that a successful candidate must have a strong statewide organization in place long before the national candidates even show up.

Even if a candidate can get on the ballot in most states, the winner-take-all nature of presidential elections makes it nearly impossible to win any electoral votes. Under the electoral college system, a state's electoral votes go to the winning candidate, and the winning candidate alone. That means having a strong national campaign is not enough. Candidates must have a strong presence in enough states to put together a winning total.

Even though Texas billionaire Ross Perot spent over $60 million of his money in 1992 to create a national party from scratch, and won 20 percent of the popular vote, he failed to win a single state in the electoral college. And lacking any semblance of state or local party organizations, he did not win a single state-level victory. He did even worse in 1996.

One of the reasons third-party candidates fare so poorly over time is that the Democratic and Republican parties often move just far enough to either recapture their wayward supporters or

Supporters of third-party presidential candidate Ross Perot in 1992, many of whom were getting involved in politics for the first time in their lives. Perot ran again in 1996 and lost.

create a new coalition of old and new voters. After the 1968 election, for example, Republicans successfully wooed the white anti-civil rights, anti-crime voters that had supported the third-party campaign of Alabama Democrat George Wallace, creating a strong Southern base that eventually helped sweep Republicans to a new majority in Congress in 1994.

Sometimes, however, the effort to absorb a third party does not work. After the 1992 election, for example, Democrats and Republicans alike went after Perot voters, both claiming to share the billionaire's commitment to a balanced budget and clean government. Their efforts were not enough to prevent Perot from mounting another run at the presidency in 1996, however.

Traditionally, third parties have served as a wake-up call for the Democratic and Republican parties. They give voters a chance to voice their anger, but often end up strengthening the two-party system. Even the most successful third party, therefore, will likely succeed by forcing one of the other two parties out of the system.

Nevertheless, third-party activity may be on the rise, in part because the public is so hungry for alternatives to what they see as the tired existing parties. Perot's Independence Party was joined on the 1996 California ballot by the Green Party, led by public interest advocate Ralph Nader. Although Nader did not expect to win the presidency, if only because his third party was on the ballot in less than half the states, he hoped the existing parties would make a greater commitment to environmental protection. In that regard, Nader's third party was playing a time-honored role in pushing the two parties toward change.

A Brief History of the Two-Party System

The Founders may have sowed the seeds of the two-party system by creating the electoral college system. Recall that Americans do not vote for president at all, but for competing slates of electors, who, in turn, vote for president as part of the electoral college.[9]

Under the Constitution, the method for awarding electoral votes is up to each state—Article II states that "each state shall appoint, *in such manner as the legislature thereof may direct,* a number of electors, equal to the whole number of Senators and Representatives to which the state may be entitled in the Congress. . . ." Although the states could easily decide to award their electoral college votes proportionally—that is, giving each candidate a percentage of electoral votes equal to his or her share of the popular vote—all but two states (Maine and Nebraska) today assign every electoral vote to the winner, no matter how close the popular vote.

As implemented by most states, the electoral college is a plurality rules, **winner-take-all system.** Whoever ends up with the most votes wins all the electoral votes. In 1992, for example, Bill Clinton lost Florida to George Bush by exactly 100,130 votes out of 5.3 million cast, but got none of Florida's twenty-five electoral votes. In a similar vein, Bush lost Georgia to Clinton by 13,714 votes out of 2.3 million cast, but got none of Georgia's thirteen electoral votes. Under such a system, third parties are well advised to join with a major party to reach a winning alliance.[10]

The electoral college is only one of several reasons why America developed a two-party system. Most elections today are contested in **single-member districts,** meaning there can be one winner for each election, and one winner only, no matter how many candidates. Unlike **multimember districts,** in which a large group of candidates compete for several seats (for example, a park board), single-member districts create a winner-take-all mentality among candidates. Under such a system, two parties and two parties only have a chance to win.[11]

Even without these electoral pressures toward a two-party system, Americans tend to be creatures of habit. Because party loyalties are learned early in life, the fact that the first party system happened to be a two-party system matters. Had the Federalists and Anti-Federalists of the late 1700s been joined by a third party—say, the "In-Between Federalists"—America might be a three-party system to this day.

Five Eras in Party History. The evolution of the two-party system was hardly smooth. There have been times when the two parties have been highly competitive, as in 1800 and 1824, when the electoral college was deadlocked, thereby throwing the election to the House of Representatives, and again in 1876 and 1888, when one candidate won the popular vote only to lose the electoral college balloting.

There have also been times when one party has been much stronger than the other, as in 1932 through 1948, when Democrats won five straight presidential elections. And there have been times when control has been in flux, as one party began to decline and another to rise.

Every election does not involve a great battle between the two parties. Indeed, the past two hundred years have witnessed a blend of balanced two-party competition, one-party dominance, and periods of transition between the two.[12] The past forty years, for example, would be characterized as competitive—the two parties split control of government several times, with Democrats primarily in charge of Congress (at least until 1994), and Republicans primarily in charge of the presidency (at least until 1992).

The blends of party competition fall into five distinct **party eras** since 1800, a party era being a period in which either one party is dominant or competition is stable. Party eras tend to begin and end with either a whimper or a bang— that is, one party will slowly fade from view as its followers leave, or the entire system will be rocked by some great issue that forces the two parties to reshuffle positions. (See Box 4–4 for a history of the five party eras.)

BOX 4-4

The Five Party Eras

First Party Era	1788–1824	Federalists vs. Democratic/ Republicans	Parties emerge in 1790s; one party dominant after 1800, but sharply divided internally
Second Party Era	1828–1854	Democrats vs. Whigs	Balanced two-party competition; Democrats mostly dominant throughout period
Third Party Era	1856–1896	Democrats vs. Republicans	Republicans dominant to 1874; balanced two-party competition until 1896; parties increasingly divided by geography (Democrats South; Republicans North)
Fourth Party Era	1896–1928	Democrats vs. Republicans	Republicans dominant except in 1912, when the party is split by a third party; parties continue to be divided by geography
Fifth Party Era	1932—	Democrats vs. Republicans	Democrats dominant until 1968; Democratic New Deal coalition weakens steadily thereafter

Source: Adapted from John Bibby, Politics, Parties, and Elections in America *(Chicago: Nelson-Hall, 1992), p. 22. Bibby did not end the fifth party era in 1994.*

Era One.   The first party era began in 1800 when Thomas Jefferson created the first Republican Party (the second was created in 1856 and remains active today). At some point in the early 1800s, his opponents managed to label the party as the Democratic-Republicans in an effort to link Jefferson with democratic radicals in France.

Much as he opposed parties in principle, Jefferson created the Republican Party as a counterweight to Alexander Hamilton's Federalist Party, which had been formed in 1796. Although these two great leaders had worked together in founding the new republic, they soon parted ways on just how strong the new government should be. Hamilton believed in a very strong national government, while Jefferson kept a more limited vision.

The two parties met first in the 1800 election, one of the most bitter contests in American history. Jefferson was the first of countless presidential candidates to argue for smaller government and lower taxes, suggesting that the Federalists had become the party of the rich and satisfied.

Jefferson also was one of the first candidates to speak directly to the people through advertising. One of his campaign posters even reminded voters of the Revolutionary War by labeling the Federalists as Tories, or British sympathizers: "Republicans: Turn out, turn out and save your country from ruin! From an Emperor– from a King—from the iron grasp of a British Tory Faction. DOWN WITH THE TORIES, DOWN WITH THE BRITISH FACTION, Before they have it in their power to enslave you, and reduce your families to distress by heavy taxation."

Energized by Jefferson's rhetoric, voters rejected John Adams and the Federalists, giving solid control to the Democratic-Republicans for the next five elections. So complete was the Democratic-Republican control that James Monroe ran unopposed in 1820, winning all but one electoral college vote. For this one brief moment, known as the "era of good feelings," America actually had a one-party system in which the public had little input into selecting candidates for office. Presidential candidates were selected by a small band of congressional leaders that earned the name "King Caucus."

Era Two.   The "era of good feelings" ended in 1824 with a brutal campaign among five candidates, all running as Democratic-Republicans. Each one represented a different faction within a single party. The two dominant candidates were John Quincy Adams (son of Federalist John Adams, Founder and second president of the United States) and War of 1812 hero General Andrew Jackson. Once again, as it had been in 1800, the contest was between a representative of the status quo (Adams) and a champion of the people (Jackson).

Just as his father had done almost thirty years earlier, Adams ran strong in the well-to-do Northeast, while a third candidate, House Speaker Henry Clay, and Jackson split the South and new states of the West, where concerns about a heavy-handed Washington, D.C., played well. Because no candidate secured a majority of electoral college votes, the election was thrown into the House. There, Clay threw his support behind Adams, denying Jackson the presidency. Adams rewarded

Clay by appointing him as secretary of state (the deal was immediately known as the "Corrupt Bargain"), creating a campaign theme for Jackson's next run.

The bitter rematch between Adams and Jackson came in 1828, as the Democratic-Republicans split in half. Jackson carried the Democratic-Republican label into the election, while Adams called himself a National Republican to link himself to the strong national government advocates of the old Federalist Party. Although Adams actually ran well in his Northeast base, he lost every state west and south of Maryland, including the nine new states added since 1789, five of which were slave-holding states of the South. Jackson became the first American president who was neither a Virginian nor an Adams.[13]

The next three decades were characterized by balanced two-party competition. By 1832, both major parties were choosing their candidates by national conventions, thereby laying the basis for strong state parties and local machines. By 1836, the Democratic-Republican label was gone from national politics, leaving Jackson's Democratic Party on one side of the electoral system, and a new party called the Whigs on the other. The Whigs were built from the same well-to-do social and economic groups that had once supported the Federalists—indeed, the name "Whigs" was a call back to colonial days, when patriots wore whigs to distinguish themselves from British sympathizers.

Era Three.   The third era began in 1856 as slavery forced a national crisis that would lead to civil war. Jackson's once-powerful Democratic Party was doomed by its strength in both the North and South, leaving it unable to choose between its antislavery supporters in the North and proslavery supporters in the South. Torn between the two sides, the party decided to take no position on slavery at all, nominating a succession of weak candidates in the hopes that the slavery issue would disappear.

The Whigs had no such trouble opposing slavery. Their party was so weak as it entered the 1850s that highly energized antislavery forces easily won control of the party. Just as activists often force today's Democratic and Republican parties toward strong stands, northern antislavery Whigs wrested control of the national convention in 1856, driving southern Whigs who favored slavery out of the party.

Cut free from its southern base, the Whig Party was now free to absorb the "Free Soil" antislavery movement, which had won 10 percent of the popular vote in 1848, and to make slavery the centerpiece of the next national elections. To emphasize the break, activists cast off the Whig label, calling themselves Republicans. Campaigning hard on the antislavery platform, the party emerged from the 1858 congressional elections with a dominant edge in the North. As northern Democrats left their party to join the fight against slavery as Republicans, southern Whigs left the new Republican party to join the fight for slavery as Democrats.

Two years later, with virtually no support in the South, Republicans won the White House. Abraham Lincoln won only 40 percent of the popular vote in 1860, but captured enough states to secure the electoral college victory. Following the bloody Civil War between the blue and the gray, America became a nation of two great parties, one of the North (Republican) and one of the South (Democrat). Democrats controlled the South all the way up to the 1960s, when their support for civil rights began to erode southern support. The 1994 congressional elections finally ended Democratic control of the South.[14]

Era Four.   The fourth era began in the economic tensions surrounding the 1896 election of Republican William McKinley. Democrats and Republicans had taken turns controlling the White House and Congress during the thirty years following the Civil War as the country struggled with an economic depression and an expanding western frontier. Democrats came to represent an angry mix of western farmers and eastern reformers; Republicans a base of financial interests and blue-collar workers scared of losing their jobs.

By 1896, the Democratic Party had been captured by radical farmers, who nominated William Jennings Bryan for president. With a party agenda devoted largely to attacking big business and advocating radical reform of the U.S. currency, Bryan was outspent by a margin of $21 to $1.[15] Although the South remained strongly Democratic, the Republicans strengthened their northern base and continued to control national politics for nearly forty years.

So great was the Republican dominance that the Democratic Party was actually at risk of disappearing completely in 1912. It was rescued by Republican Theodore Roosevelt (cousin of future Democratic icon Franklin Roosevelt), who had succeeded to the presidency after McKinley's assassination in 1901 and won election in his own right in 1904. After serving nearly two terms, Roosevelt gave up the presidency in 1908, turning the office over to his handpicked Republican successor, William Howard Taft, only to reenter politics in 1912. Having lost his effort to unseat Taft as his party's presidential nominee, Roosevelt created the Bull Moose Party, which ran the most successful third-party campaign in history, only to so split the Republican base that Democrat Woodrow Wilson, a former college professor at Princeton University, won the presidency with just 42 percent of the vote.

Era Five.   The fifth era began in 1932 with the election of Democrat Franklin Delano Roosevelt in the wake of a deep economic depression. Democrats were propelled into office by the sense that Republican President Herbert Hoover had done little to help the millions of Americans thrown out of work following the October 1929 stock market crash.

Having promised America a "New Deal," Roosevelt won every state west and south of Pennsylvania. This **New Deal coalition**—which was composed of workers, southern farmers, southern Democrats, liberals, Catholics, Jews, and African Americans—lasted through the 1960s.

During its prime, the New Deal coalition was nearly unbeatable. Democrats won five straight presidential elections from 1932 through 1948, and controlled one or both houses of Congress for all but four years (1947–1948 and 1953–1954) out of the next sixty. Yet, just as slavery unraveled the Democratic party of the

1850s, the civil rights movement divided the party again. This time, the effort to improve the lives of minorities came from the Democratic, not Republican party, with similar results in the South. Southern Democrats began to desert the party, moving toward the Republicans. By 1994, the South was no longer in Democratic hands.

Changing Eras.   As this very brief history suggests, two of the five party eras faded away with the simple passage of time: the Republican era that followed the Civil War and the New Deal era. The other three ended with what political scientists call a **critical election** or **realigning election.** Such an election involves a lasting shift in the underlying loyalties of voters, and is usually caused by a major issue that disrupts the traditional party lines. In the 1850s, that issue was slavery; in the late 1920s, it was the Great Depression.

The two existing parties face three choices when such great dividing issues arise: (1) they can ignore the issue, thereby taking the risk that they will fall by the wayside as new parties emerge; (2) one or both can absorb the issue into their existing platform, unless the issue is so disruptive that it cannot fit; or (3) one or both can modify or even reject their past positions to assemble a new party coalition. The most recent realigning election occurred in 1932, when Republicans decided to stand firm in the midst of the economic crisis, while Democrats absorbed the deepening public concerns into their existing platform to create a much larger party.

Although the New Deal coalition had largely disappeared by 1992, it is not clear a new era has begun. Democrats and Republicans are clearly battling each other for national control, but neither has yet to win a decisive final victory. The 1994 congressional elections, while dramatic, did not produce a deep enough change in party loyalty to be classified as a realignment. Thus, it may be that America has entered an era that is best called a party *de*alignment. Neither party seems able to generate the kind of lasting voter loyalty that might form the basis of a distinctive era.

The Party System in Transition?

The question is whether there will be a new era of renewed party identification, or whether parties will simply fade away as meaningful players in American political life. High levels of party loyalty are a form of consent to be governed, giving the parties the permission to recruit candidates, run campaigns, and organize the government. As such, declining party identification may weaken the legitimacy of the parties as key go-betweens between the governed and the government.

This declining loyalty shows up in more than just the raw numbers on overall party identification (see Box 4–2). The past thirty years have also witnessed a decline in **straight-ticket voting,** in which voters cast votes with their party for every office on the ballot, and a corresponding increase in **split-ticket voting,** where voters cross back and forth between parties all the way down the ballot. The number of Americans who voted for the presidential candidate of one party and the House candidate of the other grew from 13 percent in the 1952 election to 22 percent in 1992, while the number who split parties between Senate and House candidates jumped from 9 percent to 25 percent, and the number who split parties among state and local offices doubled from 26 percent to 52 percent.[16]

This unparty-like behavior has led some experts to wonder whether the parties are becoming irrelevant to how voters decide. "The two parties remind me of those old French Foreign Legion movies," says Ann Lewis, a past political director of the Democratic National Committee. "You see this fort, and it looks fine from the outside. But when you go through the gate, almost everyone inside is dead."[17]

Whether the party forts will ever thrive again depends in part on whether the public continues to see meaningful differences between the two parties. The more the public sees such differences between the two party "products," whether in the candidates, platforms, or kinds of voters each party attracts, the more likely the public is to identify with one or the other—rather like being able to taste the difference between Diet Coke and Diet Pepsi.

At least for now, the evidence is that the public can taste the difference between the two parties. In 1994, for example, roughly 75 percent of Americans saw at least a "fair amount" of difference between the two parties. That number has been increasing ever so slightly over the past decade or so, suggesting that the two parties are actually drawing firmer lines between each other.[18]

The two parties also attract very different kinds of voters. Democrats have traditionally drawn support from certain social and economic groups; Republicans from others; independents tend to be from still others. Because people have three choices in most polls on party identification—Democrat, Republican, or independent—it is sometimes best to ask who is *not* a Democrat or Republican to see the differences in social and economic backgrounds. (See Box 4–5 for a comparison.)

Some of these differences in loyalty have been remarkably stable over the past fifty years. Republicans are still more likely to be better educated and affluent; Democrats are still more likely to be African American, live in cities, and belong to labor unions.[19] Once again, the figures are less important than the general trend: the two parties still appeal to particular groups of voters.

At the same time, there has been a shift toward the Republicans among certain social groups, a shift that may have started in the late 1960s when southern Democrats began turning away from their party. By 1994, Republicans had become the preferred party for white southerners (35 percent to 20 percent), white, Non-Hispanic Catholics (47 percent to 46 percent), and white born-again Christians (38 percent to 28 percent).[20] Not only do born-again Christians now constitute almost a quarter of the U.S. adult population, they are much more likely

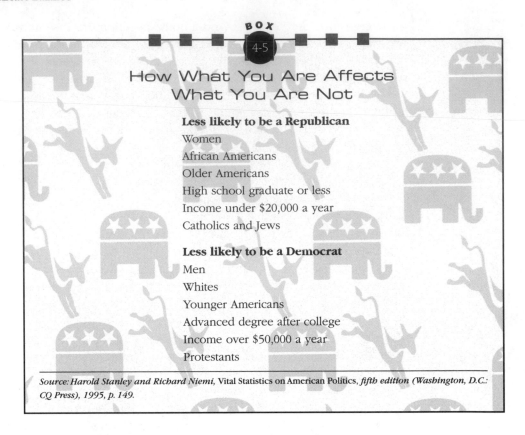

BOX
4-5

How What You Are Affects What You Are Not

Less likely to be a Republican

Women

African Americans

Older Americans

High school graduate or less

Income under $20,000 a year

Catholics and Jews

Less likely to be a Democrat

Men

Whites

Younger Americans

Advanced degree after college

Income over $50,000 a year

Protestants

Source: Harold Stanley and Richard Niemi, Vital Statistics on American Politics, *fifth edition (Washington, D.C.: CQ Press), 1995, p. 149.*

to vote in elections than the traditional Democratic base. Their votes were a significant part of the Republican victory in 1994.

Where neither party has done particularly well of late is among younger Americans. The largest party among young Americans is no party at all. Young Americans are far more likely than older Americans to say there ought to be a third major political party. Over 60 percent of people under age thirty say "yes" to the idea, compared with just 36 percent of those over age sixty-five.[21] This does not mean, however, that a third party is about to spring forth around Generation X, rather that party loyalty is less likely to influence the vote than some other factor.[22]

The question is what might be causing the shift away from the parties. It is most certainly not because the parties have somehow become irrelevant to contesting elections or organizing government. They have never been stronger, as the party unity scores in Congress suggest. Nor is it because there is some flashy new third-party product available to tempt voters. Third parties remain notoriously unable to hold party loyalty over time.

Rather, it may be that Americans simply no longer have to rely on the two parties for information or influence. They can always tune into the new media or join an organized interest instead. Just as Americans have turned away from network television and national newspapers and toward the new media, perhaps they are also turning away from the two parties and toward more specialized sources of influence. As we will see, organized interests are doing better at winning the lasting loyalty of Americans than the two parties. And, in doing so, they may be contributing to the steady erosion of the two-party system.

ORGANIZED INTERESTS

America has always been a nation of joiners. Traveling across America in the 1830s, French aristocrat Alexis de Tocqueville may have been the first to notice just how seriously Americans take their voluntary associations, or groups. Writing in *Democracy in America,* Tocqueville attributed America's success to those associations: "Americans of all ages, all stations in life, and all types of disposition are forever forming associations. There are not only commercial and industrial associations in which all take part, but others of a thousand different types—religious, moral, serious, futile, very general and very limited, immensely large and very minute. . . . Nothing, in my view, deserves more attention than the intellectual and moral associations in America."[23]

A century and a half later, America is still a nation of joiners. According to the *Encyclopedia of Associations,* there were nearly 23,000 formal associations in 1995, a number that had grown by ten a week since the early 1970s. The list runs the gamut from A to Z: from the Automotive Booster Clubs International to the ZZ Top International Fan Club.

Americans do not just join formal associations for help with their gardens, however. They also join to influence who gets what, when, and how from government. Such associations are called organized interests. The ZZ Top Fan Club would only be classified as an organized interest if it suddenly decided to take a stand against music censorship and began **lobbying** government. The term *lobbying* covers efforts to influence government, whether by providing information, building public support, or influencing elections.

Americans may say that Washington lobbyists wield too much power, but many of those lobbyists work for them. Roughly half of all Americans belong to an organization that lobbies government in some form or another. Even people who swear they would never join a lobbying group may be far more active than they think. Even people who buy Girl Scout cookies make a small contribution to the organization's effort to stop government from taxing charities.[24]

Interest Groups or Organized Interests?

Before turning to why organized interests form and what they do, there are two essential points to remember about the term *organized interests.* First, as noted earlier, not all voluntary associations are organized interests. A voluntary association only becomes an organized interest if it attempts to influence government.

Second, not all organized interests are voluntary associations. The term *organized interests* actually includes two different kinds of organizations: (1) traditional interest groups, and (2) a new breed of single-member organizations. Even though it is perfectly acceptable to use the term *interest group* to describe the wide range of organizations seeking to influence government, it is no longer quite as precise.

Interest Groups. Until recently, the standard American government textbook would have titled this section of the book "Interest Groups." The term **interest groups** refers to membership organizations that focus specifically on influencing government. Using the word *group* implies that such organizations have more than one member. The membership might consist of a specific kind of person (the National Association for the Advancement of Colored People, the National Organization for Women), a collection of professionals (the Clowns of America, American Academy of Sports Physicians, American Nurses Association), a group of businesses (the National Association of Home Builders, the Chamber of Commerce, National Association of Manufacturers), or even a federation of other interest groups (the American Federation of Labor and Congress of Industrial Organizations, or AFL-CIO).

The list also includes public interest groups, which are composed of people who join together to influence government for the common good. People who care about the environment might join the 650,000 members of the Sierra Club or the 5.6 million members of the National Wildlife Federation; people who believe in an unfettered right to bear arms might join the 2.6 million members of the National Rifle Association; people who support campaign finance reform might join the 270,000 other members of Common Cause or one of the state Public Interest Research Groups (PIRGs) set up by consumer advocate Ralph Nader in the 1970s; people who oppose abortion might join one of the 3,000 local chapters of the National Right to Life Committee; those who support abortion might join the 450,000 members of the National Abortion Rights Action League; those who worry about clean food might join the Pure Food Campaign, which includes superchefs Wolfgang Puck, Julia Child, and Alice Waters as members.[25] As the list suggests, public interest groups can be either liberal or conservative.

Single-Member Organizations. Interest groups are not the only organizations trying to influence government today, however. The 1970s and 1980s witnessed an explosion in the number of interest groups with just one member, usually a corporation. Although individual corporations often band together in traditional membership associations such as the Chamber of Commerce, National Association of Home Builders, and even the Bow Tie Manufacturers Association, many also have their own Washington offices expressly for advancing their individual concerns. Because one member does not a group make, some political scientists now use the term *organized interests* to describe such organizations.

Interestingly, colleges and universities constitute one of the fastest growing kinds of organized interests. Like corporations, colleges and universities still band together in broad membership groups such as the American Association of Higher Education. But they increasingly try to influence Congress on their own because their is money at stake. In the 1993 federal budget, for example, Congress awarded $763 million to individual colleges and universities for research of one kind or another. The University of Alaska led the list with $45 million, followed by Boston University at $29 million, Michigan State University at $23 million, the University of Maryland at $22 million, and tiny Wheeling Jesuit College in West Virginia at $21 million, which is in the home state of Democratic Senator Robert Byrd, a powerful member of the Senate Appropriations Committee, which makes many of the key decisions on who gets what, when, and how by way of federal spending. Because so much is at stake, many colleges and universities now have lobbyists in Washington.[26]

A DIFFERENT LIGHT

WHO DOES NOT JOIN?

People with social and economic resources are not the only Americans with a stake in what government does, of course, but they are much more likely to join an organized interest. People who receive welfare benefits from government are the least likely of all Americans to belong to an organized interest of any kind, as are people who are feeling the economic pinch of a tightening economy; in this case, the struggle to pay the rent seems to exhaust any extra resources the individual might have to participate in an organized interest.

Moreover, people who get government benefits do not join organized interests in equal numbers. Americans who receive government benefits on the basis of need are far less likely to join an organized interest than those who get government benefits on the basis of service in the armed forces or from Social Security. Paradoxically, the more one seems to need special help from government, the less likely one is to join an organized interest to get it. (See Box 4–6 for a list of differences in who joins and who does not.)

This does not mean poor Americans have no representation in Washington. They are often represented through charitable groups such as the Children's Defense League, the Salvation Army, or the American Public Welfare Association, all of which lobby government in one way or another. Nevertheless, when it comes time to make budget cuts or make another run at welfare reform, the people least likely to be at the table are the people most likely to be affected.

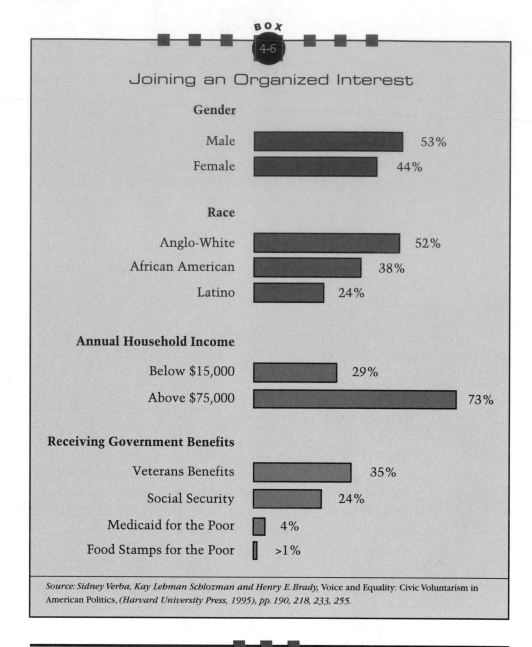

BOX
4-6

Joining an Organized Interest

Gender

Male — 53%
Female — 44%

Race

Anglo-White — 52%
African American — 38%
Latino — 24%

Annual Household Income

Below $15,000 — 29%
Above $75,000 — 73%

Receiving Government Benefits

Veterans Benefits — 35%
Social Security — 24%
Medicaid for the Poor — 4%
Food Stamps for the Poor — >1%

Source: Sidney Verba, Kay Lehman Schlozman and Henry E. Brady, Voice and Equality: Civic Voluntarism in American Politics, *(Harvard University Press, 1995), pp. 190, 218, 233, 255.*

Why Organized Interests Form

Organized interests do not spring up by accident. Some are formed by entrepreneurs who create a new organization and build public support for action, and only then start recruiting their members. Others start with public support for action, which then draws an entrepreneur, who builds an organization. Still others start with a single member, again usually a corporation, who has a demand for action, say to pass a special tax break or fund a promising technology, and builds an organization and only then hires an entrepreneur (perhaps a former member of Congress in need of work) to make the case.

Whichever comes first, political scientists agree that most organized interests emerge from social or economic upheaval. According to **disturbance theory,** organized interests tend to form in periods of social upheaval—the industrial revolution, the advent of new technologies, the Great Depression.[27] Then, and mostly then, are the conditions right for entrepreneurs to emerge, public demands to arise, and organizations to find the members to survive.

Social or economic disturbances may also lead members of already existing organized interests to create their own distinct groups. Computer manufacturers and chip makers did not exist as a distinct economic force much before the late 1960s, and felt reasonably well-represented by traditional business associations until a decade or so later. That is clearly not the case today. For example, as the information superhighway moves from an abstract fantasy toward reality, computer makers, chip designers, and information specialists have created their own lobbying operations, including the American Software Association (founded in 1982), the Interactive Multimedia Association (1988), and the Computer Literacy Council (1992).

As American society becomes more complex, the number of disturbances can only increase. That means, in turn, that the community of organized interests will inevitably expand, even as the interests represented by each new group become more narrow. The ability of big interest groups such as the National Association of Manufacturers to hold their membership may weaken, and smaller industries break off.

Once established, organized interests cannot survive unless they provide benefits to their member(s). Members join organized interests in search of one or more of four benefits: (1) a *material benefit* that comes back to members, such as tax breaks, higher benefit payments, government protections, even new roads; (2) a *social benefit,* which some political scientists also call a *solidary benefit,* that gives members the simple pleasure of working together, (3) a *civic benefit* that gives members a sense that they are doing something good for their nation, and (4) a *policy benefit,* which some political scientists call an *expressive* or *purposive benefit,* that comes from actually influencing government in a way that helps the nation as a whole.

According to political scientists Sidney Verba, Kay Lehman Schlozman, and Henry Brady, most Americans do not join organized interests for policy benefits. Rather, most people join either for the material benefits that come back to them as individuals or for the civic benefits that come from fulfilling a sense of civic duty.[28] (As we will see in Chapter 5, these benefits also affect why people participate in other political activities, including voting, giving money to campaigns, and writing letters to members of Congress.)

ACT UP protestors put pressure on the 1992 presidential candidates for action on AIDS. People join ACT UP in part to gain the material benefits that might come from more funding for research and treatment (the slogan "VOTE AS IF YOUR LIFE DEPENDS ON IT" is very much about material benefits). They can also reap social benefits by working together with others affected by the disease, civic benefits by doing something good for the nation, and policy benefits by actually influencing government decisions for those who will get AIDS in the future.

Getting a member or members to join an organized interest involves more than offering a simple list of benefits, however. As economist Mancur Olson has shown, a truly rational person would never join a group if he or she can get the benefits for free. (Economists call this the **free rider problem.**) Why buy the cow of government influence, or so to speak, when the milk of benefits is free? According to Olson, a rational person would only join an interest if (1) the organized interest is so small that one more member would truly enhance the interest's power, (2) the benefits are clearly reserved for the member or members, or (3) the organization can force the member to join, say to get a professional credential or license.[29]

Although the argument is compelling in many cases, economists may underestimate the role of altruism in explaining why people join groups. After all, some people join groups just because they believe in the cause. Nevertheless, the theory helps explain why organized interests try to limit **collective benefits,** which are available to everyone in society regardless of their membership in the organized interest.

Some collective benefits are inevitable, of course. All elderly prosper when the American Association of Retired Persons (AARP) wins a Social Security benefit increase, for example; all nature lovers benefit when the Sierra Club wins greater protection for the national parks. Neither benefit can be denied to nonmembers, making it a collective good. If such collective benefits are too great, however, every potential member will prefer to be a "free rider," getting the benefits without the cost, even if such selfish behavior eventually kills the organized interest itself.

Since organized interests cannot avoid collective benefits completely, they often control for the free rider problem by offering an attractive inventory of **selective benefits.** Selective benefits are available only to members. The better the selective benefits are, the more rational being a member becomes.

Providing selective benefits is exactly how AARP got to be 32 million members strong. A yearly membership fee of just $5 entitles any American over the age of fifty to a host of discount services: automobile and travel clubs, life and health insurance, a prescription drug service, discounts on magazine subscriptions, even a mutual fund. Most members join for the selective material benefits they get as individuals, not for the government influence they get as part of a collective whole.

A History of Organized Interests

Organized interests tend to grow in waves rather than in a steady flow.[30] Political scientists have identified at least three great waves of growth.[31] The first began in 1830 and lasted roughly forty years. The key disturbance was the general upheaval over the rapidly growing nation, which gave rise to the American Medical Association (AMA)(1847), the Young Men's Christian Association (founded in 1851), the National Grange (which represents farmers and was founded in 1867), the Elks (1868), and a host of antislavery groups (which can be counted among America's first public interest groups).

The second wave began in the 1880s and also lasted forty years. (Some political scientists divide this second wave in two: the 1880s, and 1900–1920.) The key disturbance was the industrial revolution, which uprooted many Americans and brought wave after wave of new immigrants to America. Many of today's most familiar interests were formed during the period: the American Red Cross (1881), the National Association of Manufacturers (1895), the Veterans of Foreign Wars (1899), the National Association for the Advancement of Colored People (NAACP) (1909), the U.S. Chamber of Commerce (1912), the American Cancer Society (1913), and the American Farm Bureau (1919).

The third and current wave began in the 1960s and has yet to end. The key disturbances were the civil rights movement and Vietnam War. The success of the civil rights movement led directly to the formation of a host of public interest groups on everything from the environment to handgun control. As new laws regulating business and society were passed, America's corporate sector responded by organizing its own groups. The Business Roundtable was created as a counterforce in 1972, followed by a number of smaller, more specialized lobbies.

There is no better example of the link between social divisions and organized interests than the women's movement. With more and more women entering the workforce during the 1960s, concern about gender discrimination grew. Although Congress protected women against employment discrimination in the Civil Rights Act of 1964, complaints about uneven enforcement led a small group of women to found the National Organization for Women (NOW) in 1966. According to Betty Friedan, author of the *Feminine Mystique,* a major influence on feminist thinking, and one of the Founders of NOW, the goal of the new organization was simple: "to take action to bring women into full participation in the mainstream of American society, *now.*"[32]

NOW was only the first of a long list of women's groups—from the Women's Legal Defense Fund and the National Association of Working Women in the early 1970s to the Fund for a Feminist Majority in 1987. Not all the groups were in favor of women's liberation, however. As NOW and other feminist groups launched their campaign for the Equal Rights Amendment (ERA), which would have prohibited discrimination on the basis of gender, a host of anti-ERA groups formed—STOP-ERA, Females Opposed to Equality (FOE), American Women Against the Ratification of ERA (AWARE), and Happiness of Motherhood Eternal (HOME).

As the third wave continued into the 1980s, it began to generate a rather different kind of interest around single issues such as abortion and ERA. These **single-issue groups,** which focus on one issue, reflect a splintering of American social groups. Single-issue groups have emerged to promote auto safety (Center for Auto Safety) and prevent drunk driving (Mothers Against Drunk Driving); to protect animals (the Fund for Animals) and reduce pesticide abuse (the National Coalition Against the Misuse of Pesticides); to reduce violence in television (Action for Children's Television), and even improve the way members of Congress organize their offices (the Congressional Management Foundation).

The longer the third wave continues, the larger the organized interest community becomes. The community appears to be infinitely elastic, able to absorb any number of new organizations. Although figures on the exact numbers are not perfect, political scientists generally agree that there are roughly four times as many organized interests operating in Washington today as there were in the late 1940s.

Influencing Government

Efforts to influence who gets what, when, and how from government are as old as the government itself. Indeed, the term *lobbyist* was in usage as early as the

1830s to describe individuals or groups who waited outside government chambers (in the lobbies) to plead for their clients.

Lobbyists were in the hallways of the very first Congress in 1789. "After each legislative day, hogsheads of wine and port poured freely at sumptuous meals of mutton, pork, duck, and turkey," writes reporter Jeffrey Birnbaum in *The Lobbyists*. "The dinner linens were snowy white, the cutlery was burnished and English, and the check was paid by the wealthy merchants of the day."[33] (A hogshead is an obscure measure roughly equivalent to eight "pony" kegs of beer.)

Although the tactics have become much more sophisticated over the years, lobbying still depends in large measure on creating goodwill with Congress. Lobbying involves far more than just showing up at a senator's or house member's office to make the case on behalf of the elderly or a local college, however. Rather, it involves a host of efforts, small and large, to focus legislative attention on a specific issue, none of which will matter to the final outcome if the organized interest does not have the two basic ingredients of success: (1) resources, and (2) the tools to make them stick. Each will be discussed below.

Resources of Influence.   An organized interest's influence depends on several broad measures of strength, including size, intensity, and money. There is clearly power in sizes. In theory, or so the largest interests argue, size translates into votes on election day. Many divide their membership lists by congressional district, all the better to show Congress just what might be at stake on a given issue in a future election. Many also publish box scores of key legislative votes to remind Congress that someone is watching.

It is AARP's 32 million members, for example, that give its lobbyists such influence in the halls of Congress. The AARP's new Washington headquarters employs a full-time lobbying staff of eighteen, and generates so much mail both in and out that it has earned its own zip code. The AARP also has 251,000 legislative volunteers located across the country ready to organize a letter-writing campaign on the latest Social Security or Medicare crisis.[34]

Size is useless, however, if members are not intensely committed to the cause. Groups that are small but intense may be much more successful than ones that are large but ambivalent. Large groups may have particular difficulty reaching agreement on what they want, and may be unable to hold their members around controversial positions.[35] To keep members happy, they often adopt the least controversial positions, and may have particular problems deciding to act at all.

Moreover, large groups may be particularly sluggish when it comes time to make compromises on major legislation. It is like turning an aircraft carrier in rough seas. Being a very big ship creates certain advantages—not the least of which is the fear it strikes into the enemy—but also limits mobility.

Beyond a group's intensity, money makes the organized interest world go round. Whether raised through dues, magazines (the Consumers Union, for example, publishes *Consumer Reports*), or grants from private foundations and government,

President Clinton addresses the American Association of Retired Persons. Its more than 30 million members give AARP significant influence on aging policy.

money pays for the essentials of organizational survival: staff, rent, lobbyists, advertising, printing, mail, heat, and light. Half of AARP's $300 million yearly budget comes from $5 membership dues, the other half from member fees for the discount pharmacy, travel clubs, and money market funds.

Tools of Influence.   Gone are the days when a hogshead is enough to secure a member's support. According to a survey of Washington representatives by political scientist Robert Salisbury, organized interests do many things to lobby government, some of which they do regularly (alerting clients about issues), others they do sparingly (filing an **amicus brief,** which is from the term *amicus curiae* meaning friend of the court, to make their position known to the Supreme Court), still others they do just once every few years (providing money to campaigns). (See Box 4–7 for the list of activities.)

All of these activities are designed for but one purpose, however: *to glue an organized interest's resources to a specific position on who gets what, when, and how from government.* Members of Congress can hardly help an organized interest if they do not know what the organized interest wants. Although all of the activities involve an effort to focus government attention, the list can be collapsed into three basic activities: (1) providing information, (2) building public support, and (3) influencing elections.

BOX
4-7

What Organized Interests Do

Activity	Frequency*
Alerting client about issues	4.3
Developing policy or strategy	4.3
Maintaining relations with government	3.8
Making informal contacts with officials	3.7
Monitoring proposed changes in rules and laws	3.7
Providing information to officials	3.5
Preparing testimony or official comments	3.4
Commentary for press; public speaking	3.2
Mobilizing grassroots support	3.0
Monitoring interest groups	2.8
Testifying	2.7
Drafting proposed legislation or regulations	2.7
Making contacts with opposition	2.6
Making contacts with allies	2.5
Resolving internal organizational disputes	2.5
Litigation	2.1
Arranging for political contributions	2.0
Writing briefs to the Supreme Court	1.6

*1=never; 5=regularly

Source: Robert H. Salisbury, "The Paradox of Interest Groups in Washington—More Groups, Less Clout," in Anthony King, ed., The New American Political System (Washington, D.C.: American Enterprise Institute Press, 1990), p. 228.

Providing Information. Most legislative decisions begin with simple information about a problem and its potential solutions. That is why organized interests spend so much time trying to educate Congress, the presidency, and the Supreme Court on the issue.

Nowhere is the effort to inform more aggressive than on Capitol Hill. Lobbyists often supply the first draft of the bills, provide most of the witnesses that testify before committees, and write the background papers that find their way into floor speeches by members. Congress simply could not operate without help from lobbyists.

Lobbyists do not restrict their focus to Congress, however. Many provide background arguments to the courts on key cases. Amicus briefs are designed to help a given court sort through the issues in a case. Not all of the briefs are on the same side, of course. In 1984, for example, the U.S. Supreme Court case of

Sony Corporation of America v. Universal City Studios turned on the question of whether Americans were free to tape television programs with their VCRs. In all, 140 amicus briefs were filed, most from corporations involved in the high stakes decision (which was ultimately decided in favor of free taping), but some from free speech groups such as the American Civil Liberties Union.[36]

Building Support. As already noted in Chapter 3, Washington, D.C., likes nothing better than a good public opinion poll. Members of Congress and presidents clearly pay attention to what the people think, if not to make final decisions, then at the very least to help set the agenda of issues they will address. That is why organized interests spent so much energy building and showing public support for their issues.

If the organized interest is large enough, of course, the action of its own members is often enough to get attention. Letter writing campaigns, telegrams, telephone trees, petitions, and marches are all time-honored methods for demonstrating member interest. Merely producing a million form letters is far less effective than generating highly personalized, handwritten requests. The latter is seen as true grassroots interest, while the former is often dismissed by Congress as manufactured, or astroturf, support. The more personal and individual the letter, the more likely Washington is to take it seriously.

For smaller organized interests or on highly controversial issues in which more than one organized interest might be involved, having a mail campaign may not be enough. Many organized interests have started to use paid advertising to convince the American public of its cause, hoping that public opinion polls will create momentum behind their preferred option. This *advocacy advertising,* as it is sometimes labeled, was particularly visible during the 1993–1994 debate over health care reform. Americans were treated to a media barrage, including advertisements featuring "Harry and Louise," a sympathetic couple who wondered what government involvement might do to their health care.

Influencing Elections. Once an organized interest convinces a member of Congress or a president to support its cause, nothing could be worse than to lose that supporter in the next election. That is why many organized interests endorse candidates for office, and why they often encourage members to participate in party politics. The 16 million members of America's labor unions, for example, constitute a highly motivated resource for the Democratic Party, whether as voters or party workers.

Keeping supporters in office is also why so many organized interests create **political action committees (PACs).** A PAC is a legally distinct organization that raises and spends money on election campaigns, whether by giving money directly to candidates and political parties, or by spending money indirectly for campaign activities such as advertising and get-out-the-vote efforts.

The first PACs were created in 1973 under sweeping campaign finance reform legislation. Because this legislation altered the campaign finance system across the board, it will be discussed in more detail in Chapter 6. For the time being, suffice

it to note that organized interests are prohibited from making cc
candidates through any other device but PACs, and are limited in ho
can give to any one candidate in any one election campaign, primary

There is no question that PACs have become a significant player i
tion process. The number of PACs has grown from 722 in 1975 to ne   +,000
in 1995, while the amount of money raised by PACs has risen from $54 million
to $391 million by 1994.[37] Even as the numbers increased, the mix of interests
remained relatively stable. (See Box 4–8 for the mix of PACs.)

There are two other points to remember about the mix of PACs. First, corporations account for the largest percentage of PACs. They also happen to give the

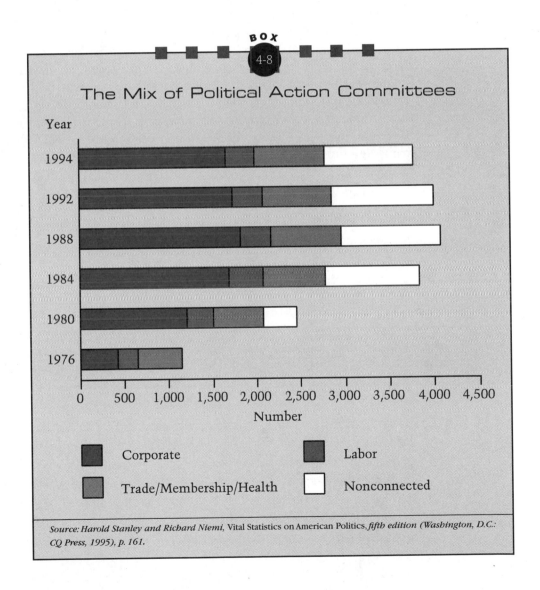

BOX

4-8

The Mix of Political Action Committees

Source: Harold Stanley and Richard Niemi, Vital Statistics on American Politics, *fifth edition (Washington, D.C.:*
CQ Press, 1995), p. 161.

greatest amounts of money. In 1994, for example, corporate PACs gave roughly $70 million to candidates, while trade, membership, and health groups (which include substantial numbers of corporations among their memberships) came in second with nearly $53 million, and labor came in third with just under $42 million. Nonconnected groups, a term that includes public interest groups, came in a distant fourth at just $18 million.

Second, the number of nonconnected groups has grown the fastest over the years. However, not all public interest groups have PACs. Many prefer to earn their influence the old fashioned way, by providing information and building public support. AARP does not have a PAC, for example, nor does the National Wildlife Federation, the Children's Defense League, Mothers Against Drunk Driving, or Common Cause.

Over the past two decades, PACs have become the number one source of funding for reelection campaigns, accounting for almost 50 cents of every dollar raised by incumbents.[38] Yet, just because PACs spend large amounts of money hardly guarantees they can swing the legislative debate one way or the another. PACs tend to give their money to politicians who already support their position, making it difficult to determine which came first: the PAC money or the member's favorable position. Moreover, PAC money constitutes a relatively small share of campaign funding from year to year, barely topping a third of total dollars raised in 1990 and 1994.

The problem with the access, however, is that Congress loses time to think about issues, write legislation, and reflect about the public good. As such, the real cost of PAC money may not be in the declining public trust that goes with the appearance of special influence, but in the fact that members of Congress and candidates must spend so much of their time raising it.

IN A DIFFERENT LIGHT

THE 1995 GIFT BAN

Before the 1940s, there were few rules on what lobbyists could do to influence government. Although outright bribery was against the law, lobbyists could and often did give members of Congress and other high-ranking officials "gifts" of one kind or another, including speaking fees, free travel, and entertainment. By the early 1990s, most lobbyists were spending between $5,000 and $15,000 a year alone taking members of Congress and their staffs out for free meals.[39]

Although Congress tightened some of the excess in 1946, it was not until 1995 that both houses banned most gifts. Because each house controls its own members, the two versions of the gift ban were slightly different. The Senate put a $50 limit on all gifts, including entertainment and meals, while the House banned all gifts regardless of amount.

In theory, the gift bans were designed to end all appearances that lobbyists were buying access through gifts. However, because each ban contained its own loopholes, they may have created a whole new industry in Washington just interpreting what constitutes a free meal. "If you stand at a bar and pay for a drink, that's OK," said a senior House lawyer in explaining the new rules to lobbyists. "But if you're sitting down, ordering rounds of drinks and hot hors d'oeuvres and cold hors d'oeuvres, that's beginning to look an awfully lot like a meal. And a meal is ba-a-a-ad."

As long as the food is on a toothpick, according to the "Toothpick Rule," it is exempt from the ban on free meals. Once food lays on a plate or is covered by gravy, which means that it must be eaten with a fork or spoon, it becomes a meal. Breakfast is a particularly tough meal to regulate, according to the rules. "Coffee and doughnuts are OK. Croissants are probably all right. But I get a lot of questions about bagels and what you can put on them. Lox may be pushing it."[40]

The question is why bother with trying to regulate gifts at all. What is so bad about a free lunch at an upscale Washington restaurant? The answer is that the rules are not so much about meals or travel or speaking fees, but about changing the relationship between lobbyists and government. Lobbyists do not give members of Congress a free breakfast, a trip to Bermuda, or a $2,000 honoraria for delivering a speech out of the goodness of their hearts. They give gifts to get something in return.

That "something" in return is not a specific vote on a bill, however. No member of Congress can be bought for a plate of fresh fruit or a bagel. Rather, what lobbyists get is better access at key moments in the legislative process. A member may not remember what he or she ate at that lunch with the lobbyist six weeks before the key vote, but just might make time for a ten minute briefing on the pros and cons of the issue. With only so much time in the day, members of Congress may make their toughest decisions on who they will see. And who they see may have a significant impact on a final vote.

Even if gifts have no bearing whatsoever on what members of Congress do, they create the appearance of **conflict of interest.** Such conflicts arise whenever elected or appointed officials have a personal stake in an issue they must decide, for example, because they own stock in a company regulated by their agency, have a family member who works for a company up for a major federal contract, or know the defendant in a criminal case. Members of Congress who accept large amounts of gifts may create the image that they have a personal stake in favoring a given position, leading the public to conclude that government is run for the benefit of special interests.

By itself, a gift ban is not enough to restore public confidence that government is run for the benefit of the people, if only because one of the largest gifts a lobbyist can give, campaign money, continues to flow. Moreover, lobbyists had already found ways around the ban within days of its passage—the House allows free travel and meals at "widely attended events," meaning that members will likely start eating with lobbyists at larger tables. Nevertheless, the gift ban is a step toward reducing the appearance of conflict of interest. If that means pricey Washington restaurants face a bit of an economic slowdown, it may be a small price to pay.

■ ■ ■

CONCLUSION

If the Founders wanted ambition to counter ambition, they got their wish. The number of organized interests has never been larger, nor has the potential for stalemate ever seemed greater. Indeed, as the number of organized interests has grown, it has fragmented into ever smaller parts, rendering all of the community less capable of coming together to capture government.[41] Gone are the days when huge interests such as the American Medical Association can dictate to their members. There are now literally hundreds of groups involved in health policy, and dozens in most other issues. More groups has come to equal less clout for everyone.

There are at least two reasons to believe that the growth of organized interests is far from over. First, population and social trends suggest growing conflict in the future. America is growing older, more women are working, the society is becoming more diverse, the traditional two-parent, two-child family is in decline, and the distance between the haves and have-nots continues to expand. The result is a nation with more reasons to join organized interests.

Second, there is some evidence that public boredom with the parties is fueling some of the growth in organized interests. As Americans increasingly define themselves by their memberships in organized interests, they may feel less need to define themselves by their party. They may see differences between the two parties, and still identify with one or the other party at any given point in time, but may see less of a reason to stay loyal. After all, they can always join an organized interest to have their voice heard in Washington.

The Founders might be deeply concerned by the amount of ambition. Much as Madison and his colleagues hoped that interests would cancel each other out, they most certainly would not have wanted ambition to eventually cancel out action altogether. They wanted a government that would be just strong enough, not one that would become so paralyzed by multiple interests that it could not work at all.

Unfortunately, the current condition of government may yield few other outcomes. Lacking the clout to drive ideas forward, organized interests may have little choice but to favor stalemate. And, given the Founders' design of separate powers, interests and layers, and checks and balances, it is a choice with a very high probability of success. Almost any organized interest can win a battle somewhere in the system—if not in the House, then perhaps in the Senate; if not in the Congress, then perhaps in an executive agency; if not in the executive branch, then perhaps in a lower court; if not in the federal government, then perhaps in a state or local government. That is, of course, part of the beauty of the constitutional design, but it is also part of its great risk. As the number of groups increases, the pressure toward stalemate also increases.

The Founders might conclude that a strong two-party system is essential to stemming the effects of so many organized interests. Although they saw parties and organized interests as two sides of the same coin of faction, the Founders might well recognize that parties play a significant role in building coalitions across the divides created by organized interests. They might admire how parties work to discipline the House and Senate, and how they help recruit candidates and contest elections. They might even agree that the parties can play a critical role in putting the Humpty-Dumpty of government back together after it cracks under the weight of so many organized interests.

THE BASICS

■ The Founders expected parties and organized interests to exist outside government, if only because it is human nature to form such factions. They designed government to control the effects of faction by counteracting ambition with ambition. In theory, the more factions, the better. What would surprise them is how important both have become as go-betweens in the space between government and the people.

■ The very first political parties appeared almost immediately after ratification of the Constitution. Alexander Hamilton formed the Federalist Party in 1796, while Thomas Jefferson formed the Republicans in 1800. The Founders had expected these two parties to disappear once the battle over ratification was resolved.

■ Today's parties perform three essential roles in democratic life: (1) contesting elections, (2) organizing government, and (3) helping voters decide. In fulfilling these roles, party organizations exist at three levels—federal, state, and local. Party platforms are one glue that holds the three roles together. Platforms are a product of the national conventions, which also nominate the presidential and vice presidential candidates, often form the basis for legislation, and signal voters on what the parties believe.

■ America is a nation of joiners, and organized interests are one kind of organization people can join. What makes organized interests different from other kinds of organizations is the effort to influence who gets what, when, and how from government. The term *organized interest* includes traditional membership-based interest groups, as well as a new breed of single-member organizations.

■ Organized interests form during social or economic disturbances, and exist to provide one or more of four basic benefits: (1) material, (2) social, (3) civic, or (4) policy. Most organized interests focus on material benefits for their members, and prevent the free rider problem of collective benefits by offering selective benefits available to their member(s) and their member(s) only.

KEY CONCEPTS

■ The Federalist Party did, in fact, disappear early in the 1800s, leaving the Democratic-Republicans as the single party during the so-called Era of Good Feelings. That era came to an end, however, in the 1820s when the Democratic-Republicans divided into three splinter parties. America has had a two-party system ever since, in part because the *winner-take-all* nature of elections appears to encourage such a system. Altogether, there have been five party eras, three of which ended in critical or realigning elections. The fifth and current era appears to be coming to a close with no realignment yet in sight.

■ The two parties are doing very well by way of both contesting elections and organizing government. Party unity scores in Congress are at a recent high. However, the two parties appear to be weakening as devices for helping voters decide. The number of Americans who split their votes between parties is up, and the number who have anything either good or bad to say about the parties is down. Although voters still see differences between the two parties, there is growing evidence that party no longer shapes the vote as it once did.

■ Organized interests seek to influence, or lobby, government in three ways: (1) providing information, (2) building public support, and (3) influencing elections. Their success in doing so depends on their size, intensity, and financial resources. The most controversial lobbying tactic involves giving money to campaigns through political action committees, or PACs. The largest amounts of money come from corporate PACs, with nonconnected (or public interest group) PACs giving the least. Whatever their interest, however, most PACs tend to give money to incumbents.

■ The past 30 years have produced a remarkable increase in the number of organized interests, creating concerns about whether government is still strong enough to do its job. Every organized interest can win some battle somewhere in the Founders' government of separate powers, interests and layers, and checks and balances. Ironically, the Founders might view a strong two-party system as addressing some of the effects of organized interests.

129

IN A DIFFERENT LIGHT

■ People who show up for the national party conventions are very different from the rest of the public. They tend to be much more ideological than Americans in general and other members of their own party. The result is that presidential candidates must often move toward the extremes of their party to win the nomination. The party platforms are also likely to be out of touch with the general public.

■ Third parties have very poor chances of actually winning a presidential election, in large part because they do not have the organizational strength needed to win. The closest a third party has ever come to the White House is the Bull Moose Party of Theodore Roosevelt, which ran the most successful third-party campaign in history in 1912, but mostly succeeded in throwing an otherwise easy Republican election to the Democratic Party (and in doing so may have saved the Democratic Party from complete collapse!). Third parties are almost always absorbed by the existing parties.

■ Not all Americans have the resources or information to join an organized interest. People with higher socioeconomic status are the most likely to be members of an organized interest, while those with what appears to be the greatest need for help are the least likely to be represented by a lobbying group.

■ In 1996, the House and Senate both passed bans on receiving gifts from lobbyists. The bans are anything but simple, and often involve almost silly rules about what gets classified as a meal (the "Toothpick Rule" and the "Gravy Rule"). The purpose of the gift ban is to eliminate the appearance of conflict of interest that comes when members of Congress and their staffs accept free meals, travel, and speaking fees from organized interests.

OPEN QUESTIONS

■ Why have so many Americans become less willing to identify with one or the other political party? Is their reluctance just a passing fad or does it somehow fit with other changes in politics? If Americans are not using party to help make their voting decisions, just what are they using? To what extent are candidates for office also distancing themselves from their parties?

■ If Americans are so critical of special interests, why are they so active as members? Are they being overly critical or is there something else happening in the polling numbers? Is it possible, for example, that individual Americans think very highly of the groups they join, but less so of the corporate lobbyists or others associated with the kinds of conflicts of interest involved in the gift ban?

■ How does the rise of organized interests fit with the decline of party loyalty? Are the two related, and if so, just how? Would America be better off abandoning the two-party system and opting for parties built around organized interests (recall that Ralph Nader ran for president as the candidate of the Green, or environmental, Party in 1996)? Just as Americans have learned to use new media, is it time for new parties?

TERMS TO REMEMBER

political party	critical election
organized interest	realigning election
party committees	straight-ticket voting
party platforms	split-ticket voting
national party conventions	lobbying
party machines	interest groups
congressional campaign committee	disturbance theory
party identification	free rider problem
independents	collective benefits
winner-take-all system	selective benefits
single-member districts	single-issue groups
multimember districts	amicus brief
party eras	political action committees (PACs)
New Deal coalition	conflict of interest

Endnotes to Chapter 4

▶ 1. Jefferson and Washington quoted in James Roger Sharp, *American Politics in the Early Republic: The New Nation in Crisis* (New Haven, CT: Yale University Press, 1993), p. 9; Adams quoted in A. James Reichley, *The Life of the Parties: A History of American Political Parties* (New York: The Free Press, 1992), p. 17.

▶ 2. Paul Allen Beck and Frank J. Sorauf, *Party Politics in America* (New York: HarperCollins, 1992), pp. 11–12.

3. Beck and Sorauf, *Party Politics in America,* p. 105.

4. *New York Times*/CBS News Poll, reprinted in *New York Times,* August 26, 1996, p. A12.

▶ 5. See Steven Smith, *The American Congress* (Boston: Houghton Mifflin, 1995), p. 162.

6. Harold W. Stanley and Richard G. Niemi, *Vital Statistics on American Politics* (Washington, DC: CQ Press, 1995), p. 198.

7. Drawn from Stanley and Niemi, *Vital Statistics,* p. 146.

8. Times Mirror Center for The People & The Press, *The People, the Press and Politics: The New Political Landscape,* September 21, 1994, p. 58.

▶ 9. Not all scholars accept this view. For an excellent critique, see James Caesar, *Presidential Selection: Theory and Development* (Princeton, NJ: Princeton University Press, 1979).

10. Reichley, *The Life of the Parties,* pp. 36–37.

11. See John Bibby, *Politics, Parties, and Elections in America* (Chicago: Nelson-Hall, 1992).

12. Bibby, *Politics, Parties, and Elections in America,* p. 39.

13. Kenneth C. Davis, *Don't Know Much About History* (New York: Avon Books, 1990), p. 119.

14. For a detailed history of party change from the early 1800s to the present, see James Sundquist, *Dynamics of the Party System: Alignment and Realignment of Political Parties in the United States,* revised ed. (Washington, DC: Brookings Institution, 1983).

15. Davis, *Don't Know Much About History,* p. 213.

16. Stanley and Niemi, *Vital Statistics,* p. 136. The figure on split-ticket voting for state and local offices is for 1984.

17. James Perry, "Win or Lose, Perot Proves One Can Run without Major Parties," *Wall Street Journal,* July 14, 1992, p. A1.

18. Times Mirror Center, *The New Political Landscape,* p. 54.

19. Times Mirror Center, *The New Political Landscape,* p. 48.

20. Times Mirror Center, *The New Political Landscape,* p. 48.

21. Times Mirror Center, *The New Political Landscape,* p. 58.

22. See Michael MacKuen, Robert Erikson, and James Stimson, "Macropartisanship," *American Political Science Review*, volume 83, number 4 (Winter 1989), pp. 1125–42.

23. Alexis de Tocqueville, *Democracy in America,* ed., J. P. Mayer, trans. George Lawrence (Garden City, NY: Harper Perennial, 1988), pp. 513–17.

24. David Segal, "Main Street America Has Advocates Aplenty," *Washington Post,* July 10, 1995, p. A6.

25. See Marian Burros, "Chefs' Environmental Politics Is Making the Kitchen Hotter," *New York Times,* September 30, 1992, p. B1.

26. Thomas Toch and Ted Slafsky, "The Scientific Pork Barrel," *U.S. News & World Report,* volume 114, issue 8, March 1, 1993, pp. 58–59.

27. See Robert Salisbury, "An Exchange Theory of Interest Groups," *Midwest Journal of Political Science,* vol. 13, no. 1 (February, 1969), pp. 1–32; see also Ronald Hrebenar and Ruth Scott, *Interest Group Politics in America* (Englewood Cliffs, NJ: Prentice-Hall, 1990), p. 14, for a summary.

▶ 28. Sidney Verba, Kay Lehman Schlozman, and Henry E. Brady, *Voice and Equality: Civic Voluntarism in American Politics* (Cambridge, MA: Harvard University Press, 1995), p. 122.

▶ 29. Mancur Olson, *The Logic of Collective Action* (Cambridge, MA: Harvard University Press, 1965), pp. 64–65.

▶ 30. See David Truman, *The Governmental Process* (New York: Knopf, 1971).

31. James Q. Wilson, *Political Organizations* (New York: Basic Books, 1975), p. 198.

32. Quoted in Ethel Klein, *Gender Politics: From Consciousness to Mass Politics* (Cambridge, MA: Harvard University Press, 1984), p. 23.

▶ 33. Jeffrey Birnbaum, *The Lobbyists: How Influence Peddlers Work their Way in Washington* (New York: Times Books, 1993), p. 8.

34. These figures are drawn from Ron Suskind, "Whose Side Are They On, Anyway?" *SmartMoney,* February 1993, p. 98.

35. See Mancur Olson, *The Logic of Collective Action,* pp. 9–36, for a discussion of the problems of large groups.

36. See Henry J. Abraham, *The Judicial Process,* sixth edition (New York: Oxford University Press, 1993), p. 239.

37. Stanley and Niemi, *Vital Statistics,* pp. 161, 164.

38. These numbers come from Frank Sorauf, *Inside Campaign Finance: Myths and Realities* (New Haven, CT: Yale University Press, 1992), p. 71.

39. See Peter H. Stone, "Lobbyists on a Leash," *The National Journal,* February 3, 1996, p. 245.

40. Eric Schmitt, "Order for Lobbyists: Hold the Gravy," *New York Times,* February 11, 1996, p. 30.

41. See Robert Salisbury, "The Paradox of Interest Groups in Washington: More Groups, Less Clout," in Salisbury, ed., *Interests and Institutions: Substance and Structure in American Politics* (Pittsburgh: University of Pittsburgh Press, 1992).

PARTICIPATION AND VOTING

CHAPTER 5

Just as America has always been a nation of joiners, it has also always been a nation of political participators. "No sooner do you set foot upon American ground than you are stunned by a kind of tumult," Tocqueville wrote upon his return to France after his visit to a young America 150 years ago. "[A] confused clamor rises on every side, a thousand voices are heard at once. . . . To take a hand in the government of society and to talk about it is [the] biggest concern and, so to say, the only pleasure [an American] knows."[1] Participating is part of what Tocqueville labeled "the habits of the democratic heart."

Tocqueville would still hear the clamor today, whether in million-man marches on Washington or battles for the school board. Citizens are still contacting their president and members of Congress, still voting in elections, still working together as volunteers to address public problems in their own communities, still creating a kind of tumult with their activity. Even though the Founders would be surprised to see so many women and minorities involved in politics (recall that the Constitution did not envision a role for either in politics or voting), they would probably view the participation as a consent to be governed, an expression of the broad commitment to a government of the people.

Habits of the Democratic Heart

Not all the news is good, however. Even though large numbers of Americans may participate in politics, the engagement is uneven across society. Some Americans cannot participate at all because they simply do not have the resources or civic skills to be effective; others are checking out because they have grown alienated from politics; still others are becoming "checkbook activists," in which their sole activity is writing a check to a candidate or organized interest.

As we will see, Americans have ample cause for not participating. There is not enough time in the day, taking care of the kids comes first, and politics is a dirty business (Jay Leno jokes that the word *politics* comes from the Greek *poly* meaning many and *ticks* meaning blood suckers). But even if the reasons are good, the voices are still lost and the base of participation is still narrowed.

In the rest of this chapter we will explore these problems of participation in more detail, first by looking at the options for participating in general, then at voting specifically. Many of the reasons Americans may be checking out involve declining resources and skills for participating. Every act of participation costs something in time and energy. Even the least expensive act of all, voting, takes more than a moment's notice.

PARTICIPATING IN POLITICS

Participating in politics is very much an act of consent to be governed. By showing up to vote, citizens not only endorse a specific candidate, but also endorse representative democracy. By writing a letter to their leaders, they not only convey a specific message, but also acknowledge the legitimacy of the institution for deciding who gets what, when, and how from government. And by volunteering to help others in their communities, they not only improve their communities, but also express their broad commitment to the common good.

By any measure, Americans are still giving their consent to be governed. Roughly 80 percent of Americans do some kind of political participating every year, from volunteering with their neighbors to address some community problem such as crime or traffic to showing up for jury duty, signing a petition, working in a campaign, talking about politics with their friends or family, voting in an election, or watching the evening news.[2] Americans do participate.

Lost in this tumult, however, are very real differences among Americans in the amount that they participate. Not all Americans can afford to give money to campaigns and not all can find the time to register to vote. And because politics is run by those who show up, these differences matter to who gets what, when, and how from government. Before turning to these differences, it is first important to inventory the options for participating and understand more about why Americans participate at all.

Options for Participating

With over a half million elected officials to contact, over 85,000 units of government (national, state, and local) to petition, nearly 18 million public employees to talk to, and thousands upon thousands of membership groups to join, Americans have a nearly infinite list of opportunities for engagement.

Although the options are many, political scientists often winnow the list down to eight basic acts that are open to most Americans:

1. Voting
2. Working as a volunteer for a candidate running for office
3. Giving money to a campaign
4. Contacting government by mail or in person
5. Taking part in a protest, march, or demonstration of some kind
6. Working with others to address community problems
7. Joining a local governmental board such as the school board or city council
8. Joining or giving money to an organized interest.[3]

The average American participates in two of these eight acts per year. (Count your own level of participation by checking off the questions in Box 5–1.)

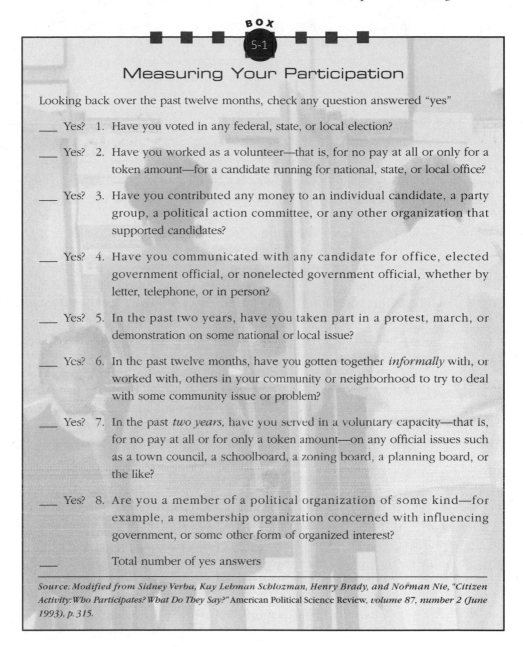

BOX 5-1

Measuring Your Participation

Looking back over the past twelve months, check any question answered "yes"

___ Yes? 1. Have you voted in any federal, state, or local election?

___ Yes? 2. Have you worked as a volunteer—that is, for no pay at all or only for a token amount—for a candidate running for national, state, or local office?

___ Yes? 3. Have you contributed any money to an individual candidate, a party group, a political action committee, or any other organization that supported candidates?

___ Yes? 4. Have you communicated with any candidate for office, elected government official, or nonelected government official, whether by letter, telephone, or in person?

___ Yes? 5. In the past two years, have you taken part in a protest, march, or demonstration on some national or local issue?

___ Yes? 6. In the past twelve months, have you gotten together *informally* with, or worked with, others in your community or neighborhood to try to deal with some community issue or problem?

___ Yes? 7. In the past *two years,* have you served in a voluntary capacity—that is, for no pay at all or for only a token amount—on any official issues such as a town council, a schoolboard, a zoning board, a planning board, or the like?

___ Yes? 8. Are you a member of a political organization of some kind—for example, a membership organization concerned with influencing government, or some other form of organized interest?

___ Total number of yes answers

Source: Modified from Sidney Verba, Kay Lehman Schlozman, Henry Brady, and Norman Nie, "Citizen Activity: Who Participates? What Do They Say?" American Political Science Review, *volume 87, number 2 (June 1993), p. 315.*

All options for participating are not equal, however. They differ in their publicness, frequency, acceptability, personal cost, and sharpness of the message sent to government. We will tackle each difference in order.

Publicness. The options for participating vary greatly in visibility, or "publicness." Some Americans like to participate in private, others in public. Nothing is more visible, for example, than serving on a school board. The decisions are often highly controversial, particularly when it comes time to raise taxes or cut programs. Nothing is less visible, perhaps, than volunteering with others to solve some community problem. Millions of Americans do so every day, with no acknowledgment asked and none given.

Voting is both the least and most visible act of all. *How* a person votes is completely invisible—that is, after all, the point of a secret ballot. But *whether* a person votes is a very public act. Showing up at the polling booth is an admittedly old-fashioned way of showing the consent of the governed. As we will see later in this chapter, the movement toward voting by mail reduces the publicness of voting, perhaps weakening the act as a shared expression of consent.

Frequency.   The options for participating come in two basic frequencies: acts that occur only on occasion versus those that permit nearly infinite activism. Voting is clearly fixed by law and practice. Elections take place only on occasion, and every voter gets just one vote, unless, of course, one wants to risk going to jail for voter fraud. In a similar vein, serving on local government boards is limited by the number of openings and the election process itself.

The rest of the options for participating are unlimited. Americans are free to telephone Congress as long as their fingers can dial, e-mail the president as long as their computer keyboards still work, march on Washington as long as their shoes hold up, and contribute to campaigns as much as their bank accounts will cover. And the more that Americans participate in these activities, the more influence they can have. For sure, the more money a citizen gives to campaigns, the more campaigns will court that citizen; the more visible a citizen becomes in local politics, the more responsive government is likely to be. Although the relationship between activity and influence is not perfect, rare is the citizen who has influence by staying at home.

Acceptability.   Americans do not believe all forms of participation are civically acceptable, a judgment that is usually based on whether a given act fits with what the nation defines as being a good citizen. Not surprisingly, voting is seen as the most **conventional participation,** or civically acceptable act. Americans are so certain that it is their civic duty to vote that they feel guilty when they do not.

What Americans do not like are protests of one kind or another, which are considered **unconventional participation,** or civically unacceptable acts. Only 15 percent approve of consumer boycotts, and just 11 percent approve of lawful demonstrations and marches, both of which are guaranteed under the right to peaceful assembly in the First Amendment, and both of which contributed to the founding of the nation two hundred years ago. They are even less supportive of breaking the law to advance a cause: just 1 percent approve of blocking traffic, painting slogans on walls, engaging in personal violence, and damaging property.[4]

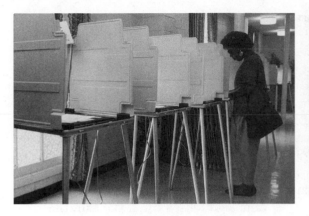

Conventional and unconventional participation. Voting (left) is considered civic duty, while protesting (right) is considered less acceptable.

Cost.   Every option for participating in politics carries a cost, whether in time, information, or money. Americans cannot give money to a campaign, for example, without having money to give. They cannot give time to an organization without having time to give. Recognizing that participation has a cost is essential for understanding why some Americans participate more than others.

Voting is a simple example. In most states, citizens cannot vote unless they are registered, which requires at least some effort to figure out where and how to register, and even more effort to actually go through the act of registering itself. Voters also have to know when the election will take place, which means paying at least some attention to the news, and where to vote, which usually means at least a quick glance at the inside pages of a newspaper or election guide.

Once election day arrives, voters have to find the time and energy to actually go to the polling place. If **voter turnout,** which is the number of registered voters who actually vote, is high, they might have to wait in line to be checked off the registration list, then wait in line to pick up their ballot, then wait in line for the next open voting booth, and only then cast their ballots.

Just getting past the mechanics is tough enough for many Americans. However, if they wish to make their choices on something other than party identification or whether the candidate has a familiar last name, voters must spend at least some time before the election listening to advertisements, reading newspaper and magazine articles about the candidates, watching debates, and paying attention. Being informed is not "cheap" in either time or energy, particularly in the United States where elections are frequent, party differences are sometimes minimal, and voting registration laws differ state by state. No single act takes more than a few minutes, but each act adds up.

Sharpness of the Message.   Every option for participating conveys some sense of what a citizen wants in return—for example, lower taxes, safer streets, or some personal benefit. It is just that some of the information is clear, and some foggy.

Voting in presidential elections is the bluntest form of communication of all. With 50 to 60 million votes cast on his or her behalf, the winning candidate is free to interpret the election as a mandate for a range of ideas. But even local elections give little opportunity to send a clear message. Voters can only say "yes" or "no" to a given candidate, and have little chance to tell their candidate why they voted as they did. Other than referenda and initiatives, where voters voice a "yes" or "no" on a specific policy issue, voting is a very blunt tool for communicating, indeed.

In theory, contributing to a campaign is almost as blunt. In the flood of small contributions that pay the bulk of the campaign bills, a candidate can barely remember who gives, let alone what a giver might want. Nevertheless, especially large contributions often convey a clear message about what an individual or political action committee wants. After all, people and organized interests give money to campaigns as a tool of influence. Although the small contributions of $100 here and there will be forgotten soon after the election, the large contributions may be long remembered.

Of all the options for participating, none is sharper than contacting government directly. Letter writers can tell their officials exactly what they want and when they want it. They can pinpoint specific decisions they care about, and offer unmistakable opinions about their preferences.

 ## IN A DIFFERENT LIGHT

BOWLING ALONE

Few political scientists are more identified with concern about declines in public participation than Harvard University's Robert Putnam, who wrote a paper in 1994 titled "Bowling Alone: Democracy in America at the End of the Twentieth Century."[5] The paper earned him a discussion with President Clinton and a story in *People* magazine.

Putnam made three broad arguments about the state of civic engagement in America. First, he argued that civic participation has declined over the past two decades. Since 1973, the number of Americans who attended a political rally or speech in the previous year fell by over 30 percent, the number who have attended a public meeting on town or school affairs fell by almost 40 percent, and the number who have worked for their political party fell by almost 50 percent.

Second, Putnam argued that Americans have been pulling away from the traditional civic organizations that once held the nation together. Membership in the Boy Scouts dropped 26 percent between 1970 and 1993, the League of Women Voters declined 42 percent, and the Red Cross fell 62 percent. Membership in men's clubs such as the Elks, Lions, and Moose also dropped.

Putnam's most whimsical evidence of the decline in civic engagement was bowling. "More Americans are bowling today than ever before," Putnam wrote, "but *league* bowling has plummeted in the last ten to fifteen years. Between 1980 and 1993 the total number of bowlers in America increased by 10 percent, while league bowling decreased by 49 percent.... The rise of solo bowling threatens the livelihood of bowling proprietors because league bowlers consume three times as much beer and pizza as solo bowlers, and the money in bowling is in the beer and pizza, not the balls and shoes."

Third, Putnam argued that Americans have become less trusting of not just government and politics, but of each other. The number of Americans who say most people can be trusted has fallen from 58 percent in 1960 to 34 percent in 1994. A majority of Americans now believe most people will take advantage of others if given the chance. If they do not trust their neighbors, it is no surprise that Americans do not trust their government.

Not everyone agrees with Putnam's assessment, however.[6] Research shows that certain kinds of participation are actually going up, not down. PTA membership has increased over the past two decades as the 75 million baby boomers born between 1946 and 1964 have focused on raising their children. Soccer leagues and softball leagues are also way up, more than offsetting the drop in beer and pizza sales.

Americans also are giving more money to charity and reporting increased volunteering, including a dramatic surge in crime watch patrols. And, as the old civic organizations decline, Americans are building a new generation of organizations such as COOL (Campus Outreach Opportunity League) and Habitat for Humanity in place of the League of Women Voters and the Elks Club.

Nevertheless, given the nation's need, Americans may not be participating enough. America needs more than just an offset to league bowling. It needs a substantial boost in activism if it is to care for an aging society and reduce drug abuse, crime, and urban decay. Participation is no less important today than it was when Tocqueville visited the nation 150 years ago.

Why Americans Participate

The choice of one option for participating over another depends on the benefits each option provides. Americans seek the same benefits from participating in politics as they seek in joining organized interests: (1) a *material benefit* that comes back to individual citizens, such as tax cuts, higher benefit payments, better streets, or new schools; (2) a *social benefit* that comes from the simple pleasure of working together; (3) a *civic benefit* that comes from fulfilling one's duties as a citizen; and (4) a *policy benefit* that comes from actually influencing government in a way that helps the nation as a whole.

The degree to which a given option provides any of these benefits largely depends on the publicness, frequency, acceptability, cost, and sharpness of the message, as discussed above. Not all options offer the same level or kind of benefit.[7]

Consider voting first. Since voting does not allow individual citizens to tell candidates what they want, it is an exceptionally poor vehicle for providing material benefits. And since voting is so infrequent and done in private, it is also a poor source of social benefits. Casting one vote every year or two is hardly the way to get a sharp message heard, especially since elected officials have no way to know just how an individual voted.

Consider working in campaigns and volunteering in the community next. Neither is a particularly potent source of material benefits. It is hard to see how working on a Habitat for Humanity house would redound to the volunteer's favor at the Internal Revenue Service, or how licking envelopes for a candidate would help with a government contract. Like voting, both activities offer enormous civic benefits, giving participants a sense that they are doing something good for their nation. But unlike voting, both activities offer high social benefits. There is nothing quite so rewarding as working with others in building a house for a deserving family or serving a bowl of hot soup to a homeless person, nothing quite so energizing as working together for a candidate in whom one believes.

Contacting government actually offers a mix of benefits, depending upon the nature of the contact. Some people who write to their leaders do so in search of material benefit for themselves by asking for government help, whether in finding a missing Social Security check or pushing an application to West Point. Members of Congress have staffers called **congressional case workers** to handle just such requests. Other people write in search of policy benefits by taking a position on some pending legislative decision. Still others simply think writing their members of Congress is the right thing to do as a citizen. What contacting government cannot provide is much of a social benefit. It is more a private experience.

Protesting is just the opposite. It provides enormous social benefits to those who march. Participants may not remember exactly what was said by the speakers, but they will long remember the sense of solidarity that came from linking arms together for a cause. Indeed, there is some evidence that people who participated in the antiwar marches of the late 1960s and early 1970s were marked for life. They tend to remember the marches vividly, and have been more active in politics ever since.[8] The same holds for many of the individuals involved in the civil rights marches of the 1950s and early 1960s. People who heard Martin Luther King speak of his dream will never forget the experience.

Finally, contributing money offers different benefits depending on the size of the check and where it goes. People who give to individual candidates in small amounts (as we will see, federal law limits the amount that a citizen can give to any one candidate in any single election campaign) appear to do so for the civic benefits. In contrast, people who give money to an issue organization appear to

A 1963 civil rights march on Washington, D.C. The civil rights movement was guided by a commitment to nonviolent action, and included many peaceful protests.

do so for policy benefits, putting their dollars where their policy beliefs are, while people who give money to a political action committee appear to do so for the material benefits that will eventually come back to them as individuals.

Levels of Participation

Given the reasons for participating, it should not come as a surprise that not all Americans participate in every act. Not all Americans want or need material benefits, not all seek social or civic rewards. Recalling the eight options in Box 5–1, political scientists Sidney Verba, Kay Schlozman, and Henry Brady found that voting was the most popular form of participation. (See Box 5–2 for a chart of the activities.)

Americans put their activities together in many ways. Indeed, political scientists often describe six different types of participators. Roughly 20 percent of Americans are *inactives* who do not participate at all: no voting, no contacting, certainly no joining. Another 20 percent are *voting specialists* who vote and do nothing else. Roughly 5 percent are *parochial participants* who contact public officials on their own behalf only, and otherwise stay out of politics completely. Another 20 percent are *communalists* who get involved in public life to improve their communities, usually vote, but otherwise stay out of politics. Another 15 percent are *campaigners* who get involved in campaigns, but otherwise stay away

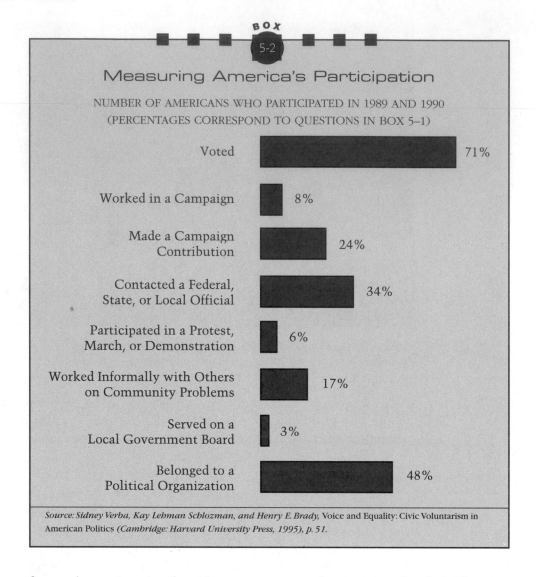

BOX 5-2

Measuring America's Participation

NUMBER OF AMERICANS WHO PARTICIPATED IN 1989 AND 1990
(PERCENTAGES CORRESPOND TO QUESTIONS IN BOX 5–1)

Voted	71%
Worked in a Campaign	8%
Made a Campaign Contribution	24%
Contacted a Federal, State, or Local Official	34%
Participated in a Protest, March, or Demonstration	6%
Worked Informally with Others on Community Problems	17%
Served on a Local Government Board	3%
Belonged to a Political Organization	48%

Source: Sidney Verba, Kay Lehman Schlozman, and Henry E. Brady, Voice and Equality: Civic Voluntarism in American Politics *(Cambridge: Harvard University Press, 1995), p. 51.*

from volunteering. Another 10 percent are *complete activists* who do it all: write, call, attend, vote, campaign, and contribute. (The last 10 percent do not fit any category.)

Regardless of the option for participating, the central question is whether participation, and the consent that goes with it, is up or down. There are two ways to answer: (1) by comparing the level of participation to other democracies, and (2) by comparing the level of participation to the past. Both comparisons suggest that Americans are still giving their consent to be governed, albeit in changing numbers.

Start by looking abroad, where other democracies outpace America in several important measures of political participation. America trails most other western democracies in voter turnout, for example. Between 1980 and 1989, for example, Belgians (94 percent), Austrians (92 percent), Australians (90 percent), Swedish (88 percent), Germans (87 percent), Italians (84 percent), Israelis (79 percent), Greeks (78 percent), British (74 percent), Irish (73 percent), Canadians (72 percent), and Japanese (68 percent) all turned out at higher rates than Americans (53 percent). Indeed, America trails all established democracies but one: Switzerland (49 percent).[9]

This does not mean Americans are behind in all areas of participation, however. America tends to lead the free world in campaign volunteering, contacting government, and community work, and is near the top in the number of its citizens who attend political meetings.[10] Even if America could do better in getting voters to the polls, which is not clear, it has become an international leader in getting people to take their communities seriously.

Continue the comparison by looking back over time. The evidence from the past three decades suggests that Americans are becoming more active in some areas and less active in others. Participating in elections is off sharply since the 1950s and 1960s, whether measured by voting in national or local elections. Efforts to influence others in making their election decision also appears to be off, as is working in campaigns and for the local political party. The only area in which the numbers have gone up is giving money to campaigns.

Where the numbers are way up is in contacting government directly. The number of letters, calls, faxes, and e-mail sent to Congress and the White House has exploded over the past two decades, in part because organized interests have become much more skilled at generating grassroots action. Looking back to the 1960s for comparison, the number of Americans who contact local officials in any given year has increased by over 70 percent, while the number who contact state or federal officials has doubled.

Not that the letters are always real, however. As political scientist Sidney Verba notes:

> There is nothing so spontaneous in America, so reflective of the genuine initiative of citizens that it cannot be converted into a money making organized activity. There are companies that will produce a spontaneous outburst, and technologies that allow them to avoid the obviously canned letter or post-card campaign that legislators so easily recognize and generally discount. There are computer programs that vary the message, that simulate actual signatures, that make typographical errors. As someone put it, the spontaneity of the grass roots gets replaced by astro-turf.[11]

Consulting firms will even dial the phone numbers. For a small fee per call, the Clinton Group—no relation to the president—will call a voter, explain an issue, then ask whether that voter wants to be transferred to the White House or their member of Congress. If the answer is "yes," the Clinton Group merely transfers the call. The voter never even dials and most certainly does not pay for the call.[12]

Explaining the Differences

Americans have many reasons for not participating. Nearly 40 percent of political inactives say they do not have enough time to participate, and almost as many argue they should take care of themselves and their families before worrying about the community or nation. Nearly 20 percent say the important things in their lives have nothing to do with politics, and almost as many say they never thought of being involved, politics is uninteresting or boring, politics cannot help with their personal or family problems, politics is too complicated, and one individual cannot have an impact.[13]

These explanations are closely related to three underlying causes of low participation: *age, resources,* and *skills.* Together, these three causes help explain who has the strongest voice in influencing who gets what, when, and how from government.

Age.   Younger Americans spend less time in conventional participation than older Americans. They are less likely to vote (in part because they move so often that they do not know the time or place to register), and are far less likely to attend hearings, write letters, or donate money to political campaigns (in part because they have less money to give). (See Box 5–3 for a summary of the relationship between age and participation.)

There are two theories about why young people participate less. Under the **life-cycle theory of participation,** people become more involved in politics as they age. As they settle down, register to vote, have children, and start worrying about their paychecks, taxes, and future retirement, they start to see participating in politics as more important to their lives. Thus, age is important to participation because it generally predicts how anchored people are in their families and communities.

Under the **generational theory of participation,** people born into the same generation (for example, the baby boom or Generation X) learn the same lessons about the costs and benefits of participation. What matters is not age, but the events that shape a generation's attachment to the political process early in life. Once alienated from politics, always alienated from politics, or so the theory would suggest.

It is not clear which theory will hold for today's young Americans. From a life cycle view, younger Americans are likely to see more reasons to participate if and when they put down roots in communities. From a generational view, however, they may always feel less confident that government can be trusted. Having grown up in a period of great distrust, they may be marked for life.

Not all the figures show that young Americans are completely disengaged from participating in politics. They are as likely as middle-aged and older Americans to sign petitions and attend political rallies, and much more likely to engage in unconventional participation. According to one count, 20 percent of eighteen to

BOX 5-3

Participation by Age

Activity	Age					
	18–24	25–29	30–34	35–49	50–64	65+
Wrote letter to elected official	23%	27%	32%	41%	42%	40%
Wrote letter to the editor	14	14	16	15	15	10
Signed or circulated petition	52	51	58	62	52	34
Attended a public hearing	26	27	30	42	41	28
Boycotted a company	26	27	30	29	16	9
Took part in a public demonstration	20	12	13	9	5	2
Attended a political meeting or rally	20	20	22	30	31	22
Donated tax dollars to campaign fund	18	21	23	28	30	23

Source: *Times Mirror Center for The People & The Press, "The People, the Press, and Politics, Campaign '92: The Generations Divide," July 8, 1992, p. 44*

twenty-four year olds said they had taken part in a public demonstration in 1992, compared to just 9 percent of thirty-four to forty-nine year olds, and only 2 percent of people over age sixty-five.[14]

Moreover, there is growing evidence that campus activism is up. As author Paul Loeb found in his travels around college campuses in the early 1990s, there appears to be a quiet trend back toward campaign activism and renewed political involvement.[15]

Resources.   Participating in American politics takes more than a simple desire to act. As already noted, even voting, which may be the easiest way to participate in American politics short of answering a public opinion poll or listening to talk radio, takes some minimum amount of effort.

Thus, the role of resources in political participation is clear: resources pay the costs of participation outlined above. And the two key resources are education and income. Education gives people the skills and confidence to be effective; income gives them a greater stake in getting involved, as well as the ability to purchase time (through babysitters, extra help around the house, etc.) to engage in more expensive activities.

The relationships are borne out in the list of eight options noted earlier in this chapter. People with household incomes over $75,000 a year are twice as likely as those with incomes less than $20,000 to contact government (50 percent to 25 percent), more than twice as likely to join an organized interest (73 percent to 29 percent), nearly three times as likely to volunteer in their communities (38 percent to 13 percent), four times as likely to work in a campaign (17 percent to 4 percent), six times as likely to belong to a local government board (6 percent to 1 percent), and nearly ten times as likely to make a campaign contribution (56 percent to 6 percent).

Income also affects relatively inexpensive participation. People with upper incomes are also much more likely to vote (86 percent to 52 percent), and more likely to join a protest (7 percent to 3 percent). In short, there is absolutely no form of participation, cheap or expensive, visible or private, frequent or infrequent, where people with lower incomes have the edge in making their case about who gets what, when, and how from government.[16]

Skills.   Regardless of socioeconomic levels, Americans need certain skills to participate. It is not enough just to have money to give a campaign contribution. A citizen must know where to send the check, whom to contact, and how to satisfy the laws on how much to give. Nor is it enough to want to volunteer for a campaign. A citizen must know something about how a campaign works, how to interact with others, and where to make the connection.

Luckily, civic skills are taught in many places. Many Americans start learning how to participate early, whether in classrooms or student councils. Young Americans can learn a great deal about how to participate from Sunday schools, Boy and Girl Scouts, sports leagues, and a host of other nonpolitical activities.

Once again, people with more education and higher incomes are likely to have the noncivic experience that leads to civic skills. People with family incomes of more than $75,000 a year are more than twice as likely to learn civic skills on the job than those with incomes under $20,000. They are also twice as likely to learn civic skills in nonpolitical organizations such as clubs and alumni groups.[17]

Civic skills are related to greater **political efficacy,** which is simply an individual's sense that he or she can influence government. The more practice people have in participating, the more likely they are to say that government officials care about what they think. In turn, the more that people say government officials care about what they think, the more likely they are to actually participate in politics. Because income and education affect skills, and skills affect efficacy, it should come as no surprise that people with higher socioeconomic status feel the most confident, or efficacious, about participating in politics.

Missing Voices

The combined impact of resources and skills create a twofold bias in participation. The first bias is that government tends to hear most from people who are already doing quite well. People who receive government benefits based on the lack of income are far less likely to participate than people who get government benefits based on their age or prior military service.

Again think back to the eight activities noted earlier—voting, campaign work, contributing money, contacting government, protesting, volunteering in the community, belonging to a government board, and joining an organized interest. People who get veterans' benefits, student loans, Medicare (government's health program for the elderly), or Social Security are much more likely to engage in politics than people who get welfare, Medicaid (government's health program for poor people), housing support, or food stamps.[18]

The question is why people doing well would participate more than people in trouble. One answer is that the people doing well can buy the time and information needed to participate. They also have the resources to contribute to campaigns and the education to target their contacts most effectively. At the same time, poor people do not have equal access to the resources and skills to participate at all. They may need the attention more—people who delay medical care and rent to make ends meet would seem to have a good case for government attention—but may not know who to contact, let alone how to be heard.

The second bias is that government tends to hear different messages from different people. When lower-income Americans contact government, they tend to focus on their own needs—that is, a lost Social Security check, ways of making their housing better, help for a small business, and efforts to make the streets safer; in short, all issues of material need. By comparison, when upper-income Americans contact government, they tend to focus on broader policy concerns such as a clean environment, equality, and help for the poor. They have the luxury to think about broader issues. Because lower-income Americans participate less to begin with, the result may be that their messages get lost in the process, easily dismissed as self-centered or, worse yet, ignored in the flood of more elegant messages from those with greater resources and skills.[19]

These biases are only likely to increase with growing attention to e-mail and other interactive participation. While as many as a third of American homes currently have computers, only 5 percent, at most, are on line.[20] The current craze for high tech forms of participation, whether electronic town halls or the information superhighway, often ignores the vast majority of Americans who cannot pay the tolls.

VOTING

Voting deserves special attention in a book about American government. Not only is it the most common form of participation, it was also the Founders' preferred tool for giving consent. Although contacting government is certainly covered in the Bill of Rights—through the First Amendment's right to petition government, for example—it is voting that provides the central test of a citizenry's commitment to democracy.

Voting and Democracy

Voting may be cherished as essential to the Founders' democracy but it has been declining over time. Turnout in national elections has fallen from a high of over 80 percent in the late 1800s to barely 50 percent today, while voting in local elections has dropped even further.

Comparisons over such a long time are risky, however, if only because daily life has changed so much over the years. It is not clear, for example, whether the voters of 1876, who set the all-time turnout record of 82 percent, set a record worth admiring.

As we will soon see, turnout is not a pure measure of consent. It can only reflect how many *eligible* voters actually show up. Restrict eligibility to upper-income Americans, and turnout will jump dramatically, perhaps to the same level as when only property owners could vote. Expand it to include citizens of every kind, and turnout will naturally fall. High turnout may look good on paper, but not if it comes at the price of exclusion.

So noted, there is still cause for concern in the recent trends. Voting clearly dipped during the early 1900s, rose a bit during the 1930s to 1960s, then dipped again sharply during the 1970s and 1980s. In 1960, 62.8 percent of eligible voters turned out to cast votes in the presidential election; by 1988, the number had dropped to 50.2 percent. Although the number rebounded to 55.2 percent in 1992, it resumed its long decline in 1996, falling below 50 percent for the first time since 1924. With Clinton far ahead throughout the campaign, some Americans may have concluded that their votes did not matter.

The fact is that 1992 was a nearly perfect election for getting people out to vote. America had an older, more educated and skilled voting population; the presidential candidates represented very different views of the future; the campaign was close; media attention was intense; the presidential debates were engaging; the rest of the campaign had a very high number of close races for the House, Senate, and state governorships; and many states had made it easier for their citizens to register and vote—yet the election produced only a 55 percent turnout.[21] This may mean that 55 percent is about as high as it will ever get in today's electorate.

Those who do not vote may be sending one of two messages. On the one hand, they may be perfectly happy with whomever gets elected, expressing their general satisfaction with government and its leaders by not voting at all. On the other hand, they may be extremely unhappy with the choice of candidates, withholding their votes as a sign of absolute dissatisfaction.

Which message is the electorate sending? Most Americans (84 percent) say that voting in all elections is a very effective or fairly effective way of trying to influence the way the government is run and which laws are passed, and even more (93 percent) say they have a duty to vote. As noted earlier, large numbers (70 percent) even feel guilty when they stay at home.[22] This deep sense of civic duty can be viewed as a form of consent to be governed. It does not matter if the people do not vote, or so the notion goes, as long as they feel they should vote.

Moreover, it is not clear that voting is always worth the time. Some political scientists argue that it is perfectly rational not to vote if the benefits of the election do not outweigh the cost of voting. It takes time to register, time to follow the campaigns closely enough to know something about the choices, time to get to the polling place. American elections are always held on Tuesdays, right in the middle of the workweek. That means taking time after work, a particularly high cost for single parents.[23]

Nonvoting may also be a referendum on the candidates and a voter's own self-confidence. Asked why they stay home from elections, nearly two-thirds of nonvoters say they do not know enough about the candidates to vote and sometimes just do not like any of the candidates. Roughly a third of nonvoters say that it does not matter that much who gets elected, and a quarter say they just do not want to involve themselves in politics. Only a quarter say it is difficult to get to the polls to vote, and just a tenth say it is too complicated to register.[24]

IN A DIFFERENT LIGHT

VOTERS AND NONVOTERS

Although nonvoting may raise concerns about the consent of the governed, people who stay at home on election day would have voted pretty much the same as those who turned out. As voting expert Ruy Teixeira asks, "What if they gave an election and everybody came? Would it make a difference? The answer, it turns out, is not much."[25] Getting more people out on election day would mostly increase the margin of victory for the winner.[26]

Yet, much as they might agree on their choice of candidates, voters and nonvoters are anything but identical. The two groups clearly differ by population characteristics. In 1994, for example, nonvoters tended to be younger (only 6 percent of 1994 voters were under age thirty, compared to almost 40 percent of all nonvoters), less well off financially (only 35 percent of voters had incomes under $30,000, compared to nearly 50 percent of all nonvoters), much more mobile (only 7 percent of voters had moved within the last two years, compared to nearly 25 percent of nonvoters), and more likely to be minorities (only 7 percent of voters were African American, compared to 16 percent of nonvoters).[27]

Voters and nonvoters also differ on attitudes toward the parties and government. Nonvoters in 1994 were more likely to favor the creation of a new political party, slightly more in favor of outlawing abortion, slightly more in favor of increased federal spending to help minorities, and slightly less in favor of increased spending on the environment. Nonvoters were also more likely than voters to receive welfare of one kind or another, and to be economically or socially disadvantaged.

The Mechanics of Voting

What makes voting so powerful as a tool of consent is that it is the great equalizer. It may be a relatively private, blunt form of participation when compared to volunteering in a campaign or serving on a neighborhood council, but everyone over the age of eighteen except for convicted felons has a clear right to do it.

Voting is an almost entirely private act, thanks to the secret ballot. Recall from Chapter 4 that the political parties once printed all the ballots, each party listing only its candidates. "Party hawkers" would stand outside the polling place promoting their party's ballot to voters. Because each party's ballot came in a different color and on different sized paper, and because voters dropped their ballot in voting boxes out in the open, rather than in closed booths, it was easy to spot who was voting for whom.[28] And because voters could deposit one ballot and one ballot only, it was nearly impossible to split a ticket.

The movement toward secret ballots began in 1888 when Massachusetts printed the first **Australian ballot.** An Australian ballot is printed by government, lists all the candidates, and is cast in secret—for example, in a voting booth. In less than eight years, 90 percent of the states had followed suit.[29] Voting turnout began to decrease almost immediately. Some political scientists argue that the high turnouts of the late 1800s were primarily a result of corruption—that is, that the parties were not only printing and promoting their own ballots, but were actually dropping ballots in the voting box for citizens who did not show.

For the most part, voting is much simpler today. Only citizens of the United States can vote, and most must register to vote with states, usually through their county registrar. Assuming they have passed these two simple tests of citizenship and registration, they show up at their designated polling place on election day and cast their secret ballot.

Just because voting is a simple process does not mean it is entirely without restrictions. Consider five questions about the mechanics of voting: (1) who makes the rules? (2) who gets to vote? (3) where are the district lines? (4) what is the voting about? and (5) how are the votes counted to determine who wins? We will address each question in order.

Who Makes the Rules? States have the greatest say over the basic rules of voting. Under Article I, Section 4 of the Constitution, "The Times, Places and Manner of holding Elections for Senators and Representatives, shall be prescribed in each state by the Legislature thereof, but the Congress may at any time by Law make or alter such Regulations, except as to the Places of choosing Senators."

Under the provision, states decide who gets to register to vote, when elections occur, and even how many votes it takes to win a given contest. Almost all states currently have winner-take-all, plurality-rules election systems—that is, the candidate who wins the most votes wins the election.

The Constitution does not give states complete control, however. Article I also gives Congress the right to determine how its own members are selected, a right that can influence how states behave. In 1971, for example, Congress decided to allow eighteen to twenty year olds to vote in *national* elections.

The only problem was that most states had long ago set the minimum voting age at twenty-one. Faced with the administrative cost of issuing two separate ballots, one for eighteen to twenty year olds listing just the national contests and another for everyone twenty-one and over listing state and local contests, states quickly complied with the federal law. (A similar strategy led to major voting reforms under the Voting Rights Act of 1965, which banned a number of discriminatory practices used by states to deny the vote to minorities.)

Still other rules are set jointly under constitutional amendments. The Fifteenth Amendment, ratified in 1870, gave the right to vote to all races; the Seventeenth Amendment, ratified in 1913, allowed for the direct election of senators (the Constitution had originally required that senators be elected by state legislatures); the Nineteenth Amendment, ratified in 1920, gave the right to vote to women; the Twenty-Fourth Amendment, ratified in 1964, prohibited use of the poll tax in national elections; and the Twenty-Sixth Amendment, ratified in 1971, changed the minimum voting age to eighteen.

Over the years, differences in federal and state laws have created a complex set of rules governing elections. Some rules are common across the country: people over eighteen are allowed to vote, and national general elections are held the first Tuesday after the first Monday in November. Other rules vary: some states elect their governors and legislators in odd years, some in even; some states use primaries to select candidates, others use caucuses, or conventions, of party delegates; still others use both.

Who Gets to Vote? Under the amendments discussed above, the Constitution is now quite clear on just who is eligible to vote: voters have to be at least eighteen years of age and citizens of the United States.

However, states still have considerable say in who gets to vote by setting the basic rules of *voter registration*. Voter registration was originally designed to prevent election fraud by requiring voters to prove their eligibility by showing up some days in advance to prove their residency, citizenship, and age.

Many states have also used voter registration to deny the vote to certain people. Almost immediately after African Americans were given the right to vote, Southern states began creating barriers to registration. Some states used a poll tax, which required citizens to pay for the privilege of voting. In some states, citizens not only had to pay for the election in which they wanted to vote, but also for all elections they had missed. In 1964, the Twenty-Fourth Amendment made the poll tax unconstitutional.

Other states used literacy tests, which asked citizens to prove their knowledge or moral character. Mississippi required applicants for registration to be able to "read and write any section of the constitution of this state and give a reasonable interpretation thereof to the country registrar," while Louisiana required citizens to "understand the duties and obligations of citizens under a republican form of government," and present two voters to vouch for him or her.

Southern states were not the only ones with such tests. Idaho imposed a test of moral character that barred prostitutes, people who "habitually resort to any house of prostitution or of ill fame," gays and lesbians, and advocates of bigamy and polygamy.[30] All such tests were outlawed by the 1965 Voting Rights Act.

Many states continue working to ease the burdens of voting. Minnesota, Maine, and Wisconsin, for example, allow voters to register on the same day and in the same place as they vote. All voters in these three states must do is have some form of identification—a driver's license, an electric bill—to prove they live where they say.[31] North Dakota is the only state that does not require registration at all.

Other states keep their citizens on the registration rolls even if they do not vote in election after election. In contrast to states that automatically cancel registration if a voter fails to vote in just one general election (Arizona, Hawaii, and Nevada) or two (Colorado, Delaware, Kansas, New Hampshire, Rhode Island, and Virginia), at least nine states never purge, or clean, their rolls of nonvoters. Such states clearly make voting much easier.[32]

Finally, most states now allow volunteers to register voters on the state's behalf. Instead of requiring people to register only at the county seat, most allow volunteer deputy registrars, as they are called, to go where the voters are, which means setting up registration booths on college campuses, in housing projects, shopping malls, and just about anywhere else potential voters can be found.

Where Are the District Lines?   The House of Representatives has not always had 435 members, nor the Senate 100. The growth of the Senate is simple: the Senate added two members with each new state admitted to the union, reaching 100 with Hawaii and Alaska in the late 1950s.

The growth of the House is more complex. From 1790 to 1830, Congress had one member for every 30,000 citizens, growing from 196 to 242 members. If the same number, or apportionment of seats to citizens, applied today, Congress would have over 7,500 members! Congress raised the number of citizens per member of Congress to 70,680 in 1840, then decided in 1850 that it would merely set the number of seats in advance and divide it into the total population determined in the census (conducted under constitutional order in the first year of every decade). By 1910, Congress had reached 435 seats, and decided to stop growing.[33] From then on, the size of the districts, not Congress, would have to grow. By 1990, each member of Congress had an average of 570,000 constituents.

The problem for drawing the district lines is that America does not grow at the same rate in every state. Some states are expanding rapidly, while others are shrinking. In the last reapportionment, California (plus seven), Texas (plus three), and Florida (plus four) all gained congressional seats in 1990, while New York (minus three), Michigan (minus two), and New Jersey (minus one) all lost seats. Montana also lost one, leaving it with more senators (two) than House members (one).

Changes in total population mean that every state, except those with only one member of Congress (Alaska, Delaware, Montana, North Dakota, South Dakota, Vermont, and Wyoming), must redraw its districts every ten years. Congress may determine how many members it has, but the states say which people vote in what district—that is, they apportion the population into House districts. Since state legislatures and governors have the ultimate authority to draw the lines, subject to federal court review in cases where voting rights might be affected, there is considerable room to shape and reshape district lines to benefit one party or the other.[34]

Efforts to draw favorable lines have existed since the early 1800s when Massachusetts Governor Elbridge Gerry and his party machine redistricted the state into a patchwork of odd-shaped districts, one of which looked like a salamander. To this day, such efforts are labeled **gerrymandering** (Gerry plus salamander).[35]

During the early 1990s, apportionment was used to help racial minorities. The goals of redistricting had changed—from favoring one party over another to increasing the odds for electing minority candidates—but the result still looked the same: voting districts that make little geographic sense.

This **racial gerrymandering,** which produces **majority-minority districts,** was the product of the 1982 amendments to the 1965 Voting Rights Act. Under the 1982 amendments, states were allowed to draw district lines to prevent minority votes from being "diluted" by large white populations. Working with the new population figures from the 1990 census, several Southern states used race-based redistricting to create more than a dozen majority-minority districts. The best example was North Carolina's Twelfth District, a long thin district that runs 160 miles along Interstate 85 from Gastonia to Durham, including Charlotte, Greensboro, and Winston-Salem. It was one of two North Carolina districts drawn to pool African American votes. (See Box 5–4 for a map of the North Carolina district).

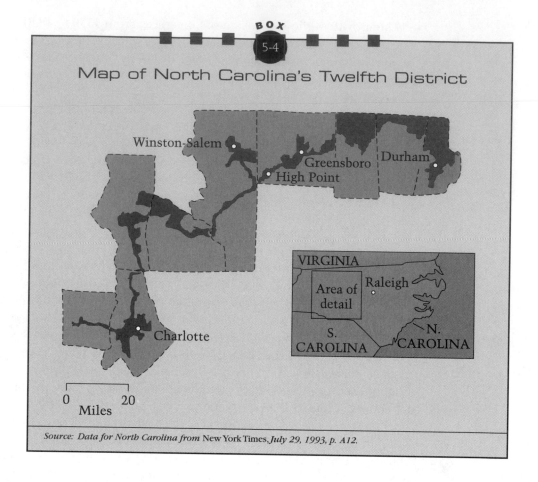

Map of North Carolina's Twelfth District

Winston-Salem • Greensboro • High Point • Durham

VIRGINIA
Area of detail • Raleigh
S. CAROLINA • N. CAROLINA

Charlotte

0 ___ 20
Miles

Source: Data for North Carolina from New York Times, *July 29, 1993, p. A12.*

Indeed, with North Carolina's 78 percent white and 20 percent African American population, defenders claim racial gerrymandering is the only way to enhance African American representation. Kenneth Spaulding, a Durham lawyer, who was one of four African Americans who had repeatedly lost to whites in the old 2nd congressional district, said, "How a district looks, I'm not concerned about. I'm concerned about how a congressional delegation looks. What everyone seems to be missing is any mention of the history of an all white male congressional delegation."[36]

Other states also created majority-minority districts, including Georgia's Eleventh, Louisiana's Fourth, and Texas' Eighteenth, Twenty-ninth, and Thirtieth. Voting rights experts suggest that racial redistricting may have accounted for the election of thirteen additional African Americans and six Hispanics in 1992 alone.[37]

It is important to note that majority-minority districting concentrates heavy numbers of typically Democratic voters in single districts, thereby increasing the likelihood of Republican victories elsewhere. It may be an entirely valid strategy for increasing minority representation in the House, but perhaps at the risk of reducing the total number of Southern districts in which Democratic candidates, whether minority or not, might be competitive.

Moreover, given its enormous impact on who votes where, majority-minority districting prompted a number of lawsuits alleging reverse discrimination. Whites who became the minority in some racially gerrymandered districts sued in federal court to have many of the new districts declared unconstitutional. The challenges produced a mix of results in the lower courts. Louisiana's Fourth District, all three Texas districts, and Georgia's Eleventh District were all declared unconstitutional by the lower courts, but North Carolina's Twelfth was not. The Supreme Court reconciled the differences in three decisions, two of which involved the North Carolina district. The first in 1993 with *Shaw v. Reno;* the next in 1995 with *Miller v. Johnson;* and the most recent in 1996 with *Shaw v. Hunt.*

Ruth Shaw was a voter in North Carolina's Twelfth Congressional District, and Janet Reno was the attorney general, who, under the 1965 Voting Rights Act, was responsible for approving the redistricting plan that created North Carolina's Twelfth. Shaw and several other white citizens sued Reno (and the federal government she represented) to overturn the district on the grounds that it was so extremely irregular in shape that it could only be viewed as a effort to segregate races for voting, and therefore violated the Fourteenth Amendment's **equal protection clause**—which says that no state can deny any person equal protection of the laws—by creating reverse discrimination against whites.

After a federal district court rejected the argument, Shaw appealed. Although the Supreme Court did not declare the North Carolina district unconstitutional at the time, it did send the case back to the lower court for another review on a 5 to 4 vote. The majority opinion was written by Justice O'Connor:

> Racial classifications of any sort pose the risk of lasting harm to our society. They reinforce the belief, held by too many for too much of our history, that individuals should be judged by the color of their skin. Racial classifications with respect to voting carry particular dangers. Racial gerrymandering, even for remedial purposes, may balkanize us into competing racial factions; it threatens to carry us further from the goal of a political system in which race no longer matters—a goal that the Fourteenth and Fifteenth Amendments embody, and to which the Nation continues to aspire. It is for these reasons that race-based districting by our state legislatures demands close judicial scrutiny.[38]

In 1995, the Supreme Court took the next logical step on the issue in *Miller v. Johnson,* ruling that Georgia's Eleventh Congressional District was unconstitutional.[39] The 5–4 majority argued that using race as the predominant factor in drawing a new district line is almost always going to be unconstitutional, carrying forward O'Connor's argument from *Shaw v. Reno.* Within hours of announcing the decision, the Supreme Court accepted two other redistricting cases, one from Texas and the old one from North Carolina. In 1996, the Supreme Court finally overturned North Carolina's Twelfth District and three more districts from Texas.[40]

What Is the Voting About?   What voters vote about most frequently is candidates. Candidates vary by the *level of office* involved (federal, state, and local), as well as by the *stage of the campaign* (primary and general). General elections have the highest turnout, particularly when they fall in a presidential year—they create the greatest interest and draw the highest public interest. Primary elections have the lowest turnout, particularly when they fall in odd years or involve local offices only—they generate only passing interest.

Many, though not all voters, also get to vote about policy issues. Most Western states also allow voters to make decisions on policy. Twenty-five states have the **referendum,** which allows the legislature to put bills on the ballot for public decision; twenty-three have the **initiative,** which allows citizens to put legislation on the ballot through petitions signed by roughly 5 to 10 percent of eligible voters; and fifteen have the **recall,** which allows voters to remove elected officials from office in special elections, again through petitions. Finally, all states except Delaware require voters to ratify changes to their constitutions.[41]

A protest in 1994 against California's Proposition 187, an initiative that proposed to ban public assistance for illegal immigrants and their children. The proposition passed, but was immediately declared an unconstitutional denial of equal protection by the federal courts.

Whatever the Founders might think of these occasions for direct democracy, there has been a dramatic increase in the number of ballot initiatives over the past decade. Roughly 50 percent of the nearly 2,000 initiatives ever considered in U.S. history have been on the ballot in the last fifty years, with nearly 25 percent in just the last decade, and almost 10 percent in 1994 alone.

Ballot initiatives now run the gamut of topics: crime, gambling, taxes, term limits for elected officials, and bans on gay and lesbian rights. Efforts to limit tax increases are almost always on the ballot somewhere, as are efforts to strengthen crime control. Term limits have been a more recent wave, spurred by voter distrust toward government. Since 1990, twenty-two mostly western states have passed some sort of term limits on members of Congress, all of which were rendered unconstitutional in 1995 when the Supreme Court declared that limits constitute a new qualification for holding national office. Because the Founders decided that age and citizenship would be the only qualifications for office, the only way to impose such a new qualification would be through a constitutional amendment. Voters in nine states responded to the Supreme Court decision by passing initiatives in 1996 that will ask future federal candidates to pledge their support for term limits. Those who refuse will be listed as opposed on the ballot.

Term limits were not the only initiatives on the 1996 ballot. In a record-setting year, citizens were asked to vote on over ninety initiatives, including affirmative action in California, river boat gambling in Ohio, conservation and protection of the Everglades in Florida, legalization of marijuana for medical use in Arizona and California, limits on clear-cutting of forest land in Maine, and bear hunting in Idaho. (See Box 5–5 for a sampling of the 1996 initiatives.)

Because initiatives are often controversial, they can increase voter turnout. However, because they do so by stimulating popular passions, they may fuel the faction that so worried the Founders. California's Proposition 209, which was designed to abolish affirmative action programs in state and local government, including the state's higher education system, provoked intense opposition across racial lines in 1996 and passed with 54 percent of the vote.

Nevertheless, direct democracy is a growing business. Private firms will do virtually everything needed to pass an initiative, from "harvesting" the citizen signatures needed to put an idea on the ballot to the advertising and direct mail needed to get it passed. Signature harvesters—students, part-timers, and homeless people—are paid anywhere from 35 cents per valid signature in California to $6 a signature in Nevada.[42]

How Are the Votes Counted?   As noted above, almost all elections are won or lost on the basis of total votes. Although several states require runoff elections when the top candidate does not win a majority of all votes cast, most states merely require the winner to have a plurality—that is, the winner is the candidate with the largest number of votes, even if that number is not an absolute majority.

BOX 5-5

The Voters Speak, 1996

Affirmative action: California voters amended the state's constitution to abolish affirmative action in state and local government, including employment, education, and contracting.

Campaign finance: Maine voters agreed to provide state funding for candidates who voluntarily accept spending limits in their races for statewide office. California voters approved restrictions on campaign contributions.

Environment: Florida voters rejected a 1 cent per pound tax on raw sugar grown in the Everglades as a device for funding conservation of the endangered wetlands, but passed two other measures to protect the area.

Gambling: Voters in five states rejected measures that would have permitted gaming casinos or other gambling. Michigan voters approved gambling casinos with the condition that all tax revenues from the gambling be used for crime prevention, economic development and public education.

Hunting: Voters in three states voted to restrict the use of hounds, traps, or bait in hunting. Idaho voters prohibited the use of dogs or bait to hunt black bears; Massachusetts voters prohibited the use of steel-jaw leg traps to hunt bears.

Crime: Arizona voters approved an initiative that will try juveniles, fifteen years old and older, as adults for armed robbery, murder, or rape.

Family values: Colorado voters rejected a constitutional amendment declaring that parents have the "inalienable right" to control "the upbringing, values, and discipline of their children."

Marijuana use: Arizona and California voters approved the use of marijuana for medicinal purposes.

Term limits: Voters in nine states approved measures that require candidates to pledge their support for term limits or risk being listed on the ballot as having refused.

Victims' rights: Voters in eight states approved initiatives on behalf of crime victims.

Taxes: Colorado voters approved a measure that eliminates tax exemptions on property used for religious purposes, profit-making schools, and certain other charitable purposes.

There are only two offices at the national level that are elected on the basis of anything but the number of popular votes: president and vice president. Recall from Chapter 2 that they are elected by members of the *electoral college,* a curious invention of the Founders designed both to cool the passions of the public, and assure that the president was not just the leader of the American people, but of the separate states.

Because the Constitution sets the number of electors by adding Senate and House seats, it clearly encourages presidential candidates to concentrate their energies on winning the big states. Why bother with Delaware, South Dakota, or Idaho? And because the system awards final votes on a winner-take-all basis, it also almost always inflates the margin of victory for the winner. In 1980, for example, Ronald Reagan won just 51 percent of the popular vote, but took 91 percent of the electoral college; in 1992, Bill Clinton won just 43 percent of the popular vote, but 69 percent of the electoral vote.

As a result, the winner-take-all system creates the very real possibility that a president can be elected without having won the popular vote. It is simple mathematics: if a candidate can win New York (33 electoral college votes) and Pennsylvania (23) in the northeast; take Ohio (21), Michigan (18), and Illinois (22), in the midwest; go south to pick up Texas (32), Florida (25), North Carolina (14), and Georgia (13); then head west for California (54) and Washington (11); and throw in just one small state such as Hawaii (4) along the way, that candidate can become president of the United States after winning just twelve out of fifty states.

Fear of such an election has prompted calls for abolishing the electoral college in favor of using a simple national vote. Candidates would mount a national campaign, instead of fifty separate state campaigns. Under the notion that "if it ain't broke, don't fix it," however, it is unlikely that the nation would approve such a reform until the worst case actually occurs. After all, the last time a candidate won the election but lost the electoral college was in 1888, when Grover Cleveland won the popular vote by 48.6 percent to 47.8 percent, but lost the electoral vote by 168 to 233—not even close.

IN A DIFFERENT LIGHT

MAKING VOTING EASIER

Efforts to make voting easier peaked in the 1960s and early 1970s with passage of the Voting Rights Act and ratification of the Twenty-Sixth Amendment. However, the 1990s have produced two efforts to encourage greater electoral participation, both of which may make voting easier.

A voter registration effort at the University of California, Santa Barbara. Allowing deputy registrars to register voters is one way to lower the barriers to voting. Allowing citizens to register when they get other government services such as a driver's license and allowing them to vote-by-mail are two others.

The first is a nationwide effort designed to give citizens more opportunities to register. Under the so-called **motor voter law,** which was passed by Congress in 1993, states must let voters register whenever they get other state and local services such as a driver's license (hence, the term *motor voter*) or welfare check.

According to early estimates, nearly 40 million new voters will be registered under the law by 1998. Although most of the new voters will register at driver's license bureaus, 10 to 20 percent will sign up at public welfare agencies. By reducing the costs of registering for these poor Americans, the motor voter law helps reduce some of the bias in the current registration system. Contrary to early expectations that these new voters would likely register as Democrats, neither party has benefited from the easier registration. If anything, Republicans have done slightly better under the law.

If there is a problem with the motor voter law, it is for young people. Most Americans get their first driver's license at age sixteen, but cannot register to vote until eighteen. Because most states do not require a license renewal for six years, young people do not get the benefit of the motor voter law until after their first election, at the very earliest. That is why Florida is considering allowing students to register to vote when they register for college classes. The proposal, called "Register Once," was developed by the Florida Student Association, an organized interest that lobbies on behalf of students at state universities and community colleges.[43]

The second effort to encourage greater participation is designed to reduce the personal costs of voting by allowing citizens to vote by mail. Oregon tried the idea in a special U.S. Senate election in early 1996. The state sent every registered voter a ballot and prepaid return envelope twenty-one days before election day. Voting simply meant sealing the secret ballot in its prepaid return envelope and dropping it in the mail. In all, 66 percent of registered voters returned their ballots, producing a much higher turnout than would have occurred otherwise. At the same time, the state saved $1 million by not having to open the polling places on election day.

Vote-by-mail produced both positives and negatives for participation. On the positive side, it sharply lowered the cost of participating. Voters did not have to find babysitters or take time off from work, nor did they have to find the polling place. And turnout increased. On the negative side, vote-by-mail may have altered the conduct of the election campaign. Because most voters sent in their ballots within five days of receiving them, there was no final election day. As one observer argued, vote-by-mail made "the process the equivalent of picking an NBA champion the week before the finals begin."[44] Vote-by-mail may also increase the chances of fraud by leaving so many ballots in circulation for so long. More troubling perhaps, vote-by-mail eliminated all chances that citizens would run into each other in this most central act of democracy, furthering the privatization of participation discussed earlier in the chapter.

CONCLUSION

America may still be a nation of participators, but there are warning signs on the horizon. The clamor of a thousand public voices that greeted Tocqueville 150 years ago may soon become the eerie quiet of a thousand individual letters and e-mails dropping quietly on congressional desks.

The first question about these trends is whether having Americans participate is essential to a healthy democracy. Although some political theorists argue that apathy is a good measure of consent, the declining participation may reflect a steady fraying of America's democratic fabric. The same forces that lead people to stay at home on election day may also lead them to avoid their neighbors on the street, ignore community problems such as drugs and crime, and even excuse themselves from caring for their children. Such a lonely nation can easily transform a government designed to be just strong enough into one that does not have the consent to govern at all.

The next question is what might be done about the decline in participation. America may have reached the maximum in conventional participation such as voting and contributing. If only 55 percent vote in an election like 1992, when the stakes are high and the options clear, motor voter and vote by mail are not going to raise the numbers much higher. It may be that the only way to raise participation is to encourage what some political scientists call **participatory**

democracy, a hybrid of representative and direct democracy in which citizens are encouraged to work together to solve community problems.[45] (Recall that less than one in five Americans currently do so.)

Participatory democracy involves more than cheerleading for community problem solving, however. It can also involve creation of formal neighborhood governments that give citizens real power to manage their own problems. Such governments already exist in a number of cities, from Birmingham, Alabama, where neighborhood officers are elected every two years, to Dayton, Ohio, where a system of seven priority boards link neighborhoods to the city government; from Portland, Oregon, which has a citywide system of independent neighborhood associations, complete with staffs and budgets to help citizens make decisions on local problems, to St. Paul, Minnesota, which has seventeen elected district councils that have substantial power over what the city docs in their neighborhoods, and San Antonio, which has a nonprofit community group called Communities Organized for Public Service (COPS) to energize citizens to solve their own problems.

It is not clear, however, that participatory democracy helps rebuild participation, particularly among Americans who have otherwise checked out. The best available research suggests that creating formal networks of neighborhood associations does not necessarily draw more people into the process. Getting together with neighbors to solve community problems such as crime demands both time and energy.

Nevertheless, participatory democracy does offer significant benefits for enhancing the consent to be governed. People who engage in neighborhood problem solving are more likely than people who do not to say that government pays a great deal of attention to what people think, and that the government would give serious attention to their views about a major neighborhood problem. The effects are particularly dramatic for poor people, who are the least likely to participate in politics generally.

Obviously, participatory democracy is not a cure-all for American politics. But by reducing distrust and rebuilding the public's sense that they can make a difference, it gives officials the chance to hear from neighborhoods drowned out in traditional politics—the poor, the disadvantaged, the people in trouble. Neighborhood associations may not create greater numbers of participants per se, but they do give the disadvantaged an equal voice in shaping policy. That can only help increase the sense that government is listening.

THE BASICS

■ America has always been a nation of political participators. Although the Founders did not want a government of the people, they did want the people to give their consent to be governed. Americans give their consent in many ways: voting, volunteering for campaigns, giving money, contacting government, taking part in protests, working informally with others to address community problems, joining a local governmental board, or joining a political organization. The options for participating vary by visibility, frequency, civic acceptance, cost, and sharpness of the message sent.

■ Americans choose one form of participation over another based on the benefits it provides: (1) material benefits that come back to the individual participant, (2) social benefits that come from working together, (3) civic benefits that arise from fulfilling one's civic responsibilities, and (4) policy benefits that arise from influencing a specific government decision on behalf of the nation as a whole.

■ Voting merits special attention as the Founders' preferred tool for giving consent. There have been a number of changes in voting over history, including adoption of the Australian ballot in the late 1800s. The Fifteenth, Seventeenth, Twenty-Fourth, and Twenty-Sixth Amendments have all made voting either easier (by outlawing the poll tax) or expanded the electorate (by allowing former slaves, women, and eighteen to twenty year olds to vote).

■ Beyond who sets the basic rules, the mechanics of voting also involve questions about who gets to vote, which most states determine by requiring citizens to register; where the district lines are set, which some states have occasionally determined through gerrymandering; what the voting is about, which is determined by the level of the contest (federal, state, or local), the stage of the campaign (primary or general election), and whether a given state allows the referendum, initiative, or recall; and how the votes are assembled, which usually involves a winner-take-all, plurality system.

KEY CONCEPTS

■ Participating in politics is uneven across society. Age, resources, and civic skills help explain much of the unevenness. Younger Americans are less likely to participate because they are at an early stage of the life cycle, and, therefore, may not have the community ties that lead older Americans to join in. Less-educated and lower-income Americans are less likely to participate because they cannot afford the costs of engaging that are easily absorbed by those with higher socioeconomic status. And less skilled Americans may not have the practice to feel confident in their abilities to participate.

■ Efforts to increase participation by minorities have led some states to undertake racial gerrymandering, which alters the shape of districts to assure a greater chance that minority candidates will be elected. The Supreme Court has recently ruled that drawing such districts predominantly to benefit a particular race is unconstitutional.

■ Even with the unevenness in participation, America is one of the most active democracies in the world. America leads most established democracies in campaign volunteering, contacting government, and community work, but trails in voter turnout. Indeed, 55 percent appears to be about the maximum turnout America can expect in presidential campaigns. Over time, giving money to campaigns and virtually all other forms of election participation has declined. At the same time, contacting government is up dramatically.

IN A DIFFERENT LIGHT

■ There is some evidence that Americans are disengaging from participating in politics together. Just as more Americans are bowling alone, more Americans are participating alone: writing private letters to their government, but not attending rallies; joining specialized interest groups, but not the Elks or League of Women Voters.

■ Because voters and nonvoters share similar views of the candidates, getting more nonvoters to the polls probably would not alter the final results. However, voters and nonvoters are very different in other respects. Nonvoters tend to be younger, less well off financially, more mobile, and more likely to be members of a minority group. They also have different political views.

■ The 1990s have witnessed several promising efforts to make voting easier. Passage of the motor voter law allowed Americans to register to vote almost anywhere they get state or local government services, most visibly the driver's license bureau, while the 1996 Oregon vote-by-mail experiment allowed voters to cast their ballots at home at any point during the three weeks before the final election. Although both efforts have positives, motor voter does not address the registration problems facing younger Americans (most of whom get their driver's licenses at sixteen and do not renew until twenty-two), while vote by mail may dramatically alter the conduct of campaigns.

OPEN QUESTIONS

■ Should America worry about participation? What messages do people who do not participate send their government? Does the fact that so many Americans stay at home on election day weaken the legitimacy of government?

■ How hard should America work to increase voter turnout? What are the positives in efforts to improve voter turnout by easy voter registration? Even if Americans still do not vote, is it important for government to keep trying to encourage them to vote? What about efforts to encourage greater participation by redrawing district lines to favor people who historically do not participate, such as young people or the poor?

■ How politically active is your campus? How much of the time are you participating in politics these days? And how much of your participation is alone or with others? What might explain the sharp increase in the number of Americans contacting government in private? Does that increase relate to the decline in voting? What could you do to start participating with others and what kind of resources and skills would you need to do so? Does your college or university offer any help in getting those resources and teaching those skills? And if not, should it?

TERMS TO REMEMBER

conventional participation

unconventional participation

voter turnout

congressional case workers

life-cycle theory of participation

generational theory of participation

political efficacy

Australian ballot

gerrymandering

racial gerrymandering

majority-minority districts

equal protection clause

referendum

initiative

recall

motor voter law

participatory democracy

Endnotes to Chapter 5

▶ 1. Alexis de Tocqueville, *Democracy in America* ed., J. P. Mayer, trans., George Lawrence (Garden City, NY: Harper Perennial, 1988), pp. 242–243.

2. The 80 percent figure is drawn from the discussion later in this chapter about the six types of political participants. Only 20 percent of the American public can be labelled as absolutely inactive in politics.

▶ 3. This list is drawn from Sidney Verba, Kay Lehman Schlozman, and Henry Brady, *Voice and Equality: Civic Voluntarism in American Politics* (Cambridge, MA: Harvard University Press, 1995).

4. Samuel Barnes and Max Kasse, eds., *Political Action: Mass Participation in Five Western Democracies* (Beverly Hills, CA: Sage, 1979), p. 545.

▶ 5. "Bowling Alone: Democracy in America at the End of the Twentieth Century," paper prepared for delivery at the Nobel Symposium "Democracy's Victory and Crisis," Uppsala, Sweden, August 27–29, 1994; the paper was published as "Bowling Alone: America's Declining Social Capital," *Journal of Democracy,* volume 6, number 1 (January 1995), pp. 65–78.

▶ 6. For dissenting views of the state of civic life in America, see Nicholas Lemann, "Kicking in Groups," *Atlantic,* April 1996, pp. 22–26; Frank Riessman and Erik Banks, "The Mismeasure of Civil Society," *Social Policy,* Spring 1996, pp. 2–5; and Katha Pollitt, "For Whom the Ball Rolls," *The Nation,* April 16, 1996; see also the defense of Putnam in response to Pollitt's scathing editorial from Benjamin Barber, *The Nation,* July 1, 1996, pp. 2, 24.

7. The following discussion draws heavily on data presented by Verba, Schlozman, and Brady, *Voice and Equality,* p. 115.

8. See M. Kent Jennings and Richard G. Niemi, *Generations and Politics: A Panel Study of Young Adults and Their Parents* (Princeton, NJ: Princeton University Press, 1981).

▶ 9. Ruy Teixeira, *The Disappearing American Voter* (Washington, DC: Brookings Institution, 1992), p. 8

10. Verba, Schlozman, and Brady, *Voice and Equality,* p. 70.

11. Sidney Verba, "The 1993 James Madison Award Lecture: The Voice of the People," *PS: Political Science and Politics,* volume 26, number 4 (December 1993), p. 679.

12. See Stephen Engelberg, "A New Breed of Hired Hands Cultivates Grass-Roots Anger," *New York Times,* March 17, 1993, p. A11.

13. Verba, Schlozman, and Brady, *Voice and Equality,* p. 129.

14. Times Mirror Center for The People & The Press, *The People, The Press and Politics, Campaign '92: The Generations Divide,* July 8, 1992, p. 44.

▶ 15. Paul Loeb, "Greeks and Granolas and Steeps and Slackers," *Mother Jones,* September/October 1994, pp. 58–59.

16. Verba, Schlozman, and Brady, *Voice and Equality,* p. 190.

17. Verba, Schlozman, and Brady, *Voice and Equality,* p. 319.

18. Sidney Verba, Kay Lehman Schlozman, Henry Brady, and Norman Nie, "Citizen Activity: Who Participates? What Do They Say?" *American Political Science Review,* volume 87, number 2 (June 1993), p. 305.

19. Verba, et al., "Citizen Activity," p. 312.

20. See Barbara Kantrowitz and Debra Rosenberg, "Ready, Teddy. You're Online." *Newsweek,* September 12, 1994, pp. 60–61.

▶ 21. See Ruy Teixeira, "Turnout in the 1992 Election," *Brookings Review,* Spring 1993, p. 47.

22. Times Mirror Center, *Campaign '92,* p. 40.

23. Anthony Downs, *An Economic Theory of Democracy* (New York: Harper & Row, 1957).

24. Times Mirror Center, *Campaign '92,* p. 42.

25. Teixeira, *The Disappearing American Voter,* p. 95.

26. See Teixeira's analysis in *The Disappearing American Voter,* pp. 95-97.

27. These 1994 data are from the *New York Times*/CBS News Poll, reported in a chart carried by the *New York Times,* November 9, 1994, p. B4.

28. See Jerrold G. Rusk, "The Effect of the Australian Ballot Reform on Split Ticket Voting: 1876-1908," in Richard G. Niemi and Herbert F. Weisberg, *Classics in Voting Behavior* (Washington, DC: CQ Press, 1993), p. 313.

29. Rusk, "Australian Ballot Reform," p. 313.

30. The tests are listed in *Congressional Quarterly Almanac* (Washington, DC: CQ Press, 1965), p. 539.

31. Teixeira, *The Disappearing American Voter,* p. 108, see also Raymond Wolfinger and Steven Rosenstone, *Who Votes?* (New Haven: Yale University Press, 1980).

32. Harold W. Stanley and Richard G. Niemi, *Vital Statistics on American Politics* (Washington, DC: CQ Press, 1994), pp. 37-39.

33. This history is easily found in David Butler and Bruce Cain, *Congressional Redistricting: Comparative and Theoretical Perspectives* (New York: Macmillan, 1992), p. 19.

34. See Richard Miniter, "The Computer that Defeated A Congressman," *Washington Post National Weekly Edition,* September 28-October 4, 1992, p. 24.

35. Butler and Cain, *Congressional Redistricting,* p. 17.

36. Ronald Smothers, "Fair Play or Racial Gerrymandering," *New York Times,* April 16, 1993, p. B9.

37. See Smothers, "Fair Play," p. B9.

38. *Shaw v. Reno,* 61 U.S.L.W. 4818 (1993).

39. *Miller v. Johnson,* 63 U.S.L.W. 4726 (1995).

40. *Shaw v. Hunt,* S.Ct. Docket No. 94-923.

▶ 41. For a history of initiative and referendum, see David Magleby, *Direct Legislation: Voting on Ballot Propositions in the United States* (Baltimore: Johns Hopkins University Press, 1984).

42. James Sterba, "Politicians at All Levels Seek Expert Advice, Fueling an Industry," *Wall Street Journal,* September 1, 1992, p. A1.

43. See "Florida May Take Motor Voter Step Further," special to the *New York Times,* February 25, 1996, p. 39.

44. Norman Ornstein, "A Vote Cheapened," *Washington Post,* February 8, 1996, p. A19.

▶ 45. Jeffrey M. Berry, Kent E. Portney, and Ken Thompson, *The Rebirth of Urban Democracy* (Washington, DC: Brookings Institution, 1993), p. 3.

CAMPAIGNS AND ELECTIONS

CHAPTER

6

Election campaigns are the feast of democracy, the only time the Founders truly wanted the people and their representatives to "dine" together. For their part, voters consume vast quantities of information about candidates, issues, and the state of the nation, picking through the offerings in search of a decision about how to vote. And for their part, candidates consume vast quantities of information about what voters think, building a menu of ideas that might motivate more of their supporters to go to the polls than their opponent's, which is, after all, why campaigns exist in the first place.

Together, this feast of information and ideas is maybe the single most important event in American democratic life, a rare opportunity for Americans to simultaneously give their consent to be governed and hold their representatives accountable for what they have or have not done since the last election. There is good evidence that Americans take the opportunity seriously. Even when they think a campaign is dull and boring, as half the public described the presidential campaign in 1996, the vast majority of Americans still pay a lot or some attention to the ebb and flow of events.

Nevertheless, the Founders might be worried about how long and expensive election campaigns have become, and how dependent candidates have come to

The Feast of Democracy

be on political consultants and television. They might be disturbed, for example, to discover that candidates for office spend so much time raising money, and would likely wonder why campaigns have to be so long. They might also be puzzled at how much candidate image appears to matter to the final vote. Much as they would agree that campaigns are still a feast of democracy, they might wonder why so much junk food gets served.

This is not to say that the Founders would disapprove of campaigning per se. The Founders were practical politicians who knew that candidates had to campaign to get elected. When George Washington first ran for office in 1757, for example, he is said to have provided the "customary means of winning votes": 28 gallons of rum, 50 gallons of rum punch, 34 gallons of wine, 46 gallons of beer, and 2 gallons of cider royal. Given that there were only 319 voters in his district, Washington spent 2 quarts per vote.[1]

Rather, what would trouble the Founders is how winning elections has become less a test of a candidate's virtue, and more a test of a candidate's ability to just look good out there. They might ask whether a George Washington could get elected today, or whether he would be painted as too old and stuffy, whether an investigative reporter might find some scandal in that long winter at Valley Forge (why didn't he win the Revolutionary War in less time?), or whether he could stand the bright lights of television.

As the rest of this chapter will show, modern campaigns are anything but simple affairs. There are complex rules governing elections, complex organizations for conducting campaigns, and complex strategies for persuading voters. Yet, as this chapter will also show, the final decision that each voter makes may be anything but complex. In the end, most voters cast their ballots for the candidate they like the most, or the one they dislike the least.

CAMPAIGNING FOR OFFICE

Running for political office is one of the most challenging tasks in America. It means intense public scrutiny, a nearly constant search for campaign money, and moments of great drama. It is not a decision to be taken lightly, for it involves hard rules and tough choices.

Rules of Engagement

The Constitution provides few details on who gets to run for national office. Besides setting simple qualifications such as age and citizenship for holding office, the Constitution leaves the specifics to the states. The result is a patchwork of rules across the nation.

Recognizing these differences, reaching office almost always involves winning at least two separate contests: a **nomination** and a **general election.** The first is to get on the ballot itself; the second is to win the office outright.

Under Article I, Section 4, states have considerable influence over how nomination contests are decided, often using one system for selecting nominees for congressional and state offices and a second, different system for choosing delegates to the national party conventions. States also have considerable influence over how general elections are conducted, and sometimes set the dates for state elections in odd-numbered years to keep national politics out of the debate. Many states also give their localities similar freedom to set the dates.

Choosing Congressional and State Nominees. The most frequently used method for selecting congressional and state nominees is by **primary election,** in which voters decide who gets to run as a party's nominee. Most primary elections take place several months before the **general election,** which determines who gets to hold the office. All fifty states use some kind of primary election either as the sole method for selecting nominees (thirty-seven states) or as part of a more complicated nomination process (thirteen states) that involves local and/or state party conventions.

All states give the people a say somewhere in the process, but they vary greatly in defining who gets to vote in a primary. The vast majority of states use a **closed**

primary, in which only party members are allowed to cast ballots in their party's primary. These states require voters to declare their party preference when they register to vote. Republicans are allowed to vote only in Republican primaries, Democrats only in Democratic primaries. Some states allow independents to chose one or the other primary on election day, others prohibit independents from participating altogether.

A much smaller number of states use an **open primary,** in which voters are allowed to cast ballots in any party primary they wish. But once a voter decides the party primary in which to participate, that voter must stay in that party's ballot. Because voters are not required to declare their preference until they arrive to vote, Republicans and Democrats are free to crossover and vote in the other party's primary, while independents are free to vote in whichever primary they wish. Such crossover voting is more likely if one party has a particularly exciting contest.

An even smaller number of states use a blanket primary, in which voters receive a ballot listing all candidates of both parties and are free to move back and forth across party lines all the way down the ballot.

Of the three, closed primaries do the most to strengthen the role of the parties in choosing nominees. Because independents and voters from the opposition party cannot crossover to vote in a closed primary, candidates must appeal to their party's faithful if they are to win.

Choosing Delegates to the National Conventions.

States also set the rules for selecting delegates to the national party conventions with broad guidance from the national parties.[2] The national Democratic Party requires, for example, that all state delegations be split equally between men and women.

As with congressional and state offices, most of the states use a primary system for selecting presidential delegates, and most of those that do use a closed primary in which only party voters are allowed to choose among competing candidates. (A small number of states use a delegate selection primary in which party voters are only allowed to vote for the names of specific delegates who are pledged to different candidates. Like the electoral college, voters only get to cast ballots for the delegates who then get to vote for the candidate.) By tradition, New Hampshire holds the first presidential primary in February of every fourth year.

Although the number of primaries continues to grow, a quarter of the states still use a **caucus system,** in which delegates are selected through a series of party meetings that usually begin at the local level (*caucus* is simply a term that means convention). In contrast to a primary, which involves a brief moment of participation, local caucuses are intense face-to-face events, often running late into the night as friends and neighbors talk about the future of their party. By tradition, Iowa hosts the first major party caucus, again in February of every presidential election year.

Because the purpose of these primaries and caucuses is to select delegates to the national conventions, the states must decide how to allocate seats to each

Candidate Clinton talks with the voters on the eve of the New Hampshire primary in 1992.

candidate. Under national Democratic Party rules, all states must allocate their Democratic delegates using a **proportional voting system,** in which delegates are divided up according to the final votes in the primary or caucus. A candidate who won 40 percent of the final vote would get 40 percent of the delegates. Roughly half of all Republican primaries are winner-take-all, in which the top vote-getter wins all the delegates.

Because the Democratic Party has more minority members to begin with and has rules encouraging the selection of minority and women delegates, its delegates are likely to be more diverse than Republican Party convention goers. In 1992, for example, about 50 percent of Democratic delegates were women, 14 percent were African Americans, and 45 percent were attending their first convention. Although almost as many Republican delegates were women, only 4 percent were African Americans, and far fewer were attending their first convention. What both conventions shared was higher education. Half of all Democratic delegates had a postgraduate degree, as did a third of Republicans.[3]

The past fifty years have witnessed two important changes in the nomination process. First, the number of delegates selected through primaries has steadily increased, rising from roughly 40 percent of all delegates in the early 1900s to over 80 percent today. Primaries were seen as a way to give citizens a greater role in the selection process, which they most certainly did. More than 30 million Americans participated in the 1996 Democratic and Republican primaries.

Second, the number of early primaries and caucuses has steadily increased. It used to be that only small states liked to go early, on the theory that they get greater influence by helping sort out the early candidates, while larger states liked to go late, on the theory that they would get attention through sheer size alone. New Hampshire and Iowa came first, California last.

In 1996, however, California decided to move its primary up from June to March in an effort to compete with the growing number of smaller states going earlier. "March Madness" is no longer just a term for the NCAA national basketball tournament. Roughly two-thirds of the 1996 presidential delegates were picked during March, a compression of the nominating process that was caused by what experts call front-loading. The front-loading clearly reduces the time spent in a given state, and tends to favor candidates who have more money for paid advertising.

Deciding to Run

The most important decision candidates make is to enter the campaign in the first place. Candidates need what some call a "fire in the belly" to survive the process, particularly once they enter national politics. In 1996, for example, General Colin Powell decided early on that he simply did not have the ambition needed to mount a serious campaign for the Republican presidential nomination. Neither did his fellow Republicans Jack Kemp and William Bennett. Nevertheless, all three were serious contenders for the vice presidential nomination, which eventually went

Ret. Gen. Colin Powell says "no" to a presidential bid in 1996 as his wife looks on. In announcing his decision not to run, Powell said that a campaign requires "a calling I do not yet hear."

to Kemp. He may not have had the fire for the presidential nomination, but proved an energetic campaigner on behalf of the Republican ticket.

Most candidates for office are motivated by a commitment to public service. They believe they can accomplish something worthwhile, most believe in the democratic process, and most have a strong sense of purpose. "Who sent us the political leaders we have?" asks journalist Alan Ehrenhalt in his book *The United States of Ambition.* "There is a simple answer to that question. They sent themselves. And they got where they are through a combination of ambition, talent, and the willingness to devote whatever time was necessary to seek and hold office."[4]

Nevertheless, there is some evidence that the kinds of candidates who decide to run today are different from those who ran earlier. Because campaigns are longer, the sacrifices demanded of family are greater and the demands for fund-raising skills are much more intense. Physical endurance is clearly more important today than ever before, as is an ability to communicate through television. A commitment to public service is still essential, but is clearly no longer enough. Candidates must also have well-developed campaign skills. And those skills may have little to do with actually governing once in office.

Building an Organization

Putting together an effective campaign for election starts with the basics: an organization. At a very minimum, a campaign must have a legally established organization to receive and spend campaign contributions. But the organization is also the home for a host of other essential activities.

The key question in building an organization is whether the campaign organization is going to do everything for itself or let the national, state, or local party committee do some of the work. In a **party-centered campaign,** the candidate runs as a representative of the party. All messages focus on reminding voters of their party identification, all fund-raising and polling come from the party organization, and the hard work of getting voters to the polls is done by the party field staff, which operates through state and local committees. What matters is not so much whether the candidate wins, but how strongly the candidate is tied to the party. For long after the election is over, the party organization will endure.

In contrast, a **candidate-centered campaign** is of the candidate, for the candidate, and by the candidate. The focus is on whatever it takes to get the candidate elected. If that means abandoning all ties to the party, so be it. All messages focus on electing the candidate, all fund-raising and polling come from the candidate's own organization, and the get-out-the-vote effort is handled by the candidate's own field staff. The candidate-centered organization is a temporary shelter for dozens of specialized staff who might be out of a job as soon as the last ballot is counted.[5] (Box 6–1 shows the organization chart for today's candidate-centered presidential campaign.)

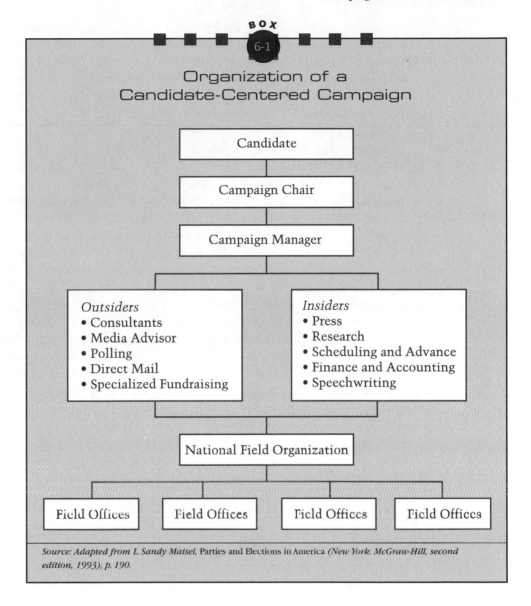

BOX 6-1

Organization of a Candidate-Centered Campaign

Candidate

Campaign Chair

Campaign Manager

Outsiders
- Consultants
- Media Advisor
- Polling
- Direct Mail
- Specialized Fundraising

Insiders
- Press
- Research
- Scheduling and Advance
- Finance and Accounting
- Speechwriting

National Field Organization

Field Offices   Field Offices   Field Offices   Field Offices

Source: Adapted from L. Sandy Maisel, Parties and Elections in America *(New York: McGraw-Hill, second edition, 1993), p. 190.*

Most of the outsider jobs in Box 6–1 were once done by the party. In today's candidate-centered campaign, they are now performed by consultants and specialists of one kind or another. The most visible outsider post belongs to the lead campaign consultant, the individual most responsible for developing the broad campaign strategy. Unlike the campaign manager, who handles the day-to-day details of *how* the campaign runs, the consultant helps make broad decisions about *what* the campaign does, and brings a pure focus on doing whatever it takes to win.

Creating a candidate-centered campaign makes perfect sense given the decline of party loyalty and the rise of the new media. Candidates no longer need to rely on the parties or traditional media to get their message out. Indeed, many candidates see the party label as a liability. Running against Washington is also "in," even for long-time Washington insiders. It is no small trick to portray oneself as an agent of change after serving in Congress for twenty years, but incumbents do it all the time. Once back in office, these members may have much less incentive to work together to make government run at all.

Hiring a Consultant

Hiring a lead political consultant may be the single most important decision a campaign makes. Just as hiring an architect is essential for building a home, so, too, is hiring a consultant for creating an effective campaign. The consultant draws the blueprints, and often hires the specialists. The general contractor (campaign manager) may make sure every nail goes in on time, but the consultant often tells the contractor where each nail should go.

Consultants are different from other campaign staff in that they have no lasting loyalty to the candidate. They come to the campaign because the pay is good and the candidate has a chance to win. Although most consultants work only for one party or the other, some are perfectly comfortable working with both.

Consultants have existed since the dawn of politics. Niccolo Machiavelli was a consultant of a kind when he wrote *The Prince* in the fifteenth century, giving advice to his prince on how to manipulate the political process.

What makes the current period different is both the rise of consulting as an organized industry in American politics and its enormous influence over what candidates do. A survey by political scientist Mark Petracca shows that the number of firms has grown so fast that half of those in business in 1989 were not in business in 1980.[6] An estimated 12,000 Americans earned part or most of their living from political consulting by the end of the 1980s.[7]

That number reflects dramatic growth over the 1980s. There are now consultants to do just about anything a campaign needs. One consulting firm once advertised that "We know how to handle indictments, arrests, or a candidate that simply falls down stairs a lot."[8]

The growth of the consulting industry is clearly tied to the decline of the parties, although it is not quite clear which came first. Whatever the order of events, candidates have come to rely less and less on the parties to organize the campaign, importing expertise in the form of political consultants instead. According to Roger Stone, a top Republican consultant, "what has happened is that in many ways, the political consultants have replaced political parties and the party leaders." His Democratic counterpart, Robert Squier agrees: "There was an accidental timing of technologies. There was the mass production of the automobile, the television set, and the creation of the suburbs. People drove out from under the existing political systems, which really existed only in the cities. . . . Suddenly there were no block captains, people had to make decisions for themselves. . . . It basically knocked whatever strength there was out of our party system."[9]

The consulting industry also grew because there was money to be made in campaign consulting. There were 500,000 offices up for election in 1992, although most did not involve much campaign spending, and the totals add up. A few thousand here for a county commissioner's job, a few hundred thousand there for a U.S. House seat, and suddenly campaigns are a $3 *billion* biannual industry.[10] No wonder people are getting into the business. If they can get just the tiniest fraction of that money, they can make a very nice living. Moreover, there are virtually no start-up costs for a consulting firm—no licenses to get, no fancy equipment.

This single-minded commitment to winning has its cost, of course. Consultants have a very strong stake in making sure that those in power stay in power. Incumbents are always going to make good clients, in part because they raise and spend more money, in part because they have a very high chance of winning, thereby making a consultant's won-lost record better. But they also make *known* clients who return a consultant's phone calls. They tend to work with those they already know.

More troubling, consultants may be contributing to the increasing public distrust with democracy. Consultants have pioneered the art of negative "attack" ads, and have also perfected the art of "voter suppression," in which campaigns discourage unfriendly voters from showing up for the election. Political scientist Larry Sabato minces no words regarding the impact of consultants on the electoral process: "Political consultants, answerable only to their client-candidates and independent of the political parties, have inflicted severe damage upon the party system and masterminded the modern triumph of personality cults over party politics in the United States."[11] They may also be increasing the tendency that government just strong enough cannot act at all.

Creating a Strategy

Having decided to run, built a campaign staff, and hired a consultant, a candidate's election campaign must develop and execute a credible strategy for winning. A campaign strategy tells the candidate which issues to highlight, what messages to emphasize, and where the most supportive voters can be found. Its purpose is to match what the candidate says and does with the prevailing mood of the electorate.

A winning strategy need not be complex, however. In 1992, for example, Bill Clinton won the presidency with a one-sentence strategy printed on a huge sign at campaign headquarters: "It's the Economy, Stupid!" Every campaign stop, every message, and every advertisement reminded voters of the poor economic performance under incumbent president George Bush.

Because no candidate is perfect, a campaign strategy also addresses candidate strengths and weaknesses, playing up the things voters might like, and playing down the things voters might dislike. As we will see in Chapter 7, incumbent members of Congress have a host of advantages over challengers, not the least of which is that they have already won at least one election, and have a certain level of name recognition. They also do many of the things that voters like, including casework on behalf of individual constituents.

Incumbents also have remarkable access to campaign funding. In 1994, for example, incumbents had, on average, a 5:1 advantage over their challengers, and an 8:1 advantage in cash on hand going into the final weeks of the election.[12] The fact is that most contributors like to bet on a winner. The average Democratic House incumbent spent nearly $600,000 in the 1994 campaign, compared to just $230,000 for the Republican challenger; the average Republican House incumbent spent nearly $450,000 against just $150,000 for the challenger. In contrast, Democratic and Republican challengers for open seats spend roughly $550,000 each, about as even as it gets.[13]

The most important step in creating a campaign strategy is to take stock of these strengths and weaknesses. Take the presidency as an example. Some historians even argue that incumbent presidents can tell if they are going to win reelection by asking thirteen simple questions at the start of the campaign. When the answers to six or more are false, the challenger will win. (See Box 6–2 for the thirteen keys.)

The thirteen keys worked well for predicting the 1996 election. Bill Clinton's party entered the presidential campaign in deep trouble. Republicans won 52 seats in the House, eight in the Senate, and the first congressional majority in over forty years. Not a single Republican incumbent who ran for reelection in the House or Senate lost—give Clinton his first "false"; his party was clearly in decline.

At the same time, Clinton had no opposition in winning his party's nomination—give him his first "true"—and was running for reelection—give him another "true." He got all the benefits of being presidential; that is, the seal of office, the military pomp and circumstance, the chance to sign popular legislation such as an increase in the minimum wage. Although Ross Perot ran again for the presidency, he was left out of the presidential debates and was never considered a serious candidate—give Clinton another "true."

The economy was not in a recession in 1996—another "true" for Clinton—and had improved significantly since 1992 with the stock market setting an all-time record just before the election—yet another "true." On national policy, Clinton had a mixed record. His national health insurance plan never came to a formal vote in either chamber of Congress, but a number of lesser initiatives such as family leave passed—give him a third "false" on the list.

Moving down the keys, there was no civil unrest during the administration—a "true"—no major failure in foreign or military affairs—another "true"—and a major foreign policy success in restoring democratic rule to Haiti—still another

BOX
6-2

The Thirteen Keys to Predicting
a Presidential Election

True/False: The sitting president's party has more seats in the House of Representatives today than it had four years ago.

True/False: There is no serious contest for the nomination of the sitting president's party.

True/False: The president is running for reelection.

True/False: There is no significant third-party or independent candidate such as Ross Perot.

True/False: The economy is not in a recession during the presidential campaign.

True/False: The economy has been as strong or stronger during the sitting, or incumbent, president's term of office as it was before.

True/False: The sitting president has been able to make major changes in national policy such as national health insurance.

True/False: There has been no sustained social unrest during the sitting president's term such as the 1965 race riots (the 1991 Los Angeles riots would not count since they did not spread and were quickly contained).

True/False: There has been no major scandal such as Watergate or Whitewater.

True/False: There has been no major failure in foreign or military affairs such as the Vietnam War.

True/False: There has been a major success in foreign or military affairs such as the Persian Gulf War or the Haiti invasion.

True/False: The sitting party's candidate is a charismatic leader or a national hero such as retired General Colin Powell.

True/False: The challenger is a *not* a charismatic leader or a national hero.

Source: Allan Lichtman and Ken DeCell, The 13 Keys to the Presidency *(Lanham, MD: Madison Books, 1990), p. 7.*

"true." Although the administration was tainted by a series of scandals—a third "false"—the lapses did not seem to matter in the 1996 election because Clinton was so charismatic—another "true"—and because his opponent, Bob Dole, was not—another "true." According to the thirteen keys, Clinton was destined to win, ten "trues" to just three "falses."

Although campaign strategy cannot turn a weak economy into a strong one, it can compensate for weaknesses and build upon strengths. Dole might have addressed public concerns about the Clinton scandals more directly or he might have raised the broad "character" issue earlier in the campaign. More importantly perhaps, the Republican Party might have been more successful if it had picked a presidential candidate who could match the president's charisma smile for smile. As it was, Dole often looked old and mean in his debates with Clinton and overly negative in his television advertising.

IN A DIFFERENT LIGHT

BASELINE, TRACK, PUSH, AND ATTACK

Public opinion polls are essential tools of modern election campaigns. Early in a campaign, candidates use **baseline polls** to take stock of strengths and weaknesses and test possible campaign themes. They ask voters about the issues that matter most to the election, and try to anticipate possible weak points in their campaigns.

Candidates use **tracking polls** to measure their standing day to day and to show trends in support over time. Tracking polls are designed to interview two or three hundred likely voters every day, adding the fresh respondents to those interviewed the day before, while subtracting the respondents interviewed the day before that. The result is a statistically accurate sample that can tell candidates exactly where they stand with the people who are most likely to show up on election day.

In recent years, some candidates have also started conducting **push polls** late in the campaign. Push polls are not scientific polls at all, but have earned the name because they are often disguised as legitimate polls. The purpose of a push poll is simple: give voters such negative information on the other candidate that they will either change their vote or not show up to vote at all. The negative information is designed to persuade, or push, voters away from their preferred candidate; hence, the name *push polls.* Such polls are part of a what experts sometimes call *voter suppression campaigns* whose sole purpose is to keep the opponent's voters home.[14]

Because push polls are only used in the very last days of a campaign, they are almost impossible to trace to the originating campaign, and difficult if not impossible to counterattack in time to weaken their impact. One of the most famous push polls came in the hotly contested 1994 Florida governor's contest when the Democratic candidate, Lawton Chiles, authorized at least 70,000 calls to senior citizens claiming that the Republican candidate, Jeb Bush (son of President George Bush), wanted to abolish Social Security and Medicare. Chiles won by a few thousand votes, in part because at least some of those senior citizens stayed home or switched their votes.

Push polls are troubling innovations in modern campaign tactics. By casting negative information in a legitimate light or by misleading voters entirely, they are versions of old-fashioned "whisper campaigns," in which campaign workers would ride at the back of elevators whispering lies to each other about the opponent hoping other riders would listen and spread the lies as truth. Most push polls are not discovered until it is too late, and are often conducted using phony organizations as fronts. Candidates who use such tactics may win election, but do little to increase public confidence in the governments they get to lead.

Raising Money

Money pays for just about everything a campaign does, from building an organization to hiring a consultant and persuading voters. It even pays for raising more money. "There are two things that are important in politics," said Mark Hanna, the father of modern campaigning, in 1895. "The first is money and I can't remember what the second one is."[15]

Most candidates for federal office will attest that raising money is the most difficult thing they do. Calling strangers to ask for money is hard enough, but calling hundreds of strangers a day is even tougher. Candidates call it "trolling for dollars." "I felt like a total whore, running after rich people begging with your tin cup," said Colorado Democrat Patricia Schroeder, who ran briefly for the Democratic presidential nomination in 1988.[16] (The special problem of presidential financing will be covered at the end of this section.)

Campaigns clearly cost more today than they did even twenty years ago. That much is obvious from the figures. In 1972, according to campaign finance expert Frank Sorauf, all congressional candidates put together spent barely $77 million. By 1986, the total had jumped to $450 million. Even adjusting for inflation, the increase was over 100 percent.[17] By 1996, the total had increased to $800 million.

The conventional wisdom is that an effective House campaign today needs to raise roughly $600,000 to be competitive: $150,000 for two broad mailings to every home in the district; $100,000 to produce and run three television commercials and six radio spots; and another $350,000 for consultants, polling, office rental, and travel. Given the fact that the average congressional campaign actually averaged barely half of the ideal in 1994, Sorauf suggests that "one can make a plausible argument that candidates spend too little, not too much, in congressional campaigns."[18] As for the Senate, no one won a Senate race in 1994 spending less than $1 million.

Like most averages, this one disguises enormous variation. Congressional campaigns in large states such as California are "media intense," with heavy television advertising and direct mail, and can cost millions to win; campaigns in small states such as South Dakota, with ample amounts of "free media" coverage, remain within reach of a challenger with but a few hundred thousand dollars.

This does not mean campaigns in small and midsize states always come cheap. Until 1994, the state spending record was North Carolina's $26.5 million 1984 Senate race between incumbent Senator Jesse Helms and Governor Jim Hunt. It was not broken until California's $43 million senatorial contest in 1994 between Michael Huffington and Dianne Feinstein. Together, the two Californians spent roughly $100,000 a day during the year, most of it for buying television time.

Raising money also has an impact on the democratic process. At the very minimum, fund-raising takes time away from other activities. Assume that a congressional candidate has to call fifty potential donors a day to find ten who are willing to contribute; also assume the candidate has to spend five minutes on each call making the pitch and closing the deal, including asking the donor to get the check in the mail right away.[19] That comes to 250 minutes a day, or four solid hours that could be used for something else.

California Senate candidates Dianne Feinstein and Michael Huffington appear on *Larry King Live* in October 1994, in a rare opportunity for free media in the most expensive Senate campaign of the year. Together, the two candidates spent $43 million dollars, or $100,000 a day during the campaign, most of it going for paid media. Feinstein won.

Time is hardly the only casualty of expensive campaigns, however. A candidate's ability to raise money becomes a key qualification for running, displacing a host of what might be more important qualifications for serving—for example, leadership, civic-mindedness, intelligence, and experience. Moreover, good candidates may decide they would rather not run than spend four hours a day raising money, leaving the candidacies to those whose major attribute is either the ability to dial for dollars or the willingness to spend huge amounts of their own money.[20] The result may be a Congress of either the very wealthy, who are willing and able to spend great quantities of their own money to win a seat, or great fund-raisers, who can pry $1,000 out of even the most reluctant contributor, but have very little else to offer in terms of skills.

A Brief History of Campaign Spending.   Until the 1970s, raising campaign money was a relatively simple enterprise. Candidates got most of their money from two sources: very large individual contributors and people who wanted jobs in government (before 1884, almost all federal jobs were given on the basis of political connections, or patronage). The number of fund-raising calls a candidate had to make was small, the size of the individual contributions very large. (See Box 6-3 for a brief history of campaign fund-raising.)

The 1896 election ushered in the modern era of large individual contributions from America's wealthiest citizens and corporations. This dependence upon large contributors, and the sense that elections were being bought and sold, eventually prompted a wave of campaign finance reform. The first wave of reform actually came in the early 1900s when Congress banned all direct campaign contributions by banks and corporations, followed by a second wave in the early 1940s, which banned contributions by labor unions. All three groups now make their contributions through political action committees. (See Chapter 4 for a basic introduction to PACs.)

As the cost of presidential campaigns grew, the reform wave continued to gather momentum, culminating in the early 1970s with passage of three separate election campaign acts—the first was the *Federal Election Campaign Act of 1971,* which established full disclosure of congressional and presidential campaign contributions and spending; the second was the *Revenue Act of 1971,* which created a checkoff on the tax form that allows taxpayers to contribute to the presidential campaign fund; and the third was the *Federal Election Campaign Act of 1974,* which placed limits on how much individuals and political committees (parties and PACs) could contribute to a single campaign. The 1974 act also created the Federal Election Commission, which monitors campaign spending.

Together, the 1974 act and its later amendments created three different systems of campaign finance law: one that covers candidates for the two houses of Congress, a second that covers candidates for the presidential nominations, and a third that covers candidates for the presidential general election. Candidates for the House and Senate receive no public funding, candidates for the presidential

BOX
6-3

A History of Campaign Finance

1789–1820   Because the electorate was small, campaign costs were low. Candidates themselves, friends, and family usually paid for campaigns. No laws regulating campaign fund-raising were necessary.

1820s–1830s   Campaign costs began to rise due to a growing electorate and the arrival of the two-party system. The first presidential campaign managers appeared in 1828, and the practice of buying votes began. Uncommitted voters earned $22 for their votes in the 1838 New York City mayoral race.

1840s–1880s   Campaign costs continued to rise, as did fund-raising. The first federal campaign finance regulation was passed in 1867 prohibiting officers and government employees from soliciting money from naval yard workers. The Civil Service Reform Act of 1883 protected all federal employees from being solicited.

1880s–1920s   Referred to as "the golden age of boodle," the late 1800s and early 1900s ushered in a new era of very large campaigns. Direct election of senator and the expansion of the electorate to include women pushed the cost of running for office upward. Bans on direct contributions from banks and corporations were enacted, but remained mostly unenforced.

1930s–1940s   More elections, including the advent of primaries, as well as a growing electorate, and greater government involvement in the economy combined to increase costs. Labor unions became significant contributors to Democratic candidates. Franklin Delano Roosevelt raised more than $500,000 from the Congress of Industrial Organizations for the 1936 election. The CIO formed the first political action committee in 1944 to circumvent contribution limits passed in 1940 and 1943.

1950s–1970s   With growth in the electorate starting to slow, television took over as the leading cause of increasing campaign costs. The 1972 election produced a long list of illegal contributions, including a $200,000 contribution delivered in cash to the Committee to Reelect the President. The Watergate scandal revealed further abuses of power, leading to a broad reform effort.

1980s–1990s   Campaign costs have continued upward, driven by the rising number of candidate-centered campaigns, in which candidates run without strong ties to their party. Money is much easier to track under the Watergate-era legislation. States have led the effort to control campaign spending.

Source: Center for Responsive Politics, A Brief History of Money in Politics *(Washington, DC: Center for Responsive Politics, 1995).*

nominations receive matching dollars, and candidates for the final run to the White House receive full public funding.[21]

The result is an intricate, and often puzzling set of rules governing campaign finance that affects individual givers, congressional candidates, and the presidential candidates. (The rules are summarized in Box 6–4).

Because congressional and presidential campaigns are covered by different rules, they must be treated separately. Before turning to each, it is useful to note that the 1974 law succeeded in reducing contributions from wealthy individuals and corporations. Neither can give more than $25,000 a year total to federal candidates, party committees, or PACs.

There are only two exceptions to the impacts. First, large contributors are free to spend as much as they want on behalf, but independent, of a given candidate. In 1976, the Supreme Court declared such **independent spending** to be a form of free speech, and therefore not subject to limits.[22] The only restriction is that the spending cannot be coordinated with the campaign, but the word *independent* is usually interpreted loosely. Second, large contributors are free to give as much as they want to the national party committees for party building and get-out-the-vote campaigns. Such contributions are called **soft money** because they are not restricted by hard limits.

Congressional Campaigns.   Raising money is particularly important for congressional campaigns, where there are four, and only four, sources of money for congressional candidates: (1) individual donors, (2) the political parties, (3) political action committees (PACs), and (4) the candidates themselves. Of the $611 million raised for the 1994 congressional campaigns, individual donors gave the largest share at $336 million (55 percent), with PACs second at $169 million (28 percent), loans and contributions from candidates to themselves at $82 million (13 percent), and the rest from the parties and other loans.[23]

BOX
6-4

Rules Governing Campaign Spending

	A Person May Give	A PAC May Give	A Party May Give
Each federal candidate per election	$ 1,000	$ 5,000	$ 1,000
Each national party committee per year	20,000	15,000	20,000
Each PAC per year	5,000	5,000	5,000
Limit on total contributions per year	$25,000	unlimited	unlimited

The easiest way to raise money is to give it to yourself—that is, to be rich enough to back your own campaign. The First Amendment protects free speech, and giving money to one's own campaign has been defined by the Supreme Court as a form of free speech. (As we will see, presidential candidates who accept public financing also accept voluntary limits on putting their own money into their campaigns. Because congressional candidates receive no public financing, they face no such limits.)

Although individual donors and the candidates themselves are obviously major sources of congressional financing, PACs have received the greatest attention in recent years, in part because their numbers have grown so quickly (the number of PACs increased from just a few hundred in the early 1970s to roughly 4,000 today), and in part because they give so much of their money to incumbents. In 1991–1992, for example, PACs gave 71 cents out of every dollar to incumbents; by 1993–1994, the figure had grown to 89 cents out of every dollar.[24]

The numbers on PAC giving in 1993–1994 confirm two trends. First, business and trade associations connected with business are the big givers, accounting for nearly 65 cents of every dollar given in PAC money, while labor accounts for just 25 cents, and issue groups the rest. (See Box 6–5 for two top ten lists on how much different kinds of PACs have given to candidates over the past decade.)

BOX
6-5

PAC Top Tens

Top Ten PACS by Industry, 1985–1995		Top Ten Individual PACS, 1993–1994	
Banking and Finance	$56 million	United Parcel Service	$2.6 million
Energy	51 million	Teamsters Union	2.5 million
Agriculture	49 million	American Medical Association	2.5 million
Transportation Unions	45 million	American Federation of State, County,	
Insurance	42 million	and Municipal Employees (AFSCME)	2.5 million
Real Estate	41 million	National Education Association	2.3 million
Media	38 million	Association of Trial Lawyers of America	2.2 million
Government Employee		United Auto Workers	2.2 million
Union	37 million	National Rifle Association (NRA)	1.9 million
Medical	37 million	National Association of Realtors	1.9 million
Transportation Firms	30 million	National Auto Dealers Association	1.8 million

Ranked by contributions to congressional races.

Sources: For top ten over the 1985–1995 period, Time, August 14, 1995, p. 20; for top ten PAC sponsors in 1993–1994, Center for Responsive Politics, The Price of Admission, (Washington, D.C.: Center for Responsive Politics, 1995), p. 17.

Second, PACs are hardly risk takers in spending their money. They tend to give their dollars to winners, which mostly means giving to incumbent members of Congress. In 1993–1994, for example, PACs gave $101 million to House incumbents and only $11 million to challengers, yielding a 9:1 ratio. In the Senate, where elections are more hotly contested, PACs gave about $25 million to incumbents and $5 million to challengers, for a 5:1 ratio.[25]

This does not mean PAC money always goes to incumbents regardless of the election trends. Business money started moving away from Democratic incumbents and toward Republican challengers late in the 1994 congressional campaigns when it started to look like Republicans just might do the impossible and take control of the House. Once the election was over, the trend reverted to form. Only now the Republicans, not the Democrats, were the beneficiaries. In the first three months of 1993, with Democrats in charge of both houses, AT&T gave 64 percent of its PAC money to Democrats; in the first three months of 1995, with Republicans now in charge, AT&T gave 79 percent of its dollars to Republicans.[26] The only thing that had changed was the incumbent party.

Presidential Campaigns. Modern presidential campaigns are very different from all other campaigns. First, they are much longer than any other campaigns. Presidential campaigns start well before Iowa and New Hampshire. Candidates must be up and raising money at least six months earlier if they are to survive the early nomination tests, and many run informally for several years before, taking repeated trips to Iowa and New Hampshire to test the presidential waters.

Second, presidential campaigns are intense, becoming more so over the past few elections. The intensity is particularly clear in the compression of the nomination season. In 1992, for example, the candidates had 113 days between the first Iowa caucus and the critical California primary in June. In 1996, they were separated by just forty-three days; roughly three-quarters of all delegates to the national party conventions were selected between the Iowa caucuses on February 12 and the California primary on March 26. If the candidates do not have their financing on hand to start rolling in early February, they will never find the time to raise it later.

Once past the conventions, presidential campaigns become even more intense. Although successful candidates need not compete in all fifty states, the District of Columbia, Puerto Rico, and the American territories to win, they must contest the major sources of electoral votes. Even states that are almost automatic for one or the other party—Texas was nearly guaranteed to George Bush in 1992—cannot be neglected, lest the opposing candidate make a surprise run.

Third, not surprisingly given the length, intensity, and the number of states involved, presidential campaigns are extraordinarily expensive. Twenty million dollars was considered the minimum needed for a Republican to be competitive in the 1996 nomination campaigns, an amount that had to be raised in $1,000 or $5,000 contributions. For a little-known candidate such as Tennessee Republican

Lamar Alexander, who started his campaign in January 1995, the $20 million target meant raising $77,000 every business day of the campaign.[27]

Fourth, presidential campaigns are funded mostly with public money raised through the $3 checkoff on the income tax form. The money comes in two installments: the first involves matching money for the nomination campaign, the second involves full public funding for the general election campaign.

The public funding is part of a quid pro quo, or promise, candidates make: In return for public funding, they agree not to use more than $50,000 of their own money in the campaign season. If they do not agree to the personal limit, they do not get the public funds. In 1996, for example, Steve Forbes refused the public funds, spending $25 million of his own money in his failed bid for the Republican nomination.

During the nomination season, the first payment of public funds is only available to candidates who raise $5,000 in at least twenty states in contributions of no more than $250. Once a candidate meets this simple test, he or she gets dollar-for-dollar matching up to a preset spending ceiling. In 1992, for example, candidate Bush received almost $11 million in matching dollars for his nomination campaign, far outdistancing his nearest Republican rival, former Nixon speechwriter Patrick Buchanan, at $5.2 million. With $12 million, candidate Clinton also bettered his party rivals, leading former California Governor Jerry Brown at $4.1 million, and former U.S. Senator Paul Tsongas at just under $3 million.[28]

Once past the nomination, all the money is public, provided the candidate accepts voluntary limits on personal spending. In 1996, for example, the two major-party candidates divided $120 million for the campaign. Just because the two party candidates are spending public money does not mean private money is banned from presidential campaigns, however. As noted earlier, organizations and individuals are free to spend as much money as they want independent of the two presidential campaigns. Such money can finance get-out-the-vote efforts, direct mail to potential voters, and even extensive television advertising.

IN A DIFFERENT LIGHT

SOFT MONEY AND BUNDLING

Despite the 1974 Federal Election Campaign Act, large contributions still flow into federal campaigns. Money in campaigns is very much like mercury—push it here and it goes there; push there and it goes here. Even the tightest campaign finance law leaves gaps where the money can flow.

During the 1980s, parties and candidates developed two new techniques for exploiting those loopholes. The first involves soft money gifts to the national parties. Under 1979 amendments to the 1974 law, individuals and corporations may contribute unlimited amounts of money to the parties as long as the money goes into the administrative accounts for party-building activities such as voter registration drives and get-out-the-vote campaigns.

As large contributors discovered the loophole, the money started to flow. Between 1991 and 1994, the Republican National Committee raised $95 million in soft money, or roughly one-fifth of its total budget; the Democratic National Committee raised $75 million, or one-sixth of its budget. Among the givers were Hard Rock Cafe owner Peter Morton, who gave $100,000 to the Democrats; Wall Street investment banker and future Clinton Secretary of the Treasury Robert Rubin, who gave $275,000 to the Democrats; and Dwayne Andreas and his Archer Daniels Midland Company (a huge agricultural conglomerate), who gave $227,500 to the Republicans.

The two parties have clearly been strengthened by the soft money, giving them added leverage with members of Congress and state officials in enforcing greater party discipline. That is likely a good thing, particularly as a counterweight to the growing number of organized interests. However, the soft money may deepen public beliefs that government is run for the special interests.

It can hardly strengthen trust, for example, when the two national party committees create special clubs for donors who give $100,000 or more in soft funding—the Republicans call them members of "Team 100," the Democrats call their $100,000 givers "Trustees" and their $200,000 givers "Managing Trustees." A $100,000 contributor in 1996 got two meals with President Bill Clinton, two meals with Vice President Al Gore, a slot on a foreign trade mission with Democratic National Committee leaders, and a host of smaller benefits, including a party staffer assigned to address the contributor's "personal requests."[29]

The second technique for raising more money outside the constraints of campaign finance laws is known as **bundling.** Bundling involves nothing more than collecting large numbers of individual checks and turning them over to a candidate or candidates. Each check is made out to the candidate, not the person or organization doing the bundling. Technically, the bundler is not making a contribution at all.

EMILY's List (*Early Money Is Like Yeast*) is one of the most effective bundling operations currently in operation. Established to help women candidates get desperately needed early funding for their campaigns, EMILY's List proved so successful that it became one of the largest sources of money for House and Senate candidates in 1993–1994 at $7.5 million, making it the second largest spender of all.[30] Technically, however, EMILY's List did not give any money at all, and does not show up on any inventory of the top campaign givers or PACs. All it did was drop nearly 75,000 individual checks on campaign '94, all of which were bundled together to help individual candidates.

Although soft money and bundling are both perfectly legal techniques for raising campaign dollars, they may undermine public trust nonetheless. Exploiting loopholes, whether legal or not,

President Clinton greets former Texas Governor Ann Richards at an EMILY's List event in 1995. EMILY's List gives its bundled dollars only to women candidates and usually early in a campaign. The acronym EMILY stands for Early Money Is Like Yeast.

may create the appearance of conflict of interest, adding to the public's anger with government and its leaders. The money simply may not be worth it.

■ ■ ■

Persuading Voters

The ultimate purpose of a campaign is simple: get more supporters to the polls than opponents. That means reinforcing the things voters already like about the candidate, while emphasizing the things voters dislike about the opponent; it also means minimizing the things voters dislike about the candidate, and making them question the things they like about the opponent.

These likes and dislikes can involve the candidate's party, issue positions, or image as a leader. As we will see later in this chapter, voters appear to make their decision by adding up their likes and dislikes and voting for the candidate who comes out on top. Becoming the most liked candidate is always the preferred strategy, but being the least disliked candidate will also do.

The media play a central role in shaping these likes and dislikes, with television the undisputed key. Nearly two-thirds of Americans say they often do not become aware of political candidates until they see the candidate's advertising on television; more than half say they get some sense of what candidates are like through their commercials; and three-quarters say they like to have a picture of a candidate in their mind when they go to vote.[31]

Not surprisingly, therefore, getting the candidate on television is the center-piece of the strategy, whether through **paid media** such as advertising or **free media** such as news programs and talk shows.

Paid Media.   Television advertising is viewed as the most effective form of paid media. It is also by far the most expensive. According to media analysts Stephen Bates and Edwin Diamond, authors of *The Spot: The Issue of Political Advertising on Television,* "a dollar spent on TV advertising may reach as many voters as $3 worth of newspaper ads or $50 worth of direct mail. Banning spots would probably *increase* campaign spending, by diverting candidates to less efficient forms of communication."[32] The greatest cost in a media campaign is not in making the advertisement itself, but in buying the television or radio time.

Whether designed for television or radio, a media campaign must decide whether to go with positive or negative advertisements. (See Box 6–6 for examples of each from the 1996 Republican primaries.)

Positive advertisements come in four basic types: (1) the "sainthood spot," which builds up the candidate's life and accomplishments before voters really know anything else; (2) the "testimonial spot," in which real people claim the candidate can accomplish almost anything; (3) the "bumper-sticker-policy spot," which is very short and allows the candidate to tout one vague idea on a noncontroversial topic; and (4) the "feel-good spot," which praises people, the land, and so forth and promises the candidate will protect them all.[33] Positive ads are designed to increase what voters like about the candidate.

The problem with positive ads is that the public tends to believe the worst about their candidates. "In August, we spent about $1.2 million running positive ads, basically detailing her accomplishments as a senator—getting guns out of schools, the assault weapons ban, and so on," said Dianne Feinstein's campaign director about the heated 1994 California Senate race. "But the public's cynicism about politics and politicians is such that whatever you assert positively about your candidate, it is almost impossible to get beyond the cynicism. The reaction is, 'Who can believe anything that a politician says about themselves?'"[34]

This distrust is what makes *negative advertisements* so effective. Negative ads focus on raising dislikes, and come in six types: (1) the "flip-flop spot," which shows the candidate as inconsistent; (2) the "compare-and-contrast spot," which compares candidates' stands or records; (3) the "comedy spot," which makes fun of the opponent as incompetent or not worthy of consideration; (4) the "not-on-the-job spot," which attacks voting and attendance records; (5) the "hit-and-run spot," which ties candidates to unrelated candidates or issues; and (6) the "frontal assault," which is a pure attack on a given candidate with no comparison and contrast.[35]

BOX 6-6

Going Positive/Going Negative

Going Positive	Going Negative
TYPE: Sainthood Spot	TYPE: Frontal Assault
PURCHASER: Pat Buchanan	PURCHASER: Bob Dole
LENGTH: 30 seconds	LENGTH: 30 seconds
IMAGES: Old photos of President Richard Nixon boarding a helicopter, President Reagan speaking to a crowd, the space shuttle Challenger explosion, a battle scene from the Vietnam War	IMAGES: Pictures of opponent Steve Forbes, the White House, World War II troops, militant Muslims, and gravestones at the Arlington National Cemetery
BACKGROUND NOISE: Patriotic music	BACKGROUND NOISE: Eerie, windy music
KEY NARRATIVE: "The convictions I learned from my parents, work, family, faith, character, have served me well. I've never been afraid to speak my mind. I will never be afraid to lead."	KEY NARRATIVE: "A look at his past indicates he is largely untested in making big decisions."
LASTING POINT: Pat Buchanan will not compromise.	LASTING POINT: Forbes cannot be trusted with the job of being president.
HIDDEN POINT: Front-runner Bob Dole will compromise.	HIDDEN POINT: Front-runner Bob Dole can be trusted.
MISSING INFORMATION: Pat Buchanan has never held elected office, and never served in Vietnam.	MISSING INFORMATION: Bob Dole appears nowhere in the ad even though he paid for it.

Negative ads tend to last longer in the voter's mind than positive ads. A positive ad may have to run ten times before it makes its mark, while a negative and may only need to be on once or twice. In large states where advertising is more expensive, negative ads are more prevalent because they deliver a bigger bang per buck. "Everyone wants to say that stuff doesn't work," says Eddie Mahe, a Republican attack ad expert, "but the fact is that everywhere in the country I've gone on the attack, I've made progress."[36] Attack ads in politics work for the same reason the Pepsi taste test works in selling soda pop: Voters seem to believe negatives more than positives, and they learn from comparisons. Candidates may hate attack ads, said Senator William Cohen (R-ME), but "what they hate worse is losing."[37]

Free Media.   Campaigns are not only interested in paid television advertising, of course, especially if they do not have much money. They also seek free coverage whenever they can get it, whether from newspapers, radio stations, or television. (Recall from Chapter 3 the role of talk shows in the 1992 campaign.) Free coverage is not only important in reinforcing campaign messages, it also confers legitimacy on a candidate's message. The local news anchor is often one of the most trusted figures in a community.

Like so much in modern campaigns, however, getting free television coverage is becoming a very sophisticated business. Major campaigns today routinely feed local television stations prepackaged video news releases and candidate "actualities" that provide brief soundbites—short, highly quotable segments from a speech or news conference that are specifically designed to grab public attention—for convenient unedited use on the evening news. Campaigns are also more than willing to pay for satellite time to give local television stations "exclusive, live" interviews with the candidate.

The techniques are catching on, in part because local news budgets are too tight to cover national campaigns directly. The local station looks like it has landed an exclusive interview with a presidential candidate, when, in fact, hundreds of stations have received the same material. The only difference is that each local anchor "dubs" or "voices over" the interview questions. The number of local stations using such video news releases increased four-fold between 1988 and 1992.[38]

The blurring of the lines between free and paid advertising may help explain the growing public distrust toward the media. People may not know that the live interview with the candidate is being bought by the campaign, but may suspect something sinister is going on nonetheless.

As campaigns have become more sophisticated in using the media, the media has come under greater pressure to be more careful about how they cover campaigns. CBS News adopted a rule in 1992 requiring that all candidate soundbites be at least thirty-seconds long (they have been averaging less than ten seconds in recent years), while most newspapers began running "truth in advertising" stories questioning false or misleading campaign ads. Many newspapers now run ad watches in which they dissect specific campaign messages for accuracy and fairness.

Whether such efforts will improve either the quality of advertising or reporting is not known—after all, even the most misleading spot can have a devastating impact the one time it is aired, often because it can generate free news coverage of its own. As for efforts to show more of what the candidate says, CBS' thirty-second rule had two immediate impacts: reporters either paraphrased candidate positions or the candidates were never shown at all.

HOW VOTERS DECIDE

Deciding how to vote is easy. Most voters come to the polling place having thought a bit about all their likes and dislikes toward the leading candidates and the two parties—likes and dislikes that come from advertisements, images, issues the voter cares about, the debates, whatever. Weighing the likes and dislikes equally, voters cast their ballots for the candidate with the greatest net number of likes. If no candidate has an advantage, and a given voter has a party identification, he or she typically votes with the party. If the voter has no party identification, he or she may vote on the basis of some particular like or dislike (a fleeting memory from a campaign debate, a momentary image of a negative advertisement).[39]

All in all, it is a very simple process that raises two questions about how voters decide. First, do campaigns matter to the list of likes and dislikes? Second, how do voters come to have likes and dislikes in the first place? Each question will be addressed in order.

Do Campaigns Matter?

Given all the hard work that goes into running for office, candidates and their supporters have to believe that campaigns matter. Otherwise, why abandon all semblance of a normal life for the campaign trail? The fact is, however, that most campaigns do not change the outcome of elections. As in a chess match, candidates will almost certainly lose if they do not move. But even the most brilliant campaign cannot win the election if the candidate starts the game with a weaker position—say, a struggling economy, a declining party, or an angry electorate.

Nevertheless, belief in the power of campaigning is hard to shake. According to Bill Clinton's chief 1992 political consultants James Carville and Paul Begala, having a good campaign staff is definitely not the reason most candidates for any office win. "Bill Clinton could have taken his staff and defeated George Bush's, or he could have taken Mr. Bush's staff and beat his own. The single best strategic decision we made as political consultants was to go to work for Bill Clinton in the first place."[40] But what Carville and Begala fail to note is that Clinton could not have taken George Bush's record as the incumbent and won. As the thirteen keys discussed earlier suggest, Bush's fate was cast long before the first television advertisement ran.

Consider the presidential debates as a test of whether campaigns matter. The first challenge is to get Americans to watch. Although debates historically attract large audiences, the 1996 debates were among the least watched in history, largely because most Americans saw little drama in the campaign. The second challenge is to change votes, something debates have rarely been able to do.[41] "Like so many things in the campaign," writes *Washington Post* pollster Richard Morin, "they entertain and occasionally inform. They solidify existing preferences, making people feel good about their choices and give more reasons not to vote for the other guy. They mark a milestone in the campaign season, and represent the only opportunity to see both candidates together. But they don't push around a lot of votes."[42]

The reason debates do not move more votes is that a high percentage of voters make up their minds long before the presidential debates even take place. In 1992, for example, over half of the voters said they made their decision either before (39 percent) or during (14 percent) the conventions, while 45 percent decided during the general election campaign. Of those late deciders, almost half waited until the last two weeks, in large measure because Ross Perot's third-party candidacy so upset the normal track of the two major campaigns.[43]

Bill Clinton could not have won the presidency without a campaign, of course. He needed to remind independent and Republican voters why they were mad at George Bush, and offer them a credible reason for voting Democratic. Hence, the campaign slogan "It's the Economy, Stupid!" He also needed to remind Democratic voters to get to the polls to do what was already on their minds—that is, vote for a Democratic candidate.

Campaigns do more than simply reinforce preexisting likes and dislikes, however. They often add new issues to the contest, and clearly have some impact on what issues voters think are most important.[44] Moreover, media coverage and advertising often create new likes and dislikes, as they did in 1992 when Clinton's draft record and marital infidelity became part of his credibility problem.

Finally, even if all but a handful of voters have made up their minds long before the election is held, campaigns clearly shape what that handful thinks. Elections are often won and lost at the margins—that is, among voters who add a few percent one way or the other to the total. Woe be to the candidate for any office who assumes that an election cannot be lost, particularly in a winner-take-all system that awards nothing for getting close.[45]

Indeed, history is replete with the names of candidates who lost despite a favorable climate. In 1948, for example, Republican Thomas Dewey was so confident of victory that he slowed down his campaign in the week before the election. The *Chicago Daily Tribune* was so confident, too, that it set its "Dewey Defeats Truman" headline before the results were in. The only problem, of course, was that Truman continued campaigning, and won by 5 percent of the popular vote. If equal efforts cancel out, unequal efforts matter. That is why incumbents do so well—they have higher name recognition and much more money than most of their challengers. Even then, a few always lose.

Even the most effective campaign cannot alter economic and political reality. "There is no doubt that the campaign was important in 1992," write political scientists Paul Quirk and Jon Dalager. "But, more than anything, the 1992 campaign represented the unfolding of the fundamental political strengths and weaknesses that the two major party candidates had going into it. A presidential campaign depends above all on the appeals the candidates are in a position to make—in

Victorious candidate Harry Truman holds an early edition of the *Chicago Daily Tribune* headline heralding his defeat. Pollsters had stopped tracking voter sentiment in the last two weeks of the campaign assuming that Republican Thomas Dewey would be easily elected.

short, their ammunition. In 1992 the Democrats had more ammunition."[46] As we will see, they had more ammunition in 1996, too.

How Voters Make the Final Choice

Once the curtain closes behind a voter, the final decision gets made on the basis of three sources of likes and dislikes: party loyalty, policy issues, and candidate images.

Party Loyalty.   In the 1950s and early 1960s, party loyalty was everything to the voting decision. The authors of *The American Voter* talked of a "funnel of causality" that shaped how voters behave.

At the wide end of the funnel were all the long-term factors that influence party identification: childhood socialization, past votes, income, education, race, and ideology. At the narrow end were all the short-term factors unique to a particular election: the condition of the economy, the candidates, debates, campaign advertising, and so forth. As the funnel narrowed over the life of a campaign, party identification helped voters make sense of all the information and events. Democrats would view short-term forces as favorable to Democrats; Republicans as favorable to Republicans. The short-term forces had to be very powerful, therefore, to break the force of party identification in determining the vote.[47]

For many Americans today, party loyalty no longer resides at the open end of the funnel. In fact, it may actually have moved past those short-term forces to the very narrowest point in the funnel. For these voters, party loyalty is less a predictor of how they will vote than a simple way to remember what they did in the most recent election.

There is no question that party loyalty still carries great influence over voting decisions, particularly among older Americans with lifelong ties. However, the decline of party loyalty increases the number of Americans who make their decisions later in the campaign, making their choices less predictable and much more responsive to what candidates say and do.

Policy Issues.   In a perfectly informed electorate, candidates would carefully outline their positions on the issues, voters would be highly informed about where the candidates stand, and elections would be determined by **issue voting.** Voters would start each campaign with their own list of "most important problems" facing the country. The candidates would then provide voters with detailed positions on each of the top issues. The voters would measure their distance from the candidates, and give their vote to the one who came closest to their views. Everything would be perfectly rational.

But the electorate is not perfect. Most voters do not meet the requirements for truly rational voting.[48] Voters might not know their own self-interest, and might not follow the campaigns closely enough to know where the candidates stand; indeed, candidates might not provide the information needed to allow voters to measure distances.[49]

Yet, a kind of issue voting can occur under less exacting circumstances. What if voters only have to take stock of how they think the country is doing, or whether they feel that change is needed, or even whether they feel better off today than they did four years ago? That would be a less elegant form of issue voting—no careful assessments of position papers and candidate speeches here—but it would be issue voting of a sort.

This kind of general referendum on the past may be the closest most Americans can get to the issue-voting ideal. Instead of thinking about the future and all the promises candidates are making, perhaps they are quite rational to think back over the past year or two and ask how they are doing. If they are doing well, they vote for the incumbent party. If they are doing poorly, they vote for change. "Citizens are not fools. . . .," political scientist Morris Fiorina notes in his theory of **retrospective voting.** "They need *not* know the precise economic or foreign policies of the incumbent administration in order to see or feel the *results* of those policies. And is it not reasonable to base voting decisions on results as well as on intentions?"[50]

If party loyalty continues to weaken, this kind of simple retrospective voting may take on an even larger role in explaining voting decisions. Indeed, Ronald Reagan built much of his 1980 campaign around the simplest retrospective theme by asking voters whether they were better off in 1980 than they had been in 1976, and using something he called a "misery index" to prove that inflation, income, and unemployment were all worse after four years of Jimmy Carter than before. It was a theme Bill Clinton picked up in 1992, asking voters whether their economic lives were any better after twelve years of Ronald Reagan and George Bush than before. In a similar vein, Bob Dole urged voters to ask whether their economic lives were any better after four years of Bill Clinton than before. Apparently, the answer was mostly "yes."

Candidate Image. The Founders clearly wanted presidential elections to reflect voter impressions of the candidates. Since they opposed political parties, and did not believe candidates should make promises about the future course of the nation, the Founders hoped voters would pick their candidates on the basis of virtue and ability to lead the nation.

Image still matters to campaigns at all levels. It is the only factor for voters who have no party identification and no knowledge of the issues. Moreover, today's candidate-centered campaigns tend to focus on giving voters evidence that a candidate has the ability to lead. Voters look for *human qualities* such as compassion for others, sincerity, and high ethical standards; *political qualities* such as experience in Washington, party loyalty, and political saavy; and *leadership qualities* such as consistency, forcefulness, and sound judgment in crisis. Together, these qualities create a general sense of a candidate's competence. (See Box 6–7 for what Americans valued in a president at the start of the 1996 campaign.)

Voters do see differences between candidates on these qualities. In 1992, for example, Bill Clinton was seen as relatively weak on human qualities. Although voters thought he was in touch with ordinary people, they had lingering doubts about his moral character and his overall courage, in part because of negative advertisements reminding them of his draft record and the Whitewater scandal. At the same time, Clinton was seen as very strong on decision-making qualities. Although voters thought he waffled too much on the issues and wondered whether he had enough experience as the governor of a small Southern state to be president, they had no doubt about his intelligence. More importantly, they thought he was much more in touch with ordinary people, and believed he had the capacity to inspire the nation, qualities they saw lacking in George Bush.

There is some evidence that voter confidence in the candidates has been falling in recent years.[51] Just as Americans think little of politicians in general, they think little of their candidates specifically. Part of the explanation rests with attack ads. Candidates who are ahead know that "going negative" is a way to keep the other candidate down; candidates in trouble know that one way to get back in a race is to sling as much mud as necessary to increase their opponent's negative ratings.

BOX 6-7

What Americans Want in a President

Sound Judgment in a Crisis	76%
High Ethical Standards	67%
Compassion	63%
Sincerity (Saying What One Believes)	59%
Consistency	51%
Forcefulness and Decisiveness	50%
Willingness to Compromise	22%
Political Savvy and Know-How	31%
Experience in Public Office	30%
Loyalty to One's Party	25%
Experience in Washington	22%

Source: Times Mirror Center for The People & The Press, "Voter Anxiety Dividing GOP; Energized Dems Backing Clinton," Nov. 14, 1995, p. 22.

However, something deeper may be going on than just a deluge of negative advertising. It may be that political campaigns are increasingly attracting individuals who are just not as likable. The kinds of skills that make for a *successful* candidate—the ability to raise money, the willingness to go negative, the focused ambition to stay on the road month after month, and the readiness to sacrifice one's friends and family—may not make for a very *likable* candidate.

IN A DIFFERENT LIGHT

DOES NEGATIVE ADVERTISING WORK?

Negative advertising has been part of campaigning for office since the beginning of the republic. (Recall Thomas Jefferson's attack on the British sympathizers in the 1800 campaign.) According to one history, Abraham Lincoln was called almost every name in the book in his two runs for the presidency: "Ape, Buffoon, Coward, Drunkard, Execrable, Fiend, Ghoul, Hopeless, Ignoramus, Jokester (in the face of war tragedies), Knave, Lunatic, Murderer, Negro, Outlaw, Perjurer, Robber, Savage, Traitor, Usurper, Vulgar, Weakling."[52]

History noted, there has been a recent increase in both the number and intensity of negative advertising. Fully half of all political advertisements emphasize the weaknesses of opponents rather than the strengths of the sponsoring candidate.[53] The "infection" of hard ads is not restricted to politics, however. Over half of today's consumer product ads are negative, too.

The reason candidates go negative, of course, is that they think the strategy works. There is new evidence that they may often be wrong, and may be wreaking havoc with public confidence in government as a result. According to a series of carefully designed experiments conducted by political scientists Stephen Ansolabehere and Shanto Iyengar, negative advertisements have three effects.

First, negative advertisements have different impacts among party loyalists. Negative advertising clearly hurts the sponsoring candidate among Democrats, perhaps because Democrats want to believe more in government's ability to do good. In contrast, negative advertising clearly helps the sponsoring candidate among independents and Republicans, perhaps because these voters are predisposed to think the worst about government. As with campaigns in general, however, negative advertisements do not appear to change many votes. They tend to reinforce what voters already believe about their candidates and government.

Second, negative advertising tends to polarize the electorate into angry camps. "On election day," write Ansolabehere and Iyengar, "the electorate speaks with a highly partisan vote, for that is the mindset reinforced by the candidates' campaign messages."[54] Negative advertising may not change many votes, but it most certainly makes both sides angrier.

Third, and most troubling, negative advertising appears to weaken the public's willingness to participate. According to the experimental evidence, roughly 5 percent of Americans stay home purely because of negative advertising. According to Ansolabehere and Iyengar's analysis, the negative campaigns run by Senate candidates in 1992 led over six million eligible Americans to stay home and another one million voters who did show up to skip the Senate election on their ballots.[55] Hence, even as the motor voter law and vote by mail make voting *easier,* the growing tide of negative advertising may make voting *less attractive* as an act of democratic participation.

This is not to argue that negative advertising should be banned. Candidates are entitled to the same protection of free speech that the rest of Americans enjoy. Moreover, certain kinds of negative advertising can be very helpful to voters, particularly the "compare-and-contrast" ads that show the two candidates and their issue positions side by side. The problem appears to be the growing tide of "frontal assault" spots—that is, spots that are designed solely to weaken a given candidate's support without giving voters any alternative. Such spots may help the sponsoring candidates win, but—as with so many of the new techniques (recall push polls)—they may weaken public confidence in the offices they seek.

The 1996 Election

The 1996 election is perhaps best described as uneventful. Although there were tight races for the Senate, the House, and local offices in every state, the final outcome was no surprise. Republicans gained a bit in the Senate and lost a bit in the House, but still maintained a majority in both chambers of Congress for another two years; Bill Clinton ended up with just 49 percent of the popular vote, up from 43 percent four years before, and 379 electoral votes, up just six.

After a long, expensive, and, some would argue, nasty campaign, many Americans remained bored by it all. Turnout sagged to just 49 percent, setting a seventy-year low. Whether by intent or accident, voters endorsed divided government for a second straight election, giving Democrats control of the presidency for another four years (the first time a Democrat had won a second term since Franklin Roosevelt) and Republicans control of the Congress for a second two years (the first time a Republican majority was continued since 1930).

All three factors that shape the simple act of voting—issues, party, and image—came into play in giving Democrats and Republicans alike cause to claim victory.

On party, Democrats and Republicans both did reasonably well in holding their loyalists at the top of the ticket. Eighty-four percent of Democratic voters cast their ballots for Clinton; 80 percent of Republican voters went for Dole; and independents split their vote total 43 percent for Clinton, 35 percent for Dole, and 17 percent for Perot.[56]

Clinton and Dole also did well among their party's core demographic groups. (See Box 6–8 for a summary of how different groups of voters split in the 1996

BOX 6-8

Dividing the Electorate, 1996

Group	All Voters	Bill Clinton	Bob Dole	Ross Perot
Gender				
Male	48%	43%	44%	10%
Female	52	54	38	7
Race				
White	83%	43%	46%	9%
African American	10	84	12	4
Hispanic	5	72	21	6
Asian	1	43	48	8
Other	1	64	21	9
Age				
18 to 29	17%	53%	34%	10%
30 to 44	33	48	41	9
45 to 59	26	48	41	9
60 or over	24	48	44	7
Education				
No high school	6%	59%	28%	11%
High school graduate	24	51	35	13
Some college	27	48	40	10
College graduate	26	44	46	8
Post-graduate	17	52	40	5
Family Income				
Less than $15,000	11%	59%	28%	11%
$15,000 to $30,000	23	53	36	9
$40,000 to $59,999	27	48	40	10
$60,000 to $74,999	21	47	45	7
$75,000 to $100,000	9	44	48	7
$100,000 and up	9	38	54	6
Religion				
Protestant	38%	41%	50%	8%
Catholic	29	53	37	9
Other Christian	16	45	41	12
Jewish	3	78	16	3
No religion	7	59	23	13
Party Identification				
Democrat	39%	84%	10%	5%
Republican	35	13	80	6
Independent	26	43	35	17
Political Ideology				
Liberal	20%	78%	11%	7%
Moderate	47	57	33	9
Conservative	33	20	71	8

Source: Courtesy of CNN/TIME AllPolitics and Voter News Service.

election.) Clinton ran strongest among women, where there was a large gender gap, as well as among African Americans and Hispanics, younger and older Americans, those with less education, Catholics and Jews, and lower-income groups. Dole ran strongest among men, whites, the middle aged, college graduates, Protestants, and upper-income groups. Perot did not do particularly well in any demographic group, and did not even win a majority of those who had voted for him in 1992—a plurality went for Dole.

Of the groups, women gave Clinton his margin of victory. Clinton ran well among working women, who gave him a 57 percent endorsement, as well as homemakers, who gave him 49 percent. Clinton also did well among "soccer moms," the relatively well-to-do suburban women who received so much attention during the campaign.[57]

On issues, Americans were clearly more satisfied with the economy in 1996 than they had been when George Bush was defeated for reelection in 1992. A majority said the country was headed in the right direction, of which almost three-quarters voted for Clinton. To the extent the election was a referendum on Clinton's policy leadership, the outcome was an endorsement, albeit lukewarm. Clinton also did well on education, where those who cited the issue as a top concern went 78 percent for the president and only 16 percent for his challenger. The issue was particularly important to young female college graduates and singles.

Clinton did not win all of the policy issues, of course. Dole won almost three-quarters of voters who listed taxes as their top issue, and held a majority among those who worried most about foreign policy, the federal budget deficit, and crime and drugs. But Dole was never able to wake the public from its basic satisfaction with the economy. A third of voters said their family finances had gotten better since 1992 (of which two-thirds voted for Clinton), almost half said their finances were about the same (of which only 46 percent voted for Clinton, compared to 45 percent for Dole, and 8 percent for Perot), and just 20 percent said their finances had gotten worse (of which just 27 percent voted for Clinton, 57 percent for Dole, and 13 percent for Perot).

At the same time, many Americans linked Dole to House Speaker Newt Gingrich, easily one of the most unpopular politicians in 1996. Nearly 60 percent of all voters had an unfavorable opinion of Gingrich, of which nearly 70 percent voted for Clinton, while nearly half said that worries about Gingrich affected their vote for the House.

On image, Clinton did worse than he had hoped. Fifty-four percent of voters said Clinton was neither honest nor trustworthy, and 60 percent said he was not telling the truth about the Whitewater scandal. Yet, in spite of Dole's nearly constant attack on Clinton's character during the final weeks of the campaign, only one out of five voters said honesty was the top factor in their vote. (Not surprisingly, of course, the vast majority of those voters went for Dole.)

Consider two possible reasons why character never worked for Dole. First, Americans may have devalued the presidency itself. They may not have thought Bill

Clinton was honest or trustworthy in *general*, but most certainly believed he was honest and trustworthy *enough* to be president of the United States.

Second, Dole had his own character problems, not in honesty or trust, but in his age and perceived meanness. A third of voters said they believed Dole's age would affect his performance as president, and a similar number said Dole had attacked his opponent unfairly.

Voters also seemed to like Clinton as a person more than they liked Dole. Asked just for fun in June 1996 to imagine going into business with either Clinton or Dole, most Americans thought Dole would devote more time and energy to making the business a success, and most wanted Dole to keep the books, but it was Clinton who they most wanted out there selling the product. Asked again just for fun to imagine giving their car keys to Clinton or Dole, roughly equal numbers thought the two candidates would know where to go, but it was Clinton with whom they said they would most enjoy the ride.[58]

Two questions emerge from this analysis of party, issues, and image. First, did the campaign matter to the final outcome? The answer is mixed. As noted earlier in this chapter, Clinton entered 1996 as an incumbent president with a strong economy. The polls showed him with a commanding lead from March 1996 all the way to election day, suggesting the great difficulty Dole confronted in unseating a reasonably popular president and a mostly satisfied public.

Nevertheless, there is some consensus among scholars and pundits that Dole might have done better had he waged a more effective campaign. He never quite settled into a message, moving from tax cuts to teenage drug use to character and back again almost day to day, and never seemed quite sure of how hard to hit Clinton on the character issue.

Still, the final result may have been preordained. Although he did well in both presidential debates (which most voters still thought Clinton won), and mounted a heroic 96-hour nonstop dash to the finish line that likely improved Republican chances in key Senate and House contests, there are few scenarios under which he could have broken Clinton's momentum.

Second, did the campaign give either party a mandate to govern? The answer is "no." With voter turnout at a modern low and distrust edging higher with the huge amounts of soft money and independent expenditures coursing through the campaigns, neither party could claim much of an endorsement for action. Given their doubts about Clinton and the House Republicans, voters seemed to be sending a message that a bit of gridlock might not be bad for the nation.

CONCLUSION

Campaigns and elections have changed dramatically over the past half century. Campaigns have grown more candidate-centered, and have become a multibillion-dollar industry. Once the totals are in, campaigns will have raised and spent almost $4 billion in 1996 alone, most of it going into television and consultants.

The rules governing campaigns have also changed. Raising and spending money is now closely regulated, and the role of wealthy individuals and corporations weakened somewhat. At the same time, PACs have grown in importance, and big givers have found other ways around the contribution limits. Money is still a powerful factor in elections, and raising it is still a central campaign activity.

Not all elections and campaigns are created equal, of course. The rules governing presidential campaigns are different from House and Senate campaigns, as are the timetables and logistics. Nevertheless, if there is a common trend regardless of office, it is the rise of the candidate-centered campaign.

Although winning the party nomination remains an essential step to the White House and Congress, the parties are no longer as actively involved in the day-to-day operation of most campaigns, whether federal, state, or local. Presidential candidates in particular tend to run separate from the national parties, establishing separate headquarters (Clinton's 1992 headquarters was in Little Rock, Arkansas, not Washington) and recruiting separate staff.

The cost of candidate-centered campaigns is not just in a weakened role for the parties, however. They may also isolate citizens even more from the process. Elections are increasingly conducted from a television studio, with fewer and fewer opportunities to actually meet and greet real voters. Citizens may get to see more of their candidates on television, but may be pushed ever farther from the kind of direct contact that encourages deeper public participation. American campaigns may still be the feast of democracy, but the food is less nourishing.

Moreover, candidate-centered campaigns may weaken a government's ability to do its job. By focusing mostly on image, candidate-centered campaigns rarely generate much consensus on what government should do. And if candidates are elected on their own unique platform, not on any shared loyalty to one or the other party, they may wind up in government with no reason to work together. In the Founders' system of checks and balances and separate powers, this lack of common ground may increase the difficulty of reaching agreement on what constitutes a foreign or domestic threat, which can change a government just strong enough into one that can rarely work at all.

All is not pessimistic, however. Americans still pay a great deal of attention to campaigns, and show a remarkable interest in what candidates say and do. Trust in government may be down, but Americans still bother to watch, perhaps giving their consent to be governed by turning on the television. Candidates who misuse this attention by polarizing the electorate do more than damage their own campaigns. They turn the feast of democracy into little more than a food fight, and belittle the enormous respect Americans still have for what remains the most important event in democratic life.

THE BASICS

■ Campaigns for election offer an opportunity for Americans to give their consent to be governed and to hold their representatives accountable for what they have or have not done. Americans follow campaigns closely, and pay attention to key events such as television advertising and candidate debates, particularly in more visible races for state offices, Congress, and the presidency.

■ America may have more elections than any other established democracy, in large part because reaching office usually involves winning at least two contests: a nomination and a general election. States have the greatest say over the rules governing nominations, often using one system for their own officers and Congress, and another for the presidency. Most states use primary elections to select candidates, some of which are closed to all but registered party members, others of which are open to any voter regardless of party identification. Delegates to the national party conventions are also selected by the states under broad guidance from the national parties. Most states use primaries here, too, but at least one-quarter use a caucus system. Whatever the states use, the Democratic Party requires all of its delegates to be selected through proportional voting. The Republican Party has no such rules.

■ Campaigns for office are one of the most exciting events in democratic life, and follow a natural cycle. They usually start with a candidate's decision to run, continue with efforts to build an organization, hire a consultant, create a campaign strategy, raise money, and persuade voters by reinforcing the things they already like about a candidate, while emphasizing the things voters dislike about the opponent. Becoming the most liked candidate is always the preferred outcome, but becoming the least disliked candidate will also do.

■ A voter's final decision is influenced by three separate sources of likes and dislikes: (1) party loyalty, (2) policy issues, and (3) candidate image. As party identification weakens, a growing number of Americans may be using a form of issue voting called retrospective voting. Although they do not always know the fine details of major policy issues such as the economy or foreign policy, they most certainly can feel the results, and may cast their votes as a kind of informal referendum on the incumbent president or party.

KEY CONCEPTS

■ The past few decades have witnessed an increase in candidate-centered campaigns, and a parallel decline in party-centered campaigns. The focus of a candidate-centered campaign is to get the candidate elected at all costs, even if that means abandoning party labels altogether. Because officials elected through candidate-centered campaigns owe no allegiance to their party, such campaigns may weaken government's ability to do its job once the election is over.

■ Money has become increasingly important to campaigns for office. Although raising money has always been part of politics, the amounts needed to wage a competitive campaign have increased over the past half century, as have the rules governing what candidates and contributors can and cannot do. The ultimate cost of raising money may come in the lost time for other campaign duties such as talking with voters or reflecting on issues. The ability to raise money may also become a primary qualification for running.

■ Raising money for Congress is a very different exercise from raising money for the presidency. Congressional candidates do not receive any public funds, but are required to report all contributions and expenditures. In contrast, presidential candidates receive matching public financing during the nomination season, and full pub-

lic financing in the general election campaign, provided they agree to limits on how much of their own money they can contribute. Because congressional candidates do not receive public financing, they face no limits on the amount of their own money they can put into their campaigns. Individuals and PACs are restricted in the amount they can give to all federal campaigns.

■ The media play a central role in shaping candidate likes and dislikes. Many Americans report that they do not even become aware of a candidate until they see that candidate on television. There are two kinds of media, paid and free, each of which plays an important role in the campaign. Paid media consists of advertisements, whether positive or negative, most designed to reinforce likes of the candidate or dislikes of the opponent. Free media consists of news coverage.

■ It is not clear that campaigns do much to change voter decisions about the candidates. Voters enter campaigns with predispositions to like or dislike the candidates, and usually vote on the basis of how those likes and dislikes add up. Therefore, most campaigns are designed to reinforce what voters already believe going into the election. However, campaigns can add new issues to the contest, while media coverage and advertisements often create new likes and dislikes.

[IN A DIFFERENT LIGHT]

■ Polling is an essential tool of modern campaigning, particularly in establishing baselines on what the public thinks and tracking daily changes late in the campaign. Recent years have also witnessed an increase in push polls, which manipulate public opinion by communicating misleading or untruthful information to the electorate late in the campaign in an effort to encourage an opponent's supporters to stay home.

■ As the rules governing campaign fund-raising have tightened, parties and candidates have invented new techniques for exploiting loopholes in the Federal Election Campaign Act. One such technique is called *soft money,* and involves unlimited gifts to the national parties for party-building activities. The other is called *bundling,* and involves the collection of large numbers of small checks into bundles to give to individual candidates. Both techniques are perfectly legal, but may create public suspicions about special interest influence nonetheless.

■ Negative advertising has been part of campaigning for office since the beginning of the republic. Recent evidence suggests that negative advertising does not work very well in changing votes, but may divide the electorate into angry camps while suppressing turnout. Even as America is working to make voting easier, negative campaigning may make voting less attractive.

OPEN QUESTIONS

■ What would make for a good campaign in a healthy democracy? How would one know a good campaign if it occurred? Through turnout? Citizen trust in government? A close election? A unanimous choice? What would make for a bad campaign? What do you think the current balance between good and bad is, and what can the nation do to ensure more good campaigns and less bad?

■ How would you raise money for a campaign if you were the candidate or manager? What kinds of promises would you be tempted to make to contributors in return for their support? Can a $1,000 contribution from an individual affect what a member of Congress or president does once in office? Can a $5,000 contribution from a PAC? Does soft money or bundling change how money influences politics?

■ How should voters make their final decisions? Is it healthy that so many Americans still rely on their party identification? What about the large number who use candidate image? Is issue voting the ideal way to decide? And, if so, are Americans really capable of the kind of issue voting Americans seem to admire most? (Recall how little Americans know about the issues from Chapter 3.) What might the Founders think of issue voting?

■ Would you ever run for office? If so, why? If not, why not? Are the best people running for office these days? And are the skills needed to win a long campaign the same ones needed to govern wisely once in office?

...TERMS TO REMEMBER

nomination

general election

primary election

closed primary

open primary

caucus system

proportional voting system

party-centered campaign

candidate-centered campaign

baseline polls

tracking polls

push polls

independent spending

soft money

bundling

paid media

free media

issue voting

retrospective voting

Endnotes to Chapter 6

1. See George Thayer, *Who Shakes the Money Tree? American Campaign Financing Practices from 1789 to the Present* (New York: Simon and Schuster, 1973), p. 25.

▶ 2. See Stephen Wayne, *The Road to the White House, 1992: The Politics of Presidential Elections* (New York: St. Martin's Press, 1992), p. 99, for a discussion of how the national parties influence state nomination procedures.

3. Data from *New York Times,* July 13, 1992, p. B6.

▶ 4. Alan Ehrenhalt, *The United States of Ambition: Politicians, Power, and the Pursuit of Office* (New York: Times Books, 1992), p. 19.

5. For background on the candidate-centered campaign, see Stephen Salmore and Barbara Salmore, *Candidates, Parties, and Campaigns: Electoral Politics in America* (Washington,

DC: CQ Press, 1985), p. 17; see also Martin Wattenburg, *The Rise of Candidate-Centered Politics: Presidential Elections of the 1980s* (Cambridge, MA: Harvard University Press, 1990).

6. Mark Petracca, "Political Consultants and Democratic Governance," *PS: Political Science and Politics,* volume 22, number 1 (March 1989), p. 12.

7. Walter De Vries, "American Campaign Consulting: Trends and Concerns," *PS: Political Science and Politics,* volume 22, number 1 (March 1989), p. 21.

8. James Sterba, "Democracy Inc. Politicians at All Levels Seek Expert Advice, Fueling an Industry," *Wall Street Journal,* September 21, 1992, p. A1.

9. Quoted in Thomas Edsall, "Taking the Money and Helping Others Run." *Washington Post National Weekly Edition,* December 13–19, 1993, p. 11.

10. These figures are drawn from Sterba, "Democracy Inc."

▶ 11. Larry Sabato, *The Rise of Political Consultants: New Ways of Winning Elections* (New York: Basic Books, 1981), pp. 8, 3.

12. Stephen Labaton, "Con the Money Trail, Most 'Insiders' Had the Advantage," *New York Times,* November 9, 1994, p. B1.

13. Federal Election Commission, "1994 Congressional Spending Sets Record," news release, December 22, 1994.

14. Ann Devroy, "Push Becomes Shove in Political Polling with Negative Phone-Bank Tactics," *Washington Post,* February 13, 1996, p. A9.

▶ 15. Quoted in Center for Responsive Politics, *A Brief History of Money in Politics* (Washington, DC: Center for Responsive Politics, 1995), p. 3.

16. Quoted in Richard Berke, "To Campaign (v): To Beg, to Borrow, to Endure," *New York Times,* February 5, 1995, p. D6.

17. Frank J. Sorauf, *Money in American Elections* (New York: HarperCollins, 1988), p. 1.

▶ 18. Frank Sorauf, *Inside Campaign Finance: Myths and Realities* (New Haven, CT: Yale University Press, 1992), p. 189.

19. For a story on calling for cash, see Richard Berke, "Before Asking for Votes, Candidates Ask for Cash," *New York Times,* April 10, 1994, p. 1.

20. Sorauf, *Inside Campaign Finance,* p. 188.

21. Sorauf, *Money in American Elections,* p. 6.

22. The case was *Buckley v. Valeo,* 424 U.S. 1 (1976).

23. Federal Election Commission news release, December 22, 1994, p. 4.

24. Larry Makinson, *The Cash Constituents of Congress* (Washington, DC: Center for Responsive Politics, 1992), p. 3.

25. Federal Election Commission news release, December 22, 1994, p. 4.

26. Jonathan Salant and David Cloud, "To the '94 Election Victors Go the Fundraising Spoils," *Congressional Quarterly,* April 15, 1995, p. 1057.

27. Jason DeParle, "The First Primary," *New York Times Magazine,* April 16, 1995, p. 30.

▶ 28. See Anthony Corrado, *Paying for Presidents: Public Financing in National Elections* (New York: Twentieth Century Fund Press, 1993).

29. See Charles Lewis, *The Buying of the President* (New York: Avon, 1996), p. 29.

30. Harold W. Stanley and Richard G. Niemi, *Vital Statistics on American Politics* (Washington, DC: CQ Press, 1995), p. 166.

31. Times Mirror Center for The People & The Press, *The People, the Press, and Politics, Campaign '92: The Generations Divide,* July 8, 1992, p. 51.

32. Stephen Bates and Edwin Diamond, "Damned Spots," *The New Republic,* September 7 and 14, 1992, p. 14.

33. Jerry Hagstrom, *Political Consulting: A Guide for Reporters and Citizens* (New York: Freedom Forum Media Studies Center, 1992), pp. 14–16.

34. Robin Toner, "Bitter Tone of the '94 Campaign Elicits Worry on Public Debate," *New York Times,* November 13, 1994, p. A14.

35. See Hagstrom, *Political Consulting,* pp. 18–20, for the first five types.

36. Andrew Rosenthal, "A Battle of the Negatives," *New York Times,* October 31, 1992, p. A7.

37. Toner, "Bitter Tone," p. A14.

38. John Pavlik and Mark Thalhimer, "From Wausau to Wichita: Covering the Campaign Via Satellite," *Covering the Presidential Primaries* (New York: Freedom Forum Media Studies Center, 1992), p. 36.

39. This list is modified from Stanley Kelley Jr., and Thad Mirer, "The Simple Act of Voting," *American Political Science Review,* volume 68, number 2, (June 1974), pp. 572–91.

40. James Carville and Paul Begala, "It's the Candidate, Stupid!" *New York Times,* December 4, 1992, p. A15.

41. Richard Berke, "Debating the Debates: John Q. Public Defeats Reporters," *New York Times,* p. A13.

42. Richard Morin, "The Effects of Debates Are Debatable," *Washington Post National Weekly Edition,* September 28–October 4, 1992, p. 37.

▶ 43. See William Flanigan and Nancy Zingale, *Political Behavior of the American Electorate* (Washington, DC: CQ Press, 1994), p. 164.

▶ 44. For a discussion of how campaigns affect elections, see Marion R. Just, Ann N. Crigler, Dean E. Alger, Timothy E. Cook, Montague Kern, and Darrell M. West, *Crosstalk: Citizens, Candidates, and the Media in a Presidential Campaign* (Chicago: University of Chicago Press, 1996).

45. Flanigan and Zingale, *Political Behavior of the American Electorate,* pp. 162–63.

46. Paul Quirk and Jon Dalager, "The Election: A 'New Democrat' and a New King of Presidential Campaign," in Michael Nelson, *The Elections of 1992* (Washington, DC: CQ Press, 1993), p. 83.

47. Angus Campbell, Philip Converse, Warren Miller, and Donald Stokes, *The American Voter* (New York: John Wiley and Sons, 1960), pp. 24–32.

48. Flanigan and Zingale, *Political Behavior of the American Electorate,* p. 180.

49. See Benjamin Page and Robert Shapiro, *The Rational Public: Fifty Years of Trends in America's Policy Preferences* (Chicago: University of Chicago Press, 1992), p. 387, for a counterargument; they suggest that voters do not need large amounts of information to make rational choices.

50. Morris Fiorina, *Retrospective Voting in American National Elections* (New Haven, CT: Yale University Press, 1981), p. 5.

51. Flanigan and Zingale, *Political Behavior,* pp. 171–72.

52. See Bruce Felknor, *Dirty Politics* (New York: W. W. Norton, 1966), p. 27.

▶ 53. See Stephen Ansolabehere and Shanto Iyengar, *Going Negative: How Political Advertisements Shrink and Polarize the Electorate* (New York: Free Press, 1996), p. 90.

54. Ansolabehere and Iyengar, *Going Negative,* p. 96.

55. Ansolabehere and Iyengar, *Going Negative,* p. 112.

56. These figures come from the presidential exit poll posted on the Internet by Allpolitics (www.allpolitics.com), a news service of CNN and *Time,* November 7, 1996, located at atl.exit.poll/index2.html.

57. See Gerald Seib, "Women's Vote Proved to Be Key in Clinton's Victory Over Dole," *Wall Street Journal,* November 7, 1996, p. 11.

58. These figures are drawn from "Revealing Opinions on the Presidential Contest," *The American Enterprise,* volume 7, number 6 (November/December, 1996), p. 101.

CONGRESS

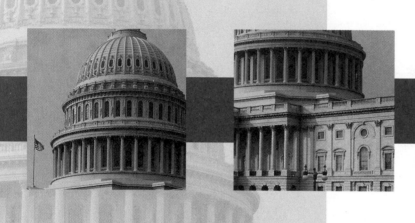

CHAPTER

7

T he Founders created Congress to do two jobs: make the laws and represent the people. The first job is defined in the very first sentence of Article I in the Constitution, which vests all lawmaking powers in a Congress of the United States. The second job is confirmed through the use of elections to select senators and representatives.

There are times when the two jobs are perfectly compatible, particularly when threats to the nation affect every citizen regardless of where they live. That is why votes to declare war are so often unanimous. There was only one dissenting vote to declare World War II, and that was from a member of the House who simply believed that no such votes should be unanimous.

More often than not, however, the two jobs are in conflict. Because making the laws is how Congress determines who gets what, when, and how from government, senators and representatives fight hard to protect their states or districts. Making the laws is the most obvious example of the delicate balance that underpins the Constitution. Congress must be united enough to protect the nation as a whole, but never so united that it threatens the individual liberties of Americans.

Maintaining this balance was essential to the Founders, who worried about how to keep Congress from being too strong. Making the laws was no small power

To Make the Laws

to give any institution, particularly one as close to the people as the House of Representatives, which was to be elected directly by the people. (Recall that the Founders gave the House the power to raise revenue precisely to assure that there would be no taxation without representation, a rallying cry of the Revolution.)

The question, therefore, was how to prevent Congress from abusing its power without exposing the young nation to peril. "In framing a government which is to be administered by men over men," wrote Madison in *Federalist Paper No. 51,* "the great difficulty lies in this: you must first enable the government to control the governed; and in the next place oblige it to control itself."[1] As we will see, the answer was to split Congress into two chambers, giving each enough power to check the other and enough reason to do so.

Take 1995 as an example. It was a record-setting year in modern congressional history. With a new Republican majority in control of both houses for the first time in four decades, and a beleaguered Democrat in the White House, Congress was as sharply divided as it has been since *Congressional Quarterly* first started tracking congressional performance in the 1940s. President Clinton won barely one-third of the congressional votes on which he took a position, a modern record in presidential frustration. At the same time, a majority of one party in Congress voted against a majority of the other nearly three-quarters of the time, another modern record. Although Congress took more votes on legislation than at any time in American history, 1995 produced fewer new laws than in any year since the early 1930s.[2] It was a year of great activity, even greater conflict, but very little product. No wonder the public is disapproving.

Yet it was also a year in which the Constitution worked exactly as designed. Clinton did poorly precisely because the people changed their minds about which party should be in control of Congress; Congress did poorly precisely because the House and Senate often disagreed on who should get what, when, and how from government; Congress took so many votes precisely because it took its job seriously. Lost in all the press coverage about conflict and the failure to pass legislation is the real story: American government was a spectacular success in 1995 precisely because it did *not* produce huge volumes of legislation. The American public was protected from great swings in the laws by a system that sets very high odds against quick action.

This chapter will examine just how Congress works to simultaneously make the laws and represent the public. The first section will examine the Founders' original intent in designing a two-chambered Congress in the first place, and in giving each house its own duties and qualification. The second section will examine the real Congress today, looking at the internal structure of the institution, the reasons for the changing complexity, and the process for making the laws.

THE IMAGINED CONGRESS

The Founders came to Philadelphia with plenty of legislative experience. Some had served in the Continental Congress, which was a single chambered, or **unicameral legislature.** Others served in the Confederation congress established under the Articles of Confederation, which was also unicameral. Still others had served in their state congresses, most of which were two chambered, or **bicameral legislatures.** As a result, they most certainly knew what they were doing in creating Congress.

The Constitutional Convention also served as an introduction to how the Founders hoped the future Congress would act. With fifty-five delegates, it was as large as the Continental Congress (which had fifty-six delegates), and operated under a series of careful legislative rules that covered everything from who could speak to how votes were to be taken.[3] Similar rules govern the House and Senate to this day.

The Founders also established **norms,** or informal rules governing behavior. Delegates were to address each other with respect, never descending into personal attack. They were to defer to the Committee on Detail that did the hard work of refining the various planks of the Virginia Plan that had been adopted early in the convention. And they were to remember always the broad national interest, even as they represented their individual states; a point reinforced when the convention unanimously selected George Washington, who was already recognized as a national leader, as its chair on its first day in session. As we will see, similar norms have held throughout most of history, but are clearly changing today.

A Divided Branch

There was never any doubt among the Founders about which branch would be first in the Constitution. It was to be Congress, for lawmaking was to be the essential activity. That is where it was on the third day of the Constitutional Convention when the Founders made the decision to create a national government consisting of "a supreme legislative, judiciary and executive." And that is where it was when the convention adjourned three months later.

Although they never discussed their reasons for putting Congress first, the Founders clearly considered Congress to be closest to the people. Neither the presidency nor the judiciary were directly accountable to the public. As South Carolina Representative John Calhoun observed in 1817, "This, then, is the essence of our liberty; Congress is responsible to the people immediately, and the other branches of Government are responsible to it."[4]

This is not to say that all the details involved in creating Congress were agreed upon easily. It took nearly three months for the Constitutional Convention to resolve all the disagreements over how members should be elected.

Immediately after deciding to create a supreme legislature, the Founders divided Congress into two bodies, the House of Representatives and the Senate. Having given Congress the job of making the laws, the Founders immediately created one of the single most important obstacles to doing so. As James Madison noted, they enabled government to control the governed, then obliged it to control itself.

The Founders obliged Congress to do so through a number of devices, from different terms to different constituencies, but none was more important than dividing the Congress into two chambers. Worried about the tendency for the legislative branch to dominate government, they made the two chambers "as little connected with each other as the nature of their common functions and their common dependence on the society will admit."[5]

The Founders were absolutely clear about having a bicameral Congress. Indeed, bicameralism is the most distinctive organizational feature of the U.S. Congress. Each chamber has its own place to meet in separate wings of the Capitol Building; each has offices for its members on separate ends of North and South Capitol Street; each has its own committee structure, its own rules for considering legislation, and its own record of proceedings (even though the record is published jointly as *The Congressional Record*); and each sets the rules governing its own members (recall from Chapter 4 that the ban on gifts from lobbyists applies differently in each chamber).[6]

It is hardly surprising that the Founders split the legislature. Bicameral legislatures had been standard practice in most of the colonies. Moreover, a split Congress was seen as essential to a government that would prevent strong-willed majorities from oppressing individual Americans.[7] Having a two-house legislature was merely one more way to assure that government would be just strong enough to act, but not so strong as to threaten liberty. As James Madison put it, "in order to control the legislative authority, you must divide it."[8]

The Duties of Congress

Article I of the Constitution begins quite simply: "All legislative powers herein granted shall be vested in a Congress of the United States, which shall consist of a Senate and House of Representatives." In theory, that single statement gives all lawmaking power to Congress. Almost everything Congress does by way of its internal structure and operations is intimately connected to this one duty.

As if to emphasize the point, the Founders gave the longest list of express powers to Congress. Because it was closest to the people, Congress would have the first say about taxes and finances—that is, the power to raise and spend taxes. It would also have the power to organize government by creating the departments and agencies of the executive branch, as well as the entire federal court system (which it used to create the first federal courts in 1789). It would also be responsible for protecting the nation against foreign threats by declaring war, raising armies, building navies, and ratifying treaties negotiated by the president, as well as for protecting against domestic threats by regulating commerce and immigration, providing for the creation of state militia to maintain the peace, and controlling the power to borrow and coin money. Finally, Congress would be responsible, in part, for holding the nation together by establishing post offices and building roads. (To this day, the interstate highways are federal, while all other roads are state or local. The interstate highway system binds the nation together as no state or local road can.)

Just in case the list was not enough to allow Congress to do the job, the Founders added an *elastic clause,* allowing Congress to "make all laws which shall be necessary and proper for carrying into execution the foregoing powers, and all other powers vested by this Constitution in the government of the United States, or any department or officer thereof." Congress also had complete authority to set its own rules (see Article I, Section 5 of the Constitution).

Yet even as they gave Congress these duties, the Founders fueled future conflict by creating a list of specific powers for each chamber. The House, and only the House, would be given the authority to originate all tax bills, reassuring large states that small states would not be able to impose an unfair share of the burden on their bigger neighbors.

The Senate, and only the Senate, would have the authority to ratify treaties (by a two thirds vote of all senators who are present and voting) and presidential appointments (by a simple majority) to executive offices and the courts. Recall that senators were originally selected at arms length from the public, thereby assuring a greater wisdom in making these difficult decisions.

Finally, the Founders split the power to impeach the president—the House would vote the articles, or charges, of impeachment for high crimes and misdemeanors, while the Senate would make the final decision to acquit or convict.

Once again, the Founders had divided enough of the power to make governing just a bit more difficult. By requiring that all bills for raising revenue had to come from the House, the Founders assured virtually ceaseless conflict. The Senate may be the incubator of great policy ideas, for example, but the House has considerable say over where the money for great policy ideas comes from. By giving the Senate the power to ratify treaties (by a two-thirds majority of all senators present and voting) and the authority to confirm all presidential appointees, the Founders added more reason for conflict. The House may decide where the money comes from, but the Senate has a great deal of say over who gets to spend it.

Qualifications for Office

The Founders set different minimums for serving in the House and Senate. House members have to be at least twenty-five years old, while senators have to be at least thirty; House members have to be U.S. citizens for at least seven years; senators for at least nine. Other than age and citizenship, there are no other qualifications for office. (See Box 7–1 for a comparison of the backgrounds of members in the First Congress versus the 100th Congress two hundred years later.)

It is no secret why the Founders set the age limits: they simply did not trust their "Generation X". As Virginia delegate George Mason argued, age was a way of "measuring the deficiency of young politicians;" particularly since "political opinions at the age of 21 were too crude & erroneous to merit an influence on public measures."[9]

As for the different requirements for the House and Senate, part of the justification flowed from the Senate's treaty-making power (the Founders wanted even more wisdom), and part flowed from images of the House as a more unpredictable chamber. The Founders may have called the House the "first branch," but they still worried about the impact of direct election. By setting the Senate's requirements higher and giving its members a six-year term, the Founders hoped the Senate would be the enlightened body. Concerned about the "fickleness and passion" of the House of Representatives, Madison in particular saw the Senate as "a necessary fence against this danger."[10] One hundred years later, a Princeton professor named Woodrow Wilson endorsed the notion as follows:

> It is indispensable that besides the House of Representatives which runs on all fours with popular sentiment, we should have a body like the Senate which may refuse to run with it at all when it seems to be wrong—a body which has time and security enough to keep

BOX 7-1

Congress Then and Now

	First Congress		100th Congress	
	House	Senate	House	Senate
Size	65	26	435	100
Average Age	44	46	51	54
Race				
White	100%	100%	92%	100%
Black	—	—	5	—
Hispanic	—	—	3	—
Sex				
Male	100%	100%	95%	98%
Female	—	—	5	2
Occupation				
Planters	36%	48%	5%	5%
Lawyers	38	38	42	62
Business/Banking	17	14	33	28
Public Service	5	0	22	20
Clergy	5	0	—	—
Educators	—	—	9	12
Journalists	—	—	5	8
Other	—	—	6	8
Education				
No College	49%	41%	11%	6%
Some College Only	3	3	—	—
College Graduate Only	48	56	28	15
Graduate Degree	—	—	61	79

Source: Adapted from a chart titled "Congress: The First and the 100th," New York Times, January 5, 1987, p. A14.

its head, if only now and then and but for a little while, till other people have had time to think.[11]

One qualification the Founders did not adopt was a limit on the total number of terms a House member or senator could serve. It was a decision that led to the term limit movement two hundred years later. By the mid-1990s, over half the states had adopted term limits on their House members and senators, most of which involved twelve years of service total (six House terms or two Senate terms).

The Founders clearly knew about term limits. The Articles of Confederation had prohibited anyone from being a member of Congress for more than three years out of six, and the idea came up again in connection with the great debate over the length of House and Senate terms.[12]

The Founders briefly considered the idea of limiting terms under the Constitution, but rejected it unanimously and without debate. It was not that term limits had been a failure in the Confederation Congress. They most certainly forced some members out. It was more that those members happened to be very talented, leaving the Continental Congress less effective and souring the Founders on the idea.

Thus, when the Supreme Court was asked to rule on the constitutionality of term limits in 1995, it concluded that the Founders' voice still held force today. Much as states argued that they could impose term limits under their Article I power to set the manner, places, and times of elections, the 5–4 majority ruled otherwise. Writing for the majority, Justice John Paul Stevens made the case overturning Arkansas's three-term limit on House members and two-term limit on senators as follows:

> The Framers decided that the qualifications for service in the Congress of the United States be fixed in the Constitution and be uniform throughout the Nation. That decision reflects the Framers' understanding that Members of Congress are chosen by separate constituencies, but that they become, when elected, servants of the people of the United States. They are not merely delegates appointed by separate, sovereign states; they occupy offices that are integral and essential components of a single National Government. In the absence of a properly passed constitutional amendment, allowing individual States to craft their own qualifications for Congress would thus erode the structure envisioned by the Framers, a structure that was designed, in the words of the Preamble to our Constitution, to form a more perfect Union.[13]

Under the ruling, all other state term limits on federal officers were rendered unconstitutional.

IN A DIFFERENT LIGHT

THE CHANGING FACE OF CONGRESS

Although race, gender, and wealth were not used as qualifications for office, the Founders clearly expected Congress to be a white, male, mostly propertied institution. After all, women and slaves could not vote.

The changing face of Congress. A portrait of the Senate in 1850 (top) and a picture of new members of the House in 1992 (bottom).

The Founders would be surprised at the face of Congress today. The 104th Congress in 1995–1996 had the largest number of women and minorities ever elected, including the first African American woman ever elected to the Senate, Carol Moseley-Braun (D-IL), and the first Native American, Ben Nighthorse Campbell (R-CO). The 104th also had the largest number of African American and Hispanic House members in history.

The changing face of Congress reflects more than just the changing demographics of society. It also reflects the growing effectiveness of women and minority candidates. Running as the ultimate outsiders, for example, women candidates offered an option to voters who saw Congress as out of touch with ordinary Americans. "People rejected candidates who appeared not to know what a grocery scanner was, while welcoming those who knew the price of milk and hamburger," pollster Celinda Lake explained. "Female candidates were seen as populist outsiders who could make government work for ordinary people—a powerful profile in today's political environment."[14] Voters also judged women to be more honest than men by 5 to 10 percentage points, more caring by 5 points, and less tied to special interests.[15]

The changing face of Congress also reflects the rising number of majority-minority districts. Of the sixteen new African Americans elected to Congress in 1992, all but three came from the new districts forged after the 1990 census. There were similar gains for Hispanics in Texas and California. It remains to be seen whether the gains will hold given the Supreme Court's decisions in *Shaw v. Reno, Miller v. Johnson,* and *Shaw v. Hunt.* (Recall the discussion of majority-minority districts in Chapter 5.)

These new voices have clearly made a difference in both how and what Congress decides. Women legislators are more likely than men to oppose abortion limits and the construction of nuclear power plants, for example. They are also more likely to support equal rights for women, and are generally more liberal on economic issues.

Women and minority legislators can also bring a different agenda to Congress. Consider how first-year Senator Carol Moseley Braun changed the Senate's mind on patenting the logo of the United Daughters of the Confederacy, a logo that showed a laurel wreath around the Confederate flag. The Senate had initially given its blessing to the logo on a fifty-two to forty-eight vote.

It was not until Moseley-Braun took the floor to attack the provision that the Senate began to understand just how offensive the logo was. (The South fought the Civil War under the Confederate flag.) "On this issue there can be no consensus," Moseley-Braun reminded them. "It is an outrage. It is an insult. It is absolutely unacceptable to me and to millions of Americans, black or white, that we would put the imprimatur of the United States Senate on a symbol of this kind of idea."

Moseley-Braun then moved that the Senate rescind its earlier decision, and the Senate overwhelmingly agreed as twenty-seven Senators changed sides from their earlier vote. "We must get racism behind us. We must move forward," explained Senator Ben Nighthorse Campbell as he changed his vote. "We must realize we live in America today." Even Alabama Democrat Howell Heflin changed his mind, saying his grandfathers, both of whom served in the Civil War, "might be spinning in their graves" because of his flip-flop, but he would change his vote nonetheless.[16]

Although the face of Congress may be changing, its pocketbook is not. Almost one-third of the Senators who served in the 104th Congress were millionaires, and lawyers remain vastly over-represented compared to the rest of society. Moreover, old customs die hard. Even with the Democratic senator from Washington, Patty Murray, sitting on his Appropriations Committee, chairman Robert Byrd still referred to the members as "Gentlemen."[17] However, with new sources of money for women and minority candidates and a growing list of successes, the Senate and House are likely to continue changing.

THE REAL CONGRESS

Time has not stood still on Capitol Hill. As with so much that happens in legislative life, the devil is not in the broad outline but in the details. Over the years, Congress has grown larger, more complicated, and, as 1995 suggests, more divided over the issues of the day.

Before turning to the details of the institutional Congress today and how a bill becomes a law, it is important to recognize that the future complexity was apparent in the First Congress that convened in 1789. The Founders did not believe Congress would convene and somehow produce legislation by magic. Just as they had used rules and committees to force decisions in the Constitutional Convention, the Founders expected the First Congress to use structure and rules in making laws.

The First Congress

The first task in the First Congress was to organize itself to do business. After all, the Constitution had merely specified that each house was to set its own rules, keep its own journal of proceedings, and meet at least once a year. (Note that Congresses are numbered in two-year terms; the First Congress was elected in 1788 even as the Constitution was still being ratified, and served to 1791, when the Second Congress, which was elected in 1790, came into office. Hence, the 105th Congress came into office precisely 208 years after the First Congress.)

Everything else had to be invented from scratch—the leadership, the committees, and the rules. And that is exactly what the fifty-nine members of the first House and the twenty-two members of the first Senate did. (Note that the Senate had only twenty-two members because North Carolina and Rhode Island had not yet ratified the Constitution and had not selected members.)

Almost all of the first members of Congress had served in their state legislatures, one-half in either the Continental or Confederation Congresses, and one-fourth in the Constitutional Convention itself. These were legislative experts who drew upon their prior experience in federal or state government, as well as lessons from the British Parliament, which had (and still has) a House of Commons (akin to the U.S. House) and the House of Lords (akin to the U.S. Senate).

Because of its size, the first House needed to quickly create a basic structure and rules. Members acted immediately to select a **Speaker of the House** to keep individual members from tying up the body by talking too much or introducing too many bills. The Speaker was also given authority to appoint members of the temporary committees that came and went with specific bills, an approach that resembled use of the Committee of Detail to flesh out the fine points of the Constitution. The First Congress acted unanimously in picking James Madison as its first Speaker.

The House membership had nearly tripled in size by 1810. And as it grew, so did the House structure and rules. After relying on hundreds of ad hoc committees in its first six years, the House had created four permanent, or **standing committees** by 1795, and had added another six by 1810. The powerful House Ways and Means Committee was formed in 1802, and remains to this day the first stop for all tax proposals in Congress.[18]

The political parties also began playing a more significant role in organizing both the House and the Senate during the period. "The existence of the two parties in Congress is apparent," wrote Senator John Taylor of Virginia in 1794. "The fact is disclosed almost upon every important question. Whether the subject be foreign or domestic—relative to war or peace, navigation or commerce—the magnetism of opposite views draws them wide as the poles asunder."[19] By 1800, the Speaker of the House had become the top job for the majority party, and officers were in place for the minority.

Because of its small size, the Senate adopted a structure and rules much more slowly than did the House. The Senate had fewer than fifty-nine members (the size of the first House) until 1848 when Wisconsin entered the Union; by that time, the House had grown to 237 strong. Moreover, the Founders had taken it upon themselves to establish the Senate's leadership structure by creating a president of the Senate (who would always be the vice president of the United States), and a president pro tem (or temporary president) who would lead the chamber in the vice president's absence (which is almost always). They had also resolved the greatest procedural problem the Senate could ever face: the president of the Senate would cast the deciding vote whenever there was a tie among the Senate's always even-numbered membership.

The Founders might also feel that the Senate has less need for rules because it would be populated by a "cooler" kind of representative. In contrast to the passionate House, the Founders expected the Senate to be a bastion of decorum and civility. Even when the Senate did adopt rules, they were less about how to pass a bill and much more about how individual senators should treat each other. One of the rules adopted in the first Senate prohibited senators from reading newspapers during debates; another prevented members from speaking twice in any one debate on the same day.

As for establishing permanent committees, the Senate had little need for such structure early on. Its first committees were ad hoc and dissolved as soon as a legislative issue was resolved. When the Senate finally began creating permanent committees in the early 1800s, it was more to accommodate the growing activity in the House than to control its own members. (The House membership was capped at 435 in 1911 when Congress passed a reapportionment act ordering the states to stop drawing new districts, a perfectly legal act of Congress allowed under Article I, Section 4 of the Constitution. The Senate kept growing by twos as each new state was added, most recently Alaska and Hawaii during the 1950s.)

The Institutional Congress

Today's House and Senate can be as different from each other as they are from the presidency and the Supreme Court. The Senate prides itself on being an incubator of ideas, a place in which individual members can take the floor on behalf of an oppressed minority and hold it forever; the House prides itself on being the voice of the people, a place in which former House Speaker Thomas "Tip" O'Neill once remarked "all politics is local." (See Box 7–2 for a list of the key differences.)

The two chambers are no more complex, however, than the society they have come to represent and the government they must oversee. It was far easier to control the 59 House members and 22 Senators who represented only white male property owners in 1789 than the 435 House members and 100 Senators who represent the diverse America of today; far easier to write legislation for the tiny government in 1789 than for the $1.5 trillion government today. In the 1790s, a handful of permanent committees could handle the entire task of making the laws and checking government. As we will soon see, today's Congress has more than two hundred committees and subcommittees of one kind or another.

Despite the many differences between the House and the Senate, being in the same business produces important similarities. Both chambers have leadership, committees and staff, albeit in rather different numbers. Understanding how the two chambers are organized is an essential step in learning how a bill becomes a law.

Leadership. Every organization needs leaders, if only to gavel a meeting to order. In Congress, that leadership is picked by the two parties at the start of every two-year period. Only party members may participate in the election of the party leaders of the House and Senate.

Once selected, everything the party leaders do is aimed at getting the 218 votes in the House and 51 in the Senate needed to pass most legislative proposals, or **bills.** "The only thing that counts is 218 votes," House Minority Leader Richard Gephardt (D-MO) once explained, "nothing else is real."[20] En route to a majority, however, the parties do everything from selecting administrative employees

BOX
7-2

Key Differences between the House and Senate

Size

The House has 435 members, number from each state varies by population

The Senate has 100 members, two from each state

Terms

House members serve for two years

Senators serve for six years

Elections

House members are elected by districts; all come up for election every two years

Senators serve their entire state; one-third of the Senate comes up for election every two years; the two senators from the same state do not come up for election at the same time

Rules

The House has 700 pages of rules governing itself, largely because of its size

The Senate has 100 pages of rules governing itself, again largely because of its size

Leadership

The House has more layers of leadership, and more leaders at each layer

The Senate has fewer layers of leadership, and fewer leaders at each layer

Legislative Passage

The House operates under a simple majority rule: bills come to the floor for final passage under a strict "rule," or ticket, that sets limits on debate and amending activity

The Senate operates mostly under unanimous consent: bills usually come to the floor with the consent of every member; final passage is also by simple majority rule

Role of Individual Members

Individual House members have little power to influence legislation

Individual Senators have great power to influence legislation, including the ability to hold the floor indefinitely

(including members of the Capitol Hill police) to scheduling floor business, influencing members, and working with the president to shape legislation.

Members do not get to be party leaders unless they have a certain level of **seniority,** or length of service in the chamber. But seniority is not the only criterion for picking leaders. If it were, South Carolina Republican Senator Strom Thurmond, and not Kansas Senator Bob Dole, would have been the Senate majority leader in 1995. After all, Thurmond was first elected to the Senate in 1956, twelve years before Dole. What made the difference for Dole in 1995 was his reputation for getting things done and his connections within the Republican party.

Because it is easier to lead 100 senators than 435 House members, it is best to think of four parties in Congress: two in the Senate (majority, minority), and two in the House (majority, minority). Together, these four parties determine virtually everything that happens in making the laws and representing the public.

In the House, the majority party meets to select the Speaker, its **majority leader,** and its **whip,** whose job is literally to whip up support on the floor. At roughly the same time, the minority party selects its **minority leader** and its whip. The two parties each select their own **committee on committees** for making assignments to all committee and subcommittee slots.

The Speaker of the House may be the single most important position in the entire Congress, for it concentrates power in one individual far beyond any other post in either chamber. The Speaker schedules all legislation, presides over debates, chairs the committee that decides who sits on all committees, decides which committees will consider what legislation, and, as the chief administrative officer of the House, even determines which members get the best offices. These powers help explain why Newt Gingrich became a household name as the new Speaker of the House in 1995.

House Speaker Newt Gingrich. When his party recaptured the House in 1994 after forty years in the minority, Gingrich became one of the most visible leaders in America. His popularity fell in 1996 as Americans began to believe that the Republican "Contract with America" had gone too far in cutting domestic programs.

Over in the smaller, more informal Senate, the party leadership is much less important. Despite its constitutional origins, the president pro tempore is largely a ceremonial position. Instead, the majority leader occupies the single most powerful position in the Senate, followed by the minority leader. If not as important as the Speaker of the House, the Senate majority leader is often the most visible political leader in the country after the president. It is often the leader of the opposition party in the Senate who gives the response to the president following the State of the Union address, for example.

Compared to the House, however, the Senate party leadership has relatively little power. The majority leader cannot strip a member of a committee assignment, force a bill from the calendar, or make a committee act. "Many times I've wished I could simply impose my will and do what I want done without the need to consult and explain," said Senate Majority Leader George Mitchell in 1991. Instead, Mitchell had to build "the best-developed patience muscle in America."[21] Because rules are much weaker in the Senate, the majority leader is often at the mercy of strong-willed colleagues. "All of us are entrepreneurs," said one senator. "The leadership has no handle on us. They can't really do anything for us or to us."[22]

No matter these differences in power, the two chambers have both produced increasingly complex leadership structures. There are now more layers of party leaders in each chamber, and more leaders at each layer. (See Box 7–3 for a comparison of the majority party leadership in 1960 and 1992.)

One reason the congressional party leadership structure has grown more complex is that members have so many demands on their time, which, in turn, makes the job of the House and Senate whips so important. The job of the whip is simple: get party members to vote for the party. As former congressional staffer Christopher Matthews notes, "the job of party whip in the Senate resembles that of a shop steward on the factory floor. This person looks out for the members' endlessly developing problems and interests. If they need to have the schedule changed because of an important event back home, it is the whip's job to see whether something can be done."[23] As one senator once remarked about his whip's function, "If you took out a pencil, he'd sharpen it."[24]

Committees. Congressional committees exist to fulfill both jobs of Congress. On the one hand, committees are a key tool for making the laws. They hold the legislative hearings that define the problems, draft the bills that provide the solutions, lead the fights for final passage, and make sure the executive branch is faithfully executing the laws.

On the other hand, committees provide important opportunities for members to speak on behalf of their **constituents,** that is, the people who live and vote in their district or state. Members of Congress from farm states tend to gravitate toward the agriculture committees, members from high tech districts to energy and commerce.

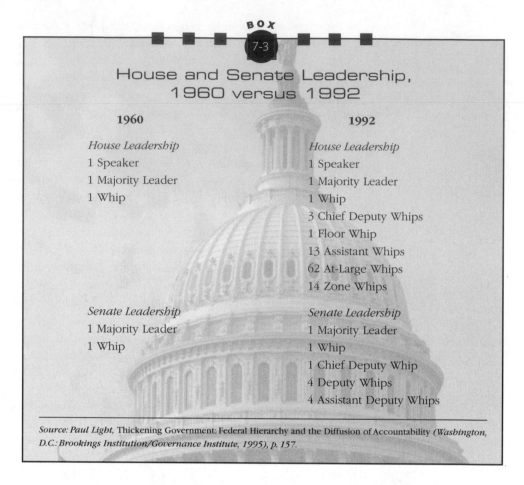

Source: Paul Light, Thickening Government: Federal Hierarchy and the Diffusion of Accountability *(Washington, D.C.: Brookings Institution/Governance Institute, 1995), p. 157.*

Like the leadership and staff of Congress, the committee structure has become ever more complex over time. Starting from just four standing committees in the 1790s, the number and jurisdiction of committees has expanded steadily thereafter. By the 1940s, committees were so numerous that Congress undertook a sweeping reorganization designed to both reduce the total number and strengthen the power of committee chairs. The 1970s brought another effort to make the committee structure somehow more rational, as did the first days of the 104th Congress under the new Republican House majority, when three full committees and over thirty subcommittees were abolished.

Most committees today have subcommittees to cover specific areas of legislation. The Senate Commerce, Science, and Transportation Committee, for example, has subcommittees on aviation, communications, consumer affairs, oceans and fisheries, space, and surface transportation/merchant marine. The House and Senate appropriations committees, which allocate money to federal programs, each have thirteen subcommittees, one for each of the thirteen major spending bills that must be enacted every year.

Compared to the 1800s, the number of committees and subcommittees today is staggering. However, the complexity is not so much in the number of committees and subcommittees, which now number two hundred for Congress as a whole, but in the number of assignments each member receives. The average House member now sits on five committees and subcommittees, a level roughly that of the 1950s, while the average senator sits on eleven, a number up by half from the 1950s.

Understanding the congressional committee structure involves answering three questions: (1) what kinds of committees are there, (2) how do members get assigned, and (3) what kind of committee is a conference committee? Each will be addressed in order below before turning to a brief discussion of conference committees as a special device for making laws.

Kinds of Committees. All congressional committees are not created equal. *Standing committees* and their *subcommittees* are permanent and are the sources of most bills. *Select* and *special committees* reflect temporary priorities of Congress and rarely author legislation. *Joint committees* have members from both bodies and exist either to study some issue of interest to the entire Congress or to oversee congressional support agencies such as the Library of Congress or the U.S. Government Printing Office.

The Senate Armed Services Committee holds a hearing on gays in the military in the wake of President Clinton's "don't ask/don't tell" policy. Clinton's policy allowed gays to serve in the military provided they keep their sexual preference a secret.

Standing committees and subcommittees are clearly the most important arenas for making laws and representing constituents, and fall into four different types: authorizing, appropriations, rules (just in the House), and revenue. (See Box 7–4 for a list of the standing House and Senate committees in 1995.)

Authorizing committees pass the basic laws that tell government what to do. The House and Senate education and labor committees, for example, are responsible for setting the basic rules of the Pell Grant student loan program—who can apply, how much they can get, where the loans come from, and how defaults are handled. In 1995–1997, there were fifteen authorizing committees in the House and thirteen in the Senate.

Authorizing committees do more than author legislation, however. They also conduct *oversight hearings* on the current operation of government. Some of the

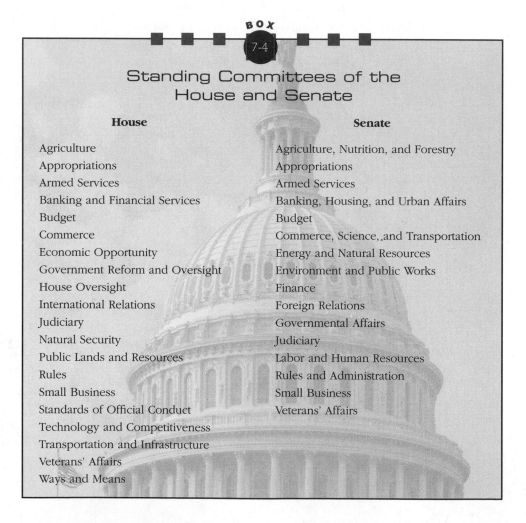

BOX
7-4

Standing Committees of the House and Senate

House	Senate
Agriculture	Agriculture, Nutrition, and Forestry
Appropriations	Appropriations
Armed Services	Armed Services
Banking and Financial Services	Banking, Housing, and Urban Affairs
Budget	Budget
Commerce	Commerce, Science, and Transportation
Economic Opportunity	Energy and Natural Resources
Government Reform and Oversight	Environment and Public Works
House Oversight	Finance
International Relations	Foreign Relations
Judiciary	Governmental Affairs
Natural Security	Judiciary
Public Lands and Resources	Labor and Human Resources
Rules	Rules and Administration
Small Business	Small Business
Standards of Official Conduct	Veterans' Affairs
Technology and Competitiveness	
Transportation and Infrastructure	
Veterans' Affairs	
Ways and Means	

hearings are designed to ask whether programs are working well; others to ferret out fraud, waste, or abuse in an agency of government; still others to conduct investigations of some major scandal. But whatever the focus of the hearing, the amount of oversight is clearly increasing. Political scientist Joel Aberbach found, for example, that just 8 percent of all legislative hearings focused on oversight in 1961 compared to over 25 percent just two decades later.[25]

Appropriations committees determine just how much money government gets to spend for each program—for example, how much money students will actually get in Pell Grants. There is just one appropriations committee in each chamber. Because money talks, the appropriations committees have great power to undo or limit decisions by the authorizing committees. The education and labor committees authorized Pell Grants to rise as high as $3,700 a year in 1992, but the appropriations committees only provided enough money for $2,300.

Rules and *administration committees* determine the basic operations of the two houses—for example, how many staff individual members get. The House Rules Committee has special responsibility for giving each bill a rule, or ticket, to the floor of the House, and determines what, if any, amendments to a bill will be permitted. Under an *open rule,* any amendment can be considered; under a *closed rule,* only amendments that the rules committee approves can be considered. It is an extraordinarily powerful committee.

Revenue and *budget committees* deal with how much money government can raise, and the broad targets that shape the federal budget. The House Ways and Means Committee is arguably the single most powerful committee in the U.S. Congress, for it is both an authorizing committee responsible for making basic decisions on the huge Social Security and Medicare programs, and a revenue committee responsible for setting basic tax policy. It is the committee responsible for assuring the constitutional requirement that all revenue bills originate in the House.

Getting Assigned. Winning a good committee assignment is one of the most important campaigns a new member of Congress mounts. A good assignment can make or break the next election, either allowing the new member to claim great influence over issues that matter in his or her home district; a bad assignment can allow the challenger to point out how little influence the member has.

New members work hard to make their preferences for committee assignments known. As newly elected Representative Sam Coppersmith (D-AZ) said of the few seats open in 1995 on the exclusive committees, "There would be a certain poetic justice if they just threw three juicy steaks into a room full of 65 hungry dogs and see which three dogs come out with the steaks. It would be an amazing labor-saving device."[26]

All of the decisions on appointments to House and Senate committees are made by the parties. Although the majority party sets the ratio of majority to minority seats on each committee, it has no say on who the minority party appoints to its slots. Each party in each chamber appoints its own committee on committees, which, in turn, appoints all committee members. As a general rule, all reelected members can keep their old assignments. If they decide to change committees, however, they must get approval from the committee on committees, which almost always honors such requests.

Each committee on committees has a somewhat different set of rules for keeping the process fair. New House Democrats who are assigned to an "exclusive," or especially powerful committee such as Appropriations, Ways and Means, or Rules, usually do not get another standing assignment; no member gets a second "major" committee assignment until all other members have a major assignment of their own; and new members who are likely to face a particularly tough first reelection campaign may get an extra boost where possible.

Conference Committees. It is impossible to discuss the role of committees in legislation without a brief review of an entirely different kind of congressional committee: **conference committees.** (Recall the discussion in Chapter 2.)

Unlike standing committees, conference committees are anything but lasting. They come together for a brief moment in legislative time to accomplish one goal: find agreement when the House and Senate pass different versions of a proposed law. What the Founders had set asunder through separate powers and interests, conference committees put together.[27]

"When I came to Congress I had no comprehension of the importance of conference committees which actually write legislation," a member said. "We all know that important laws are drafted there, but I don't think one person in a million has any appreciation of their importance and the process by which they work."[28]

Conference committees derive their power from striking the final deal between the House and Senate. Conference committee members are appointed from both chambers, but each chamber has but one vote to cast on behalf of the bill. The goal is simple: instead of passing a bill back and forth between chambers until one or the other back down, conference committees take the House and Senate versions of a bill and, if successful, *report,* or send back, a single compromise.

Technically, the compromise does not have to resemble either version of the original bill, a political reality that once prompted President Reagan to note, "You know, if an orange and an apple went into conference consultations, it might come out a pear."[29] If a conference committee cannot reach a two to nothing vote, the original bills cannot advance, unless, of course, one chamber backs down and passes the other's version.

Congressional Staff. The institutional Congress also includes the thousands of staffers who make sure the members and committees are well equipped to do their two jobs. It is the staff who write most of the bills, draft most of the questions that get asked at hearings, produce the legislative reports that support final action, and generate much of the flowery language used on the floor. They also write most of the letters back home to the district and do the vast majority of casework with the executive branch on behalf of constituents.

Congressional committees and member offices are best seen as small businesses in which often anonymous employees do the basic work of producing the final product under the company's label. As such, consider three different kinds of staff that together make Congress work: personal, committee, and support agency.

Personal office staffs exist primarily to help members represent their constituents. The hierarchy of the average office is simple: legislative correspondents at the bottom answer the letters; legislative assistants at the middle handle the constituent needs; legislative directors just near the top keep track of the key bills; and the administrative assistant/chief of staff makes sure that the member is always informed.

In the 1930s, there were fewer than 1,500 House and Senate personal staffers *total;* today, there are well over 11,000.[30] The average House office is between fifteen and twenty staffers strong; the average Senate office is now over forty staffers. The cost of running Congress has increased accordingly. It cost $343 million to pay the salaries of members and staff in 1970, $1.2 billion in 1980, and $2.8 billion in 1992; a seven-fold increase over just twenty years.[31]

The proportion of personal staff that works in the home district or state has increased as well. Roughly half of House and one-third of Senate staffers are now located back home.[32] These staffers maintain a constant election presence and provide immediate access whenever "some poor, aggrieved constituent becomes enmeshed in the tentacles of an evil bureaucracy and calls upon Congressman St. George to do battle with the dragon," as political scientist Morris Fiorina describes it.[33]

Committee and *subcommittee staffs* exist largely to help make the laws. Split into majority and minority staffs, they schedule the hearings, conduct the investigations, markup the bills, and write the legislative reports.

Here, too, the hierarchy is simple: interns and staff assistants at the bottom do the routine work; professional staff handle the specific bills and hearings, the committee clerk keeps track of the schedule; legislative counsels make sure the language of each bill is clear; and the staff director makes sure the committee chair is always informed. The majority staff is always larger than the minority, and has the offices with windows.

Committee and subcommittee staffs have also grown over the years. It was not until the 1940s that Congress had any permanent committee staff at all; today, there are over 3,000.

Alongside personal and committee staffers, Congress has three large *support agencies* that support its legislative work: (1) the General Accounting Office (GAO), which oversees executive agencies and audits the performance of specific programs; (2) the Congressional Research Service of the Library of Congress, which does basic research on policy issues; and (3) the Congressional Budget Office (CBO), which was established in 1974 to give Congress its own source of information on the federal budget and spending. Together, over 10,000 people work in these three agencies.

Why Congress Changed

Much of the growing complexity in Congress reflects the increasing length of congressional careers. Long gone are the days when members of Congress came to Washington for a term or two and went home.[34] During the first one hundred years or so, being a member of Congress was definitely a part-time job. Members came to Washington for a few terms, averaged less than five years of continuous service, and quickly returned to their careers. Congressional pay was low, and Washington was still a long ride from home.

The pattern began to change in the late 1800s. Congress started to meet more frequently, pay increased, and being a member of Congress became increasingly attractive.[35] In the 1850s, roughly half of all House members retired or were defeated at each election; by 1900, the number was down to roughly one-quarter.

Turnover remains low to this day. Even in the 1994 congressional elections when Republicans won the House majority for the first time in forty years, 90 percent of House members who ran for reelection won. The Republicans took control of the House by winning a remarkable share of the open seats created by Democratic retirements, by defeating just enough incumbent Democrats, and by reelecting all but one of their own party members.

By the 1950s, being a member of Congress had become a lifelong profession and a full-time job. Members came to Washington to stay, and began to exploit the natural advantages that come with running for reelection as an **incumbent,** or sitting member, of Congress: name recognition, service to constituents, the lion's share of PAC money, and nearly unlimited free mailings back home. Back in 1954, for example, members of Congress sent 44 million pieces of mail back home. By 1992, the number had increased ten-fold to nearly 460 million.[36]

Having professional members of Congress clearly affects how Congress operates. Members think about their constituents constantly and worry about how to keep their jobs. As one political scientist argues, congressional elections are *Unsafe at Any Margin*.[37] If the Speaker of the House can be defeated, as Democratic Speaker Thomas Foley (D-WA) was in 1994, any member can be defeated.

It just makes sense, therefore, for even the most junior member to establish visibility back home as quickly as possible. If that means getting to the floor as quickly as possible at the start of a career, even if it means trampling on seniority and apprenticeship, so be it. Today's new member of Congress cannot wait to be seen *and* heard.

The result is a Congress filled with mavericks and entrepreneurs—that is, members who may care more for their reelection and policy goals than the overall institution itself. Just as premed students cannot afford to fail introductory biology, and prelaw students cannot afford to fail constitutional law, members of Congress who want to stay in the profession cannot afford to fail an election. That means having more opportunities to serve constituents, which, in turn, means having more committee slots to chair and more staff to develop legislation and help constituents. As noted in Chapter 6, it also means candidate-centered campaigns—members cannot risk their jobs in a party-centered effort. In turn, the changing electoral needs of individual members puts ever greater pressure on the leadership of Congress as it seeks to find enough consensus among members to forge legislation.

A funny thing happened on the way to the reelection, therefore: Congress abandoned many of the norms that once guided its members.[38] The old norms were simple. Members were once supposed to specialize on a small number of issues (the norm of specialization); defer to their elders (the norm of seniority); never criticize anyone personally (the norm of courtesy); and wait their turn (the norm of apprenticeship). New members were to go along to get along, to be seen and not heard, and to wait their turn.

The norms began to die with a surge of younger liberal Democrats elected in the late 1950s. These first-term members of Congress were no longer willing to wait their turn. The norm of apprenticeship steadily declined throughout the 1960s as new members became much more visible participants in the lawmaking process. So, too, did the norm of specialization recede, as even the most junior members gained enough staff to weigh-in on just about any issue at just about any point in the legislative process. And, as apprenticeship and specialization fell, so, too, did the norm of seniority. By the 1970s, except for the norm of courtesy, the old norms no longer dictated how Congress ran.

As a result, today's member of Congress is much more independent and entrepreneurial than at any time in history. As Burdett Loomis writes in his book *The New American Politician:* "Beginning with the class of '74, a new generation of leaders rushed to the fore of American politics and brought with them a new way of doing business. . . . They have established an issue-oriented, publicity-conscious style that differs dramatically from that produced within the seniority dominated Congress of the 1950s."[39] With many members driven to obtain publicity, Congress has no time for the old norms of specialization, courtesy, seniority, and apprenticeship. Members must take care of themselves first.

One example of the entrepreneurship in Congress is the rising number of informal committees, or **caucuses,** that individual members join to promote their legislative interests. Unlike organized interests, caucuses are composed of the members of Congress themselves.

Congress has always had caucuses of one kind or another, starting with caucuses built around the rooming houses where most of the early members stayed during the brief sessions of the part-time Congress. But what makes the current list of caucuses different is their number, diversity (more of just about every interest is represented among the 130 caucuses), character (many have paid staff, dues-paying members, and offices), and ability to monitor legislative actions that affect their interest.[40] There are caucuses for House members only, for Senators only, and for members of both chambers together. By the 1990s, according to one count, House members actually served on more informal caucuses than on committees and subcommittees.[41]

The growing diversity of the caucuses parallels the rest of society. There is a Black Caucus, Hispanic Caucus, Women's Issues Caucus, Rural Health Caucus, Children's Caucus, Cuba Freedom Caucus, Pro-Life Caucus, Homelessness Task Force, Urban Caucus, and Ethiopian Jewry Caucus. The diversity also parallels the fragmentation of organized interests, with caucuses on nearly every business and public interest issue—from the B-2 stealth bomber, steel, beef, bearings, high tech, computers, mushrooms, mining, gas, sweeteners, wine, footwear, and soybeans to animal welfare, the Chesapeake Bay, clean water, drug enforcement, adoption, the arts, energy, military reform, AIDS, and antiterrorism. There are also friends of the Caribbean Basin, of the Animals, of Human Rights Monitors, and of Ireland.

Although the Republican majority cut funding for the caucuses in 1995, it appears that many will survive by raising outside money from lobbyists. Such fundraising merely confirms the link between the caucuses and the organized interests they often serve.

IN A DIFFERENT LIGHT

DO MEMBERS CARE TOO MUCH?

Taking care of the folks back home is one of the best ways a member can increase the odds of winning reelection. That is why many members travel home every weekend to talk about the issues, why they send out bales of newsletters and press releases touting their success, why they work to solve constituent problems with government, and why they struggle to ensure the home district gets its share of federal spending.

The reason they offer this level of service is obvious: members must be reelected to maintain their careers. Woe be to the member blinded by the bright lights of Washington. As political scientist Richard Fenno observes, "Representatives and prospective Representatives think about their constituencies because they seek support in their constituencies. They want to be nominated and elected, and then renominated and reelected. For most members of Congress most of the time, this electoral goal is primary. It is the prerequisite for a congressional career and, hence, for the pursuit of other member goals. And the electoral goal is achieved—first and last—not in Washington but at home."[42]

Each member of Congress even has what Fenno calls a unique **home style**—that is, a way of simultaneously developing trust with his or her constituents and explaining votes in Congress.

That home style usually includes some way of advertising their successes, claiming credit for the good things happening back home, and creating a sense that they are still connected to the district. But if that home style does not include helping constituents solve problems, which is called **casework,** that member will not be a member of Congress for long. Home style and casework help explain why Americans are so distrusting toward Congress as an institution, yet so very trusting of their own member.[43]

It is to build trust that the average House member answers 10,000 letters a year, sends a quarterly newsletter to each of the 200,000 to 250,000 homes in the district, and handles 10,000 constituent requests for help a year. Such casework might involve a late Social Security check, a passport problem, a question about welfare, or a nomination to the military academies (which can only be made by members of Congress).

At some point, of course, this concern for the folks back home may distract members from the national good. Being too concerned about constituents is exactly what the Founders worried about. And it is something many members readily acknowledge. "We're too much in touch," said Senator Warren Rudman (R-NH) before retiring in 1993. "People here are traumatized by the polls, by the focus groups, by all of that." His colleague Richard Lugar (R-IN) calls Congress a "hyper weather vane" blowing one way and the other with the latest wind of opinion.[44]

In short, the more members stay in touch with the district, the more they may be unwilling to cast tough votes for the national interest. They may end up giving the district the final say, asking themselves not what the people *need,* but what the people *want.* Had the Founders known members would work so hard to serve the people, they might well have reconsidered their vote against term limits.

Forging Legislation

As noted in Chapter 2, the odds against action in Congress are great. Congress may be spending more time in session and casting more votes than ever, but it is definitely producing fewer laws. Almost twice as many bills were introduced in the late 1940s than in the mid-1990s, and more than four times as many actually passed in the 1940s than in the 1990s.

One of the reasons it is so hard to pass a bill is that the process provides ample chances for defeat. A bill must win many small contests on the way to final passage.[45] Consider eight steps from beginning to end: (1) having an idea, (2) writing a bill, (3) receiving a hearing, (4) marking up, (5) reaching the floor, (6) passing twice, (7) surviving conference, and (8) getting the president's signature. (See Box 7–5 for the standard chart on how a bill becomes a law.)

Having an Idea. The legislative process starts with an idea for a bill, an idea that might involve a visit from a constituent, a call from an organized interest, or

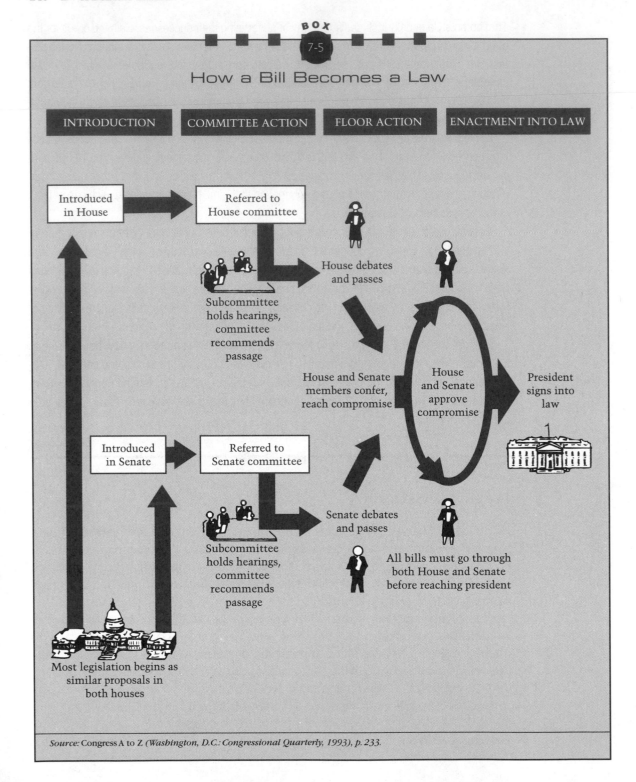

BOX
7-5

How a Bill Becomes a Law

| INTRODUCTION | COMMITTEE ACTION | FLOOR ACTION | ENACTMENT INTO LAW |

Introduced in House

Referred to House committee

Subcommittee holds hearings, committee recommends passage

House debates and passes

House and Senate members confer, reach compromise

House and Senate approve compromise

President signs into law

Introduced in Senate

Referred to Senate committee

Subcommittee holds hearings, committee recommends passage

Senate debates and passes

All bills must go through both House and Senate before reaching president

Most legislation begins as similar proposals in both houses

Source: Congress A to Z *(Washington, D.C.: Congressional Quarterly, 1993), p. 233.*

an event covered by the media. Whatever the source, members of Congress are constantly looking for ways to express their concerns about the issues of the day. The average member introduces roughly fifteen bills a year.

Ideas generally emerge from one or more of four basic goals that members bring into office. The first is *reelection*. Not surprisingly, most farm bills come from members who represent farm states; most bills to help cities come from members who represent cities. Even if it never passes, authoring a bill allows a member to claim credit back home. Members do care about the country, and do worry about how to help their constituents for more than just the next campaign.

The second goal of members of Congress is *good policy*. Contrary to public opinion about the role of special interests, most members of Congress do care about the national interest. As Democratic Representative Tim Penny of Minnesota said of his decision to run for Congress, "I was young and idealistic, and I went into politics at a relatively early age. I was enough of a true believer that I ran for office. I wanted to be part of it. I wanted to show people that government can work and that partisanship doesn't have to be the dominant force in politics, that interest groups don't have to be a deciding factor on every vote."[46]

The third goal is *higher office*. House members may develop ideas that generate statewide results in the effort to establish credibility for a future run at the Senate or governor's office; senators may push ideas that establish credibility for a future run at the White House.

The fourth goal is *personal*. Members often carry deeply personal concerns into office. "Politicians are human beings," said Massachusetts Representative Joe Kennedy, II. "When there is a degree of very personal pain that one feels toward an issue—it might be gun control [Kennedy's father, Bobby Kennedy, was assassinated with a handgun] or my uncle's interest in fighting cancer [Senator Ted Kennedy's son had bone cancer]—the commitment level is higher and your willingness to compromise is lower."[47]

Writing a Bill. Under a law passed in 1871, every bill begins the very same way. Its title is always "A BILL for the establishment. . . ." and its first sentence is always "Be it enacted by the Senate and House of Representatives of the United States of America in Congress assembled, That, ..."

Writing a bill is not difficult. Once past the enactment sentence, all bills instruct government to do something, whether to launch a new program, spend a certain amount of money, or stop a program.

Once a bill is finished, House members introduce it for consideration by placing a copy in the mahogany box (called the *hopper*) on a desk at the front of the House chamber, while senators can either hand the bill to the clerk of the Senate or rise from the floor to introduce the bill in a speech. A bill that comes from the House is always designated *H.R.* followed by its number, and a bill from the Senate is always listed *S.* followed by its number. The number is listed at the top of the first page, followed by the date, and the chief sponsor and any cosponsors. In theory, the longer the list of cosponsors, the greater the chance of passage. Unless the member has a special request for a number—S. 1 and H.R. 1 are reserved for the majority party's top priorities—the bill is simply given the next available number in line.

It is important to remember that all bills that do not pass die at the end of each two-year period. They can always be reintroduced again, but nothing carries over from one Congress to the next.

Receiving a Hearing. Once a bill is introduced in either chamber, it is "read" into the record as a formal proposal and referred to the appropriate committee—tax bills to Ways and Means or Finance, farm bills to Agriculture, technology bills to Science, Space, and Technology, small business to Small Business, and so forth.

Although most bills are referred to a single committee, particularly complex bills may be referred to multiple committees at the same time. President Bill Clinton's 1,364 page proposal for national health insurance went to sixteen House and Senate committees simultaneously. In the House, for example, Ways and Means, Banking, Budget, Energy and Commerce, Government Operations, Judiciary, Small Business, Science, Space, and Technology, and Veterans Affairs all received jurisdiction over some aspect of the bill.

Once received by a committee, a bill often gets further referred to a subcommittee. Whether in the full committee or a subcommittee, a serious bill usually receives a hearing in which witnesses speak to its pros and cons. (Some bills simply die in committee at the end of a session without a hearing or any action beyond the referral.) This committee or subcommittee hearing is part of the **legislative record** that the executive agencies and courts use later to interpret what Congress wants, and it is usually carefully scripted so that witnesses speak to particularly important questions that might influence future implementation.

Marking Up. Once a committee or subcommittee decides to pass the bill, it holds a *markup* to clean up and/or amend its version of the bill. The term *markup* refers to the pencil marks that members make on the final version of the bill.

At the end of the markup, the bill must be passed by the committee or subcommittee and forwarded to the next step of the process. If it is passed by a subcommittee, for example, it is forwarded to the full committee; if it is passed by a full committee, it is forwarded to the full chamber. Of the 9,800 bills introduced in the 103rd Congress, perhaps 2,000 were reported out of subcommittee and committee.

Reaching the Floor. Once reported to the full chamber, a bill will either be scheduled for floor action or dropped entirely. Whether a bill gets scheduled depends on what the leadership wants and the amount of time left in the session. The busiest time of the year is right before the end of a session, usually in late September or early October. (See Box 7–6 for a list of the bills up for consider-

BOX 7-6

The Legislative Calendar
Week of March 4, 1996

In the House

H.R. 2778: A bill to provide that members of the Armed Forces performing services for the peacekeeping effort in the Republic of Bosnia and Herzegovina shall be entitled to certain tax benefits.

H.R. 2853: A bill to authorize the extension of nondiscriminatory treatment (most-favored-nation status) to the products of Bulgaria.

H.R. 497: A bill to create the National Gambling Impact and Policy Commission.

H.R. 994: A bill to require the periodic review and automatic termination of federal regulations.

H.R. 927: Cuban Liberty and Democratic Solidarity Act of 1995 (Conference Report).

H.R.___: Debt Ceiling Limit.*

In the Senate:

H.R. 2546: Fiscal Year 1996 District of Columbia Appropriations (Conference Report).

H.R. 927: Cuban Liberty and Democratic Solidarity Act of 1995 (Conference Report).

S. 343: Comprehensive Regulatory Reform Act of 1995.

* The Debt Ceiling bill had no number when it was scheduled. The Speaker only knew that it would be coming.

ation during the week of March 4, 1996, a not particularly busy week in congressional time. The list shows that the Senate was considering two bills that had passed first in the House—a bill retains the number given by the chamber that passes it first.)

Given their different sizes, it should not be surprising that the House and Senate floors work differently. No bill gets to the floor of the House without a rule, or ticket, which can only be granted by the Rules Committee. The rule tells the House when the legislation will be allowed to come up, and what amendments are to be in order, or permitted, for consideration. Once the House leadership decides to act, there are few surprises.[48]

The Senate, in contrast, is far less predictable. Senators have far greater freedom to call a bill up for consideration, and have nearly unlimited authority to propose amendments to any bill. As we will see, they also have nearly unlimited opportunity to talk, and sometimes use that freedom to talk a bill to death.

In general, the Senate calendar is set by the majority and minority leaders who work together to find an agreeable time for specific bills. The schedule is then presented to the full Senate for unanimous consent—a requirement that asks all senators to agree in advance on how a bill will be debated. Almost all bills passed are so noncontroversial that unanimous consent is easy. If, however, a bill is so controversial that unanimous consent is impossible to achieve, it can be brought up for action with a simple majority vote.

These differences in floor procedure can make the House and Senate look very different: one is efficient, one not; one a well-oiled legislative machine, the other a wandering conversation. May 7, 1994, is as good an example of how the two chambers work as any, a day *New York Times* reporter David Rosenbaum summarized well in a piece titled, "A Day in the House Equals a Week in the Senate".

> On Thursday, the House had two and a half hours of crisp debate on whether to ban semiautomatic assault weapons. Almost every seat was filled. Most representatives spoke for a minute or two. No one spoke for more than five.
>
> Then, before 5 P.M., they voted. The excitement built as the running tally was registered on the electronic scoreboard overhead. After 15 minutes, the opponents of the ban were ahead, 214 to 213. Then a Congressman switched, and the proponents were ahead. Two more voted yes. One voted "no." And that was it. The bill was approved by the narrowest of margins, 216 to 214, and the House went on to other matters.[49]

Over in the Senate, Rosenbaum reported, most of the day was spent on delaying action. Technically, the Senate can only remain in session if a majority of members are present, and any member can request a quorum call just to make sure. Then "from 7 P.M. to 10 P.M. the Senate was paralyzed," wrote Rosenbaum. "Several Senators were at a black tie dinner for the Prime Minister of Malaysia. Nothing could be done without them. . . . It is routine for the Senate to interrupt its work for the convenience of one or two members."[50]

Passing Twice. After all the hard work that goes into getting a bill to the floor, voting for passage is easy. House members vote electronically by inserting a magnetic card and their personal code number into one of the many automatic voting machines on the floor; senators must still cast their votes in person as their names are read in alphabetical order by the clerk. Unless the bill is an amendment to the Constitution, which requires a two-thirds vote for passage, almost all other legislation needs only a simple majority for passage.

Members cast their votes on the basis of at least four different influences. The first is *constituency interest*. Members clearly worry how a given vote will affect their standing back home, and sometimes poll their constituents on particularly difficult votes.

The second is *ideology*. Just as the public splits between liberal, moderate, and conservative, so do members of Congress. In 1995, for example, Patrick Leahy (D-VT) was the most liberal member of the Senate, and Bill Clay (D-MO) the most liberal member of the House, while Bob Smith (R-NH) was the most conservative member of the Senate, and Dave Weldon (R-FL) the most conservative member of the House.[51]

Unlike the public, however, Congress may be losing its center. Of the twenty senators who ranked in the center in 1995, for example, eight (four Democrats and four Republicans) stepped down at the end of 1996.

The third influence is *party*. And, in modern history, party differences have never been greater. In 1995, for example, a majority of House Democrats voted against a majority of House Republicans a record 73.2 percent of the time, while a majority of Senate Democrats voted against a majority of Senate Republicans 68.8 percent of the time. The tension was particularly intense in the House, where the new Republican majority pushed one party vote after another in the first one hundred days of the session. All totalled, seventy-nine of the first one hundred votes taken in the 104th House were party line.[52] At least since the 1950s, such party line votes have been far less frequent.

Although ideology and party are closely related, some Republicans are more liberal than some Democrats, and vice versa. In 1995, for example, New England Republican senators, John Chafee and Jim Jeffords, were more liberal than Alabama's sole Democrat, Howell Heflin. In the House, Maryland Republican Constance Morella was more liberal than Texas Democrat Ralph Hall.

The final influence is *the president* of the United States. Presidents take positions on many issues up for a final vote, and those positions do matter to how members of Congress vote, particularly if those members belong to the president's own party.

Obviously, presidents do worse when their party is in the minority, as Bill Clinton did in 1995 in facing the new Republican majority. Clinton took a position on 123 votes, and won on just 36 percent, a record low for a third year of a presidency. By comparison, Dwight Eisenhower won 75 percent of his votes, Richard Nixon 75 percent, and George Bush 54 percent, even though all three were also working with a minority party.[53] Part of Clinton's problem goes back to the ideological fervor of new House Republican majorities in both chambers.

Surviving Conference. If both chambers have passed the same version of the same bill, the bill goes on to the president. But if they have passed different versions of the same bill, they must agree on a final compromise. Under the Founders' original design, the chambers would pass a bill back and forth until one finally said okay to the other's version.

Starting with the First Congress, however, the two chambers began using conference committees as a shortcut. As noted earlier, each chamber appoints its own slate of conferees, who are usually drawn from the majority and minority membership of the originating committees. It does not matter how many conferees get appointed, for each chamber in the conference committee has just one vote. If the House and Senate sides cannot agree, the bill dies. If the conference committee agrees to a final version, it produces a conference report that describes the bill. When both chambers approve the report, usually an automatic given the hard work involved, the bill is ready to move on for the president's signature.

Getting the President's Signature. Once a bill is passed in final form by both chambers, it is printed, or enrolled, on parchment paper and hand carried by congressional messenger to the White House for the president's signature. The president's decision to sign or veto a bill will be discussed in more detail in Chapter 8. For now, suffice it to say that the president's signature makes the bill a public law. Once signed, the enrolled bill is forwarded to the Archivist of the United States where it is assigned a public law number that begins with the number of the Congress in which it passed—hence, laws passed in the 105th Congress, 1997–1998, are numbered 105–XX. The law then becomes part of the federal statute books that tell the American people who gets what, when, and how from government.

Looking back over the eight steps, it seems fair to ask how any bill can pass. The answer is that important legislation passes even under the most difficult circumstances. As political scientist David Mayhew shows, the president and Congress are able to work together whether they are divided by party or not. Republican presidents get legislation out of Democratic Congresses, and vice versa.[54]

In fact, some of the most important laws in recent history were passed during periods of divided party control—that is, when Congress and the presidency were controlled by different parties. America's first civil rights act was passed in 1957, for example, when both ends of Pennsylvania Avenue were controlled by different parties. Although such periods rarely produce as much legislation as periods of unified control, Americans need not despair that the nation will completely collapse when different parties occupy these two branches of government.

IN A DIFFERENT LIGHT

HOW TO KILL A BILL

Although legislation can die in both chambers of Congress, there is no more lethal a place to legislative survival than the U.S. Senate. While an individual House member has very little influence on the floor, every individual senator has the ultimate power to talk a bill to death through a **filibuster.** The only way to end a filibuster is to invoke **cloture,** which requires a supermajority vote of the entire Senate—that is, sixty members total rather than three-fifths of whoever is present and voting. As a result, according to Richard Fenno, "Every member of the Senate has an atomic bomb that can blow up the place."[55]

(It is useful to note that filibusters were not part of the constitutional design. The first filibuster occurred in 1841 as part of sweeping debates over slavery and the role of national government in economic affairs. It was not until 1917 that the Senate finally created a rule for invoking cloture.)

It used to be, for example, that filibusters were physically exhausting events—rent a copy of the movie *Mr. Smith Goes to Washington* for the classic Hollywood rendition. South Carolina Republican Strom Thurmond still holds the individual endurance record, talking for 24 hours and 18 minutes straight in killing a 1957 civil rights bill.

Today's filibusters are less stressful physically but do carry occasional moments of drama. For example, in 1988, Senate Majority Leader Robert Byrd (D-WV) kept the Senate in session for three days straight in an effort to break a Republican filibuster against a Democratic campaign finance bill. Republicans were so angry at the pressure that they finally stopped coming to the chamber in protest. Byrd, in turn, ordered the Senate Sergeant at Arms to arrest the absent Republicans and bring them to the Senate floor, a power that had not been used for forty years. Former Senator Robert Packwood (R-OR) resisted arrest, or so to speak, and had to be physically carried to the Senate floor at 1:19 A.M. Despite Byrd's efforts, the Democrats could not break the filibuster. After losing the eighth cloture vote to limit debate, Byrd was forced to withdraw the bill from Senate consideration.

Except for such rare exceptions, filibusters are not dramatic events. By the 1970s, according to journalist Hendrik Hertzberg, "the production was automated. It is no longer actually necessary to conduct a filibuster; it suffices merely to announce one, and the Senate moves on to other business until the required sixty votes can be assembled or the targeted bill dies. No muss, no fuss, no embarrassing Cleghorns in string ties reading excerpts from the telephone directory far into the night."[56]

In part because filibusters have become easier, their use has grown. There were no filibusters during the 1700s; sixteen in the 1800s; sixty-six from 1900 to 1950; twenty in the 1960s; fifty-two in the 1970s; eighty in the 1980s; and, if current trends hold, there will be more than two hundred in the 1990s.

Filibusters are not the only way to kill a bill, however. Senators are always free to place a **legislative hold** on a bill, which expresses their personal objection to a given proposal. Since much of the Senate's business is conducted by unanimous consent—all senators must agree to allow a bill to come to a vote—a single senator's objection can doom a proposal. The only way to challenge a legislative hold is to force a formal vote to proceed, a rare occurrence in the more courteous Senate.

These delaying tactics can seem undemocratic, particularly when a majority of senators want action. But by allowing a single senator to delay or kill a bill, the filibuster and its cousins give minorities an extra source of protection. The problem is that they are being used on a host of less than significant issues. "The threat of a filibuster is now a regular event in the Senate, weekly at least, sometimes daily," argued an exasperated Senate Majority Leader George Mitchell in his last term in office. "It is invoked by minorities of as few as one or two Senators and for reasons as trivial as a Senator's travel schedule."[57]

CONCLUSION

Congress has rarely worked harder than it does today. It holds more votes, stays in session longer, and works its members harder. When in session, members average eleven-hour days.

Yet, Congress may be producing less and less by way of legislation. The number of bills introduced is down, even as members have more staff. The number of bills marked up for final consideration is down, even though committees and subcommittees spend more time in session. And the number of bills passed and enrolled on parchment paper for the president's signature is down, even though there is more time in debate.

One reason for the decline in congressional productivity may involve the breakdown of congressional comity—that is, the ability of members to get along with each other on a personal level. Americans who tune into C-SPAN to watch live Senate or House debate are more likely than not to hear stinging personal attacks rather than stirring policy debates. Although Congress was never designed to be a haven for politeness and good manners, neither was it created as a cauldron for name-calling and bitterness. Members who cannot agree to disagree respectfully may find it difficult to produce much of anything by way of major policy breakthroughs.

A second reason for the decline involves Congress itself. The increasingly complicated institutional structure provides many more opportunities to defeat a bill. Another reason is the conduct of modern campaigns. Candidate-centered efforts do little to build the bridges that might help members find consensus once in office. Still another reason lies outside Congress, in the sharp disagreements Americans have about who should get what, when, and how from government.

Congress is caught in a remarkable Catch 22: when it does act, Americans think it causes more problems than it solves, but when it fails to act, Americans think it is not doing its job.

The question is whether the declining output is somehow endangering government's ability to protect either the nation as a whole or American citizens as individuals. The answer is that Congress still seems quite capable of producing legislation on pressing national issues, whether in supporting the use of U.S. troops as peacekeepers in Bosnia, providing dollars to hire more police for America's cities, or funding essential services for the disadvantaged. Indeed, some supporters of free speech might even argue that Congress was much too capable in threatening individual liberties by passing the "cybersmut" provisions under the 1996 telecommunications law.

Where Congress may be failing is in producing legislation *on time*. It is one thing to finally agree to rescue Social Security or Medicare from impending crisis, and quite another to do so in time to prevent the crisis in the first place. In many policy areas, Congress has become addicted to crisis as the device for making the system work. Unable to find common ground early in a debate, Congress often waits until the last minute to act, which can, in turn, confirm the public's sense that members are out of touch with the rest of the nation.

The Founders set a very high threshold for getting legislation passed, and likely would not lower it today. The fact that Congress passed only a few hundred of the nearly 10,000 bills introduced in 1995–1996 would be taken as a sign of success, not failure. Although good legislation was no doubt lost as a result, bad legislation was surely denied passage. It is always tempting to measure Congress by its legislative output, but there are times when less is clearly better, particularly when society is so sharply divided on what to do. During such times, a Congress that is just strong enough may be just what America needs.

THE BASICS

■ The Founders gave Congress two essential jobs: making the laws and representing the people. Toward the first, they gave Congress a long list of enumerated powers, including the power to raise and spend taxes, declare war, regulate commerce, establish post offices, and build roads. Toward the second, they assured that House members would be elected directly by the people and senators indirectly by the state legislatures. (The Seventeenth Amendment changed the selection of senators to direct election.)

■ Because the Founders worried about Congress having too much power, they divided the chamber into two bodies, creating a bicameral legislature. As James Madison argued, "in order to control the legislative authority, you must divide it." Toward that end, the Founders created a host of differences between the chambers—size, terms, and elections—which, in turn, create a host of related differences—rules, leadership, legislative passage, and the role of individual members in the legislative process.

■ The First Congress in 1789 established a number of precedents that hold to this day. The House acted immediately to create a Speaker of the House to preside over the floor, and soon invented standing committees to handle legislation. Although the Senate was slow to follow suit, both chambers had established party organizations by the turn of the century, and both had at least some rules governing how a bill becomes a law.

■ Congress today is a complex institution, composed of leaders, committees, and staff.

■ The parties still choose the leadership in both chambers. Although only the House has a Speaker, both chambers have majority and minority leaders, as well as majority and minority whips (for whipping up support for specific bills). Both chambers also have committees on committees for assigning their party members to committee slots.

■ Congress has a complicated committee structure that consists of standing (permanent), special or select (temporary), joint (on which members of both chambers serve), and conference (specific to resolving differences between the two chambers on specific legislation) committees. Most committees have subcommittees. There are four kinds of standing committees: (1) authorizing, (2) appropriations, (3) rules and administration, and (4) revenue and budget.

- Congress has staff support for both representing the people and making the laws. Personal office staff support the former, while committee staff support the latter. In addition, Congress can draw on three support agencies (the General Accounting Office, Congressional Research Service, and Congressional Budget Office).

- The lawmaking process consists of eight steps: (1) having an idea, (2) writing a bill, (3) receiving a hearing, (4) marking up, (5) reaching the floor, (6) passing at least twice, (7) surviving conference, and (8) getting the president's signature. Each step has its own rules and odds against passage. Of the nearly 10,000 bills introduced in the 104th Congress in 1995–1996, only a few hundred survived to become public laws. The legislative record that emerges from this long process helps the executive branch and the courts interpret what Congress wants.

KEY CONCEPTS

- The Founders did not want Congress to be an efficient institution, and they divided power precisely to create obstacles to quick action. Although Congress sometimes frustrates the public by not acting, the Founders intended the legislative process to be difficult. In 1995, that process created one of the least productive Congresses in modern history. But the Founders would likely see the lack of legislation as a success.

- Getting assigned to the right committee is one of the most important campaigns a new member of Congress makes—it is essential to a successful first reelection. Members campaign for the right assignment with their party's committee on committees, which makes every effort to accommodate all requests.

- For the first 150 years of Congress, members came for short stays and went home to resume their former careers. Today, being a member of Congress has become a long-term career—that is, members stay as long as possible. The trends started to change in the late 1800s and have continued to the present. One reason members are able to stay longer is that they have enormous advantages as incumbent, or sitting, members. (Recall from Chapter 6 that incumbents get the lion's share of PAC money.)

- The legislative process starts with an idea for change. Having that idea can involve the goal of reelection, a desire for good policy, a hope for higher office, or a personal issue that a member carries into office. Although reelection is obviously one of the most important concerns of members—not getting reelected is the surest way of losing influence over legislation—it is important to remember that members care about more than just the next campaign.

IN A DIFFERENT LIGHT

■ The face of Congress has changed dramatically since the 1700s when all members were white, male, and mostly property owners. The number of women and minorities in Congress reached record levels in the 104th Congress, reflecting a mix of good campaigning, a rising amount of campaign funding, and the impact of majority-minority districts. These new faces clearly make a difference both in how Congress operates and what it does.

■ There is ample evidence that members of Congress care about their constituents. Members spend a great deal of time courting their constituents, whether through the mails, a unique home style, or casework. As a result, most Americans trust their members of Congress much more than they trust the institution of Congress as a whole. The question is whether members care too much for their constituents, losing sight of the national good as they seek to stay in touch with the folks back home. They may end up asking less what the people need and more what the people want.

■ There is no more threatening a place to legislation than the U.S. Senate. While the House has clear rules governing debate, the Senate operates largely through unanimous consent. Starting in the 1840s, Senators began using filibusters to delay and/or kill legislation. The only way to end a filibuster is to invoke cloture, which requires a three-fifths vote of the Senate (sixty votes). Filibusters have become easier and, therefore, more frequent. Whereas they were once designed to highlight great national issues, they are now used for sometimes trivial subjects.

OPEN QUESTIONS

■ Should Congress be more efficient than it is? What might be done to make it faster and more effective in passing legislation? Would it be good to eliminate some of the rules that get in the way of action, including the Senate filibuster? If so, what might happen to the country?

■ How much do you trust your own member of Congress? Do you recall having received any mail from your member of Congress over the years? Who would you call if your student grant got hung up? Who would you call if your passport got lost? Does all the constituent casework provided by Congress help the country or hurt? Should Congress simply tell everyone to get in line with the rest of the country, or continue to help anyone who figures out how to call? What is the bias in using Congress to solve such problems?

■ Should Congress pass a term limits amendment? What might happen as a result? Would the unelected representatives get more or less power? Would the public get better or poorer representation? How might the Founders reframe the question if they were to suddenly return? Would they drop the idea of term limits without debate or still think it is a bad idea?

■ Who do you think would make the best president: a House member or a senator? Given the role of the government in protecting the nation as a whole and Americans as individual citizens, which chamber does a better job on each? Knowing that more senators get to be president than do representatives, is the country better off as a result?

TERMS TO REMEMBER

unicameral legislature
bicameral legislature
norms
Speaker of the House
standing committees
bills
seniority
majority leader
whip
minority leader
committee on committees

constituents
conference committees
incumbent
caucuses
home style
casework
legislative record
filibuster
cloture
legislative hold

Endnotes to Chapter 7

1. Roy P. Fairfield, ed., *The Federalist Papers* (Baltimore: Johns Hopkins University Press, 1981), p. 160.
2. These results are from Jeffrey Katz, "A Record Setting Year," *CQ*, January 27, 1996, p. 195.
3. See Max Farrand, ed., *The Records of the Federal Convention of 1787*, volume I (New Haven, CT: Yale University Press, 1966).

4. Quoted in Charles O. Jones, *The United States Congress: People, Place, and Policy* (Homewood, IL: The Dorsey Press, 1982), p. 6.

5. Fairfield, *The Federalist Papers,* p. 160.

▶ 6. See Roger Davidson and Walter Oleszek, *Congress and Its Members,* fourth edition (Washington, DC: CQ Press, 1994), p. 24.

▶ 7. Richard Fenno, *The United States Senate: A Bicameral Perspective* (Washington, DC: American Enterprise Institute, 1982), p. 1.

8. James Madison, *Notes of Debates in the Federal Convention of 1787* (New York: W. W. Norton, 1969), p. 127.

9. Max Farrand, *The Records of the Federal Convention of 1787,* volume I, p. 375.

10. Charles Warren, *The Making of the Constitution* (Boston: Little, Brown and Company, 1928), p. 195.

11. Woodrow Wilson, *Congressional Government* (1885, reprinted by Cleveland Meridian, 1956), p. 154.

12. Congressional Quarterly, *Origins and Development of Congress* (Washington, DC: CQ Press, 1982), pp. 53–54.

13. *U.S. Term Limits v. Thornton,* 63 U.S.L.W. 4430 (1995).

14. Celinda Lake, "Women Won on the Merits," *New York Times,* November 7, 1992, p. A15.

▶ 15. For a review of why it is so difficult to elect women to Congress, see Wendy Kaminer, "Crashing the Locker Room," *The Atlantic Monthly,* July 1992, pp. 59–70.

16. Adam Clymer, "A Daughter of Slavery Makes the Senate Listen," *New York Times,* July 23, 1993, p. A10.

17. In Kaminer, "Crashing the Locker Room," p. 65.

18. Congressional Quarterly, *Origins and Development of Congress,* p. 107.

19. Congressional Quarterly, *Origins and Development of Congress,* p. 205.

20. Quoted in Davidson and Oleszek, *Congress and Its Members,* p. 167.

21. Quoted in Davidson and Olezsek, *Congress and Its Members,* p. 167.

22. Quoted in Davidson and Oleszek, *Congress and Its Members,* p. 177.

▶ 23. Christopher Matthews, *Hardball: How Politics is Played by One Who Played the Game* (New York: Harper and Row, 1988), p. 54.

24. Quoted in Matthews, *Hardball,* p. 54.

25. Joel Aberbach, *Keeping a Watchful Eye: The Politics of Congressional Oversight* (Washington, DC: Brookings Institution, 1990), p. 33. Aberbach's data excludes hearings by appropriations, administration, and rules, but do include budget and the revenue committees.

26. Clifford Krauss, "Vying for Committees, Freshmen Mimic Elders," *New York Times,* November 30, 1992, p. A9.

▶ 27. Lawrence Longley and Walter Oleszek, *Bicameral Politics: Conference Committee in Congress* (New Haven, CT: Yale University Press, 1989), p. 30.

28. Quoted in Longley and Oleszek, *Bicameral Politics,* p. 3.

29. Quoted in Longley and Oleszek, *Bicameral Politics,* p. 1.

30. The House and Senate figures are both from Stanley and Niemi, *Vital Statistics,* p. 217.

31. Carla Fried, "How Congress Perks Up Its Pay," *Money,* August 1992, p. 132.

32. Norman Ornstein, Thomas Mann, and Michael Malbin, *Vital Statistics on Congress 1995–1996,* (Washington, DC: Congressional Quarter, 1996), pp. 135–36.

33. Morris Fiorina, *Congress: Keystone of the Washington Establishment,* second edition (New Haven, CT: Yale University Press, 1989), p. 42.

▶ 34. For a history of the first Congresses, see James Sterling Young, *The Washington Community, 1800–1828* (New York: Columbia University Press, 1966).

35. Davidson and Oleszek, *Congress and Its Members,* p. 30.

36. Ornstein, Mann, and Malbin, *Vital Statistics,* p. 170.

37. Thomas Mann, *Unsafe at Any Margin: Interpreting Congressional Elections* (Washington, DC: American Enterprise Institute, 1978).

38. Herbert Asher, "The Learning of Legislative Norms," *American Political Science Review*, volume 67, number 2 (June 1973), pp. 499-513.

▶ 39. Burdett Loomis, *The New American Politician: Ambition, Entrepreneurship, and the Changing Face of Political Life* (New York: Basic Books, 1988), p. 28.

40. See Davidson and Oleszek, *Congress and Its Members*, p. 310.

41. Davidson and Oleszek, *Congress and Its Members*, p. 307.

42. Richard Fenno, *Home Style: House Members in Their Districts* (Boston: Little, Brown, 1978), p. 31.

43. Davidson and Oleszek, *Congress and Its Members*, p. 444.

44. Helen Dewar, "The Trees Get in the Way of the Forest," *Washington Post National Weekly Edition*, June 15-21, 1992, p. 13.

▶ 45. There are dozens of wonderful case studies of how a bill becomes a law. For a sampling, see Gary C. Bryner, *Blue Skies, Green Politics: The Clean Air Act of 1990* (Washington, DC: Congressional Quarterly, 1993); Janet M. Martin, *Lessons from the Hill: The Legislative Journey of an Education Program* (New York: St. Martin's Press, 1994); and Steven Waldman, *The Bill: How the Adventures of Clinton's National Service Bill Reveal What Is Corrupt, Comic, Cynical—and Noble—About Washington* (New York: Viking, 1995).

46. Lloyd Grove, "How a Bright Penny Just 'Wore Down,'" *Washington Post National Weekly Edition,* August 30-September 5, 1993, p. 12.

47. Clifford Krauss, "How Personal Tragedy Can Shape Public Policy," *New York Times,* May 16, 1993, p. 16.

▶ 48. Steven Smith, *Call to Order: Floor Politics in the House and Senate* (Washington, DC: Brookings Institution, 1989), p. 253.

49. David Rosenbaum, "A Day in the House Equals a Week in the Senate," *New York Times,* May 8, 1994, p. A6.

50. Rosenbaum, "A Day in the House Equals a Week in the Senate," p. A6.

51. Richard Cohen and William Schneider, "Voting in Unison," *National Journal,* January 27, 1996, pp. 179-201.

52. Dan Carney, "As Hostilities Rage on the Hill, Partisan-Vote Rate Soars," *CQ,* January 27, 1996, p. 199.

53. Jon Healy, "Clinton Success Rate Declined to a Record Low in 1995," *CQ,* January 27, 1996, p. 193.

▶ 54. David Mayhew, *Divided We Govern* (New Haven, CT: Yale University Press, 1991).

55. Quoted in Adam Clymer, "In House and Senate, Two Kinds of G.O.P.," *New York Times,* November 15, 1994, p. A12.

56. Hendrik Hertzberg, "Catch-XXII," *The New Yorker,* late August, early September, 1994, pp. 9-10.

57. Quoted by Davidson and Oleszek, *Congress and Its Members*, p. 348.

THE PRESIDENCY

CHAPTER

8

T he Founders created the presidency to do three jobs: execute the laws, represent the nation as a whole, and check Congress from becoming too powerful. The Founders did not imagine the presidency as the all-powerful center of government, but neither did they think government could protect the young nation if it had the kind of weak state and federal executives that had followed the Revolution.

Unlike Congress, where the Founders decided to divide power to control it, they decided to unify power in a single president as a way to ensure that government would be just strong enough to act. The Founders came to believe that only a single person could act with the "energy, dispatch, and responsibility" needed in such an emergency, said Pennsylvania's James Wilson.

That is not where the Founders started, however. They spent far more time talking about Congress, and actually had agreed upon a relatively weak executive until rather late in the Constitutional Convention. By the end of the summer, however, advocates of "energy in the executive" at the Constitutional Convention had worn down the opposition, in part because many of the Founders had come to worry about how to control the Congress they had created.

No one was more important to the campaign for a strong executive than New

Mission Impossible

York delegate Alexander Hamilton, who worked to strengthen the office at every turn. As Hamilton defended the presidency in *Federalist Paper No. 70*, a strong executive was essential to good government. "A feeble Executive implies a feeble execution of the government. A feeble execution is but another phrase for bad execution; and a government ill executed, whatever it may be in theory, must be in practice a bad government."[1] (Hamilton's version of a strong president is often labeled the Hamiltonian model.)

Indeed, the presidency was so strong compared to previous experience that some opponents characterized it as an American king. Hamilton rebutted the charges in *Federalist Paper No. 69*, emphasizing that the president was to be elected into office, not born, and would serve for four years, not life. Moreover, even though the president would have the power to faithfully execute the laws, veto legislation, wage war, run the government, and make treaties, all of these powers would be checked by Congress. The president's word would be anything but final. The presidency would be strong enough, but not too strong, thus well-suited to a government that was just strong enough.

The rest of this chapter will examine the founding of the presidency in more detail, while asking how the presidency works today. The first section on the imagined presidency will discuss the reasons underpinning the Founders' decision to create a single, independent executive, and will review the duties and qualifications of the office. The second section on the real presidency will examine how the Founders' decisions have played out over time, starting with the precedents set by George Washington in America's first presidency, and continuing with a discussion of the institutional structure and operation of the presidency today. The final section will ask how the tactics of presidential leadership have changed, focusing on the increasing tendency of presidents to go directly to the public for support of their programs.

THE IMAGINED PRESIDENCY

Just as the Founders had plenty of experience with legislatures, they also had plenty of experience with executives. On the one hand, they had all experienced the great tyranny inflicted by the all-powerful British king, and most certainly did not want a similar concentration of unlimited authority in the American presidency.

On the other hand, most of the Founders came from states with weak governors, and all had witnessed the paralyzing weakness of the executive created under the Articles of Confederation. Most governors were appointed by their state legislatures for single terms lasting but a year, obviously making the governors enormously dependent on keeping the legislatures happy. And the president created under the Articles was nothing more than a presiding officer of Congress.

The lone exception to this history of weak executives was the governor of New York, a single executive elected directly by the people for a three-year term. Unlike the governors of other states, who could only serve one term, the governor of New York could serve as long as the public voted for reelection. It was New York where Alexander Hamilton learned his lessons about the value of a strong executive. And, as already noted, it was Hamilton who became the greatest champion of a strong presidency.

In the end, Hamilton's vision prevailed at the Constitutional Convention. The Founders made a number of decisions that strengthened the office as a counterweight to the Congress, most important among them the creation of a single executive selected by the people (albeit only through the electoral college), not the Congress itself. They also gave the presidency just enough power to create a central focus on protecting the nation as a whole. These decisions will be discussed below.

A Single Executive

It is safe to argue that the Founders' single most important decision about the presidency was also their first. Meeting on June 1, 1787, the Constitutional Convention decided that there would be a single executive. The proposal for "a single vigorous executive" came from Pennsylvania's James Wilson. Even though nine of the thirteen states already had a single executive, Wilson's proposal was met by intense opposition from delegates who wanted a plural executive—that is, a kind of presidential clerkship in which three individuals would share the job of running the government.

Despite worries that a single president might become what Virginia's Edmund Randolph called the "fetus of monarchy," the Founders eventually concluded that the new government needed energy in the executive. They were willing to increase the risk of tyranny in return for some efficiency. Much as the delegates feared an American version of the English king, they feared foreign and domestic threats more. They also knew that a weak version of the single executive had failed under the Articles of Confederation, and believed that a plural executive would be more of the same.[2]

The delegates eventually voted seven states to three in favor of a single executive, with the Founders' hoped-for first president, George Washington, voting "aye." Apparently, it was easier to vote for a single executive believing Washington might be the first to serve.

An Independent Executive

Having decided on a single executive, the Founders had to decide just how independent that executive would be, which, in turn, meant finding an appropriate method of selection or election. The convention was initially divided on the question. A small number of the delegates favored direct election by the people, which Pennsylvania's James Wilson thought would assure that the president was completely independent of Congress.

An equally small number favored selection by Congress, tying the president more closely to the legislative branch. Those who favored selection by Congress also supported a single seven-year term to keep the president from bribing Congress to assure reelection. Yet by making the successful candidate dependent on Congress, the proposals would have sharply weakened the presidency as a check against congressional tyranny.

Despite Wilson's earlier success in winning approval of a single executive, the convention never seriously considered his proposal for direct election. Virginia's George Mason said, "It would be as unnatural to refer the choice of a proper character for chief Magistrate to the people, as it would to refer a trial of colours to a blind man."

Selection by Congress fared better over the summer, and was actually adopted at several points. The problem was the single, seven-year term. A good president would be out after one term and a bad president would never feel the heat of reelection. In the end, the convention rallied around the cumbersome electoral college, in which voters cast their ballots for competing slates of electors who, in turn, cast their electoral votes for president. It might be called a form of indirect direct election. They also opted for a four-year "renewable" term—that is, the president would be able to serve as long as the public wanted.

The final outline was hardly perfect, however. Along the way, the Founders decided that the candidate who received the most electoral college votes would become president, while the candidate who came in second would become vice president. In short, the runner-up only received the vice presidency by failing to win the presidency.

Since the Founders imagined a country without political parties, this runner-up rule made perfect sense. Surely great candidates would be able to work together after the election. But imagine if this runner-up rule had been in place in 1996. America would have inaugurated President Clinton and Vice President Dole, a rather unworkable combination given their sharp disagreements over national and international issues.

It did not take long for the Founders to experience the problem for themselves. The 1796 election produced Federalist President John Adams and Democratic-Republican Vice President Thomas Jefferson. Because the two disagreed so sharply about the future of the country, Jefferson was rendered virtually irrelevant to government. Indeed, speaking of Jefferson during the 1796 campaign, Adams said "I am almost tempted to wish he may be chosen Vice-President. . . . For there, if he could do not good, he could do no harm." Adams got his wish and Jefferson was banished to serve his term in complete isolation from his president. A similar fate might have befallen Bob Dole had he been forced into office as Bill Clinton's vice president.

If the runner-up rule created an awkward pairing in 1796, it created an outright electoral stalemate in 1800. The election could not have been more important, for it occurred during a time of rising public anger about the nation's direction. Two Democratic-Republicans, Thomas Jefferson and Aaron Burr, emerged from the 1800 election with exactly seventy-three electoral votes each, while Federalist John Adams received just sixty-three. Under the Constitution, a tie vote of the electoral college forces the election of the president into the House of Representatives. It took thirty-six House ballots before Jefferson was elected. His vice president? None other than Aaron Burr, whom he had just defeated.

It was in response to these two early elections that the states ratified the Twelfth Amendment in 1804. Under the amendment, electors were required to cast separate votes for the offices of president and vice president, thereby creating the incentive for presidential and vice presidential candidates to run together as a **presidential ticket.**

Having decided how a president would enter office, the Founders also decided how a president would leave. Short of defeat, death, resignation, or retirement, the only other way out was through impeachment for treason, bribery, or other high crimes and misdemeanors. Recall that the House votes the articles of **impeachment,** which list the charges against the president, and the Senate votes to impeach, or convict, the president.

Over the years, constitutional amendments have added two other ways for presidents to leave office. The Twenty-Second Amendment (ratified in 1951) prohibited presidents from being elected to office more than twice, while the Twenty-Fifth Amendment (ratified in 1967) established a process for removing the president for disability. The Twenty-Second Amendment was enacted in a backlash against Franklin D. Roosevelt, whose four consecutive terms violated the two-term tradition established by George Washington. The Twenty-Fifth Amendment was adopted because medical technology had created the very real possibility that a severely disabled president might survive a stroke or assassination attempt, but be unable to discharge the powers and duties of the office. (See Box 8–1 for a list of how presidents leave office today.)

BOX
8-1

Seven Ways to Leave the Presidency

Once someone has been elected president of the United States, there are seven ways to leave office.

1. The president can lose a bid for reelection (Ford, Carter, and Bush).

2. The president can choose not to run for a second term (Johnson).

3. The president can serve out the two full terms permitted under the Twenty-Second Amendment and leave undefeated (Truman, Eisenhower, and Reagan).

4. The president can die in office (Roosevelt, Kennedy).

5. The president can resign (Nixon), automatically elevating the vice president to be president.

6. The president can be declared either temporarily or permanently unable to discharge the powers and duties of the office under the Twenty-Fifth Amendment, which was ratified in 1967. No president has yet to leave office under this amendment.

7. The president can be impeached and convicted by Congress for what the Constitution calls "Treason, bribery, or other high Crimes and Misdemeanors." Impeachment requires a majority vote by the House upholding the charges made against the president. The Senate then must hold a trial and can only convict the president by a two-thirds vote. Andrew Johnson is the only president ever to be impeached. He survived conviction by one vote. However, Nixon resigned to avoid impeachment and a likely conviction for his involvement in the Watergate scandal.

The Duties of the Presidency

Article II of the Constitution begins even more simply than Article I: "The executive power shall be vested in a President of the United States of America." The problem comes in trying to define just what the executive power means.

Some scholars argue, for example, that the executive power covers just about everything not listed under Congress. Compare the first sentence of Article II against the first sentence of Article I: "All legislative powers *herein granted* shall be vested in a Congress of the United States." By not using the same "herein vested" language in Article II, perhaps the Founders meant the presidency to rely more on implied, rather than express powers. The Founders were hardly sloppy writers and might have meant something by the difference.

At the same time, the Founders also gave the presidency a short list of express powers, thereby suggesting that the president be bounded by specifics. The president's powers fall into two broad categories, one dealing with what appear to be mostly exclusive powers to run the executive branch, and the second dealing with shared powers on making the laws. After examining the two sets of duties, we will turn to a brief discussion of how Congress and the presidency continue to share power today.

Executive Powers. Unlike the long list of duties for Congress, the Constitution provides only the briefest sketch of executive powers.[3] Leaving some of the duties unspecified helped the Founders accept the notion of a strong executive. This is not to argue that the presidency was left powerless. Although thin on detail, Article II did speak to foreign threats and the day-to-day operations of government, establishing the president's authority to play three central roles in the new government: (1) commander in chief, (2) negotiator in chief, and (3) administrator in chief.

Commander in Chief. The president's first duty is to be commander in chief of the army and navy. It is a fundamental expression of the president's role in protecting the nation as a whole. The question was never who would command the armed forces, but who would initiate and make war.[4] Under the Virginia Plan, the Founders had initially agreed that Congress would make war, raise armies, build and equip fleets, enforce treaties, and suppress and repel invasions.

By the end of the convention, however, the list of congressional responsibilities in war had been shortened, and the term "make war" had been changed to "declare war." In making the change, the Founders agreed that it would be the Congress's responsibility to initiate war and the president's to repel invasions and protect citizens. But the specifics were not carried forward into the Constitution itself. President Clinton used this power in ordering troops to invade Haiti, arguing that the continued suppression of democracy threatened the U.S.

Negotiator in Chief. By enumerating the power to make treaties, Article II also makes the president negotiator in chief. (It is a power reinforced elsewhere in

Article II in the power to appoint U.S. ambassadors and receive ambassadors from other countries.)

Once again, the Founders appeared to change their minds over time. As late as August 1787, the Founders assumed that the Senate, not the president, would have the treaty making power. By the end of the month, however, the Founders shifted back to the president, giving the Senate a secondary role by requiring a two-thirds vote of consent. Along the way, the Founders defeated a motion by James Madison that would have given the Senate its own treaty making power separate from the presidency. Presidents eventually expanded the treaty power through the use of **executive agreements,** which are simple agreements between the heads of countries. Not quite treaties, these agreements can cover a range of issues, from student and cultural exchanges to commitments on international trade.

Administrator in Chief. By enumerating the president's authority to appoint the officers of government (for example, the heads of departments, ambassadors, U.S. marshals) and compel their opinions in writing, Article II clearly makes the president administrator in chief. Although this might seem to be the least controversial of the president's enumerated powers, it provoked enormous debate at the convention. The Founders worried about favoritism in the appointment process, and struggled with ways to ensure that the very best people would be asked to serve. At one point, for example, the Founders wanted the Senate to appoint ambassadors; at another, they wanted Congress as a whole to appoint the secretary of the treasury.

In the end, the Founders gave the president the appointment power, provided that the Senate would confirm all individual nominees through simple majority votes. It is important to note, however, that Congress, not the president, is responsible for creating all appointive positions through its lawmaking power. Congress creates the departments and agencies, judgeships, and ambassadorial slots by law, while the president makes the final appointments with the Senate's confirmation. It is a sharing of power that guarantees no one branch will ever be in complete control.

Beyond giving the president the enumerated roles of commander, negotiator, and administrator in chief, the Founders also provided a broad implied power in the **take care clause.** Located at the very end of Article II is the simple statement that the president "shall take Care that the Laws be faithfully executed. . . ." Short though it may be, the clause gives the president ultimate authority to implement the laws. This power is particularly important if Congress is fuzzy about what it wants. And since fuzzy language is sometimes the best way to pass a bill, the president ends up with broad authority to execute the legislation once it is signed.

Lawmaking Powers. The president's legislative powers reflect the Founders' concern with protecting the nation as a whole and checking Congress. Although Congress has the greater role in writing the specifics of a given law, presidents have a substantial say in defining the **legislative agenda,** that is, the informal list of issues Congress will address. This agenda-setting role is part of the president's duty to represent the nation as a whole, and is contained in the Article II requirement that the president "from time to time give to the Congress Information of the State of the Union, and to recommend to their Consideration such Measures as he shall judge necessary."

The state of the union requirement is an example of how the presidency and Congress share the power to make the laws. Over the years, the phrase "time to time" has come to mean "annually," while the phrase "information on the State of the Union" has come to be known as the **State of the Union Address.** Until the early 1900s, the address was not an address at all, but an annual message delivered to Congress on paper. Today, the address is delivered orally before a joint session of both chambers, and is carried live on the major television networks and many cable channels.

It is important to note that not all of the president's legislative powers are found in Article II. Under Article I, the president has the power to veto legislation passed by Congress. Under the veto power, the president has ten days (not counting Sundays) from the time a bill reaches the White House to make one of three choices: (1) sign the bill into law, (2) veto the bill by returning it to Congress with a list of objections, or (3) do absolutely nothing, letting the ten-day clock expire.

President Ronald Reagan delivers his 1982 State of the Union Address to a joint session of Congress. Behind him is Vice President George Bush (left) and House Speaker Thomas P. "Tip" O'Neill (right).

If the ten-day clock runs out while Congress is still in session, the bill automatically becomes a law. If, however, the clock runs out after Congress has formally adjourned to go home (as opposed to just taking a short recess, or break), the bill is automatically killed under a **pocket veto.**

The process is not necessarily over with the formal veto, however. Except for pocket vetoes, which occur after members have gone home at the end of a session and therefore do not allow for any further action, Congress has the option to override the veto, provided it can muster a two-thirds vote in each house. The bill then becomes law over the president's veto. Thus does the president have a check on Congress, and Congress a check back on the president.

The Ebb and Flow of Shared Power.   The presidency and Congress share many of the essential powers for governing the nation. Neither can quite paralyze the other, but neither has absolute power to act on its own. Congress and the presidency are, as political scientist Richard Neustadt once observed, separate institutions sharing power.[5]

Over the years, the relative strength of the two institutions has ebbed and flowed. From the 1870s through the early 1900s, for example, Congress was the dominant institution, far eclipsing the presidency in national visibility and impact. The Speaker of the House was regarded as the most important national figure of the era.

By the 1930s, however, the presidency was ascendant, easily eclipsing Congress as the nation battled the Great Depression. The presidency reined supreme as the centerpiece of government for the next forty years. Congress attempted to reverse the tide in the early 1970s with the passage of two major laws.[6]

The first involved an effort to restrain the president's war making power. Under the 1973 **War Powers Resolution,** which was passed into law over President Richard Nixon's veto, presidents are required to consult with Congress whenever there is a chance that U.S. troops will be involved in hostilities. The law also requires the president to report to Congress within forty-eight hours of sending those troops into harm's way, and must withdraw those troops if Congress does not declare war within sixty days.

Although the law sounds tough in theory, it has been routinely ignored in practice. Presidents have argued that the War Powers Resolution is an unconstitutional infringement on their authority as commander in chief. Moreover, Congress has always had the power to bring an end to any troop deployment by cutting off funds through the appropriations process. That it has never done so suggests the great difficulty in stopping a war once the fighting begins. No one wants to be accused of undermining the morale or support of troops in battle.

The second law involved an effort to strengthen congressional influence over the federal budget. Under the **Budget and Impoundment Control Act** of 1974, Congress made three major changes in how the budget process works: (1) it sharply limited the president's authority to impound, or refuse to spend, legally appropriated funding; (2) it created its own independent source of budget information in the form of the Congressional Budget Office; and (3) it established a new budget process designed to help the many committees and subcommittees involved in raising and spending money keep track of the bottom line.

With the passage of this law, Congress was much more successful in swinging the pendulum back toward the legislative branch. Although congressional committees and subcommittees still have trouble keeping their eyes on the bottom line—witness the continuing difficulties reducing the huge federal budget deficit—Congress is doing a better job of informing itself on key budget issues, and presidents no longer have unlimited freedom to impound.

Qualifications for Office

Just as the Founders set minimums for serving in Congress, they established minimums for the presidency. However, the Founders came to the discussion of qualifications for the presidency late in the convention.

During the first part of the summer of 1787, the Founders had generally assumed that Congress would be choosing the president, making a discussion about qualifications mostly irrelevant. Congress would not select a president who did not meet the minimums for service in the House or Senate. In addition, the Founders assumed that George Washington would be the first president, thereby establishing a rather impressive standard against which to measure future presidential candidates.

However, once the Founders gave the public a voice in picking the president, establishing minimum qualifications became essential. Even once removed from direct election by the electoral college, the public would still have a say about who would serve as president.

Therefore, to further protect the office from popular passion, the Founders created three qualifications. The president had to be: (1) over thirty-five years old; (2) a natural born citizen as opposed to an immigrant who becomes a citizen by applying to the U.S. government for naturalization; and (3) a resident of the United States for at least fourteen years. These qualifications were the stiffest of any in the three branches of government.

The citizenship and residency requirements reflected a variety of concerns. The Founders worried that the public might drift toward a popular foreign war hero such as Prussian General Baron Frederick von Steuben, drawn to such leaders out of a longing for the "good old days" of a foreign monarchy. The citizenship requirement also ended rumors that the Founders were somehow plotting to import a European monarch to take the presidency—Prince Henry of Prussia and Frederick, Duke of York, who was King George III's second son, were supposedly on the list. The residency requirement was designed to keep British sympathizers out of the new government. Colonists who had fled to England during the Revolutionary War would be ineligible for election.

IN A DIFFERENT LIGHT

A PLACE IN HISTORY

Presidents are motivated by the same goals as members of Congress: reelection (every first-term president wants to win a second term), good policy (every president enters office with at least some commitments to broad policy achievements), and personal concerns (Lyndon Johnson's experiences as a school teacher shaped his commitment to federal funding for education). Since most presidents see no higher office than the presidency itself (although William Howard Taft left the presidency in 1913 later to become the chief justice of the Supreme Court), they often focus on their place in history as the ultimate goal.[7]

Winning a high place in rankings by historians and political scientists involves a mix of leadership skills, crisis management, legislative accomplishments, political skills, and character. The top of the list of America's greatest presidents is never a surprise: Abraham Lincoln, Franklin Roosevelt, George Washington, Theodore Roosevelt, Thomas Jefferson, Andrew Jackson, Woodrow Wilson, Harry Truman, Dwight Eisenhower, and William McKinley.[8]

Note that nine of the ten were involved in one way or the other in America's great wars—Lincoln, McKinley, Wilson, Franklin Roosevelt, and Truman were all presidents during wartime, and Theodore Roosevelt was a hero in the Spanish-American War. Also note that all were involved in managing the great crises of their times—the Revolutionary War, the 1800 election, the Civil War, the industrial revolution, the Great Depression, World War II, and the Cold War after World War II. Finally, also note that all had an impact on expanding the role of government—Jefferson engineered the purchase of the Louisiana territory, Theodore Roosevelt helped the United States become an international power.[9]

The bottom of the list is also no surprise: William Harrison, Warren Harding, James Buchanan, Franklin Pierce, Richard Nixon, James Garfield, Andrew Johnson, Millard Fillmore, and Ulysses Grant. Some earned their position through scandal—Nixon and Watergate, Harding and Tea Pot Dome. Others just happened to serve during the wrong era—for example, during the decades of congressional dominance in the late 1800s. Still others had the misfortune to follow great presidents—Andrew Johnson followed Lincoln. Obviously, being a war hero is not enough by itself to guarantee greatness. Otherwise, Grant would be near the top.

It is not yet clear where America's most recent presidents will end up. Jimmy Carter, Ronald Reagan, and George Bush are generally placed in the middle of the rankings, but their final place is still uncertain. Harry Truman was very poorly rated in the first two decades following his presidency, often dismissed as having been too much of a common man for the top of the charts. Truman has aged well, and is now routinely ranked near the top. Nevertheless, as Vice President Walter Mondale once said, political reputation is like cement: "You can stir it and stir it for a while, but pretty soon it becomes harder to stir and then it's set."[10]

Franklin Roosevelt is the most highly rated of the twentieth-century presidents. In fact, he is regarded by many scholars as the first modern president. Inside the presidency, Roosevelt had

President Richard Nixon waves goodbye to his White House staff after resigning in disgrace from the presidency. Secret tape recordings of key White House meetings in which Nixon discussed a cover-up of the Watergate scandal ultimately proved his downfall. The tape recording system was originally installed to help Nixon keep accurate records for his memoirs.

a profound impact in creating the Executive Office of the President, which, as we will see later, is the nerve center of the executive branch. He succeeded in winning much greater staff support for the president, and was thereby able to vastly increase the supervisory power that Washington had originally established in the 1790s.

Outside the presidency, Roosevelt set a precedent for aggressive government involvement in the economy. Roosevelt's first one hundred days in office in 1933 produced a staggering inventory of federal intervention in fighting the Great Depression, and much of his New Deal agenda for helping working and poor Americans is still on the statute books today. From free school lunches for poor children to Social Security for the aged, unemployment insurance for those out of work to federal aid to families with dependent children (AFDC, or welfare), Roosevelt made the federal government an unmistakable presence in American life. Moreover, as already noted in Chapter 2, Roosevelt expanded the role of the federal government in cooperating with state and local government, launching the era of cooperative, or marble-cake, federalism.

The problem with lists of great presidents is that sitting presidents can take them too seriously. The best way to earn a place in history is to focus on solving problems and representing the nation in the present. Presidents who devote too much time to their future may find that history deals a harsh judgment. At the same time, worrying about one's place in history is one way for presidents to remind themselves that satisfying public demands in the present is not the only path to success.

THE REAL PRESIDENCY

Time has not stood still at 1600 Pennsylvania Avenue any more than it has on Capitol Hill. The presidency has grown bigger, more complicated, and infinitely more visible than the Founders could have imagined. And, as we will see later in this chapter, presidents today also go public much more often.

Nevertheless, today's presidency reflects precedents set in the very first presidency of George Washington. The Founders could not have anticipated the kinds of foreign and domestic threats that now so occupy the office—from the war on drugs to international trade—but they would recognize the importance of the president in representing the nation as a whole.

The First Presidency

As with the First Congress, America's first presidency created important precedents for the future. It established a precedent on just how the president would be addressed in public. Vice President John Adams argued that the president should be called "His Highness the President of the United States and protector of Their Liberties," a title the popularly elected House immediately rejected. The president of the United States would be called "The President of the United States."

Much more importantly, America's first presidency established George Washington as the model against which to measure future presidents. And Washington, for his part, helped establish the legitimacy and basic authority of his office. He negotiated the new government's first treaty, appointed its first judges and

George Washington in a painting by George Hicks. Washington set precedents that stand to this day.

department heads, received its first foreign ambassadors, vetoed its first legislation, and signed its first laws.

Washington also established a host of lesser precedents for running the presidency that still hold today. He started by assembling the first White House staff.
It was hardly large, composed of just two clerks, but it was an office nonetheless. (Washington never used federal dollars to cover his office budget; he paid
for staff and expenses out of his own pocket. Today's president could not afford
such generosity: the budget for the White House staff, including travel expenses,
mail, and security, runs almost $200 million a year.)

Washington also appointed the first department secretaries. His choices for the
top jobs were impeccable: Thomas Jefferson became secretary of state and
Alexander Hamilton secretary of the treasury. With James Madison as the floor
leader of the House, Washington was able to develop a smooth liaison with Congress, establishing precedents for communicating between the two branches
that continue to this day.

Washington may have set his most important precedent in establishing the president's *sole* authority for supervising the executive branch. He was absolutely clear
about the division of executive and legislative powers. Congress could appropriate money, confirm appointees, conduct oversight hearings, and always change
the laws, but it could not run the departments. That was the president's job.

Congress did not give up control easily. In creating the Treasury Department,
for example, Congress required the new secretary to report to both branches simultaneously, a requirement that stands in law to this day, but which is ignored
in practice. Congress also tried to limit Washington's power to fire his own political appointees. Because Congress was responsible for confirming presidential
appointees, or so the argument went, it only stood to reason that Congress would
be responsible for removing appointees.

Washington argued just the opposite. Confirming appointees was an appropriate check on executive power, but removing appointees was an essential tool for
supervising the daily work of the departments. Nevertheless, legislation requiring prior congressional approval of all firings nearly passed the very first Senate,
and was only defeated when Vice President John Adams cast the tiebreaking vote.

The war over the presidential removal power was not over. Congress tried again
to limit the president's removal power in 1868, this time under the Tenure of Office Act, which required the president to submit all removals to the Senate for
approval. This time, however, the battle occurred with a far less popular president, Andrew Johnson, in the White House. It was Johnson's decision to fire his
secretary of war that led the House to pass a bill of impeachment indicting the
president for high crimes and misdemeanors. Although Johnson was eventually
acquitted after a six-week trial in the Senate, the struggle over executive power
is never far from the surface to this day. Congress routinely requires, for example, that federal departments keep offices open in the districts of particularly powerful senators and House members.

Washington's final contribution to the evolution of the presidency came in his decision to retire after two terms. His decision was motivated in part by the continuing worries about an American king. Although he would have been easily reelected to a third term, Washington felt two terms was enough, and returned to his Mount Vernon estate in 1796.

The Institutional Presidency

The structure that helps presidents do their jobs is referred to as the **institutional presidency.** Like the Congress, the presidency has its own leadership. Like the Congress, the presidency has its own organizations for making decisions. And like the Congress, the presidency has its own staff to provide advice and to faithfully execute the president's decisions. Each will be considered in order.

Leadership. The leadership of the presidency is both simple and complex. It is simple because there is only one leader who counts, the president. It is complicated because that leader has so many different sources of advice on what to do.

The **Executive Office of the President (EOP)** is where presidents get most of their advice. As noted earlier, Franklin Roosevelt created the EOP to give presidents more tools to supervise a fast-growing government. The term "Executive Office of the President" refers just to the small number of offices that serve the president directly, not the executive branch as a whole, which contains all of the departments and agencies that execute the laws. As such, the Executive Office of the President is part of the executive branch, but not vice versa.

The EOP brought the Bureau of the Budget (now called the Office of Management and Budget) directly under the president's control. It provided a home for future growth of the president's staff, which rose from roughly 700 staff at the height of World War II in the mid-1940s to nearly 1,600 today. As the EOP grew over the years, it became a key source of presidential control over the rest of government. As Box 8–2 shows, it also became a rather complicated organization.

If the EOP is the nerve center of the presidency, the president is the nerve center of the EOP. Although the offices contained within the EOP are set by law, presidents have great latitude to organize the flow of advice to fit their personal style. Over the past three decades, presidents have used three very different models for running the EOP: competitive, collegial, and hierarchical.

Among modern presidents, Franklin Roosevelt and Lyndon Johnson both used the competitive approach, in which presidents allow their aides to fight each other for access to the Oval Office. It is survival of the fittest. Johnson frequently gave different staffers the very same assignment, hoping that the competition would produce a better final decision.

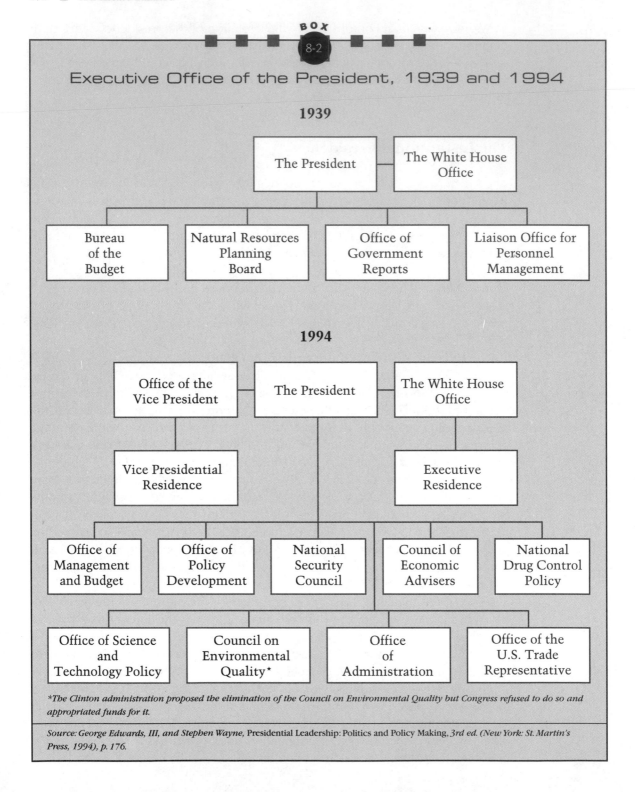

BOX 8-2

Executive Office of the President, 1939 and 1994

1939

- The President
- The White House Office
  - Bureau of the Budget
  - Natural Resources Planning Board
  - Office of Government Reports
  - Liaison Office for Personnel Management

1994

- Office of the Vice President
- The President
- The White House Office
  - Vice Presidential Residence
  - Executive Residence
  - Office of Management and Budget
  - Office of Policy Development
  - National Security Council
  - Council of Economic Advisers
  - National Drug Control Policy
  - Office of Science and Technology Policy
  - Council on Environmental Quality*
  - Office of Administration
  - Office of the U.S. Trade Representative

*The Clinton administration proposed the elimination of the Council on Environmental Quality but Congress refused to do so and appropriated funds for it.

Source: George Edwards, III, and Stephen Wayne, Presidential Leadership: Politics and Policy Making, 3rd ed. (New York: St. Martin's Press, 1994), p. 176.

Franklin D. Roosevelt (seated) meets with his Cabinet and several members of Congress. Roosevelt favored the competitive approach to running the White House.

In contrast, John Kennedy, Jimmy Carter, and Bill Clinton all used the collegial approach, in which presidents encourage aides to work together toward a common position. It is a much friendlier way to work than the competitive approach, but may have serious drawbacks in what some social psychologists call *groupthink*. Groupthink is simply a term that describes the tendency of small groups to stifle dissent in the search for happier common ground.[11]

It was groupthink, for example, that led the Kennedy administration to launch the Cuban Bay of Pigs invasion in 1961, a disastrous effort to unseat Cuba's communist government. Looking back over the decision, Kennedy realized that few of his advisers had actually supported the invasion, but wanted to agree so badly that dissenters did not speak up in opposition.

Kennedy worked to prevent groupthink two and a half years later in the Cuban missile crisis. Having discovered secret Soviet nuclear missile bases on Cuban soil in 1962, Kennedy made sure dissenters were given an opportunity to speak as the thirteen days of intense debate continued. In the end, Kennedy and his aides decided to impose a naval blockade of Cuba that eventually led the Soviets to withdraw their missiles.[12]

Jimmy Carter and his advisors in 1977. Carter favored the collegial approach to running the White House. In the foreground left is Vice President Walter Mondale, who set important precedents in making the vice president a key member of the president's inner circle.

Finally, Dwight Eisenhower, Richard Nixon, Ronald Reagan, and George Bush all used the hierarchical model, in which presidents establish tight control over who does what in making decisions. A hierarchy is a form of organization that looks very much like a pyramid—one leader at the top, two right underneath, three or more right underneath the two, and so on down the organization. The chief advantage of a hierarchy is in reducing the number of people the leader sees—the tighter the hierarchy, the fewer the contacts. Most hierarchies depend upon a "gatekeeper," usually the **chief of staff,** near the very top who enforces the tight discipline on who sees the president.

Advisory Offices. Just as committees in Congress exist to make the laws, the EOP's political and policy offices exist to shape presidential decisions. Staffed by people chosen for their loyalty, these offices act as agents on the president's behalf. Unlike the Congress, where committees have substantial power to shape final decisions, the president's advisory offices are just that: advisory. The final decision is always the president's.[13]

Political Offices. Political offices are designed to help the president both run for reelection and represent the public. Almost all of the president's political advice comes from the White House Office: the Congressional Relations Office handles the president's legislative agenda and lobbies for passage on Capitol Hill; the president's attorney provides legal advice on executive authority and is closely involved in the choice of presidential appointees to department and agency positions; the Public Liaison Office keeps in touch with key constituencies that are important to the president's reelection; the Intergovernmental Affairs Office keeps in touch with state and local governments; and the Office of Communications coordinates media strategy and includes the press secretary's office.

The Office of Public Affairs is the newest of the advisory units, created by Ronald Reagan as a trusted source of support on winning reelection. This office reflects the nearly constant campaigning that now goes on in the presidency. Bill Clinton, for example, began airing reelection advertisements well over a year before the 1996 campaign. The Public Affairs Office merely confirms in organizational terms what presidents and their staffs have long known: the only way to be a truly successful first-term president is to win a second term. As noted, reelection is never far from the mind of today's first-term president.[14]

Policy Offices.   Policy offices are designed to give substance to the president's foreign and domestic agenda. Like congressional authorizing committees, policy offices collect information and write legislation. What they do not do, of course, is hold public hearings and markups, or pass bills. They must rely on the president to forward their ideas to the Congress. They also have substantial influence when it comes time for the president to sign or veto a law.

The president's policy offices fall into three broad categories: (1) those that deal with the economy and budget, (2) those that deal with domestic issues such as transportation, education, or energy, and (3) those that deal with foreign policy and national defense.

Economic policy is shaped by four key EOP offices: the *Office of Management and Budget* (OMB), which is responsible for monitoring all federal spending; the three-member *Council of Economic Advisers,* which keeps track of current economic trends; the *Office of the U.S. Trade Representative,* which handles international trade issues; and the *National Economic Council,* which was created by Clinton in 1993 to bring together economic advice from across government. Of the four offices, OMB is by far the largest. Preparing the president's budget, while keeping track of a nearly $2 trillion federal budget, takes a staff of almost five hundred.

Making domestic policy involves a mix of several EOP offices: a very small *Domestic Policy Council* staff, which has traditionally handled social policy such as health care and welfare reform; the tiny *Office of Environmental Policy,* which provides coordination among the many federal agencies involved in protecting the environment; the *Office of National Drug Control Policy,* which was designed to coordinate the war on drugs and is headed by the nation's "drug czar;" and again OMB, which has a stake in most domestic policy decisions through the federal budget.

In contrast to both economic and domestic policy, which involve a mix of different offices, foreign policy is supposed to be shaped by a single unit, the *National Security Council* (NSC). Created by law in 1947, the council consists of the president, vice president, the secretaries of defense, state, and treasury, the U.S. ambassador to the United Nations, and three White House aides: the chief of staff, the national security assistant, and the economic policy assistant.[15]

Advisors. There are three levels of presidential staff. In order of their closeness to the president, they are (1) the inner circle of intimate advisers; (2) the White House staff, which exists solely to serve the president; and (3) the cabinet, composed of the heads of the fourteen departments of government—thirteen department secretaries and one attorney general, who heads the Department of Justice.

The Inner Circle. The term **inner circle** refers to the president's most loyal and trusted advisors. Sometimes called the "kitchen cabinet" because of its informality, the inner circle is usually engaged in every key decision. Members of the inner circle can include particularly loyal heads of departments, White House staffers, even personal friends who have special White House passes. Whoever they are, they have at least one factor in common: they are intensely loyal to the

Clinton and two of the inner circle: Vice President Al Gore (left) and former Chief of Staff Leon Panetta (right).

president. Bill Clinton's 1995 inner circle included the chief of staff (Leon Panetta), the First Lady (Hillary Clinton), and Vice President Al Gore, plus one or two other trusted advisors, depending on the issue.

For the most part, members of the inner circle have immediate access to the president and can be called upon on a moment's notice. A map of office space in the West Wing of the White House is a good indicator of whether or not someone is in the inner circle. Typically, the closer an adviser sits to the president, the more power that person has. As Vice President Walter Mondale once remarked, being in the Old Executive Office Building just across the alley from the West Wing is like being in Baltimore. The best space is just down the hall from the Oval Office, where the president works. That is where the chief of staff, national security adviser, vice president, press secretary, and the communications director all work. (See Box 8–3 for a map of the White House office assignments in 1995.)

One job that appears to be a fixed ticket to the inner circle is the vice presidency. It was not always that way. After all, the job was once described by Vice President John Nance Garner, who served under Franklin Roosevelt, as not being worth a warm bucket of spit. As America's very first vice president, John Adams, once wrote, "my country in its wisdom has contrived for me the most insignificant office that ever the invention of man contrived or his imagination conceived; . . . I can do neither good nor evil."[16]

Through most of American history, vice presidents have been a necessary nuisance. After all, they had but one real job beyond casting tiebreaking votes in the Senate: to take the president's place in the case of death or resignation.

To this day, the vice presidential nominees are still usually picked for geographic or ideological balance (northerners tend to pick southerners, liberals tend to choose conservatives), even though they might add a percent or two at best to their ticket's total votes. Moreover, the vice president can create enormous embarrassment for the president, as Dan Quayle did with his insistence that *potato* was spelled *potatoe*. It was one of several gaffes that prompted Bush to consider dropping Quayle from the ticket in 1992.

Nevertheless, the vice presidency had changed by the 1980s. Vice presidents now have their own aircraft (Air Force Two) instead of the windowless cargo plane that once carried Spiro Agnew (Nixon's first vice president) on his foreign travels. They also have their own song ("Hail Columbia"), seal of office (thanks to Ford's vice president, Nelson Rockefeller, who paid for the design out of his own pocket), an office in the West Wing of the White House just down the hall from the president, access to all the paper flowing in and out of the Oval Office, regular private meetings with the president, and a growing staff of nearly one hundred.

Being vice president has turned into a very good political job, indeed, and is now the most frequent launching pad for future presidents. Four of the past eight presidents were vice presidents before taking the presidential oath of office (Johnson, Nixon, Ford, and Bush), three were governors (Carter, Reagan, and Clin-

BOX
8-3

A Map to the Stars, 1995

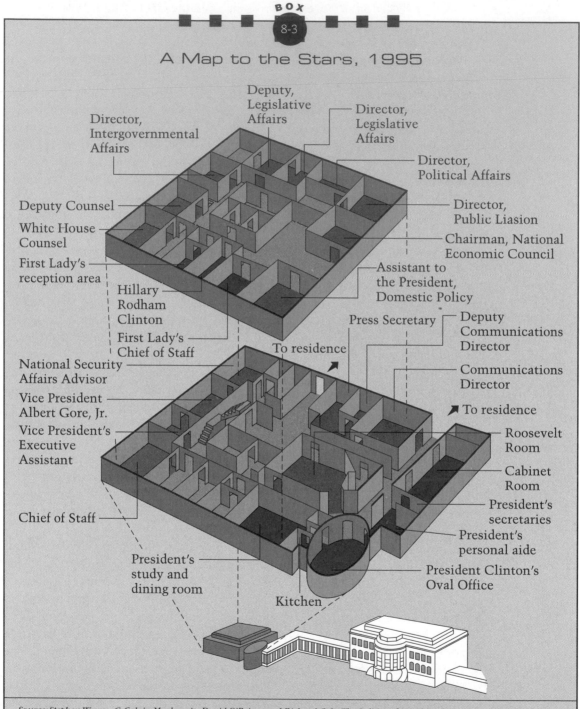

Source: Stephen Wayne, G. Calvin Mackenzie, David O'Brien, and Richard Cole, The Politics of American Government (New York: St. Martin's Press, 1995), p. 479. Adapted from the Washington Post, February 5, 1993, p. A23.

ton) and only one was a senator (Kennedy). Although being vice president is no guarantee of nomination, let alone an inaugural, it does position a politician as a nearly automatic front-runner. Having stood in the limelight, albeit always a bit in the president's shadow, vice presidents are immediately credible as presidential timber. They are also able to do the kind of political favors that future nominating convention delegates are likely to remember, whether getting a picture with the president or securing a new highway bridge for a congressional district.

The White House Staff. The president relies on sixty or so advisers to help manage the day-to-day details of the presidency. These advisers are all handpicked by the president for their loyalty, and are referred to as the **White House staff.**

Most of these advisers, however, are housed in the Old Executive Office Building just across the alley from the White House. Once used to house all the federal departments in the early 1800s, the Old Executive Office Building now holds only presidential and vice presidential staff. These staffers must be available to brief the president on a moment's notice, and often serve as a buffer between the president and the heads of the departments and agencies.

The White House staff is supported by nearly 350 permanent employees, including clerical staff, communication aides (the president is kept in constant contact with the Departments of State and Defense in case of an international crisis), schedulers, event planners, and even a webmaster to maintain the White House homepage.

In theory, the White House staff exists for one purpose, and one purpose only: to advise the president. Yet, a presidential adviser cannot help but revel in the power. There is no job quite like it. As Reagan speechwriter John Podhoretz remembers, the top of the line is having a White House West Wing office and parking space:

> Political staffers who have made it to the West Wing have achieved a rare condition of the soul: They do not wish to be anybody else, do not wish to be anywhere else. This is as good as it gets for people in politics who do not have it in them to run for public office themselves. Real proximity to real power produces a special high, one made up of equal parts self-congratulation (I have finally made it) and anxiety (They'll figure out I'm really an incompetent nobody and come and take it all away). If parasites could fear, this is what their fear would be: expulsion from the host.[17]

Gone are the days, however, when presidential staffers were invisible to the public. Some White House staffers are as visible as the president. Some even cultivate political careers of their own: Republican presidential hopeful Patrick Buchanan began his career as speechwriter to Vice President Spiro Agnew.

The Cabinet. The **cabinet** is composed of the heads of the departments of government, all of whom are appointed by the president and confirmed by the Senate. The term *cabinet* itself was created in 1793 when George Washington called the first meeting of the "Heads of the Great Departments" as a source of advice on the issues of the day.[18] Although cabinet secretaries are appointed by the president, their loyalties are not always with the White House. Many enter office with strong constituencies of their own, and sometimes become strong advocates for their departments in the annual budget process. Rare indeed is the cabinet secretary ready to support deep cuts in his or her budget, regardless of what the president might want.

There are currently fourteen cabinet departments, up from just two at the end of Washington's first term, and ten in 1960. All cabinet departments are not created equal. As we shall see in Chapter 9, the departments vary by size (the Department of Defense has nearly a million employees, while the Department of Education has barely 5,000) and budget (the Department of Health and Human Service has a budget of well over $200 billion, while the Department of State barely hits $10 billion).

They also vary by their influence in the White House. Presidents tend to pay the greatest attention to the oldest and most visible of the departments: Defense, Justice, State, and Treasury. These four departments are often called the inner cabinet because they are so important to the president's foreign and domestic success. The economy (Treasury), crime (Justice), and international affairs (State and Defense) are rarely far from the top of the president's agenda of policy concerns. As such, presidents almost always appoint very close allies to head the *inner cabinet,* even if those allies do not always have the best credentials for the jobs.

The other departments are generally called the *outer cabinet,* largely because they are more distant from the day-to-day worries that occupy the president and White House staff. The Department of Veterans Affairs, for example, is rarely in the headlines, even though its 250,000 full- and part-time employees make it the second largest department in government. (See Box 8–4 for the organization chart of the U.S. government.)

IN A DIFFERENT LIGHT

THE FIRST LADY AS FIRST ADVISOR

The president's inner circle has always included the First Lady to one extent or the other. Woodrow Wilson's wife is said to have actually run the presidency after Wilson suffered a stroke in his last year in office.

In recent decades, however, the First Lady has become much more visible as a policy adviser to the president, in part because the media is so much more aggressive in covering the White House. And no First Lady has been more visible than First Lady Hillary Clinton. Hillary Clinton is not listed on any White House organization chart, but is clearly first among presidential advisers on almost every policy issue.

BOX
8-4

Organization Chart of Government

THE CONSTITUTION

LEGISLATIVE BRANCH	EXECUTIVE BRANCH	JUDICIAL BRANCH
THE CONGRESS	**THE PRESIDENT**	The Supreme Court of the United States
Senate　　House	**Executive Office of the President**	United States Courts of Appeals
Architect of the Capitol	White House Office	United States District Courts
United States Botanic Garden	Office of Management and Budget	United States Sentencing Commission
General Accounting Office	Council of Economic Advisors	United States Court of International Trade
Government Printing Office	National Security Council	Territorial Courts
Library of Congress	Office of the U.S. Trade Representative	United States Court of Military Appeals
Office of Technology Assessment	National Critical Materials Council	United States Court of Veterans Appeals
Congressional Budget office	Council on Environmental Quality	Administrative Office of the U.S. Courts
Copyright Royalty Tribunal	Office of Science and Technology Policy	Federal Judicial Center
	Office of Administration	United States Tax Court
	Office of National Drug Control Policy	
	THE VICE PRESIDENT	

Department of Agriculture	Department of Commerce	Department of Defense	Department of Education	Department of Energy	Department of Health and Human Services	Department of Housing and Urban Development

Department of the Interior	Department of Justice	Department of Labor	Department of State	Department of Transportation	Department of the Treasury	Department of Veterans Affairs

INDEPENDENT ESTABLISHMENTS AND GOVERNMENT CORPORATIONS

ACTION
Administrative Conference of the United States
African Development Foundation
Central Intelligence Agency
Commission on Civil Rights
Commission on National and Community Service
Commodity Futures Trading Commission
Consumer Product Safety Commission
Defense Nuclear Facilities Safety Board
Environmental Protection Agency
Equal Employment Opportunity Commission
Export–Import Bank of the U.S.
Farm Credit Administration
Federal Communications Commission
Federal Deposit Insurance Corporation
Federal Election Commission

Federal Emergency Management Agency
Federal Housing Finance Board
Federal Labor Relations Authority
Federal Maritime Commission
Federal Mediation and Conciliation Service
Federal Mine Safety and Health Review Commission
Federal Reserve System
Federal Retirement Thrift Investment Board
Federal Trade Commission
General Services Administration
Inter-American Foundation
Interstate Commerce Commission
Merit Systems Protection Board
National Aeronautics and Space Administration
National Archives and Records Administration
National Capital Planning Commission

National Credit Union Administration
National Foundation on the Arts and the Humanities
National Labor Relations Board
National Mediation Board
National Railroad Passenger Corporation (Amtrak)
National Science Foundation
National Transportation Safety Board
Nuclear Regulatory Commission
Occupational Safety and Health Review Commission
Office of Government Ethics
Office of Personnel Management
Office of Special Counsel
Panama Canal Commission
Peace Corps
Pennsylvania Avenue Development Commission
Pension Benefit Guaranty Corporation
Postal Rate Commission

Railroad Retirement Board
Resolution Trust Corporation
Securities and Exchange Commission
Selective Service System
Small Business Administration
Tennessee Valley Authority
Thrift Depositor Protection Oversight Board
Trade and Development Agency
U.S. Arms Control and Disarmament Agency
U.S. Information Agency
U.S. International Development Cooperation Agency
U.S. International Trade Commission
U.S. Postal Service

Source: U.S. Department of Commerce, Statistical Abstract of the United States *(Washington, D.C.: U.S. Government Printing Office, 1994), p. 326.*

Her strong policy role has come as no surprise to those who have followed Bill Clinton's career. The couple had worked so closely together in the Arkansas governor's office that the two became known as "Billary." James Carville, Clinton's campaign consultant, described her influence in very clear terms: "If the person that has the last word at night is the same person who has the first word in the morning, they're going to be important. You throw in an IQ of a g'zillion and a backbone of steel, and it's a pretty safe assumption to say this is a person of considerable influence."[19]

Other First Ladies have also played important roles in the presidency. Eleanor Roosevelt was highly public and influential in her husband's presidency from 1933 to 1945. Lady Bird Johnson became a champion of beautifying the nation's highways and cities. Betty Ford and Rosalyn Carter both supported the Equal Rights Amendment. Carter also sat in on cabinet meetings and represented the president in foreign countries, which led some observers to criticize the extent of her power in the White House.

But what made Hillary Clinton different early in her husband's administration was her highly visible policy role. She headed the president's health care task force, and emerged as a key player on a host of other issues. She clearly had the experience and the credentials for the job: she graduated first in her Yale law school class, just ahead of the future president, and was headed for a career in law and public service long before Bill Clinton came along.

Eleanor Roosevelt (left) and Hillary Clinton (right). Two of the most influential First Ladies in history.

The problem with Hillary Clinton's early role was that many Americans simply do not want the First Lady to be a strong policy advisor. They want the First Lady to be gracious, elegant, a wonderful hostess, and even a strong advocate for issues such as highway beautification, children, and the arts. But when it comes to taking strong positions on issues such abortion or health care, some Americans believe the First Lady is better off being seen and not heard. They view the First Lady as something of a national treasure, somehow above the messy business of real politics.

Hillary Clinton will not be the last First Lady to enter office with substantial credentials of her own, however. Indeed, Elizabeth Dole promised to return to her job as president of the American Red Cross whether or not her husband was elected president in 1996. Moreover, it cannot be much longer before America elects its first First Gentleman.

Why the Presidency Changed

The presidency changed for many reasons, not the least of which was the rise of candidate-centered campaigns. Presidents now do things inside the White House—for example, polling and campaign planning—that once were either unnecessary or were the responsibility of the national party committees. Winning reelection, not to mention passing the president's legislative program, means that the White House must often operate like a public relations firm. And, as the president's agenda has grown, so has the firm.

Essential to the change was the public's very high expectations of what the president should do, expectations that have led some political scientists to write of a "cult of the Presidency."[20] The cult celebrated the presidency as the salvation of democracy, a unifying voice in an increasingly complex world.

Evidence of the cult can be found in a host of places, from surveys of children showing that the president was uniformly liked and trusted to college American government textbooks heralding the president as the engine of freedom. In 1964, for example, William Young's *Essentials of American Government* described the president as "without question, the most powerful elected executive in the world . . . (a)nd his power and responsibility are increasing."[21] In 1960, Clinton Rossiter's introductory presidency text described the office in even more glowing terms: "He is, rather, a kind of magnificent lion who can roam widely and do great deeds so long as he does not try to break loose from his broad reservation." Rossiter continued, "He reigns, but he also rules; he symbolizes the people, but he also runs their government."[22]

It is no surprise that the cult blossomed during the 1950s and early 1960s. Soviet nuclear missiles had been deployed in communist Cuba just ninety miles off the Florida coast, the Vietnam War was heating up, and the Berlin Wall dividing East and West Germany had just been built. Americans desperately wanted to believe that somebody was in charge.

The cult of the presidency began to collapse, however, when confronted with the realities of Vietnam and Watergate. The president was not all-knowing after all, nor was the office necessarily the source of democratic integrity.

Even some of the cult's strongest leaders began to doubt their vision of the presidency, perhaps no one more so than historian Arthur Schlesinger. Having written so admiringly of Kennedy's strong presidency in his 1966 best-seller *A Thousand Days,* Schlesinger attacked the Nixon administration in *The Imperial Presidency,* another best-seller just seven years later: "In the last years presidential primacy, so indispensable to the political order, has turned into presidential supremacy. The constitutional presidency—as events so apparently disparate as the [Vietnam] War and the Watergate affair showed—has become the imperial presidency and threatens to be the revolutionary presidency."[23]

The problem all along was that Americans allowed their confidence in *individual presidents* such as Roosevelt and Kennedy to influence their support for a more powerful *institution of the presidency.* The two are not the same thing. The Founders were acutely aware of this fact as they tried to structure the office of the Presidency all the while expecting George Washington, in whom they had complete confidence, to be the first president. Being president is a temporary job. What permanence there is lies in the institution of the presidency, which continues on as a collection of powers, duties, hopes, and expectations regardless of the individual who happens to be president. As such, the presidency was most certainly not the engine of the Founders' government. It was to be just one of three parts of a government that would be just strong enough.

Even though the cult is now mostly dead—witness the high levels of public distrust toward the president—Americans still have a lingering hunger for someone to come to the country's rescue. They still say they would like a strong leader to take charge. These expectations make being president a nearly impossible job. Indeed, Americans seem to know they are asking for too much. When asked "just for fun" at the end of a 1993 *Washington Post*/ABC News poll, "Would you rather serve one term as president or one week in jail?" about half of the respondents opted for a week in the jailhouse rather than four years in the White House.[24]

This does not stop Americans from hoping for some magic figure to somehow take hold of power and fix all that ails the nation. The problem with such public expectations is two-fold: first, as already suggested, the presidency has never had the kind of absolute power needed to meet the public's hopes, and second, the presidency may be even less able today than ever before to convert its limited powers into action.

Making Presidential Decisions

As presidents struggle to meet public expectations, assure their own reelection, win good policy, and find that magical place in history, they face enormous time pressures. As Lyndon Johnson said at the start of his first full term in 1965, "I keep hitting hard because I know this honeymoon won't last. Every day I lose a little more political capital. That's why we have to keep at it, never letting up. One day soon, I don't know when, the critics and the snipers will move in and we will be at stalemate. We have to get all we can now, before the roof comes down."[25]

Cycles that Affect Policy Making.   The pressure to move quickly is shaped by two cycles. The first is called the **cycle of decreasing influence:** Presidents tend to lose public and congressional support over time. The second is called the **cycle of increasing effectiveness:** Presidents almost always get better at their jobs over time.

The cycle of decreasing influence reflects patterns in two basic forms of presidential support: public approval and party seats in Congress. At least for presidents since 1960, public approval tends to be at its highest at or near the start of the first term, falling more or less steadily over the next two years, rebounding in the fourth year with the presidential campaign, and, if the president is reelected, falling again from the fifth year on. Remember, of course, that only one president, Ronald Reagan, among the seven immediately before Bill Clinton actually made it through the full eight years. The ones who did not make it showed consistent declines in approval from the first year onward.[26]

Just because a president's approval is higher at the beginning of the term and lower at the end does not mean it can never go up in between. Drawn on a chart, the general decline is often interrupted by occasional jumps in approval. Presidents almost always get a boost from American military action abroad, even if the action fails. Kennedy got a 5 percent boost in public approval following the failed Bay of Pigs invasion.

The public tends to "rally 'round the flag" during foreign crisis. These **rally points** are particularly strong when military action such as an invasion or bombing is both short and successful. Gerald Ford's approval ratings jumped 11 percent after he sent special troops to rescue the crew of a merchant ship called the Mayaguez, which had been seized by the Cambodian government; George Bush's jumped nearly as much when he ordered U.S. troops into Panama to capture dictator Manuel Noriega. (See Box 8–5 for a sampling of rally points over the past forty years.)

Not all rally points involve foreign crisis, however. Clinton's approval rose immediately following the Oklahoma City bombing, in large part because Americans turned to him for leadership in the crisis. Presidential approval can also rise during periods of great national pride. Reagan's public approval (and reelection chances) jumped during the 1984 Olympic Games as the U.S. won one gold medal after another, in part because the Soviet Union and its Eastern European allies boycotted the event.

The problem with rally points is that they evaporate rather quickly once the crisis eases. Bush's public approval hit 89 percent at the height of the Gulf War in 1991 only to plummet to barely 30 percent eighteen months later. The Gulf War turned out to be rather like a television miniseries that slowly faded from memory as the season wore on. Moreover, as Box 8–5 shows, not all rallies are positive.

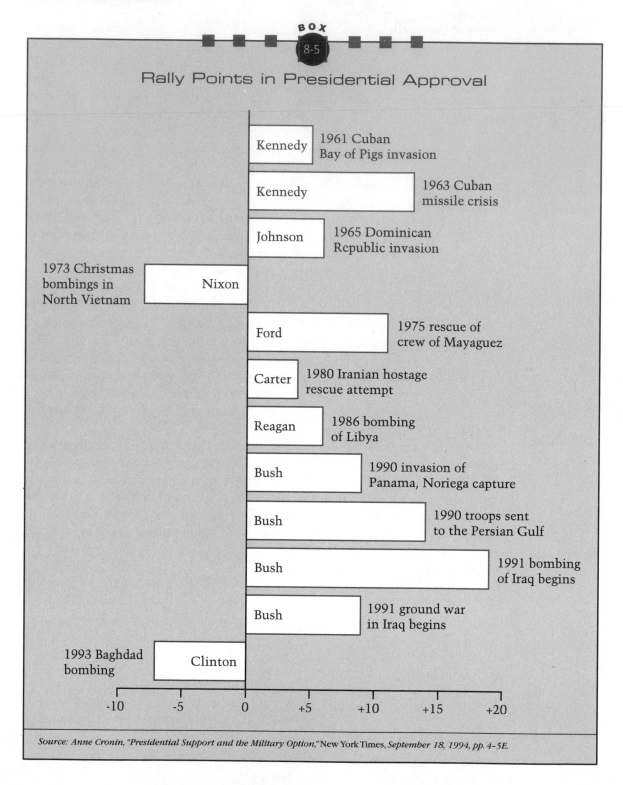

BOX
8-5

Rally Points in Presidential Approval

Kennedy — 1961 Cuban Bay of Pigs invasion

Kennedy — 1963 Cuban missile crisis

Johnson — 1965 Dominican Republic invasion

1973 Christmas bombings in North Vietnam — Nixon

Ford — 1975 rescue of crew of Mayaguez

Carter — 1980 Iranian hostage rescue attempt

Reagan — 1986 bombing of Libya

Bush — 1990 invasion of Panama, Noriega capture

Bush — 1990 troops sent to the Persian Gulf

Bush — 1991 bombing of Iraq begins

Bush — 1991 ground war in Iraq begins

1993 Baghdad bombing — Clinton

-10   -5   0   +5   +10   +15   +20

Source: Anne Cronin, "Presidential Support and the Military Option," New York Times, September 18, 1994, pp. 4–5E.

Alongside the decline in public approval, presidents almost always lose seats in Congress in the midterm elections. Indeed, there have been only two elections since 1862 in which the president's party has gained seats in the House. The worst of the recent defeats came in 1994 when Clinton's Democrats lost fifty-two seats, eclipsing the 1974 election that followed the Watergate scandal when Republicans lost forty-eight seats. Much as members of Congress try to make campaigns about local issues, the midterm elections have traditionally been an opportunity for the public to hold a referendum on the president. Because presidents rarely accomplish all that they promise, the losses are inevitable.

Together, public approval and seats in Congress form the president's **political capital.** As Mondale once described the term, "a president, in my opinion, starts out with a bank full of goodwill and slowly checks are drawn on that, and it's very rare that it's replenished. It's a one-time deposit."[27] Some presidents start with more capital than others—they win by a landslide and their parties have large congressional majorities—but regardless of where they start, political capital almost always goes down. They spend some of it on specific bills and lose some of it when they make mistakes.

Even as presidents tend to lose influence over time, they begin to benefit from the cycle of increasing effectiveness. They steadily become better at their jobs. Just as students in an American government course should know more at the end than at the beginning, presidents know more in the fourth year of the term than in the first. This cycle means that presidents should become more effective at spending their political capital over time. They may have less capital to work with, but should be able to make the most of what they have.

Thus, Bill Clinton was a much better president at the end of 1996 than at the beginning of 1993. He had learned painful lessons about how Congress worked, and reshuffled his White House staff to bring in much greater experience. Out went his old Arkansas friend Thomas "Mac" McLarty as chief of staff, in came former long-time House member Leon Panetta; out went many of the twenty-somethings who came into the White House directly from their first presidential campaign, in came old hands such as former Jimmy Carter legal adviser Lloyd Cutler.

IN A DIFFERENT LIGHT

A NO-WIN PRESIDENCY?

Put together, the two cycles of policy making create a dilemma for a new administration: presidents are most influential when they are least knowledgeable, most knowledgeable when they are least powerful. In a sense, they are in a "no-win" situation. If they move too quickly, they make mistakes; if they move too slowly, they lose momentum. As Clinton adviser George Stephanopoulos argued, "We're always stuck in the small crawl space between 'must win' and 'can't lose.'"[28]

Because presidents are rarely willing to admit they do not know enough about their jobs to make policy decisions and because they face enormous pressure to take advantage of their popularity while they still have it, they tend to pay much more attention to the cycle of decreasing influence. As a result, presidents are tempted to follow five rules at the start of the term: move it or lose it, learning must wait, take the first alternative, avoid details, and reelection comes first.

Move it or lose it. If presidents hope to use what little honeymoon they have, they must set the agenda early and repeat it often. Because this agenda-setting process determines what issues will be at the top of the president's list of concerns, it is the key first step of the policy-making process. If the agenda is not set quickly, Congress will turn its attention to its own list of priorities.

Learning must wait. Presidents do not have time to learn during their first year in office. If they do not know the issues coming into office, they just have to take the staff's word on it. Again, the risk is major policy mistakes. Knowing that the clock was ticking, Clinton pushed his highly complicated national health insurance proposal onto the agenda barely six months into the term, and was criticized even then for being late. With the proposal in tatters by the end of the year, Clinton's advisers privately admitted they should have spent more time working through the details.

Take the first alternative. If presidents have no time to think through innovations, they are pressed to take whatever programs are lying around at the start of the term and call them their own. Thus, much of what presidents propose is merely repackaging of ideas already floating around the Congress. Going with the available ideas is a safe way to get success, but hardly fits a candidate who comes into office promising great change.

Avoid details. The fast-moving president has little time for digging into the details of legislation. The result, again, can be hastily drafted bills that may collapse under close public scrutiny. Yet, presidents who stop to read the details either slow the process down or burn out. The less reading the president does, the better.

Reelection comes first. As presidents survey their territory after their first inauguration, most are struck by the remarkably short amount of time they truly have. The first year is for setting the agenda and appointing the key staff and department officers, the second for a tough midterm election, the third and fourth for reelection. And even if they win a second term, presidents have at best a year to a year and a half before the media and Congress start talking about the next presidential election. As such, presidents are "lame ducks," or powerless, by the end of their sixth year in office.[29]

THE CHANGING TACTICS OF PRESIDENTIAL LEADERSHIP

Contrary to the cult of the presidency, the world does not live on presidential leadership alone. The country has survived weak presidents as well as strong ones, dishonest presidents as well as honest ones. Congress has passed legislation under a government divided between the two parties and under a government unified.

As political scientist Charles Jones argues, there are very real dangers in exaggerating the importance of presidential leadership: "The natural inclination is to make the president responsible for policies and political events that no one can claim a legitimate right to control. Presidents are well advised to resist this invitation to assume a position of power as though it conveyed authority. Rather they need to identify and define their political capital, and must do so repeatedly in a search for the limits of their influence."[30]

Despite Jones's advice, recent presidents have followed the more tempting course. They have fought the decline of the parties, the increasing complexity of Congress, and the changing nature of public opinion through two leadership tactics that emphasize their personal skills to a far greater degree than ever before: the first is their increasing use of the power to persuade and the second is the tendency to "go public" on issues that once would have been negotiated with Congress.

The Power to Persuade

The president's constitutional powers guarantee very little by way of real power. As Lyndon Johnson once remarked, "you can tell a man to go to hell, but you can't make him go."[31] Johnson simply believed that a president's constitutional powers guarantee little by way of actual influence, and he was right. The president's constitutional powers add up to little more than a job as America's most distinguished office clerk. It is a president's ability to persuade others that spells the difference between being a clerk and being a national leader.[32] And that power to persuade resides in two places: resources and skills.

Lyndon Johnson takes a breather after leading a legislative fight as Senate Majority Leader in the 1950s. Lyndon Johnson used his legislative skills in becoming one of the most persuasive presidents in recent American history.

Presidential Resources. A president has two kinds of resources for using the power to persuade: external (meaning political capital) and internal (meaning time, energy, and information). As noted above, the president's political capital is composed of public approval and party seats in Congress, and gets spent over time.

Not only does political capital lead Congress to pay attention to what the president says, it helps enhance a president's reputation for influence. The more the president is seen as powerful, the more the president will actually be powerful. Just as sports teams try to "psych out" their opponents, presidents try to psych out Congress.

A president's power to persuade also rests on three internal resources: time, energy, and information. Presidents cannot make their case without some of each. The first two internal resources, time and energy, run out over the term and are difficult to replace. Unlike members of Congress, presidents have only so much time to make their mark. Since they can only serve for two consecutive terms, and since they are lame ducks by the end of the sixth year, they must make every day count.

In a similar vein, presidents and their staffs have only so much energy to give. As Gerald Ford remarked, "It's a hard job being President. . . . Anybody who walks in there thinking he can punch a time clock at 9 in the morning and leave at 5 has got another thought coming. We do not elect Presidents who want that kind of a life." While 300-pound William Howard Taft could nap three hours each afternoon in 1910, today's president simply cannot rest. Nor can the president's staff. Johnson apparently considered it something close to treason for a staff member to spend Sundays with his or her family.[33]

Even as presidents lose time and energy, they tend to gain information. They learn more about their jobs and the issues, and almost always leave office smarter than they entered. In a sense, the presidency is the nation's most intense American government course. One way presidents can increase their learning is to take "prerequisites" before entering office—that is, by holding offices such as the vice presidency or a governorship that are similar to being president or by studying issues as a senator or member of the House that are central to the president's constitutional duties.

Presidential Skills. A president's raw personal ability to lobby, persuade, convince, argue, and plead are clearly important to ultimate success. However, those skills can never be a substitute for political capital.[34] A president who enters office with low public approval and a party minority on Capitol Hill will always be less persuasive than one who enters with high approval and a strong majority.

But skills are hardly irrelevant to a president's success either, especially in a Congress filled with mavericks and entrepreneurs. Perhaps no skill is more important for converting scarce political capital into legislative success than the ability to focus public and congressional attention on the president's top priorities. This **focusing skill** consists of two specific tactics: timing and lobbying. The first part of focusing is timing, which involves a president's ability to set the legislative agenda early in the term, while avoiding unnecessary delays caused by overloading in key congressional committees and unproductive controversy.[35]

The second part of focusing is lobbying pressure. The president must make his or her priorities known and keep the pressure on. As Lyndon Johnson argued, "Merely placing a bill before Congress is not enough. Without constant attention from the administration, most legislation moves through the congressional process at the speed of a glacier."[36] Presidents can offer a number of rewards for their allies on Capitol Hill, not the least of which are invitations to elegant events called state dinners and special White House tours for a favored member's constituents. More tangibly, presidents still have a great say about where their party invests its campaign money, and a presidential visit back home can spell the difference between a candidate's victory or defeat in the next election.

Whatever the tactic, the purpose of focusing is to let the public and Congress know what the president wants, to make sure the list of priorities is not too long, and to keep the pressure on. Presidents who focus attention can make their political capital go farther—rather like shopping with coupons.

Going Public

One of the reasons presidents spend so much time these days measuring public opinion is that they are much more willing to "go public" in the contest with Congress. One way to build a fire on Capitol Hill in favor of the president's program is to light a match in the congressional districts. Going public simply means that the president is doing the talking in the congressional districts instead of the individual members of Congress.

Presidents have been communicating with the public from the very beginning of the Republic, when presidents even created their own newspapers to communicate their policies. What is different today is that presidents are communicating much more often and for a very different purpose: to light a fire under Congress.[37]

There is no question that recent presidents are going public more frequently. They are making more prime-time television appearances, giving more speeches, and spending more time out of the White House. According to Samuel Kernell, the number of major and minor presidential addresses has grown from just a dozen or so in the first three years of the Hoover administration (1929–1931) to well over a hundred in the first three years of the Bush presidency almost sixty years later. The greatest growth came in the number of minor addresses before specialized audiences—trade associations, college graduations, advocacy groups.

According to Kernell, the number of public appearances has also jumped significantly. Whereas Herbert Hoover made barely two dozen appearances in his first two years, George Bush made over 150. Travel outside Washington is also up. During his first three years, Hoover was barely out of town for one week total; Bush, in contrast, spent nearly ten weeks out of Washington, including frequent travel abroad.[38] Part of the reason for the increase in travel involves declining trust in government—presidents cannot afford to be seen as Washington insiders and sometimes travel just to get media exposure outside the interstate beltway that surrounds the capital city. Of course, the paradox is that knowledge of Washington is essential if a president is going to get anything done. Thus, the most successful president is likely to be an insider who looks like an outsider.

The advantage of going public is simple: The president gets to control the setting and the content, deciding who gets to attend and what he or she will say. Given this desire for greater control, it is not surprising that presidents have cut back on their press conferences. Whereas Franklin Roosevelt held almost seven press conferences a month during his twelve years in office, Reagan, Bush, and Clinton (at least through 1994) averaged barely one per month.[39]

The reason for the sharp decline in the number of presidential press conferences may be simple. Presidents have much greater control over the news if they, not reporters, set the agenda. And the rise of the new media—CNN, C-SPAN, MTV, and so forth—gives them outlets beyond the traditional television networks and newspapers. They would much rather meet with the local press outside Washington than inside, much rather give exclusive interviews than face a roomful of unpredictable reporters, and much rather use live satellite feeds to remote stations to get their message across than deal with the *Washington Post, New York Times,* or *Wall Street Journal.*

Going public clearly fits with changes in the electoral process. Presidents now have the staff, the technology, and the public opinion research to tell them how to target the message and the nearly instant media access to go public easily. And, as elections have become more image-oriented and candidate-centered, presidents have the incentive to use these tools to operate a permanent White House campaign. Unable to count on their party to deliver the voters, presidents go public because it is one of the few strategies that promises success. Presidents are still welcome to bargain and persuade, to focus congressional attention and twist arms, but members of Congress may only pay attention with pressure coming from the voters back home.

IN A DIFFERENT LIGHT

WHITE HOUSE POLLING

Public opinion polls are playing an increasingly important role in the presidential policy process. Presidents now have instant access to virtually every poll taken in the country. Indeed, according to political scientists Lawrence Jacobs and Robert Shapiro, the White House has become a "veritable warehouse of polling."[40] The fascination with polls is easy to understand. Nothing is more important to going public than public opinion polls because polls tell the president exactly where to go and what to say.

Although the presidential fascination with public opinion polls can be traced all the way back to Dwight Eisenhower in the 1950s, it was Richard Nixon who established many of the precedents that persist to this day. It was Nixon, for example, who began using secret polls in 1969 to make key presidential choices, including whether to pardon Lieutenant William Calley of war crimes committed during the Vietnam War.

Nixon was also a trendsetter in hiring special White House advisers to monitor public opinion. Instead of just tracking the latest numbers from Gallup or Harris, Nixon's survey research experts conducted secret surveys for his eyes only. It was Nixon who began using tracking polls to follow day-to-day movement in candidate standing, a practice that is now common in almost all campaigns. And it was Nixon who established the first Office of Communications to house his polling operation, an office that remains one of the most important in shaping the president's message.

The Founders might ask just how presidents use the polling information. Do presidents make the hard choices first and then use polls to shape a persuasive message, or measure the opinion and then take the most popular option? The first is a form of presidential leadership, the second a form of direct democracy that would worry the Founders greatly. There is growing evidence that presidents increasingly measure the opinion first, and only then make the decision.

Beyond creating a kind of direct democracy based on polling, the damage from paying too much attention to the latest tracking polls is two-fold. First, presidents can end up moving back and forth from one policy position to another as the winds of opinion change. This flip-flopping is especially likely on fast-changing issues such as U.S. involvement in the 1991 Gulf War. Moreover, the less the public knows about an issue, the more likely opinions will change rapidly.

Second, presidents can lose track of the big picture as they watch their daily approval ratings move up and down like a stock market. Caught in a tidal surge of polling information, presidents may end up taking the easy way out of tough questions. Public opinion leads the president instead of the president leading the public. Although it is always tempting to tell the public what it wants to hear, leadership sometimes involves telling the public just the opposite. Having the polling numbers easily available can tempt presidents to ignore the national interest by favoring one faction of Americans over another.

■ ■ ■

CONCLUSION

The Presidency has never had the power needed to satisfy the cult of the presidency. Although the Founders certainly wanted something stronger than the executive under the Articles of Confederation, they saw the presidency as part of a government that would be strong enough to answer foreign and domestic threats, but not so strong as to ever threaten liberty. As such, the presidency was an essential part of the Founders' government that would be just strong enough.

Yet, there is ample evidence that the presidency has lost ground over the past decades, in part because the government has become so much more complicated. Presidents tend to believe that adding more staff offices and political appointees will somehow strengthen their leadership in these difficult times.

The idea that more leaders equals more leadership is evident throughout the president's advisory system. In 1960, for example, Kennedy's budget office had just three levels of political appointees: a director, a deputy director, and eight assistant directors. By 1996, Clinton's budget office had eight levels: a director, a principal deputy director, a deputy director for management, two excecutive associate directors, eight associate directors, twelve deputy associate directors, four assistant directors, and three deputy assistant directors. Similar thickening occurred in every corner of the White House, from the president's personal staff to the Office of the Vice President. In 1960, there was no Office of the Vice President at all. By 1996, the office had five levels and nearly 100 staff.

However, the strength of a president's leadership is not likely to be found in the number of polls conducted or the number of appointees hired to help the president or oversee the executive branch. Nor is it likely to emerge from a president's focusing skill, management style, or seating chart. Rather, a president's leadership rests in the clarity of his or her vision, the articulation of cause, and the value produced by what government does. Leadership is in action, not in the simple perks of office. As such, a president's leadership might be strong with fewer polls, less going public, and a thinner staff. And it most certainly resides in setting reasonable expectations for the public. No president is going to be able to solve all the nation's problems, feel all the nation's pains, or answer all the nation's prayers. To expect so is to reject the Founders' design for a government just strong enough.

Presidents face a simple choice in bridging the gap between expectation and reality that exists in today's presidency. They can either adopt the rules outlined earlier in this chapter—move it or lose it, learning must wait, take the first alternative, and so forth—or they can embrace the reality that America has a system of separate institutions sharing power and a government that would be just strong enough to meet foreign and domestic threats without becoming so strong as to threaten individual liberty.

This second course suggests a much more cautious form of presidential leadership. As Charles Jones argues, newly elected presidents can start by acknowledging that learning comes *first,* knowing their strengths and weaknesses, paying far less attention to the monthly public approval polls, and, most importantly, recognizing that there is a Congress. "Solo triumphs for presidents in the separate system are, and should be, rare."[41]

If presidents take Jones's advice, and there is much in this chapter that argues they should, Americans will simply have to adjust their expectations and figure out ways of solving more of their problems on their own. This does not mean Congress and the president can never help—there is a far greater potential for shared success if presidents help the public understand that the Founders wanted a government just strong enough, not one that would solve every problem and answer every want.

THE BASICS

■ The Founders created a single, independent executive to do three basic jobs: (1) execute the laws, (2) represent the nation as a whole, and (3) check the Congress from becoming too powerful. The Founders clearly wanted an executive that was stronger than the weak state and federal executives that had followed the Revolutionary War. The more the Founders talked about the presidency over the summer of 1787, the stronger the presidency became. Alexander Hamilton was a key advocate for strengthening the presidency, arguing for energy in the executive.

■ The presidency has a shorter, less detailed list of duties than the Congress. Nevertheless, the list of express powers gives the president substantial executive and lawmaking duties. The president's executive duties involve a role as commander in chief, negotiator in chief, and administrator in chief, while the president's legislative duties involve responsibility for reporting on the state of the union and checking Congress through the veto power.

■ The president's veto power resides in Article I on Congress. Under that power, the president has ten days (excluding Sundays) to sign the bill, veto the bill, or do nothing. If the ten-day clock runs out before Congress adjourns, bills not signed by the president automatically become law. If, however, the ten-day clock runs out after Congress adjourns, bills not signed are automatically killed under a pocket veto.

■ George Washington set a number of precedents for the presidency that hold to this day. He assembled the first White House staff and appointed nationally respected leaders as his department secretaries. Washington also established the president's authority to supervise the executive branch.

■ The presidency today is a complicated institution, composed of leadership, advisory offices, and staff.

■ The leadership of the presidency is both simple and complex—simple because there is only one leader, the president, that matters, complex because the president gets so much advice on what to do. The Executive Office of the President is the nerve center of the presidency, and the president is the nerve center of the EOP.

■ The president's advisory offices are organized into political and policy duties. The political offices help support the president's goals of winning reelection, lobbying Congress, or reaching out to the nation, while the policy offices help develop ideas for economic, domestic, and foreign policy. In general, the political offices are part of the White House Office, and can be organized and reorganized as the president wishes. The policy offices are established by law, meaning Congress has a say in how they work.

■ The president has three sources of staff advice for making key decisions and executing the laws: (1) an inner circle of intimate advisers that includes the chief of staff, vice president, and first lady; (2) the White House staff that centers on the sixty or so aides who are handpicked for their loyalty; and (3) the Cabinet that is composed of the heads of the fourteen departments of government.

KEY CONCEPTS

■ Congress and the presidency share a number of duties, including executive and lawmaking powers. The president commands the armed forces, but Congress declares war; Congress writes the laws, but the president helps set the agenda and has the veto power. It is best to think of Congress and the presidency as separate institutions sharing power. Over the years, the balance between Congress and the presidency has ebbed and flowed. Congress has recently tried to constrain the president's war-making power through the War Powers Resolution and the president's budget-making dominance through the Budget and Impoundment Control Act.

■ One reason the presidency has become more complex is that the public expects so much from the occupant. Some scholars use the term "cult of the presidency" as a way of talking about how much the public expects from their presidents. The cult views the presidency as the most important branch of government and as a source of great leadership for the nation and world. The cult emerged in the 1950s

as America faced a much more dangerous world. Although the cult collapsed as a result of the Vietnam War and Watergate, Americans still expect great leadership from the White House, making being president a mission impossible.

■ Presidential policy making is governed by two basic cycles. The cycle of decreasing influence reflects the erosion of the president's political capital over the term, while the cycle of increasing effectiveness reflects the steady growth in the president's ability to do the job.

■ A president's influence does not rest in the formal powers of the Constitution, but in the power to persuade. This ability to convince Congress and the public of the rightness of a cause rests, in turn, in the president's resources and skills. In recent years, presidents have been "going public" as part of building public support for their programs. Instead of allowing members of Congress to interpret their proposals, presidents are increasingly going to key districts to make their case in person.

IN A DIFFERENT LIGHT

■ Alongside their goals of reelection, good policy, and personal commitments, presidents also seek a place in history. Earning a high ranking from historians and political scientists involves a mix of leadership skills, crisis management, legislative accomplishments, political skills, and character. Those who make the top of the list of great presidents tend to have been involved in wars or leading the nation through crises. Franklin Roosevelt is among the very top presidents because he is generally considered the first modern president—he influenced the inside of the presidency through creation of the EOP, and the outside by giving government a powerful role in influencing the economy.

■ The First Lady has become the first advisor, that is, a significant source of policy advice. Although First Ladies have always had an important role as part of the president's inner circle, no one has done more to elevate the visibility of that job than Hillary Clinton. The problem is that many Americans do not seem comfortable having a First Lady be anything other than ladylike. The question is whether the backlash will continue long into the future, and whether it will apply to the first First Gentleman.

■ Under the cycles of presidential policy making, presidents are most influential when they are least experienced, and most experienced when they are generally least influential. Hence, they are in a "no-win" presidency. Given a choice between waiting to learn or taking advantage of their limited political capital, presidents tend to follow a set of simple rules for succeeding in today's policymaking process: (1) move it or lose it, (2) learning must wait, (3) take the first alternative, (4) avoid details, and (5) reelection comes first.

■ Recent presidents have built an impressive polling empire inside the White House. They have never been more in touch with the public pulse. The problem appears to be that presidents are making more decisions on the basis of what the public wants, which means that they may be following public opinion more than leading it. The question is whether such attention to the public is good for making the tough choices that face the nation today.

OPEN QUESTIONS

■ Just what is it about the presidency that makes it part of the Founders' government that would be just strong enough? What are the checks on presidential power that make the job so difficult? And what can a president do, if anything, to be more effective in office?

■ Do Americans expect too much from the presidency today? Do they understand how limited the duties of the presidency are? Would it make sense for presidents to make an effort to explain their jobs better to the public? Can any president succeed given the complexity of the job and the competing cycles that appear to govern the term? Would it make sense to go back to the plural executive that the Founders once wanted?

■ Does the president get too much advice? Does the White House staff make presidents think that they are truly the engine of democracy? To what extent do all the people who serve the president build up the public's hope that the president will solve all their problems?

...TERMS TO REMEMBER

presidential ticket

impeachment

executive agreements

take care clause

legislative agenda

State of the Union Address

pocket veto

War Powers Resolution

Budget and Impoundment Control Act

institutional presidency

Executive Office of the President (EOP)

chief of staff

inner circle

White House staff

cabinet

cycle of decreasing influence

cycle of increasing effectiveness

rally points

political capital

focusing skill

Endnotes to Chapter 8

1. Roy P. Fairfield, ed., *The Federalist Papers* (Baltimore: Johns Hopkins University Press, 1981), p. 198.

▶ 2. See Sidney Milkis and Michael Nelson, *The American Presidency: Origins and Development, 1776–1990* (CQ Press, 1990), pp. 30–31, for a discussion of this key decision.

▶ 3. Richard Pious, *The American Presidency* (New York: Basic Books, 1978), p. 29.

4. This history of presidential powers draws heavily on Milkis and Nelson, *The American Presidency.*

▶ 5. Richard Neustadt, *Presidential Power,* second edition (New York: Free Press, 1990).

6. See James Sundquist, *The Decline and Resurgence of Congress* (Washington, DC: Brookings Institution, 1981).

7. See Bruce Miroff, "The Presidency and the Public: Leadership as a Spectacle," in M. Nelson, ed., *The Presidency and the Political System* (Washington, DC: Congressional Quarterly, 1988).

8. See Stephen J. Wayne, "Great Expectations: What People Want from Presidents," in Thomas Cronin, ed., *Rethinking the Presidency* (Boston: Little, Brown, 1982).

▶ 9. For a discussion of different kinds of modern presidents, see Fred I. Greenstein, ed., *Leadership in the Modern Presidency* (Cambridge, MA: Harvard University Press, 1988).

10. Personal conversation with the author, 1993.

11. See Irving Janis, *Groupthink* (Boston: Houghton Mifflin, 1982).

▶ 12. See Graham Allison, *Essence of Decision: Explaining the Cuban Missile Crisis* (Boston: Little, Brown, 1971).

13. For a history of many of these offices, see Charles E. Walcott and Karen M. Hult, *Governing the White House: From Hoover through LBJ* (Lawrence, KS: University of Kansas Press, 1995).

14. See John A. Maltese, *Spin Control: The White House Office of Communications and the Management of Presidential News,* second edition (Chapel Hill, NC: University of North Carolina Press, 1994).

15. John Hart, *The Presidential Branch from Washington to Clinton* (Chatham, NJ: Chatham House, 1994), p. 68.

16. Quoted in Paul Light, *Vice Presidential Power: Advice and Influence in the White House* (Baltimore: Johns Hopkins University Press, 1984), p. 12.

17. John Podhoretz, "Little Shop of Horrors," *The Washingtonian,* November 1993, p. 52.

18. Milkis and Nelson, *The American Presidency,* p. 74.

19. Maureen Dowd, "Hillary Clinton's Debut Dashes Doubts on Clout," *New York Times,* February 8, 1993, p. A10.

20. See Thomas Cronin, *The State of the Presidency* (Boston: Little, Brown, 1980).

21. William Young, *Essentials of American Government,* ninth edition, (New York: Appleton-Century-Crofts, 1964), p. 251.

22. Clinton Rossiter, *The American Presidency,* revised edition (New York: New American Library, 1960), p. 250, 84, 68–69, 17; in Cronin, *The State of the Presidency,* pp. 28–29.

23. Arthur Schlesinger, *The Imperial Presidency* (New York: Popular Library, 1973), p. 10.

24. Richard Morin, "Vox Populi," *Washington Post National Weekly Edition,* July 5–11, 1993, p. 37.

25. Quoted in Jack Valenti, *A Very Human President* (New York: W. W. Norton, 1975), p. 144.

26. Howard W. Stanley and Richard G. Niemi, *Vital Statistics on American Politics* (Washington, DC: CQ Press, 1995), p. 261.

27. Quoted in Paul Light, *The President's Agenda: Domestic Policy Choice from Kennedy to Carter,* second edition (Baltimore: Johns Hopkins University Press, 1991), p. 13.

28. Quoted by Elizabeth Drew, *On the Edge: The Clinton Presidency* (New York: Touchstone, 1994), p. 345.

29. This list is modified from Light, *The President's Agenda,* pp. 217–22.

▶ 30. Charles O. Jones, *The Presidency in a Separated System* (Washington, DC: Brookings Institution, 1994), p. 281.

31. Lyndon Johnson, *The Vantage Point: Perspectives on the Presidency, 1963–1969* (New York: Holt, Rinehart & Winston, 1971), p. 461.

32. The term "power to persuade" is from Neustadt, *Presidential Power,* p. 7.

33. Doris Kearns, *Lyndon Johnson and the American Dream* (New York: Harper and Row, 1976), p. 252.

34. See George Edwards, *Presidential Influence in Congress* (San Francisco: W. H. Freeman, 1980), p. 202.

35. See Paul Light, "The Focusing Skill and Presidential Influence in Congress," in C. Deering, *Congressional Politics* (Homewood, IL: Dorsey Press, 1989), p. 256.

36. Johnson, *The Vantage Point,* p. 448.

37. See Jeffrey Tulis, *The Rhetorical Presidency* (Princeton, NJ: Princeton University Press, 1987).

38. Samuel Kernell, *Going Public* (Washington, DC: CQ Press, 1993), pp. 92, 102.

39. Stanley and Niemi, *Vital Statistics,* p. 53.

40. Lawrence Jacobs and Robert Shapiro, "Disorganized Democracy: The Institutionalization of Polling and Public Opinion Analysis during the Kennedy, Johnson, and Nixon Presidencies," paper presented at the annual meetings of the American Political Science Association, New York, New York, September 1–4, 1994, p. 3.

41. Jones, *The Presidency in a Separated System,* p. 295.

THE FEDERAL BUREAUCRACY

CHAPTER

9

The **federal bureaucracy** is composed of fourteen departments, eleven independent regulatory commissions, sixty agencies, three to four dozen government corporations, and almost two million full-time employees, but exists for one purpose: deliver on the promises that others make. Although its primary job is to help the president execute the laws, the federal bureaucracy also helps make the laws by providing information to Congress.

Nevertheless, the Founders did not spend much time worrying about the administrative structure of government. They most certainly knew the new executive branch would have departments and officers (otherwise why give the president the power to require the written opinions of the officers of government?), and believed the bureaucracy would be "a complicated piece of machinery,"[1] but left the fine print to the First Congress and the first presidency nonetheless.

The federal bureaucracy was the least of the Founders' worries as they struggled to draft the Constitution. On the one hand, they saw the day-to-day operation of government to be far less controversial than the balance of power among the three branches. On the other hand, they most certainly expected the new government bureaucracy to be small. The new government would hardly have the

A Complicated Piece of Machinery

money to pay off its Revolutionary War debt, let alone hire large numbers of employees.

Two hundred years later, the federal bureaucracy is anything but small. It is a $1.5 trillion, 2 million employee operation, with "outlets" across the nation. It owns trillions of acres of land—parks, military bases, and forests—and occupies more square feet of office space than any single corporation in the world. As for those who criticize the "bureaucrats in Washington," only one out of ten federal employees work in the nation's capitol; the rest work in regional and local offices, including every state of the union, from a few thousand in South Dakota to over 250,000 in California.

Unlike the Founders, Americans have plenty to say about the federal bureaucracy. Roughly 70 percent of Americans believe that almost anything run by the federal bureaucracy is bound to be inefficient and wasteful,[2] that the federal bureaucracy controls too much of their daily lives and is much too large and powerful, that dealing with a federal agency is often not worth the trouble, and that big bureaucracy in general is the biggest threat to the country's future.[3] Little wonder that public administration scholar Charles Goodsell describes bureaucracy as a great "hate object."[4]

Yet, Americans like much of what bureaucracy delivers—from smoother roads to benefit checks, environmental protection to national defense. Americans will

Applying for Food Stamps, which is a welfare program that helps poor people. Americans vastly overestimate how much money the federal government spends on welfare. They also overestimate the number of minorities on welfare. The majority of welfare recipients are white.

probably never come to love the Internal Revenue Service agent who collects their taxes, but most report high levels of satisfaction whenever they meet the federal bureaucracy face to face. And they appear to want more of virtually everything government does, even if it costs money. Ask Americans if they support a constitutional amendment requiring the federal government to balance its budget and overwhelming numbers of them will say "yes." Ask them if they support the amendment if it means cutting popular programs such as Social Security and almost half will change their minds and vote "no."[5]

The rest of this chapter will provide an introduction to the federal bureaucracy at three levels. First, it will look back to the Founders' imagined bureaucracy, asking just what the Founders had in mind as they mostly ignored the bureaucracy in their constitutional debates. Second, it will examine the real federal bureaucracy, showing how Congress and the presidency shaped the first bureaucracy and providing a broad introduction to the institutional bureaucracy of today. This second section will also ask whether the federal bureaucracy is too big. Third, the chapter will provide an inventory of how Congress and the presidency seek to control the federal bureaucracy.

THE IMAGINED BUREAUCRACY

The Founders never used the word *bureaucracy* to describe the executive branch—the term was invented by sociologists in the late 1800s. But they most certainly knew something about administering programs. George Washington had run the Continental Army, and many of his colleagues at the Constitutional Convention had run banks, businesses, and farms. Most would not have been in Philadelphia had they not been at least moderately successful at running organizations of one kind or another.

Nevertheless, as already noted, the Founders devoted little time to discussing the federal bureaucracy. There is some evidence that the Founders simply expected Congress to establish the same departments that had existed under the Articles of Confederation, which is precisely what Congress did in creating the Departments of State, War, and Treasury in 1789.[6] There is also some evidence that the Founders expected good administration to flow naturally from the same virtue and wisdom that they hoped would characterize America's first elected leaders.

Whatever the reason, the federal bureaucracy remains American government's undefined branch, but one with great duties nonetheless. Before turning to those duties, it is first useful to consider two key decisions that reveal at least some of the Founders' intentions on just who was to run the future bureaucracy.

The Undefined Branch

The federal bureaucracy may have been mostly undefined by the Constitutional Convention, but the Founders did make two decisions that continue to shape the bureaucracy today. Both decisions reinforced the president's responsibility for executing the laws.

First, the Founders clearly decided not to allow members of the House and Senate to hold executive branch positions. They drew a very sharp line on the issue in Article I, Section 6 of the Constitution: "No Senator or Representative shall, during the Time for which he was elected, be appointed to any civil Office under the Authority of the United States, which shall have been created, or the Emoluments whereof shall have been increased during such time, and no Person holding any Office under the United States, shall be a Member of either House during his Continuance in Office." The provision prevented members of Congress from creating jobs for themselves in the executive branch, a common form of corruption in England prior to the Revolutionary War.[7] The Founders also worried that simultaneous service in both branches would weaken the separation of powers.

Second, the Founders decided not to give Congress the power to appoint the treasurer of the United States (now called the secretary of the treasury). For much of the summer of 1787, appointing the treasurer was first on the list of the legislature's express powers, reflecting the convention's deep concern about the financial stability of the new nation. It was not until the third to last working day of the convention that the Founders deleted the provision in an effort to reaffirm the president's authority to supervise the officers of government.

Despite their limited debate, the Founders clearly wanted public administration to be efficient. Part of having a government strong enough to protect the nation as a whole and American citizens as individuals was to make sure that the departments and agencies worked well. The Founders obviously had a very high tolerance for frustration in the making of public policy, where they wanted ambition to counteract ambition. But they had no such plans for what would become the federal bureaucracy. Once the laws were written, they were to be executed faithfully and efficiently.

The Duties of Bureaucracy

By not naming any of the departments in the Constitution, the Founders left the future of bureaucracy up to Congress and the presidency. Congress would authorize the departments and agencies of government, determine which presidential appointments would be subject to Senate confirmation, and appropriate the money to act. Only then could the president order those departments and agencies to work. Thus, the duties of the federal bureaucracy are not to be found in the Constitution but in the individual laws that describe who gets what, when, and how from government; laws that also say just where in government a program will be run.

As the laws have accumulated over the years, the federal bureaucracy has become a vast enterprise. It runs the national parks and national forests, watches hurricanes, and helps small businesses get started. It operates the air traffic control system, oversees the stock markets, collects the national census every ten years, and issues crop forecasts. It enforces laws for cleaning up the air and water, investigates and prosecutes a host of federal crimes such as kidnapping and counterfeiting, and provides the first line of defense against viruses like ebola and HIV. It helps prevent accidents on the job, protects workers and citizens from toxic chemicals, runs a national railroad, and writes checks to millions upon millions of Americans, including 35 million Social Security recipients.

Even though it is sometimes less efficient than the private sector, its responsibilities are almost always greater. Federal Express is faster with overnight packages in part because it does not have to deliver everywhere, a requirement only the U.S. Postal Service must meet. Congress often sets other requirements that make bureaucracy less efficient than it might otherwise be, not the least of which is that government must be fair in its decisions about who it helps.

By leaving the duties of bureaucracy to the future, the Founders assured that Congress and the presidency would create the bureaucracy one department and agency at a time. The result is that the bureaucracy can often look hopelessly confused. The Department of Agriculture runs the national forests, but the Department of Interior runs the national parks; the Department of Health and Human Services runs Aid to Families with Dependent Children (a cash assistance program for poor families) but the Department of Agriculture runs Food Stamps (a program that gives those same families coupons to buy food). By 1995, the federal bureaucracy had 163 separate job training programs located in 55 different departments or agencies, 90 early childhood programs located in 31 places (the Department of Health and Human Services ran 28, the Department of Education ran 34), and 35 food safety laws administered in 12 different agencies.[8]

IN A DIFFERENT LIGHT

IS BUREAUCRACY UNRESPONSIVE?

The federal bureaucracy may have grown so large and complex over the decades that it has lost touch with the public. With employees spread out in thousands of offices across the country, the federal bureaucracy may be so big that no one can truly know everything it is doing, least of all the public. Moreover, as the sole provider of essential services such as national defense, it will stay in business whether citizens like what it does or not.

Reformers argue that there are two ways to make the federal bureaucracy more responsive to the public. The first is to expose the bureaucracy to market pressure by converting some of its services into private businesses (privatization) or by having the bureaucracy compete with private businesses to deliver the same services. In theory, the market should make the federal bureaucracy more sensitive to its customers, the citizens of the United States. Although the idea has worked at the local level of government where cities have privatized everything from garbage collection to city jails, some federal services simply cannot be privatized. It is difficult to imagine the chaos created by having a private army, air force, and navy, for example.

A second way to make the federal bureaucracy more responsive to the public is to make it look like the public. By creating a **representative bureaucracy,** at least in terms of race and gender, the federal bureaucracy increases the chances that it will have some connection to the people it serves.

There is no question that the face of the federal bureaucracy has changed over the past two decades. There have never been more women and minorities in federal jobs. Women accounted for 43 percent of all federal jobs in 1990, while minorities comprised over 27 percent of the federal workforce.[9]

Even though the number of women and minorities in the federal workforce had increased by 1990, there are two other problems with creating a representative bureaucracy. First, women and minorities are not equally represented across all departments and agencies. Women and minorities tend to concentrate in departments with strong social service missions such as Education, Health and Human Services, Housing and Urban Development, and Veterans Affairs (which runs the VA hospital system and its mostly female nursing corps), all of which have more than 50 per-

The changing face of the bureaucracy. Minorities hold 27 percent of all federal jobs, but only a very small percent of the very top posts. Here, a federal worker checks newly printed U.S. currency for the U.S. Mint.

cent women. Military and technical departments such as Defense, Energy, NASA, and Transportation have far less. Health and Human Services has 65 percent women, while transportation has just 25 percent; 50 percent of the Department of Education's employees are minorities, compared to just 16 percent of Agriculture.

Second, women and minorities are not represented at all levels of the federal system. Women held roughly 35 percent of all professional and administrative jobs in 1990, where the higher paying management posts are, but 70 percent of the lower paying technical and clerical positions. Minorities were also heavily represented in the lower paying jobs. Together, women and minorities held almost half the jobs at the bottommost level of the federal pay system in 1990, and just 10 percent of the posts at the top.[10] Thus, if the federal bureaucracy is to become more representative, it has a very long way to go.

THE REAL BUREAUCRACY

There is no question that the federal bureaucracy is larger than the Founders could have ever imagined. The federal bureaucracy has grown from a handful of clerks to a complicated network of public and private employees who work to administer the laws.

The Founders might be surprised to find, for example, that not all federal jobs are done by federal employees.[11] In all, there may be as many as four private employees under contract to the federal government for every one public employee on the federal payroll. Private contractors build the airplanes and ships for the Department of Defense, program the computers for Commerce and Treasury, run welfare programs for the Department of Health and Human Services, prepare the space shuttle for NASA, and operate America's nuclear weapons plants for the Department of Energy.

The Founders might also be surprised to discover just how active the federal government is in American life. There is hardly a minute that goes by when Americans do not have direct or indirect contact with government, most of it for the good.

This is not to say that the Founders would recoil at the size and scope of today's federal bureaucracy. They knew society would become more complex, and fully expected Congress to write laws on a host of emerging issues. Nor is it to say that the Founders would think government is too big. They might note that many organizations in American society have gotten bigger over time, including state and local bureaucracies and private companies. (See Boxes 9–1 and 9–2 for two ways of looking at the size of the federal bureaucracy).

**BOX
9-1**

Comparing Federal Departments and Private Corporations by Size of Budget/Sales

Rank	Corporation/Department	Sales/Budget*
1.	Department of Health and Human Services	$399.8
2.	Department of Defense	318.3
3.	Department of the Treasury	230.6
4.	General Motors Corporation	126.9
5.	Ford Motor Company	96.1
6.	Exxon Corporation	86.7
7.	California State Bureaucracy	66.9
8.	IBM	62.7
9.	General Electric	54.6
10.	Sears, Roebuck	53.8

All figures are for 1990 and are stated in billions of dollars.

Source: *James Fesler and Donald Kettl,* The Politics of the Administrative Process *(Chatham, NJ: Chatham House Publishers, 1991), p. 5.*

■ ■ ■ ■ **BOX 9-2** ■ ■ ■ ■

Comparing Federal Departments and Private Corporations by Number of Employees

Rank	Corporation/Department	Employees*
1.	Department of Defense (civilian only)	1,051
2.	U.S. Postal Service	788
3.	General Motors Corporation	775
4.	Sears, Roebuck	510
5.	New York City Bureaucracy	412
6.	IBM	385
7.	Ford Motor Company	367
8.	California State Bureaucracy	366
9.	K Mart	360
10.	New York State Bureaucracy	305

*All figures are for 1990 and are stated in thousands of employees.

Source: James Fesler and Donald Kettl, The Politics of the Administrative Process (Chatham, NJ: Chatham House Publishers, 1991), p. 6.

The First Bureaucracy

The first bureaucracy was anything but large. As public administration scholar Leonard White once wrote, the entire federal bureaucracy of 1790 consisted of nothing more than a "foreign office with John Jay and a couple of clerks to deal with correspondence from John Adams in London and Thomas Jefferson in Paris; . . . a Treasury Board with an empty treasury; . . . a 'Secretary at War' with an authorized army of 840 men; . . . [and] a dozen clerks whose pay was in arrears."[12]

Creating the first departments was not without controversy, however. Congress not only wanted to restrict the president's removal power for all officers, it also continued the Constitutional Convention debate over who should run the Department of the Treasury. Having lost the power to appoint the secretary in the last days of the convention, the first Senate pressed to have the new department headed by a board rather than a single secretary, and briefly succeeded in requiring the secretary to submit all plans for implementing certain financial plans to Congress for approval. Both of the Senate's proposals would have sharply limited the president's authority to execute the laws, and were eventually defeated on close votes.

Once past the legislative disputes, the first departments came on line rather smoothly. Washington made three excellent first appointments: Thomas Jefferson at the Department of State, Alexander Hamilton at the Department of the Treasury, and Henry Knox at the War Department. All three were easily confirmed, and quickly went about the business of running their departments. At roughly the same time, Congress also created the Post Office Department and allowed for the appointment of a U.S. attorney general.

Even though the federal bureaucracy was but the tiniest fraction of its current size, it was not long before the country was demanding smaller government. Jefferson made smaller government a centerpiece of his first inaugural address in 1801, promising "a wise and frugal government, which shall restrain men from injuring one another, shall leave them otherwise free to regulate their own pursuits of industry and improvement, and shall not take from the mouth of labor it has earned." Jefferson wanted a government that worked better and cost less, one that taxed lightly, paid its debts on time and in full, and sought "economy in the public expense."

Ultimately, Jefferson's promise of smaller government far outweighed his actual success. Despite tax cuts and a reduction in the size of the armed forces, Jefferson's Louisiana Purchase doubled the size of the nation, requiring a rapid expansion of the General Land Office, which was responsible for granting deeds to western land. Most of the deeds were handled by career government employees who stayed in office regardless of the president. Many of them took bribes to set aside the best parcels of land.

It was corruption in the General Land Office that fueled the western anger that swept Andrew Jackson and the two-party system into office in 1828. In turn, Jackson decided that the way to stop corruption was to fill *all* government jobs with presidential appointees who would be fired at the start of a term and replaced by individuals loyal to the president and his political party.

Jackson called this system "rotation in office," meaning that no one would stay in a public job long enough to be corrupted. Most political scientists call it the "spoils system," that is, "to the victor belong the spoils." If someone wanted a job in the federal government, whether delivering the mail or registering deeds, first they would have to join the party.[13]

Although the spoils system quickly became corrupt itself (it was not long before party workers began selling government jobs), Jackson saw the change as a way to return power to the people. "They regarded their administrative handiwork, not as an attempt at modernization, but as the restoration of something old and respectable," political scientist Matthew Crenson wrote in quoting Jackson. "They aimed to purify the federal establishment of all its newfangled complexity, to restore 'the government to its original simplicity in the exercise of all its functions.'"[14]

Jackson did not stop reforming government with the employment system, however. He also reorganized the federal departments to make them more efficient, created accounting systems to track spending, and established codes of ethics to regulate the behavior of government workers. In a sense, he was the first president to truly worry about making government work better. (See Box 9–3 for a sampling from the code of ethics at the Post Office Department in Jackson's time.)

America emerged from Jackson's presidency with the outlines of today's federal bureaucracy. The federal bureaucracy had grown from a few thousand employees to over 30,000, and was well on its way to becoming a major presence in daily life.

The Institutional Bureaucracy

Paging through the *U.S. Government Manual,* a reference book that provides brief descriptions of every department and agency in government, is like an archaeological dig through the sands of time. Because the federal bureaucracy was created one unit at a time over two hundred years, no two agencies are quite alike. Some such as the Department of Defense are collections of huge agencies in their own right. The Defense Department contains the Departments of the Army, Navy, and Air Force, each with its own separate duties (as if to confirm how Congress sometimes divides responsibilities, the Army has its own air corps, and the

BOX 9-3

Rules for Government Conduct in 1830

Every clerk will be in his room, ready to communicate business, at nine o'clock A.M., and will apply himself with diligence to the public service until three o'clock P.M. . . .

Newspapers or books must not be read in the office unless connected directly with the business at hand, nor must conversation be held with visitors or loungers except upon business which they may have with the office. . . .

The acceptance of any present or gratuity by any clerk from any person who has business with the office, or suffering any such acceptance by any member of his family, will subject any clerk to instant removal. . . .

Strict economy will be required in the use of the public stationery or other property. No clerk will take paper, quills, or anything else belonging to the government for the use of himself, family, or friends.

Source: Matthew Crenson, The Federal Machine: Beginnings of Bureaucracy in Jacksonian America *(Baltimore: Johns Hopkins University Press, 1976), pp. 77-78.*

Navy has its own army, the Marines). Others such as the Department of Education are tiny by comparison, with but a handful of employees and a relatively limited set of duties.

Nevertheless, all departments and agencies share at least three basic features. Each has leadership, an organization chart, and employees. Each of these institutional characteristics will be discussed below.

Leadership. Every department and agency of the federal bureaucracy is headed by a **presidential appointee,** either subject to confirmation by the Senate, or appointed on the sole authority of the president. As political officers, presidential appointees serve at the pleasure of the president, and generally leave their posts at the end of their president's term in office.

In turn, presidential appointees work closely with **senior executives** who are at the very top of the career federal workforce. As career professionals, senior executives continue in their jobs regardless of whomever is in the White House, and are selected on the basis of merit, not political connections. Presidents have very little say over who serves as a career executive.

Together, these two types of executives—political and career—constitute the leadership of the federal bureaucracy. All totaled, there are 10,000 executives: 3,000 political and 7,000 career. Of the 3,000 political, roughly 600 are subject to Senate confirmation, while the rest are appointed solely by the president. The number has grown dramatically over the past three decades as the federal government has "thickened" with more layers of leadership and more leaders at each layer.[15] (See Box 9–4 for a comparison of the average department leadership in 1960 versus 1992.)

Thus, whereas President Kennedy selected 10 department secretaries in 1960, President Clinton picked 14 in 1992; Kennedy 6 deputy secretaries, Clinton 21; Kennedy 14 under secretaries, Clinton 32; Kennedy 81 assistant secretaries, Clinton 212; Kennedy 77 deputy assistant secretaries, Clinton 507; Kennedy 52 deputy administrators, Clinton 190. Adding up all the layers, the total number of senior executives and presidential appointees grew from 451 in 1960 to 2,393 in 1992, a 430 percent increase.

The cost of this thickening is not in the salaries of all the managers. Adding more layers to the federal hierarchy is not particularly expensive—federal salary costs are a very small part of the overall budget. Rather, the cost appears to be in the diffusion of accountability that comes in a nearly infinite number of decision points throughout the administrative machinery of bureaucracy. Almost by definition, thickening increases the number of officers who must be involved in any decision, thereby raising the costs of executing the laws.

Organizations. Public administration scholars use four terms to classify the organizations of government: (1) departments, (2) independent regulatory commissions, (3) independent agencies, and (4) government corporations.

BOX 9-4

The Thickening of Government, 1960 and 1992

	1960	1992
Secretary	𝄞	𝄞
Chief of Staff to Secretary	—	𝄞
Deputy Secretary	—	𝄞𝄞
Under Secretary	𝄞𝄞	𝄞𝄞
Deputy Under Secretary	—	𝄞𝄞𝄞𝄞
Assistant Secretary	𝄞𝄞𝄞𝄞𝄞𝄞𝄞𝄞𝄞	𝄞𝄞𝄞𝄞𝄞𝄞𝄞𝄞𝄞𝄞𝄞𝄞𝄞𝄞𝄞
Principal Deputy Assistant Secretary	—	𝄞𝄞𝄞𝄞𝄞𝄞
Deputy Assistant Secretary	𝄞𝄞𝄞𝄞𝄞𝄞𝄞𝄞	𝄞𝄞𝄞𝄞𝄞𝄞𝄞𝄞𝄞𝄞𝄞𝄞𝄞𝄞𝄞𝄞𝄞𝄞𝄞𝄞𝄞𝄞𝄞𝄞𝄞𝄞𝄞𝄞𝄞𝄞𝄞𝄞𝄞𝄞𝄞𝄞𝄞
Associate Deputy Assistant Secretary	𝄞𝄞	𝄞𝄞𝄞𝄞𝄞𝄞𝄞𝄞𝄞𝄞𝄞𝄞𝄞𝄞𝄞𝄞𝄞𝄞𝄞𝄞
Deputy Associate Deputy Assistant Secretary	—	𝄞𝄞𝄞𝄞𝄞𝄞𝄞𝄞𝄞
Assistant General Counsel/Inspector General	—	𝄞𝄞𝄞𝄞𝄞𝄞𝄞𝄞𝄞𝄞𝄞𝄞𝄞𝄞𝄞
Deputy Assistant General Counsel/Inspector General	—	𝄞𝄞𝄞𝄞
Administrator	𝄞𝄞𝄞𝄞𝄞𝄞𝄞𝄞𝄞	𝄞𝄞𝄞𝄞𝄞𝄞𝄞𝄞𝄞
Deputy Administrator	𝄞𝄞𝄞𝄞𝄞	𝄞𝄞𝄞𝄞𝄞𝄞𝄞𝄞𝄞𝄞𝄞𝄞𝄞𝄞𝄞
Associate Administrator	—	𝄞𝄞𝄞𝄞𝄞𝄞𝄞𝄞
Assistant Administrator	𝄞𝄞𝄞𝄞𝄞𝄞	𝄞𝄞𝄞𝄞𝄞𝄞𝄞𝄞𝄞𝄞𝄞
Deputy Assistant Administrator	—	𝄞𝄞𝄞𝄞𝄞

𝄞 = One Person

Source: *Paul Light,* Thickening Government: Federal Hierarchy and the Diffusion of Hierarchy *(Washington, DC: Brookings Institution/Governance Institute, 1995), p.12.*

Originally, the terms were used to describe different sizes and missions of organizations. Departments were to be the largest organizations of all, agencies the smallest, independent regulatory commissions free of political control, and government corporations the most businesslike—hence, the term corporations.

Over time, however, some of the distinctions have blurred. The Department of Education, a department with less than 5,000 employees, is smaller than many independent agencies, while the Social Security Administration, an independent agency with 65,000 employees, dwarfs all but the largest of departments.

Departments.   Cabinet **departments** are the most visible organizations in the federal bureaucracy. Today's fourteen departments of government employ more than 70 percent of all federal civil servants and spend 93 percent of all federal dollars. Thirteen of the departments are headed by secretaries, while the fourteenth, Justice, is headed by the attorney general.

The largest department by far is the Department of Defense, followed by Veterans Affairs (which runs the VA hospital system), Treasury (which contains the Internal Revenue Service and its vast collection of local field offices), Justice (which contains the Federal Bureau of Investigation), and Health and Human Services (which operates Medicare and most welfare programs).

The smallest department is the Department of Education, which was created in 1979. It was originally part of the Department of Health, Education, and Welfare, but was split into a separate department as a way to show support for America's teachers.

The greatest expansion in the number of departments occurred between 1945 and 1990: Health, Education, and Welfare (HEW) was created in 1953; Housing and Urban Development (HUD) in 1965; Transportation in 1966; Energy in 1977; and Veterans Affairs (VA) in 1989. In addition, HEW was divided in two in 1979 to create two new departments, Health and Human Services and Education.

These fourteen departments represent two very different approaches to department building. One approach is to use a department to bring a number of related programs under one broad umbrella, or conglomerate. The Department of Transportation was created by combining a number of smaller, independent agencies, including the National Highway Administration, the Federal Aviation Administration, and the Federal Railroad Administration. The Departments of Agriculture, Commerce, and Defense also reflect a conglomerate approach.

The other approach is to use a department to give added visibility to a popular issue such as education, housing, or energy, or to a large group of Americans such as the elderly or labor. These departments are not conglomerates at all, but highly specialized voices for a specific group of Americans. Not surprisingly, these departments are often closely tied to organized interests. In 1988, for example, veterans groups pushed Congress to change the Veterans Administration from an independent agency to a cabinet department as a way to show support for the nation's 10 million veterans.

Independent Regulatory Commissions.   Size and age are not the only ways to compare units within the federal bureaucracy. Power, or impact on daily life, is also important. Indeed, when Americans complain about bureaucracy being on their backs, they are often talking about the federal bureaucracy's **independent regulatory commissions.**

Yet, the federal government's eleven independent regulatory commissions were mostly set up to do just that: "get on the backs" of people and corporations, whether to protect consumers (the Consumer Product Safety Commission), regulate stock markets (the Securities and Exchange Commission), oversee interstate trucking (the Interstate Commerce Commission), monitor television and radio (the Federal Communications Commission), regulate business (the Federal Trade Commission), or control the supply of money (the Federal Reserve Board).

The commissions may be small in budget and employees (just $70 million and 1,200 employees total for all eleven combined), but their influence over American life is large. Indeed, according to some experts, the chairman of the Federal Reserve Board may be the second most influential person in the nation, second only to the president.[16]

The key difference between commissions and other departments and agencies is the president's appointment power. All independent regulatory commissions are governed by boards or commissions that cannot be removed by the president or Congress without cause—that is, unless a member is found guilty of "inefficiency, neglect of duty, or malfeasance in office," a phrase that essentially means "unless a member has broken the law."

This is not to say that the president and Congress have no authority whatsoever over these agencies. The president appoints board members to vacancies, which the Senate then confirms, and Congress most certainly has a say over budgets. But once the appointments are made and confirmed, board members are independent.

Independent Agencies. The word *independent* means at least two things in the federal bureaucracy. When it is linked to the words *regulatory commission,* it means an agency that is independent of presidential control. When it is just linked to *agency* or *administration,* it creates a much looser term that merely means "standing alone." Whereas independent regulatory commissions do not report to the president, **independent agencies** most certainly do.

As a general rule, independent agencies are small federal bureaucracies that serve specific groups of Americans or work on specific problems. Becoming an agency is often the first step toward becoming a department. The Department of Veterans Affairs is basically the same organization that once existed as the Veterans Administration. The Department of Transportation was created as an umbrella for the old Federal Aviation Administration and the Federal Highway Administration.

Independent agencies are usually headed by an administrator, which is the second most senior title in the federal bureaucracy behind secretary/attorney general. There are roughly sixty such agencies today, including the Environmental Protection Agency (EPA), the Central Intelligence Agency (CIA), the National Aeronautics and Space Administration (NASA), the Federal Emergency Management Agency (FEMA), the General Services Administration (GSA), and the Small Business Administration (SBA).

As noted earlier, independent agencies do not have to be small. NASA, for example, has an annual budget of over $11 billion and a workforce of over 23,000 employees, not to mention all the private contractors who help put the space shuttle into orbit. Indeed, NASA's budget puts it ahead of four cabinet departments (Justice, Interior, State, and Commerce).

Moreover, independent agencies can be more important to the president than some cabinet departments. There are times, for example, when the director of the CIA or the administrator of EPA gets a higher place on the president's agenda than the secretary of HUD or Agriculture. And both usually have a seat at the cabinet table. Although being a cabinet secretary certainly conveys some visibility, it is no guarantee of attention from the president or Congress.

(It is useful to note that independent agencies are not the only government organizations that call themselves agencies. There are a number of highly visible agencies that actually exist within departments, including the Forest Service (located in the Agriculture Department), the National Park Service (located in the Department of the Interior), the Occupational Safety and Health Administration (located in the Labor Department), and the Census Bureau (in the Commerce Department). What makes these agencies different from the independent agencies described above is that they report to the president only through a cabinet secretary.)

Government Corporations.   Perhaps the least understood organizations in the federal bureaucracy, **government corporations** are designed to act more like businesses than like traditional government departments and agencies. They are generally given more freedom from the assorted rules that control what agencies do by way of hiring and firing employees, purchasing goods and services, and accounting for spending. And they are most certainly encouraged to make money.[17]

Yet, no two government corporations are quite alike. The term is so loosely used that no one knows exactly how many corporations the federal bureaucracy has. What experts do know is that the number is between thirty-one and forty-seven, including the Corporation for Public Broadcasting (which runs PBS television), the U.S. Postal Service, the Tennessee Valley Authority (TVA), the Railroad Passenger Association (better known as AMTRAK), and Americorps (which runs the new national service program), along with a host of financial enterprises that make loans of one kind or another. Once again, just because these organizations are not departments does not mean they are small actors. The U.S. Postal Service employs almost 800,000 employees, making it the second largest organization in the federal bureaucracy.

Employees.   The federal bureaucracy currently employs roughly 2 million civil servants, or employees. (This number does not include the soldiers who serve in the armed forces or U.S. Postal Service workers who are covered by a different personnel system.) Members of the **civil service** are selected on the basis of merit, or qualification for the job, and continue to serve regardless of who is president. To protect against political interference in the execution of the laws, the civil service system is designed to make firing difficult.

The civil service was created in 1883 to address corruption in the spoils system. Recall that Andrew Jackson had created a system in which federal jobs were filled on the basis of political connections. In essence, all federal positions were political. Job seekers had to either know someone or pay someone to get a job. Actual ability to do the work had almost nothing to do with an appointment.

Also recall that the spoils system gave the president's party complete control over almost every government job, from cabinet secretaries all the way down to post office clerks. This political job system became known as *patronage*—patronize, or support, the president's party, and get a job.

It was a disappointed job seeker who started the federal bureaucracy down the road toward today's civil service system. Unfortunately for President James Garfield, that job seeker happened to be both disappointed and a good shot. Garfield's assassination prompted Congress to pass the Pendleton Act in 1883, which began a sixty-year effort to cover all federal jobs under the merit principle. The merit principle simply means that jobs are awarded on the basis of ability to do the work, not political connections.

Continuing concerns about merit led Congress to pass "An Act to Prevent Pernicious Political Activities" in 1939 precisely to remove any hint that political loyalties might influence public employees. The act, usually called the Hatch Act in honor of its sponsor, Senator Carl Hatch, flatly prohibited career civil servants from taking part in any form of political activity, all the way from running for office down to wearing a campaign button. Employees were free to vote, of course, but any other overt acts were off-limits.

Congress repealed the Hatch Act in 1994, giving federal employees the same rights to participate in public life as other Americans. The final vote was anything but unanimous, however. Democrats favored the measure because federal employees tend to favor Democratic candidates; Republicans opposed the measure for the same reason. As such, repeal of the Hatch Act rekindled a long-standing debate about whether Republicans can trust federal employees to faithfully execute the laws when Republicans happen to be in charge.

Is the Federal Bureaucracy Too Big?

There is no question that government has gotten bigger over the past two hundred years. There are more leaders, more departments and agencies, and more employees. However, it is not clear that the federal bureaucracy is too big. Consider two ways to ask the bigness question.

Is the Federal Bureaucracy Growing Too Fast?   Compared to the 1940s, the
federal bureaucracy is not growing very fast at all. Indeed, the total number of
federal employees mostly stopped growing in the 1950s. The number has grown
by a few hundred thousand here and there over the years, but it is barely larger
than it was when Republicans held the Congress and the White House in the early
1950s. Further, it is scheduled to get almost 275,000 employees smaller by 1999,
dropping below 2 million civilian employees for the first time in three decades.
(See Box 9–5 for a chart on growth trends.)

State and local government is the place where bureaucracy is growing. In the
1940s, total state and local employees accounted for roughly three million jobs—
teachers, police and firefighters, hospital workers, and prison guards (most of America's one million prisoners are in state and local jails).

By 1992, there were almost sixteen million state and local employees, a growth
rate of almost 500 percent. The total number of state employees grew by almost
900 percent; county employees by almost 700 percent, school district employees
by 400 percent, and city employees by 300 percent.

BOX 9-5

Growth Trends in the Size of the Federal Bureaucracy

Year	Employment (thousands)	Budget in 1987 Dollars (billions)	Budget as a Percent of GDP
1940	699	$ 96.8	9.9%
1945*	3,370	812.6	43.7
1950	1,439	241.4	16.0
1955	1,860	300.0	17.8
1960	1,808	392.1	18.3
1965	1,901	446.1	17.6
1970	2,203	596.1	19.9
1975	2,149	698.5	22.0
1980	2,161	832.1	22.3
1985	2,252	1,001.4	23.9
1990	2,250	1,110.4	22.9
1995	2,018	1,168.1	21.9

*The figures for 1945 were high because of World War II; fighting a world war is an extraordinarily expensive
proposition.*

Source: *United States Office of Management and Budget,* Budget of the U.S. Government, Fiscal Year, 1996,
Historical Tables *(Washington, DC: United States Government Printing Office, 1996), p. 17.*

The specific numbers are far less important than the trend: the state and local workforces have been growing steadily since the 1940s, while the federal workforce has remained roughly level since the early 1950s. Indeed, compared to total U.S. population, the federal bureaucracy has actually gotten much smaller. In 1950, for example, there was one federal employee for every fifty Americans; by 1990, there was one for every eighty. In a similar vein, state and local employment has gotten much larger. In 1950, there was one state or local employee for every forty Americans in 1950; by 1990, there was one for every sixteen.

Changes in how the federal bureaucracy delivers programs may have been responsible for much of the growth in state and local employment, however. One way the federal bureaucracy has managed to stay slim is by pushing much of the administrative load downward.[18]

Is the Federal Bureaucracy Spending Too Much? The federal bureaucracy is hardly about to shrink into nothingness. The number of employees may be down, but the budget is way up. The increase is particularly striking looking back to the 1930s. Viewed as a percentage of Gross Domestic Product (GDP), which is a measure of total economic activity, the federal budget has more than doubled since then. Since 1975, however, overall federal spending in dollars has almost doubled, rising fastest during the Reagan Administration. (See Box 9–5 for the trends in spending).

More important, a considerable share of the federal budget does not go to new programs but to **uncontrollable spending**—defined as programs that (1) Congress and the president have been unwilling to cut, and (2) rise in cost nearly automatically. Although candidates for federal office often promise they will go to Washington and balance the budget, the share of the federal pie they can cut in any given year is quite small. (See Box 9–6 for the figures.) Even programs such as defense, which is technically subject to yearly control, may be almost impossible to cut without controversy, leaving even less room for reducing the budget.

The largest share of uncontrollable spending comes from Social Security and Medicare, which are guaranteed to any American who has paid taxes into the program for enough years. The aging of America means more older people will qualify for Social Security and Medicare—hence, uncontrollable spending will most certainly rise over the next two decades.

Another, much smaller share of the uncontrollable budget involves welfare for the poor, which is linked to economic performance. More unemployment, for example, means more federal unemployment insurance; more poverty means more food stamps, job training, Aid to Families with Dependent Children (AFDC), and other income support programs. It is important to note, however, that welfare for the poor is not the only welfare in the federal budget. There is a substantial amount of welfare for American business, too. (See Box 9–7 for a sample of "corporate welfare" programs.)

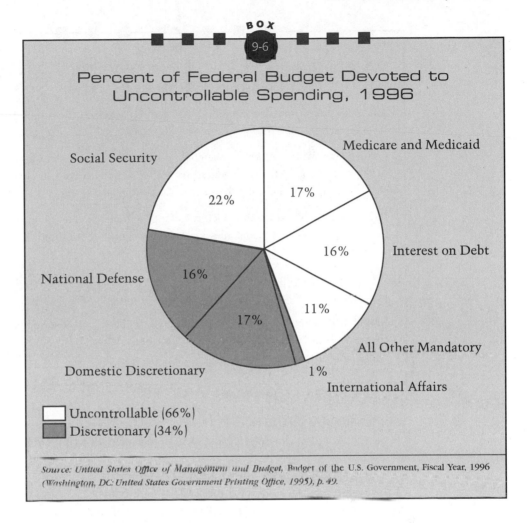

BOX 9-6

Percent of Federal Budget Devoted to Uncontrollable Spending, 1996

Social Security

Medicare and Medicaid

22%

17%

16% — Interest on Debt

National Defense — 16%

17%

11%

All Other Mandatory

Domestic Discretionary

1%

International Affairs

☐ Uncontrollable (66%)
▨ Discretionary (34%)

Source: United States Office of Management and Budget, Budget of the U.S. Government, Fiscal Year, 1996 (Washington, DC: United States Government Printing Office, 1995), p. 49.

What makes these uncontrollable programs similar is that they guarantee benefits to anyone eligible; hence, these programs are often called **entitlements.** All totaled, these automatic programs cost the federal government $762 billion in 1992–1993, accounting for over half of all spending.

The uncontrollable budget is not growing just because more people are eligible for entitlements, however. Many of these entitlements are subject to **indexing—** that is, they grow automatically with inflation, regardless of how the economy is doing. *Indexing* affects a growing list of federal programs, again leaving Congress and the president with little control over year-to-year increases. The number of programs indexed to automatic cost of living adjustments, or COLAs, grew from seventeen in 1966 to more than ninety in 1980.[19]

Ironically, Congress originally started indexing programs as a way to stop itself from spending even more. The Social Security program was indexed to rise

BOX 9-7

A Sampling of Corporate Welfare Programs in the Federal Budget

American drug manufacturers do not have to pay taxes on their operations in Puerto Rico and other U.S. territories. Cost: $4 billion a year.

Airlines and owners of private planes do not pay for the costs of running the Federal Aviation Administration, including air traffic control, even though they make substantial profits from using the system. Cost: $2 billion a year.

The Agriculture Department, which runs the U.S. forest system, builds roads primarily to help private logging companies remove timber from the forests. Cost: $150 million a year.

The federal government artificially raises the cost of sugar to help the domestic sugar industry. Cost to consumers: $300 million a year in higher sugar prices.

Mining companies are allowed to extract minerals from U.S. government lands free of charge. Cost: $200 million a year in lost revenues.

Source: Kirk Victor, "Takin' on the Bacon," National Journal, May 16, 1995, p. 1084.

with inflation in the early 1970s mostly to stop Congress from giving huge increases in benefits during election years, and a host of other programs soon followed suit.

Together, entitlements and indexing have moved a steadily increasing share of the federal budget out of the hands of elected officials and into the hands of unforeseen events. In the early 1960s, uncontrollable spending accounted for less than thirty cents of every federal dollar spent. There was no Medicare program back then, no automatic cost of living adjustment for Social Security, no automatic increase for veterans benefits. By 1996, in part because of changes in these three programs, the number was up to sixty-six cents. Candidates who want to balance the federal budget have a much smaller piece of the pie with which to work. Most of the pie is already divvied up.

The fastest growing category of uncontrollable spending is neither an entitlement nor an indexed program, however. It is interest on the federal debt. Just like individual citizens, the federal bureaucracy must pay for the money it borrows. People who buy U.S. Treasury Bonds, which cover the federal debt, must be paid interest. Again in the early 1960s, interest on the debt weighed in at $7 billion, or less than 7 percent of the entire federal budget. By 1990, interest was up to almost $200 billion a year, or almost 15 percent of the budget.[20] Much of the increase came in the 1980s when federal taxes went down and defense spending went up. The shortfall was covered by borrowing, and, like any loan or credit card debt, the interest has to be paid.

Whether uncontrollable or not, at least this spending is visible to the public. However, a large part of the budget is completely invisible to most Americans. By allowing taxpayers to deduct certain items on their annual income tax, the federal bureaucracy loses revenue, thereby "spending" money it would have had. These **tax expenditures,** as economists label the spending, are just as important as a tool of public policy as direct expenditures; they totaled almost $400 billion in income taxes *not* paid in 1992. Each year, for example, the federal bureaucracy loses almost $50 billion in revenue by allowing taxpayers to deduct interest on home mortgages, $36 billion by permitting them to deduct their state and local taxes, $17 billion by letting them deduct their contributions to charity, and $50 billion by allowing businesses to deduct their contributions to employee pension funds.[21]

IN A DIFFERENT LIGHT

IS BUREAUCRACY IMMORTAL?

One reason bureaucracy may seem too big and expensive to the average citizen is that bureaucratic organizations so rarely disappear. Take the Federal Helium Reserve as an example. Using underground caves as storage space, the reserve was created in the 1920s to assure a steady supply of helium for the nation's fleet of blimps. Although the armed services had long ago replaced blimps with airplanes and helicopters, and despite private sources of helium for industrial uses, the reserve stayed in business until it was closed in 1995.

The Federal Helium Reserve is hardly the only agency to linger on long after its mission was over. Indeed, as political scientist Herbert Kaufman discovered in writing his book *Are Government Organizations Immortal?*, many agencies that long ago lost their reason for being are still alive, in large part because they fight so hard to keep going.[22] "They are not helpless, passive pawns in the game of politics as it affects their lives," wrote Kaufman, "they are active, energetic, persistent participants."[23]

Presidents quickly find that even the weakest agency has enormous resources available to fight an attack, not the least of which are the presidential appointees who head the agency. "Once aroused, they have a large arsenal of weapons to employ in their agencies' defense," Kaufman wrote about the heads of imperiled agencies. "They cultivate their allies and the mass media. Covertly and openly, they attack and try to embarrass their adversaries. They strike bargains to appease the foes they cannot overcome. If this sounds like warfare, it is—at least a type of warfare, a struggle for organizational existence."[24]

Although every agency will not live forever, Kaufman's research shows that most agencies can expect to live a very long time. Of 175 agencies that existed in 1923, Kaufman found that 148, or 85 percent, were still alive fifty years later.

Some survivors were barely alive when Kaufman conducted his research, while others had changed status—that is, they had been demoted to a less visible position in the executive branch. Nevertheless, according to Kaufman, "the chances that an organization in the 1923 sample would not only be alive in 1973 but in virtually the same status were quite good; 109 of the original 175 (over 62 percent, or better than three out of five) were in this situation."[25]

Moreover, even as large numbers of old agencies were surviving the test of time, there were an even larger number of births. During the fifty years Kaufman studied, the federal bureaucracy celebrated the birth of 246 new units, an average of five per year. Together, the birth and survival rates means the number of federal agencies has grown dramatically since the early 1920s.

The birth and survival rates also raise troubling questions about the ultimate size of the federal bureaucracy. Can government ever close a program? Should there be automatic "sunsets," or end dates, for departments and agencies? Is this another example of the antidemocratic bias of bureaucracy? If current trends hold, for example, the next century will witness the creation of over five hundred new units. These new units will likely have important new duties but there may be some limit to how many organizations the president can supervise without losing all hope of democratic accountability.

CONTROLLING THE BUREAUCRACY

Rare is the president who enters office without promising to make the federal bureaucracy work. Indeed, Jimmy Carter, Ronald Reagan, and Bill Clinton all made bureaucratic reform a central part of their presidential campaigns. Carter promised to create a government as good as the American people; Reagan promised a war on waste; Clinton promised to reinvent government.

Yet if all presidents enter promising change, almost all leave office frustrated by their lack of success. As political scientist James Q. Wilson states, "Almost every president in modern times has admitted to his advisors, if he has not shouted from the rooftops, that he rued the day a 'disappointed office seeker' killed President Garfield, thereby energizing the civil-service reform movement. Presidents see much of the bureaucracy as their natural enemy and always are searching for ways to bring it to heel."[26]

Presidents are not the only ones who want to control the bureaucracy. Congress clearly worries about making bureaucracy work better. Together, the two branches have four basic tools of control: (1) laws and executive orders, (2) the budget, (3) presidential appointees, and (4) oversight by Congress and presidential agencies. Each one will be considered in order before asking how Bill Clinton's vice president, Al Gore, proposed to reinvent the federal bureaucracy.

Laws and Executive Orders

The first way to control bureaucracy is to tell it precisely what to do through laws of one kind or another. Congress and the president have passed dozens of statutes to do just that over the years. All totaled, there have been at least 141 major management bills passed since 1946 alone.[27] These bills have tried just about every approach known for improving the federal bureaucracy.

In addition to laws, presidents can control the federal bureaucracy through **executive orders.** An executive order carries the same force of a federal law except that it can only apply to the executive branch and its employees. Although an order can always be repealed by a future president, it does give the president an important tool for making immediate changes in bureaucracy. Truman used an executive order to integrate the armed services in the late 1940s—prior to his order, African American soldiers were kept separate from white.[28]

Executive orders also can give the president an opportunity to send important messages to the bureaucracy and nation. On his first day in office, Clinton issued four executive orders (1) lifting the restrictions on abortion counseling at federally financed clinics, restoring the right to perform abortions at American military hospitals overseas, and allowing the use of fetal tissue in federally sponsored research; (2) ending restrictions on American financial aid to United Nations family planning and population control programs; (3) imposing new ethics guidelines that barred senior government officials from lobbying the federal agency in which they work for five years after leaving the federal bureaucracy; and (4) abolishing a Bush administration program that gave businesses a way to obtain exemptions from federal regulations. He also used an executive order several weeks later to lift the ban on gays and lesbians in the military, an order that caused enormous controversy for the new administration.

The Federal Budget

The federal budget is generally viewed as the most powerful tool presidents have for controlling the bureaucracy. In an era of nearly constant budget cutting, money talks and the bureaucracy listens. The process for setting budget priorities is controlled from the Office of Management and Budget (OMB), which is headed by a highly trusted presidential aide, and involves an eighteen-month process of negotiation between the bureaucracy and the White House.

The first nine months of the process occur in the presidency. It starts in March when OMB prepares its general forecast of future revenues and spending, continues in the spring when OMB asks departments and agencies for future plans, and comes to a head in the summer when OMB provides the general estimates that guide the budget.

These estimates form the basis for a series of one-on-one hearings with each department and agency. Although each unit gets to defend its estimates and make its case for any increases, it is not clear that the hearings make any difference whatsoever in the final decisions OMB makes in early fall.

Once the departments and agencies get their final budget "marks," or specific targets, they redo their estimates and resubmit their budget. They can always appeal any cuts to the president, but almost always lose. The final budget requests are merged into a massive document that becomes the draft *Budget of the United States* for the fiscal year, which starts on October 1 and ends the following September 30. (The fiscal year, which is merely a term that covers the twelve months of actual spending, is numbered by the year in which it ends—thus, fiscal year 1996 ended on September 30, 1996.) By law, the president is required to submit a budget plan to Congress at the beginning of each calendar year.

The budget process does not stop with the presentation of the president's budget plan, however. The nine-month congressional process begins in February when

Closed for business. A budget stalemate between Congress and the president in 1995 caused the closing of the federal government, including all national parks.

the Congressional Budget Office (CBO) offers its analysis of the president's budget, and continues when the House and Senate Budget Committee holds hearings. It moves forward in March with the **budget resolution** that sets broad revenue and spending targets. The resolution also contains "reconciliation instructions" designed to force Congress to raise revenues or cut spending to make the budget totals add up to the targets.

In theory, the budget process should keep the authorization, appropriations, and revenue committees from overspending or undertaxing. Indeed, the desire for greater coordination is exactly why Congress designed the new budget process in the first place in 1974. Before the Budget and Impoundment Control Act, there had been no coordination across the assorted committees that influence what the federal bureaucracy spends. Under the new budget process, or so the authors hoped, the entire Congress would be working toward the same targets, creating a greater likelihood that authorizing and appropriations committees would not spend more money than the revenue committees would raise.

In reality, the process has never worked that way. The appropriations process has rarely been completed early enough in the legislative year to be subject to the discipline of reconciliation. In most years, the thirteen spending bills are not completed until the very last days of the session, if then.

Congress has tried other ways to close the gap between spending and revenues, most recently enacting the Gramm-Rudman-Hollings budget process in 1985, so named for its three authors, Phil Gramm (R-TX), Warren Rudman (R-NH), and Ernest Hollings (D-SC), which promised automatic cuts if Congress did not meet unbendable targets for cutting the deficit. But the "unbendable" targets always seem to get bent. Even a balanced budget amendment to the Constitution would not necessarily discipline the system. Most of the proposals give Congress and the president just enough room to keep spending if the economy turns sour.

Presidents received a small measure of increased influence over the budget in 1996 when Congress passed the **line item veto.** Unlike the constitutional veto which requires the president to either sign or veto a bill in its entirety, the new line item veto gives the president limited authority to strike specific spending categories from appropriation bills.

Presidential Appointees

Presidential appointees are more than just the leaders of bureaucracy. They are also key controllers of what agencies do. They push the president's orders downward into the federal bureaucracy, oversee the execution of the laws, and represent their departments and agencies on Capitol Hill.

Presidents usually start looking for these appointees long before the election occurs, and may even promise some of the key jobs in exchange for political support. Once the president is in office, the search process is led by the White House, where almost every appointee must be cleared, or approved, by the senior staff. Job seekers can expect to be asked their party identification and how they voted in the election, and are given extra points if they worked in or gave money to the campaign.

There is no guarantee, however, that presidential appointees will do exactly what the president wants. Some appointees represent strong interest groups (farmers, veterans, teachers, oil companies, big business, etc.) who have different views of the president's priorities; others are quickly "captured," as the White House calls it, by their departments, becoming strong advocates for whatever the department wants; and still others will simply mislead the president on what they believe in order to get a top job.

As a result, presidents have become increasingly cautious about who they appoint to the top jobs. It may not be appropriate to ask Supreme Court nominees for advance commitments on abortion and other issues that might come before the Court, but presidents are most certainly welcome to impose such *litmus tests* on their own appointees. Richard Nixon and Ronald Reagan, for example, both tried to put their own ideological stamp on the bureaucracy.[29] No one was to be appointed who did not pass muster as a true conservative.

Beyond appointing their own people to key administration posts, presidents can also try to isolate or remove career civil servants who get in the way. The Nixon administration, for example, used at least four strategies for moving what it saw as disloyal career officers out of the way. These strategies were uncovered during the congressional investigations of the Watergate scandal.[30]

The first strategy was to remove the offending employee from government completely, either through what the Nixon staff called the *frontal assault* ("You simply call an individual in and tell him he is no longer wanted"), the *transfer technique* ("By carefully researching the background of the proposed employee-victim, one can always establish that geographical part of the country and/or organizational unit to which the employee would rather resign than obey and accept transfer orders"), or the *special assignment technique (the traveling salesman)* ("especially useful for the family man and those who do not enjoy traveling").

The second strategy was to build a wall of loyalists around the offending executive. By creating new layers of management both above and below the problem officer, "You have thus layered into the organization into key positions your own people, still isolating your roadblocks into powerless makeshift positions. In all likelihood they will probably end up resigning out of disgust or boredom."[31]

The third strategy was to strip an agency of its duties, rendering the unit unable to do much of anything offensive at all. Using none other than Franklin Roosevelt as its example, the Nixon team argued that the technique was expensive (creating a new agency is no small cost), but was essential for isolating and by-passing "an entire organization [that becomes] so hopeless that there is an immediate desire to deal with nobody in the organization at all."[32]

The final strategy, called "wholesale isolation and disposition of undesirable employee-victims," was to draw disloyal employees to a glamorous new unit. Once safely transferred into the new unit, these employees would find that they had jobs of no real consequence. This technique was "designed to provide a single barrel into which you can dump a large number of widely located bad apples."[33]

Today's presidents do not have to use such extreme and clearly unethical tactics. The Senior Executive Service (SES), for example, was created in 1978 precisely to give presidents more freedom to move career executives from post to post. The Reagan administration, for example, used these and other tools to control the bureaucracy in a host of controversial areas: the Environmental Protection Agency reduced its hazardous waste inspections; the Food and Drug Administration reduced its seizures of unsafe products; the Office of Surface Mining reduced its efforts to stop "outlaw" mining from damaging the earth.[34]

Oversight

Congress and the president spend a great deal of energy watching what the federal bureaucracy does. The hope is that **oversight,** or the process of monitoring day-to-day decisions, will somehow encourage agencies to perform better, or, at the very least, deter them from worse performance.

Presidents have a number of tools for keeping a watchful eye: presidential appointees, the White House staff, even blue-ribbon commissions. However, they tend to use OMB for most routine oversight. Departments and agencies must get OMB approval before sending any testimony to Congress, collecting any survey information from the public, or imposing any new paperwork burdens on the private sector. They must also get OMB's approval before sending any legislation to Congress. Under this **central clearance** system, OMB forwards legislation to Congress under three categories: "in accordance" with the president's program (reserved for the president's top priorities), "consistent with" the president's program (indicating the president's second-tier priorities), or "no objection." If the president has an objection, of course, OMB simply does not forward the legislation to Congress. OMB also conducts oversight as it assembles the president's budget plan.

Congress also has a number of tools for oversight, not the least of which are the individual members of Congress themselves, who are free to ask agencies for detailed information on just about any issue. Former Wisconsin Senator William Proxmire conducted oversight of a sort in giving his monthly "Golden Fleece" award to an agency or program that wasted the most money.

Members and committees are also free to ask the General Accounting Office to conduct a study or investigation of a particular program. The GAO also undertakes oversight work on its own. Under the direction of the comptroller general, the GAO and its 5,000 employees produce hundreds of reports each year, on everything from how new weapons systems operate to the effectiveness of environmental protection. The comptroller general is appointed by the president, but serves for a fixed term of fifteen years to protect the agency from political interference.

Congress uses these and other sources of information as a basis for committee and subcommittee hearings on specific agencies or programs. Congress is holding more oversight hearings than ever before. In the 1960s, for example, both chambers held a grand total of 157 days of oversight hearings; by the early 1980s, the number had more than tripled to 587. The greatest increase occurred in the 1970s, fueled in part by the increasing number of legislative staff and in part by the growing independence of individual members.[35]

Together, Congress and the president conduct two basic types of oversight. One is what can be called "police patrol" oversight, in which the two branches watch the bureaucracy through a routine pattern. They read key reports, watch the budget, and generally pay attention to how the departments and agencies are running. If they happen to see a "crime" in progress, all the better. But the general goal of the patrol is to deter the problem before it arises. The other can be called "fire alarm" oversight, in which the two branches wait for citizens, organized interests, or the press to find a major problem and pull the alarm. The media plays a particularly important role in such oversight, often uncovering the scandal before a police patrol can spot it.[36]

IN A DIFFERENT LIGHT

REINVENTING GOVERNMENT

Although every administration since 1932 has campaigned for better government, none of the efforts was more visible than the "reinventing government" campaign launched in 1993. Led by Vice President Al Gore, the effort promised a new era of high performance. "Washington is filled with organizations designed for an environment that no longer exists," Gore's 1993 report to the president stated, "bureaucracies so big and wasteful they can no longer serve the American people."[37]

Gore proposed four ways to make the federal bureaucracy work. First, he wanted the federal bureaucracy to cut most red tape and rules by half. His notion was that federal employees spend far too much time filling out paperwork, and not enough time doing their jobs—the Defense Department spends more money on monitoring employee travel than on the travel itself. (For an example of a needlessly complex rule, Box 9–8 provides an excerpt from the Defense Department's rule on making brownies.)

BOX 9-8

Making Brownies at the Department of Defense

Excerpts from the 22-page Defense Department rule governing fudge brownies:

The texture of the brownie shall be firm but not hard.

Pour batter into a pan at a rate that will yield uncoated brownies which, when cut such as to meet the dimension requirements specified in regulation 3.4(f), will weigh approximately 35 grams each.

The dimensions of the coated brownie shall not exceed 3 1/2 inches by 2 1/2 inches by 5/8 inch.

Shelled walnut pieces shall be of the small piece size classification, shall be of a light color, and shall be U.S. No. 1 of the U.S. Standards for Shelled English Walnuts. A minimum of 90 percent, by weight, of the pieces shall pass through a 4/16-inch-diameter round-hole screen and not more than 1 percent by weight, shall pass through a 2/16-inch-diameter round-hole screen.

Source: John Kohut, Stupid Government Tricks *(New York: Plume, 1995), pp. 4–6.*

Second, Gore wanted departments and agencies to establish customer service standards against which to measure their performance. The Social Security Administration, for example, promised to answer its 800-number telephone lines faster; the Internal Revenue Service promised to be more courteous to taxpayers. Gore's hope was that federal bureaucrats would start thinking of citizens as customers, just as private companies do.

Third, Gore wanted the federal bureaucracy to give its frontline employees more freedom to solve their customer's problems. (Frontline employees are the ones who actually deliver the basic services of government: the air traffic controllers, VA hospital nurses, forest rangers, Social Security claims representatives.) Gore argued that the bureaucracy's midlevel managers were spending too much time getting in the way, and proposed a deep cut in the number of midlevel jobs.

Finally, Gore wanted the federal bureaucracy to spend less money on wasteful programs. He proposed over $100 billion in budget cuts, including a reduction of nearly 275,000 federal jobs and cuts in dozens of popular programs.

Gore campaigned hard for implementation of his reinventing government agenda. He even appeared on *The David Letterman Show* to break a government-issue ashtray as an example of a silly federal rule. Although Congress did adopt the federal job cut and made important changes in how departments and agencies buy products such as office supplies and computers, it was

Vice President Al Gore appears on the *David Letterman Show* to promote his campaign for reinventing government. Gore smashed a government ash tray to illustrate the needless rules required to purchase government supplies. Under federal rules, an ash tray must shatter into a fixed number of pieces when smashed with a hammer and chisel.

much less favorable toward giving federal employees more freedom to do their jobs. Congress worried that such freedom would make the bureaucracy even less accountable to the people, and rejected many of Gore's recommendations for cutting popular programs.

The key problem in reinventing government is that Congress and the president often disagree about just how to make bureaucracy better. Presidents tend to want more freedom to direct the bureaucracy, while Congress tends to want tighter rules. Both might agree that agencies should become more customer friendly, but may disagree sharply on just who the customers are and which ones come first. Because Congress relies on the bureaucracy to do casework for constituents, it is extremely sensitive about any changes that might weaken its place as the government's most important customer.

CONCLUSION

Complaints about government inefficiency and red tape are hardly new. Scholars have even found evidence of bureaucracy in ancient Egypt in a message from a Roman officer in 288 C.E. complaining about the number of persons who "have invented titles for themselves, such as comptroller, secretary, or superintendent, whereby they procure no advantage to the Treasury but [to] swallow up the profits." The message may also represent one of the very first attempts to reinvent bureaucracy: "It has therefore become necessary for me to send you instructions to arrange a single superintendent of good standing to be chosen for each estate on the responsibility of the local municipal council, and to abolish all remaining offices, though the superintendent elected shall have power to choose two, or at most three, assistants."[38] Cutting bureaucracy was in fashion then, too.

It is important to remember, however, that the federal bureaucracy has not grown larger in terms of either the number of its employees or its relative size to the total population. It has almost the same number of employees today as it did two decades ago, and has actually shrunk when compared to the total U.S. population. It is state and local bureaucracy that has grown the fastest. As for the budget, it is uncontrollable spending that is the fastest growing share of the increasing federal debt—and that uncontrollable spending includes huge entitlement programs such as Social Security and Medicare that the American people steadfastly refuse to cut.

It is also useful to note that the federal bureaucracy is not the largest government bureaucracy in the world. Measuring its budget as a percent of gross domestic product (GDP), all of America's governments (federal, state, and local) add up to a total equal to just over 35 percent of the nation's GDP. That is less than Sweden (which spends over 60 percent), Denmark (almost 60 percent), Belgium (over 50 percent), France (over 50 percent), Norway (over 50 percent), Italy (over 50 percent), West Germany (over 45 percent), Canada (over 45 percent), and Britain (over 40 percent), and barely above Japan (33 percent).[39]

Nevertheless, Americans are convinced that the federal bureaucracy is too big, wasteful, and powerful. Part of the reason they feel this way is that bureaucracy has never been popular, not in 288 C.E., not today. Another reason is that Americans have always been distrusting of big institutions—the departments and agencies of bureaucracy may not be big in absolute terms, but may appear to be big enough to the American people. Remember, too, that Congress and the president have very few tools to control what bureaucracy does, and some of the tools they use—such as thickening the number of presidential appointees—can make the federal bureaucracy even more difficult to run.

There are times when the federal bureaucracy is too slow and cumbersome, whether in approving new drugs at the Food and Drug Administration or regulating cancer-causing chemicals at the Occupational Safety and Health Administration or Environmental Protection Agency. There are also times when the federal bureaucracy is wasteful, whether in paying $800 for a hammer at the Department of Defense or maintaining ancient computers at the Federal Aviation Administration (the air traffic control system still runs on vacuum-tube technology from the 1950s). Finally, there are times when the federal bureaucracy simply does not care what the American people think, particularly in imposing needless paperwork on an already burdened society.

However, many of the federal bureaucracy's problems reflect decisions made by Congress and the presidency on behalf of the public. Making sure every job is filled by merit adds time and cost to the system, but is essential for fairness. Making sure that citizens have freedom of information about what government does also adds delays, but is essential for public accountability. Making government fair and open also makes it less efficient than it could otherwise be.

THE BASICS

■ The Founders did not spend much time debating the federal bureaucracy. Although they had considerable experience running businesses and farms, they left the future of the administrative apparatus of government up to the future. There is some evidence that they expected Congress to establish the same departments that had existed earlier under the Articles of Confederation, which is exactly what Congress did. This does not mean the Founders did not care about the administration of government. Although they expected Congress and the presidency to debate the substance of public policy, they wanted the administration of those policies to be efficient and smooth.

■ Although the bureaucracy is the "undefined branch," the Founders did make at least two decisions that shaped the future of the bureaucracy: (1) they prohibited members of Congress from serving as well as an officer or employee of the executive branch, and vice versa, and (2) they decided not to let Congress select the secretary of the treasury. Both decisions strengthened the president's control over the bureaucracy.

■ Although the federal bureaucracy has a reputation for bigness and has several of the largest organizations (by size of budget and number of employees) in America, public or private, there are large organizations in the private sector as well. The Founders would be surprised at both the size and reach of the federal bureaucracy, but would not necessarily conclude that the government is too big.

■ Today's federal bureaucracy consists of three basic components: leadership, organizations, and employees.

■ The leadership of the bureaucracy is composed of presidential appointees and senior career executives, who together occupy roughly 10,000 top-level jobs. Presidential appointees are divided between those that are subject to Senate confirmation, and a much larger number who are appointed solely on the president's authority. Most presidential appointees serve at the president's pleasure.

■ The organizations of the bureaucracy can be divided into four categories: (1) departments, which are the largest and most visible of the organizations; (2) independent regulatory commissions, which were created by Congress to insulate administration from politics; (3) independent agencies, which are usually smaller and less visible than departments, but serve directly under the president's supervision nonetheless; and (4) government corporations, which are set up to be much like private businesses. In general, departments were to be the largest organizations in the federal bureaucracy, agencies the smallest, independent regulatory commissions insulated from political control, and government corporations the most businesslike. Over time, these distinctions have blurred.

■ The vast number of employees of government are career civil servants who serve regardless of who is president. The civil service was invented in 1883 to address corruption in the spoils system created by Andrew Jackson. Under the merit principle, jobs are awarded on the basis of ability, not political connections. Continuing concerns about merit led to efforts in the 1930s to restrict the political activities of federal employees. Under the Hatch Act, federal employees were prohibited from taking part in any political activity, including wearing campaign buttons. The act was repealed in 1994.

KEY CONCEPTS

■ Because the Founders left the administrative apparatus of government to the future, they ensured that departments and agencies would be created one at a time. The result is that the structure of the federal bureaucracy often reflects conflict between Congress and the presidency over just who gets what, when, and how from government. Many departments have responsibility for similar programs, for example.

■ The first bureaucracy was tiny by comparison with today's collection of departments and agencies. Over the decades, Congress and the president created the departments one by one, adding departments and agencies as the job of the federal government grew. The greatest expansion in the number of departments occurred after 1945.

■ There are two philosophies in creating departments of government. One is to use a department to bring a number of related programs under one broad umbrella. The other is to create a department to give attention to a particular issue such as education, housing, or energy. Congress and the president have used both approaches in recent years.

■ The federal bureaucracy has thickened with an increasing number of executives. There are more layers of executives in the departments and agencies, and more executives at every layer. The cost of this thickening is in the loss of accountability that comes with so many layers and leaders, raising questions about who is responsible when things go right or wrong in the bureaucracy.

■ Although politicians often argue that the federal bureaucracy is too big, there are at least two questions that must be asked before drawing a conclusion. First, is the federal government growing too fast? The answer is definitely "no." Federal employment has been remarkably stable over the years. It is state and local government that is expanding rapidly. Second, is the federal bureaucracy spending too much? The answer is complicated. Much of the federal budget goes to "uncontrollable" spending—programs whose costs rise automatically. Entitlements, indexed programs, and interest on the national debt are all examples of uncontrollable spending. Almost $200 billion of the federal government's $1.5 trillion annual budget goes to interest on the debt.

■ Congress and the presidency have four tools for controlling the bureaucracy. The first is laws and executive orders, which tell the bureaucracy what Congress and the president want government to do. An executive order carries the weight of federal law except that it only applies to the employees of the executive branch. The second tool is the federal budget, which tells the bureaucracy what it can spend. The process for controlling the federal budget process is controlled by the Office of Management and Budget. The calendar for setting the budget begins eighteen months before the actual money gets spent. The first nine months of the process involve the development of the president's draft budget, while the second nine months involve congressional action guided by a budget resolution. The third tool is presidential appointees, who tell the bureaucracy what the president wants. Although presidents count on their appointees to follow the administration's policies, there is no guarantee that appointees will do what the president wants. The fourth tool is oversight, which gives Congress and the president an opportunity to inspect the activities of the bureaucracy. There are two types of oversight: police patrol, in which the two branches watch the bureaucracy on a regular schedule, and fire alarm, in which the two branches wait for citizens and others to find a major problem and pull the alarm.

■ The concept of bureaucracy has been and likely always will be unpopular. Americans do not trust bureaucracy; they think it causes more problems than it solves and they worry that it is getting so big that it is becoming a threat to liberty. Nevertheless, Americans tend to applaud the bureaucrats who help them in their daily lives.

IN A DIFFERENT LIGHT

■ Scholars argue that there are two ways to make the federal bureaucracy more responsive to the public. The first is to expose the bureaucracy to market pressure, which might make its employees more sensitive to their customers, the citizens of the United States. The second is to make the bureaucracy look more like the public. Having a bureaucracy that is representative of the rest of society in terms of race and gender may increase the chances that it will have some connection to the people it serves.

■ One reason Americans may be so distrustful of bureaucracy is that few departments and agencies ever go out of business. In fact, the survival rates of government organizations are so high that bureaucracy can even be thought of as immortal. Bureaucratic organizations fight hard to stay alive and are generally successful in outliving most threats to their abolishment.

■ President Clinton began one of the most aggressive efforts in the past fifty years to reinvent government in 1993. Led by Vice President Al Gore, the campaign involved a series of changes designed to reduce government red tape, increase customer satisfaction, free frontline employees to do their jobs, and reduce unnecessary expenditures. As of 1996, the effort had produced important gains mostly in reducing red tape and cutting the size of the federal workforce, but Congress had proven reluctant to give the bureaucracy more freedom to do its job. Congress still sees itself as government's number one customer, and appears to have worried that giving employees more freedom would weaken casework and constituent service.

OPEN QUESTIONS

■ Is there any way to increase the public's confidence in bureaucracy? Cut more government jobs? Make it easier to fire government employees? Would it help to have more federal agencies think of Americans as customers? What might the Founders think of calling citizens "customers"? Would they want government officers thinking of how to satisfy the customer?

■ Is there any reason to believe that the federal bureaucracy is too small or that it spends too little money? Do America's political leaders spend too much time criticizing big government, particularly given that people hate bureaucracy, but love their bureaucrats?

■ Does knowing that the federal government spends over $200 billion a year paying interest on its debt increase support for cutting the federal deficit? Thinking back to Chapter 3 on public opinion, do most Americans know where the money goes? Would they be more likely to support a balanced budget amendment to the Constitution if they knew more about where the dollars go?

■ Is the federal bureaucracy becoming more, or less, controllable by presidents and Congress as it gets smaller? Does holding the number of federal employees steady, while increasing the number of third-party providers make the bureaucracy more, or less, accountable to the public?

■ What is the best way to make the federal bureaucracy more responsive to the public? What makes the bureaucracy more responsive today? Are there ways to give citizens a greater say in what government does? If so, what would the Founders think of such devices?

... TERMS TO REMEMBER

federal bureaucracy

representative bureaucracy

presidential appointee

departments of government

independent regulatory commissions

independent agencies

government corporations

civil service

uncontrollable spending

entitlements

indexing

tax expenditures

executive orders

budget resolution

line item veto

oversight

central clearance

Endnotes to Chapter 9

1. Quoted in Catherine Drinker Bowen, *Miracle at Philadelphia: The Story of the Constitutional Convention, May to September 1787,* (Boston: Little, Brown, 1966), p. 234.

2. Times Mirror Center for the People & the Press, *The People Press & Politics: The New Political Landscape* (Times Mirror Center, September 21, 1994), p. 24.

3. Times Mirror Center for the People & the Press, *The People Press & Politics: The New Political Landscape* (Times Mirror Center, September 21, 1994), p. 24.

▶ 4. Charles Goodsell, *The Case for Bureaucracy: A Public Administration Polemic,* second edition (Chatham, NJ: Chatham House, 1985), p. 11; see also and Linda Bennett and Stephen Bennett, *Living with Leviathan: Americans Coming to Terms with Big Government* (Lawrence, KS: University of Kansas Press, 1990).

5. David Rosenbaum, "In Loss, Republicans Find Seeds of Victory," *New York Times,* March 5, 1995, p. E16.

6. See Stanley Elkins and Eric McKitrick, *The Age of Federalism* (New York: Oxford University Press, 1993), pp. 50–51.

▶ 7. See John A. Rohr, *To Run a Constitution: The Legitimacy of the Administrative State* (Lawrence, KS: University Press of Kansas, 1986).

8. See General Accounting Office, "Government Reorganization: Issues and Principles," Statement of Charles Bowsher, Comptroller General of the United States, GAO/T-GGD/AIMD-95-166, (Washington, DC: U.S. General Accounting Office, May 17, 1995).

9. General Accounting Office, "The Changing Workforce: Demographic Issues Facing the Federal Government," Report no. GAO/GGD-92-38 (Washington, DC: U.S. General Accounting Office, March, 1992).

10. General Accounting Office, "The Changing Workforce."

▶ 11. See Donald F. Kettl, *Sharing Power: Public Governance and Private Markets* (Washington, DC: Brookings Institution, 1993).

12. Leonard White, *The Federalists* (New York: Macmillan, 1956), p. 1.

13. Matthew Crenson, *The Federal Machine: Beginnings of Bureaucracy in Jacksonian America* (Baltimore: Johns Hopkins University Press, 1975), p. 3.

14. Crenson, *The Federal Machine,* p. 66.

15. See Paul Light, *Thickening Government: Federal Hierarchy and the Diffusion of Accountability* (Washington, DC: Brookings Institution/Governance Institute, 1995).

16. Donald Kettl, *Leadership at the Fed* (New Haven, CT: Yale University Press, 1986), p. 1.

▶ 17. James Fesler and Donald Kettl, *The Politics of the Administrative Process* (Chatham, NJ: Chatham House Publishers), 1991, p. 68.

18. John DiIulio and Donald F. Kettl, *Fine Print: The Contract with America, Devolution, and the Administrative Realities of American Federalism* (Washington, DC: Brookings Institution Center for Public Management, March 1, 1995), p. 16.

19. Kent Weaver, *Automatic Government: The Politics of Indexation* (Washington, DC: Brookings Institution, 1988), p. 1.

▶ 20. Harold W. Stanley and Richard G. Niemi, *Vital Statistics on American Politics* (Washington, DC: CQ Press, 1995), p. 425.

21. Michael Wines, "Taxpayers Are Angry. They're Expensive, Too," *New York Times,* November 20, 1994, p. E5.

22. Herbert Kaufman, *Are Government Organizations Immortal?* (Washington, DC: Brookings, 1976).

23. Kaufman, *Are Government Organizations Immortal?,* p. 9.

24. Kaufman, *Are Government Organizations Immortal?,* p. 10.

25. Kaufman, *Are Government Organizations Immortal?,* p. 34.

▶ 26. James Q. Wilson, *Bureaucracy: What Government Agencies Do and Why They Do It* (New York: Basic Books, 1989), p. 257.

27. These figures are from Paul Light, *The Tides of Reform: Federal Management Reform and the Confusion of Accountability, 1946–1994* (New Haven, CT: Yale University Press, 1997).

28. See Paul Light, *The President's Agenda: Domestic Policy Choice from Kennedy to Carter,* second edition (Baltimore: Johns Hopkins University Press, 1991), p. 117.

29. Wilson, *Bureaucracy,* p. 261.

30. U.S. Senate, Select Committee on Presidential Campaign Activities, *Use of Incumbency-Responsiveness Program,* 93rd Cong. 2nd sess., vol. 19 (Washington, DC: U.S. Government Printing Office, 1974), p. 8907 ff.

31. *Use of Incumbency-Responsiveness Program,* pp. 9009–9011.

32. *Use of Incumbency-Responsiveness Program,* p. 9012.

33. *Use of Incumbency-Responsiveness Program,* p. 9014.

▶ 34. B. Dan Wood, and Richard Waterman, "The Dynamics of Political Control of the Bureaucracy," *American Political Science Review,* vol. 85, no. 3 (September 1991), pp. 801–28.

35. See Steven Smith, *The American Congress* (Boston: Houghton Mifflin, 1995), p. 217–18; see also Joel Aberbach, *Keeping a Watchful Eye: The Politics of Congressional Oversight* (Washington, DC: Brookings Institution, 1990).

36. See Matthew McCubbins and Thomas Schwartz, "Congressional Oversight Overlooked: Police Patrols versus Fire Alarms," *American Journal of Political Science,* vol. 2, no. 1 (February 1984), pp. 165–79.

▶ 37. Vice President Al Gore, *From Red Tape to Results: Creating a Government that Works Better and Costs Less,* Report of the National Performance Review (Washington, DC: U.S. Government Printing Office, 1993), p. 3.

38. Marshall Dimock, *Administrative Vitality: The Conflict with Bureaucracy* (New York: Harper and Brothers, 1959), p. 116.

39. Figures from Fesler and Kettl, *The Politics of the Administrative Process,* p. 2.

THE FEDERAL JUDICIARY

The **federal judiciary** is the branch of government created both to enforce and to interpret federal laws. By enforcing the laws, the judiciary assures that Americans obey what Congress and the presidency have decided. By interpreting the laws, the judiciary ensures that what Congress and the presidency have decided is constitutional—that is, that neither branch has exceeded its authority or violated basic rights and liberties. And in doing both jobs, the federal judiciary must simultaneously protect the nation as a whole and Americans as individual citizens.

A judiciary is essential in a nation governed by laws. Some of the laws come from Congress and the presidency. Public laws reside in the statute books and are labeled **statutory law.** Other laws come from judicial interpretations of statutory law and of previous judicial opinions. These judge-made laws reside in the decisions themselves and are labeled **common law.**

Whatever the source, laws convey the rules that govern society. Some of the laws govern relationships between individuals as private citizens and sometimes relationships between individuals and government, and are collectively labeled *civil law;* others govern the behavior of individuals as members of society, and are labeled *criminal law;* still others involve the actions of the bureaucracy as it

The Least Dangerous Branch

executes the laws, and are labeled *administrative law;* and still others involve questions surrounding interpretations of the Constitution, and are labeled *constitutional law.*

In creating the federal judiciary, the Founders assured that the common law would be insulated from both public opinion and the other branches of government. First, they decided that federal judges would not be elected by the people, which had been the case in many colonial courts and remains the case to this day in many states and localities. Instead, the Founders decided that federal judges would be nominated by the president and confirmed by the Senate, with no role for the House. Second, the Founders decided that federal judges would not serve for specific terms of office, but during good behavior, which ordinarily means for life. Lacking terms of office, judges do not have to be reappointed, thereby insulating them from the presidency and the Senate. Finally, the Founders decided that Congress and the presidency would never be allowed to cut a judge's pay after that judge was nominated and confirmed, thereby removing financial pressure as a source of possible interference in the judiciary's independence.

These decisions were essential for protecting what the Founders saw as the least dangerous branch. As Hamilton wrote, "The Executive not only dispenses the honors, but holds the sword of the community. The legislature not only commands the purse, but prescribes the rules by which the duties and rights of every citizen are to be regulated. The judiciary, on the contrary, has no influence over either the sword or the purse."[1] To play its role as a check against the other two branches, the judiciary had to be insulated from both the sword and the purse. Hence, the lack of terms in office and the protection against cuts in pay.

Lacking the sword or the purse, the judiciary has only one tool for doing its job: its judgment. The federal judiciary has no army or police force to enforce its will, no credible threat to make the people obey. It can order the federal government or individual citizens to act, but has no sword or purse to extract obedience. To a much greater extent than Congress or the presidency, the judiciary must rely on the consent of the governed to accept its decisions on the merits.[2]

The challenge is to maintain this consent while tackling the very tough issues that America faces. In its proudest moments, the federal judiciary must often reject entirely what the public wants, striking down laws that most Americans support or protecting individuals that most Americans cannot abide.

In this chapter we will examine the job of the federal judiciary in more detail. In the first section, we will ask what the Founders intended as they designed the third branch of government, looking specifically at the duties of the judiciary and qualifications for appointment. In the second section, we will examine the real judiciary today, looking at the first federal courts created in 1789, then turning to the modern institutional judiciary and the process for finding and appointing federal judges. In the third section, we will take a much closer look at how the Supreme Court works.

THE IMAGINED JUDICIARY

The Founders arrived in Philadelphia with substantial legal experience. Thirty-one of the fifty-five delegates were lawyers, including James Madison and Alexander Hamilton, and many had experience in the state and local courts of the prerevolutionary days. Almost all knew something about the complicated British court system, which had nearly one hundred different kinds of courts, including ones just dealing with the English royalty. As they had done with Congress and the presidency, the Founders drew upon this experience in designing the new federal judiciary, drastically simplifying the British system even as they accepted its common-law tradition. Before turning to the decisions made in Philadelphia, it is first useful to understand a bit more about the basic legal framework the Founders brought with them.

The Basic Framework

Whether by training as lawyers or through their personal contact with the law as property owners, bankers, or merchants, the Founders had reached a number of decisions about the future of the federal judiciary long before the Constitutional Convention began. They most certainly had a sense of how the judiciary should look and act, and clearly accepted the principles of English common law, most importantly the notion of **stare decisis.** Under this principle, which means "let the decision stand," every judicial decision today must be linked to a decision made yesterday. Judges are thereby bound by **precedents**—the decisions made in previous cases—which ensure that most legal disputes have predictable outcomes. Judges make law by making decisions, which, in turn, establish precedents that bind future judges to the past.

In 1992, for example, the Supreme Court upheld the right to abortion established under *Roe v. Wade,* in part because the justices felt that a "terrible price would be paid for overruling" the 1973 decision. As the majority wrote, "A decision to overrule *Roe*'s essential holding under the existing circumstances would address error, if error there was, at the cost of both profound and unnecessary damage to the Court's legitimacy, and to the Nation's commitment to the rule of law. It is therefore imperative to adhere to the essence of *Roe*'s original decision, and we do so today."[3]

This acceptance of English common law was nearly inevitable. As one historian puts it, English common law was as central to day-to-day life as the English language itself.[4] Although the public had no love of lawyers, particularly since many had been British sympathizers during the war, common law was essential to America's survival. It was the way the colonies had governed society, and was the backbone of the economy.

Given this experience, the Founders naturally assumed there would be at least two kinds of courts, trial and appellate, each with a separate jurisdiction that would determine the cases it could resolve. As courts of original jurisdiction, **trial courts** would hear all cases for the first time and make the first decision resolving blame or innocence. Appeals from the trial courts would be heard by **appellate courts,** which would make their decisions not on the facts of the original case (for example, who did what to whom?), but on the legality of the trial (for example, was the trial court fair?).

Both trial and appellate courts had existed in the colonies before the war, and in the states after the war. It was no surprise, therefore, that the Founders imagined such a structure for the new judiciary, creating the Supreme Court as the highest appellate court of all, while leaving the rest of the federal judiciary to Congress and the presidency.

Finally, the Founders assumed there would be separate systems of federal, state, and local courts. Just as the colonies had been divided by state and local courts, and the government as a whole had been divided into a federal system, so, too, did the Founders craft a judiciary that allowed for several different layers of courts. As we will see later, there are three distinct layers of federal courts—district courts, courts of appeal, and the Supreme Court—as well as multiple layers of state and local courts.

Before turning to a more detailed discussion of the federal judiciary today, it is first important to know more about what the Founders intended. Although they drew heavily on precedent in building the third branch of government, the Founders made a number of decisions that made the federal judiciary a strong force in both refining the work of Congress and the presidency and acting as a check against the capture of government by strong-willed majorities intent on oppression.

The Third Branch

Compared to the Founders' summer-long struggle over Congress, the invention of the judiciary was easy. As Alexander Hamilton later explained in *The Federalist Papers,* the judiciary would be least able to "annoy or injure" the basic rights of the Constitution, and could "take no active resolution whatever. It may truly be said to have neither FORCE nor WILL, but merely judgment. . . ."[5]

This is not to say the Founders were in complete agreement on the precise outlines of the judicial branch. They certainly agreed that there should be a judicial branch and that it should have a single, or supreme court at the top. But that is where the agreements ended. Advocates of giving the states more power wanted just one federal court—the Supreme Court—as the court of last resort (or final appeal) for appeals upward from the states, while advocates of a stronger national government argued that state courts could not be trusted to faithfully administer national laws.

Like the rest of the constitutional debates, the question was resolved by compromise. Article III begins quite simply by vesting the judicial power of the United States in one supreme court, "and in such inferior Courts as the Congress may from time to time ordain and establish." It would be up to the First Congress to decide just how many lower courts would be needed, how they would operate, and where they would be located.

Because the Founders knew that laws would be made at each layer of government—federal, state, and local—they decided to make clear that the laws and treaties of the federal government would come first as "the supreme Law of the Land." As noted in Chapter 2, this *supremacy clause,* which can be found in Article VI of the Constitution and was affirmed in *McCulloch v. Maryland,* establishes federal laws as the strongest laws of all. When federal and state laws conflict, the federal law generally wins, unless the federal law is clearly exercising a power reserved for the states.

The Duties of the Federal Judiciary

Article III is the briefest of the three articles establishing the institutions of government. The judicial power was to be vested in a single supreme court, which would be the court of last resort, the one that would make the final decision, and any other "inferior" courts as Congress "may from time to time ordain and establish." Brief as it is, Article III does divide into two sections, one giving the judicial power to the courts, and a second outlining judicial limitations.

Judicial Power. Article III never defines the judicial power, however. There is no list of express powers, no hints of implied authorities. As Hamilton argued, the courts are to protect the Constitution against the "ill humors" that create "dangerous innovations in government and serious oppressions of the minor party in the community."[6] The courts are to be passive, not active.

Thus, Article III does not offer a definition of judicial power, but a long list of the kinds of cases reserved for the federal judiciary: ". . . —to Controversies to which the United States shall be a Party;—to Controversies between two or more States;—between a State and Citizens of another State;—between Citizens of different States;—between Citizens of the same State claiming Lands under Grants of different States, and between a State, or the Citizens thereof, and foreign states, Citizens or Subjects." And even this brief list was almost immediately changed under the Eleventh Amendment, ratified in 1795, which prohibits the federal courts from hearing cases in which a state is sued by a citizen of another state.

The debate over Article III had its moments of controversy, however, most importantly over whether the federal judiciary would be allowed to enforce and interpret the Constitution itself. Once again, the fight was between those who favored giving the states greater power and those who favored a strong national government. Those in favor of a stronger state role wanted to restrict federal jurisdiction to cases arising under the laws passed by Congress and signed by the president.

Article III leaves no doubt about who won the argument: the judicial power extends to not just all national laws, but to "all cases arising under this Constitution, the laws of the United States, and treaties made." The Founders ensured that the federal judiciary would be allowed to resolve conflicts over the Constitution itself. It is not clear, however, just how far the Founders wanted the federal judiciary to go in resolving such conflicts. Some, such as Alexander Hamilton, believed that the judiciary would have the duty to "declare all acts contrary to the manifest tenor of the Constitution void."[7] Although the Supreme Court waited over a decade to use this power of **judicial review,** Hamilton clearly believed the judiciary needed the power to grind government to a full and complete halt.

Other Founders were less sure about giving the judiciary such a significant power, and the issue was never completely resolved in the Constitutional Convention. Unlike the power of the purse or the power of appointments, which are both mentioned explicitly, the power of judicial review is neither defined nor mentioned in the Constitution.[8]

It was left to Chief Justice John Marshall to make the first assertion of judicial review in the 1803 case *Marbury v. Madison.* Recall from Chapter 2 that Marbury

John Marshall in a painting by James R. Lambdin. Marshall wrote the opinion in *Marbury v. Madison* that established the power of judicial review.

had been offered a federal judgeship in late 1800 by President John Adams, but that his papers of commission had not been delivered before the new president, Thomas Jefferson, was inaugurated. Since the two presidents were members of different parties, it is hardly surprising that Jefferson would order his secretary of state, James Madison, not to deliver the late papers.

As allowed under the Judiciary Act of 1789, Marbury went directly to the Supreme Court with his complaint, asking the Court to issue a *writ of mandamus* directing government officials (in this case, Secretary of State James Madison) to act (deliver the papers). In filing his case first with the Supreme Court, he called on the Court to exercise original, not appellate jurisdiction.

In *Marbury v. Madison,* Marshall reasoned that the Constitution had been quite specific in limiting the Supreme Court's original jurisdiction only to cases affecting ambassadors, foreign ministers, and states. In all other cases, the Founders clearly stated that the Supreme Court would only have appellate jurisdiction. Thus, when Congress added writs of mandamus to the Supreme Court's original jurisdiction under Section 13 of the 1789 Judiciary Act, it did so against the clear intent of the Founders. The expansion was, therefore, unconstitutional and held no effect. Since the Supreme Court had no power to issue a writ of mandamus as a court of original jurisdiction in Marbury's case, he never got his papers. At the same time, the Supreme Court got an essential power to review and declare acts of Congress unconstitutional. By the early 1900s, the Supreme Court had overturned 141 others acts of Congress, plus 919 state laws and 105 local laws.[9]

Judicial Limitations.   Even as the Founders insulated the judiciary against Congress and the presidency, they gave the two branches several limited checks. As already noted, they gave Congress the power to create the inferior, or lower, federal courts in the first place. They also allowed Congress to restrict the judiciary's appellate jurisdiction.

Stronger checks were hardly necessary given the judiciary's natural weakness. Federal courts are often described as passive, not active, institutions—that is, they can only make decisions on cases that are brought before them. Unlike members of Congress or presidents, judges cannot "invent" policy out of thin air. They must first have a "case or controversy," as former Chief Justice Earl Warren once observed, and that case must raise a **justiciable issue**—that is, it must involve a real dispute that the federal courts, and only the federal courts, can resolve. The courts do not waste their time on hypothetical issues or on cases where one side is unwilling to fight.

As a result, any case before the federal judiciary must pass at least three tests: (1) it must have **adverseness,** that is, a real dispute and not some hypothetical issue invented just to get an advisory opinion from a court; (2) the parties involved must have **standing to sue,** that is, the individuals who bring the case must be truly injured; and (3) it must be **ripe for decision,** that is, it cannot come too early in the process or come so late that it is **moot,** meaning the issues in the case have already been answered elsewhere.[10] The Supreme Court adds a fourth criteria to the list in setting its agenda: the case must involve a controversy worth deciding.

Qualifications for Appointment

Unlike Congress and the presidency, the Constitution sets absolutely no minimums for serving on the Supreme Court, nor did the First Congress when it created the federal lower courts. Since judges were to be appointed by the president with the advice and consent of the Senate (as a check against political favoritism by the president), perhaps the Founders simply assumed that judges would be at least as old as the president and appointed on merit.

As for additional qualifications, the Founders clearly assumed that federal judges would be persons of great integrity, though the Constitution does not set any particular requirements. As Hamilton explained, the judiciary would attract good judges because "there can be but a few men in the society who will have sufficient skill in the laws to qualify them for the stations of judges. And making the proper deductions for the ordinary depravity of human nature, the number must be still smaller of those who unite the requisite integrity with the requisite knowledge."[11] Hamilton was the consummate elitist. Few would want to be judges; fewer still would fit his qualifications.

The question for the Founders was less how to assure high quality judges, and more how to protect the independence of the courts and assure some kind of accountability to the national good. As already mentioned, they decided to prohibit any cuts in pay for sitting federal judges and to give judges permanent appointments as long as they showed good behavior.

This does not mean judges are immune from their own acts, however. Once in office, they can be removed by impeachment and conviction for the same treason, bribery, and other high crimes and misdemeanors that allow impeachment of all officers of the United States government under Article II. It is a device used only in extreme cases. In the entire history of the courts, only forty-five judges have been impeached, of which only nine faced Senate trials and only four of them were convicted.

Although impeachment is more than a hollow threat, it is not the primary source for ensuring "good behavior" on the part of federal judges. More than most elected politicians, judges behave in the national interest because that is simply the right thing to do. They pay attention to what their colleagues on the bench think, and they worry about their reputation in the legal community. They also care about their place in history—that is, where they will rank among others who have come before and who will serve after.[12]

IN A DIFFERENT LIGHT

THE CHANGING FACE OF THE JUDICIARY

The very devices that insulate the judiciary from public pressure can create an antidemocratic bias. Where many states and localities allow for the direct election of judges, the federal judiciary remains conspicuously above the political fray. Thus, the question is how the judiciary can know enough about the ordinary lives of Americans to keep its perspective as it makes life-and-death decisions about their future.

As with the federal bureaucracy, one answer is to have a representative judiciary, which simply means to assure that the demographic face of the judiciary is not so far off from the face of the public. The first courts made no such effort, of course. The only Americans who got to be judges were those who got to be lawyers. And the only Americans who got to be lawyers were white, male property owners.

Over the past thirty years, however, the face of the federal judiciary has changed. The Founders would clearly be surprised to find that there are now two women (Sandra Day O'Connor and Ruth Bader Ginsberg) and an African American (Clarence Thomas) on the Supreme Court, and to learn that the lower courts—a term used to cover both the circuit and district courts—have also become less white and less male. As the first African American on the Supreme Court, Thurgood Marshall, remarked during the bicentennial of the Constitution, the Founders "could not have imag-

The Supreme Court in 1994. Front row, from left, are Associate Justices Antonin Scalia and John Paul Stevens; Chief Justice William Rehnquist; and Associate Justices Sandra Day O'Connor and Anthony Kennedy. Back row, from left, are Associate Justices Ruth Bader Ginsburg, David Souter, Clarence Thomas, and Stephen Breyer. O'Connor was the first woman ever appointed to the Supreme Court; Ginsburg was the second.

incd, nor would they have accepted, that the document they were drafting would one day be construed by a Supreme Court to which had been appointed a woman and the descendant of an African slave."[13]

No president has placed a higher premium on changing the face of the judiciary than Bill Clinton. Less than a third of Clinton's first forty-eight judicial nominees were white males, compared to thirty out of Jimmy Carter's first thirty-four, forty-one out of Ronald Reagan's first forty-five, and seventeen out of George Bush's first twenty-three. Thus, the federal judiciary is becoming more representative of the public it serves. (See Box 10–1 for the racial and gender composition of court appointees by the last seven presidents.)

However, merely appointing more women and minority judges does not assure that the courts will become suddenly connected to ordinary America. After all, the only Americans who get to be judges today are still lawyers. There may be more women and minority candidates, but it still takes a college degree, three years of law school, and a bar exam to get a ticket to the federal bench. And usually it takes much more. Most federal judges have substantial legal experience with the nation's top law firms, which means substantial personal wealth. Thus, even though the demographic face of the judiciary appears to be changing, the socioeconomic face remains virtually unchanged from two hundred years ago.

BOX
10-1

Diversity on the District and Appeals Courts

Appointing President (number of appointees)	Johnson (162)	Nixon (224)	Ford (64)	Carter (258)	Reagan (368)	Bush (185)	Clinton (129*)
Gender							
Male	98.1%	99.6%	98.4%	84.5%	92.4%	80.6%	69.0%
Female	1.9	0.4	1.6	15.5	7.6	19.4	31.0
Ethnicity or Race							
White	93.8%	96.0%	90.6%	78.7%	93.5%	89.2%	65.9%
Black	4.3	2.7	4.7	14.3	1.9	6.5	24.0
African American	1.9	0.9	1.6	6.2	4.1	4.3	8.5
Asian	0.0	0.4	3.1	0.8	0.5	0.0	0.8
Native American	0.0	0.0	0.0	0.0	0.0	0.0	0.8

* *Clinton's total is through 1994.*

Source: Modified from David M. O'Brien, "Clinton's Legal Policy and the Courts: Rising from Disarray or Turning Around and Around," in The Clinton Presidency: First Appraisals, *ed. by Colin Campbell and Bert A. Rockman (Chatham, NJ: Chatham House, 1996), p. 137.*

THE REAL JUDICIARY

Today's federal judiciary bears a close resemblance to the Founders' imagined branch. Although the Founders might be pleasantly surprised that the Supreme Court finally got its own building in 1935—designed as a replica of an ancient Greek temple, with the words "Equal Justice Under Law" carved above its massive bronze doors—they would not be surprised by what happens inside. Unlike Congress and the presidency, which have been profoundly altered by television, the Supreme Court, indeed all federal courts, still operate pretty much as they always have, mostly as a consequence of the common-law tradition.

What has changed, however, is the workload. The federal judiciary is handling more cases than ever, and the Supreme Court is making tougher choices about what cases it will hear. And even though the Supreme Court has not grown dramatically in the number of justices, the rest of the federal court system has continued to expand as new laws and a growing crime rate require more judges. A rapidly changing society has meant more disputes, and more laws have meant more conflicts suitable for courts. And if television has not penetrated the workings of the federal judiciary, as it has in many state and local courts, it certainly has raised the visibility of what the courts do.

Before turning to the structure of the modern judiciary and questions about what judges do, it is useful to examine the rise of the first courts. Recall that the Founders left the structure of the lower courts entirely to Congress and the president. They also left the internal workings of the Supreme Court to the future. Although Article III established one Supreme Court, it did not specify how many justices would sit on this highest "bench" of all.

The First Courts

Today's federal judiciary was outlined in the very first act passed by the very first Congress. Numbered as the very first bill considered by the very first Senate (S. 1), the Judiciary Act of 1789 laid out a three-tiered system composed of a *Supreme Court* with a chief justice and five associate justices, three *courts of appeal* with two Supreme Court justices "riding" the circuit with a single district court judge, and thirteen *district courts* each with a single district court judge. As we will see later, this three-tiered court system exists to this day, supplemented by a number of *specialty courts* that handle the special needs of veterans, taxpayers, and others.

Although Congress struggled with many of the same questions raised in the Constitutional Convention, practical politics decided the shape of the judiciary. Figuring out how to pay for the new system clearly affected the final bill, leading to a much simpler system than had existed under the British.[14]

The Supreme Court was placed at the very *top* of the newly created system, the district courts at the *bottom,* one for each state, and the courts of appeal in the *middle.* (As we shall see later, Congress finally created a separate appeals court system with its own judges in 1891.) The courts of appeal originally were called circuit courts for the circuit, or map of towns, that the three judges would follow to hear cases. Given the transportation system of the late 1700s, it was much easier for the judge to go to the case than for the case to go the judge. (See Box 10–2 for the basic structure of the federal judiciary today.)

The first courts were far less visible than either the First Congress or Washington's presidency. The first Supreme Court was headed by John Jay, the least-known author of *The Federalist Papers*. The first term, or year, of the Jay Supreme Court was barely noticed. As one historian described it: "The first President immediately on taking office settled down to the pressing business of being President. The first Congress enacted the first laws. The first Supreme Court adjourned."[15]

Only four of the six members could make it to Philadelphia for the term, and the term itself lasted only ten days. Lacking cases to decide, the Court had little to do but select a clerk, choose a seal, and give several lawyers permission to present cases at some as yet undefined point in the future. As the final court of

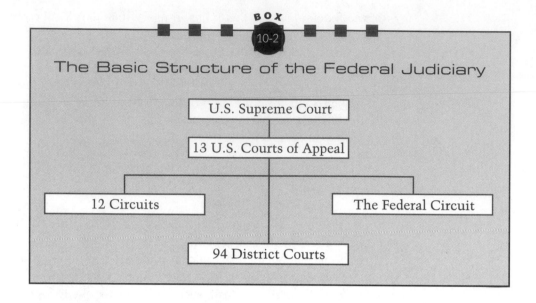

BOX 10-2

The Basic Structure of the Federal Judiciary

```
            U.S. Supreme Court
         13 U.S. Courts of Appeal

  12 Circuits              The Federal Circuit

            94 District Courts
```

appeal, the Supreme Court had to wait for cases to work their way up from the bottom.

The Institutional Judiciary

Today's judiciary remains far less visible than Congress or the presidency. Most Americans know little about the operation of the federal judiciary, let alone the divided responsibilities between federal, state, and local courts. Most hear about the judiciary at one of two levels: either in connection with highly visible local criminal cases such as the O. J. Simpson murder trial, or when the Supreme Court makes a well-publicized decision on an issue such as flag burning or abortion.

Nevertheless, as we will see in Chapter 11, the federal judiciary plays a prominent role in American life. Name an issue, and the federal courts have likely had some say. The courts have done their share of lawmaking over the decades, often moving far ahead of Congress and the presidency in addressing the controversial issues of the day. Freed from public pressure, they broke the "color" barrier in the public schools, drew the lines between church and state on religion, took a stand on abortion, and continue to struggle with the rights of criminals. Much of what the courts do is highly unpopular, but most Americans agree that the courts have shown great courage over the years.

Unlike Congress and the presidency, which are highly complicated institutions, the federal judiciary is actually quite simple. It consists of two components: judges and the courts in which they work. Although the federal judiciary does have a small staff of law clerks and administrators, these employees play a far less important role than do staff in Congress and the presidency.

Judges. The federal judiciary is led by more than eight hundred federal judges. As of 1993, there were 9 judges on the Supreme Court (one chief justice and eight associates), 167 on the courts of appeal, and 649 on the district courts.

The job of every judge is the same: to render justice. But how a judge does so depends very much on the kind of court involved. Trial court judges render justice largely by being a referee between the plaintiff and the defendant. The plaintiff is the party who alleges that a wrong has been committed, while the defendant is the party who allegedly committed that wrong. In criminal cases, the government acts on behalf of the public as a whole by acting as the prosecution. In the American legal system, every defendant is to be considered innocent until proven guilty beyond a reasonable doubt.

In contrast, appellate judges render justice by reviewing the decisions of trial courts. Their job is to ask whether the plaintiff and/or defendant received a fair trial, evidence was presented correctly, and punishment was appropriate to the act. They can void a trial court decision on several grounds, including everything from violations of procedural fairness to a breach of constitutional protection.

Every judge, whether trial or appellate, has a somewhat different courtroom presence. Some are strict disciplinarians who enforce every rule to the letter, others are willing to give one side or the other greater latitude in the give-and-take of a trial. Although they are all bound by the same law, every judge has enough discretion, whether in admitting evidence or conducting the trial, to shape the outcome.

As such, judging is much more an art than a science. As we will see at the end of this section, Congress has from time to time tried to limit discretion, particularly by restricting a judge's authority to impose sentences. In theory, a judge is to fit the sentence, or punishment, to the crime. But under legislation passed in the 1980s, punishments for certain kinds of crimes are preset by Congress.

Courts. Judges do their work in courts, which are nothing more than devices for handling cases. Although courtrooms are designed to reinforce the legitimacy of the institution, with the judge usually perched high above the proceeding, the American judicial system is relatively simple. It consists of two basic levels, federal and state, each with at least three levels within.

Federal Courts. As noted above, the federal judiciary is composed of district courts, courts of appeal, and the Supreme Court. Under Article I, Congress also has the power to create specialty courts to handle specific issues such as taxes or veterans. These four types of courts will be discussed in order below.[16]

DISTRICT COURTS. District courts handle the largest number of cases, and originate the vast majority of the work that reaches the Supreme Court for final appeal. District courts have original jurisdiction over all crimes against the United States; all civil cases arising under the Constitution; federal laws, or treaties; and cases involving citizens of different states.[17] District courts conduct all trials involving federal law, some with juries, others without. There is at least one district court in every state.

As the number of laws has grown, and the number of states has increased, the number of district courts had to increase. Congress created thirteen districts under the 1789 Judiciary Act, and provided funds for just thirteen district court judges in 1789. By 1993, the number was up to 94 districts and nearly 650 judges. The growth was clearly a response to the number of cases pending before the district courts. (See Box 10–3 for the trends in workload.) As that workload has expanded, so have delays. Congress became so concerned about the slowdowns that it passed the Speedy Trial Act in 1974 requiring that all criminal trials be started within one hundred days of charges being filed, which federal courts abide by today.

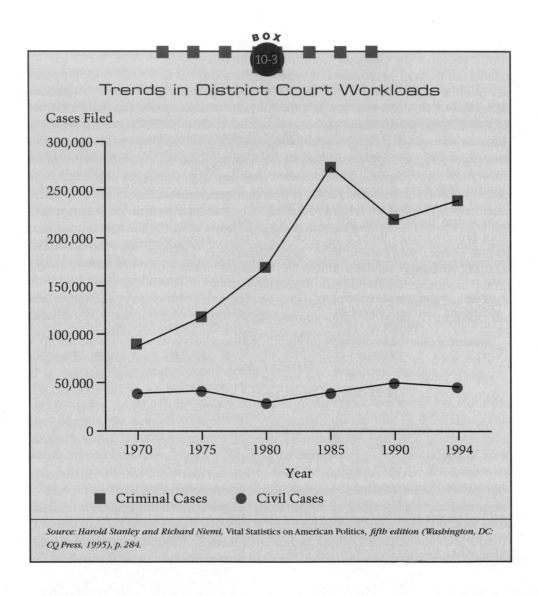

BOX 10-3

Trends in District Court Workloads

Cases Filed

■ Criminal Cases ● Civil Cases

Source: Harold Stanley and Richard Niemi, Vital Statistics on American Politics, *fifth edition (Washington, DC: CQ Press, 1995), p. 284.*

COURTS OF APPEAL. The modern appellate court system was created in 1891, when Congress established nine separate courts of appeal with funds for a total of twenty judges. Prior to 1891 individual justices of the Supreme Court rode different circuits as the first layer of appellate review. As the district courts have expanded, so have the courts of appeals. There are now 13 courts and 167 judges. Although individual Supreme Court justices are still assigned to specific circuits, they rarely participate in any proceedings.

Courts of appeals conduct no trials, and are only allowed to make decisions on facts in the existing record. The number of judges in a given circuit depends upon the workload, with the smallest circuit having four judges and the largest twenty-eight. Most decisions are made by panels of three judges who review the given district court record to assure that the original decision was fair. Each court of appeals has a chief judge to handle the administrative workload and assign cases to panels. On particularly important cases, the chief judge may decide to create a panel composed of the entire membership, which is called hearing a case *en banc.*

As with the district courts, there has been a dramatic increase in the court of appeals workload. In 1915, there were less than 1,500 cases filed for appeal; by 1993, the number had grown to nearly 50,000. Unlike the district courts, the courts of appeals are under no obligation to act quickly. Because the Supreme Court cannot reach down to the district court level to select cases it wants to hear, it must wait for the courts of appeals to act, thereby giving this intermediate layer of appeal enormous responsibility for both the timing and content of the Supreme Court agenda.

THE SUPREME COURT. Of the three levels of the federal judicial system, the Supreme Court has changed the least since 1789. There are nine Supreme Court justices today (eight associate justices and one chief justice), compared to six in 1789, and oral argument proceeds in much the same way as it did two hundred years ago. The Supreme Court is still sharply limited in what cases it can hear. Unlike Congress and the presidency, which can manufacture their own agendas from whole cloth, the Supreme Court can only react to cases brought before it.

Today's Supreme Court is a much more active institution than it once was. It fashions its docket, or agenda, of cases from a much larger number of appeals. Whereas the average district court judge hears 40 cases per year, and the average court of appeals judge hears 30, the nine Supreme Court justices together hear 100–120.

Not surprisingly, the Supreme Court has added more staff to keep up. Back in 1930, there were just fifty staff positions to help the justices dispose of their cases. By 1993, there were nearly 350.

SPECIALTY COURTS. Under Article I, Congress has the power to create "tribunals," or courts, inferior to the Supreme Court. Unlike **constitutional courts,** which are created by Congress under Article III and therefore give their judges the full protection of life tenure, **legislative courts** are created under Article I's elastic clause, which allows Congress to do whatever is necessary and proper to exercise its powers. Judges on legislative courts serve for specific terms of office, not life, and can only be reappointed through the normal confirmation process. Two examples of legislative courts are the U.S. Tax Court, which resolves disputes between taxpayers and the Internal Revenue Service, thereby helping Congress exercise its authority to lay and collect taxes; and the Court of Veterans Appeals, which reviews benefit decisions made by the Department of Veterans Affairs, thereby helping Congress exercise its authority to provide for the general welfare. Both courts handle cases that would not ordinarily appear before the constitutional courts.

It is important to note that district and appeals courts are not the only constitutional courts that have been created by Congress over the years. Congress created the U.S. Customs Court to handle disputes arising over the appraisals of imported goods by the Customs Service. Judges on such constitutional courts serve for life, and can be removed only through impeachment and conviction.

The point here is not to memorize long lists of constitutional and legislative courts, however. Rather, it is merely to note that the federal judiciary should not be seen as a single, sleek pyramid rising from district courts on up to the Supreme Court, but as what one pair of legal scholars describe as "an eroded mountain range."[18]

State Courts. In the Founders' federalist system, state courts were guaranteed a continued role in providing justice. Just as state and local bureaucracies are much larger than the federal, so, too are state and local courts larger than the federal. Indeed, the real explosion in workload has been in the states. As Federal Appeals Court Judge Frank Coffin notes, "it is in state courts that by far most of the nation's litigation is decided; the huge size of the state court component of our dual system is seldom appreciated."

According to Coffin's estimates, state trial courts handle nearly 32 million cases a year, accounting for 99 percent of all cases heard by federal and state courts combined, an estimate that would swell if he counted courts of limited jurisdiction (juvenile courts, domestic relations, wills) where 18,000 judges handle over 73 million cases a year. There are now 23 state courts for every one federal trial court; 14 state judges for every one federal; 113 state cases for every one federal.[19]

In general, most civil and criminal law is handled by the state courts (murder, drug selling, and burglary, for example, are almost always state offenses). Federal courts also handle civil and criminal law, but of a different kind (counterfeiting is a classic federal offense; states cannot coin their own money). Civil cases make up the bulk of the district court workload, accounting for more than 80 percent of the caseload in 1992. Almost all state court decisions on these cases are final with no room for appeal upward into the federal system.

There are times, however, when federal law provides alternative paths to justice. The 1992 Rodney King case is one example. King was an African American motorist beaten by four white Los Angeles police officers after being stopped

The Federal Judiciary ▲ 359

Rodney King beaten by police in Los Angeles after being stopped for a traffic violation (left) and released three days later from jail (right). The four officers who were tried on charges of assault were found not guilty by a California court. The acquittals sparked the Los Angeles riots. Two of the four acquitted officers were later found guilty of violating King's civil rights.

for a routine traffic violation. Despite an amateur video tape showing the beating in brutal detail, all four officers were acquitted of assault charges by a trial jury under California state law. It was a decision that sparked the Los Angeles riots.

Two of the four officers were later convicted in a federal court for violating King's civil rights. Although the officers could not be tried twice for the same offense—the Constitution expressly forbids double jeopardy, which means government gets one chance, and just one chance, to make its case—they could be tried twice under different laws. Federal prosecutors were able to prove that the officers had used excessive and unnecessary force with the intent of denying King's civil rights.

The federal courts can also hear appeals from state and local courts involving violations of constitutional law (the death penalty is sometimes imposed as a penalty in criminal cases by state courts but it is contested in federal courts as a cruel and unusual punishment prohibited under the Eighth Amendment).

Why the Judiciary Changed

The growing judicial workload is tied to changes in society. More people means more relationships; changing families, increasing divisions between the rich and poor, and the changing economy all contribute to more stress in those relationships; more stress creates pressure for more laws and regulations to govern behavior; more laws and regulations generate greater efforts at enforcement; and the results end up in the workload. As Federal Appeals Court Judge Stephen Reinhardt writes, "There are more and more people in this country, and Congress passes more and more laws affecting the quality of life. Thirty years ago, we had no environmental laws, no Civil Rights Act of 1964, no right to challenge many forms of arbitrary action. The 1960s changed all that. There is no going back."[20]

The workload also reflects both the public's fear of crime, and law enforcement's increased activity. Violent crime (murder, rape, robbery, and aggravated assault) increased nearly five times between 1960 and 1991 from 161 to 758 crimes per 100,000 Americans; property crime (burglary, larceny, and car theft) jumped more than three times from 1960 to 1991 from 1,887 to nearly 6,000 crimes per 100,000.[21]

As the rates have increased, the federal government has written tougher and tougher laws, broadening the death penalty to a number of new offenses and requiring judges to impose tougher sentences on certain kinds of crimes. Whether these tougher laws actually deter crime is in some dispute, but there is no question that they increase the judicial workload. (See the "In a Different Light" discussion "Three Strikes and You're Out.")

The judicial workload also reflects America's tendency to sue, a tendency that may be linked to the rising number of lawyers. In 1850, there was one lawyer for every 1,000 Americans; today, there is one for every 350 or so.[22] As the number of lawyers has grown, so, too, has their search for business. The more Americans bump into each other, both figuratively and literally (two-thirds of state and local cases deal with traffic violations or accidents), the more they decide to sue.

Much as the courts have struggled to keep up, the average delay in handling criminal cases in the federal district courts increased from just under four months in 1980 to almost six by 1992.[23] Merely adding more judges is not necessarily the answer to the problem. As the number of judges has increased, so has the amount of administrative work involved in actually deciding cases. And as the administrative backlogs have increased, so have the delays in coming to decisions. The result is a steady increase in the backlog of civil and criminal cases.

IN A DIFFERENT LIGHT

THREE STRIKES AND YOU'RE OUT

As Americans have grown increasingly worried about crime, Congress, state legislatures, and voters have pushed for harsher sentences for a host of crimes. Many of these sentences are mandatory, meaning that a judge has no choice but to impose a certain penalty if a given defendant is convicted of a particular crime. New York state law, for example, requires a mandatory minimum sentence of fifteen years to life for anyone involved in the sale of two or more ounces of cocaine, whether that sale was their first or their hundredth.

One of the most popular forms of mandatory sentencing is called "three strikes and you're out." Under such laws, anyone convicted of three violent crimes is sentenced to life in prison without the chance of early release through parole. In 1993, voters in Washington state approved an initiative establishing the nation's "three-strikes-and-you're-out" legislation requiring life in prison for repeat lawbreakers. In 1994, thirteen other states followed suit, as did the federal government. Almost 80 percent of Americans favor laws imposing such tough mandatory sentences, even if doing so means that state and federal taxes must go up to build new prisons.[24]

Such laws have had at least two impacts on the judicial system. The first is an apparent decline in the number of plea bargains in criminal cases. Under such agreements, government reduces the charges against a defendant in return for a guilty plea. The defendant gets less jail time, government saves trial costs, and the judicial workload stays down.

Defendants are clearly less willing to plea bargain when a guilty plea constitutes the third strike, especially if the third strike means life in prison. The stiffer the mandatory sentence, the more likely the defendant will take his or her chances in court. Before its "three-strikes" law took effect, 90 percent of California's more serious crimes were plea bargained. By March, only 14 percent of "second-strike" cases, and only 6 percent of "third-strike" cases were plea bargained, meaning the rest of the cases were now plugging up the judicial system awaiting trial.[25] Given the high penalty involved, many of the cases that do go to trial will be appealed, meaning more workload higher up in the judicial system.

The second impact of three-strikes and other mandatory sentencing laws is a growing number of Americans in jail. By the end of 1994, the U.S. prison population exceeded 1 million inmates for the first time in history. Prison construction is one of the fastest growing items on state and local budgets, having grown nearly five-fold over the past fifteen years, from $6 billion a year in 1980 to well over $30 billion today.

Judges are particularly concerned about the rise in mandatory sentences, largely because such laws reduce their ability to fit the punishment to the circumstances of a particular crime. "Mandatory minimums are frequently the result of floor amendments to demonstrate emphatically that legislators want to get tough on crime," said Supreme Court Chief Justice William Rehnquist in 1993. "It seems to me that one of the best arguments against any more mandatory minimums, and perhaps against some of those that we already have, is that they frustrate the careful calibration of sentences, from one end of the spectrum to the other. . . ."[26] Because mandatory sentences are particularly popular in the war on drugs, a first-time cocaine dealer can get fifteen years without parole, while a first-time rapist can get much less time in prison.

Nevertheless, there is some evidence that three-strikes and other mandatory sentencing laws may reduce crime. Having repeat offenders in jail means they are not on the streets. One recent study suggested that California's three-strikes law will reduce violent crimes by as much as one-third. Whether spending $20 billion to build the twenty-six new prisons needed to house California's third strike criminals for life is the only way to get the cut in crime is not quite so clear.

As one expert argues, "if you want to deter crime, you have to increase the certainty of punishment, not the severity." In other words, catching more criminals is likely to be more effective in reducing crime than putting a relatively small number of repeat offenders in prison for life.[27]

Appointing Judges

As the number of judgeships has grown with the workload, so, too, has the pressure to find talented people for judgeships. Federal court appointments are governed by the same language that applies to all presidential appointments. Under Article II, the president nominates all judges by and with the advice and consent of the Senate. Because most federal judges serve for life, a president can have impact on the courts long after leaving office.

George Washington established the two basic criteria for the selection process. He first tried to make sure that his appointees would be political and ideological allies (all of Washington's judgeships went to Federalists), and second that every state would be represented on some court somewhere. Thus, from the very beginning, the courts were instruments of practical politics. (Jimmy Carter added a third test for judicial nominations: racial and gender diversity. It was a test dropped under Reagan and Bush and revived under Clinton.)

Both of Washington's precedents still hold today. Presidents nominate judges who are most likely to agree with them on the key issues before the courts. Democrats nominate Democrats; Republicans nominate Republicans. (See Box 10–4 for the figures over the past fifty years.) In a similar vein, presidents routinely rely on the senators in a given state to provide recommendations for federal judges, thereby meeting Washington's second test of state representation. (See Box 10–5 for the steps involved in the Supreme Court nomination process.)

Presidents who make predictions of court decisions based on ideology are often disappointed, especially at the Supreme Court level. President Eisenhower appointed Chief Justice Earl Warren expecting conservative leadership only to watch as Warren led the civil rights revolution with *Brown v. Board of Education,* which ended racial segregation of public schools. Eisenhower later called his appointment of Warren "the biggest damn-fooled mistake" he had ever made.[28]

Truman felt the same way about his appointment of former Attorney General Tom Clark. Having been nominated to the Supreme Court as a friend of the president's, Clark sided against Truman in a key case involving the president's war power, even though he had sided with Truman on the same issue as attorney general. "Whenever you put a man on the Supreme Court he ceases to be your friend," Truman later reflected. "I'm sure of that. Tom Clark was my biggest mistake. No question about it. . . . I don't know what got into me. He was no damn good as Attorney General, and on the Supreme Court . . . it doesn't seem pos-

BOX
10-4

Judicial Appointments from the President's Party

Franklin Roosevelt (Democrat)	96.4%
Harry Truman (Democrat)	93.1%
Dwight Eisenhower (Republican)	95.1%
John Kennedy (Democrat)	90.9%
Lyndon Johnson (Democrat)	95.2%
Richard Nixon (Republican)	93.7%
Gerald Ford (Republican)	81.2%
Jimmy Carter (Democrat)	94.8%
Ronald Reagan (Republican)	94.4%

Source: Henry Abraham, Justices and Presidents *(New York: Oxford University Press, 1992), p. 68.*

sible, but he's even been worse. He hasn't made one right decision that I can think of."[29]

Presidents also worry about the Senate where confirmation is anything but certain. Although all of George Washington's Supreme Court appointments were quickly confirmed, it was a precedent that did not stand: 28 of the next 142 were rejected, the most recent defeat coming in 1987 with Reagan's nomination of Robert Bork. Bork was defeated as the result of a campaign launched by abortion-rights groups who feared that he would become the swing vote in reversing *Roe v. Wade.*

Supreme Court nominations have always been controversial to one degree or another—John Tyler, who served as president for one term from 1841–1845, lost five nominees. The difference between then and now is that judicial nominations were once handled almost completely out of public view. For many years,

BOX 10-5

Steps in Becoming a Supreme Court Justice

1. *Find the Candidate*. Most presidents have delegated that responsibility to someone in their administration, most likely in the attorney general's office. Recommendations might be solicited from White House staff, Congress, governors, bar associations, sitting and retired justices, and personal sources.

2. *Make a Short List*. The president makes a first cut of candidates based on the political impact of their appointment and their fitness to serve. Those that are found acceptable are placed on a short list.

3. *Investigate the Candidates*. Each candidate on the short list is thoroughly investigated by the Federal Bureau of Investigation and formally reviewed by the American Bar Association, which rates candidates either Well Qualified, Qualified, or Not Qualified.

4. *Pick the Nominee*. Weighing a host of political and ideological factors, as well as the chances for Senate confirmation, the president formally nominates a candidate for Senate confirmation.

5. *Hold a Hearing*. The nominee meets informally with members of the Senate Judiciary Committee; the committee holds a formal hearing, takes a vote, and passes the nomination onward to the full Senate.

6. *Confirm the Nominee*. The full Senate approves or rejects the nomination by a simple majority vote. Twenty-nine nominees have been rejected or withdrawn since 1790; only twelve of the twenty-nine actually came to the Senate floor for a final vote.

Supreme Court nominees did not even appear before the Senate Judiciary Committee for hearings. As a result, Senators could support or oppose a president's choice with little fear of election consequences. The public either did not follow the process or did not care.

Those days of nearly invisible review are long gone, in large part because organized interests in Washington have come to see the appointment of federal judges as a key opportunity to shape what government does. Pro-choice and women's rights groups mounted a successful national campaign against the nomination of Robert Bork, and nearly succeeded in stopping the nomination of Clarence Thomas.[30]

The Founders would be concerned about the role of public opinion in the appointments process. Much as they might applaud the seriousness with which the Senate continues to take the confirmation process, they would worry that public opinion might make government work too well, propelling the courts to approve highly popular laws in spite of constitutional concerns.

THE SUPREME COURT AT WORK

Although the Supreme Court is only one part of a much larger judicial system, it would be a mistake to underestimate its impact on American life. Its total number of cases may be small, but they are the most important cases heard and decided. Not only is the Supreme Court the final word in specific cases, it has the ultimate power to overturn acts of Congress, state laws, local ordinances, and even its own past decisions.

This power means that even the most insignificant Supreme Court decision can create a ripple effect across the nation. Declaring one state's law unconstitutional usually means that all similar state laws are unconstitutional; requiring one school or university to open its doors to women usually means that all similar schools must open their doors to women; requiring a single prisoner be given decent cell space usually means that all prisoners must be given decent cell space.

That power, and its increasing use in recent years, also means that the Supreme Court has become a much more significant check on Congress and the presidency. Whether the Founders intended the federal judiciary to become such a dominant player is a question best left to constitutional scholars.

Making Opinions

The Supreme Court is nothing if not predictable. It starts each term on the first Monday in October and usually finishes by the end of June. Each week from the start of the term through April, the justices follow the same schedule: oral arguments for three or four hours each Monday, Tuesday, and Wednesday; private conferences attended by all nine justices each Friday. The justices spend the rest of the time working on opinions, most of which are released in the spring and summer. On the next first Monday in October, the process starts all over again.

Because so much is at stake when the Supreme Court decides, its process deserves special attention. The process involves four steps: (1) receiving the request for appeal, (2) deciding which requests to accept, (3) hearing the case, and (4) making the decision and writing the opinion. We will examine each step.

Receiving the Request for Appeal. Besides its very limited original jurisdiction, the Supreme Court can only make decisions on requests for appeal from below. Almost all such requests come to the Supreme Court docket, or agenda, from either a state supreme court or a federal court. (See Box 10–6 for the two paths upward.)

Reaching the Supreme Court is no small feat. In the state courts, a case can rise through three different levels before exiting for the Supreme Court:

Step 1. A case starts out in any one of several courts with original jurisdiction: a state or local administrative agency might say an adult bookstore cannot open near a church or

BOX
10-6

How a Case Reaches the Supreme Court

SUPREME COURT OF
THE UNITED STATES

THE STATE ROUTE	THE FEDERAL ROUTE

Decisions can be appealed if
they raise a constitutional
question

Rulings can be appealed

50 State Supreme Courts

11 Courts of Appeal;
Court of Appeals for
the District of Columbia;
Court of Appeals for
the Federal Circuit (which
hears only tax, patent, and
international trade cases)

Further appeal for ruling by
highest court in the state

Appeals of rulings of district
courts and decisions by
independent regulatory
commissions and
administrative agencies

Intermediate Courts of Appeal

Defendant loses and appeals

State Trial Courts

94 District Courts
(in all states and the
District of Columbia)

Cases involving state law
are tried

Cases involving federal law
are tried in federal district court

Source: David M. O'Brien, Storm Center: The Supreme Court in American Politics, *(New York: W.W. Norton & Co., 1993), p. 209.*

preschool, a specialized court might take a baby away from his or her adoptive parents in favor of a long-lost grandparent, a municipal court might order all Amish to put safety triangles on their horse-drawn carriages, even though such "decorations" violate their religion, or a superior court might convict a murderer on the basis of a DNA bloodtest.

Step 2. Once decided, the case can go up on appeal to a state court of appeal, which can consider state constitutional questions governing any decision and often must review any appeal of a superior court conviction.

Step 3. Once decided again, the case can go up for one last appeal to the state supreme court, which makes the absolute final decision in all but the cases permitted to go into the federal system under the Constitution.

When a case involves a constitutional question (such as freedom of speech for an adult bookstore, freedom of religion for the Amish, or due process for a murderer), it is a likely controversy for the Supreme Court. Roughly one in five Supreme Court requests come up from the state supreme courts; almost all the rest come up from the federal courts of appeals (cases from federal agencies can get to the Supreme Court more directly under certain circumstances).

In the federal courts, the same pattern holds, but for just two levels:

Step 1. Once again, the case starts out in a court of original jurisdiction: the Federal Communications Commission (which is a regulatory agency) might deny a radio license to a religious broadcaster, the Department of Commerce (an administrative agency) might fire a federal employee, or a district court might convict someone of violating a federal law (recall that the four police officers involved in the Rodney King beating were first acquitted in a state court, then later convicted on a different charge in a federal court).

Step 2. Once again, the case moves up to a court of appeals. Anyone who loses a case in a district court has an absolute right to appeal upward for review. However, as noted earlier, the appeal can only address the fairness of the process, not the facts of the case. As a result, most district court decisions are not appealed.

Whatever the route, nearly every case comes to the Supreme Court docket under a petition for a **writ of certiorari,** a Latin term meaning "made more certain" or "better informed." The petition asks the Supreme Court to order a lower court to produce the record of the case—a writ is merely a term meaning "order."

These petitions do not have to be neat or even written by lawyers to be granted. Indeed, it was a handwritten petition on yellow legal paper from Florida state prisoner Clarence Gideon that led the Court to hear *Gideon v. Wainwright.*[31] (The 1963 case established the right to a court-appointed attorney for all poor persons accused of felonies.) When the Supreme Court is willing to hear a case after considering a petition for writ of certiorari, it grants cert. (which is the commonly used abbreviation for certiorari). When it chooses not to hear the case, it denies cert.[32]

The Supreme Court will not hear just any case. Under its own rules, it will only grant certiorari in one or more of the following situations: (1) when a federal court of appeals has rendered a decision in conflict with the decision of another federal court of appeals on the same matter; (2) when a federal court of appeals has rendered a decision in conflict with a state supreme court; (3) when a federal court of appeals has departed from the accepted and usual course of judicial proceedings; (4) when a state supreme court has decided a federal question in conflict with another state supreme court or with the federal courts; or (5) when a state or federal court of appeals has decided an important question of federal law that should have been settled by the U.S. Supreme Court.[33]

Deciding Which Requests to Accept.   As its five tests suggest, the Supreme Court does not take ordinary cases. As Justice Felix Frankfurter once stated, "importance of the outcome merely to the parties is not enough."[34] The Supreme Court reserves its limited time and energy for the kind of controversies described just above. Lower courts and lawyers should be able to interpret past decisions well enough to determine what the law means. Thus, the Supreme Court's power *not to decide* can be as important as many of its formal decisions.

The Supreme Court decides not to decide in denying certiorari in 85 to 90 percent of the requests without explanation. "I would guess that somewhere between one and two thousand of the petitions for certiorari filed with the Court each year are patently without merit," writes Chief Justice William Rehnquist of the process; "even with the wide philosophical differences among the various members of the Court, no one of the nine would have the least interest in granting them."[35]

The justices grant certiorari through a rather informal process of assigning, reading, and debating potential cases. If even one justice thinks a petition is worth discussing, it is put on the agenda for the regular weekly conference of all the justices. About one quarter of all requests are discussed at one point or another. They use a **Rule of Four** to make the decisions on granting certiorari—four justices must agree to grant the request.

As the number of requests for Supreme Court action have increased, the percentage of petitions granted has gone down. That is only to be expected as the workload has increased. A Supreme Court of nine members had to pare back. In the 1920s, roughly 20 percent of all petitions for certiorari were granted; by 1992, the rate was down to just 3 percent.

But it is not just the proportion of requests granted that went down. The absolute number fell, too. In spite of all the growth trends discussed above, the Supreme Court granted just 97 writs of certiorari in 1992, down from a high of 299 in 1971, and compared to 117 in 1926.[36] President Reagan's appointment of a large number of conservative judges has certainly made a difference, as did his reluctance to sign the kinds of statutes that produce significant court cases. The Reagan judges also seem far less likely than their peers to see the kinds of controversy that have typically attracted the Court's attention.

Hearing the Case.   Once cert. has been granted, the case is scheduled for oral argument usually at least three months away. Both sides submit briefs explaining their views of the case, law clerks prepare possible lines of questioning for their justices, the nine assemble at their places on the bench (the chief justice in the middle, the least senior justices at the two far ends), and the hour of argument begins, with one-half hour for each side. Although a half hour of time may seem short, the Supreme Court rarely grants exceptions. The purpose of oral argument is not to restate the case, but to give the justices a chance to probe specific questions about the record.[37]

The arguments may be short compared to floor debates in the House and Senate, but they appear to matter—Justice Douglas argued that "oral arguments win or lose the case."[38] Also unlike the House or Senate, all the members are present. Questioning is often tough; the back-and-forth between the justices clear. The informal rules governing oral argument are clear: be brief, do not read from a prepared text, and be quick in answering questions. There is no time to waste.

All lawyers who speak before the Court do not speak with equal authority. First among them is the **solicitor general,** who represents the United States government. Appointed by the president and confirmed by the Senate, the solicitor is a senior officer of the Department of Justice. The solicitor decides which cases the government will ask the Court to review, which cases the government will appeal, and what positions the United States will take in each case. Roughly half the cases before the Supreme Court involve the U.S. government. As former Reagan administration Solicitor General Charles Fried explains,

> . . . the Solicitor General's job has hardly changed since 1870 [when it was created by statute]. He still goes to the Supreme Court in morning coat and striped trousers as the principal spokesman there of the government. It is his job to approve what the government will say in any appellate court in the country. His staff is small (about twenty lawyers), and he takes personal, not just bureaucratic, responsibility for every decision, every brief he signs. In a real sense the Solicitor General is responsible for the government's legal theories, its legal philosophy.[39]

The solicitor general can appear before the court in at least three different roles: representing the defendant when someone sues the federal government, as a plaintiff when the federal government sues a state or individual, or as a friend of the court when the federal government takes a position on a case in which it is neither defendant nor plaintiff. This third role involves filing an **amicus brief,** which literally translates into "friend of the court." (Recall that organized interests often submit amicus briefs as part of their efforts to influence Supreme Court decisions on behalf of their member or members.)

Making the Decision and Writing the Opinion.   The justices do not rely solely, or even primarily, on oral arguments in making their final decisions. They read the original record, consult the law journals, and read the increasing number of

amicus briefs submitted on one side or the other of the case. Although the solicitor general is an important source of these briefs, they can also be submitted
by just about anyone with the resources and interest to draft a formal statement.

It is useful to note that the number of amicus briefs has risen dramatically in
recent years. In the 1920s and 1930s, for example, less than 2 percent of all Supreme
Court cases involved any amicus briefs at all.[40] In 1988 alone, over 80 percent of
all cases had at least one amicus brief, and some particularly controversial cases
had many more. *Webster v. Reproductive Health Services,* a 1989 case that challenged a Missouri antiabortion law, generated seventy-eight amicus briefs representing over four hundred different organizations.[41]

Formal decisions involve far more than careful reading and reflection by individual justices, however. They actually evolve through an ongoing conversation between the justices, whether in ones and twos or in full conferences.

The most important votes on a case are taken at these conferences. These votes
determine who will be in the majority and minority. Although the votes are not
absolutely final, they clearly direct the general tone of the Court's final opinion.
Under Rehnquist, the chief justice votes first, followed by the most senior justice,
moving down one by one to the most junior justice.

These conferences rarely change opinions, however. The docket is just too big
to argue each case through in the short time available. As Justice Scalia remarked
after two years on the Court, "To call our discussion of a case a conference is really something of a misnomer. It's much more a statement of the views of each
of the nine Justices, after which the totals are added and the case is assigned. I
don't like that. Maybe it's just because I'm new. Maybe it's because I'm an academic. Maybe it's just because I am right."[42]

After the conference votes, the most senior member of the majority is asked
to either write the opinion or delegate it to another justice. When the chief justice is in the majority, he or she either writes the opinion or assigns it to another
justice. Chief Justice Earl Warren decided to write the 1954 *Brown v. Board of
Education* opinion that overturned school segregation because of the enormous
controversy it involved. As he remembered almost twenty years later,

> I assigned myself to write the decision, for it seemed to me that something so impor-
> tant ought to issue over the name of the Chief Justice of the United States. In drafting
> it, I sought to use low-key, unemotional language and to keep it short enough so that
> it could be published in full in every newspaper in the country. I kept the text secret (it
> was locked in my safe) until I read from the bench.[43]

(To this day, most opinions are read out loud by the author from the bench—
in criminal cases, Rehnquist not only reads his decisions, but recounts the details of the crime.)

Once a majority opinion is drafted, justices have a mix of choices. They can
simply sign onto the majority opinion, which is the simplest option. They can
write a concurring opinion that reaches the same conclusion as the majority but

through different legal reasoning. They can join with other justices in signing such a concurring opinion. They can write a dissenting opinion explaining why they disagree with the majority. Or they can join with other justices in signing such a dissenting opinion.

Concurring opinions were exceedingly rare until the 1940s, when the number began to rise to its current level of roughly 40 percent of all decisions.[44] Dissenting opinions show the same pattern: rare until the 1940s, but now attached to about 60 percent of all decisions. Although roughly two-thirds of all *decisions* in the 1993–1994 term were unanimous, and only one-sixth by a 5–4 or 6–3 vote, the Court appears to be increasingly unable to reach consensus on the actual majority *opinions* it writes.[45]

This process definitely produces winners and losers. In the 1993–1994 term, for example, Justice Kennedy seemed to hold the balance of power on close cases (5–4 and 6–3 votes), joining the winning side on 85 percent of the cases, while Justice Blackmun was the most isolated, appearing on the winning side in just 35 percent of the cases.[46]

Shortcuts to Decision.   Making a decision and writing an opinion clearly take a certain amount of time, too much so for cases such as final appeals from death row inmates about to be executed. Petitions for immediate relief in such cases are sometimes handled under a **Rule of One**—that is, a single justice can decide to issue a writ ordering immediate action until the rest of the Supreme Court can meet. A **writ of habeas corpus** allows all courts, federal and state, to protect people who are falsely imprisoned. Technically, the term *habeas corpus* means "to produce the body." Legally, it is a request for an immediate review to determine whether a person is unlawfully imprisoned or detained.

Whatever the writ is called, almost all carry an *injunction* ordering or delaying a specific act. An injunction to stay, or delay action, is particularly important to prisoners on death row seeking to have their cases reviewed at the eleventh hour. Because of the life and death nature of these cases, the Court has special procedures for reviewing the requests. As retired Justice Harry Blackmun explained on *Nightline,*

> The justices have scattered and gone home probably. We know in advance about scheduled executions. There is at least one clerk from each chamber who is here, perhaps all night, if necessary. My clerk is on the phone probably several times as papers are being filed and we talk about them . Nearly always the vote is by telephone. On occasion, we have a conference call where we all get on the line. But it is kind of like a death march.[47]

From the summer of 1993 through January 1994, the Court received fifty-four applications for emergency relief; thirty-six were denied; eighteen were granted, including seven from death row prisoners. The eighteen that were granted involved a stay of some kind until the rest of the Supreme Court could consider the question.

The Rise of Judicial Activism

One reason for the growing tension on the Supreme Court, which is reflected in the number of concurring and dissenting opinions, involves the increasing role of the judiciary in making broad national policy. As all levels of government struggle to deal with an increasingly complex, often divided society, the Constitution is being tested in areas of daily life the Founders could hardly imagine—from the right to die to genetic testing. The result has been an increasing number of laws and precedents overturned, alongside a growing role for the courts in running everything from schools to prisons.

It is important to note that judicial activism is not exclusive to either a liberal or a conservative position. The ideological tone all depends on the precedents in place at the start of a given era. Conservative Supreme Courts can be just as active in overturning acts of Congress or precedents if those acts and precedents happen to come from a liberal era. Thus, activism is largely in the eye of the beholder—liberals see conservative courts as too activist; conservatives see the opposite. (See Box 10–7 for the history of activism.)

If activism were just a liberal tool, for example, a conservative Supreme Court would never overturn past precedents. But, as Box 10–7 clearly shows, the Rehnquist Court, which is generally seen as conservative, overturned twenty-one precedents in its first five years, 1986–1991, many of them eroding liberal precedents established under the Warren Court two decades before. The difference between a liberal and a conservative Supreme Court is not in activism, but in ideology.

It is not clear what the Founders would think of this activism. On the one hand, the Founders certainly saw the courts as an important check on legislative power. Recall Alexander Hamilton's vision of the courts as a last brake against public passion. Lacking a strong check, Congress would be free to repudiate the Constitution at will.

On the other hand, the Founders also might argue that the lawmaking power clearly resides in Article I and the legislature. Much as Hamilton defended the courts in *Federalist Paper No. 78* as "the bulwarks of a limited Constitution against legislative encroachment," recall that he also argued that the courts should not "substitute *WILL* instead of *JUDGMENT*," nor "substitute their own pleasure to the constitutional intentions of the legislature."[48]

Some legal scholars interpret this language of "will" and "judgment" to argue that the courts should always interpret the Constitution in the strictest possible terms. If a power or right is not written in the Constitution, or so the argument goes, judges should not write it now. Others argue that the courts should not become "super legislatures," substituting their judgments for the rightful decisions of duly elected officials. As judicial scholar Henry Abraham argues, however, there is a fine line between Hamilton's "judgment" (sometimes labeled **judicial restraint**) and "will" (often labeled as **judicial activism**).[49] Like all fine lines, whether one

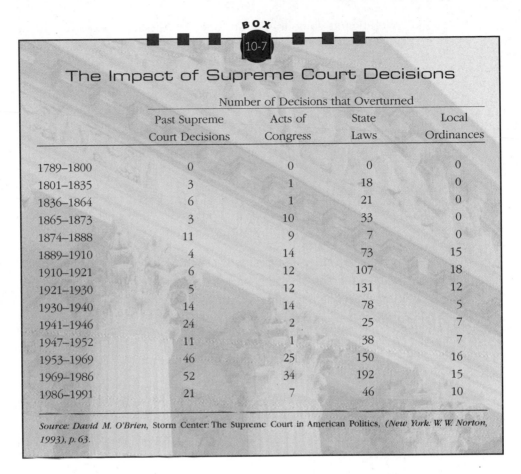

BOX 10-7

The Impact of Supreme Court Decisions

	Number of Decisions that Overturned			
	Past Supreme Court Decisions	Acts of Congress	State Laws	Local Ordinances
1789–1800	0	0	0	0
1801–1835	3	1	18	0
1836–1864	6	1	21	0
1865–1873	3	10	33	0
1874–1888	11	9	7	0
1889–1910	4	14	73	15
1910–1921	6	12	107	18
1921–1930	5	12	131	12
1930–1940	14	14	78	5
1941–1946	24	2	25	7
1947–1952	11	1	38	7
1953–1969	46	25	150	16
1969–1986	52	34	192	15
1986–1991	21	7	46	10

Source: David M. O'Brien, Storm Center: The Supreme Court in American Politics, (New York: W. W. Norton, 1993), p. 63.

sees restraint or activism often depends on one's ideological lens. What looks like making laws to conservatives may be restraint to liberals, and vice versa depending upon who happens to be making the decision.

Again, it is hard to know where the Founders would draw the fine line. They might applaud the aggressive use of the courts to protect the rights of minorities. After all, one of the judiciary's prime duties was to protect Americans from each other. But they might also worry that the federal judiciary, by its very decisions, is becoming too intimately involved in actually making the laws.

There is no question, however, that judicial activism has driven some of the key decisions of recent history. A passive judiciary never would have ordered that the Topeka School Board integrate its schools, for example, or that every person charged with a crime is entitled to legal counsel.[50]

No matter what it is labeled, all courts make laws. As former Chief Justice Earl Warren once remarked, "It doesn't make it consciously, it doesn't do it by intending to usurp the role of Congress but because of the very nature of our job. When two litigants come into court, one says the act of Congress means this, the other says the act of Congress means the opposite of that, and we say the act of Congress means something—either one of the two or something in between. We are making law, aren't we?"[51] Given their embrace of the English common-law tradition, and its history of judge-made law, the Founders would likely agree.

IN A DIFFERENT LIGHT

THE IMPORTANCE OF BEING ANONYMOUS

The federal judiciary is a mystery to most Americans. In an age of Court TV and *The People's Court,* Americans know surprisingly little about how the federal courts work, and can do better at identifying the Three Stooges than the nine justices of the Supreme Court. (See Box 10–8 for the name recognition of the nine current justices of the Supreme Court.)

BOX 10-8

Members of the Supreme Court, 1995

	Year Appointed	President	Percent Recognized
Chief Justice			
William H. Rehnquist	1972	Nixon	8%
Associate Justices			
John P. Stevens	1975	Ford	1
Sandra Day O'Connor	1981	Reagan	31
Antonin Scalia	1986	Reagan	6
Anthony M. Kennedy	1988	Reagan	4
David H. Souter	1990	Bush	4
Clarence Thomas	1991	Bush	30
Ruth Bader Ginsburg	1993	Clinton	7
Stephen Breyer	1994	Clinton	1

Source on public recognition: Joan Biskupic, "Has the Court Lost Its Appeal?" Washington Post, *October 12, 1995, p. A23.*

Being anonymous is just fine with the Supreme Court, however. The justices know that the legitimacy of their decisions depends in part on maintaining anonymity. The public's willingness to obey a judicial decision must always reside in the decision itself, not the personality or clothes of the judge. The less the public knows about a given judge, the better.

The Supreme Court does not act in secret, however. All Supreme Court decisions are public, and all oral argument occurs in the open. There may not be television cameras in the chamber, but every American is free to wait a turn in line to watch the nine justices perform without a safety net: "Power and vulnerability exist side by side. No aides hand the Justices follow-up questions to ask the lawyers; no chairman gavels a recess when things get sticky. The atmosphere is businesslike. The Justices make nothing so clear as that every second counts. Showmanship is disfavored; when an inexperienced lawyer makes a florid presentation, a chill almost visibly settles on the bench."[52]

What makes Supreme Court justices and other federal judges different from other political leaders is that they seek anonymity, creating a "cult of the robe" in which judges use their anonymity to distance themselves from the public. The justices cannot allow themselves to become celebrities. They would never appear on *The David Letterman Show* to discuss a decision, as Vice President Gore did in late 1993 to promote his reinventing government agenda, nor would they show up on one of the Sunday morning talk shows to argue a case.

This anonymity, and the mystery that goes with it, is not necessarily bad for justice. If Americans knew the real justices, or so the notion goes, they would start to think of the Supreme Court as just another collection of politicians, and might lose respect for the Supreme Court's decisions. Being anonymous is a fundamental basis for public trust.

The fact is that all courts, from the Supreme Court down to local traffic court, have little else beyond legitimacy to enforce their rulings. Again, they have no army or police force to make the country behave. They can order a Nativity display dismantled, but cannot tear it down; they can order an African American child to an all-white school, but cannot escort her to class; they can order a child rapist released into the community, but cannot unlock the cell. All the courts can do is issue orders and hope the public will obey.

Obviously, judges can become celebrities despite their best intentions. Supreme Court justices do get noticed from time to time—that is how the public learned that Justice Ginsberg reads her mail by flashlight at the movies; "I don't care much for commercials and previews," she explained.[53] Lance Ito became a public figure merely by being the next superior court judge in line for a murder trial when the O. J. Simpson case came up.

But it is one thing for a judge to become known, and quite another to seek celebrity in the first place. If judges were to suddenly start endorsing candidates, lending their names to causes, or appearing as regular guests on the Sunday news shows, their courts would lose some of their mystery. And that might weaken their ability to protect Americans from their government and each other, both subjects of the next chapter of this book.

CONCLUSION

The federal judiciary has never been more important to a government that must be just strong enough to protect the nation as a whole, but never so strong as to become a threat to liberty itself. It has become a key referee between Congress and the presidency, and has come to use the power of judicial review as a clear check on the other two branches. As America continues to grow and divide against itself, the judiciary also plays an increasing role in protecting us against ourselves—ensuring our civil liberties and protecting our civil rights; hence, the steady growth in the number of laws, cases, and courts.

Despite these changes, the federal judiciary more closely resembles the original constitutional design than either Congress or the presidency. There may be more courts, cases, and procedure than the Founders could have predicted, and more women and minority judges than the Founders could have expected. But even where the courts have been more active than Alexander Hamilton and his colleagues might like, they have acted mostly to protect us from ourselves, guarding the Constitution from encroachment, confirming basic rights embedded in the Founders' original design.

This does not mean the courts are always going to be popular. Protecting us from ourselves is hardly popular, nor is protecting the rights of the accused. Removing Nativity displays, prohibiting prayer in school, opening the Citadel to women cadets, overturning death penalties, upholding flag burning, allowing adult bookstores, protecting racists, and permitting abortion are hardly the kinds of decisions that make all Americans happy.[54] Every decision makes someone, often many someones, angry.

Nor does it mean the courts are always right. American history is filled with examples of flawed judicial decisions and poor judgment, not the least of which involve the nation's long delay in honoring the Declaration of Independence's pledge that all people are, indeed, created equal. Point to any area of the law, and one can find some example where history eventually proved the federal judiciary wrong. Being composed of human beings, the courts inevitably make mistakes—mistakes that can take decades to repair.

The more the crime issue grips the public—as it did in being the number one or near number one issue in both the 1994 and 1996 elections—the more the courts will come under fire. Indeed, it is public dissatisfaction in part that has led to the recent efforts to impose mandatory sentences for a host of federal and state crimes. Not knowing exactly how to solve the crime problem, legislators increasingly see their role as imposing strict limits on judicial discretion; hence, the rising tide of laws that require life sentences for three-time offenders. Such three-strikes-and-you're-out laws give judges little freedom to shape the sentence to the facts of the case.

Ultimately, these efforts are designed to somehow make the judiciary more responsive to public demands for action, which is exactly what the Founders hoped to avoid. They wanted the courts to be perfectly insulated from public opinion, and gave federal judges life tenure. The more Americans pressure the courts, the more they threaten their own freedom. By making the courts more sensitive to public opinion, Americans risk uncloaking the mystery that makes the judiciary legitimate. To the extent that justice becomes merely another expression of popular consent, every American becomes more vulnerable to oppression. This is one area where a government very much *not* of the people may be absolutely essential.

THE BASICS

■ The Founders arrived in Philadelphia with substantial legal experience. Thirty-one of the fifty-five delegates to the Constitutional Convention were lawyers, and most had at least some contact with the state and local court system that had existed in pre-Revolutionary War days. The Founders drew upon their legal experience in creating a system that continues to draw heavily upon the English common-law tradition—that is, law that resides in the decisions of judges. Having created Congress and the presidency to make and execute statutory law, the Founders had some confidence that the federal judiciary would follow many of the precedents already established in common law, including stare decisis, trial and appellate courts, and a system of federal, state, and local courts.

■ The Founders viewed the federal judiciary as the least dangerous branch of government, for it had neither the power of the sword nor the power of the purse. Although the Founders clearly agreed that there should be one supreme court at the very top of government, they were not quite sure just what kinds of courts should exist below. They agreed to let Congress make the key decisions, which it did in the Judiciary Act of 1789. Under that act, the federal judiciary was composed of a Supreme Court at the top, thirteen district courts (one for each state) at the bottom, and a court of appeals in the middle. The Founders protected this least dangerous branch in part by giving judges life tenure.

■ Although the Founders also agreed that the judicial power of the United States should be vested in a federal judiciary with one Supreme Court, they never defined the judicial power clearly. Instead, Article III merely lists the kinds of cases the federal judiciary would be allowed to hear. Short as it is on lists of powers, Article III does give the federal judiciary the authority to hear "all cases arising under this Constitution, the laws of the United States, and treaties made," a clause that forms the basis for the power of judicial review. Recall that the Supreme Court used this power in *Marbury v. Madison* to declare an act of Congress unconstitutional for the first time in history.

■ Today's federal judiciary consists of judges and courts. The job of every judge is the same: to render justice. But judges in different kinds of courts—trial verus appellate, for example—render justice in different ways. In trials with juries, judges do not decide guilt or innocence, but act more as referees between the prosecution and defendant. At the appellate level, judges make the decision, but can only do so based on whether the initial trial was conducted legally.

KEY CONCEPTS

■ The judicial workload has increased dramatically over the past fifty years, in part because America has become a much more complex society, in part because Americans are so concerned about crime. The number of cases at all levels of the federal judiciary has increased, as has the number at the state court level. State courts are actually the hardest working courts of all, handling the vast majority of all civil and criminal cases in this country.

■ Appointing judges is one of the most important decisions a president makes. Because federal judges serve for life, a president can have impact on the courts long after leaving office. George Washington established two precedents for appointing judges that still hold today: judges had to be politically and ideologically compatible, and every state had to be represented on some court somewhere. No matter how hard they work for ideological compatibility, presidents are sometimes disappointed by their nominees.

■ The Supreme Court is America's most powerful court. Its decisions have ripple effects throughout society, and are weighed carefully by the nine justices. The Supreme Court makes its opinions through a four-step process: (1) receiving the requests for appeal, (2) deciding which requests to accept, (3) hearing the case, and (4) making the decision and writing the opinion. Although cases only reach the Supreme Court on appeal from below, the number of requests, called writs of certiorari, has grown so dramatically that the Supreme Court is now down to accepting just 3 percent of the total requests.

■ The federal judiciary has become increasingly active in shaping public policy (who gets what, when, and how from government). This judicial activism, as it is often labeled, reflects the growing complexity of society. One way to measure activism is to track the number of laws that the federal judiciary declares as unconstitutional. Whether the courts are exercising judicial restraint or judicial activism often depends on the ideology of the observer. The fact is that all courts make laws, which is part of the common-law tradition the Founders so clearly embraced.

IN A DIFFERENT LIGHT

■ One way to deal with the antidemocratic bias of the federal judiciary is to pursue greater demographic diversity among federal judges. This is clearly what President Clinton did early in his term by increasing the number of women and minorities nominated for federal judgeships. Although the face of the judiciary is changing as a result, the fact remains that all federal judges are still lawyers, and being a lawyer is hardly a guarantee that a judge will stay in touch with the lives that ordinary Americans lead.

■ As crime rates grew during the 1980s, Congress, state legislatures, and voters have pushed for laws that require mandatory sentences for certain crimes. One of the most popular forms of mandatory sentencing requires that repeat violent offenders be put in prison for life without a chance for parole. Such "three-strikes-and-you're-out" laws appear to increase the judicial workload while filling the prisons. Whether they also reduce crime is in some doubt. Many judges are opposed to mandatory sentencing because it weakens their ability to fit the punishment to the circumstances of the crime.

■ Federal judges value anonymity. They believe that the less the public knows about them as people, the more likely the public is to obey their decisions. They often cultivate a "cult of the robe," in which judges use their anonymity to distance themselves from the public. The federal courts have little else beyond legitimacy to enforce their rulings.

OPEN QUESTIONS

■ Would it have been better had the Founders required federal judges to be selected through direct election? Would direct election make justice more likely? Does it make any sense to have federal judges selected through the nomination and appointment process, while so many state and local judges are elected? If the Founders were so right about protecting judges from public pressure, should states and localities change their systems of selection?

■ To what extent has the Founders' least dangerous branch become too active over time? Would the Founders still see the judiciary as so harmless, so unable to annoy? Does the fact that Congress is passing so many mandatory sentencing laws suggest that the federal judiciary is not working so well, or that Congress is working too hard?

■ What makes a good judge? Should demographic diversity be part of the answer? What about wisdom and intellect? How much weight should be given to having some connection with the ordinary Americans whose lives are affected by what the federal judiciary does? And, if the weight should be great, how might law schools and law firms make such connection more likely?

...TERMS TO REMEMBER

federal judiciary

statutory law

common law

stare decisis

precedents

trial courts

appellate courts

judicial review

justiciable issue

adverseness

standing to sue

ripe for decision

moot

constitutional courts

legislative courts

writ of certiorari

Rule of Four

solicitor general

amicus brief

Rule of One

writ of habeas corpus

judicial restraint

judicial activism

Endnotes to Chapter 10

1. Roy P. Fairfield, ed., *The Federalist Papers* (Baltimore: Johns Hopkins University Press, 1981), p. 227.
2. Fairfield, *The Federalist Papers,* p. 227.
3. David O'Brien, *Supreme Court Watch 1993* (New York: W. W. Norton, 1994), pp. 243–44.
4. Lawrence M. Friedman, *A History of American Law* (New York: Simon and Schuster, 1973), p. 95.
5. Fairfield, *The Federalist Papers,* p. 227.
6. Fairfield, *The Federalist Papers,* p. 231.
7. Fairfield, *The Federalist Papers,* p. 228.
8. See Alexander M. Bickel, *The Least Dangerous Branch* (New Haven, CT: Yale University Press, 1962), p. 1.
▶ 9. The figures are from David O'Brien, *Storm Center: The Supreme Court in American Politics* (New York: W. W. Norton, 1993), p. 63.

10. O'Brien, *Storm Center*, pp. 210–20.

11. Fairfield, *The Federalist Papers*, p. 233.

12. See David O'Brien, *Storm Center: The Supreme Court in American Politics* (W. W. Norton, 1986), p. 100.

▶ 13. Thurgood Marshall, "Reflections on the Bicentennial of the United States Constitution," *Harvard Law Review* (1987), volume 101, number 1, p. 2.

14. See Maeva Marcus and Natalie Wexler, "The Judiciary Act of 1789: Political Compromise or Constitutional Interpretation," in M. Marcus, ed., *Origins of the Federal Judiciary: Essays on the Judiciary Act of 1789* (New York: Oxford University Press, 1992), p. 14.

15. John Frank, *Marble Palace* (New York: Knopf, 1968), p. 9.

16. Most of the statistics on federal workload discussed below are from Harold W. Stanley and Richard G. Niemi, *Vital Statistics on American Politics* (Washington, DC: CQ Press, 1995), pp. 281–85.

▶ 17. Henry J. Abraham, *The Judicial Process*, sixth edition (New York: Oxford University Press, 1993), p. 156.

▶ 18. Robert Kastenmeier and Michael Remington, "A Judicious Legislator's Lexicon to the Federal Judiciary," in Robert Katzmann, ed., *Judges and Legislators: Toward Institutional Comity*, (Washington, DC: Brookings Institution, 1988), p. 60.

▶ 19. Frank Coffin, *On Appeal: Courts, Lawyering, and Judging* (New York: W. W. Norton, 1994), pp. 46, 56.

20. Stephen Reinhardt, "Are 1,000 Federal Judges Enough? No. More Cases Should be Heard," *New York Times*, May 17, 1993, p. A11.

21. Stanley and Niemi, *Vital Statistics*, p. 407.

22. See Richard Abel, *American Lawyers* (New York: Oxford University Press, 1989), p. 280.

23. Stanley and Niemi, *Vital Statistics*, p. 305.

24. Margaret Edwards, "Mandatory Sentencing," *CQ Researcher*, May 26, 1995, p. 473.

25. Fox Butterfield, "California's Courts Clogging Under Its 'Three Strikes' Law," *New York Times*, March 23, 1995, p. A.1.

26. Quoted in David B. Kopel, "Prison Blues: How America's Foolish Sentencing Policies Endanger Public Safety," Cato Institute, Policy Analysis No. 208, pp. 18–19.

27. Edwards, "Mandatory Sentencing," p. 471.

28. Quoted in O'Brien, *Storm Center*, p. 81.

29. O'Brien, *Storm Center*, p. 81.

▶ 30. See Mark Silverstein, *Judicious Choices: The New Politics of Supreme Court Nominations* (New York: W. W. Norton, 1994).

▶ 31. The case can be found at 372 U.S. 335 (1963); see Anthony Lewis, *Gideon's Trumpet* (New York: Random House, 1964), for the story of the case.

32. Abraham, *The Judicial Process*, p. 175.

33. Rule 17 of the Supreme Court's Review Process, in Lee Epstein, Jeffrey Segal, Harold Speth, and Thomas Walker, *The Supreme Court Compendium* (Washington, DC: CQ Press, 1994), p. 53.

34. Quoted in Abraham, *The Judicial Process*, p. 176.

35. William H. Rehnquist, *The Supreme Court: How It Was, How It Is* (New York: Morrow, 1987), p. 264.

36. Linda Greenhouse, "High Court Opens Its Fall Session by Refusing Cases," p. A10.

37. See Abraham, *The Judicial Process*, p. 192.

38. Quoted in the *Philadelphia Inquirer*, April 9, 1963, cited in Abraham, *The Judicial Process*, p. 191.

39. Charles Fried, *Order and Law: Arguing the Reagan Revolution: A Firsthand Account* (New York: Simon and Schuster, 1991), p. 14.

40. Epstein, et al., *The Supreme Court Compendium,* p. 581.

41. See O'Brien, *Storm Center,* p. 45.

42. Quoted in the *New York Times,* February 22, 1988, p. A16.

43. Quoted in the *New York Times,* July 11, 1974, p. A35.

44. Epstein, et al., *The Supreme Court Compendium,* p. 158.

45. Joan Biskupic, "The Supreme Court's Emerging Power Center," *Washington Post National Weekly Edition,* July 11–17, 1994, p. 31.

46. Joan Biskupic, "The Supreme Court's Emerging Power Center," p. 31.

47. Joan Biskupic, "11th-Hour Stay Requests Are Business as Usual for the High Court," *Washington Post,* January 16, 1994, p. A10.

48. Fairfield, *The Federalist Papers,* p. 230.

49. Abraham, *The Judicial Process,* p. 316.

▶ 50. Walter Murphy and C. Herman Pritchett, *Courts, Judges, and Politics: An Introduction to the Judicial Process* (New York: Random House, 1979), p. 37.

51. Quoted in the *New York Times,* June 27, 1969, p. 17.

52. Linda Greenhouse, "Life and Times," *The New York Times Magazine,* March 7, 1993, p. 84.

53. Linda Greenhouse, "A Talk with Ginsburg on Life and the Court," *New York Times,* July 7, 1994, p. B11.

54. These cases will be discussed in Chapter Eleven.

CIVIL LIBERTIES
AND CIVIL RIGHTS

CHAPTER

11

American government has always required a delicate balance. On the one hand, it has to be strong enough to protect the nation from foreign and domestic threats, which means government must have the power to force individual Americans to obey the laws. On the other hand, it cannot be so strong as to threaten individual liberty.

The Constitution provides two kinds of protection for Americans as individual citizens. It protects **civil liberties,** which guarantee freedoms such as speech, press, and religion, and **civil rights,** which provide protection against discrimination on the basis of individual characteristics such as race, gender, and disability.

One way to distinguish the two types of protection is to remember that civil liberties protect individual citizens against government (government is prohibited from establishing a national religion, for example), while civil rights generally protect individual citizens from each other (businesses cannot discriminate against women or minorities in the hiring process, for example).

Most of the protection resides in the first ten amendments to the Constitution. Recall that the final draft of the Constitution did not contain a bill of rights—the Founders believed that separate powers, interests and layers, and checks and bal-

Protect Us from Our Government and Each Other

ances were more than enough to protect the public against a tyranny of the majority. Moreover, most states already had bills of rights in their constitutions.

Also recall that most citizens of the young nation did not share the Founders' confidence in Articles I, II, and III as their sole sources of protection.[1] Facing opposition to ratification, the Founders promised that the First Congress would enact a bill of rights. Working through a list of nearly two hundred proposals, that Congress eventually proposed twelve amendments, of which ten were eventually ratified by the states. (Recall that one of the two lost amendments, regulating congressional pay, was ratified as the Twenty-Seventh Amendment in 1992.)

The Bill of Rights is best viewed as a statement of limits, that is, of what the federal government cannot do to the public. As such, it provides a basic list of civil liberties, which protect individuals from their government, not a list of civil rights, which protect individuals from each other. (See Box 11–1 for a brief summary of the limits of the ten amendments; the full text of each amendment can be found in Appendix B.)

Americans received additional protections from each other under the Fourteenth Amendment, which was ratified following the Civil War in 1868. Under the amendment, no state shall "deny to any person within its jurisdiction the equal protection of the laws." Under this **equal protection clause,** all citizens, whether former slaveholders or slaves, have the same rights to be protected from each other.

BOX
11-1

Limits on Government in the Bill of Rights

Passed by Congress on September, 25, 1789.
Ratified on December 15, 1791.

Limits on Congress

I: Congress shall not establish a religion or limit the free exercise of religion. It shall not limit the freedoms of speech, press, peaceful assembly or the right to petition government for a redress of grievances.

Limits on the Executive Branch

II: The government shall not interfere with the right to keep and bear arms, "a well regulated militia, being necessary to the security of a free state."

III: The government shall not arbitrarily force citizens to allow soldiers to live in their homes.

IV: The government shall not search or seize evidence without first proving to a court that the search and seizure are reasonably linked to a crime.

Limits on the Federal Courts

V: The government shall not try someone for a crime unless there is a finding such person might reasonably have committed that crime; try someone twice for the same crime; force someone to testify against himself or herself; punish someone without due process of law; or take private property without paying a fair amount for it.

VI: The government shall not try someone for a serious crime unless the trial is speedy and public; the accused is informed of the charges; the accused is allowed to confront opposing witnesses and compel supporting witnesses to testify; the trial is held where the crime was committed and heard by an impartial jury; and an attorney is available to help with the defense.

VII: The government shall not deny the accused a trial by jury.

VIII: The government shall not impose excessive bail, unreasonable fines, or cruel and unusual punishments.

Limits on the Federal Government in General

IX: The federal government shall not assume the people have only those rights specified in the Constitution.

X: The federal government shall not exercise powers not delegated to it by the Constitution, because those powers belong to the states, unless the Constitution denies those powers to the states, or to the people.

No state could deny individuals within its borders privileges due to them as citizens of the United States, nor could it deprive them of life, liberty, or property without giving them **due process of law,** meaning a fair and open procedure. States were also required to ensure that every person within its jurisdiction was given equal protection under the law, meaning that they could not single out certain groups of citizens for special treatment or punishment.

The problem with all these protections is that they can frustrate the will of the majority. Indeed, some of the most famous Supreme Court cases have pitted a single individual against the majority of Americans—a single African American who objects to sitting at the back of the bus, a single high school student who objects to a graduation prayer, a single individual who objects to a Christmas pageant at a local school.

Ultimately, this power to frustrate can lead the majority of Americans to long for a government in which no individual citizen can stand in the way of what the majority sees as progress. At the same time, it can also lead minorities to wonder whether government will ever act at all—after all, it took four score and seven years for Abraham Lincoln to issue the Emancipation Proclamation freeing the slaves, and another three score years for Congress to grant women the right to vote. And many would argue that America has yet to make things right with the Native Americans who occupied this land long before the first foreign immigrants arrived.

But even as those delays frustrate majority and minority alike, they also protect. What has taken so long to achieve is also extremely difficult to undo. Rights won through hard work over the decades earn the protections of the Founders' government that would be just strong enough.

In the rest of this chapter we will examine the protection of civil liberties and civil rights today. Before turning to a separate discussion of these liberties and rights, we will consider how the Bill of Rights came to cover so much of American life. Originally, it was designed just to cover Americans as national citizens, leaving the state and local governments to impose their own rules restricting liberties and rights as they wished. One case at a time over the decades, the Bill of Rights was steadily pushed downward to cover every corner of state and local life.

NATIONALIZING THE BILL OF RIGHTS

The most significant events in the evolution of America's civil liberties and civil rights involve what judicial scholars call the **nationalization of the Bill of Rights.** Nationalization is the slow, but steady effort to broaden coverage of the Bill of Rights to state and local government and to the actions of individual citizens against each other.

For the first one hundred years of the Bill of Rights, the ten amendments did not apply to the states, just to actions by the federal government. In 1789, the public did not worry about the states—states were seen as protectors of civil rights and liberties, not as threats. Indeed, many state constitutions at the time contained lists of basic rights, some of which were much more detailed than the Bill of Rights itself. Instead, people wanted a Bill of Rights to protect them from the federal government.

Given a chance to expand the Bill of Rights to the states in *Barron v. Baltimore* in 1833, the Supreme Court declined. John Barron owned a cargo wharf just off the deepest water in Baltimore Harbor. His business prospered until the city of Baltimore dumped so much sand into the water that ships could no longer reach Barron's wharf. Barron's business was ruined.

Barron sued the city under the Fifth Amendment. Although best known for its protections against self-incrimination—individuals cannot be forced to testify against themselves—the Fifth Amendment also protects citizens from unreasonable "takings" of property. Simply put, government may not take something of value from a citizen without providing reasonable compensation. In Barron's view, government (the city of Baltimore) had taken something of very great value (his wharf) without paying anything at all. The trial court agreed with the argument and awarded him $4,500. The city of Baltimore appealed to the Supreme Court.

Barron's case was doomed by one fact: Baltimore was not seen as part of the national government, but of the state of Maryland. Under this logic, Barron was a *dual citizen,* first of the state of Maryland, and only then of the United States of America. If Maryland did not provide protection against takings of property, Barron would have to suffer the consequences. Chief Justice John Marshall made the point in simple terms: "The Constitution was ordained and established by the people of the United States for themselves, for their own government, and *not for the government of their individual states.*"[2] Having concluded that the Bill of Rights did not apply to the states, in part because the states already had such strong bills of rights of their own, the Marshall Court voided Barron's award.

Fast forward to 1994 and a small business owner in Tigard, Oregon, a tiny suburb of Portland. Florence Dolan wanted to expand her store and pave her parking lot, a relatively simple business decision. But under Tigard land-use regulations, she could only do the work if she agreed to set aside about one-tenth of her two acre property for a bike path and small public park.

Dolan sued her local government arguing that the land-use requirement constituted the same kind of taking that had so angered Barron. Despite having already lost three times—first at the local planning board, second at an Oregon appeals court, and third at the Oregon Supreme Court—Dolan appealed to the U.S. Supreme Court. There she won a 5–4 decision forcing the city to reargue its taking.[3] The specifics of *Dolan v. Tigard* are far less important than the simple fact that the Supreme Court felt quite comfortable intervening in a local decision.

What happened between 1833 and 1994? The answer is that the federal judiciary slowly expanded coverage of the Bill of Rights to the states, eventually allowing Dolan to use the federal courts to sue Tigard. Like Barron, Dolan was still a dual citizen, but unlike Barron, she was a citizen of the United States first, and of Oregon second.

The breakthrough in Dolan's case actually came with the ratification of the Fourteenth Amendment over one hundred years before Tigard took its action. With the end of the Civil War, southern states, not the federal government, became the greater threat to liberty. The Reconstruction Era, which lasted until the late 1800s, was one of the most divisive periods in history. It spawned the white-hooded Ku Klux Klan (KKK), which spreads its message of hate to this day, and a host of political devices for denying rights to the four million former slaves. The Fourteenth Amendment gave them the broad outlines of protection as they built new lives.

As we will see later, the amendment did not suddenly nationalize the Bill of Rights. Rather, it merely laid the groundwork for one hundred years of Supreme Court decisions.[4] The key sentence in the amendment is simple enough: "No state shall make or enforce any law which shall abridge the privileges or immunities of citizens of the United States; nor shall any State deprive any person of life, liberty, or property without due process of law; nor deny to any person within its jurisdiction the equal protection of the laws." As such, the Fourteenth Amendment made clear that the Fifth Amendment's due process clause applies to the states.

The nationalization of the Bill of Rights was hardly over with the Fourteenth Amendment, however. The federal judiciary had to decide whether the Fourteenth Amendment applied just to the Fifth Amendment's due process provisions or to the entire Bill of Rights. At least in the beginning, the Supreme Court took the narrow view that the Fourteenth Amendment did not automatically bring the states under any part of the Bill of Rights. Indeed, in its very first decision on the issue, the Supreme Court had actually decided not to incorporate the states under the Bill of Rights at all.

Under *The Slaughterhouse Cases,* a collection of cases assembled together for a single decision in 1873, the Supreme Court had been asked to apply the equal protection clause to several New Orleans slaughterhouses located along the Mississippi River.[5] The state of Louisiana had passed a law prohibiting the slaughter of livestock near the Mississippi River to protect the public from the spread of deadly cholera. The slaughterhouse owners sued, arguing that they had been deprived of their livelihood without due process. (Note the similarities to Barron's complaint, the difference being the use of the Fourteenth Amendment, not the Fifth, as the base for the slaughterhouses' suit.) The Supreme Court disagreed, concluding that the Fourteenth Amendment was only concerned with protecting former slaves, and thereby denying the applicability of the amendment to other citizens.

The *Slaughterhouse Cases* were only the beginning of a long trail of cases leading to nationalization, some that blocked nationalization for a period, others that advanced it.

If the Bill of Rights was to be nationalized, change would have to come one case at a time. Some citizen would have to find a state law that violated some part of the Bill of Rights—say, freedom of speech or the right to a speedy trial—then file a case using the Fourteenth Amendment as a basis to argue that a state law is unconstitutional. By favorable rulings in such cases, the federal courts could slowly expand the Bill of Rights to incorporate the states. (See Box 11–2 for a list of the key nationalization cases.[6])

BOX 11-2

Nationalizing the Bill of Rights, Step-by-Step

Year	Right (Amendment)	Case that extended the right to the state or local level
1897	Fair payment for property (V)	*Chicago, Burlington & Quincy RR v. Chicago*
1927	Freedom of speech (I)	*Fiske v. Kansas*
1931	Freedom of the press (I)	*Near v. Minnesota*
1932	Counsel in capital cases (VI)	*Powell v. Alabama*
1937	Assembly and petition (I)	*DeJonge v. Oregon*
1940	Exercise of religion (I)	*Cantwell v. Connecticut*
1947	Establishment of religion (I)	*Everson v. Board of Education of Ewing Township*
1948	Public trial (VI)	*In re Oliver*
1949	Unreasonable search and seizure (VIII)	*Wolf v. Colorado*
1958	Association (I)	*NAACP v. Alabama*
1961	Exclusion of evidence from unreasonable search and seizure (IV)	*Mapp v. Ohio*
1962	Freedom from cruel and unusual punishment (VIII)	*Robinson v. California*
1963	Counsel in felony cases (VI)	*Gideon v. Wainwright*
1964	Self-incrimination (V)	*Malloy v. Hogan*
1965	Confront opposing witnesses (VI)	*Pointer v. Texas*
1965	Privacy (I,III,IV,V,IX)	*Griswold v. Connecticut*
1966	Impartial jury (VI)	*Parker v. Gladden*
1967	Speedy trial (VI)	*Klopfer v. North Carolina*
1967	Obtain supporting witnesses (VI)	*Washington v. Texas*
1968	Jury trial in nonpetty cases (VI)	*Duncan v. Louisiana*
1969	Double jeopardy (V)	*Benton v. Maryland*
1972	Counsel in criminal cases involving a jail term (VI)	*Argersinger v. Hamlin*

Source: David M. O'Brien, Constitutional Law and Politics: Civil Rights and Liberties, *(New York: W. W. Norton, 1991), pp. 280–81.*

That is exactly what has happened over the years as the cases have come before the Court. Slowly but surely, the Fourteenth Amendment has become the vehicle to nationalize the Bill of Rights. By the late 1920s, the federal judiciary was beginning to accept the notion that there were fundamental rights of every citizen, regardless of where they lived. States could no longer violate the freedom of speech as of 1927, freedom of the press as of 1931, freedom of religion as of 1940, or the separation of church and state as of 1947. Nor would they be free to deny the accused a public trial as of 1948, deny protection from self-incrimination as of 1964, deny the right to privacy as of 1965, deny a speedy trial as of 1967, try the accused twice for the same crime (double jeopardy) as of 1969, or deny a lawyer in all criminal cases involving a jail term as of 1972.[7] By 1972, the expansion was mostly over.

There are still pieces of the Bill of Rights that do not apply to the states. The right to bear arms has never been pushed downward, for example, nor has the right against excessive fines. On the other hand, some states are ahead of the Constitution in granting certain rights to their citizens. For example, the right to privacy is not specifically written into the U.S. Constitution, and the Supreme Court had to infer it from other constitutional amendments in order to establish the right to privacy in 1965. Some states have included the right to privacy as a separate constitutional amendment.

Just because the Bill of Rights has been almost fully nationalized does not mean the Supreme Court cannot reverse the trend. In 1995, for example, the Supreme Court issued two 5–4 decisions that reflected growing support for reversing decades of federal dominance. One case overturned a federal law requiring states to ban the possession of firearms near local schools, while the other rejected a federal law requiring states to either regulate low-level radioactive waste (of the kind produced in medical facilities) or "take title" to the waste and dispose of it properly.[8]

IN A DIFFERENT LIGHT

CREATING A RIGHT TO DIE

Until April 2, 1996, thirty-two states had bans on physician-assisted suicide, a practice in which physicians help their terminally ill patients end their lives. Although terminally ill patients argue that they, and they alone, should decide when and how to die, these states felt that physicians should not be given such power.

On April 2, the U.S. Court of Appeals for the Second Circuit (which covers twelve states including New York) voided New York's version of the ban in *Quill v. Vacco*.[9] The case was filed by three physicians, one of whom was Timothy Quill, who wrote the *New England Journal of Medicine* in 1991 to admit that he had once prescribed a lethal dose of sleeping pills to a terminally ill patient. The defendant was the attorney general of New York responsible for enforcing the ban, Dennis C. Vacco. "Doctors have been doing this," another of the physicians in the case, Howard Grossman, said of assisted suicide, "but they have been isolated, alone and terrified, afraid to reveal their secret even to the person they sleep next to every night."[10]

The three physicians were joined by three of their terminally ill patients, one of whom was Rita Barrett, a physical education teacher who had thyroid cancer and wanted her doctor to prescribe painless medication to help her end what had been a painful battle with an inevitable end. None of the three patients lived to hear the decision. "She had this sense that this would be her legacy," said Barrett's daughter. "When she told me she joined the suit, she told me that it was the right thing to do, that people shouldn't be made to suffer just because they were terminally ill."

The plaintiffs argued that state restrictions on assisted suicide denied personal liberties without due process and equal protection under the Fifth and Fourteenth Amendments. Under New York law, a patient had the right to ask physicians to stop all efforts to prolong life—for example, by forbidding heroic efforts to resuscitate life during a heart attack or stroke. But under the same law, a patient had no right to ask a physician to hasten death. If a patient can commit suicide by refusing treatment, the appeals court argued, "they should be free to do so by requesting appropriate medication to terminate life during the final stages of terminal illness."

Dr. Jack Kervorkian, highly visible advocate of assisted suicide. By 1996, Kervorkian had assisted more than forty people take their own lives.

By a unanimous decision, the court struck down most of New York's ban, concluding that such bans "are not rationally related to any legitimate state interest." "What interest can the state possibly have in requiring the prolongation of a life that is all but ended?" the court asked. "And what business is it of the state to require the continuation of agony when the result is imminent and inevitable?"

Although the court made its decision based on the Fifth and Fourteenth Amendments, it stopped short of nationalizing the right to die. The court was quite clear that states had the authority to specify the conditions under which a physician could help a terminally ill patient end life.

Even though the ruling applied only to the twelve states covered by the Second Circuit, there was little doubt that other physicians and patients in other parts of the country would use the decision as a basis for challenging their state bans. Even before the Second Circuit acted, the Ninth Circuit in San Francisco (which covers Arizona, California, Idaho, Montana, Nevada, Oregon, and Washington) had already overturned a Washington state law on privacy grounds, arguing that individual Americans have the same right to choose when and how to die that they do in deciding whether to have an abortion.

Moreover, with or without a legal blessing, the quiet practice of assisted suicide may go on nonetheless. According to a study released just before the Second Circuit's decision, requests for such help are not rare, and are honored for one out of four patients. As such, the federal courts may be confirming a practice already well on its way to being accepted as a tragic, but frequent fact of modern medical life.[11]

PROTECT US FROM OUR GOVERNMENT

The Declaration of Independence, which launched the Revolutionary War in 1776, asserted the basic right of every American to "Life, Liberty, and the pursuit of Happiness," a right not granted by government, but by the "Creator." In many ways, therefore, the Bill of Rights is best seen as a restatement of what many Americans already held to be "self-evident," that all people are created equal.

The most familiar of these rights are found in the First Amendment, which guarantees freedom of religion, press, and speech. Americans accused of crimes have significant protections under the Bill of Rights, too. And, as we will see shortly, the courts have even found a right to privacy in between the other rights in the first ten amendments. We will examine each of these rights—religion, press, speech, the rights of the accused, and privacy—below.

Freedom of Religion

Freedom of religion is the most basic civil liberty guaranteed by the Bill of Rights. It comes before freedom of speech and freedom of assembly in the First Amendment: "Congress shall make no law respecting an establishment of religion. . . ." Indeed, Jefferson called it "the most inalienable and sacred of all human rights."[12]

Americans may not be the most religious people compared to other nations, but religion remains prominent in American life nonetheless. Not only do almost two-thirds of Americans say that religion is very important in their own lives, they also believe that religion is still relevant to all or most of today's problems.[13] Presidents go to church regularly; the Senate and House of Representatives start each day with prayer; the back of a dollar bill carries the motto "In God We Trust"; and between 60 and 70 percent of Americans support some form of school prayer. Moreover, religion has clearly played a prominent part in political history, most recently with the role of born-again southern, white Christians in lifting Republicans to victory in the 1994 congressional campaigns.[14]

Thus, the question is not so much whether Americans are religious, but why there is a wall between church and state. Not surprisingly, the answer goes all the way back to the founding and the evolution of the First Amendment. The amendment actually contains two clauses on religion: the **establishment clause,** which prohibits the establishment of a national religion, and the **free exercise clause,** which prohibits any government interference in the practice of religious beliefs.

Legal scholars believe that the Founders mostly wanted to prohibit creation of a *particular* religion or a *particular* church, not to ban religion from American life. They did not want to separate Americans from their religious beliefs, nor did they want to protect government from religion. Rather, they wanted to protect religion from government.[15] Toward that end, the Supreme Court has generally argued that government should neither aid nor hinder religion, simultaneously avoiding establishment and promoting free exercise.

The wall between church and state does not mean that religious groups are banned from trying to influence government, for they have the same rights to assemble peacefully and petition government as other Americans.[16] Although some Americans argue that religion has no place in government, even to the point of protesting the morning prayer that opens each day of Congress, the Founders most certainly did not intend religious Americans to be silent on the great issues of the day.

Protecting the free exercise of religion involves a careful balance. The courts cannot go so far that they discourage religious life in America, but they also cannot permit government to favor one religion over another. On the one hand, state legislatures can open their sessions with a prayer, a Nativity scene is fine as part of a larger Christmas celebration at a city park, school districts can loan textbooks to religious schools, and student religious groups can meet in public school buildings. On the other, a Christmas Nativity scene is not okay if it stands by itself on city ground, a city cannot allow churches to veto liquor licenses, states may not order schools to teach the biblical theory of creation, public schools may not send teachers to instruct students in religious school buildings nor may they give financial aid for field trips taken by religious school students.

The line between what is and is not permitted can be confusing at times, in part because the courts can only act when a specific case is presented for decision. (The Bill of Rights is not a self-enforcing document; violations can and do occur until they are challenged in the courts.) Why is it permissible, for example, to have a Nativity scene in a park, but not in City Hall? Why is it okay to loan a religious school textbooks, but not to provide instruction in religious school buildings? The answer rests in trying to prevent government from promoting a specific religion even as it goes about the business of celebrating holidays and educating students. (See Box 11–3 for a comparison of the two Christmas cases.)

BOX 11-3

Rulings on Christmas

A Nativity scene is fine as part of a Christmas celebration

Lynch v. Donnelly, 465 U.S. 668 (1984).

Pawtucket, Rhode Island, set up a Christmas display in a nonprofit owned park in the heart of the shopping district every Christmas season. It contained all of the usual Santa Claus-related decorations plus a creche. The presence of the creche was challenged as a violation of the Establishment clause. The Supreme Court ruled that "The display is sponsored by the City to celebrate the Holiday and to depict the origins of that Holiday. These are legitimate secular purposes." Furthermore, any benefit to a particular religion from the display is "indirect, remote and incidental."

But is not okay as a single display in a city office building

Allegheny County v. Greater Pittsburgh ACLU, 492 U.S. 573 (1989).

The Roman Catholic Holy Name Society donated a creche that was displayed in the Allegheny, Pennsylvania, County Courthouse. The Court ruled that the display was impermissible as a single display. Without the other secular seasonal symbols surrounding it (for example, Santa Claus, candy canes, the North Pole), the display "sends an unmistakable message that it supports and promotes the Christian praise to God that is the creche's religious message."

IN A DIFFERENT LIGHT ▬▬▬▬▬▬▬▬▬ ■ ■ ■

SCHOOL PRAYER

Freedom of religion involves hard questions about where government ends and religion begins. However, there is no more controversial issue in the debate than school prayer. The vast majority of Americans see absolutely nothing wrong with opening each public school day with a moment of silence or spoken prayer. But whether silent or spoken, printed on a wall (Tennessee once ordered that the Ten Commandments be displayed on school walls) or nondenominational, the Supreme Court has generally ruled that organized prayer in public schools violates the First Amendment.

The line against prayer in public schools was drawn in a series of cases that began in the 1960s. The first case came in 1962 when the Supreme Court ruled that New Hyde Park, New York, schools could not start the day with the following one-sentence prayer: "Almighty God, we acknowledge our dependence upon Thee, and we beg thy blessings upon us, our parents, our teachers and our Country."[17] *Engel v. Vitale* was quickly followed by a second case striking down a Pennsylvania law requiring a daily Bible reading and the Lord's Prayer.[18] As one case followed another, the courts expanded the protections to prohibit both voluntary prayer and a moment of silence at the start of each day.

One of the most recent expressions of the ban involved a prayer at a middle school graduation ceremony.[19] The case, *Lee v. Weisman,* was decided in 1992. Deborah Weisman, a student at Nathan Bishop Middle School in Providence, Rhode Island, was about to graduate when her father, Daniel Weisman, found out that a local rabbi had been asked to deliver the opening and closing prayer at the graduation ceremony.

Deborah and her father asked a district court to stop the school from including prayers in its graduation ceremony, but the court denied the request. The Weismans attended the ceremony, then filed suit again, this time to prevent school officials from arranging for prayers at future high school graduations, which would someday soon involve Deborah.

What made the prayer a problem was not just that the school had scheduled an invocation and benediction, but that it had also sent the rabbi a pamphlet outlining the elements of a good prayer—for example, that the prayer show "inclusiveness and sensitivity." Although the pamphlet was well-meaning, it meant the school (and, therefore, the state) had a hand in composing the prayer, hence favoring a religion. The district court ruled in the Weismans' favor, prompting the school district to appeal on behalf of the principal, Robert Lee. Hence *Lee v. Weisman.*

In this case, as with the others on prayer, the Supreme Court's concern was clear: government could not endorse prayer because prayer is an expression of religion. Students who did not believe in prayer would be unprotected. As Justice Anthony Kennedy, a Ronald Reagan appointee, wrote for the 5–4 majority, "the school district's supervision and control of a high school graduation ceremony places public pressure, as well as peer pressure, on attending students to stand as a group or, at least, maintain respectful silence during the Invocation and Benediction. This pressure, though subtle and indirect, can be as real as any overt compulsion."[20] The Court prohibited any further prayers at graduation.

According to news reports at the time, Deborah's peers were angered by the controversy. And not just students in New York, either. The student council president of Penn Laird High School, Virginia, vowed to include a prayer and Bible verse in his graduation address in 1993, saying "It's not an issue of Christianity. It is an issue of free speech. If a Muslim student wants to get up and pray, I'd sit there and listen."[21]

But it was not a majority that was at risk here. For many students, a prayer would have been no big deal, especially if it did not favor one religion or another. Moreover, public opinion is clearly on the side of a little school prayer. Roughly three in five Americans see nothing wrong with reading the Lord's Prayer or Bible verses in schools.[22]

But the sheer numbers of Americans who believe in school prayer is not the issue at all. The issue is whether there is a minority, even composed of but one student, who might be forced to participate against his or her will.

The school prayer debate is hardly over. Advocates of prayer in public schools have made some progress by defining prayer as freedom of speech rather than free expression of religion. In 1995, the Supreme Court appeared to give the definition some momentum in *Rosenberger v. The University of Virginia.* The 5–4 decision required the university to provide the same financial support to a student religious newspaper as it provides for any other student newspaper. In doing so, the Supreme Court noted the difficulty in knowing when, as Justice Lewis Powell once puzzled, "singing hymns, reading scripture, and teaching biblical principles cease to be singing, teaching, and reading."[23] When a public school schedules a prayer, picks the clergy, and offers instructions on how to write a proper text, it goes over the line into state establishment of religion, but when it makes space available for bible readings, it may be merely allowing religious students to do what other students already do: engage in free speech.

Freedoms of the Press and Speech

Freedoms of the press and speech also reside in the First Amendment, and cover everything from calling for the overthrow of government to protecting pornography. It is important to note, however, that the First Amendment protection is not as strong as some of the Founders hoped. James Madison, in particular, was so worried about censorship that he proposed an entirely separate amendment prohibiting the states from interfering with the press.

Like the rest of the liberties guaranteed in the Bill of Rights, these freedoms have been tested and refined over the years. Neither the press nor individual Americans can say anything they wish, for example. Free speech is unprotected when it involves a lie. Both **slander,** which is a false statement by the spoken word, and **libel,** which is a false statement by the written or electronic (television, radio) word, are grounds for lawsuit.

Even here, however, the First Amendment provides some protection. In *New York Times Co. v. Sullivan,* a 1964 case, the Supreme Court ruled that public officials at all levels of government can only sue for libel if they can prove the press published a story "with knowledge that it was false or with reckless disregard of whether it was false of not." The case revolved around L. B. Sullivan, a Montgomery, Alabama, city commissioner who argued that the *New York Times* had libeled him by printing an advertisement attacking the city of Montgomery for violating civil rights. The Supreme Court ruled that public officials have much less protection against libel, even if they are wronged (which the Supreme Court refused to determine in the Sullivan case). As Justice William O. Douglas argued, citizens and the press have "an absolute, unconditional privilege to criticize official conduct despite the harm which may flow from excesses and abuses. The prized American right 'to speak one's mind' about public officials and affairs needs 'breathing space to survive.'"[24]

This freedom to speak one's mind was not always so broadly interpreted, however. Until the 1950s, for example, the federal courts had been particularly harsh toward Americans whose free speech created a "clear and present danger" to the nation during wartime. The **clear and present danger test** was established by the Supreme Court in 1919 to uphold the conviction of Charles Schenck. As secretary of the Socialist Party during World War I, Schenck took responsibility for discouraging young men from entering the draft. That he was woefully unsuccessful in his work did not matter to the federal government. What mattered, according to *Schenck v. United States,* was that Schenck's words were "used in such circumstances and are of such a nature as to create a clear and present danger that they will bring about the substantive evils that Congress has a right to prevent."[25]

Although the ruling appeared to leave room for unpopular speech—if not advocating the overthrow of government, which is often labeled subversive speech, then at least allowing criticism of government—the federal courts allowed states to impose tough restrictions on even limited criticism until the late 1960s. It was not until 1969, in *Brandenburg v. Ohio,* that the Supreme Court finally protected all subversive speech unless it advocated an immediate, violent, and illegal action. Brandenburg was a Ku Klux Klan leader who had told a Klan rally that "it's possible that there might have to be revengeance [sic] taken" if the federal government continued to "suppress the white, Caucasian race." Brandenburg had been convicted of violating restrictions on subversive speech, but the Supreme Court overturned the conviction in requiring that subversive speech had to involve something more than a vague threat against government.[26]

The federal courts had also been harsh toward free speech (in the form of magazines and books) whose effect was to "deprive and corrupt those whose minds are open to such immoral influences and into whose hands a publication of this sort might fall."[27] This test of obscenity was so broad that it led to the ban of books by James Joyce, D. H. Lawrence, and Arthur Miller, and began to unravel in a series of cases starting in 1957. By 1969, the Supreme Court had granted protection even to hard-core pornography, provided that the hard-core pornography meets broadly defined community standards. At the same time, however, the Supreme Court allows communities to ban the sale of pornography to children, limit sexually explicit entertainment, and prohibit the location of adult book stores in certain areas of cities.

The problem in regulating obscenity starts with defining the term. While the courts have allowed communities to regulate obscenity when "to the average person, applying contemporary community standards, the dominant theme of material taken as a whole appeals to prurient interests," the standard is exceedingly difficult to use. Just what is a prurient interest? What is obscene? Is it a nude painting? An adult movie? Just certain paintings and movies? The difficulty led Justice Potter Stewart, who served on the Court from 1958 to 1981, to argue that he could not define obscenity, but "I know it when I see it."[28]

IN A DIFFERENT LIGHT

CAMPUS HATE SPEECH

The definition of what constitutes free speech continues to change in many areas of society, not the least of which is the recent ban on obscenity in cyberspace. The ban was signed into law as the Decency in Communications Act on February 8, 1996, and was challenged in the Federal District Court in Philadelphia the very same day. The suit was filed in Philadelphia to make the point about the Founders' commitment to free speech.

The definition also continues to evolve on college campuses, where speech codes against hate speech have proliferated over the past decade. The current debate about campus speech codes, for example, is intimately related to a little-noticed event in Minnesota that eventually led to a landmark Supreme Court case in 1992, *R.A.V. v. St. Paul.* Just before daybreak on June 21, 1990, a group of teenagers poured lighter fluid on a homemade cross they had planted on the lawn of a St. Paul African American family and set it afire.

This was not the first time anyone had burned a cross. Sadly, cross burnings have a long and ugly history as a way of threatening racial and religious minorities in America. But this was the first time someone violated a hate crimes law in doing so, for St. Paul had passed its Bias-Motivated Crime Ordinance to punish just such crimes. The law was simple:

Whoever places on public or private property a symbol, object, appellation, characterization or graffiti, including, but not limited to, a burning cross or Nazi swastika, which one knows or has reasonable grounds to know arouses anger, alarm or resentment in others on the basis of race, color, creed, religion or gender commits disorderly conduct and shall be guilty of misdemeanor.

Since actions such as protests, marches, even cross burnings are a form of speech, St. Paul had declared that all hate speech *on the basis of race, color, creed, religion or gender* was illegal. Many Americans would applaud St. Paul's effort.

However, at least one person did not think so highly of the new law: Robert A. Viktora (R.A.V.), who was one of the teenagers charged under the law. His complaint that the ordinance violated his freedom of speech eventually made it all the way to the Supreme Court. Although government is allowed to regulate certain kinds of speech, including "fighting words" designed to arouse anger, the St. Paul law singled out only certain kinds of fighting words—that is, just fighting words about race, color, creed, religion, or gender.

In a 1992 unanimous decision, the Supreme Court found for R.A.V. and declared the St. Paul statute unconstitutional. Simply put, it was not possible to say one set of fighting words was illegal just because it involves certain people, while other fighting words are perfectly acceptable. St. Paul was free to prohibit all fighting words, but not just the ones that offend certain people.

Writing for the majority, Justice Antonin Scalia, another Ronald Reagan appointee, expressed the Court's disgust with the basic act it was forced to defend: "Let there be no mistake about our belief that burning a cross in someone's front yard is reprehensible. But St. Paul has sufficient means at its disposal to prevent such behavior without adding the First Amendment to the fire."[29] In other words, states and localities can still stop cross burnings through other laws. Some prosecute cross burners under laws that make trespassing illegal. Others limit cross burning as a fire safety issue. Still others have even stopped cross burning by defining it is as a source of pollution.

How does a single cross burning in St. Paul relate to campus speech codes around the country? The answer rests in the First Amendment. During the late 1980s and early 1990s, many colleges and universities adopted speech codes limiting hate speech in an effort to create a more welcoming learning climate in the classroom. At the University of Michigan, for example, students and professors alike were subject to discipline for any behavior, "verbal or physical that stigmatizes or victimizes an individual on the basis of race, ethnicity, religion, sex, sexual orientation, creed, national origin, ancestry, age, marital status, handicap or Vietnam-era veteran status," if that behavior threatens or interferes with an individual's academic efforts, or creates "an intimidating, hostile, or demeaning environment for educational pursuits. . . ."[30]

Whatever the code and punishment—Yale University gave a student two years of probation in 1986 for ridiculing the gay community—almost all codes shared a singular commitment to eliminating hate speech on campus. By restricting their focus to just those fighting words involving certain students, as Michigan did, almost all of the one hundred or so codes in effect in 1992 were called into question by the Supreme Court's decision on the cross burning in St. Paul.

Once again, the Bill of Rights offers its protection even to those who say and do things many Americans cannot stand. The result may be anything but pleasant on our college campuses, for professors have been given much greater latitude to say whatever is on their minds. Yet, the decisions may benefit colleges and universities in the long run. Instead of relying on speech codes to merely punish hate speech, and possibly drive it underground, institutions of higher learning may have to address the underlying reasons that lead some professors and students to use inflammatory language. If that means tolerating hostile language in the meantime, the Bill of Rights has been interpreted to say, "so be it."

■ ■ ■

The Rights of the Accused

Having witnessed many of their fellow patriots falsely imprisoned under the British, the Founders were determined to protect the rights of the accused. Today's accused are rarely patriots, however, and include some of the most reviled people in America—rapists, murderers, drug dealers, child pornographers, kidnappers, and terrorists. Nevertheless, the rights of the accused still hold.

The Fifth Amendment requires government to make a formal charge against the accused, gives the accused the right to remain silent, and assures due process of law, which basically means that every step of the legal process must be clear and fair. The Sixth Amendment requires government to give the accused a speedy and public trial by an impartial jury, full information regarding the nature and causes of the charges, an opportunity to confront witnesses, the power to compel witnesses to testify on his or her behalf, and the right to have an attorney. The Eighth Amendment prohibits excessive bail and cruel and unusual punishments. All three amendments prohibit the kind of practices the British had used to harass the revolutionaries.

Nevertheless, it was not until *Miranda v. Arizona* in 1966 that the Supreme Court ruled that the accused actually have a right to know what these rights are in the first place. Ernesto Miranda was a twenty-three-year-old indigent who had been convicted of kidnapping an eighteen-year-old girl from a candy counter at a movie theater, driving her into the desert outside Phoenix, and raping her. His conviction came largely on the strength of his own confession, which he gave to the police after being identified by the victim. He was sentenced to forty to fifty-five years in prison.

Miranda challenged the conviction on the grounds that he confessed without being informed of his rights. The American Civil Liberties Union, which represented Miranda all the way to the Supreme Court, argued that such a confession could be considered coerced and was, therefore, a violation of the Fifth Amendment's right against self-incrimination. There was really nothing new in this, Chief Justice Warren described the decision years later, "except to require police and prosecutors to advise the poor, the ignorant, and the unwary of a basic constitutional right in a manner which had been followed by the Federal Bureau of Investigation procedures for many years. It was of no assistance to hardened underworld types because they already know what their rights are and demand them."[31]

Ernesto Miranda awaits a jury's decision in 1966 in his second trial on rape and kidnapping charges. Miranda's first conviction was overturned by the Supreme Court. The jury convicted Miranda on the basis of new evidence.

As part of its decision, the Court outlined what quickly became known as the *Miranda* rule:

> He must be warned prior to any questioning that he has the right to remain silent, that anything he says can be used against him in a court of law, that he has the right to the presence of an attorney, and that if he cannot afford an attorney one will be appointed for him prior to any questioning if he so desires. Opportunity to exercise these rights must be afforded to him throughout the interrogation. After such warnings have been given, and such opportunity afforded him, the individual may knowingly and intelligently waive these rights and agree to answer questions or make a statement. But unless and until such warnings and waiver are demonstrated by the prosecution at trial, no evidence obtained as a result of interrogation can be used against him. . . .[32]

Miranda was freed, retried on the basis of new evidence, and convicted a second time in 1966. He was eventually released on parole and died in 1976 of a knife wound incurred during a barroom fight.

Miranda was not the only convict released under the *Miranda* rule, of course. Over the years, an untold number of cases have been dismissed because of the failure to follow the Court's order, which prompted the more conservative Burger (1969–1986) and Rehnquist (1986 to the present) Courts to slowly chip away at the precedent. Nevertheless, *Miranda* still holds, prompting the occasional story about a particularly heinous crime going unpunished because of a failure to conduct a proper search or read a suspect his or her rights.

The Right to Privacy

As noted earlier, there is no explicit right to privacy in the Constitution. Rather, the right resides somewhere in what Supreme Court Justice William O. Douglas called the "penumbras," or shadows, of at least six amendments. Writing the majority opinion in *Griswold v. Connecticut,* Douglas argued that the right to privacy demanded the repeal of a 1879 law that prohibited the distribution of information about the use of contraceptives.[33] The case had involved the director of the Connecticut Planned Parenthood, Estelle Griswold, who had been convicted of dispensing contraceptives in her birth control clinic.

The Supreme Court found the right to privacy between the First, Third, Fourth, Fifth, Ninth, and Fourteenth Amendments. The First Amendment says people are free to associate with whomever they wish, including abortion doctors and clinic counselors. The Third Amendment says the government cannot force individuals to house soldiers in peacetime, putting a zone of privacy around what happens inside the home. The Fourth Amendment guarantees the people's right to be "secure in their persons, houses, paper, and effects against unreasonable searches and seizures." The Fifth Amendment says people cannot be forced to testify against themselves, creating another zone of privacy around what people do and know. The Ninth Amendment says that the "enumeration in the Constitution, of certain rights, shall not be construed to deny or disparage others retained by the people." The Fourteenth Amendment says that the state cannot deny life or liberty without due process. Mixed in there somewhere, according to the Court, is a clear right to privacy.

Today's debate about the right to privacy, and the right to abortion that goes with it, is linked to one of the most famous Supreme Court cases of all, *Roe v. Wade.* The case, decided in 1973, overturned dozens of state laws then in effect, and continues to spark political controversy to this day. January 22 is marked each year with a march on Washington by antiabortion groups.

Norma McCorvey used the name Jane Roe to remain anonymous. She lived in Texas, she was pregnant, and she wanted an abortion. But, like many states at the time, Texas only allowed abortions to save the life of the mother, and McCorvey was in no medical danger. Only five states allowed abortion on demand, another thirteen to protect the mother's physical and mental health, and thirty to save the woman's life. Three states did not permit any abortions at all.

Because her pregnancy progressed faster than the courts, Norma McCorvey had her baby and gave it up for adoption before the final decision was made. Along the way, however, she met two young lawyers, Sarah Weddington and Linda Coffee. Together, the three decided to sue Henry Wade, the district attorney in Dallas County, Texas, responsible for enforcing the ban on abortion. The case, *Roe v. Wade,* made it to the Supreme Court in 1971.[34]

The oral arguments on the case were themselves a study in contrasts. Weddington and Coffee stood before the nine members of the Court as fresh graduates of the University of Texas Law School to argue on behalf of Roe, while Texas Assistant Attorney General Jay Floyd made the case for the state. He started his argument with an entirely inappropriate aside: "It's an old joke, but when a man argues against two beautiful ladies like this, they are going to have the last word."[35]

Norma McCorvey, also known as Jane Roe, in 1989. For the first twenty years following the Supreme Court's decision in *Roe v. Wade,* McCorvey was a strong advocate of abortion rights. In the early 1990s, she became a born-again Christian and renounced her support for abortion.

The Supreme Court chambers went silent. In his introduction, Floyd had made his views of women unavoidably clear.

The case turned on whether women and men alike had the right to privacy, including the right to control their own bodies. Building upon the *Griswold* decision, the Supreme Court voided the Texas ban on abortion. "We, therefore, conclude that the right of personal privacy includes the abortion decision," Justice Harry Blackmun wrote for the seven-member majority, "but that this right is not unqualified. . . ." The state had some interest in protecting the health of pregnant women, and in "protecting the potentiality of human life." The question, therefore, was which right to protect at which point in a pregnancy.

The Court struck what might seem like an awkward solution. First, it argued that laws regulating abortion were actually of relatively recent "vintage," as Justice Harry Blackmun described them. According to Blackmun's majority opinion, antiabortion laws were enacted in part to discourage illicit sexual activity by women, in part to protect women from unsafe abortion techniques, and in part to protect the unborn child's life. The first two reasons were rendered less compelling by the advent of more effective birth control and much safer medical techniques, while the third remained a valid government concern. However, according to Blackmun, past laws had generally regulated abortion after *quickening,* the stage of a pregnancy when the unborn child starts to move inside the womb.

Armed with this history and building upon his years as the legal counsel to the Mayo Clinic, Blackmun spent months in the Supreme Court library pouring over medical journals shipped in for his use. Using his research, he convinced six colleagues that quickening could still be used to regulate abortion, albeit quickening defined with much more precision.

Under the Court's decision, the woman's right to abortion would be the strongest when the fetus was least able to survive, in the first three months of a nine-month pregnancy, while a state's interest in protecting human life would be strongest when the fetus was most able to survive, in the final three months. The state's interest in protecting the health of the mother would also grow over the length of the pregnancy. As of January 23, 1973, abortion became a constitutional right, but one that could be limited somewhat by the states.

The states began testing those limits immediately. In the year after *Roe,* state legislatures considered some 260 abortion bills, of which 39 were passed.[36] Some prohibited public funding of abortions; some forbade abortions in public hospitals; many required waiting periods; some required abortion clinics to provide information on alternatives to abortion; several required clinics to show pictures of fetuses in various stages of development; and at least two, Minnesota and Ohio, required teenagers to notify one or both parents before getting an abortion. The Supreme Court struck down most of the laws, leaving only the ban on public funding and the parental notification and waiting period statutes in place.[37] Along the way, the Court reaffirmed the basic right to abortion at every turn.

Americans remain sharply divided about abortion rights to this day. According to the Gallup Poll, roughly one-third support the unqualified right to a legal abortion, another one-sixth say it should always be illegal, while just about half say abortion should be legal only under certain circumstances.[38]

PROTECT US FROM EACH OTHER

As noted at the start of this chapter, the Founders paid little attention to protecting Americans from each other. There is no mention of equality or equal rights in the Constitution or in the first ten amendments.

Moreover, the Constitution itself separated Americans into different groups with very different rights. Recall that slaves were counted as three-fifths of a person, and women could not vote. Indeed, the story of civil rights in America is largely one of breaking such population classifications, first through the Fourteenth Amendment, then through a tangle of court cases, and finally through civil rights legislation.

Ultimately, of course, all Americans are members of groups, and are put into categories all the time: race, gender, marital status, religion, age, region, education, income, sexual preference, size, college major, and so on. However, the classifications only become significant when they are used to give someone a better job, house, mortgage rate, or the like, simply because that person happens to be white or young. This is when the equal protection clause of the Fourteenth Amendment comes into play. It forbids discrimination solely on what the Supreme Court calls "suspect classifications" that place Americans into population categories such as race, gender, and disability.

It is important to understand that the Fourteenth Amendment does not forbid *all* discrimination. The fact is that most laws discriminate against someone in some way: only people over age sixty-two can receive Social Security; married couples pay higher taxes than two single people living together; people who earn more money pay higher taxes; only people with certain college degrees can get certain kinds of jobs.

Some of these population classifications, and the discrimination they produce, are acceptable; others, according to the Supreme Court, are "suspect," meaning that they may lead to unfair discrimination. Classifications based on race, for example, are immediately suspect under the Fourteenth Amendment, while classifications based on social or economic factors such as education or income are rarely challenged.

Consider the use of age as a classification. Obviously, discriminating against young people by giving Social Security benefits only to the elderly makes perfect sense—after all, the program is designed to support retirees. However, discriminating against older people by forcing them to retire at age sixty-five or seventy may not make equal sense. When age has a bearing on performance—for example, on the ability of airline pilots to make life-and-death decisions—it can be used as a classification; when it has no such bearing, it cannot be used.

The history of civil rights is best viewed as a series of individual struggles to declare certain population classifications as suspect. What started with the fight to end racial discrimination in the 1950s and 1960s continued to women's rights in the late 1960s and 1970s; to the disabled in the 1980s; and to Native Americans, gays, and lesbians today.

Protection against Classification by Race

The search for protection against racial classification began immediately after the Civil War and continues today. The Thirteenth Amendment (abolishing slavery), the Fourteenth Amendment (creating equal protection), and the Fifteenth Amendment (giving the right to vote to minorities) all contributed to the end of racial discrimination. But, like so much of the Constitution, mere words were not enough to secure the guarantees.

In fact, ending overt racial discrimination has taken more than a century of protest, three major acts of Congress, dozens of court cases, hundreds of voter registration drives, and countless acts of courage by individuals. It has taken school children who stood up to police dogs in Birmingham, Alabama; a forty-three-year-old seamstress named Rosa Parks who refused to move to the back of the bus in Montgomery when the bus driver yelled "Niggers move back"; three young

Rosa Parks with her attorney in February 1956 after her arrest on charges of boycotting buses in a mass protest against bus segregation. (Montgomery had passed an antiboycotting ordinance in the wake of her original protest.) Parks's refusal to move to the "Negro Section" of a bus on December 5, 1955, prompted the boycott.

college students who were murdered as they tried to register minority voters in Mississippi during the "Freedom Summer" of 1964; and the civil rights leaders who gave their lives to the cause. Because the effort has lasted so long, it is best viewed in three distinct eras: 1877 to 1954, 1954 to 1978, and 1979 to the present.

Separate but Equal (1877–1954).   Although the Fourteenth Amendment was essential to the struggle for civil rights, it was hardly strong enough to ensure success on its own. The Civil War may have ended slavery, but historical barriers to full inclusion of African Americans were not so easily removed. Indeed, the equal protection clause was not fully tested as a device for ending racial inequality until 1896, three decades after ratification. And even then, it was easily brushed aside as the Supreme Court endorsed the **separate but equal doctrine,** which allowed American society to satisfy the Fourteenth Amendment's equal protection clause by merely providing separate facilities and services to each race.

The facts of the first test case, ***Plessy v. Ferguson,*** are brief. Homer Plessy, a one-eighth African American, bought a train ticket from New Orleans to Covington, Louisiana. Instead of sitting in the car marked "Colored Only," he boarded the train and took a seat in a car reserved for whites only. The only part of Plessy that mattered, however, was the one-eighth African American. He was arrested and convicted of violating Louisiana's 1890 "Jim Crow" law—the term *Jim Crow* was a way of ridiculing African Americans as lazy and stupid.

The *Plessy* case was actually set in motion by a 1883 Supreme Court decision that overturned the Civil Rights Act of 1875, which had made it a crime for public accommodations (restaurants, hotels, etc.) to deny "the full enjoyment" of their facilities on the basis of race or religion.[39] In declaring the act unconstitutional, the Supreme Court encouraged the rise of the Jim Crow laws, the first of which was created by Florida in 1877. It was one of those laws that Plessy challenged.[40]

Plessy appealed his case all the way to the Supreme Court, only to find that eight of the highly conservative justices saw nothing whatsoever wrong with the concept of separate but equal. It was not surprising that the Court rejected Plessy's argument when he challenged one of the laws created in the wake of its earlier decisions.

It was a ruthless decision nonetheless, accepting the prevailing view of African Americans as somehow below the rest of society. "If the civil and political rights of both races be equal," Justice Henry Brown concluded for the majority, "one cannot be inferior to the other civilly or politically. If one race be inferior to the other socially, the constitution of the United States cannot put them upon the same plane."[41] After all, African Americans and whites got to Covington at the same time. What difference did it make that they rode in different cars?

Not surprisingly, *Plessy v. Ferguson* invited states to pass more Jim Crow laws. African American barbers could not give whites haircuts; white nurses could not care for African American patients. Perhaps that is what Justice John Marshall Harlan, the lone dissenter, meant when he warned that the *Plessy* decision would plant the seeds of hate: "What can more certainly arouse race hate, what can more certainly create and perpetuate a feeling of distrust between these races, than state enactments which, in fact, proceed on the ground that colored citizens are so inferior and degraded that they cannot be allowed to sit in public coaches occupied by white citizens?"

The Breakthrough Decades (1954–1978).

The federal courts were reluctant to challenge the separate but equal doctrine for a half century, and even then came late to a prominent role in the civil rights movement. Leadership on civil rights, therefore, fell to the presidency and Congress. (See Box 11–4 for a timeline of key events in the civil rights movement.)

It was President Harry S. Truman who finally ordered the full desegregation of the U.S. military in 1948, splitting his Democratic party in the process, and Presidents John F. Kennedy and Lyndon Johnson who led the fight for the great civil rights legislation of the 1960s: the Twenty-Fourth Amendment banning the poll tax in 1964, the Civil Rights Act of 1964, the Voting Rights Act of 1965, the Fair Housing Act in 1968, plus a half dozen presidential executive orders forcing integration forward in the federal government along the way. It was an impressive legislative and executive agenda, indeed. The Twenty-Fourth Amendment removed one of the last southern barriers facing poor minority voters; the 1964 Civil Rights Act made it unlawful to discriminate against any individual "because of such individual's race, color, religion, sex, or national origin" in housing, schools, public accommodations, and employment; the Voting Rights Act sent federal registrars to the South; and the Fair Housing Act banned discrimination in the sale or rental of housing.[42]

BOX
11-4

Key Events in the Civil Rights Movement

1948   President Truman orders desegregation of U.S. military.

1954   *Brown v. Board of Education I* outlaws desegregation of public schools.

1955   *Brown v. Board of Education II* orders integration of public schools.

Interstate Commerce Commission bans segregation in interstate travel.

Montgomery Bus Boycott begins in December after Rosa Parks is arrested for refusing to go to the back of the bus.

1956   Montgomery Bus Boycott ends in December when the U.S. Supreme Court affirmed an appellate court ruling that outlawed segregation on the buses.

1957   Southern Christian Leadership Conference forms, with Martin Luther King as president.

First Civil Rights Act in nearly one hundred years passes Congress, creates the Civil Rights Commission.

President Eisenhower sends troops to enforce desegregation at Central High School in Little Rock, Arkansas.

1960   Student Nonviolent Coordinating Committee forms to organize the sit-ins and boycotts that are occurring all over the South and in some northern cities.

1961   Freedom Rides by over three hundred African American and white college students take place across the South to implement the law outlawing segregation on interstate transportation. Many of the students are assaulted or arrested.

1963   Nonviolent demonstrations occur in Birmingham, Alabama, and are met with police violence, including the use of fire hoses on children.

1964   Twenty-Fourth Amendment bans poll taxes in federal elections.

Freedom Summer occurs, in which white students travel to Mississippi to register African American voters for 1964 presidential election. Two white students and one African American are murdered.

Civil Rights Act of 1964 passes, and forbids discrimination based on race, color, religion, sex, or national origin.

Martin Luther King is awarded Nobel Peace Prize.

1965   Voting Rights Act of 1965 passes, and sends federal registrars to any district in which less than half of eligible minority voters are not registered.

1968   Fair Housing Act bans discrimination in the sale or rental of housing.

Source: Adapted from flyleaf from Juan Williams, Eyes on the Prize: America's Civil Rights Years, 1954–1965 *(New York: Viking, 1987).*

As the list suggests, the civil rights movement used a broad range of legislative and court action to achieve its goals. As the victories mounted, public attitudes toward discrimination also began to change. The number of African American children who went to school with white students grew from just twenty-three in 1954 to over 2 million twenty years later; the percent grew from just the tiniest fraction of a percent in 1954 to over 90 percent by 1971.[43] (See Box 11–5 for a sample of changes in public opinion on race.)

This is not to suggest the courts played no role at all in desegregation. At least one landmark decision, the 1954 ***Brown v. Topeka Board of Education,*** propelled civil rights onto the national agenda as never before. The case involved an eight-year-old girl who merely wanted to go the all-white school just down the street rather than ride a school bus to the minority school five miles away.

Bound together in 1951 with three other school desegregation cases (from Delaware, South Carolina and Virginia), *Brown* was decided after a three-year wait on the Supreme Court docket. Part of the delay involved the death of Chief Justice Fred Vinson. A new chief justice had to be nominated and confirmed before moving ahead.

Part of the wait also reflected the real politics of the decision. The justices knew their decision would provoke intense opposition in the South, and wanted to wait to announce their decision until after the 1952 election.[44] Fears of this backlash clearly influenced the new chief justice, Earl Warren, as he drafted the final opinion on the case. He wanted an opinion short enough so it could be easily reprinted in newspapers around the country, and clear enough so it could be read and understood by most Americans. Warren also wanted a unanimous opinion so the nation could hold no illusions about the strength of the Supreme Court's conviction.[45]

Once the Supreme Court turned to making its actual decision, it split the case in two: *Brown I* came in 1954,[46] and *Brown II* followed in 1955.[47] *Brown I* would

Linda Brown during her first year as the first African American at a previously all-white school.

BOX 11-5

Differences in Racial Attitudes over Forty Years

Question: Do you think white students and African American students should go to the same schools or to separate schools? (Asked of whites only)

	Same Schools	Separate Schools	Don't Know
1942	30%	66%	4%
1956	48	49	3
1985	92	7	1

Question: If African American people came to live next door, would you move? (Asked of whites only)

	Would Definitely Move	Might Move	Would Not Move	Don't Know
1958	21%	23%	56%	—
1966	13	21	66	—
1990	1	4	93	2

Question: Would you move if African American people came to live in great numbers in your neighborhood? (Asked of whites only)

	Would Definitely Move	Might Move	Would Not Move	Don't Know
1958	50%	30%	21%	—
1966	39	31	30	—
1990	8	18	68	6

Question: In *Brown v. Board of Education,* the Supreme Court ruled that racial segregation in all public schools is illegal. This means that all children, no matter what their race, must be allowed to go to the same schools. Do you approve or disapprove of this decision? (Asked of all respondents regardless of race)

	Approve	Disapprove	Don't Know
1954	55%	40%	5%
1961	63	32	5
1994	87	11	2

Source: Harold W. Stanley and Richard G. Niemi, Vital Statistics on American Politics, *(Washington, DC: CQ Press, 1995), p. 367.* Gallup Poll Monthly, *May 1994, p. 25.*

convey the Supreme Court's decision about the constitutionality of segregation, while *Brown II* would instruct the states on what to do with their segregated schools. By breaking the case in two, the Supreme Court divided the substance of its decision from implementation. Americans would have time to think about the Supreme Court's basic opinion on segregated schools before turning to the actual consequences for educating their children.

In the end, *Brown I* confronted a simple question: could a child get an equal education in a separate but equal system? This time, the Supreme Court unanimously answered "no." Although the Supreme Court did not reverse *Plessy,* nor end segregation in other areas of society such as barber shops, hotels, hospitals, and restaurants, it declared the separate but equal doctrine inherently flawed. The opinion came down to two very simple sentences in the second-to-last paragraph of the opinion: "We conclude that in the field of public education the doctrine of 'separate but equal' has no place. Separate educational facilities are inherently unequal." Using the Fourteenth Amendment as the basis for its ruling, *Brown I* concluded that Linda Brown had been denied equal protection under the Fourteenth Amendment, and *Brown II* ordered the states to desegregate their schools with "all deliberate speed."

The *Brown* cases provoked intense opposition from the South and lasting political fallout for the Democratic Party. Southern politicians, from mayors up to governors, vowed to block schoolhouse doors; southern states passed law after law ordering school districts not to comply with the Court's order; the governor of Arkansas even put 270 state troopers around Little Rock's Central High in the fall of 1957 to prevent just nine African American students from entering the school; nineteen senators and eighty-two members of Congress drafted a "Southern Manifesto" attacking the *Brown* decision, giving further aid and comfort to the "massive resistance" back home.

The acts of defiance melted away with repeated court orders and the growing civil rights movement; the governor of Arkansas backed down when President Dwight Eisenhower ordered federal paratroopers into Little Rock. But the overall strategy of delay clearly worked for most who opposed integration. Ten years after *Brown,* Justice Hugo Black would complain that "There has been entirely too much deliberation and not enough speed." Forty years later, many public schools remain just as segregated, if not by deliberate action or law (de jure segregation), then by the concentration of minority populations in the central cities. Ending segregated public schools does not necessarily lead to fully integrated public schools. It can also produce the movement of white students out of the public school system and into private schools, or out of the cities and into the suburbs. Both frustrate ultimate integration.

The Growing Backlash (1979 to the Present). The backlash era against civil rights actually began even before the *Brown* decision. It started when southern Democrats bolted the party after the 1948 national convention adopted a platform plank promising action on civil rights, and gained momentum in the 1968 election when Richard Nixon and Alabama Governor George Wallace both courted white votes in the wake of the race riots of the mid-1960s.

Although the backlash was mostly eclipsed by the civil rights movement of the 1960s, it has accelerated in recent years as moderates have joined conservatives in turning against some of the signature programs for eliminating racial discrimination. It is not that Americans are abandoning their support for racial equality, however. As political scientist Seymour Martin Lipset argues, "the old consensus in favor of civil rights and equality of opportunity remains intact. Americans, including many southern whites, categorically reject the kind of racial discrimination that was common in this country only a few decades ago."[48]

Instead, the slippage may be due to lingering resentment toward some of the basic tools of desegregation, none of which has ever been popular. Court-ordered school busing in the 1970s may have fueled white flight to the suburbs; minority "set-asides," or guaranteed shares, of government contracts have created bitterness among nonminority firms denied the chance to compete; diversity training has been ridiculed as politically correct.

Of all the tools, **affirmative action,** which gives minorities extra help up the college or job ladder, may be the most controversial of all. Affirmative action programs give protected classes of Americans such as minorities special help in advancing through society, whether in getting into college, finding a first job, getting a home loan, or landing a government contract. Some affirmative action programs set goals for the number of women and minorities to be helped, goals that are sometimes converted into quotas that reserve a specific number of slots in a college class or pool of employees for women or minorities.

Most Americans favor some form of affirmative action to help African Americans and other minority groups get a fair start in the competition for jobs and education. They also support general goals for helping more women and minorities advance. If that means giving women and minorities access to special training programs before a first job or extra financial aid in college, the public rarely objects. "But," as Lipset finds, "a large majority of whites and roughly half of all blacks draw the line at preferential treatment, at suspending standards and adopting quotas or other devices that favor citizens on the basis of their membership in groups."[49]

Americans have a particular dislike, for example, for quotas, which set aside a specific number of jobs or slots for minorities only. The problem is that quotas appear to fix past wrongs by creating new winners and losers—reserving a slot for one person means denying one to another. Some argue that the winners are permanently branded as less competent; others believe that the losers are merely new victims of discrimination.

At least one of those "losers" decided to take his anger all the way to the Supreme Court. Twice denied admission to the University of California at Davis Medical School in the mid-1970s, Alan Bakke sued the school in 1977 on the basis of two simple facts: first, that sixteen of the one hundred openings had been reserved in advance for "disadvantaged" groups—African Americans, Latinos/Chicanos, and

Allan Bakke. Bakke's case raised questions about the fairness of quota systems, which set aside a fixed number of jobs or slots for minorities. Bakke eventually won his case and enrolled for medical school in 1978.

Native Americans, thereby constituting a quota system; and, second, at least some of the sixteen successful minority applicants had lower test scores and grade point averages than Bakke.

Bakke eventually won his case, **Regents of the University of California v. Bakke,**[50] but not his campaign against affirmative action. Although the Court ordered the University of California to admit Bakke, the final opinion did not overturn affirmative action. The bare majority of five justices could agree on only one paragraph of the final opinion: that the university's quota system was unlawful, and that Bakke should be admitted. As for affirmative action, the complicated opinion seemed to say government could take race into account as long as it is only to fix past wrongs. At the same time, several justices also worried that affirmative action might damage race relations in the long run.

Ultimately, the mixed signals from *Bakke,* indeed from most of the affirmative action cases that have followed, merely confirm the Court's continued ambivalence about how fast and far to go on racial equality. In late 1994, for example, a federal appeals court rejected a University of Maryland scholarship program that was available only to African Americans, arguing that such a set-aside was going too far. "*Bakke* set a 'yes, but . . .' standard," said law professor John Jeffries Jr. "Schools have emphasized the 'yes,' not the 'but.'"[51]

This ambivalence is shared by the American public at large. Americans want integrated schools, but no busing; diverse colleges and universities, but color-blind admissions; equal opportunity in the workplace, but no quotas. According to a March 1995 *Newsweek* poll, 75 percent of Americans think that qualified African Americans should not receive preference over equally qualified whites in getting into accommodations or getting jobs. At the same time, however, 51 percent say cities should give minorities preference in hiring so that the police force would have the same racial makeup as the community, and nearly as many approve of government set-asides, which reserve contracts for minority-owned businesses.[52]

The debate over the protection of classification by race is far from over. As America continues to change, becoming ever more diverse, the pressure to address the rights of minorities will not abate. Nor will the continuing sense among minorities that race still matters. (See Box 11–6 for a discussion of how race still shapes American life.)

BOX 11-6

Does Race Still Matter?

Even though great strides have been made in extending civil rights to all Americans, substantial differences remain in how different races view society. Consider the following questions as examples of how race still divides the nation on jobs.

Asked of African Americans

Do you think blacks in this country have better or worse job opportunities than whites? *Worse opportunities:* 87%

Do you agree or disagree: When black people have good jobs, white people often think they're in these positions because of affirmative action and not because they deserve it. *Yes:* 75%

Do you think we need more government efforts to help blacks get better job opportunities, do you think government programs are adequate, or do you think that existing government programs go too far? *More programs needed:* 58%

Thinking about your present job, do you feel that affirmative action goals or programs have helped you in this job? *Yes:* 33%

Asked of Whites

Do you think blacks in this country have better or worse job opportunities than whites? *Worse opportunities:* 56%

Do you agree or disagree: When I see a black person in a good job, I often wonder whether they have the job because of affirmative action and not because they deserve it? *Agree:* 19%

Do you think we need more government efforts to help blacks get better job opportunities, do you think government programs are adequate, or do you think that existing government programs go too far? *More programs needed:* 19%

Have you personally or has someone you know ever been discriminated against because of an affirmative action program for blacks? *Yes:* 24%

Source: Reprinted from a Time/CNN Poll *conducted by Yankelovich Partners, April 24–29, 1991.*

Protection against Classification by Gender

Although the Fourteenth Amendment provides protection against classification by gender, it is not the only protection women have in the quest for equality. Women also benefited from the legislative victories of the 1960s, most importantly the 1964 Civil Rights Act.

Ironically, it was a conservative Virginia Democrat, Howard W. Smith, who added women to the 1964 legislation. He had hoped that bringing women into the statute would defeat the bill. "To the laughter of his House colleagues," writes historian Kenneth Davis, "Smith added 'sex' to the list of 'race, color, religion or national origin,' the groups that the bill had been designed to protect. Assuming that nobody would vote to protect equality of the sexes, Smith was twice struck by lightning. The bill not only passed, but now protected women as well as blacks."[53]

Women won additional protection in 1972 when the original act was amended to deny federal funding to private or public programs that discriminate on the basis of gender. The amendments also required colleges and universities to provide equal facilities and opportunities for female athletes (under Title IX), meaning equal numbers of athletic scholarships.

With these legislative victories in hand, national women's groups made a fateful decision to push for the Equal Rights Amendment (ERA) to the Constitution. The amendment itself was remarkably simple—"Equality of rights under the law shall not be denied or abridged by the United States or by any State on account of sex"—but the politics were not. Liberals argued that women could not get equal protection without the amendment; conservatives argued that the amendment would require everything from same-sex bathrooms to unisex haircuts. As with all constitutional amendments, the controversy favored the status quo. Passed by a two-thirds vote of Congress in 1972, the amendment died in 1982 just short of the thirty-eight states needed for ratification.[54] (Unlike James Madison's amendment limiting congressional pay, which took over two hundred years for ratification, ERA had an initial seven-year deadline that was extended for an additional three years before it lapsed.)

The defeat hardly ended progress toward women's rights, however. The Supreme Court continued to broaden women's rights under the equal protection clause and assorted civil rights laws. Along the way, the Court unanimously struck down several laws that favored men—from a Louisiana law allowing a husband to dispose of jointly owned property without his wife's consent to a Utah law that set the age of adulthood at eighteen for females and twenty-one for males, thereby requiring three extra years of child support for male children. During the same period, it also struck down laws that favored women—from a Social Security provision that gave widows more support than widowers to a Mississippi nursing school's policy of denying admission to qualified males.[55]

Besides abortion, which involves substantial questions of women's rights, the Supreme Court's most visible decisions on women's rights have been in the area of workplace equality. In 1986, for example, the Court ruled that merely having a formal policy against sexual harassment did not excuse a company from its responsibility to create a climate free of "intimidation, ridicule, and insult."[56] In 1987, the Court upheld a California law that required companies to provide pregnancy leaves for women.[57] And in 1993, the Court unanimously declared that women need not prove psychological harm or an inability to do their job to win a judgment of sexual harassment.

Merely uttering an insult in a hallway does not necessarily trigger civil rights protection, but neither does a woman need suffer an emotional collapse to prove damage.[58] As Justice Sandra Day O'Connor, a Ronald Reagan appointee, wrote for the unanimous Court, "A discriminatory abusive work environment, even one that does not seriously affect employees' psychological well-being, can and often will detract from employees' job performance, discourage employees from remaining on the job, or keep them from advancing in their careers."[59] When sexual harassment "pollutes" the job climate, it is covered both by federal law and the Fourteenth Amendment.

IN A DIFFERENT LIGHT

BREAKING THROUGH THE CITADEL

Although the Fourteenth Amendment was clearly designed to end racial discrimination, it has become an important tool for ending gender discrimination as well. There is no better case to illustrate the point than *Faulkner v. Jones*. Shannon Faulkner seemed to be the perfect candidate for admission to The Citadel, a South Carolina state military academy established in 1842. James E. Jones, Chairman of the Board of Visitors of The Citadel, was the first name on the long list of defendants in the case.

Faulkner was a high school honors graduate with a 4.0 grade point average, a varsity letter, and the kind of recommendations The Citadel admired. Not surprisingly given the file, Faulkner was invited to join the corps of cadets, class of 1997. There was just one problem with Faulkner's application: The Citadel was an all-male school, and Shannon Faulkner happened to be female. The application did not ask whether Faulkner was a male or female, and her name betrayed no clue. Moreover, Faulkner had removed all references to gender from her application. Based on the facts of her admission file, she was in. But once The Citadel found out her gender, it withdrew the offer of admission.

Faulkner sued the state school, and won the first round of her case on July 22, 1994, when a federal district court ordered her immediate admission to the corps. "All classifications based on sex are not unconstitutional," wrote Judge C. Weston Houck in his opinion. "The law recog-

Shannon Faulkner on her third day as a cadet at The Citadel. Faulkner waged a two-year court battle to win admission to the state-run school.

nizes that there are some real differences between men and women and permits different treatment that provides a legitimate accommodation for those differences. What the law will not allow, however, is classifications based on fixed notions, archaic and stereotypical notions, concerning the relative roles and abilities of females and males."[60] Based on his reading of the Fourteenth Amendment's protection, Houck ordered Faulkner's immediate admission to the corps.

Faulkner's case was far from over with Houk's decision, however. The Citadel immediately appealed, forcing Faulkner into a two-year court battle. The case was finally resolved when a three-judge panel of the Fourth Circuit Court of Appeals ruled 2–1 that the Citadel had violated the equal protection clause of the Fourteenth Amendment by denying her admission. Faulkner arrived on campus August 12, 1995, to begin orientation as the first woman ever admitted as a cadet.

Six days later, however, Faulkner became one of twenty-four cadets who left after the grueling first week. The male cadets she left behind were overjoyed at their victory over this one young woman, delighted with her failure to survive. To keep Faulkner's experience in perspective, consider the following comment from Army Major Carol Barkalow, who had graduated from the army's West Point Military Academy in its first class of women twenty years ago. "Even with all the other women who came, and even though we had Congress on our side, there were plenty of times when you felt very alone and against the world. It's not easy being a pioneer in any situation, and

Male cadets celebrate Shannon Faulkner's withdrawal at the end of her first week at The Citadel. Four women enrolled in The Citadel in 1996.

for two years Shannon Faulkner has pretty much fought this alone."[61] Although she could not reap the rewards of her long struggle, Faulkner made the breakthroughs that will allow some future young woman to become the first graduate of The Citadel, just as Rosa Parks could not reap all of the rewards of the whirlwind of liberty she created with a simple decision to sit at the front of the bus. In 1996, six women were admitted to The Citadel and four enrolled.

Protection against Classification by Disability

Over time, the success of minorities and women in breaking down the barriers has spread to other disadvantaged groups. In 1990, for example, Congress passed and President Bush signed the Americans with Disability Act (ADA), easily the most sweeping civil rights statute since 1964. More than 13 million Americans have impaired eyesight, another 8 million have trouble walking, another 8 million have hearing impairments, and 1.3 million plus use walkers or wheelchairs. All totaled, 14 million Americans have some kind of physical or mental disability. Yet, no federal law protected any of them from routine employment discrimination. If a business did not have wheelchair ramps, so be it. If a company wanted to fire some-one who happened to have AIDS, epilepsy, or brain cancer, so be it.

All that changed with the ADA. The impacts are visible in every sector of the economy and public life. Under the act, all properties open to the public must be accessible to disabled persons—that means wheelchair access, for example. Employers may not discriminate against qualified disabled persons in hiring, ad-vancement, pay, or training, and must fix the workplace if necessary—that means new application procedures, more access, even special computers. All new buses, trains, and subway cars must be wheelchair accessible; and all telephone companies must provide relay services allowing people with voice or hearing im-pairments to place and receive calls from ordinary telephones.[62] The cost has led some Republicans to argue for repeal.

Because the statute is complicated, the regulations that govern implementa-tion will be long in coming. Nevertheless, the ADA had immediate consequences for American business, not the least of which was a new list of "dos" and "don'ts" for the hiring process. It is a list that will affect many Americans in their next job search. "Don't ask job candidates or even their references about applicant's dis-abilities," advises the *Wall Street Journal.* "Focus on abilities. Don't ask about the following before you offer a job: medical history; prescription drug use; prior work-ers' compensation or health insurance claims; work absenteeism due to illness; and past treatment for alcoholism, drug use or mental illness."[63]

Again, passing a law is only the first step toward change. Complaints must be filed, cases won, court orders enforced, public opinions changed. The ADA is so complicated and costly that some companies even decided to wait to be sued before complying voluntarily.[64] But the cases will come. The first one was filed by the federal government in November 1992 against a small company that had fired its executive director upon learning he had terminal brain cancer. The case will eventually wind its way through the courts, and may yet become a landmark case in the history of civil rights.

CONCLUSION

Guaranteeing America's civil liberties and civil rights has been difficult from the very beginning. America in the 1790s was deeply divided by race, religious dif-ferences, geography, and income.[65] It was more a loose collection of many small communities than one United States. It was also a society trying to define itself in a new world, all the while struggling to manage deep internal divisions.

The parallels to today are unmistakable. America is still sharply divided by lo-cal and regional conflict, still trying to find itself in a changing and even more diverse world. The old Soviet Union, which defined so much of the nation's po-litical debate in recent years, is gone; the information revolution is underway; Amer-ica is desperately trying to figure out its place in a world not of two superpowers, but of many smaller powers engaged in many smaller wars; American society is becoming more fragmented. As a result, the struggle for civil liberties and civil rights is likely to continue far into the twenty-first century.

The struggle will continue to flow from two simple sources. The first source is formal: Articles I–III, the Bill of Rights, the Fourteenth Amendment, the Supreme Court decisions, and the assorted laws, executive orders, and regulations that provide the basic protections from government and other individuals. Faced with a threat to their individual rights, Americans can always invoke the equal protection clause, or call upon the legal precedent.

They might start by simply remembering the names of the people in the great Supreme Court cases: William Marbury (to support the right of judicial review), James McCulloch (to assert the supremacy of federal laws over state laws), Deborah Weisman (to protect against school prayer), R.A.V. (to support freedom of speech, no matter how ugly), Jane Roe or Norma McCorvey (to underline the right to privacy), Linda Brown (to dismiss the separate but equal doctrine), and Alan Bakke (to challenge quotas). They might also call upon key statutes: the 1964 Civil Rights Act (to demand fair treatment), Title IX of the 1972 Civil Rights Act Amendments (to protest poor athletic facilities for women), or the Americans with Disabilities Act (to demand equal access). They might even bolster their argument with an executive order or two, including Harry Truman's order integrating the armed services.

Merely invoking court cases and statutes like some ancient prayer is not enough to guarantee protection, however. The cases may be well known and the statutes well established, but this will hardly protect Americans if they are unwilling to take on the fight. Discrimination will continue unless challenged. Thus, the second source of individual civil liberties and civil rights is informal: simple *courage*.

The fact is that it does not take much to make an issue of civil liberties and civil rights. After all, Rosa Parks was simply fed up with sitting at the back of the bus; Shannon Faulkner wanted to go to the best college she knew; Florence Dolan did not want to set aside her property without a fair reason; and Homer Plessy just wanted a decent train ride to Covington. Few of them sought celebrity from their acts, and fewer still were prepared for the backlash that would eventually come from the Supreme Court's decisions. Certainly, Linda Brown and Shannon Faulkner were unprepared for the unprecedented public scrutiny. Indeed, a certain kind of infamy seems to go with the territory in taking on these causes. Just look back to the picture on page 419 for the evidence.

Nevertheless, these Americans showed the courage of their convictions in asking America to honor its constitutional commitments to liberty and fairness, as did the African Americans who marched on Washington in the 1960s, the women who campaigned for equal rights and comparable pay in the 1970s, the disabled who literally rolled through the halls of Congress in the 1980s, and those who continue their efforts to break down discrimination today. As the cases described in this chapter suggest, such efforts often begin with a single step, whether an insult on the job, a rejection in the community, or an injustice by the government.

Therein lies the true protection for individuals. If Americans sit back and wait for someone else to act, their rights will slowly wilt away. No matter what side you are on, some things are worth fighting for, even if you happen to be the only one. Most of the progress on civil liberties and civil rights has been unpopular at some time. That is what being in public life is about. Americans do not need to be president or governor to matter. Nor do they need to be a constitutional lawyer. Civil liberties and rights start with simple courage, and the commitment to carry the idea forward against the prevailing public view.

THE BASICS

■ The Constitution and its early amendments provide two kinds of protections for Americans as individual citizens. It protects individual civil liberties, which guarantee freedoms such as speech, press, and religion, and individual civil rights, which provide protection against discrimination on the basis of individual characteristics such as race, gender, and disability. One way to distinguish the two types of protection is to remember that civil liberties protect individual citizens from government (government is prohibited from establishing a national religion, for example), while civil rights protect individual citizens from each other (businesses cannot discriminate against women or minorities in the hiring process, for example).

■ Some of this protection resides in the basic structure of the Founders' government. Separate powers, separate interests, separate layers, and checks and balances all make it difficult for strong-willed majorities to impose their will on individual Americans. However, most of the protection resides in the first ten amendments to the Constitution. Although the final draft of the Constitution did not contain a bill of rights—most states already had bills of rights in their constitutions—the Founders agreed to offer a bill of rights as the very first item of business in the First Congress. The First Congress actually came up with twelve amendments, ten of which passed. Those first ten amendments are labeled the Bill of Rights. The Bill of Rights is best viewed as a statement of limits—of what the federal government *cannot* do to the public.

■ The most familiar civil liberties involve freedom of religion, press and speech, the rights of the accused, and the right to privacy.

■ Freedom of religion is the most basic civil liberty guaranteed by the Constitution, and is the very first freedom mentioned in the Bill of Rights. The First Amendment contains two clauses on religion: the establishment clause, which prohibits the establishment of a national religion, and the free exercise clause, which prohibits any government interference in the individual practice of religious beliefs.

■ Freedoms of press and speech also reside in the First Amendment. Both freedoms have grown over the past fifty years as Supreme Courts have loosened restrictions on criticizing government officials and abandoned restrictions of free speech during wartime.

■ The rights of those accused of crimes mostly reside in the Fifth, Sixth, and Eighth Amendments. However, it was not until 1966 that the Supreme Court ruled that the accused has to be notified of their rights at the time of arrest. These rights are called *Miranda* rules in reference to the Supreme Court case *Miranda v. Arizona* that required police to read suspects their rights, including the right to remain silent and the right to the presence of an attorney.

■ The right to privacy is not mentioned specifically in the Bill of Rights. Rather, according to the Supreme Court, it resides in the penumbras, or in between, the existing amendments. The Supreme Court applied the right to privacy in 1973 to strike down state bans on abortion in *Roe v. Wade*.

■ Although the Bill of Rights pays a great deal of attention to civil liberties, it is nearly silent on civil rights. It was left to the Fourteenth Amendment, ratified in 1868 after the Civil War, to create the basic tool for attacking racial discrimination. The Fourteenth Amendment forbids states from denying life, liberty, and property without due process of law, meaning a fair and open hearing, and also requires states to provide equal protection under the law, meaning that states may not single out a single group of citizens for special treatment or punishment.

KEY CONCEPTS

■ For the first one hundred years of American history, the Bill of Rights applied just to actions by the federal government. In *Barron v. Baltimore,* a 1833 case involving the owner of a shipping wharf that was being slowly put out of business as Baltimore filled its waters with sand, the Supreme Court declared that the Fifth Amendment's requirement of due process did not apply to citizens of Baltimore, and by implication to any other state or city. Under the Fourteenth Amendment, however, states were prohibited from denying due process or equal protection to any citizen, whether under state or federal laws. The Fourteenth Amendment has been crucial for the nationalization of the Bill of Rights. Over the years, case by case, most pieces of the Bill of Rights have been extended downward to cover U.S. citizens wherever they live.

■ Although the Fourteenth Amendment was a key tool in the fight for civil rights, it was not enough on its own to end all discrimination based on "suspect classifications," which put Americans into population categories such as race, gender, and disability. Many of these categories have been outlawed as a basis for discrimination one case at a time or in sweeping federal laws. One of the most important cases in ending discrimination was *Brown v. Board of Education,* which declared racial segregation in public schools unconstitutional. The case involved Linda Brown, an eight-year-old African American girl who merely wanted to attend an all-white school just blocks from her home rather than ride a bus to the minority school five miles away.

■ In recent years, Congress and the federal courts have worked to eliminate discrimination by age, gender, and disability. As the protections have been expanded, Americans have become increasingly opposed to further efforts to help minorities. Several recent Supreme Court cases have restricted the use of affirmative action as a device to give minorities and other protected classes of Americans extra help. At the same time, Congress recently passed the Americans with Disabilities Act, a sweeping law that forces the nation to make facilities more accessible to those with physical or mental disabilities.

IN A DIFFERENT LIGHT

■ Several recent federal court decisions appear to move America closer to creating a right to die. In April 1996, a federal court of appeals ruled that New York state's ban on physician-assisted suicide for terminally ill patients was an unconstitutional infringement on the Fourteenth Amendment's equal protection clause. Just one month earlier, another federal court of appeals had overturned Washington state's ban as a violation of the right to privacy.

■ There is no more controversial issue involving freedom of religion than school prayer. Most Americans believe school prayer should be allowed, whether as a moment of silence at the start or the day or as a formal prayer. However, the federal courts have generally ruled that any prayer, whether spoken or silent, violates the separation of church and state. In the most recent case on the issue, *Lee v. Weisman,* the Supreme Court ruled that an opening prayer at a public middle school graduation was unconstitutional.

■ During the late 1980s and early 1990s, many colleges and universities adopted speech codes limiting hate speech in an effort to create a more welcoming learning climate in the classroom. Some of the codes imposed penalties for any behavior that might offend an individual on the basis of race, religion, sexual orientation, age, and a mix of other suspect classifications. Almost all of the codes were rendered unconstitutional under a Supreme Court decision that voided a St. Paul, Minnesota, law that classified cross burning and other acts as forms of hate speech.

■ Civil liberties and civil rights are not guaranteed just because the Constitution says so. They must be protected in what are often unpopular cases involving lonely individuals who are ready to stand up for their cause. Shannon Faulkner is one of the most recent to do so, suing in 1993 to be admitted to The Citadel as the first women to ever attend the South Carolina state military academy. Although Faulkner eventually won her case and enrolled at The Citadel, she dropped out in the first week of classes, worn down by the intense public scrutiny that accompanied her case.

O P E N QUESTIONS

■ What rights have you enjoyed today? Thinking back to the beginning of the day, where have you benefited from someone else's fight for protection? What Supreme Court cases listed in this chapter have helped you today? Are there any cases that have hurt you?

■ What personal commitments are involved in fighting for one's civil liberties and rights? How can an individual prepare for the public rejection that so often accompanies an effort to guarantee rights such as religious freedom or free speech? Do Rosa Parks and Alan Bakke have anything in common? How would you introduce Shannon Faulkner to the cross burner from St. Paul?

■ How far can the nation go in protecting Americans as individual citizens without eventually weakening its ability to protect the nation as a whole? Do Americans have too many rights today—that is, do Americans think of themselves too frequently as members of special groups deserving protection rather than as citizens of the nation? Does the focus on individual rights sometimes make it impossible for diverse citizens to work together?

■ ■ TERMS TO REMEMBER

civil liberties

civil rights

equal protection clause

due process of law

nationalization of the Bill of Rights

establishment clause

free exercise clause

slander

libel

clear and present danger test

Miranda v. Arizona

Roe v. Wade

separate but equal doctrine

Plessy v. Ferguson

Brown v. Topeka Board of Education

affirmative action

Regents of the University of California v. Bakke

Endnotes to Chapter 11

▶ 1. James Roger Sharp, *American Politics in the Early Republic: The New Nation in Crisis* (New Haven, CT: Yale University Press, 1993), p. 2.

2. 7 Peters 243, 246 (1833). Finding a Supreme Court case is not difficult. Take each piece of the citation above in order. The number "7" refers to the volume in which the decision is printed. The name, "Peters," refers to the last name of the Supreme Court reporter who

recorded the decision. The first 90 volumes of Supreme Court decisions are listed by reporter's name; the rest are simply labeled U.S., which stands for U.S. Reports. The number "243" refers to the page number where the case begins in volume 7, and the number "246" refers to the page number where the quote resides. The last number, which is in parentheses, is the year in which the case was decided, "1833."

More recent cases can be found in several additional places. They can always be found in U.S. Reports, which remains the official location of all Supreme Court decisions. Because the official version is printed only after a term is over, private publishers have created several faster ways to get individual decisions out to the legal community, including Lawyers' Edition (L.Ed.) and Supreme Court Reporter (S.Ct.). These citations also carry the volume number first, the name of the publisher in the middle, and the page number where the case begins third, page number of a quote fourth, and the year in parentheses. Different libraries may have one or more of these sources. For more information on finding Supreme Court and other court decisions, see Albert Melone and Carl Kalvelage, *Primer on Constitutional Law* (Pacific Palisades, CA: Palisades Publishers, 1982).

3. *Dolan v. City of Tigard,* 114 S.Ct. (1994).

▶ 4. See David O'Brien, *Constitutional Law and Politics: Civil Rights and Civil Liberties* (New York: W. W. Norton, 1991), p. 277.

5. *The Slaughterhouse Cases,* 16 Wall. (83 U.S.) 36 (1873).

6. The footnotes to Box 11-2 are as follows: *Chicago, Burlington & Quincy RR v. Chicago,* 166 U.S. 226 (1897); *Fiske v. Kansas,* 274 U.S. 380 (1927); *Near v. Minnesota,* 283 U.S. 697 (1931); *Powell v. Alabama,* 287 U.S. 45 (1932); *DeJonge v. Oregon,* 299 U.S. 353 (1937); *Cantwell v. Connecticut,* 310 U.S. 296 (1940); *Everson v. Bd. of Educ. of Ewing Township,* 330 U.S. 1 (1947); *In re Oliver,* 337 U.S. 257 (1948); *Wolf v. Colorado,* 338 U.S. 25 (1949); *NAACP v. Alabama,* 357 U.S. 449 (1958); *Mapp v. Ohio,* 367 U.S. 643 (1961); *Robinson v. California,* 370 U.S. 660 (1962); *Gideon v. Wainwright,* 372 U.S. 335 (1963); *Malloy v. Hogan,* 378 U.S. 1 (1964); *Pointer v. Texas,* 380 U.S. 400 (1965); *Griswold v. Connecticut,* 381 U.S. 479 (1965); *Parker v. Gladden,* 385 U.S. 363 (1966); *Klopfer v. North Carolina,* 386 U.S. 213 (1967); *Washington v. Texas,* 388 U.S. 14 (1967); *Duncan v. Louisiana,* 391 U.S. 145 (1968); *Benton v. Maryland,* 395 U.S. 784 (1969); *Argersinger v. Hamlin,* 407 U.S. 25 (1972).

7. This is part of an exhaustive list provided in O'Brien, *Constitutional Law and Politics,* pp. 280-81.

8. See Linda Greenhouse, "Blowing the Dust Off the Constitution that Was," *New York Times,* May 28, 1995, p. D-1.

9. The case can be found at Docket No. 95-7028—F.3rd—(2nd Cir. 1996).

10. The quotes in this section are from Esther B. Fein, "The Decision Offers Relief to Plaintiffs," *New York Times,* April 3, 1993, p. B5.

11. Anthony L. Back, Jeffrey I. Wallace, Helene E. Starks, and Robert A. Pearlman, "Physician-Assisted Suicide and Euthanasia in Washington State Patient Requests and Physician Responses," *Journal of the American Medical Association,* volume 275, March 27, 1996, pp. 919-925.

▶ 12. Quoted in Stephen Carter, *The Culture of Disbelief: How American Law and Politics Trivialize Religious Devotion* (New York: Basic Books, 1994), p. 106.

13. *The Gallup Poll Monthly,* April 1994, p. 3.

▶ 14. For an analysis of religion in American politics, see A. James Reichley, *Religion In American Public Life* (Washington, DC: Brookings Institution, 1985).

15. Carter, *The Culture of Disbelief,* p. 106.

16. Carter, *The Culture of Disbelief,* p. 106.

17. *Engel v. Vitale,* 370 U.S. 421 (1962).

18. *Abington School District v. Schempp,* 374 U.S. 203 (1963).

19. *Wallace v. Jaffree,* 472 U.S. 38 (1985).

20. *Lee v. Weisman,* 112 S.Ct. 2649, 2658 (1992).

21. "Students Challenge Ban on Prayer at Graduation," *New York Times,* May 26, 1993, p. A7.

22. See "Thirty Years After the Supreme Court's School Prayer Decision," *The American Enterprise,* volume 3, number 2 (March/April 1992), for a history of public opinion on the issue.

23. *Rosenberger v. University of Virginia,* 115 S. Ct. 2510 (1995).

24. *New York Times Co. v. Sullivan,* 376 U.S. 254 (1964).

25. *Schenck v. U.S.* 249 U.S. (1919).

26. *Brandenburg v. Ohio,* 395 U.S. 444 (1969).

27. The test comes from English common law, cited in O'Brien, *Constitutional Law and Politics,* p. 284.

28. C. Herman Pritchett, *Constitutional Civil Liberties* (Englewood Cliffs, NJ: Prentice-Hall, 1984), pp. 91–92.

29. *R.A.V. v. St. Paul,* 112 S. Ct. 2538, 2550 (1992).

30. *Doe v. University of Michigan,* 721 F. Supp. 852, 856 (E.D. Mich. 1989).

31. Earl Warren, *The Memoirs of Chief Justice Earl Warren* (New York: Doubleday, 1977), pp. 316–17.

32. *Miranda v. Arizona* 384 U.S. 436 (1966).

33. *Griswold v. Connecticut,* 381 U.S. 479 (1965).

34. *Roe v. Wade,* 410 U.S. 113 (1973).

35. O'Brien, *Constitutional Law and Politics,* p. 1160.

▶ 36. See Barbara Craig and David O'Brien, *Abortion and American Politics* (Chatham, NJ: Chatham House, 1993), for an excellent history of the issue.

37. For a quick list of the key decisions, see Robin Toner, "Since Roe v. Wade: The Evolution of Abortion Law," *New York Times,* January 22, 1993, p. A12.

38. *The Gallup Poll Monthly,* January 1992, p. 6.

39. *The Civil Rights Cases,* 109 U.S. 3 (1883).

40. For a brief history of the *Civil Rights Cases,* see O'Brien, *Constitutional Law and Politics,* pp. 1277–78.

41. *Plessy v. Ferguson,* 163 U.S. 537 (1896).

42. For a history of the politics of civil rights in the Eisenhower, Kennedy, and Johnson years, see James Sundquist, *Politics and Policy: The Eisenhower, Kennedy, and Johnson Years* (Washington, DC: Brookings Institution, 1968), chapter 6.

43. Lee Epstein, Jeffrey Segal, Harold Speth, and Thomas Walker, *The Supreme Court Compendium* (Washington, DC: CQ Press, 1994), p. 621.

▶ 44. For those who want to read more about the case and the furor it caused, see Richard Kluger's excellent and readable book *Simple Justice* (New York: Vintage, 1973).

45. See O'Brien, *Constitutional Law and Politics,* p. 1306.

46. *Brown v. Board of Education of Topeka, Kansas,* 347 U.S. 483 (1954).

47. *Brown v. Board of Education of Topeka, Kansas,* 349 U.S. 294 (1955).

48. Seymour Martin Lipset, "Affirmative Action and the American Creed," *Wilson Quarterly,* volume 16, number 1 (Winter 1992), p. 53.

49. Lipset, "Affirmative Action and the American Creed," p. 53.

50. *Regents of the University of California v. Bakke,* 438 U.S. 265 (1978).

51. Joan Biskupic, "A Negative View of Affirmative Action," *Washington Post National Weekly Edition,* November 7–13, 1994, p. 34.

52. Peter Anin, "Race and Rage," *Newsweek,* April 3, 1995, pp. 23–34.

53. Kenneth Davis, *Don't Know Much About History* (New York: Avon Books, 1990), p. 362.

▶ 54. For a history of the debate, see Gilbert Steiner, *Constitutional Inequality: The Political Fortunes of ERA* (Washington DC: Brookings Institution, 1985), and Jane Mansbridge, *Why We Lost the ERA* (Chicago: University of Chicago Press, 1986).

55. See O'Brien, *Constitutional Law and Politics,* pp. 1424–27 for a list of the cases.

56. *Meritor Savings Bank, FBD v.Vinson,* 477 U.S. 57 (1986).

57. *California Federal Savings & Loan Association v. Guerra,* 479 U.S. 272 (1987).

58. *Harris v. Forklift Systems,* 114 S.Ct. 367 (1993).

59. "Excerpts from Supreme Court Ruling on Sexual Harassment in Workplace," *New York Times,* November 10, 1993, p. A14.

60. *Faulkner v. Jones,* 858 F.Supp. 552 (D.S.C. 1994), p. 563.

61. Debbi Wilforen, "First Female Cadet Leaves The Citadel," *Philadelphia Inquirer,* August 19, 1995, p. A7.

62. For a quick summary of the ADA, see Peter Kilborn, "Big Change Likely as Law Bans Bias toward Disabled," *New York Times,* July 19, 1992, p. A1; for a history of the movement toward rights for the disabled, see Robert A. Katzmann, *Institutional Disability: The Saga of Transportation Policy for the Disabled* (Washington, DC: Brookings Institution, 1986); for a history of the ADA, see Robert L. Burgdorf Jr., "The Americans with Disabilities Act: Analysis and Implications of a Second Generation Civil Rights Statute," *Harvard Civil Rights-Civil Liberties Law Review,* volume 26, number 2 (Summer 1991), pp. 413–522.

63. Joann Lublin, "Disabilities Act Will Compel Business to Change Many Employment Practices," *Wall Street Journal,* July 7, 1992, p. B1.

64. See Julie Janofsky, "Whoever Wrote ADA Regs Never Ran a Business," *Wall Street Journal,* March 15, 1993, p. A10.

65. Sharp, *American Politics in the Early Republic,* p. 3.

Making Public Policy

CHAPTER 12

A public policy involves a decision about who gets what, when, and how from government. The final decision can be conveyed to the public in many ways: in the laws passed by Congress and signed by the president, opinions issued by the Supreme Court, or rules written by the federal bureaucracy. But whatever the form, a **public policy** tells the nation what the federal government is going to do, or not do, about a specific problem.

Making public policy in a government designed to be just strong enough is rarely easy. If the Founders ever doubted that their complicated design would make decisions difficult, they learned firsthand as they struggled to make America's first public policies. Even James Madison and Alexander Hamilton, who had worked so closely together on *The Federalist Papers,* soon found themselves locked in bitter struggle over how to finance the new government.

Reducing that complicated debate to a few short paragraphs, Hamilton (America's first secretary of the treasury) wanted the federal government to create a national bank to cover the government's Revolutionary War debt. Much of the debt, which included IOUs to soldiers who fought in the war, was held by speculators, private banks, and states that had been unwilling to raise taxes to cover

Artful Work

the costs of the war. Hence, Hamilton's proposal seemed to favor those who had benefited from other's misfortune by buying up debt at less than full value, even as it appeared to punish states that had worked hard to retire their own debts.

It was a blend of classic divisions that shape the policy debate to this day. Northern states favored Hamilton's proposal, while southern states opposed it; banking and business interests supported the idea, while farmers and small businesses opposed it; wealthy Americans (including speculators) liked the idea, for it promised a healthy return on their investments, while Americans who had sold their IOUs for a few cents on the dollar saw Hamilton's bank as just another way for the rich to get richer.

Because mostly rural southern states stood to lose the most under Hamilton's proposal, Virginia's James Madison rose in opposition in the House of Representatives. After months of intense debate, which pundits might label gridlock today, Congress finally approved the Compromise of 1790: Southern states would support Hamilton's bank if Northern states would move the nation's capital from New York south to its current location on the Potomac River.[1]

Two hundred years later, it is still best not to watch the process too closely, for it remains messy and confusing. It is also still best to recognize that no public policy is perfect. The process rarely produces works of legislative art, but often involves artful work. Every public policy, no matter how carefully drafted, contains flaws. That is the nature of the process.

In the rest of this chapter we will examine three aspects of making public policy. In the first section we will review the different types of public policy, looking at foreign, economic, and social policy as separate concerns for policy makers.

In the second section we will outline the process for making public policy. We have examined pieces of that process in earlier chapters. Here we will put the various pieces of the process together in a chain of eight decisions: (1) making assumptions about the world, (2) picking the problem to be solved, (3) deciding whether to act at all, (4) deciding how much to do, (5) picking a tool for solving the problem, (6) finding someone to deliver the services, (7) making the rules for implementation, and (8) running the program.

After reviewing this chain of decisions, we will examine, the demographic and economic trends that are changing the face of America and that will shape the public policy agenda for the coming decades.

TYPES OF POLICY

America barely survived its first thirty years. It had a staggering war debt, deep internal divisions, and a long inventory of international problems, not the least of which was the continuing struggle with the British, which led to the War of 1812. Nevertheless, it seems safe to argue that the foreign and domestic threats America faces today are much more complicated, perhaps more unsolvable, than those faced but a few short decades ago.

As we will see, even with the collapse of the Soviet empire in the late 1980s, the world has become a more volatile place. America now faces a host of lesser threats from regional powers such as Iraq (which ignited the 1991 Gulf War with its invasion of Kuwait in 1990) and North Korea (which appears to be well on its way toward building nuclear weapons), not to mention the enormous potential threat from the People's Republic of China.

As for the inventory of domestic problems, there seems to be no shortage of stubborn problems facing government, from America's antiquated air traffic control system to its rising teenage pregnancy rate, declining high school test scores, increasing crime rates, growing childhood poverty, declining job security, increasing domestic terrorism (half of Americans believe the threat from domestic terrorists such as the ones who planned the Oklahoma City bombing is now greater than from foreign terrorists), aging roads and bridges, and the looming crisis in funding America's social safety net for the elderly.

This is not to say that America has been unable to make progress in solving some of its most pressing problems. Gregg Easterbrook argues, for example, that the nation has made great progress in cleaning up the environment. In 1992, he reports, 54 million Americans lived in areas that failed to meet minimum air quality standards. The number is still too high, of course, but it is undeniably lower than the 100 million who lived in dirty air in 1982. Much of this progress occurred because of public policies enacted and implemented by the federal government. "The good news should not scare anyone," writes Easterbrook, "particularly lovers of nature. Consider that recent improvements in air quality came mainly during a decade of Republican presidents—prominently Ronald Reagan, who labored under the garbled impression that trees cause more air pollution than cars."[2]

The list of lingering foreign and domestic problems merely underscores the point that American government is always under pressure to answer public problems. That pressure comes in three broad categories: foreign, social, and economic. We will tackle each in order below.

Foreign Policy

Foreign policy is concerned with simultaneously protecting America from foreign threats and promoting American values abroad. As the world has grown more complex, so, too, has meeting these two goals.

In the early years of the republic, America's foreign policy mostly consisted of efforts to protect the nation from economic and military threats. George Washington's farewell address put the focus on keeping America as separate from the rest of the world as possible: "The great rule of conduct for us in regard to foreign nations is, in extending our commercial relations, to have with them as little *political connection* as possible. . . . Trust to temporary alliances for extraordinary emergencies, steer clear of permanent alliances with any portion of the foreign world. . . . Such an attraction of a small or weak nation toward a great and powerful nation dooms the former to be the satellite of the latter."[3]

For most of its first 150 years, America heeded Washington's warning. This is not to say the young nation was completely isolated from the rest of the world, however. It occasionally expressed strong concerns about foreign involvement in its corner of the hemisphere—President James Monroe issued his Monroe Doctrine in 1823 warning Europe to steer clear of any further efforts to colonize the Americas.

Rather, to the extent possible, America wanted to be left alone. Although the nation was drawn into World War I in 1917, America soon returned to isolationism when the Senate rejected President Woodrow Wilson's proposal for a League of Nations. At least in 1919, America would have none of what would become today's United Nations.

Nevertheless, world events conspired to make America a critical partner in world affairs. As America grew from being George Washington's "small and weak" nation to being a "great and powerful nation" in its own right, its foreign policy became more complicated. In 1781, America had just seven embassies and diplomatic posts located abroad; by 1992, the number of embassies and posts had increased

President Clinton meets with U.S. peacekeeping troops in Bosnia. The world has become more volatile and foreign policy more difficult to explain after the end of the Cold War.

to 284.[4] America has never been more involved around the world, sometimes putting U.S. troops in harm's way in nations most Americans cannot identify, such as Bosnia and Somalia.

Along the way, the world has become a more dangerous place. Seventeen international agreements are currently in force just to regulate the spread, testing, or use of nuclear weapons; four more limit the use of poisonous gas, biological, or inhumane weapons; one reduces the risk of nuclear war; one limits conventional weapons in Europe; and one bans the use, development, production, and stockpiling of chemical weapons. The first such agreement came in 1925 when 130 nations signed a treaty banning the use of poisonous gas; the most recent came in 1993 when 130 nations signed the Chemical Weapons Convention. In between, 126 nations agreed to ban the use of nuclear weapons in outer space, 135 to prohibit biological weapons, and 128 to limit nuclear bomb tests.

America's foreign policy involvement is shaped by four basic goals. The first is *national security,* which involves protecting America from outside threats (including nuclear and inhumane weapons); the second is *economic interest,* which involves building foreign economic conditions that support American interests back home; the third is to promote *humanitarian or social values,* which involves America's image of what the world should look like, including efforts to encourage democracy and human rights; and the fourth is *world order,* which involves making the world less volatile.[5]

In turn, these goals shape what the policy-making process identifies as problems. The Gulf War, for example, involved a blend of all four goals. Although Iraq was much too small to ever threaten the U.S. directly, its huge army clearly menaced Israel, America's closest ally in the region and largest foreign aid recipient. To the extent that Iraq endangered Israel, it engaged both U.S. security interests and world order.

Iraq's 1990 invasion of Kuwait also threatened the American economy, which is highly dependent on oil imports. To the extent that the Iraqi invasion imperiled U.S. oil supplies, it involved U.S. economic interests. Finally, the brutality of the Iraqi invasion called upon U.S. humanitarian and social values. These assorted goals came together in the 100-hour war that drove Iraqi forces from Kuwait.

IN A DIFFERENT LIGHT

DOES THE U.S. STILL NEED A FOREIGN POLICY?

For much of this century, America's foreign policy was shaped by a great battle between democracy and communism. Communism is an ideology in which individual freedom is sharply restricted for the benefit of the nation as a whole. There is no delicate balance in a communist system. All is for the whole, nothing for the individual.

The United States and the Soviet Union emerged from World War II in 1945 both deeply committed to promoting their views of the world. For the better part of the next half century, the two waged a great "Cold War," never firing a shot at each other but constantly sparring through smaller allies. The Soviet Union and its communist neighbor, China, backed the North Vietnamese in the Vietnam War, years later the United States and its western European allies backed the rebels in the Soviet Union's "Vietnam," Afghanistan.

In a blink of history, however, the Cold War was over. Under intense economic pressure from the West, the Soviet empire began to crumble in the late 1980s, first in Poland and East Germany, then almost overnight in the rest of the Soviet Union. Only Cuba remained committed to the old Soviet communist ideal.

With no great enemy to unite the public behind international involvement, polls showed that Americans were becoming far less worried about foreign policy. Only 2 percent of Americans mentioned foreign policy issues as the most important problem facing the nation in 1995,[6] suggesting that the nation may be entering a new era of **isolationism,** in which America will steer clear of the rest of the world.

For the time being, however, most Americans still believe the nation needs a foreign policy. Americans may not see foreign affairs as a most important problem, but two-thirds want the nation to take an active part in world affairs nonetheless. The majority reject the notion that the U.S. "should mind its own business internationally and let other countries get along the best they can on their own."[7]

Nevertheless, Americans have become more precise about just when and where their nation should take an active part in world affairs. They no longer want America to be the world's police officer, and believe other nations should rely less on U.S. troops for protection. Less than one in ten Americans believe the U.S. should be the "single world leader," while three-quarters say the U.S. should play a shared leadership role with other nations.

Americans have also become more focused on foreign policy issues that have domestic impacts. Number one is stopping the flow of illegal drugs into the U.S. (89 percent of the public say it should be a very important U.S. foreign policy goal), followed by protecting the jobs of American workers (83 percent), preventing the spread of nuclear weapons (82 percent), controlling and reducing illegal immigration (72 percent), securing adequate supplies of energy (62 percent), reducing America's trade deficit with other countries (59 percent), and improving the global environment (58 percent). Traditional Cold War issues such as promoting and defining human rights in other countries, helping bring democratic forms of government to other countries, and helping improve the standard of living in less-developed countries fall far below.[8]

As a result, America is becoming a reluctant partner in world affairs, with limited public support for involvement when the going gets tough or violent. Unless a president can find a clear domestic benefit from engagement abroad, the public is likely to say "no," particularly when U.S. troops are at risk.

Economic Policy

Economic policy is concerned with increasing America's standard of living, whether measured by inflation, unemployment, the national debt, or gross domestic product. (See Box 12–1 for a brief description of these terms.) Increasing the standard of living is easier said than done, however, if only because the American economy is now part of a vast global network. America no longer controls its own economic destiny, in part because of its own success in rebuilding the devastated economies of Europe and Japan following World War II.[9] Those nations have become major competitors with the U.S., whether in cars, computers, rice, or wine.

Economic policy has always been at or near the top of the federal government's list of problems. It was economic policy, for example, that created the fight over the Revolutionary War debt in the First Congress. For the first 150 years or so, however, economic policy was generally left to the private sector. Government generally stayed out of the business of business, adopting a *laissez faire* (or leave alone) philosophy toward the economy.

BOX
12-1

A Definition of Economic Terms

Inflation: Measured by the Consumer Price Index (CPI). Shows how much more or less Americas are paying for the same "basket of goods" over time. The major components accounted for in the CPI are food, shelter, household fuel, clothing, transportation, and medical care.

Unemployment: Measures the percentage of Americans who are looking for jobs but cannot find them. Does not measure the number who have given up looking for work.

National Debt: Measures how much money the government owes—directly tied to the federal budget deficit. When federal spending exceeds taxes and other revenues, the federal government must borrow money, thereby increasing its debt. Like any consumer, the government must pay interest on any money it borrows. A growing percentage of the federal budget is simple interest on the national debt. Paying this interest has several effects. First, if there is not enough money available in the economy, government borrowing may drive up the interest rate on money, which is the simple measure of how much money costs (credit cards, for example, often carry an 18 to 22 percent annual interest rate). As interest rates rise, other consumers reduce their spending for a host of goods (houses, cars, clothing) because money is just too expensive. Second, whatever the money costs at the time, government must eventually pay back the money it borrows, meaning that future taxpayers may bear the burden for today's budget deficits.

Gross Domestic Product: Measures the size of the entire American economy by totaling all of the things the economy produces and sells and subtracting what it buys from other countries. It tells how fast the economy is growing or shrinking. It is reported quarterly by the Department of Commerce.

As America moved from being a primarily agricultural, rural economy in the 1800s to a more industrial, urban economy in the early 1900s, government began to take a more aggressive role in regulating the economy, including new rules forbidding child labor, cleaning up the meatpacking industry, improving workplace safety, and breaking up industry monopolies, or trusts. Congress also created the first independent agencies to govern a variety of economic practices, including interstate commerce. The result of this "progressive era" in American history was a government much more deeply involved in economic life than ever before.

It took the stock market crash in October 1929 and the subsequent Great Depression to drive the federal government toward a more aggressive role in trying to solve economic problems. Over the ten years leading up to World War II, the federal government became involved in virtually all areas of the economy but for one: it never nationalized, or took control, of any industries. Unlike other Western democracies, which have owned everything from airlines to television stations, or communist nations, which generally own all instruments of production from steel factories to farms, the federal government has generally resisted the temptation to own whole industries.

Nevertheless, the federal government emerged from the Great Depression and World War II convinced that it could, and should, manipulate the economy to promote four basic goals. The first is *economic growth,* which involves expanding the standard of living; the second is *full employment,* which involves finding jobs for as many Americans as possible; the third is *price stability,* which involves holding down inflation; and the fourth is *international competitiveness,* which involves keeping America atop the global economy.

The federal government has two basic options for reaching these four goals: it can use **fiscal policy,** which uses government taxes and spending as tools for stimulating or slowing the economy, or **monetary policy,** which involves efforts to change the cost and supply of money.

Congress and the president control fiscal policy. Whether intended or not, any tax or spending decision is a fiscal policy choice. Tax increases and spending cuts, for example, are seen as devices for slowing down a "hot," or inflationary economy. By taking money away from individual consumers, government reduces demand for products. As demand falls, so do prices. Conversely, spending increases and tax cuts are seen as devices for stimulating a sluggish economy. By putting money in the pockets of consumers through their purchases of goods or by cutting their taxes, the government increases demand for products. As demand rises, so does production. New jobs should naturally follow.

Ronald Reagan had a rather different theory of how federal taxes and spending interact. He believed that cutting taxes and increasing defense spending would actually result in a smaller budget deficit. His notion was simple: cutting taxes on well-to-do Americans would release their money for investments; those investments would stimulate economic growth; that growth would increase wages; those wages would generate more taxes; and those taxes would reduce the federal deficit. Unfortunately for the national debt, the theory proved wrong. The result was a massive federal budget deficit that continued into the 1990s, and led to pressure for a constitutional amendment requiring a balanced budget as one way to control fiscal policy.

Despite their considerable influence over fiscal policy, Congress and the president have little control, if any, over monetary policy. That responsibility belongs to the Federal Reserve Board, which is commonly called the Fed. Although the seven members of the Fed are appointed by the president and confirmed by the Senate, they serve fourteen-year terms, which makes them mostly independent of political pressure.

Established in 1913, the Fed determines the basic price borrowers must pay for money. The Fed sets this price through the *discount rate,* which is the interest rate the Fed charges its banks for money. Reducing the discount rate is seen as a device for stimulating a sluggish economy. By lowering interest rates, the Fed puts more money into the economy, thereby increasing demand. Conversely, increasing the discount rate is seen as a device for slowing a hot economy. By raising interest rates, the Fed makes consumers pay more for the money they borrow, hence, dampening demand.

The challenge in making fiscal and monetary policy today is that the economy sometimes does not behave as predicted. The Carter administration witnessed a new kind of economic problem in the late 1970s called stagflation, which is a combination of unemployment and inflation, two problems that are not supposed to exist at the same time. In theory, unemployment is supposed to be high when inflation is low, and vice versa. In reality, stagflation is a symptom of an increasingly complex global economy that does not yield quite so readily to U.S. fiscal or monetary decisions. In fact, much of what happens in the U.S. economy today is determined by decisions made in nations and markets abroad.

Social Policy

Social policy is concerned with protecting America's quality of life, while assuring that Americans have some protection, or a safety net, against personal hardship. Social programs of one kind or another now account for over half of all federal spending, with Social Security for the elderly by far the largest single program in the federal budget.

Until the early 1900s, however, the federal government did little to either protect the quality of life or create a social safety net. Although the federal government did provide small pensions to veterans and occasional land grants to new settlers, the rest of society had to rely on the kindness of strangers to find a way through hardship. Education was left to communities; public welfare was left to private charities or religious institutions.[10]

This informal safety net began to fray as America's cities filled with wave after wave of immigrants at the turn of the century; it unraveled completely with the Great Depression. Private charities simply could not meet the needs, putting greater pressure on the federal government to become involved in both managing the economy and preventing poverty. Congress passed the Social Security and unemployment compensation programs in 1935, and provided the first federal housing assistance in 1937. Together, these New Deal programs formed the basis for further expansion under Lyndon Johnson's Great Society, most notably Food Stamps for the poor in 1964 and Medicare for the elderly in 1965.

By the 1960s, America's social policy agenda had grown to cover three broad goals, each an umbrella for dozens of separate programs that endeavor to solve social problems. The first goal is *personal safety,* which involves everything from keeping streets safe to environmental protection, from access to decent housing to at least minimal access to health care, primarily for the elderly (through

Medicare) and the poor (through Medicaid), but not yet for the working poor, who often hold jobs without health insurance. The second goal is *income security,* which involves providing protection against downturns in economic performance through programs such as unemployment insurance, job training, disability insurance, Food Stamps, and Aid to Families with Dependent Children (AFDC), as well as support for the elderly through programs such as Social Security and regulations to protect pensions. The third goal is *civil liberties and civil rights,* which has become so important over the past thirty years that it warrants its own chapter in this book (see Chapter 11).

One way to distinguish among the many income security programs that now exist is to ask who gets the benefits. Some programs provide benefits only to Americans who have earned a right to participate through contributions earlier in life, either in the form of taxes (a financial contribution) or service to the nation (a personal contribution). These programs are called *contributory social programs.*

Other programs provide benefits only to Americans who are in trouble through accidents and events mostly outside their control, whether an act of God such as a hurricane or a personal crisis such as a divorce or teenage pregnancy. These programs are labeled *noncontributory social programs,* and include everything from disaster relief to job training. Some of these programs require proof that recipients are poor enough to merit government support. To qualify for such *means-tested* programs, recipients must prove that they lack the means to provide for themselves.

Although most income security programs are either contributory *or* noncontributory, America's Social Security system provides both kinds of benefits. Americans cannot qualify for Social Security unless they have paid at least some

Clinton swears in a class of Americorps volunteers in 1995. Americorps is an example of a contributory program in which voluntary service entitles the contributor to funding for college.

amount of taxes into the system over a minimum amount of time, making access to the program contributory. At the same time, the formula for calculating payments is set so that those with lower incomes (who paid in less) receive a greater proportion relative to those with higher incomes (who paid in more), thereby making a portion of each Social Security check noncontributory.

THE POLICY-MAKING PROCESS

As the types of policies have become more complicated over time, so has the process for making those policies. There are more participants at the policy table—witness the dramatic increase in the number of organized interests over the past half century—and there are also more "tables," or places, where policy gets made: more subcommittees in Congress, more White House staffers, more presidential appointees, more media outlets, more political consultants, indeed, more of just about every kind of participant imaginable, except, it seems, individual citizens. The result is a fragmented, often messy process that confirms the Founders' desire to counteract ambition with ambition.

Where Policy Is Made

The final choices on who gets what, when, and how from government are usually made under formal rules—only senators can vote in the Senate, only the president can issue an executive order, and so on. And they produce formal outcomes—a public law, a verdict.

Just because the process for making final decisions looks formal does not make it so, however. Final policy decisions usually involve a long string of informal decisions made in **policy networks** of political leaders and organized interests that come together to make a specific policy decision or two, then disband.[11] As such, these networks are anything but formal. They are free to convene anywhere—from a lobbyist's office to a senator's suite, from a taxi cab to a local restaurant—and can involve just about anyone with a stake in the final decision.

Policy networks are a much more flexible version of what political scientists call **iron triangles** of influence. An iron triangle is composed of three simple corners: (1) a federal department or agency, (2) a set of loyal organized interests, and (3) a House and/or Senate authorizing committee. Each side of the triangle gives and receives benefits from the other two. Congress gives money to the agency, for example, and gets campaign money and endorsements from the lobby in return; the lobby gives money and endorsements to Congress, and gets special services from the agency in return; the agency gives special services to the lobby, and gets money from Congress in return.

Making veterans policy is a classic example of how iron triangles work. (See Box 12–2 for the veterans iron triangle.) Composed of the House and Senate Vet-

The Veterans Iron Triangle

House and Senate Veterans Committees

- Write legislation creating new programs and authorizing new facilities
- Defend veterans hospital and benefits system from budget cuts
- Promote veterans agends through hearings
- Give supportive members of Congress opportunities to sponsor legislation, testify at hearings, cast proveteran votes

Department of Veterans Affairs

- Runs "veterans-only" hospital and benefits system
- Provides free space to veterans groups in all veterans facilities
- Defends veterans budget from cuts in executive-branch budget process
- Gives members of Congress credit for construction of new facilities and benefit increases
- Provides special treatment to constituent cases from key members of Congress

Veterans Lobby

- Supports members of Congress who vote for veterans programs
- Provides free advice to veterans who apply for benefits
- Organizes grassroots support for veterans programs
- Invites members of Congress to participate in key events (parades, wreath-laying ceremonies)
- Gives money, endorsements, and photo opportunities to supportive candidates

erans Committees, the veterans lobby, and the Department of Veterans Affairs, the triangle has been able to protect the $17 billion a year veterans health care system in spite of a 56 percent drop in the number of inpatients since the late 1960s. "We have the moral high ground," Veterans Affairs (VA) Secretary Jesse Brown explained in 1995. "We have God on our side. We're right. And we have the American people on our side."[12]

Brown might have added that the VA has the House and Senate Veterans Committee and the veterans lobby on its side, too. "There is no anti-veterans group," argues Brown's predecessor, Edwin Derwinski, who was fired after he proposed changes in the VA hospital system. "It's just a one way street. Now we're not talking about a hell of a big army, but it's unopposed."[13] With thousands of local posts across the United States, the veterans lobby (American Legion, Veterans of Foreign Wars, Disabled American Veterans) is able to generate huge volumes of mail for or against particular policy proposals.

Most of the other old iron triangles have been replaced by policy networks, which flourished as the number of organized interests grew. The increasing number of small, highly specialized organized interests meant that Congress and federal agencies could not identify an ongoing occupant for the third corner of the iron triangle. They had to find temporary allies depending on the issue. There is nothing "iron" about such coalitions of smaller groups. They only last as long as a given issue is hot.

The 1994 debate over national health insurance produced a remarkable collection of such short-term policy networks. (See Box 12–3 for a sampling of the members involved.) On one side in favor of reform was a network composed of organized labor (including the twenty union presidents who created the Committee for National Health Insurance), a variety of "good government" organizations (including a coalition called Healthright), smaller collections of physicians, consumers, even the League of Women Voters. On the other side was a network composed of the large physician groups, tobacco companies (which feared that health reform would be financed by a tax on cigarettes), small businesses, hospital organizations, a mix of insurance groups, and huge pharmaceutical companies. In between were a mix of lone insurance companies and health care groups that hoped for a compromise on the issues.

Such policy networks may weaken government's ability to act by forcing presidents and leaders of Congress to build separate majorities for every issue that arises, a time-consuming, often frustrating process that raises the cost of passing legislation. Given the decline of the once-powerful organized interests that dominated the policy-making process documented in Chapter 4, the only way to create a majority in support of passage is to build a coalition of smaller interests. As British political scientist Anthony King argues, "The materials out of which coalitions might be built simply do not exist. Building coalitions in the United States today is like building coalitions in the sand. It cannot be done."[14]

BOX
12-3

The Health Care Issue Network

Medical Schools
American Association of Medical Colleges

Insurance Companies
National Association of Life Underwriters
American Council of Life Insurance
AFLAC, Inc.
Prudential Insurance

Insurance Agents
Independent Insurance Agents of America

Other Health Care Providers
American Podiatry Association
American Dental Association
American Chiropractic Association
American Nurses Association
American Occupational Therapy Association
American Optometric Association

Consumer Groups
Families USA
AIDS activists
Child Welfare League
National Council of Senior Citizens

Hospitals
American Hospital Association
American Health Care Association

Doctors
American Medical Association
American College of Emergency Physicians
American Academy of Ophthalmology
American College of Physicians

Doctors
American Academy of Family Physicians
Physicians for a National Health Program

Tobacco Companies

Private Companies
American Airlines
United States Surgical Corporation

Pharmaceutical Manufacturers
Eli Lilly & Co.
Pfizer Inc.
Shering-Plough Corp.

Reform Groups
Health Care Reform Project
League of Women Voters
Healthright

Business Associations
National Association of Manufacturers
National Federation of Independent (Small) Businesses
U.S. Chamber of Commerce

Organized Labor
AFL–CIO
United Auto Workers
Committee for National Health Insurance

Department of Health and Human Services
Health Care Financing Administration

Department of Veterans Affairs
Veterans Health Administration

Department of Labor

Other Congressional Committees
House and Senate Appropriations
House and Senate Budget
House and Senate Veterans Affairs
House Energy and Commerce
House Science, Space, and Technology
House Government Operations and Senate Governmental Affairs
Senate Commerce, Science, and Transportation
Senate Aging

INNER CIRCLE

House Ways and Means
Committee

House Education and Labor Committee

House Energy and Commerce Committee

Senate Finance Committee

Senate Labor and
Human Resources Committee

Hillary Clinton's Health Care
Reform Task Force

INNER CIRCLE

OUTER CIRCLE—CON

OUTER CIRCLE—PRO

Making Policy

Every policy reflects a series of separate decisions leading to final implementation and action. From start to finish, making policy involves at least eight decisions: (1) making assumptions about the world, (2) picking the problem to be solved, (3) deciding whether to act at all, (4) deciding how much to do, (5) picking a tool for solving the problem, (6) finding someone to deliver the services, (7) making the rules for implementation, and (8) running the program. The first four decisions are mostly made by Congress, the presidency, or the courts, while the last four are mostly made by the federal bureaucracy.

What makes the process both exciting and frustrating is that it does not always start at the beginning. In fact, it is more appropriate to array the eight decisions as part of a never-ending circle. (See Box 12–4 for a simple depiction of the process.) A specific problem gets identified, a solution gets passed, implementation occurs; the problem may worsen, an amendment to the old solution gets passed, further implementation occurs, and so forth.

It is best, therefore, to think of making public policy as an often unpredictable process in which problems and solutions are loosely connected to each other. The result is a policy-making process that is often unpredictable, and almost always in flux.[15]

Making Assumptions about the World. Every government decision involves assumptions about how the world works. Is the economy going to get stronger? If so, perhaps employment will go up, and the costs of supporting the unemployed will go down. Is teenage pregnancy going to increase? If so, perhaps childhood poverty, which increases as single teenagers have babies, will continue to grow. Is world terrorism going to increase? If so, perhaps the United States needs to strengthen its border security.

The problem with making even short-term assumptions about the world is that they are often wrong. Ronald Reagan's Office of Management and Budget Director David Stockman once despaired of making assumptions even a year into the future. "I'm beginning to believe that history is a lot shakier than I thought it was," he remarked in late 1981 as the Reagan economic theory began to fail. "In other words, I think there are more random elements, less determinism, and more discretion in the course of history than I ever believed before."[16]

Making short-term assumptions is easy, however, compared to creating the seventy-five-year forecasts needed for Social Security. Because most Americans pay into the program for thirty or forty years of working life, and draw out their benefits for another twenty or thirty years of retirement, the program is very slow to change, meaning that policy makers must plan decades in advance to fix possible problems. Hence, the seventy-five-year forecasts. Knowing the future of Social Security policy today involves guesses about how many children will be

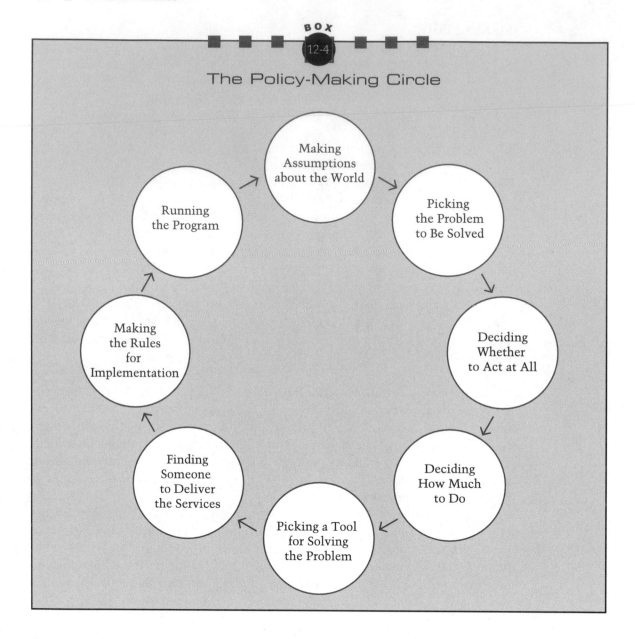

BOX
12-4

The Policy-Making Circle

- Making Assumptions about the World
- Picking the Problem to Be Solved
- Deciding Whether to Act at All
- Deciding How Much to Do
- Picking a Tool for Solving the Problem
- Finding Someone to Deliver the Services
- Making the Rules for Implementation
- Running the Program

born (more children born today means more taxpayers tomorrow), inflation (in indexed programs such as Social Security, higher inflation means higher benefit checks), and unemployment (higher unemployment means fewer people working, which means less Social Security tax being paid).

Because there is no sure way to pick among competing assumptions about such a distant future, policy makers often choose assumptions that help sell their particular views of the world. They are often pessimistic about the future when they define problems, but optimistic when they announce specific proposals to fix the problems. The result is that problems may seem much worse than they truly are, while solutions may look more likely to work than they ever can.

Picking the Problem to Be Solved.   Picking the problem to be solved is the essential decision in setting the **policy agenda.** The agenda, as political scientist John Kingdon defines it, "is the list of subjects or problems to which governmental officials, and people outside of government closely associated with those officials, are paying some serious attention at any given time."[17]

Problems reach the agenda from a variety of sources. Many come from events: an American passenger jet crashes; an earthquake hits California; an oil tanker runs aground in Alaska. Others reach the agenda because of the government's own numbers: the economy slows down; the number of children immunized against illness falls; crime rates increase.

The source of the problem clearly matters to policy makers. Some sources, particularly organized interests, have a great stake in making sure their cause reaches the agenda. That is why they exist in the first place, and most certainly why they make campaign contributions. Problems that arise from a crisis are difficult to ignore, although, as we will see, the public attention span to a crisis may be very short, indeed. Problems that are identified through numbers and analysis may be the easiest to ignore, in part because there always seem to be numbers to refute one analysis or another.

As the number of problems competing for space has grown, in large part because of the fragmentation of organized interests, policy makers have increasingly come to rely on a small number of think tanks to help winnow the list. A **think tank** is simply an organization composed of public-policy researchers. Its main products are ideas, which are usually published as books or short articles that are promoted widely in government. Because a think tank's scholars tend to have strong views about what government should or should not do, think tanks tend to be labeled as liberal or conservative.

Think tanks tend to rise and fall with the party in power. One of the most visible think tanks during the 1980s was the Heritage Foundation. Populated largely by conservative scholars, and funded mostly by conservative foundations, Heritage was deeply involved in supporting the Reagan effort to cut government. The closer it worked with the Reagan administration, the better it seemed to do in raising money from conservatives. It grew from an initial funding of just $250,000 when it was created in 1973 to $10 million ten years later. Along the way, Heritage was able to finance a $9.5 million headquarters building located near Capitol Hill.

Although most think tanks employ a rather small number of scholars, they have a significant impact. Think tanks distill information, distilling the raw numbers on foreign, economic, and social trends into meaningful advice. They often lay the intellectual and research groundwork for major legislative proposals. They supply many of the witnesses who testify before the key committees, many of the authors who write the op-ed pieces that endorse or oppose action, and many of the "talking heads" who show up on the network news. Think tanks may not come up with every proposal enacted into law, but the fact that they are studying a particular issue is an important sign that the issue is "in good currency," which is a way of saying that the issue is hot.

Deciding Whether to Act at All. Just because a problem exists does not automatically mean Congress and the president will try to solve it. Sometimes they make a *nondecision,* which is simply a deliberate decision not to act. Government may not have the money to do much of anything substantive, and a delaying device such as a commission or study may not be appropriate.

Other times, issues will simply fade from the public's mind. In fact, writes political scientist Anthony Downs, "American public attention rarely remains sharply focused upon any one domestic issue for very long—even if it involves a continuing problem of crucial importance to society." According to Downs, attention to problems follows an **issue-attention cycle** in which each problem "suddenly leaps into prominence, remains there for a short time, and then—though still largely unresolved—gradually fades from the center of public attention."[18] (See Box 12–5 for a list of the steps in the issue-attention cycle.)

Ultimately, nothing forces presidents, members of Congress, or judges to pick a problem if that problem does not further their reelection, place in history, or good policy. Some problems help policy makers achieve one or more of these goals; others do not.

Deciding How Much to Do. Once Congress, the president, or the courts decide to act, the process of actually finding a solution to a given problem is enormously complicated in its own right—recall Box 7–5 on how a bill becomes a public law. Even before a bill is introduced, however, policy makers make two basic decisions before drafting a proposal.

The first involves the size of the solution. Will it be a small step from current practice, which political scientists call an **incremental program,** or a major policy reform? Major policy reforms are generally much more difficult to pass, sometimes because they cost much more and sometimes because they cut long-established federal programs. At the same time, however, they allow Congress and the president to claim much greater credit for solving a problem.

The second decision involves how benefits are to be distributed across the various groups in society. Will the solution offer new benefits to most groups in society? Such a **distributive program** generally helps all groups in society, and shares the costs evenly. National parks, air traffic control, the interstate highway system, education funding, national defense, and Social Security are all defined as distributive in nature.

BOX
12-5

The Issue-Attention Cycle

The Pre-Problem Stage

This first stage in the cycle prevails when some highly undesirable social condition exists but has not yet captured much public attention.

Alarmed Discovery and Euphoric Enthusiasm

Stage two comes about when, as a result of some dramatic series of events . . ., or for other reasons, the public suddenly becomes both aware of and alarmed about the evils of a particular problem.

Realizing the Cost of Significant Progress

The third stage consists of a gradually spreading realization that the cost of "solving" the problem is very high indeed.

Gradual Decline of Intense Public Interest

In stage four, as more and more people realize how difficult, and how costly to themselves, a solution to the problem would be, three reactions set in. Some people just get discouraged. Others feel positively threatened by thinking about the problem; so they suppress such thoughts. Still others become bored by the issue.

The Post-Problem Stage

In the final stage, an issue that has been replaced at the center of public concern moves into a prolonged limbo—a twilight realm of lesser attention or spasmodic recurrences of interest.

Source: Anthony Downs, "The 'Issue-Attention Cycle,'" The Public Interest, vol. 28 (Summer 1972), pp. 38–50.

Or will the solution take wealth (in the form of taxes) from one group in society and convert it into benefits for another? Such a **redistributive program** tends to concentrate benefits on the less fortunate in society, and often provokes conflict between the haves and have nots. Welfare, poverty programs, Headstart for poor children, and special programs to help minority groups are often characterized as redistributive. Some political scientists call these programs *zero-sum games,* meaning that one side's gain is another's loss.

Headstart students. Headstart is a program designed to help poor children get a headstart on schooling. It is a redistributive program.

Or will, as is often the case today in cutting the federal budget, the solution ask all Americans to give up benefits they once enjoyed? Because of its controversy, such a **dedistributive program** is clearly the most difficult to pass. It is always easier for Congress and the president to sell a program that distributes benefits than to sell one that inflicts pain. The 1983 Social Security rescue is one example of a dedistributive program. It cut benefits for older Americans, raised taxes on all workers, and increased the retirement age on future retirees, all exceedingly unpopular ideas, but essential if the program was to continue to pay benefits on time.[19]

Picking a Tool for Solving the Problem.   Policy makers are not finished with formulating a solution until they pick a tool for actually solving the problem. Although there are literally thousands of federal programs now on the statute books, public-policy scholars argue that there are four basic tools available to solve most public problems: (1) making outright money payments, (2) providing goods or services directly, (3) providing protection against risk, and (4) enforcing restrictions and penalties.[20]

Outright money payments are made either directly to individuals or to agencies that provide services to them. Social Security is a direct payment to individuals; Headstart, which provides early childhood education for disadvantaged children, is funded by the federal government, and delivered by local schools.

Goods and services are provided either completely free to the public or for a price. National parks such as Yosemite or the Grand Canyon generally charge an admission fee; the National Air and Space Museum on the Washington Mall is open to the public for free; and Americans do not pay anything directly for national defense. Ultimately, of course, nothing the government does is completely free—the National Air and Space Museum is supported by general taxes, as is defense.

Protections against risk involve a range of devices to encourage activities where the private sector might otherwise not go. The most familiar protections are federal loan guarantees, under which the government promises to cover the losses in the event a student, farmer, small business, or other borrower fails to repay a debt. The federal government also provides protection against risk in the form of special exemptions from certain laws. Major league baseball, for example, is exempted from federal antitrust law. The exemption was designed to encourage the expansion of the national pastime, but was never given to professional football, hockey, or basketball.

Restrictions and penalties are designed to encourage or discourage certain behaviors. The list of laws and regulations that affect Americans is seemingly endless, and includes everything from criminal laws to cancer warnings on cigarette packages, which are required under federal law.

Finding Someone to Deliver the Services.   Once a tool is selected, Congress, the president, or the courts must decide who will actually deliver the services. The answer is no longer always federal employees.[21] With federal employment actually in decline, policy success increasingly depends on **third-party federal government,** which is defined as the use of nonfederal employees to deliver services on behalf of the federal government.

There are three major sources of third-party delivery of government services today: (1) private companies who work for the federal government under contracts; (2) state and local governments who work for the federal government under mandates; and (3) nonprofit organizations, which are sometimes called part of the independent sector, that fill in the gaps where private contractors or state and local governments are unwilling or unable to go.

Private Companies.   Private companies are a first alternative to delivery of service by federal employees. Paid under contracts with federal agencies, these profit-making businesses provide an increasing share of federal services once provided exclusively by federal employees, including everything from performing laboratory tests for the National Institutes of Health to writing congressional testimony for the secretary of the Department of Energy.[22]

As of 1993, over $200 billion, or almost one-fifth of the federal budget, went to private contractors. The top three contractors were McDonnell Douglas at $8 billion, mostly for building fighter jets; Martin Marietta at $7.5 billion, mostly for running Department of Energy laboratories; and Lockheed at $7 billion, again mostly for fighter jets. Defense contractors accounted for over two-thirds of the contracting budget, the Department of Energy another one-tenth, NASA one-fifteenth, and the rest of the domestic agencies about one-sixth. However, the share going to jets, parts, and weapons is clearly falling as more of the federal budget gets spent on services—computers, telephones, consulting, and so forth.

As the amount of contracting grows, so does the number of "shadow" federal employees—people who are basically federal employees without the ID cards. Thus, promises to shrink government by merely cutting the total number of full-time federal employees are misleading. The number of employees who work for the federal government may go down, but the number who work under federal contracts almost always goes up.

State and Local Governments.   America's vast collection of state and local governments are a second source for the delivery of services on behalf of the federal government. As noted in Chapter 9, state and local governments are growing much faster than the federal government. State and local employment has ballooned from roughly 3 million in 1950 to 16 million today, rising from just one state and local employee for every forty Americans to one for every sixteen.

The growth of state and local government is one of the most dramatic, yet least-visible trends shaping American government today. The federal government may get the attention, but state and local governments deliver an increasing share of the services. As the National Commission on the State and Local Public Service observed in making its final report to President Clinton on the condition on state and local government in 1993:

> These employees do much of the real work of domestic governance. We literally could not live without them. They provide our water, collect our trash, vaccinate our children, police our communities, and administer traffic safety, airports, and the vital systems we need to communicate with each other and other nations. They do much of the teaching, training, and counseling in our public schools, universities, and community colleges to prepare our children for fulfilling careers. They are responsible for environmental cleanup and protection programs. They design and carry out programs to lift our most needy out of poverty and into jobs and housing. They operate the hospitals that are the last hope of the uninsured. They staff most of our prisons, as well as our court system. Not a day passes during which their work does not touch and shape our lives.[23]

Part of this role involves **federal mandates,** or orders, to the states. A mandate is quite simple: the federal government merely orders a state or local government to accept some responsibility it might otherwise not accept. Because most mandates come attached to federal grants, state and local governments are hard-pressed to refuse the added responsibility.[24] Although states can always refuse the funds if they do not like the strings attached, the money has become irresistible, even habit-forming.

All mandates do not come from federal legislation, however. The Supreme Court mandated states to integrate the public schools under *Brown v. Board of Education* in 1954, for example. As political scientist Martha Derthick explains, "Until the mid-1950s, federal courts interpreting the Constitution had habitually told the states what they might *not* do. . . . But they had refrained from telling the states what they *must* do. This changed with school desegregation. . . . Once courts and litigants discovered what could be done (or attempted) in the schools, other state institutions, especially prisons and institutions for the mentally ill, became targets."[25]

As the federal budget has tightened in recent years, Congress has frequently resorted to what some experts call "mandates without money." Unlike the era of cooperative federalism, in which the federal government provided much of the funding to help states absorb new responsibilities, today's new federalism often involves nothing more than the order to act.

The Independent Sector.   The final source of third-party federal government is the *independent sector,* which is composed of tax-exempt agencies such as the Red Cross, Salvation Army, and Catholic Charities. By law, these agencies are prohibited from making a profit from their work.

The growth of the independent sector is also one of the most important trends in public policy. The number of charities is growing, as is their role in answering many of the tough problems that now plague America. By 1990, there were over 130,000 charitable organizations providing services across America. Over one-third of these agencies provided human or social services—from marriage counseling to crisis prevention. Another one-fifth provided health care services, one-sixth provided education, and one-tenth arts and culture.[26]

Charitable agencies play two important roles as third-party providers of services. First, many small social service agencies receive grants to administer federal programs of one kind or another. Second, many charitable agencies provide services in the absence of federal programs, filling the gaps in the government's safety net. These agencies are particularly important in addressing unpopular populations or unpopular problems such as drug abuse, inner city crime, AIDS, and joblessness among able-bodied adults.[27]

A DIFFERENT LIGHT

THE PROBLEM WITH THIRD-PARTY GOVERNMENT

Third-party government is almost certain to increase in the future. It is a way for Congress and the presidency to have their policy cake and eat it, too. By using third-party government to deliver services, Congress and the presidency can keep the total federal workforce relatively small, even as the budget grows steadily. They can even claim that the era of big government is over, when, in fact, the number of employees who get paychecks under federal contracts goes up.

There are three problems with using third parties in lieu of federal employees to provide services. First, third-party government may increase the unresponsiveness of bureaucracy. Federal employees may spend more time managing contracts and issuing orders than they do talking to the people they serve. As such, they may become isolated from the world they are supposed to improve, and may lose track of the basic purpose of their programs.[28]

Second, third-party government may increase the public's confusion about where the federal government ends and third parties begin. With so many different entities involved in delivering policy, Americans may not know whom to hold accountable when a contractor, state government, or nonprofit fails to implement a federal program. By increasing the number of nonfederal employees involved in implementing the laws, third-party government may assure that no one can be held accountable for what goes wrong (or right).

Finally, third-party government may hide the true size of the federal government. Contracting out or mandates may make the federal government look smaller, but no one quite knows whether they will save money or cost money. Nor is anyone quite sure just how many contractors now work for the federal government—perhaps as many as six to ten million. What is clear is that private contractors are in business to make a profit, and that the profit is paid by the taxpayer.

Third-party government is not without advantages, however. People who work for contractors, state and local governments, and nonprofit agencies are often more committed to the program goals than the federal employees who write the contracts and rules, in part because third parties are in close contact with the people they serve. Moreover, third parties have at least some financial incentive to do a good job. In theory, competition for future contracts should increase the pressure to spend money wisely.

In practice, however, there may not be enough third parties to create the competition necessary to produce savings and efficiency. In many federal programs, there are only a handful of third parties willing to do the work, reducing competition and increasing the chance that third parties will exploit their position to increase their profit.

Making the Rules for Implementation.   Almost everything the federal government does involves a **rule.** A rule is a precise legal statement about what a policy actually means. It lays out the details on exactly who gets what, when, and how—for example, by specifying the amount of sulfur dioxide that can be released from a smokestack, the required height of a wheelchair ramp in a private building, or the number of life jackets that must be on a ferryboat. As such, rules are essential for turning even the most detailed legislation into action, and rulemaking is the central device used to execute the laws.[29]

Technically, rulemaking comes at the very end of the policy-making process, and is almost invisible to most Americans. Nevertheless it is in ironing out the details that the federal bureaucracy converts the abstract ideas and language of laws, presidential orders, and court rulings into precise rules governing what the public or agencies can do.

There is no question that rules have become more important since the 1950s. Although government has been making rules since the Revolutionary War, it was not until the 1950s that the explosion in rulemaking began, driven largely by implementation of new civil rights and labor laws.

The greatest growth in rulemaking occurred in the 1970s. Congress passed 130 laws requiring some form of social or economic regulation during the decade, leading to a vast increase in the number of rules governing American society.[30] The number of pages published in the **_Federal Register,_** which is a weekly newspaper-like report that lists all new and proposed rules, jumped from just 5,000 a year in 1940 to 87,012 in 1980.[31] By the 1990s, the Office of Management and Budget estimated that Americans were spending 6.6 billion hours each year filling out paperwork required under those rules—whether IRS tax forms, Census Bureau surveys, or environmental and occupational safety and health reports.

The growth of regulation is clear in the **_Code of Federal Regulations,_** which contains every rule issued by the federal government. The _Code_ grew from 121 chapters in 1938 to 221 in 1969 to 313 in 1989. In 1938, there were no pages devoted to environmental protection; by 1990, there were 8,250 pages. In 1938, there were just 39 pages on labor law; by 1990, there were 5,721.[32]

The number of rules is not growing because it is easy to make a rule, however. It is just as complicated to draft, review, and issue a rule as it is to draft, debate, and pass a bill. The process of rulemaking involves eight separate steps. (See Box 12–6 for a quick review of how the eight steps came into play for the Department of Transportation's recent rule on the transport of hazardous materials, such as volatile chemicals, by air, sea, truck, or train.)

Step 1.   The rulemaking process starts when a bill is signed into law, and is sent to the appropriate agency for rulemaking. No bill, no rule.[33]

Step 2.   The agency starts a rulemaking process, basically deciding what to decide. This is no simple decision. Just because a law is passed does not mean it is converted into a rule, not immediately at least. Some agencies such as the Environmental Protection Agency have so many laws that need to be converted and so little staff that some rulemaking gets delayed far into the future.

Step 3.   A draft of the rule is written, including a preamble that states the basic purpose of the rule, the specific language of the rule itself, and whatever research backs up the decision.

Step 4.   The agency must post a formal "Notice of Proposed Rulemaking" in the _Federal Register._ Under federal law, those affected by the rule must be given a chance to raise their concerns.

BOX 12-6

Making an Explosives Rule

Step 1. The Explosives and Combustibles Act of 1908 is passed, giving the federal government authority to regulate dangerous and hazardous materials as they are transported.

Step 2. Over the next eighty years, regulations enforcing the Act are adopted, resulting in 1,400 pages in the *Code of Federal Regulations,* known as the Hazardous Materials Regulations (HMR).

Step 3. As society changes, the regulations become harder to follow and enforce. By the 1970s, there is a general agreement that the existing HMR is inadequate. Work on the revised HMR begins in 1981.

Step 4. The first Notice of Proposed Rulemaking appears in the *Federal Register* in April 1982. Numerous other public notices appear in the *Federal Register* inviting further comment as the process moves ahead.

Step 5. Interested parties take full advantage of the comment period as their primary chance to shape the final rules. More than 2,200 written comments are received. Each comment must be read, analyzed, and answered somewhere in the rulemaking process. The rule must also be negotiated with other departments and agencies in the federal bureaucracy. This step takes ten years.

Step 6. Twenty federal employees are engaged full-time in drafting the final rule, including analyses of the impact of the rule on the environment, small business, occupational health and safety, paperwork burdens on the public, and general cost.

Step 7. The final rule is published in the *Federal Register* on Friday, December 21, 1990.

Step 8. The rule becomes effective on October 1, 1991, over ten years after the process begins. The length of time is not unusual even for rules implementing routine legislation.

Source: Cornelius Kerwin, Rulemaking: How Government Agencies Write Law and Make Policy *(Washington, DC: CQ Press, 1994), pp. 39–42.*

Step 5. The people affected by the rule have anywhere between thirty and ninety days to register their concerns through a process called *notice and comment.* All letters and formal reactions become part of the rulemaking record.

Step 6. The formal rule is finished in response to the notice and comment.

Step 7. The formal rule is published in the *Federal Register.*

Step 8. The rule goes into effect thirty days after it is published.

The process involves a number of smaller steps along the way, including detailed review of proposed rulemaking by the president's Office of Management and Budget.[34] And it does not necessarily end after *Step 8*. Some of the people affected by the rule may decide to sue, moving the case into the federal appeals courts.

The rulemaking process is so time consuming that it can make how a bill becomes a law seem simple. Even a small delay in a federal rule—say, to clean up toxic waste dumps faster—may save an industry millions and millions of dollars. Indeed, it was meat producers who slowed down the new food labels in 1991 and 1992. Because some meats contain a very high percentage of fat, producers worried that the new labels would cut sales. They fought the process at every step, and most certainly delayed final action.

Running the Program. Implementation of public policy does not end with publishing the formal rule, however. It continues in the day-to-day tasks of running public agencies, evaluating how programs work, and dealing with ordinary citizens.

These tasks are all part of what the founder of the Children's Defense Fund, Marian Wright Edelman, once called the "nitty-gritty steps of implementation": "Passing a law or drafting a regulation or issuing an RFP [request for proposal for federal funding] is the easiest part of a change process. Making it work. Informing the public. And assisting and monitoring local enforcement, protecting budgets in a sustained manner, and getting and training sensitive and skilled personnel to administer it in a compassionate way are all important parts of the change process."[35]

Implementation involves a variety of tasks that policy makers often leave to the career public service, and includes everything from hiring the staff to do the work to writing the checks, enforcing the laws, evaluating success, and reporting to Congress. The reason most policy makers ignore implementation is that it is rarely as glamorous or exciting as actually passing the laws, but, as the old saying goes, "the devil is in the details." Implementation is where many programs fail, in part because Congress and the president often write such vague and uncertain laws that no bureaucrat or third-party provider can figure out just what government wants.

THE FUTURE POLICY AGENDA

It is not difficult to imagine the kinds of policy issues America will confront in the future. Indeed, the shape of the policy agenda of the future is already clear in five demographic and economic trends that are changing the face of America: (1) America is getting older, (2) more women are working, (3) the nation is becoming more diverse, (4) the gap between rich and poor is growing, and (5) the traditional two-parent family is in decline. Each trend will be discussed in turn.

The Aging of America

America is getting older every year. In 1990, the average American was thirty-three years old; by the year 2020, the average American will be thirty-eight. No one knows yet whether the Rolling Stones and the Eagles will still be on tour.

America is getting older for two reasons: first, fewer children are being born per woman, and second, Americans are living longer. More older people living longer plus fewer children means that the average age of America must go up.

The birth rate declined largely because of the birth control pill. At the height of the baby boom in the 1950s and 1960s, for example, 20 percent of all births were unwanted; by 1980, the number was down to 7 percent.[36] Over the period, birth rates fell from 3.4 births per woman to roughly 1.8 births per woman—2.1 is considered the number necessary for zero population growth. The result was a "baby bust." The children born during this baby bust are often labeled Generation X.

As the number of children fell, the number of elderly increased. In 1900, only one out of every twenty-five Americans was over the age of sixty-five. By 1950, the number was one in twelve. By 1985, one in nine. By 2030, one in five. In 1900, the average American lived to age forty-seven; by the year 2000, the average will be up to seventy-nine.

The increase in life span is largely due to a decline in death at early ages. More children are surviving childhood as vaccinations now prevent many of the illnesses that killed so many children in previous generations. More middle-aged Americans are living to retirement age as medical research has rendered once-deadly diseases manageable. And more sixty-five-year-olds will live into their eighties and beyond as heart attacks no longer kill quite so easily, and survival rates from cancer are inching upward.

The fact that more Americans survive the early and middle years of life assures that more will live past their seventies and eighties. Indeed, the number of "oldest old," which is defined as people over age eighty-five, is expected to double between now and the year 2020.[37] The number of oldest old will grow from just over 3 million today to almost 17 million by 2050; the number of people over 100 will jump from 45,000 today to over one million. By the year 2020, many states will look like Florida looks today, with large numbers of elderly living side-by-side with a shrinking population of younger Americans.

This rising tide of older Americans influences economic and social policy in many ways. By 2030, with the baby boom mostly retired, the number of Americans eligible for Social Security and Medicare will more than double from 40 million today to 80–90 million.[38] That means America will have to figure out a way to provide the necessary money to cover the huge increase in these two entitlement programs. As we will see in the "In a Different Light" discussion later, solving the coming Social Security crisis will be anything but easy.

Women at Work

The past three decades have witnessed a dramatic increase in the number of women who work full- and part-time. By 1992, three out of five women were working, compared with two out of five in the early 1960s. Half of the Secret Service agents who protect the president are now women.[39]

It is not as if women suddenly discovered work in the 1980s, however. "The mythical American family of the 1950s and 1960s was comprised of five people, only one of whom 'worked'—or at least did what society called work," writes sociologist Juliet Schor. "Dad went off to his job every morning, while Mom and the three kids stayed at home. Of course, the 1950s-style family was never as common as popular memory has made it out to be. Even in the 1950s and 1960s, about one-fourth of wives with children held paying jobs."[40]

Most women went to work for a simple reason: they needed the income. But many women soon found that they could not earn as much as men even for comparable work. Even in 1993, for example, women still earned only about 70 cents for every dollar earned by men. African American women earned less, 62 cents; Hispanic women even less, 54 cents.[41] Some of the gap involves different jobs—women tend to get caught, or segregated, in lower-paying positions. But some of the gap involves simple discrimination.

The pay gap, as it is sometimes called, continues up the educational ladder. Women with high school degrees earn less than men with high school degrees, women with bachelor's degrees earn less than men with bachelor's degrees, and women with law and medical degrees earn less than men with law and medical degrees. Women did catch up somewhat during the 1980s, in part because of longer hours worked and increasing seniority.[42] Nevertheless, pressure for equal pay for either equal work (the same job) or comparable work (jobs that use similar skills) is not likely to let up soon.

Even as more women enter the workforce, they still provide most of the care to their elderly parents and children.[43] It is no surprise, therefore, that economic and social policy issues such as maternity leave, daycare, and eldercare would be primary concerns for women who work.

Increasing Diversity

The workforce of the future will not look very much like today's. By the year 2000, according to a detailed projection of future hiring trends, only 15 percent of new workers will be white males, compared to almost 50 percent in the 1980s.[44] It is no longer a white male, or even white, America. In some border states such as California and Texas, the term *minority* no longer has any meaning. In one out of every four California cities, for example, no racial group is a majority.[45]

A family of illegal immigrants being processed in McAllen, Texas. Concerns about the cost of supporting illegal immigrants led to a tightening of the U.S. border with Mexico.

America is getting more diverse for two reasons: first, the number of immigrants into the United States is growing, and, second, minority populations have somewhat higher birth rates than whites.

Consider immigration first. Although America has always been a nation of immigrants, the country has been tightening its borders in recent years. The tightening began in the late 1970s with the unexpected arrival of the flood of Cuban "boat people" into the Miami area, and heightened a decade later with the rising number of illegal immigrants entering the United States from Mexico. Florida, California, and Texas have all complained about the high cost of supporting illegal immigrants who arrive in the country with limited education and job skills. These concerns have prompted proposals to deny public support to illegal immigrants and their children, even though those children become legal citizens if they are born in the United States.

Still, America admits more immigrants than all of the other industrialized nations in the world combined. From 1971 to 1990, America accepted 10.5 million immigrants, and added 2 million more in 1991. Seventy-one percent of the 1991 immigrants went to just seven states, from west to east: California (735,000), Arizona (40,000), Texas (212,000), Illinois (73,000), Florida (141,000), New Jersey (56,000), and New York (188,000).[46]

Birth rates also help explain the growing diversity of America. According to the Census Bureau, the 1980s witnessed dramatic growth among racial and ethnic groups. The white population grew the slowest over the decade at 6 percent, while the Asian and Pacific Islander population grew the fastest at 108 percent. In between were Hispanics at 53 percent, Native Americans-Eskimos-Aleut at 38 percent, and African Americans at 13 percent. White America is still growing in actual numbers—11 million of the 22 million total Americans added during the 1980s were white. However, it is the minority population of America that is increasing the fastest.

These trends are particularly visible in America's schools. By the year 2000, nearly one-third of all school-age children will be students of color. Already, forty-nine of America's one hundred largest school districts report majorities of non-white children. Most of the change mirrors the population growth discussed above, but some involves white flight to the suburbs and a growing number of mostly white private schools.

Even as schools struggle to face these changes, diversity is creating enormous conflict in foreign, economic, and social policy. Americans are fighting about dozens of issues surrounding race. Should everyone speak English? How far should affirmative action go? Are the public schools worth saving? Should ballots be bilingual? Who should be fired first as corporations downsize? What about immigration reform? All are questions being confronted in today's policy process.

Rich and Poor

The 1980s were very good years for wealthy Americans. Tax rates on the richest Americans went down, as did tax rates on corporate earnings and investment. According to the Internal Revenue Service, the number of millionaires grew 1,400 percent over the decade. In 1980, only 4,400 Americans reported $1 million in adjusted gross income (the figure listed at the bottom of the tax return); by 1990, the number was up to 63,642.[47]

Just as the number of rich people increased, so did the number of poor people. The rich got richer, and the poor got poorer. According to the Center on Budget and Policy Priorities, a liberal think tank, the average income for the top one-fifth of Americans grew nearly $14,000 over the 1980s, rising from $83,000 to $97,000, while the average income for the bottom one-fifth dropped $600, from $10,900 to $10,300.[48] Not only were the rich getting richer, the gap between the top and bottom appeared to be growing.

The gap between rich and poor is increasing for two reasons: first, the rich are keeping more of their earnings, and, second, the jobs that once supported the middle class are disappearing.

The rich got richer largely because of economic policies passed during the early 1980s. According to Donald Bartlett and James Steele, the Pulitzer Prize-winning reporters who wrote *America: What Went Wrong,* the very wealthy got the largest tax cuts of anyone—their taxes actually fell 31 percent under the 1986 tax cut, amounting to an average savings of $281,033 in 1989. Those just above poor, at $10,000 to $20,000 in annual income, got the smallest cuts—their taxes fell just 6 percent, for an average of $69. The middle class got a tax cut between 11 and 16 percent.[49]

The middle class got a smaller tax cut primarily because the nation's economy lost over 300,000 relatively high-paying manufacturing jobs over the decade. Those jobs were mostly replaced by relatively low-paying service and retail jobs. By the end of the 1980s, more Americans were working in service and retail than in manufacturing, a dramatic turnaround from the 1950s and 1960s. Many of the old manufacturing jobs that once supported America's middle class have moved abroad as global economic competition led corporations to find cheaper sources of labor.

The problem is that service and retail jobs pay far less, and almost always come without health or retirement benefits. Imagine trying to support a family on a full-time job at McDonald's, or a couple of part-time minimum-wage jobs bagging groceries and cleaning houses. Imagine taking a bus, then a subway, then another bus just to get to work in the suburbs. It happens much more frequently than most people think. It is not the unemployed who need health insurance—in fact, they already have coverage through the federal Medicaid program. Rather, it is the working poor who appear most vulnerable.

At the bottom of the economic ladder, government statistics show that the poor got poorer. By 1993, the U.S. Census Bureau reported that the number of poor people stood at nearly 37 million.[50] Poverty in American was growing faster than the population itself. (In 1995, a family of four was considered below the poverty line if it had cash income less than $14,763.) Children were particularly hard hit by the increase in poverty—by the end of the 1980s, nearly one in five children was in poverty; more than one in eight were being raised by mothers on federal Aid to Families with Dependent Children (AFDC), the nation's most visible income support program.

The growing gap between rich and poor influences economic policy in several ways. It clearly shapes tax policy, which involves discussions about who pays what (a progressive tax such as the federal income tax is one that increases the tax rate as income goes up; a regressive tax such as a sales or gasoline tax is one that lays the burden equally on all income groups). It also shapes welfare policy, which establishes the level of support society is willing to give to those in need.

The Changing American Family

There is no such thing as a "traditional" American family anymore. The two-parent, two-kid, mom-at-home, dad-at-work family that America celebrated in the 1950s with television shows such as *Leave it to Beaver* and *Father Knows Best* is increasingly rare. Most children today would say their families are much more like the Simpsons than the Cleavers.

The numbers prove the point. In 1960, at the height of the baby boom, there were just over 50 million American families. Just about half were married couples with children; another 37 percent were married couples without kids; just 6 percent were single women with kids; and fewer than 1 percent were single men with kids. By 2000, the numbers will look very different, indeed. Of the 72 million families, only 35 percent will be married couples with kids; 43 percent will be married couples without kids; 10 percent will be single women with kids; and 3 percent will be single men with kids.[51]

This general movement away from the traditional family reflects a host of other trends: the number of people who will never marry is up; divorce rates are high; the number of babies born outside of marriage is up; people are getting married later in life; gays and lesbians are having or adopting more children. All of the trends flow from what people do about marriage and divorce.

It is not just that fewer people are getting married, however. It is also that people who are getting married are getting married later in life. And once they do get married, the odds of divorce are high. Roughly 2.4 million people got married in 1990, but 1.2 million got divorced. Almost half of the people who got married in the late 1960s and early 1970s had already been divorced by 1990, and current projections show that the numbers will remain high far into the future.

These statistics on marriage, divorce, and single parenthood have created their own political divisions. Indeed, the 1992 presidential campaign helped fuel what may have been the first "family gap" in campaign history. Married voters with children between the ages of eighteen and thirty-four gave almost half their votes to President George Bush versus just 29 percent to Bill Clinton, while single voters in the same age group gave 58 percent to Clinton and only 20 percent to Bush.

Family policy is a growing focus for social policy debates in Congress and the presidency, whether in proposals to increase federal support for daycare to ease the caregiving burden on women or in efforts to make divorce more difficult in an effort to keep families with children together. Family policy also involves debates over gay and lesbian rights, foster care for children, education reform, and a host of other policies that directly or indirectly touch upon family life.

IN A DIFFERENT LIGHT

THE FUTURE OF SOCIAL SECURITY

The Social Security program, which provides income support to millions of older Americans, will enter a funding crisis in the next century as the huge baby boom generation retires. Although

Social Security is often viewed by the public as a savings program in which taxpayers put money in throughout their working lives, it is, in fact, a modified "pay-as-you-go" program. Most of the money that comes in by way of taxes from working Americans and their employers goes immediately out in the form of benefit checks to the current beneficiaries.

At the start of the program in 1940, there were almost 160 workers paying their taxes into the program for every one beneficiary receiving monthly Social Security checks. By 1995, there were 3.3 workers for every beneficiary. But by the year 2030, when the baby boom is fully retired, there will be just two workers for every beneficiary.

The result is a serious and growing gap between the money taxpayers put into the program and the money being taken out in monthly benefits. Looking far into the future and assuming that Social Security will continue to pay its current levels of benefits, the system faces a $12 *trillion* shortfall in meeting its obligations. Somewhere in the 2020s, the program will start taking in less money each year than it gives out.

There are only two ways to fix a pay-as-you-go system: increase revenues or cut benefits. One way to increase revenues is to raise the amount workers pay in FICA (Social Security) taxes, thereby putting more money into the system. Another is to allow the Social Security system to invest part of its current reserves in the stock market—under current law, Social Security taxes are invested in federal treasury bonds, which pay a very low interest rate. Neither option is particularly popular on Capitol Hill. Workers are already paying over 7.5 percent of their paychecks into Social Security, and might revolt at the kind of increase needed to address the future crisis. And allowing Social Security to invest in the stock market is risky at best—the stock market always looks good when it is going up.

The options are just as unpopular on the benefits side. One way to cut benefits is to increase the retirement age, which is already scheduled to increase from age sixty-five today to age sixty-seven in the early 2020s. Some experts argue that the retirement age should be set at seventy years old. After all, Americans are living longer. However, it is not necessarily clear that all the extra years of life are good ones. Raising the retirement age means trading the very healthiest years of retirement (which come at the beginning) for the very worst (which come just before death). Another way to cut benefits is to freeze or reduce the annual cost of living adjustment, which indexes Social Security benefits to inflation. (See Chapter 9 for a discussion of indexing.)

However unpopular the solutions are, Social Security simply cannot survive without reform. The question for the moment is whether Congress and the presidency have the political courage to act now, when the amounts of revenue increases and benefits cuts needed to close the gap have more time to add up, or wait until the very last minute, when the increases and cuts must be deeper.[52]

If Congress and the president wait to act, much of the burden will fall squarely on Generation X and its younger brothers and sisters. Americans plan for retirement decades in advance, and will not tolerate a last-second change in retirement age or Social Security investment policy. By waiting, Congress and the president also create an inevitable preference for tax increases as the tool for closing the shortfall.

The question is whether the members of Generation X will be able to pay the tax increase needed to cover the gap. It is not as if most Generation Xers are doing very well as it is. They are trailing previous generations in home ownership, starting salaries, and savings rates, but leading in college debt. "After graduation," write Neil Howe and William Strauss, "they're the ones with big loans who were supposed to graduate into jobs and move out of the house but didn't, and who seem to get poorer the longer they've been away from home—unlike their parents at that age, who seemed to get richer."[53] This poor performance creates a clear problem for the future of Social Security. Even if they want to pay higher Social Security taxes to support the baby boomers, members of Generation X may not have the income to pay as you go.

CONCLUSION

It is no surprise that making public policy is so difficult. It is all in the Founders' original design. Separated powers create doubts about just who is in charge at every step of the policy-making process. Separate interests put Congress, the presidency, and the judiciary on radically different timetables from each other, and make agreement on the policy agenda difficult. Separate layers have created a patchwork of federal, state, and local delivery units. And checks and balances keep the entire system just a little off balance.

This is not to say that American government can never act at all. Congress, the president, and the courts are quite capable of making decisions, even during periods of sharply divided government.[54] Although making policy to deal with the changing face of America will be frustrating at times, there is ample evidence to suggest that the nation and its government will be able to respond. The policies will not be perfect, if only because the problems of the future are complex. But the past suggests that the Founders' government will continue to produce artful work.

Indeed, the challenge for the future is not to become discouraged by a government that makes patience a virtue. After all, each of the decisions in making policy contains its own perils for those who want quick government action. Assumptions create impossible expectations, problems get defined out of existence, decisions to act get delayed, tools are misplaced, finding someone to deliver the program becomes fuzzy, rules are always hard to make, and implementation is often ignored. Given that policy gets made in more places than just the traditional institutions of government, it is not surprising that making policy is so difficult. It is often something of a miracle.

It would be a mistake to let fears of the future create momentum for major reform in the Founders' design. Those who argue for a more powerful presidency or a faster Congress may underestimate the continuing threats to liberty that reside in America's highly divided society. They may also lose sight of the essential purpose of American government, which is not just to protect the nation as a whole, but also to protect each individual.

The Founders could have made government very efficient, indeed, by creating a dictator or an American king. Instead, they created a government strong enough to protect the nation from foreign and domestic threats, but never so strong as to threaten Americans as individual citizens. It is far better to have a bit of delay and frustration in making policies for the future than to risk a threat to freedom. Success in the American system of government is all about maintaining the delicate balance, even when it frustrates and delays.

JUST THE FACTS

THE BASICS

■ Public policy determines who gets what, when, and how from government. As America has grown more complex as a society, so have the public policies for governing the nation. There are three basic types of public policy today: foreign policy, economic policy, and social policy.

■ Foreign policy is concerned with both protecting America from foreign threats and promoting American values abroad. As America grew from being what George Washington called a "small and weak" nation to being "great and powerful," its foreign policy became more complicated. Foreign policy today is concerned with four goals: national security, economic interest, the promotion of humanitarian or social values, and the preservation of world order.

■ Economic policy is concerned with increasing America's standard of living, whether measured by inflation, unemployment, the national debt, or gross domestic product. As the world economy has become more interconnected, American economic policy has grown more complicated. Economic policy today is concerned with four goals: economic growth, full employment, price stability, and international competitiveness. The federal government can use fiscal policy or monetary policy as tools to achieve these goals.

■ Social policy is primarily concerned with protecting America's quality of life and ensuring that Americans have some protection (or a safety net) against personal hardship. Social policy is a relatively recent addition to the federal government's agenda. Social policy today is concerned with three broad goals: personal safety (from crime to health care), economic security, and civil liberties and civil rights.

■ The policy-making process involves eight basic decisions: (1) making assumptions about the world, (2) picking the problem to be solved, (3) deciding whether to act at all, (4) deciding how much to do, (5) picking a tool to use, (6) finding someone to deliver the services, (7) making the rules for implementation, and (8) running the program. The first four decisions are mostly made by Congress, the presidency, or the judiciary, while the last four are mostly made by the federal bureaucracy.

■ The policy agenda of the future is already emerging in five demographic and economic trends that are changing the face of America. First, America is getting older, in part because women are having fewer children, and in part because Amer-

467

icans are living longer. Second, more women are working full- and part-time. By the year 2000, women will compose roughly three-fifths of all new workers hired. Third, America is becoming much more diverse, in part because the number of immigrants into the United States is growing, and in part because birth rates among minority populations are higher than among whites. Only 15 percent of tomorrow's workers will be white males. Fourth, the gap between rich and poor is growing as the rich become richer and the poor become poorer. Fifth, the American family is changing. Barely one-third of the families of the future will be married couples with children, while almost half will be married without children.

KEY CONCEPTS

■ The Founders' system of government makes the making of public policy very difficult. Separate powers create doubts about just who is in charge of everything, from making assumptions about the world to the day-to-day decisions in running programs. Separate interests make agreement on the policy agenda difficult, and often create conflicts in deciding to act, deciding how much to do, and picking a tool to use. Separate layers have created a patchwork of federal, state, and local delivery units. And checks and balances keep the entire system just a little off balance as it tries to reach judgments at every step of the process.

■ Final policy decisions usually involve a long string of informal decisions made in policy networks composed of temporary collections of political leaders and organized interests. Policy networks are a looser version of what political scientists call iron triangles of influence. Iron triangles are composed of three simple sides: a federal department, a set of loyal organized interests, and a House and/or Senate authorizing committee. Policy networks are particularly attractive in today's volatile policy process, which is popu-

lated by a large number of smaller organized interests.

■ Once Congress, the presidency, or the judiciary has decided to act and picked a tool for solving a problem, they must decide who will deliver the program. The answer is often not federal employees. Recent decades have witnessed an increase in what public administration scholars call third-party government, which involves the delivery of services by private companies that work for the federal government under contracts, state and local governments that work for the federal government under mandates, and nonprofit organizations that deliver services for the federal government when neither private contractors nor state and local governments are willing or able to do so.

■ Almost everything the federal government does involves a rule, which is a precise legal statement about what a law actually means. Rules are essential for turning even the most detailed legislation into action, and rulemaking is the central device used to execute the laws. Because rulemaking comes near the very end of the policy-making process, it is often ignored as a source of significant decisions.

IN A DIFFERENT LIGHT

■ With the end of the Cold War between the United States and the Soviet Union, many Americans began to wonder whether America still needed a foreign policy. Although only 2 percent of Americans see foreign policy as a source of the nation's most important problems, the nation is not drifting into isolationism. Rather, Americans are getting very picky about when and where America should show world leadership. They tend to believe that the most important foreign policy issues are the ones that hit close to home, with stopping the flow of illegal drugs the single most important goal that they believe America should pursue.

■ There are three problems with the rising amount of third-party government. First, third-party government tends to increase the unresponsiveness of bureaucracy, isolating federal employees from the people they serve. Second, third-party government may confuse the public about where the federal government ends and the third parties begin. Third, third-party government may hide the true size of the federal government. By using private contractors, state and local governments, and nonprofits to deliver services, the federal government can look much smaller in total employees than it truly is.

■ America's Social Security system, which provides income to millions of older Americans, will enter a funding crisis early in the next century. As the huge baby boom generation begins to retire, the system will start spending more on benefits than it can bring in through the current level of taxes. There are only two ways to fix the program: increase revenues through tax increases or cut benefits. Most of the options for fixing the program are unpopular, thereby leading Congress and the president to wait until the crisis gets bad enough to prompt reform. However, by waiting, much of the burden for fixing the program will fall squarely on Generation X. Whether members of Generation X and their younger brothers and sisters will have the incomes to pay the higher taxes to fix the program is still in doubt.

OPEN QUESTIONS

■ When is the best point in the process to stop a policy from happening? Change the assumptions to make the world look better than it already is? Push for a nondecision that takes a problem off the agenda? Stop the rulemaking process from producing an effective rule? Reduce funding for the agencies that must implement the law? Does the fact that the process has so many places to take a stand against action help or hinder the Founders' vision of a government just strong enough?

■ What kinds of changes could be made to help make the policy-making process more efficient? What kinds of authority would make the president a stronger leader when times get tough? How might Congress be strengthened? Would proposals such as limiting the number of terms a member of Congress can serve help or hurt the policy-making process? What are the potential costs of having the policy-making process work more efficiently?

. . . TERMS TO REMEMBER

public policy

isolationism

fiscal policy

monetary policy

policy networks

iron triangles

policy agenda

think tank

issue-attention cycle

incremental program

distributive program

redistributive program

dedistributive program

third-party federal government

federal mandates

rule

Federal Register

Code of Federal Regulations

Endnotes to Chapter 12

1. See James Roger Sharp, *American Politics in the Early Republic: The New Nation in Crisis* (New Haven, CT: Yale University Press, 1993), pp. 33–38.
2. Gregg Easterbrook, *A Moment on the Earth: The Coming Age of Environmental Optimism* (New York: Viking, 1995), p. xv.
3. The quote can be found in Daniel Boorstin, ed., *An American Primer* volume 1 (Chicago: University of Chicago Press, 1966), pp. 192–210; emphasis in the original.
4. Harold W. Stanley and Richard G. Niemi, *Vital Statistics on American Politics* (Washington DC: CQ Press, 1995), p. 347.
► 5. Barbara Kellerman and Ryan J. Barilleaux, *The President as World Leader,* (New York: St. Martin's Press, 1991), p. 20.
6. See Jeremy Rosner, "The Know-Nothings Know Something," *Foreign Policy,* no. 101 (Winter 1995–1996), p. 124.

7. Steven Kull, "What the Public Knows that Washington Doesn't," *Foreign Policy,* no. 101 (Winter 1995-1996), p. 103.

8. See John Rielly, "The Public Mood at Mid-Decade," *Foreign Policy* no. 98 (Spring 1995), pp. 76-93, for an inventory of public opinion on foreign policy.

9. Kellerman and Barilleaux, *The President as World Leader,* p. 13.

▶ 10. For a history of this period, see Theda Skocpol, *Protecting Soldiers and Mothers: The Political Origins of Social Policy in the United States* (Cambridge, MA: Harvard University Press, 1992).

11. Hugh Heclo, "Issue Networks and the Executive Establishment," in A. King, ed., *The New American Political System* (Washington, DC: American Enterprise Institute, 1978), pp. 87-124.

12. Bill McAllister, "VA Hospitals Refuse to Sound Retreat," *Washington Post National Weekly Edition,* May 29-June 4, 1995, p. 31.

13. McAllister, "VA Hospitals," p. 31.

14. Anthony King, "The American Polity in the 1990s," in A. King, *The New American Political System* (Washington, DC: American Enterprise Institute, second version, 1990), p. 296.

▶ 15. See John Kingdon, *Agendas, Alternatives, and Public Policy* (Boston: Little, Brown, 1984), for a description of the process.

16. William Greider, "The Education of David Stockman," *The Atlantic,* vol. 248, no. 12 (December 1981), p. 39.

17. Kingdon, *Agendas, Alternatives, and Public Policies,* p. 3.

18. Anthony Downs, "The 'Issue-Attention Cycle,'" *The Public Interest,* vol. 28 (Summer 1972), p. 38.

19. See Paul Light, *Still Artful Work: The Continuing Politics of Social Security Reform* (New York: McGraw-Hill, 1994), p. 13, for a discussion of Social Security reform as a dedistributive issue.

▶ 20. Lester Salamon and Michael Lund, "The Tools Approach: Basic Analytics," in L. Salamon, ed., *Beyond Privatization: The Tools of Government Action* (Washington, DC: The Urban Institute Press, 1989).

21. Frederick Mosher, "The Changing Responsibilities and Tactics of the Federal Government," *Public Administration Review,* volume 40, number 6 (November/December, 1980), p. 541.

▶ 22. See Donald Kettl, *Sharing Power: Public Governance and Private Markets* (Washington, DC: Brookings Institution, 1993).

23. National Commission on the State and Local Public Service, *Hard Truths/Tough Choices* (Albany, NY: National Commission on the State and Local Public Service, 1993), p. 1.

24. See John DiIulio and Donald F. Kettl, *Fine Print: The Contract with America, Devolution, and the Administrative Realities of American Federalism* (Washington, DC: Brookings Institution, 1995), p. 17.

25. Martha Derthick, "Federal Government Mandates: Why the States Are Complaining," *Brookings Review,* volume 10, number 4 (Fall 1992), p. 52.

26. Virginia Hodgkinson, Murray Weitzman, Stephen Noga, and Heather Gorski, *A Portrait of the Independent Sector: The Activities and Finances of Charitable Organizations* (Washington, DC: Independent Sector, 1993), p. 10.

27. See Michael Lipsky and Steven Rathgeb Smith, "Nonprofit Organizations, Government, and the Welfare State," *Political Science Quarterly,* vol. 104, no. 4 (Winter 1989-1990), pp. 625-648.

28. Kettl, *Sharing Power,* p. 206.

▶ 29. See Cornelius Kerwin, *Rulemaking: How Government Agencies Write Law and Make Policy* (Washington, DC: CQ Press, 1994).

30. Kerwin, *Rulemaking,* p. 14.

31. Stanley and Niemi, *Vital Statistics,* p. 253.

32. Kerwin, *Rulemaking,* p. 19.

33. Kerwin, *Rulemaking,* p. 75.

34. See Gary Bryner, "Restructuring Review in OMB," *The Bureaucrat,* volume 18, number 3 (Fall 1989), pp. 45–51, for a discussion of the OMB process.

35. Quoted in Richard Nathan, *Turning Promises Into Performance: The Management Challenge of Implementing Workfare* (New York: Columbia University Press, 1993), p. 133.

36. See Paul Light, *Baby Boomers: A Social and Political Reappraisal* (New York: W. W. Norton, 1988), pp. 149–152.

37. These figures are drawn from U.S. Department of Commerce, Bureau of the Census, *Population Projections of the United States, by Age, Sex, Race, and Hispanic Origin: 1992–2050* (Washington, DC: U.S. Government Printing Office, November 1992).

38. For a discussion of these key programs see Eric R. Kingson and Edward D. Berkowitz, *Social Security and Medicare: A Policy Primer, Governance* (Montclair, CT: Auburn House, 1993).

39. "President's Safety is Now Often a Woman's Work," *New York Times,* July 6, 1993, p. A7.

▶ 40. Juliet B. Schor, *The Overworked American: The Unexpected Decline of Leisure* (New York: Basic Books, 1992), pp. 24–25.

41. Joan Rigdon, "Three Decades After the Equal Pay Act, Women's Wages Remain Far From Parity," *Wall Street Journal,* June 9, 1993, p. B1.

42. See Sylvia Nasar, "Women's Progress Stalled? Just Not So," *New York Times,* p. F1.

43. Scc Betty Sancier and Patricia Mapp, "Who Helps Working Women Care for the Young and Old?" *AFFILIA,* volume 7, number 2 (Summer 1992), pp. 61–76.

44. These figures come from William Johnston and Arnold Packer, *Workforce 2000: Work and Workers for the 21st Century* (Indianapolis: Hudson Institute, 1987), p. xxi.

45. Peter Morrison, "Testimony Before the House Subcommittee on Census and Population," May 26, 1992, p. 3.

46. The numbers are from Tom Morganthau, "America: Still a Melting Pot?" *Newsweek,* August 9, 1993, pp. 16–25; for an excellent analysis of how immigration helps America, see Thomas Muller, *Immigrants and the American City* (New York: New York University Press, 1993).

47. See Paul Farhi, "They're In the Money," *Washington Post National Weekly Edition,* July 20–26, 1992, p. 21.

48. Numbers are rounded; see Spencer Rich, "The Rich Got Richer, Again," *Washington Post National Weekly Edition,* September 14–20, 1992, p. 37.

▶ 49. Donald Bartlett and James Steele, *America: What Went Wrong?* (Kansas City, MO: Andrews and McMeel, 1992), p. 6.

50. These figures come from Robert Pear, "Poverty in U.S. Grew Faster than Population Last Year," *New York Times,* October 5, 1993, p. A10.

51. Dennis Ahlburg and Carol J. De Vita, "New Realities of the American Family," *Population Bulletin,* (August 1992), reprinted by the Population Reference Bureau Social Issues Resources Series, volume 4, article number 96.

52. For a discussion of how Congress and the president solved the most recent Social Security crisis, see Paul Light, *Still Artful Work.*

53. Neil Howe and William Strauss, "The New Generation Gap," *The Atlantic Monthly,* volume 270, (December 1992), pp. 78–79.

▶ 54. See David Mayhew, *Divided We Govern: Party Control, Lawmaking, and Investigations, 1946–1990* (New Haven, CT: Yale University Press, 1991).

The Declaration of Independence

When in the Course of human events, it becomes necessary for one people to dissolve the political bands which have connected them with another, and to assume among the Powers of the earth, the separate and equal station to which the Laws of Nature and of Nature's God entitle them, a decent respect to the opinions of mankind requires that they should declare the causes which impel them to the separation.

We hold these truths to be self-evident, that all men are created equal, that they are endowed by their Creator with certain unalienable Rights, that among these are Life, Liberty and the pursuit of Happiness. That to secure these rights, Governments are instituted among Men, deriving their just powers from the consent of the governed. That whenever any Form of Government becomes destructive of these ends, it is the Right of the People to alter or to abolish it, and to institute new Government, laying its foundation on such principles and organizing its powers in such form, as to them shall seem most likely to effect their Safety and Happiness. Prudence, indeed, will dictate that Governments long established should not be changed for light and transient causes; and accordingly all experience hath shown, that mankind are more disposed to suffer, while evils are sufferable, than to right themselves by abolishing the forms to which they are accustomed. But when a long train of abuses and usurpations, pursuing invariably the same Object evinces a design to reduce them under absolute Depotism, it is their right, it is their duty,

to throw off such Government, and to provide new Guards for their future security.—Such has been the patient sufferance of these Colonies; and such is now the necessity which constrains them to alter their former Systems of Government. The history of the present King of Great Britain is a history of repeated injuries and usurpations, all having in direct object the establishment of an absolute Tyranny over these States. To prove this, let Facts be submitted to a candid world.

He has refused his Assent to Laws, the most wholesome and necessary for the public good.

He has forbidden his Governors to pass Laws of immediate and pressing importance, unless suspended in their operation till his Assent should be obtained; and when so suspended, he has utterly neglected to attend to them.

He has refused to pass other Laws for the accommodation of large districts of people, unless those people would relinquish the right of Representation in the Legislature, a right inestimable to them and formidable to tyrants only.

He has called together legislative bodies at places unusual, uncomfortable, and distant from the depository of their public Records, for the sole purpose of fatiguing them into compliance with his measures.

He has dissolved Representative Houses repeatedly for opposing with manly firmness his invasions on the rights of the people.

He has refused for a long time, after such dissolutions, to cause others to be elected; whereby the Legislative Powers, incapable of Annihilation, have returned to the People at large for their exercise; the State remaining in the mean time exposed to all the dangers of invasion from without, and convulsions within.

He has endeavoured to prevent the population of these States; for that purpose obstructing the Laws of Naturalization of Foreigners; refusing to pass others to encourage their migration higher, and raising the conditions of new Appropriations of Lands.

He has obstructed the Administration of Justice, by refusing his Assent to Laws for establishing Judiciary powers.

He has made Judges dependent on his Will alone, for the tenure of their offices, and the amount and payment of their salaries.

He has erected a multitude of New Offices, and sent hither swarms of Officers to harass our People, and eat out their substance.

He has kept among us in times of peace, Standing Armies without the Consent of our legislature.

He has affected to render the Military independent of and superior to the Civil power.

He has combined with others to subject us to a jurisdiction foreign to our constitution, and unacknowledged by our laws; giving his Assent to their acts of pretended Legislation.

For quartering large bodies of armed troops among us:

For protecting them, by a mock Trial, from punishment for any Murders which they should commit on the inhabitants of these States:

For cutting off our Trade with all parts of the world.

For imposing taxes on us without our Consent:

For depriving us in many cases, of the benefits of Trial by Jury:

For transporting us beyond Seas to be tried for pretended offences:

For abolishing the free System of English Laws in a neighbouring Province, establishing therein an Arbitrary government, and enlarging its Boundaries so as to render it at once an example and fit instrument for introducing the same absolute rule into these Colonies.

For taking away our Charters, abolishing our most valuable Laws, and altering fundamentally the Forms of our Governments:

For suspending our own Legislature, and declaring themselves invested with Power to legislate for us in all cases whatsoever.

He has abdicated Government here, by declaring us out of his Protection and waging War against us.

He has plundered our seas, ravaged our Coasts, burnt our towns, and destroyed the lives of our people.

He is at this time transporting large Armies of foreign Mercenaries to compleat the works of death, desolation and tyranny, already begun with circumstances of Cruelty & perfidy scarcely paralleled in the most barbarous ages, and totally unworthy the Head of a civilized nation.

He has constrained our fellow Citizens taken Captive on the high Seas to bear Arms against their Country, to become the executioners of their friends and Brethren, or to fall themselves by their Hands.

He has excited domestic insurrections amongst us, and has endeavoured to bring on the inhabitants of our frontiers, the merciless Indian Savages, whose known rule of warfare, is an undistinguished destruction of all ages, sexes and conditions.

In every stage of these Oppressions We have Petitioned for Redress in the most humble terms: Our repeated Petitions have been answered only by repeated injury. A Prince, whose character is thus marked by every act which may define a Tyrant, is unfit to be the ruler of a free People.

Nor have We been wanting in attention to our British brethren. We have warned them from time to time of attempts by their legislature to extend an unwarrantable jurisdiction over us. We have reminded them of the circumstances of our emigration and settlement here. We have appealed to their native justice and magnanimity, and we have conjured them by the ties of our common kindred to disavow these usurpations, which, would inevitably interrupt our connections and correspondence. They too have been deaf to the voice of justice and of consanguinity. We must, therefore, acquiesce in the necessity, which denounces our Separation, and hold them, as we hold the rest of mankind, Enemies in War, in Peace Friends.

We, therefore, the Representatives of the United States of America, in General Congress, Assembled, appealing to the Supreme Judge of the world for the rectitude of our intentions, do, in the Name, and by Authority of the good People of these Colonies, solemnly publish and declare, That these United Colonies are, and of right ought to be Free and Independent States; that they are Absolved from all Allegiance to the British Crown, and that all political connection between them and the State of Great Britain, is and ought to be totally dissolved; and that as Free and Independent States, they have full Power to levy War, conclude Peace, contract Alliances, establish Commerce, and to do all other Acts and Things which Independent States may of right do. And for the support of this Declaration, with a firm reliance on the protection of divine Providence, we mutually pledge to each other our Lives, our Fortunes and our sacred Honor.

The Constitution of the United States of America

We the People of the United States, in Order to form a more perfect Union, establish Justice, insure domestic Tranquility, provide for the common defence, promote the general Welfare, and secure the Blessings of Liberty to ourselves and our Posterity, do ordain and establish this Constitution for the United States of America.

[THREE BRANCHES OF GOVERNMENT]

[The legislative branch]

Article I

[Powers vested]
SECTION 1 All legislative Powers herein granted shall be vested in a Congress of the United States, which shall consist of a Senate and House of Representatives.

[House of Representatives]
SECTION 2 The House of Representatives shall be composed of Members chosen every second Year by the People of the several States, and the Electors in each State shall have the Qualifications requisite for Electors of the most numerous Branch of the State Legislature.

No Person shall be a Representative who shall not have attained to the Age of twenty-five Years, and been seven Years a Citizen of the United States, and who shall not, when elected, be an Inhabitant of that State in which he shall be chosen.

[Representatives and direct Taxes shall be apportioned among the several States which may be included within this Union, according to their respective Numbers, which shall be determined by adding to the whole Number of free Persons, including those bound to Service for a Term of Years, and excluding Indians not taxed, three fifths of all other Persons.][1] The actual Enumeration shall be made within three Years after the first Meeting of the Congress of the United

---

[1] Changed by Section 2 of Amendment XIV.

States, and within every subsequent Term of ten Years, in such Manner as they shall by Law direct. The Number of Representatives shall not exceed one for every thirty Thousand, but each State shall have at Least one Representative; and until such enumeration shall be made, the State of New Hampshire shall be entitled to chuse three, Massachusetts eight, Rhode-Island and Providence Plantations one, Connecticut five, New York six, New Jersey four, Pennsylvania eight, Delaware one, Maryland six, Virginia ten, North Carolina five, South Carolina five, and Georgia three.

When vacancies happen in the Representation from any State, the Executive Authority thereof shall issue Writs of Election to fill such Vacancies.

The House of Representatives shall chuse their Speaker and other Officers; and shall have the sole Power of Impeachment.

[*The Senate*]

SECTION 3 The Senate of the United States shall be composed of two Senators from each State, [chosen by the Legislature thereof],[2] for six Years; and each Senator shall have one Vote.

Immediately after they shall be assembled in Consequence of the first Election, they shall be divided as equally as may be into three Classes. The Seats of the Senators of the first Class shall be vacated at the Expiration of the Second Year, of the second Class at the Expiration of the fourth Year, and of the third Class at the Expiration of the sixth Year, so that one-third may be chosen every second Year; [and if Vacancies happen by Resignation, or otherwise, during the Recess of the Legislature of any State, the Executive thereof may make temporary Appointments until the next Meeting of the Legislature, which shall then fill such Vacancies][3]

No person shall be a Senator who shall not have attained to the Age of thirty Years, and been nine Years a Citizen of the United States, and who shall not, when elected, be an In-

habitant of that State for which he shall be chosen.

The Vice President of the United States shall be President of the Senate, but shall have no Vote, unless they be equally divided. The Senate shall chuse their other Officers, and also a President pro tempore, in the absence of the Vice President, or when he shall exercise the Office of President of the United States.

The Senate shall have the sole Power to try all Impeachments. When sitting for that Purpose, they shall be on Oath or Affirmation. When the President of the United States is tried, the Chief Justice shall preside: And no Person shall be convicted without the Concurrence of two-thirds of the Members present.

Judgment in Cases of Impeachment shall not extend further than to removal from Office, and disqualification to hold and enjoy any Office of honor, Trust, or Profit under the United States: but the Party convicted shall nevertheless be liable and subject to Indictment, Trial, Judgment, and Punishment, according to Law.

[*Elections*]

SECTION 4 The Times, Places and Manner of holding Elections for Senators and Representatives, shall be prescribed in each State by the Legislature thereof; but the Congress may at any time by Law make or alter such Regulations, except as to the Places of chusing Senators.

The Congress shall assemble at least once in every Year, and such Meeting shall be on the first Monday in December, [unless they shall by Law appoint a different Day][4]

[*Powers, duties, procedures of both bodies*]

SECTION 5 Each House shall be the Judge of the Elections, Returns, and Qualifications of its own Members, and a Majority of each shall constitute a Quorum to do Business; but a smaller Number may adjourn from day to day, and may be authorized to compel the Attendance of absent Members, in such Manner, and under such Penalties as each House may provide.

[2]Changed by Amendment XVII.
[3]Changed by Amendment XVII.

[4]Changed by Section 2 of Amendment XX.

Each House may determine the Rules of its Proceedings, punish its Members for disorderly Behavior, and, with the Concurrence of two thirds, expel a Member.

Each House shall keep a Journal of its Proceedings, and from time to time publish the same, excepting such Parts as may in their Judgment require Secrecy; and the Yeas and Nays of the Members of either House on any question shall, at the Desire of one fifth of those Present, be entered on the Journal.

Neither House, during the Session of Congress, shall, without the Consent of the other, adjourn for more than three days, nor to any other Place than that in which the two Houses shall be sitting.

[*Compensation, privileges, limits on other government service*]

SECTION 6 The Senators and Representatives shall receive a Compensation for their Services, to be ascertained by Law, and paid out of the Treasury of the United States. They shall in all Cases, except Treason, Felony and Breach of the Peace, be privileged from Arrest during their Attendance at the Session of their respective Houses, and in going to and returning from the same; and for any Speech or Debate in either House, they shall not be questioned in any other Place.

No Senator or Representative shall, during the Time for which he was elected, be appointed to any civil Office under the Authority of the United States, which shall have been created, or the Emoluments whereof shall have been encreased during such time; and no Person holding any Office under the United States, shall be a Member of either House during his Continuance in Office.

[*Origin of revenue bills; presidential approval or disapproval of legislation; overriding the veto*]

SECTION 7 All Bills for raising Revenue shall originate in the House of Representatives; but the Senate may propose or concur with Amendments as on other Bills.

Every Bill which shall have passed the House of Representatives and the Senate, shall, before it become a Law, be presented to the President of the United States; if he approve he shall sign it, but if not he shall return it, with his Objections to that House in which it shall have originated, who shall enter the Objections at large on their Journal, and proceed to reconsider it. If after such Reconsideration two thirds of that House shall agree to pass the Bill, it shall be sent, together with the Objections, to the other House, by which it shall likewise be reconsidered, and if approved by two thirds of that House, it shall become a Law. But in all such Cases the Votes of both Houses shall be determined by Yeas and Nays, and the Names of the Persons voting for and against the Bill shall be entered on the Journal of each House respectively. If any Bill shall not be returned by the President within ten Days (Sundays excepted) after it shall have been presented to him, the Same shall be a Law, in like Manner as if he had signed it, unless the Congress by their Adjournment prevent its Return, in which Case it shall not be a Law.

Every Order, Resolution, or Vote to which the Concurrence of the Senate and House of Representatives may be necessary (except on a question of Adjournment) shall be presented to the President of the United States; and before the Same shall take Effect, shall be approved by him, or being disapproved by him, shall be repassed to two thirds of the Senate and House of Representatives, according to the Rules and Limitations prescribed in the Case of a Bill.

[*Powers granted to Congress*]

SECTION 8 The Congress shall have power To lay and collect Taxes, Duties, Imposts and Excises, to pay the Debts and provide for the common Defence and general Welfare of the United States; but all Duties, Imposts and Excises shall be uniform throughout the United States;

To borrow money on the credit of the United States;

To regulate Commerce with foreign Nations, and among the several States, and with the Indian Tribes;

To establish an uniform Rule of Naturalization, and uniform Laws on the subject of Bankruptcies throughout the United States;

To coin Money, regulate the Value thereof, and of foreign Coin, and fix the Standard of Weights and Measures;

To provide for the Punishment of counterfeiting the Securities and current Coin of the United States;

To Establish Post Offices and post Roads;

To promote the Progress of Science and useful Arts, by securing for limited Times to Authors and Inventors the exclusive Right to their respective Writings and Discoveries;

To constitute Tribunals inferior to the Supreme Court;

To define and punish Piracies and Felonies committed on the high Seas, and Offences against the Law of Nations;

To declare War, grant Letters of Marque and Reprisal, and make Rules concerning Captures on Land and Water;

To raise and support Armies, but no Appropriation of Money to that Use shall be for a longer Term than two Years;

To provide and maintain a Navy;

To make Rules for the Government and Regulation of the land and naval Forces;

To provide for calling forth the Militia to execute the Laws of the Union, suppress Insurrections and repel Invasions;

To provide for organizing, arming, and disciplining the Militia, and for governing such Part of them as may be employed in the Service of the United States, reserving to the States respectively, the Appointment of the Officers, and the Authority of training the Militia according to the discipline prescribed by Congress;

To exercise exclusive Legislation in all Cases whatsoever, over such District (not exceeding ten Miles square) as may, by Cession of particular States, and the acceptance of Congress, become the Seat of the Government of the United States, and to exercise like Authority over all Places purchased by the Consent of the Legislature of the State in which the Same shall be, for the Erection of Forts, Magazines, Arsenals, dock-Yards, and other needful Buildings;—And

[*Elastic clause*]

To make all Laws which shall be necessary and proper for carrying into Execution the foregoing Powers, and all other Powers vested by this Constitution in the Government of the United States, or in any Department or Officer thereof.

[*Powers denied to Congress*]

SECTION 9 The Migration or Importation of Such Persons as any of the States now existing shall think proper to admit, shall not be prohibited by the Congress prior to the Year one thousand eight hundred and eight, but a tax or duty may be imposed on such Importation, not exceeding ten dollars for each Person.

The privilege of the Writ of Habeas Corpus shall not be suspended, unless when in Cases of Rebellion or Invasion the public Safety may require it.

No Bill of Attainder or ex post facto Law shall be passed.

[No capitation, or other direct, Tax shall be laid, unless in Proportion to the Census or Enumeration herein before directed to be taken.][5]

No Tax or Duty shall be laid on Articles exported from any State.

No preference shall be given by any Regulation of Commerce or Revenue to the Ports of one State over those of another: nor shall Vessels bound to, or from, one State be obliged to enter, clear, or pay Duties in another.

No money shall be drawn from the Treasury, but in Consequence of Appropriations made by Law; and a regular Statement and Account of the Receipts and Expenditures of all public Money shall be published from time to time.

No Title of Nobility shall be granted by the United States: And no Person holding any Office of Profit or Trust under them, shall, without the Consent of the Congress, accept of any present,

---

[5]Changed by Amendment XVI.

Emolument, Office, or Title, of any kind whatever, from any King, Prince, or foreign State.

[*Powers denied to states*]

SECTION 10 No State shall enter into any Treaty, Alliance, or Confederation; grant Letters of Marque and Reprisal; coin Money; emit Bills of Credit; make any Thing but gold and silver Coin a Tender in Payment of Debts; pass any Bill of Attainder, ex post facto Law, or Law impairing the Obligation of Contracts, or grant any Title of Nobility.

No State shall, without the Consent of the Congress, lay any Imposts or Duties on Imports or Exports, except what may be absolutely necessary for executing its inspection Laws: and the net Produce of all Duties and Imposts, laid by any State on Imports or Exports, shall be for the Use of the Treasury of the United States; and all such Laws shall be subject to the Revision and Control of the Congress.

No State shall, without the Consent of Congress, lay any duty of Tonnage, keep Troops, or Ships of War in time of Peace, enter into any Agreement or Compact with another State, or with a foreign Power, or engage in War, unless actually invaded, or in such imminent Danger as will not admit of delay.

[*The executive branch*]

Article II

[*Presidential term, choice by electors, qualifications, payment, succession, oath of office*]

SECTION 1 The executive Power shall be vested in a President of the United States of America. He shall hold his Office during the Term of four Years, and, together with the Vice President, chosen for the same Term, be elected, as follows:

Each State shall appoint, in such Manner as the Legislature thereof may direct, a Number of Electors, equal to the whole Number of Senators and Representatives to which the State may be entitled in the Congress: but no Senator or Representative, or Person holding an Office of Trust or Profit under the United States, shall be appointed an Elector.

[The Electors shall meet in their respective States, and vote by Ballot for two persons, of whom one at least shall not be an Inhabitant of the same State with themselves. And they shall make a List of all the Persons voted for, and of the Number of Votes for each; which List they shall sign and certify, and transmit sealed to the Seat of the Government of the United States, directed to the President of the Senate. The President of the Senate shall, in the Presence of the Senate and House of Representatives, open all the Certificates, and the Votes shall then be counted. The Person having the greatest Number of Votes shall be the President, if such Number be a Majority of the whole Number of Electors appointed; and if there be more than one who have such Majority, and have an equal Number of Votes, then the House of Representatives shall immediately chuse by Ballot one of them for President; and if no Person have a Majority, then from the five highest on the List the said House shall in like Manner chuse the President. But in chusing the President, the Votes shall be taken by States, the Representation from each State having one Vote; A quorum for this Purpose shall consist of a Member or Members from two-thirds of the States, and a Majority of all the States shall be necessary to a Choice. In every Case, after the Choice of the President, the Person having the greatest Number of Votes of the Electors shall be the Vice President. But if there should remain two or more who have equal Votes, the Senate shall chuse from them by Ballot the Vice President.][6]

The Congress may determine the Time of chusing the Electors, and the Day on which they shall give their Votes; which Day shall be the same throughout the United States.

No person except a natural born Citizen, or a Citizen of the United States, at the time of the Adoption of this Constitution, shall be eligible

---

[6]Changed by Amendment XII.

to the Office of President; neither shall any Person be eligible to that Office who shall not have attained to the Age of thirty-five Years, and been fourteen Years a Resident within the United States.

[In case of the removal of the President from Office, or of his Death, Resignation, or Inability to discharge the Powers and Duties of the said Office, the same shall devolve on the Vice President, and the Congress may by Law provide for the Case of Removal, Death, Resignation or Inability, both of the President and Vice President, declaring what Officer shall then act as President, and such Officer shall act accordingly, until the Disability be removed, or a President shall be elected.][7]

The President shall, at stated Times, receive for his Services, a Compensation, which shall neither be encreased nor diminished during the Period for which he shall have been elected, and he shall not receive within that Period any other Emolument from the United States, or any of them.

Before he enter on the Execution of his Office, he shall take the following Oath or Affirmation:—"I do solemnly swear (or affirm) that I will faithfully execute the Office of President of the United States, and will to the best of my Ability, preserve, protect and defend the Constitution of the United States."

[*Powers to command the military and executive departments, to grant pardons, to make treaties, to appoint government officers*]

SECTION 2 The President shall be Commander in Chief of the Army and Navy of the United States, and of the Militia of the several States, when called into the actual Service of the United States; he may require the Opinion, in writing, of the principal Officer in each of the executive Departments, upon any subject relating to the Duties of their respective Offices, and he shall have Power to grant Reprieves and Pardons for Offenses against the United States, except in Cases of Impeachment.

[7]Changed by Amendment XXV.

He shall have Power, by and with the Advice and Consent of the Senate, to make Treaties, provided two-thirds of the Senators present concur; and he shall nominate, and by and with the Advice and Consent of the Senate, shall appoint Ambassadors, other public Ministers and Consuls, Judges of the Supreme Court, and all other Officers of the United States, whose Appointments are not herein otherwise provided for, and which shall be established by Law; but the Congress may by Law vest the Appointment of such inferior Officers, as they think proper, in the President alone, in the Courts of Law, or in the Heads of Departments.

The President shall have Power to fill up all Vacancies that may happen during the Recess of the Senate, by granting Commissions which shall expire at the End of their next Session.

[*Formal duties*]

SECTION 3 He shall from time to time give to the Congress Information of the State of the Union, and recommend to their Consideration such Measures as he shall judge necessary and expedient; he may, on extraordinary Occasions, convene both Houses, or either of them, and in Case of Disagreement between them, with Respect to the Time of Adjournment, he may adjourn them to such Time as he shall think proper; he shall receive Ambassadors and other public Ministers; he shall take Care that the Laws be faithfully executed, and shall Commission all the Officers of the United States.

[*Conditions for removal*]

SECTION 4 The President, Vice President and all civil Officers of the United States, shall be removed from Office on Impeachment for, and Conviction of, Treason, Bribery, or other high Crimes and Misdemeanors.

[*The judicial branch*]

Article III

[*Courts and judges*]

SECTION 1 The judicial Power of the United States, shall be vested in one supreme Court, and in such inferior Courts as the Congress may from time to time ordain and establish. The Judges, both of the supreme and inferior Courts, shall hold their Offices during good Behaviour, and shall, at stated Times, receive for their Services a Compensation which shall not be diminished during their Continuance in Office.

[Jurisdictions and jury trials]

SECTION 2 The judicial Power shall extend to all Cases, in Law and Equity, arising under this Constitution, the Laws of the United States, and Treaties made, or which shall be made, under their Authority;—to all Cases affecting Ambassadors, other public Ministers and Consuls;—to all Cases of admiralty and maritime Jurisdiction;—to Controversies to which the United States shall be a Party;—to Controversies between two or more States;—[between a State and Citizens of another State;—][8] between Citizens of different States;—between Citizens of the same State claiming Lands under Grants of different States, [and between a State, or the Citizens thereof, and foreign States, Citizens or Subjects][9]

In all Cases affecting Ambassadors, other public Ministers and Consuls, and those in which a State shall be Party, the supreme Court shall have original Jurisdiction. In all the other Cases before mentioned, the supreme Court shall have appellate Jurisdiction, both as to Law and Fact, with such Exceptions, and under such Regulations as the Congress shall make.

The trial of all Crimes, except in Cases of Impeachment, shall be by Jury; and such Trial shall be held in the State where the said Crimes shall have been committed; but when not committed within any State, the Trial shall be at such Place or Places as the Congress may by Law have directed.

[Treason and its punishment]

SECTION 3 Treason against the United States, shall consist only in levying War against them,

or, in adhering to their Enemies, giving them Aid and Comfort. No Person shall be convicted of Treason unless on the Testimony of two Witnesses to the same overt Act, or on Confession in open Court.

The Congress shall have power to declare the Punishment of Treason, but no Attainder of Treason shall work Corruption of Blood, or Forfeiture except during the Life of the Person attainted.

[THE REST OF THE FEDERAL SYSTEM]

Article IV

[Relationships among and with states]

SECTION 1 Full Faith and Credit shall be given in each State to the public Acts, Records, and judicial Proceedings of every other State. And the Congress may by general Laws prescribe the Manner in which such Acts, Records and Proceedings shall be proved, and the Effect thereof.

[Privileges and immunities, extradition]

SECTION 2 The Citizens of each State shall be entitled to all Privileges and Immunities of Citizens in the several States.

A Person charged in any State with Treason, Felony, or other Crime, who shall flee from Justice, and be found in another State, shall on demand of the executive Authority of the State from which he fled, be delivered up, to be removed to the State having Jurisdiction of the Crime.

[No Person held to Service or Labour in one State, under the Laws thereof, escaping into another, shall, in Consequence of any Law or Regulation therein, be discharged from such Service or Labour, but shall be delivered up on Claim of the Party to whom such Service or Labour may be due.][10]

---

[8]Changed by Amendment XI.
[9]Changed by Amendment XI.

[10]Changed by Amendment XIII.

[*New states*]

SECTION 3 New States may be admitted by the Congress into this Union; but no new State shall be formed or erected within the Jurisdiction of any other State; nor any State be formed by the Junction of two or more States, or parts of States, without the Consent of the Legislatures of the States concerned as well as of the Congress.

The Congress shall have Power to dispose of and make all needful Rules and Regulations respecting the Territory or other Property belonging to the United States; and nothing in this Constitution shall be so construed as to Prejudice any Claims of the United States, or of any particular State.

[*Obligations to states*]

SECTION 4 The United States shall guarantee to every State in this Union a Republican Form of Government, and shall protect each of them against Invasion; and on Application of the Legislature, or of the Executive (when the Legislature cannot be convened) against domestic Violence.

[MECHANISM FOR CHANGE]

Article V

[*Amending the Constitution*]

The Congress, whenever two-thirds of both Houses shall deem it necessary, shall propose Amendments to this Constitution, or, on the Application of the Legislatures of two-thirds of the several States, shall call a Convention for proposing Amendments, which, in either Case, shall be valid to all Intents and Purposes, as part of this Constitution, when ratified by the Legislatures of three-fourths of the several States, or by Conventions in three-fourths thereof, as the one or the other Mode of Ratification may be proposed by the Congress; Provided that no Amendment which may be made prior to the Year One thousand eight hundred and eight shall in any Manner affect the first and fourth Clauses in the Ninth Section of the first Article; and that no State, without its Consent, shall be deprived of its equal Suffrage in the Senate.

[FEDERAL SUPREMACY]

Article VI

All Debts contracted and Engagements entered into, before the Adoption of this Constitution shall be as valid against the United States under this Constitution, as under the Confederation.

This Constitution, and the Laws of the United States which shall be made in Pursuance thereof; and all Treaties made, or which shall be made, under the Authority of the United States, shall be the supreme Law of the Land; and the Judges in every State shall be bound thereby, any Thing in the Constitution or Laws of any State to the Contrary notwithstanding.

The Senators and Representatives before mentioned, and the Members of the several State Legislatures, and all executive and judicial Officers, both of the United States and of the several States, shall be bound by Oath or Affirmation, to support this Constitution; but no religious Test shall ever be required as a Qualification to any Office or public Trust under the United States.

[RATIFICATION]

Article VII

The Ratification of the Conventions of nine States shall be sufficient for the Establishment of this Constitution between the States so ratifying the Same.

Done in Convention by the Unanimous Consent of the States present the Seventeenth Day of September in the year of our Lord one thousand seven hundred and eighty seven and of the Independence of the United States of America the twelfth. In witness whereof We have hereunto subscribed our Names.

[BILL OF RIGHTS AND OTHER AMENDMENTS]

Articles in addition to, and amendment of, the Constitution of the United States of America, proposed by Congress, and ratified by the several States, pursuant to the fifth Article of the original Constitution.

Amendment I [1791]

[*Freedoms of religion, speech, press, assembly*]
Congress shall make no law respecting an establishment of religion, or prohibiting the free exercise thereof; or abridging the freedom of speech, or of the press; or the right of the people peaceably to assemble and to petition the Government for a redress of grievances.

Amendment II [1791]

[*Right to bear arms*]
A well regulated Militia, being necessary to the security of a free State, the right of the people to keep and bear Arms, shall not be infringed.

Amendment III [1791]

[*Quartering of soldiers*]
No Soldier shall, in time of peace be quartered in any house, without the consent of the Owner, nor in time of war, but in a manner to be prescribed by Law.

Amendment IV [1791]

[*Protection against search and seizure*]
The right of the people to be secure in their persons, houses, papers, and effects, against un-reasonable searches and seizures, shall not be violated, and no Warrants shall issue, but upon probable cause, supported by Oath or affirmation, and particularly describing the place to be searched, and the persons or things to be seized.

Amendment V [1791]

[*Protection of citizens before the law*]
No person shall be held to answer for a capital, or otherwise infamous crime, unless on a presentment or indictment of a Grand Jury, except in cases arising in the land or naval forces, or in the Militia, when in actual service in time of War or public danger; nor shall any person be subject for the same offence to be twice put in jeopardy of life or limb; nor shall be compelled in any criminal case to be a witness against himself, nor be deprived of life, liberty, or property, without due process of law; nor shall private property be taken for public use, without just compensation.

Amendment VI [1791]

[*Rights of the accused in criminal cases*]
In all criminal prosecutions, the accused shall enjoy the right to a speedy and public trial, by an impartial jury of the State and district wherein the crime shall have been committed, which district shall have been previously ascertained by law, and to be informed of the nature and cause of the accusation; to be confronted with the witnesses against him; to have compulsory process for obtaining witnesses in his favor, and to have the Assistance of Counsel for his defence.

Amendment VII [1791]

[*Rights of complainants in civil cases*]
In suits at common law, where the value in controversy shall exceed twenty dollars, the right of trial by jury shall be preserved, and no fact tried by jury, shall be otherwise reexamined in any Court of the United States, than according to the rules of the common law.

Amendment VIII [1791]

[*Constraints on punishments*]
Excessive bail shall not be required, nor excessive fines imposed, nor cruel and unusual punishments inflicted.

Amendment IX [1791]

[*Rights retained by the people*]
The enumeration in the Constitution, of certain rights, shall not be construed to deny or disparage others retained by the people.

Amendment X [1791]

[*Rights reserved to states*]
The powers not delegated to the United States by the Constitution, nor prohibited by it to the States, are reserved to the States respectively, or to the people.

Amendment XI [1798]

[*Restraints on judicial power*]
The Judicial power of the United States shall not be construed to extend to any suit in law or equity, commenced or prosecuted against one of the United States by Citizens of another State, or by Citizens or Subjects of any Foreign State.

Amendment XII [1804]

[*Mechanism for presidential elections*]
The electors shall meet in their respective states and vote by ballot for President and Vice-President, one of whom, at least, shall not be an inhabitant of the same state with themselves; they shall name in their ballots the person voted for as President, and in distinct ballots the person voted for as Vice-President, and they shall make distinct lists of all persons voted for as President, and of all persons voted for as Vice-President, and of the number of votes for each, which lists they shall sign and certify, and transmit sealed to the seat of the government of the United States, directed to the President of the Senate;—The President of the Senate shall, in presence of the Senate and House of Representatives, open all the certificates and the votes shall then be counted;—The person having the greatest number of votes for President, shall be the President, if such number be a majority of the whole number of Electors appointed; and if no person have such majority, then from the persons having the highest numbers not exceeding three on the list of those voted for as President, the House of Representatives shall choose immediately, by ballot, the President. But in choosing the President, the votes shall be taken by states, the representation from each state having one vote; a quorum for this purpose shall consist of a member or members from two-thirds of the states, and a majority of all the states shall be necessary to a choice. [And if the House of Representatives shall not choose a President whenever the right of choice shall devolve upon them, before the fourth day of March next following, then the Vice-President shall act as President, as in the case of the death or other constitutional disability of the President.—][11] The person having the greatest number of votes as Vice-President, shall be the Vice-President, if such number be a majority of the whole number of Electors appointed, and if no person have a majority, then from the two highest numbers on the list, the Senate shall choose the Vice-President; a quorum for the purpose shall consist of two-thirds of the whole number of Senators, and a majority of the whole number shall be necessary to a choice. But no person constitutionally ineligible to the office of President shall be eligible to that of Vice-President of the United States.

Amendment XIII [1865]

[*Abolishment of slavery*]
SECTION 1 Neither slavery nor involuntary servitude, except as a punishment for crime

---

[11]Superceded by Section 3 of Amendment XX.

whereof the party shall have been duly convicted, shall exist within the United States, or any place subject to their jurisdiction.

SECTION 2 Congress shall have power to enforce this article by appropriate legislation.

Amendment XIV [1868]

[Citizens' rights and immunities, due process, equal protection]

SECTION 1 All persons born or naturalized in the United States, and subject to the jurisdiction thereof, are citizens of the United States and of the State wherein they reside. No State shall make or enforce any law which shall abridge the privileges or immunities of citizens of the United States; nor shall any State deprive any person of life, liberty, or property, without due process of law; nor deny to any person within its jurisdiction the equal protection of the laws.

[Basis of representation]

SECTION 2 Representatives shall be appointed among the several States according to their respective numbers, counting the whole number of persons in each State, excluding Indians not taxed. But when the right to vote at any election for the choice of electors for President and Vice President of the United States, Representatives in Congress, the Executive and Judicial officers of a State, or the members of the Legislature thereof, is denied to any of the male inhabitants of such State, being twenty-one years of age, and citizens of the United States, or in any way abridged, except for participation in rebellion, or other crime, the basis of representation therein shall be reduced in the proportion which the number of such male citizens shall bear to the whole number of male citizens twenty-one years of age in such State.

[Disqualification of Confederates for office]

SECTION 3 No person shall be a Senator or Representative in Congress, or elector of President and Vice-President, or hold any office, civil or military, under the United States, or under any State, who, having previously taken an oath, as a member of Congress, or as an officer of the United States, or as a member of any State legislature, or as an executive or judicial officer of any State, to support the Constitution of the United States, shall have engaged in insurrection or rebellion against the same, or given aid or comfort to the enemies thereof. But Congress may by a vote of two-thirds of each House, remove such disability.

[Public debt arising from insurrection or rebellion]

SECTION 4 The validity of the public debt of the United States, authorized by law, including debts incurred for payment of pensions and bounties for services in suppressing insurrection or rebellion, shall not be questioned. But neither the United States nor any State shall assume or pay any debt or obligation incurred in aid of insurrection or rebellion against the United States, or any claim for the loss or emancipation of any slave; but all such debts, obligations and claims shall be held illegal and void.

SECTION 5 The Congress shall have power to enforce, by appropriate legislation, the provisions of this article.

Amendment XV [1870]

[Explicit extension of right to vote]

SECTION 1 The right of citizens of the United States to vote shall not be denied or abridged by the United States or by any State on account of race, color, or previous condition of servitude.

SECTION 2 The Congress shall have power to enforce this article by appropriate legislation.

Amendment XVI [1913]

[Creation of income tax]

The Congress shall have power to lay and collect taxes on incomes, from whatever source derived, without apportionment among the several States, and without regard to any census or enumeration.

Amendment XVII [1913]

[*Election of senators*]

The Senate of the United States shall be composed of two Senators from each State, elected by the people thereof, for six years; and each Senator shall have one vote. The electors in each State shall have the qualifications requisite for electors of the most numerous branch of the State legislatures.

When vacancies happen in the representation of any State in the Senate, the executive authority of such State shall issue writs of election to fill such vacancies: *Provided,* That the legislature of any State may empower the executive thereof to make temporary appointments until the people fill the vacancies by election as the legislature may direct.

This amendment shall not be so construed as to affect the election or term of any Senator chosen before it becomes valid as part of the Constitution.

Amendment XVIII [1919]

[*Prohibition of alcohol*]

[SECTION 1 After one year from the ratification of this article the manufacture, sale, or transportation of intoxicating liquors within, the importation thereof into, or the exportation thereof from the United States and all territory subject to the jurisdiction thereof for beverage purposes is hereby prohibited.

SECTION 2 The Congress and the several States shall have concurrent power to enforce this article by appropriate legislation.

SECTION 3 This article shall be inoperative unless it shall have been ratified as an amendment to the Constitution by the legislatures of the several States, as provided in the Constitution, within seven years from the date of the submission hereof to the States by the Congress.][12]

---

[12]Repealed by Amendment XXI.

Amendment XIX [1920]

[*Voting rights and gender*]

The right of citizens of the United States to vote shall not be denied or abridged by the United States or by any State on account of sex. Congress shall have the power to enforce this article by appropriate legislation.

Amendment XX [1933]

[*Terms of executives, assembly of Congress, presidential succession*]

SECTION 1 The terms of the President and Vice President shall end at noon on the 20th day of January, and the terms of Senators and Representatives at noon on the 3d day of January, of the years in which such terms would have ended if this article had not been ratified; and the terms of their successors shall then begin.

SECTION 2 The Congress shall assemble at least once in every year, and such meeting shall begin at noon on the 3d day of January, unless they shall by law appoint a different day.

SECTION 3 If, at the time fixed for the beginning of the term of the President, the President elect shall have died, the Vice President elect shall become President. If a President shall not have been chosen before the time fixed for the beginning of his term, or if the President elect shall have failed to qualify, then the Vice President elect shall act as President until a President shall have qualified; and the Congress may by law provide for the case wherein neither a President elect nor a Vice President elect shall have qualified, declaring who shall then act as President, or the manner in which one who is to act shall be selected, and such person shall act accordingly until a President or Vice President shall have qualified.

SECTION 4 The Congress may by law provide for the case of the death of any of the persons from whom the House of Representatives may choose a President whenever the right of choice shall have devolved upon them, and for the case of the death of any of the persons from whom the Senate may choose a Vice President whenever the right of choice shall have devolved upon them.

SECTION 5 Sections 1 and 2 shall take effect on the 15th day of October following the ratification of this article.

SECTION 6 This article shall be inoperative unless it shall have been ratified as an amendment to the Constitution by the legislatures of three-fourths of the several States within seven years from the date of its submission.

Amendment XXI [1933]

[Repealing of prohibition]
SECTION 1 The eighteenth article of amendment to the Constitution of the United States is hereby repealed.

SECTION 2 The transportation or importation into any State, Territory, or possession of the United States for delivery or use therein of intoxicating liquors, in violation of the laws thereof, is hereby prohibited.

SECTION 3 This article shall be inoperative unless it shall have been ratified as an amendment to the Constitution by conventions in the several States, as provided in the Constitution, within seven years from the date of the submission hereof to the States by the Congress.

Amendment XXII [1951]

[Limits on presidential term]
SECTION 1 No person shall be elected to the office of the President more than twice, and no person who has held the office of President, or acted as President, for more than two years of a term to which some other person was elected President shall be elected to the office of the President more than once. But this Article shall not apply to any person holding the office of President when this Article was proposed by the Congress, and shall not prevent any person who may be holding the office of President, or acting as President, during the term within which the Article becomes operative from holding the office of President or acting as President during the remainder of such term.

SECTION 2 This article shall be inoperative unless it shall have been ratified as an amendment to the Constitution by the legislatures of three-fourths of the several States within seven years from the date of its submission to the States by the Congress.

Amendment XXIII [1961]

[Voting rights of District of Columbia]
SECTION 1 The District constituting the seat of Government of the United States shall appoint in such manner as the Congress may direct:

A number of electors of President and Vice President equal to the whole number of Senators and Representatives in Congress to which the District would be entitled if it were a State; but in no event more than the least populous State; they shall be in addition to those appointed by the States, but they shall be considered, for the purposes of the election of President and Vice President, to be electors appointed by a State; and they shall meet in the District and perform such duties as provided by the twelfth article of amendment.

SECTION 2 The Congress shall have power to enforce this article by appropriate legislation.

Amendment XXIV [1964]

[Prohibition of poll tax]
SECTION 1 The right of citizens of the United States to vote in any primary or other election for President or Vice President, for electors for President or Vice President, or for Senator or Representative in Congress, shall not be denied or abridged by the United States or any State by reason of failure to pay any poll tax or other tax.

SECTION 2 The Congress shall have power to enforce this article by appropriate legislation.

Amendment XXV [1967]

[Presidential disability and succession]
SECTION 1 In case of the removal of the President from office or his death or resignation, the Vice President shall become President.

SECTION 2 Whenever there is a vacancy in the office of the Vice President, the President shall nominate a Vice President who shall take the Office upon confirmation by a majority vote of both houses of Congress.

SECTION 3 Whenever the President transmits to the President pro tempore of the Senate and the Speaker of the House of Representatives his written declaration that he is unable to discharge the powers and duties of his office, and until he transmits to them a written declaration to the contrary, such powers and duties shall be discharged by the Vice President as Acting President.

SECTION 4 Whenever the Vice President and a majority of either the principal officers of the executive departments, or of such other body as Congress may by law provide, transmit to the President pro tempore of the Senate and the Speaker of the House of Representatives their written declaration that the President is unable to discharge the powers and duties of his office, the Vice President shall immediately assume the powers and duties of the office as Acting President.

Thereafter, when the President transmits to the President pro tempore of the Senate and the Speaker of the House of Representatives his written declaration that no inability exists, he shall resume the powers and duties of his office unless the Vice President and a majority of either the principal officers of the executive department, or of such other body as Congress may by law provide, transmit within four days

to the President pro tempore of the Senate and the Speaker of the House of Representatives their written declaration that the President is unable to discharge the powers and duties of his office. Thereupon Congress shall decide the issue, assembling within 48 hours for that purpose if not in session. If the Congress, within 21 days after receipt of the latter written declaration, or, if Congress is not in session, within 21 days after Congress is required to assemble, determines by two-thirds vote of both houses that the President is unable to discharge the powers and duties of his office, the Vice President shall continue to discharge the same as Acting President; otherwise, the President shall resume the powers and duties of his office.

Amendment XXVI [1971]

[Voting rights and age]

SECTION 1 The right of citizens of the United States, who are eighteen years of age, or older, to vote shall not be denied or abridged by the United States or by any state on account of age.

SECTION 2 The Congress shall have the power to enforce this article by appropriate legislation.

Amendment XXVII [1992]

[Congressional pay raises]

No law varying the compensation for the services of the Senators and Representatives shall take effect, until an election of Representatives shall have intervened.

From *The Federalist Papers,*
Nos. 10 and 51

FEDERALIST NO. 10 [1787]

To the People of the State of New York: Among the numerous advantages promised by a well-constructed union, none deserves to be more accurately developed than its tendency to break and control the violence of faction. The friend of popular governments, never finds himself so much alarmed for their character and fate, as when he contemplates their propensity to this dangerous vice. He will not fail, therefore, to set a due value on any plan which, without violating the principles to which he is attached, provides a proper cure for it. The instability, injustice, and confusion introduced into the public councils, have, in truth, been the mortal diseases under which popular governments have everywhere perished; as they continue to be the favourite and fruitful topics from which the adversaries to liberty derive their most specious declamations. The valuable improvements made by the American constitutions on the popular models, both ancient and modern, cannot certainly be too much admired; but it would be an unwarrantable partiality, to contend that they have as effectually obviated the danger on this side, as was wished and expected. Complaints are everywhere heard from our most considerate and virtuous citizens, equally the friends of public and private faith, and of public and personal liberty, that our gov-ernments are too unstable; that the public good is disregarded in the conflicts of rival parties; and that measures are too often decided, not according to the rules of justice, and the rights of the minor party, but by the superior force of an interested and overbearing majority. However anxiously we may wish that these complaints had no foundation, the evidence of known facts will not permit us to deny that they are in some degree true. It will be found, indeed, on a candid review of our situation, that some of the distresses under which we labour have been erroneously charged on the operation of our governments; but it will be found, at the same time, that other causes will not alone account for many of our heaviest misfortunes; and, particularly, for that prevailing and increasing distrust of public engagements, and alarm for private rights, which are echoed from one end of the continent to the other. These must be chiefly, if not wholly, effects of the unsteadiness and injustice, with which a factious spirit has tainted our public administrations.

By a faction, I understand a number of citizens, whether amounting to a majority or minority of the whole, who are united and actuated by some common impulse of passion, or of interest, adverse to the rights of other citizens, or to the permanent and aggregate interests of the community.

There are two methods of curing the mischiefs of faction: The one, by removing its causes; the other, by controlling its effects.

There are again two methods of removing the causes of faction: The one, by destroying the liberty which is essential to its existence; the other, by giving to every citizen the same opinions, the same passions, and the same interests.

It could never be more truly said, than of the first remedy, that it was worse than the disease. Liberty is to faction what air is to fire, an ailment without which it instantly expires. But it could not be a less folly to abolish liberty, which is essential to political life, because it nourishes faction, than it would be to wish the annihilation of air, which is essential to animal life, because it imparts to fire its destructive agency.

The second expedient is as impracticable, as the first would be unwise. As long as the reason of man continues fallible, and he is at liberty to exercise it, different opinions will be formed. As long as the connection subsists between his reason and his self-love, his opinions and his passions will have a reciprocal influence on each other; and the former will be objects to which the latter will attach themselves. The diversity in the faculties of men, from which the rights of property originate, is not less an insuperable obstacle to an uniformity of interests. The protection of these faculties is the first object of government. From the protection of different and unequal faculties of acquiring property, the possession of different degrees and kinds of property immediately results; and from the influence of these on the sentiments and views of the respective proprietors, ensues a division of the society into different interests and parties.

The latent causes of action are thus sown in the nature of man; and we see them everywhere brought into different degrees of activity, according to the different circumstances of civil society. A zeal for different opinions concerning religion, concerning government, and many other points, as well as of speculation as of practice; an attachment to different leaders ambitiously contending for preeminence and power; or to persons of other descriptions whose fortunes have been interesting to the human passions, have, in turn, divided mankind into parties, inflamed them with mutual animosity, and rendered them much more disposed to vex and oppress each other, than to cooperate for their common good. So strong is this propensity of mankind, to fall into mutual animosities, that where no substantial occasion presents itself, the most frivolous and fanciful distinctions have been sufficient to kindle their unfriendly passions and excite their most violent conflicts. But the most common and durable source of factions, has been the various and unequal distribution of property. Those who hold, and those who are without property, have ever formed distinct interests in society. Those who are creditors, and those who are debtors, fall under alike discrimination. A landed interest, a manufacturing interest, a mercantile interest, a moneyed interest, with many lesser interests, grow up of necessity in civilized nations, and divide them into different classes, actuated by different sentiments and views. The regulation of these various and interfering interests forms the principal task of modern legislation, and involves the spirit of the party and faction in the necessary and ordinary operations of the government.

No man is allowed to be a judge in his own cause; because his interest will certainly bias his judgment, and, not improbably, corrupt his integrity. With equal, nay, with greater reason, a body of men are unfit to be both judges and parties at the same time; yet what are many of the most important acts of legislation, but so many judicial determinations, not indeed concerning the right of single persons, but concerning the rights of large bodies of citizens? And what are the different classes of legislators, but advocates and parties to the causes which they determine? Is a law proposed concerning private debts? It is a question to which the creditors are parties on one side, and the debtors on the other. Justice ought to hold the balance between them. Yet the parties are, and must be, themselves the judges; and the most numerous party, or, in other words, the most powerful faction, must be expected to prevail. Shall domestic manufactures be encouraged, and in what degree, by restrictions on foreign manufactures? are questions which would be differently decided by the landed and the manufacturing classes; and probably by neither with a sole regard to justice and the public good. The apportionment of taxes, on the various descriptions of property, is an act which seems to require the most exact impartiality; yet there is, perhaps, no legislative act, in which greater opportunity and temptation are given to a predominant party to trample on the rules of justice. Every shilling, with which they overburden the inferior number, is a shilling saved to their own pockets.

It is in vain to say, that enlightened statesmen will be able to adjust these clashing interests, and render them all subservient to the public good. Enlightened statesmen will not always be at the helm: nor, in many cases, can such an adjustment be made at all, without taking into view indirect and remote considerations, which will rarely prevail over the immediate interest which one party may find in disregarding the rights of another, or the good of the whole. The inference to which we are brought is, that the *causes* of faction cannot be removed; and that relief is only to be sought in the means of controlling its *effects*.

If a faction consists of less than a majority, relief is supplied by the republican principle, which enables the majority to defeat its sinister views, by regular vote. It may clog the administration, it may convulse the society; but it will be unable to execute and mask its violence under the forms of the constitution. When a majority is included in a faction, the form of popular government, on the other hand, enables it to sacrifice to its ruling passion or interest, both the public good and the rights of other citizens. To secure the public good, and private rights, against the danger of such a faction, and at the same time to preserve the spirit and the form of popular government, is then the great

object to which our inquiries are directed. Let me add, that it is the great desideratum, by which alone this form of government can be rescued from the opprobrium under which it has so long laboured, and be recommended to the esteem and adoption of mankind.

By what means is this object attainable? Evidently by one of two only. Either the existence of the same passion or interest in a majority, at the same time, must be prevented; or the majority, having such coexistent passion or interest, must be rendered, by their number and local situation, unable to concert and carry into effect schemes of oppression. If the impulse and the opportunity be suffered to coincide, we well know that neither moral nor religious motives can be relied on as an adequate control. They are not found to be such on the injustice and violence of individuals, and lose their efficacy in proportion to the number combined together; that is, in proportion as their efficacy becomes needful.

From this view of the subject, it may be concluded, that a pure democracy, by which I mean a society consisting of a small number of citizens, who assemble and administer the government in person, can admit of no cure for the mischiefs of faction. A common passion or interest will, in almost every case, be felt by a majority of the whole; a communication and concert, results from the form of government itself; and there is nothing to check the inducements to sacrifice the weaker party, or an obnoxious individual. Hence, it is, that such democracies have ever been spectacles of turbulence and contention; have ever been found incompatible with personal security, or the rights of property; and have in general been as short in their lives, as they have been violent in their deaths. Theoretic politicians, who have patronized this species of government, have erroneously supposed, that by reducing mankind to a perfect equality in their political rights, they would, at the same time, be perfectly equalized and assimilated in their possessions, their opinions, and their passions.

A republic, by which I mean a government in which the scheme of representation takes place, opens a different prospect, and promises the cure for which we are seeking. Let us examine the points in which it varies from pure democracy, and we shall comprehend both the nature of the cure and the efficacy which it must derive from the union.

The two great points of difference, between a democracy and a republic, are, first, the delegation of the government, in the latter, to a small number of citizens, elected by the rest; secondly, the greatest number of citizens, and greater sphere of country, over which the latter may be extended.

The effect of the first difference is, on the one hand, to refine and enlarge the public views, by passing them through the medium of a chosen body of citizens, whose wisdom may best discern the true interest of their country, and whose patriotism and love of justice, will be least likely to sacrifice it to temporary or partial considerations. Under such a regulation, it may well happen, that the public voice, pronounced by the representatives of the people, will be more consonant to the public good, than if pronounced by the people themselves, convened for the purpose. On the other hand the effect may be inverted. Men of factious tempers, of local prejudices, or of sinister designs, may by intrigue, by corruption, or by other means, first obtain the suffrages, and then betray the interest of the people. The question resulting is, whether small or extensive republics are most favourable to the election of proper guardians of the public weal; and it is clearly decided in favour of the latter by two obvious considerations.

In the first place, it is to be remarked that, however small the republic may be, the representatives must be raised to a certain number, in order to guard against the cabals of a few; and that however large it may be, they must be limited to a certain number, in order to guard against the confusion of a multitude. Hence, the number of representatives in the two cases not being in proportion to that of the constituents, and being proportionally greatest in the small republic, it follows, that if the proportion of fit characters be not less in the large than in the small republic, the former will present a greater option, and consequently a greater probability of a fit choice.

In the next place, as each representative will be chosen by a greater number of citizens in the large than in the small republic, it will be more difficult for unworthy candidates to practise with success the vicious arts, by which elections are too often carried; and the suffrages of the people being more free, will be more likely to centre in men who possess the most attractive merit, and the most diffusive and established characters.

It must be confessed, that in this, as in most other cases, there is a mean, on both sides of which inconveniences will be found to lie. By enlarging too much the number of electors, you render the representatives too little acquainted with all their local circumstances and lesser interests; as by reducing it too much, you render him unduly attached to these, and too little fit to comprehend and pursue great and national objects. The federal constitution forms a happy combination being referred to the national, the local and particular, to the state legislatures.

The other point of difference is, the greater number of citizens, and extent of territory, which may be brought within the compass of republican, than of democratic government; and it is this circumstance principally which renders factious combinations less to be dreaded in the former, than in the latter. The smaller the society, the fewer probably will be the distinct parties and interests composing it; the fewer the distinct parties and interests, the more frequently will a majority be found of the same party; and the smaller the number of individuals composing a majority, and the smaller the compass within which they are placed, the more easily will they concert and execute their plans of oppression. Extend the sphere, and you take in a greater variety of parties and interests; you make it less probable that a majority of the whole will have a common motive to invade the rights of other citizens; or if such a common motive exists, it will be more difficult for all who feel it to discover their own strength, and to act in unison with each other. Besides other impediments, it may be remarked, that where there is a consciousness of unjust or dishonourable purposes, communication is always checked by distrust, in proportion to the number whose concurrence is necessary.

Hence, it clearly appears, that the same advantage, which a republic has over a democracy, in controlling the effects of faction, is enjoyed by a large over a small republic,—is enjoyed by the union over the states composing it. Does this advantage consist in the substitution of representatives, whose enlightened views and virtuous sentiments render them superior to local prejudices, and to schemes of injustice? It will not be denied that the representation of the union will be most likely to possess these requisite endowments. Does it consist in the greater security afforded by a greater variety of parties, against the event of any one party being able to outnumber and oppress the rest? In an equal degree does the increased variety of parties, comprised within the union, increase the security? Does it, in fine, consist in the greater obstacles opposed to the concert and accomplishment of the secret wishes of an unjust and interested majority? Here, again, the extent of the union gives it the most palpable advantage.

The influence of factious leaders may kindle a flame within their particular states, but will be unable to spread a general conflagration through the other states; a religious sect may degenerate into a political faction in a part of the confederacy; but the variety of sects dispersed over the entire face of it, must secure the national councils against any danger from that source: a rage for paper money, for an abolition of debts, for an equal division of property, or for any other improper or wicked project, will be less apt to pervade the whole body of the union than a particular member of it; in the same proportion as such a malady is more likely to taint a particular county or district, than an entire state.

In the extent and proper structure of the union, therefore, we behold a republican remedy for the diseases most incident to republican government. And according to the degree of pleasure and pride we feel in being republicans, ought to be our zeal in cherishing the spirit, and supporting the character of federalists.

JAMES MADISON

FEDERALIST NO. 51 [1788]

To the People of the State of New York: To what expedient then shall we finally resort for maintaining in practice the necessary partition of power among the several departments, as laid down in the constitution? The only answer that can be given is, that as all these exterior provisions are found to be inadequate, the defect must be supplied, by so contriving the interior structure of the government, as that its several constituent parts may, by their mutual relations, be the means of keeping each other in their proper places. Without presuming to undertake a full development of this important idea, I will hazard a few general observations, which may perhaps place it in a clearer light, and enable us to form a more correct judgment of the principles and structure of the government planned by the convention.

In order to lay a due foundation for that separate and distinct exercise of the different powers of government, which to a certain extent, is admitted on all hands to be essential to the preservation of liberty, it is evident that each department should have a will of its own; and consequently should be so constituted, that the members of each should have as little agency as possible in the appointment of the members of the others. Were this principle rigorously adhered to, it would require that all the appointments for the supreme executive, legislative, and judiciary magistracies, should be drawn from the same fountain of authority, the people, through channels, having no communication whatever with one another. Perhaps such a plan of constructing the several departments would be less difficult in practice than it may in contemplation appear. Some difficulties however, and some additional expense, would attend the execution of it. Some deviations therefore from the principle must be admitted. In the constitution of the judiciary department in particular, it might be inexpedient to insist rigorously on the principle; first, because peculiar qualifications being essential in the members, the primary consideration ought to be to select that mode of choice, which best secures these qualifications; secondly, because the permanent tenure by which the appointments are held in that department, must soon destroy all sense of dependence on the authority conferring them.

It is equally evident that the members of each department should be as little dependent as possible on those of the others, for the emoluments annexed to their offices. Were the executive magistrate, or the judges, not independent of the legislature in this particular, their independence in every other would be merely nominal.

But the great security against a gradual concentration of the several powers in the same department, consists in giving to those who administer each department, the necessary constitutional means, and personal motives, to resist encroachments of the others. The provision for defense must in this, as in all other cases, be made commensurate to the danger of attack. Ambition must be made to counteract ambition. The interest of the man must be connected with the constitutional rights of the place. It may be a reflection on human nature, that such devices should be necessary to control the abuses of government: But what is government itself but the greatest of all reflections on human nature? If men were angels, no government would be necessary. If angels were to govern men, neither external nor internal controls on government would be necessary. In framing a government which is to be administered by men over men, the great difficulty lies in this: You must first enable the government to control the governed; and in the next place, oblige it to control itself. A dependence on the people is no doubt the primary control on the government; but experience has taught mankind the necessity of auxiliary precautions.

This policy of supplying by opposite and rival interests, the defect of better motives, might be traced through the whole system of human affairs, private as well as public. We see it particularly displayed in all the subordinate distributions of power; where the constant aim is to divide and arrange the several offices in such a manner as that each may be a check on the other; that the private interest of every individual, may be a sentinel over the public rights. These inventions of prudence cannot be less requisite in the distribution of the supreme powers of the state.

But it is not possible to give to each department an equal power of self defense. In republican government the legislative authority, necessarily, predominates. The remedy for this inconveniency is, to divide the legislature into different branches; and to render them by different modes of election, and different principles of action, as little connected with each other, as the nature of their common functions, and their common dependence on the society, will admit. It may even be necessary to guard against dangerous encroachments by still further precautions. As the weight of the legislative authority requires that it should be thus divided, the weakness of the executive may require, on the other hand, that it should be fortified. An absolute negative, on the legislature, appears at first view to be the natural defense with which the executive magistrate should be armed. But perhaps it would be neither altogether safe, nor alone sufficient. On ordinary occasions, it might not be exerted with the requisite firmness; and on extraordinary occasions, it might be perfidiously abused. May not this defect of an absolute negative be supplied, by some qualified connection between this weaker department, and the weaker branch of the stronger department, by which the latter may be led to support the constitutional rights of the former, without being too much detached from the rights of its own department?

If the principles on which these observations are founded be just, as I persuade myself they are, and they be applied as a criterion, to the several state constitutions, and to the federal constitution, it will be found, that if the latter does not perfectly correspond with them, the former are infinitely less able to bear such a test. There are moreover two considerations particularly applicable to the federal system of America, which place that system in a very interesting point of view.

First. In a single republic, all the power surrendered by the people, is submitted to the administration of a single government; and usurpations are guarded against by a division of the government into distinct and separate departments. In the compound republic of America, the power surrendered by the people, is first divided between two distinct governments, and then the portion allotted to each, subdivided among distinct and separate departments. Hence a double security arises to the rights of the people. The different governments will control each other; at the same time that each will be controlled by itself.

Second. It is of great importance in a republic, not only to guard the society against the oppression of its rulers; but to guard one part of the society against the injustice of the other part. Different interests necessarily exist in different classes of citizens. If a majority be united by a common interest, the rights of the minority will be insecure. There are but two methods of providing against this evil: The one by creating a will in the community independent of the majority, that is, of the society itself; the other by comprehending in the society so many separate descriptions of citizens, as will render an unjust combination of a majority of the whole, very improbable, if not impracticable. The first method prevails in all governments possessing an hereditary or self appointed authority. This at best is but a precarious security; because a power independent of the society may as well espouse the unjust views of the major, as the rightful interests, of the minor party, and may possibly be turned against both parties. The second method will be exemplified in the federal republic of the United States. While all authority in it will be derived from and dependent on the society, the society itself will be broken into so many parts, interests and classes of citizens, that the rights of individuals or of the minority, will be in little danger from interested combinations of the majority. In a free government, the security for civil rights must be the same as for religious rights. It consists in the one case in the multiplicity of sects. The degree of security in both cases will depend on the number of interests and sects; and this may be presumed to depend on the extent of country and number of people comprehended under the same government. This view of the subject must particularly recommend a proper federal system to all the sincere and considerate friends of republican government: Since it shows that in exact proportion as the territory of the union may be formed into more circumscribed confederacies or states, oppressive combinations of a majority will be facilitated; the best security under the republican form, for the rights of every class of citizens, will be diminished; and consequently, the stability and independence of some member of the government, the only other security, must be proportionally increased. Justice is the end of government. It is the end of civil society. It ever has been, and ever will be pursued, until it be obtained, or until liberty be lost in the pursuit. In a society under the forms of which the stronger faction can readily unite and oppress the weaker, anarchy may as truly be said to reign, as in a state of nature where the weaker individual is not secured against the violence of the stronger: And as in the latter state even the stronger individuals are prompted by the uncertainty of their condition, to submit to a government which may protect the weak as well as themselves: So in the former state, will the more powerful factions or parties be gradually induced by alike motives, to wish for a government which will protect all parties, the weaker as well as the more powerful. It can be little doubted, that if the state of Rhode Island was separated from the confederacy, and left to itself, the insecurity of rights under the popular form of government within such narrow limits, would be displayed by such reiterated oppressions of factious majorities, that some power altogether independent of the people would soon be called for by the voice of the very factions whose misrule had proved the necessity of it. In the extended republic of the United States, and among the great variety of interests, parties and sects which it embraces, a coalition of a majority of the whole society could seldom take place on any other principles than those of justice and the general good; and there being thus less danger to a minor from the will of the major party, there must be less pretext also, to provide for the security of the former, by introducing into the government a will not dependent on the latter; or in other words, a will independent of the society itself. It is no less certain than it is important, notwithstanding the contrary opinions which have been entertained, that the larger the society, provided it lie within a practicable sphere, the more duly capable it will be of self government. And happily for the *republican cause,* the practicable sphere may be carried to a very great extent, by a judicious modification and mixture of the *federal principle*.

JAMES MADISON

adverseness A test used to determine whether a court case involves an actual dispute between two or more parties; used by the Supreme Court to determine whether to hear a case. (See **writ of certiorari**)

affirmative action Programs designed to help women and minorities in areas where they have experienced discrimination, such as getting into college or finding a job.

amicus brief Background information provided to courts by individuals and groups who have an interest in a case.

appellate courts The second tier of the federal courts; appellate courts can only hear appeals from courts of original jurisdiction.

Articles of Confederation Adopted by the thirteen colonies in the midst of the Revolutionary War, the Articles of Confederation was America's first constitution. The national government consisted of a weak president and a unicameral legislature. Most of the power remained in the states.

Australian ballot A voting system introduced in the late 1800s in which the ballot names all candidates and the vote is cast in secret; also known as the *secret ballot*.

baseline polls Measures of public opinion taken early in a campaign to assess a candidate's strengths and weaknesses and test possible campaign themes.

bicameral legislature A two-chambered legislative body.

Bill of Rights The first ten amendments to the Constitution.

bills Legislative proposals in the form of a draft law that are considered by Congress.

block grants A grant of money from the federal government to the states with broad instructions about how to spend the money. (See **categorical grants**)

broadcasting Messages that are transmitted by the media to all viewers on a single network.

Brown v. Topeka Board of Education The 1954 Supreme Court decision that ended the practice of separate but equal and led to the end of segregated public schools.

Budget and Impoundment Control Act A 1974 act of Congress that strengthened congressional influence over the federal budget.

budget resolution A congressional statement that sets broad revenue and spending targets that govern the spending and revenue committees as they adopt the federal budget; a resolution is passed by both chambers of Congress but is not signed by the president.

bundling A technique for raising money that involves collecting large numbers of individual checks and turning them over en masse, or bundled, to a candidate.

cabinet Composed of the heads of the fourteen departments of government and selected agencies; members are appointed by the president and confirmed by the Senate.

candidate-centered campaign An election campaign that is run by the candidate with little reference to party. (See **party-centered campaign**)

casework Efforts made by congressional staff to help their representative's constituents.

categorical grants A grant of money from the federal government to the states with specific instructions about how to spend the money. (See **block grants**)

caucus system A process for nominating candidates in which delegates to the party conventions are selected through a series of meetings that usually begin at the local level.

caucuses Informal committees that individual members of Congress join to promote their legislative interests.

central clearance The process by which the Office of Management and Budget approves legislation and testimony that an agency sends to Congress.

checks and balances The constitutional powers given to the legislative, executive, and judicial branches of government to prevent the other two branches from threatening liberty.

chief of staff A key member of the White House staff and of the president's inner circle; supervises the White House staff.

civic journalism An effort by some journalists to strengthen the media's role in promoting citizen participation; also known as public journalism.

civil liberties Freedoms such as speech, press, and religion guaranteed to protect citizens against government.

civil rights Protections against discrimination on the basis of individual characteristics such as race, gender, and disability.

civil service The federal employment system that seeks to fill federal jobs on the basis of employee merit without regard to political affiliation.

clear and present danger test A standard used to determine whether speech is protected under the First Amendment; it takes into consideration the circumstances under which words are spoken.

closed primary An election in which only party members are allowed to cast ballots; voters must declare their party preference when they register to vote.

cloture A vote by sixty of the one hundred members of the Senate to end a filibuster. A successful vote is known as invoking cloture.

Code of Federal Regulations A compilation of all rules issued by the federal government

collective benefits Benefits that are available to all people regardless of their membership in an organized interest.

committee on committees The separate committee selected by the members of each party in each chamber of Congress to assign all committee and subcommittee seats.

common law Laws that come from the judicial interpretations of statutory law and previous judicial opinions; also known as *judge-made law*.

concurrent powers Those powers given to both the states and the national government under the Constitution, such as the power to raise taxes.

conference committees Temporary committees formed to resolve the differences between the House and Senate passed versions of a particular bill.

conflict of interest A situation in which elected or appointed officials have a personal stake in an issue they must decide.

congressional campaign committee The separate committee appointed by each party in each chamber to raise money for the election of its members and candidates.

congressional case workers Staff of members of Congress who handle constituent requests, such as applications to West Point or lost Social Security checks.

conservatives Americans who believe that government should play a limited role in solving the nation's problems.

constituents People who live and vote in an elected official's district or state.

constitutional courts Courts that are created by Congress under Article III of the Constitution.

conventional participation Forms of civic activity that Americans find acceptable.

cooperative federalism A structure of government in which the federal, state, and local governments work together to solve problems.

critical election An election that produces a lasting shift in the underlying party loyalties of voters; also known as a *realigning election*.

cycle of decreasing influence The tendency for presidents to lose public and congressional support over time.

cycle of increasing effectiveness The tendency for presidents to learn more about their jobs and become more effective over time.

Declaration of Independence A list of grievances against the British that announced the colonies' intent to be free; written by Thomas Jefferson and signed on July 4, 1776. (See Appendix A)

dedistributive program A government policy that requires all Americans to give up government benefits.

demographics Personal characteristics such as race, gender, age, education, and income.

departments of government The most visible organizations in the federal bureaucracy: thirteen of the fourteen departments are headed by secretaries, the fourteenth is headed by the attorney general.

devolution revolution The effort to shift power from the federal government downward to state and local governments.

direct democracy A form of democracy in which every citizen has a say in every decision that government makes.

distributive program A government program that generally helps all groups in society and that spreads the costs evenly.

disturbance theory   The view that most organized interests emerge from social or economic upheaval.

dual federalism   A structure of government in which the federal and state levels of government do not work together to solve problems.

due process of law   Fair and open legal procedures guaranteed by the Fifth and Fourteenth Amendments.

elastic clause   Found in Article I, Section 8 of the Constitution; gives Congress the power to make any laws needed to carry out its express duties and is the source of Congress' implied powers; also known as the *necessary and proper clause.*

electoral college   Created by the Founders to elect the president. The people of each state vote for slates of delegates to the electoral college who, in turn, elect the president.

elitism   An option for representative democracy in which educated, often wealthy individuals speak for the people.

entitlements   Federal programs that provide benefits to everyone who is eligible for benefits.

equal protection clause   Found in the Fourteenth Amendment, the clause declares that all citizens of the United States and the states are to be treated equally.

establishment clause   Found in the First Amendment; prohibits the establishment of a national religion.

exclusive powers   Those powers given only to the national government under the Constitution, including the power to declare war, make treaties with other governments, and create money.

executive agreements   Agreements between the heads of countries that do not require the approval of the Senate.

executive branch   The part of government created to implement the laws.

Executive Office of the President   The small number of offices that serve the president directly; includes the Office of Management and Budget, the White House staff, and the National Security Council.

executive orders   Presidential orders that carry the same force as an act of Congress except that (1) they apply only to the executive branch, and (2) they can be overturned by a future president.

express powers   The specific lists of constitutional duties found in Articles I, II, and III of the Constitution that tell each branch exactly what it can and cannot do.

federal bureaucracy   The departments, independent regulatory commissions, agencies, and government corporations that do the work of implementing the laws.

federal judiciary   The part of government created to interpret the laws.

federal mandates   Orders by the federal government to state or local governments to perform some action.

Federal Register   A weekly newspaper-like report that lists all new and proposed rules of the federal government.

federalism   The division of power between the national, state and local layers of government.

filibuster   The practice that allows a single Senator to hold the floor indefinitely in order to block a particular piece of legislation; can only be ended by cloture.

First Continental Congress   The national legislature convened by the Founders in Philadelphia in September 1774.

fiscal policy   Decisions to use taxes or spending in order to stimulate or slow the economy.

focusing skill   A president's ability to use timing and lobbying to focus attention on top legislative priorities.

free exercise clause   Found in the First Amendment; prohibits any government interference in the practice of religion.

free media   News coverage of a candidate in a campaign.

free rider problem   A problem faced by organized interests in recruiting members; by providing benefits that all Americans receive, whether members or not, an organized interest reduces incentives to join the group.

gender gap   Differences in the opinions of men and women; related to childhood socialization as well as the generally poorer economic performance of women.

general election   The election contest that determines who will hold a particular office. (See **primary election**)

general revenue sharing   A new federalism program under which states and localities receive revenues from the federal government to use with no strings attached.

generational theory of participation   The theory that people born into the same generation learn the same lessons about the costs and benefits of participation.

gerrymandering Redrawing of election district lines to favor one party over another.

government A set of institutions (Congress, the presidency, executive branch, and courts in the United States) for managing politics.

government corporations Organizations in the federal bureaucracy designed to act more like businesses than traditional governmental departments and agencies.

Great Compromise The agreement by the Constitutional Convention to have a two-house, or bicameral, legislature.

home style The way in which members of Congress develop trust with their constituents and explain their votes in Congress.

ideology Underlying views of how much government should be involved in the day-to-day activities of American society.

impeachment A process used to remove duly elected and appointed officials from office; in presidential impeachments, the House of Representatives votes the articles of impeachment, and the Senate votes to acquit or convict.

implied powers Those powers given to Congress under the necessary and proper clause of the Constitution; implied powers allow Congress to carry out its express powers.

incremental program A small change from current practice in a public policy.

incumbent A current officeholder. Incumbents may have advantages in running for office, including name recognition.

independent agencies Usually small federal bureaucracies that either serve specific groups of Americans or work on specific problems. Their heads report to the president.

independent regulatory commissions Federal agencies established to protect Americans by overseeing and regulating various industries. Governed by boards or commissions that serve for fixed terms and cannot be removed by the president or Congress without cause.

independent spending Money spent on behalf of a federal candidate that is not coordinated with a campaign and is not, therefore, subject to campaign finance limits.

independents Individuals who do not identify with a political party. Independents who say they lean toward a party behave more like strong party loyalists than those who say they are weakly identified with a party, while pure independents are barely attached to the political process.

indexing The practice of increasing the dollars spent on a benefit program automatically with inflation.

initiative An election question that is placed on the ballot by citizen petition; a form of direct democracy.

inner circle The president's most loyal and trusted advisors.

institutional presidency The leadership, organizations, and advisors who help presidents do their jobs.

interest groups Membership organizations that focus specifically on influencing government.

iron triangles A tight relationship between a federal department or agency, a set of loyal organized interests, and a congressional authorizing committee; most are now replaced by policy networks.

isolationism A foreign policy that seeks to avoid involvement with the rest of the world.

issue voting Choosing between candidates by comparing each candidate's position on a voter's list of most important problems and selecting the candidate who comes closest to that voter's views.

issue-attention cycle A pattern in how the public pays attention to an issue. Under the cycle, the public becomes alarmed or enthusiastic about an issue, realizes the cost of action, and loses interest.

judicial activism A term used to describe broad interpretation of the Constitution and congressional intent in making judicial decisions. (See **judicial restraint**)

judicial branch The part of government created to interpret the laws and protect individual rights.

judicial restraint A term used to describe narrow interpretation of the Constitution and faithful adherence to congressional intent in making judicial decisions. (See **judicial activism**)

judicial review The power of the courts to overturn an act of Congress or of the president as unconstitutional.

justiciable issue A test used to determine whether a court case involves issues that are within federal court jurisdiction and whether the case can be resolved by either the legislative or executive branches.

legislative agenda The informal list of issues Congress will address.

legislative branch The part of government created to make the laws.

legislative courts Courts that are created by Congress under Article I of the Constitution.

legislative hold A Senator's personal objection to a given proposal. Because the Senate operates largely by unanimous consent, a hold can delay or even kill a bill.

legislative record The formal hearings, legislative reports, and debates about a bill as it works its way through Congress; used by executive agencies and courts to interpret congressional intent.

libel A false statement made by the written or electronic (television, radio) word.

liberals Americans who believe that government should play an active role in solving the nation's problems.

life-cycle theory of participation The theory that people become more active in political participation as they age.

line item veto Authority given to the president (and many state governors) to strike specific items from a spending bill.

lobbying Efforts to influence government; includes providing information, building public support, and influencing elections.

majority leader Elected to lead the majority party in each chamber of Congress.

majority-minority districts Election districts created to enhance the odds of electing minority representatives.

majority rule A way to make public decisions that allows the majority (50 percent plus one) the greatest say. (See **minority rights**)

minority leader Elected to lead the minority party in each chamber of Congress.

minority rights Constitutional protections designed to assure that minorities are not oppressed by majority rule. (See **majority rule**)

Miranda v. Arizona A 1966 Supreme Court decision that stated that all accused persons have a right to know their rights.

moderates Americans who see the benefits of government activism on some issues and of limited government on others.

monetary policy Decisions to change the supply of money in order to stimulate or slow the economy.

moot A test used to determine whether a case has already been resolved outside the judicial proceeding; used by the Supreme Court to determine whether to hear a case. (See **writ of certiorari**)

motor voter law Passed by Congress in 1993, requires states to allow citizens to register to vote at the same time they apply for other state and local services such as a driver's license.

multimember districts Electoral districts in which a large group of candidates compete for several seats in an election, such as a park board election.

narrowcasting Messages transmitted by specialized media to select viewers.

national party committees The governing bodies of the national party organizations; composed of members from every state party committee.

national party conventions Meetings of party delegates every four years to nominate each party's presidential and vice presidential candidates.

nationalization of the Bill of Rights The extension of the Bill of Rights to cover the actions of state and local governments.

necessary and proper clause Found in Article I, Section 8 of the Constitution; gives Congress the power to make any laws needed to carry out its express duties and is the source of Congress' implied powers; also known as the *elastic clause*.

New Deal coalition The groups that supported the Democratic Party from the 1930s through the 1960s, including workers, southern farmers, southern Democrats, liberals, Catholics, Jews, and African Americans.

new federalism A term first used in the early 1970s to describe efforts to shift federal responsibilities and dollars back to the states and localities.

New Jersey Plan A plan for organizing the new federal government offered in response to the Virginia Plan; outlined a weak national government, leaving most power to the states.

nomination The formal party endorsement of a candidate for office.

nonattitudes Public opinion based on a lack of information; often created when the public is asked polling questions about which little is known.

norms Informal congressional rules that govern behavior; includes apprenticeship and specialization.

open primary A primary election in which voters are allowed to choose the party primary in which to vote at the time of balloting; voters may not switch back and forth to the other party on specific contests. (A primary that allows switching is called a *blanket primary*.)

organized interests Organizations that exist for the purpose of influencing government for the benefit of its member or members.

oversight Presidential and congressional monitoring of the day-to-day decisions and activities of the federal bureaucracy.

paid media Campaign advertising on radio and television designed to reinforce public likes of the candidate or dislikes of the opponent.

participatory democracy A hybrid of representative and direct democracy in which citizens are called to engage in community problem solving.

party eras Periods in which either (1) one political party is dominant or (2) the competition between two parties is stable.

party identification A voter's sense of attachment to a particular political party.

party machines Consisting of a party boss, workers, and money to buy votes, these organizations once dominated big city politics and were key to successful local, state, and national campaigns.

party platform The statement of policies that a national political party supports.

party-centered campaign An election campaign during which the candidate runs as a representative of the party. (See **candidate-centered campaign**)

Plessy v. Ferguson A 1896 Supreme Court decision endorsing the separate but equal doctrine which divided Americans by race; overturned by *Brown v. Topeka Board of Education*.

pluralism An option for representative democracy in which organized interests speak for the people.

pocket veto Presidential power to kill legislation passed by Congress by allowing the ten-day period for bill signing to expire without the president having signed or vetoed the measure; can only be used if Congress formally adjourns during the ten-day period.

policy agenda The issues to which Congress and the president are paying attention.

policy networks Political leaders and organized interests that form alliances around a specific policy decision and then disband.

political action committees (PACs) Formal organizations that raise and contribute money to election campaigns and political parties. PACs are regulated under federal campaign finance laws.

political capital The assets that presidents have when they take office, such as public approval and the number of seats held by their party in Congress.

political efficacy An individual's sense that he or she can influence government.

political party A broad membership organization designed to win elections, organize government, and influence voters.

politics How people decide who gets what, when, and how in society.

polling The collection of public opinion by taking a random sample of individuals who represent the public as a whole.

political socialization The process by which children and adolescents form underlying beliefs about politics and government.

precedents Judicial decisions made in previous cases.

presidential appointee An employee of the executive branch who is either subject to confirmation by the Senate or appointed on the sole authority of the president.

presidential ticket The joint listing of presidential and vice presidential candidates on the same ballot, as required by the Twelfth Amendment.

primary election The election that determines who will run as a party's nominee for a particular office in the general election. (See **general election**)

proportional voting system A system of counting votes in which delegates are split among all candidates according to the final votes in a primary or caucus. (See **winner-take-all system**)

public administration How government implements and manages public policy once the decisions are made.

public opinion The collected views of Americans on government, politics, and society.

public policy Decisions about what government does.

push polls Highly negative information distributed at the end of a campaign in the form of a public opinion poll; designed to discourage voters from going to the polls.

racial gerrymandering Redrawing of election district lines to increase the odds of electing minority candidates in what are often labeled majority-minority districts.

rally points The increase (and occasional decrease) in public approval that presidents tend to experience during periods of foreign crisis.

random sample A small number of people who are chosen by pure chance to represent the views of the entire population; each person must have an equal chance to be selected.

ratification The final stage in adopting the Constitution or its amendments. Three-fourths of the states must approve the proposal, either in the state legislatures or in constitutional conventions.

realigning election An election that produces a lasting shift in the underlying party loyalties of voters; also known as a *critical election.*

recall The process by which voters may call a special election by petition to remove elected officials from office.

redistributive program A government program that takes wealth from one group in society and transfers it into benefits for another.

referendum A specific election question placed on the ballot by the state legislature; a form of direct democracy.

Regents of the University of California v. Bakke A 1978 Supreme Court decision that stated that quotas were not permissible even to achieve affirmative action goals.

representative bureaucracy A method to increase the federal bureaucracy's responsiveness to the public by making it look like the nation in terms of race and gender.

representative democracy A form of democracy in which the people vote for leaders who make the decisions on their behalf.

republic A society in which the people give their consent to be governed through the election of representatives.

reserved powers Those powers specifically given to the states under the Constitution, including the power to regulate commerce within state borders, police the public, and prosecute most crimes.

retrospective voting A form of voting in which voters choose between candidates on the basis of past performance. Voters ask whether they are better off since the last election; if "yes," they vote for the incumbent; if "no," they vote against the incumbent.

Revolutionary War The war that established America's independence from England; lasted from 1775 to 1783.

ripe for decision A test that asks whether an injury claimed in a case is imminent and whether judicial action is the last likely obstacle; used by the Supreme Court to determine whether to hear a case. (See **writ of certiorari**)

Roe v. Wade A 1973 Supreme Court decision that legalized abortion.

rule A precise legal statement from the federal bureaucracy about what a policy actually means.

Rule of Four The Supreme Court requirement for granting a petition for writ of certiorari; four of the nine justices must agree to hear a case in order to grant cert. (See **writ of certiorari**)

Rule of One The Supreme Court rule allowing a single justice to order immediate relief until the rest of the Court can consider the request; most visibly used in death penalty cases.

sampling error A measure of the potential for inaccuracy in polling data. The percentage by which the opinions of the random sample might differ from the opinions of the entire population.

Second Continental Congress The national legislature convened by the Founders in Philadelphia in May 1775, which ultimately produced the Declaration of Independence.

selective benefits Benefits that are available only to members of an organized interest—for example, discount insurance and travel clubs.

seniority Length of service by a member of Congress in the House or the Senate; used as one of several criteria for selecting party leaders and committee and subcommittee chairs.

separate but equal doctrine An interpretation of the equal protection clause that permitted separate facilities and services for each race; confirmed in *Plessy v. Ferguson* and overturned in *Brown v. Topeka Board of Education.*

separate interests Used in the Constitution to ensure that the three branches of government would remain independent of each other by giving the branches different voters and terms of office.

separate layers Used in the Constitution to limit the power of the national government by dividing power between the state and national governments, creating what is called a federalist system of government.

separate powers Used in the Constitution to ensure that no single branch of government is able to control decisions about who gets what, when, and how from government.

single-issue groups Interest groups formed around one specific issue, such as abortion or gun control.

single-member districts Electoral districts in which there can be only one winner for each election, no matter how many candidates there are.

slander False statement by the spoken word.

socioeconomic status A combination of education and income.

soft money Money donated to the national party committees for "party-building activities" under federal campaign finance laws; includes money for voter registration and get-out-the-vote campaigns.

solicitor general The Justice Department appointee who represents the federal government before the Supreme Court.

Speaker of the House Elected as the leader of the House of Representatives; presides over the business of the House.

split-ticket voting Voting for candidates of different parties for different offices on the same ballot.

standing committees The permanent congressional committees created to manage legislation.

standing to sue The legal status to bring a lawsuit, meaning that the individuals who bring the case must be truly injured or subject to injury.

stare decisis Literally, "let the decision stand," which means that every judicial decision today must be linked to a decision made in the past.

State of the Union Address Annual presidential statement to Congress on how things are going and what the president plans to do about it.

states' rights A view of federalism that emphasizes states as having the primary role in a federal system. (See **dual federalism**)

statutory law Laws that come from Congress and the president.

straight-ticket voting Voting for the candidates of one party for every office on the ballot.

supremacy clause Found in Article VI of the Constitution, the clause gives federal laws precedence over state or local laws when they conflict.

take care clause Found at the end of Article II of the Constitution, the clause gives the president ultimate authority to implement the laws.

tax expenditures Items that taxpayers are allowed to deduct from their annual income tax, such as charitable contributions or mortgage interest.

think tank An organization composed of public policy researchers.

third-party federal government The use of nonfederal employees (private companies, state and local governments, and nonprofit organizations) to deliver services on behalf of the federal government.

three-fifths compromise An agreement reached by the Constitutional Convention that calculated each slave as three-fifths of a person toward the total population of a state in determining the allocation of seats in the House of Representatives.

tracking polls Measures of public opinion taken to check a candidate's standing day to day and to show trends in support over time.

trial courts Courts of original jurisdiction. The first courts in the judicial system to hear a case.

uncontrollable spending Money spent on programs that (1) Congress or the president have been unwilling to cut, and (2) rise in cost nearly automatically.

unconventional participation Less acceptable forms of civic activity, such as breaking the law to advance a cause.

unicameral legislature A single-chambered legislative body.

veto The power to reject laws passed by another branch of government. Presidents exercise the veto by returning a bill to Congress with a message stating the reasons for not signing it.

veto override The power of the legislative branch to overturn or reject a veto by a two-thirds vote in each chamber.

Virginia Plan Drafted by James Madison as a model for the new government, the plan outlined a government with three branches: legislative, executive, and judicial.

voter turnout The number of registered voters who actually vote in a particular election.

War Powers Resolution A 1973 act of Congress adopted to restrain the president's war making power.

whip A party position filled in each chamber of Congress to win support for and "whip" members into line behind party legislation on the floor of Congress.

White House staff The members of the Executive Office of the President who work in the White House and serve the president's daily needs.

winner-take-all system A method of counting votes that gives all of the delegates or electors at stake to the candidate who gets the most votes, even if by the narrowest margin.

writ of certiorari An order by the Supreme Court to a lower court requesting the record of a case that the Supreme Court has agreed to review. Granting a petition for writ of certiorari (also known as *granting cert.*) places a case on the Supreme Court's calendar to be heard.

writ of habeas corpus An order by the Supreme Court to a lower court requesting the record of a case to determine whether a person is unlawfully imprisoned or detained.

Acknowledgments

Box 3–1: From "Reality Check: The Politics of Mistrust (Politics Quiz)." From the *Washington Post,* January 29, 1996, p. A6. Copyright © 1996 Washington Post Writers Group. Reprinted with permission.

Box 3–2: From "Clinton Ratings Hold: Balanced Budget a Public Priority, But Few See Personal Payoff," from The Pew Research Center for the People and the Press News Release, January 18, 1996, pp. 11–12, 16–17.

Box 3–3: From *Vital Statistics on American Politics* by Harold W. Stanley and Richard G. Niemi. (Washington, DC: CQ Press, 1992), p. 150, and the General Social Survey by the National Opinion Research Center, University of Chicago, p. 150.

Box 3–4: From "The People, the Press and Politics: The New Political Landscape," from the Times Mirror Center for the People and the Press News Release, September 21, 1994, p. 110.

Box 4–1: "Win or Lose, Perot Proves One Can Run without Major Parties" by James M. Perry. From the *Wall Street Journal,* July 14, 1992, p. A11. Copyright © 1992 Dow Jones & Company, Inc. All rights reserved worldwide.

Box 4–2: From the *New York Times,* August 26, 1996, p. A12. Copyright © 1996 by The New York Times Company. Reprinted by permission.

Box 4–3: From *Vital Statistics on American Politics* by Harold W. Stanley and Richard G. Niemi. (Washington, DC: CQ Press, 1992), p. 146.

Box 4–4: Adapted from *Politics, Parties, and Elections in America* by John Bibby. (Chicago, IL: Nelson-Hall Publishers, 1992), p. 22.

Box 4–5: From *Vital Statistics on American Politics,* 5th edition, by Harold W. Stanley and Richard G. Niemi. (Washington, DC: CQ Press, 1995), p. 149.

Box 4–6: From *Voice and Equality: Civic Voluntarism in American Politics* by Sidney Verba, Kay Lehman Schlozman, and Henry E. Brady. (Cambridge, MA: Harvard University Press, 1995), p. 190–fig. 7.2, p. 218–fig. 7.12, p. 233–table 8.1, p. 255–fig. 8.4. Reprinted with permission by The President and Fellows of Harvard College.

Box 4–7: From "The Paradox of Interest Groups in Washington—More Groups, Less Clout" by Robert H. Salisbury, from *The New American Political System* ed. by Anthony King. (Washington, DC: American Enterprise Institute Press, 1990), p. 228.

Box 4–8: From *Vital Statistics on American Politics,* 5th edition, by Harold W. Stanley and Richard G. Niemi. (Washington, DC: CQ Press, 1995), p. 161.

Box 5–1: From "Citizen Activity: Who Participates? What Do They Say?" by Sidney Verba, Kay Lehman Schlozman, Henry E. Brady, and Norman Nie, as it appeared in *American Political Science Review,* vol. 87, no. 2 (June 1993), p. 315.

Box 5–2: From *Voice and Equality: Civic Voluntarism in American Politics* by Sidney Verba, Kay Lehman Schlozman, and Henry E. Brady. (Cambridge, MA: Harvard University Press, 1995), p. 51–fig. 3.1. Reprinted with permission by The President and Fellows of Harvard College.

Box 5–3: From "The People, the Press and Politics, Campaign '92: The Generations Divide" (Survey VIII), from the Times Mirror Center for the People and the Press News Release, July 8, 1992, p. 44.

Box 5–4: Adapted from *The Politics Of American Government* by Stephen Wayne. (New York: St. Martin's Press, 1995), p. 349.

Box 6–1: From *Parties and Elections in America,* 2nd edition, by L. Sandy Maisel. (New York: McGraw-Hill, 1993), p. 190.

Box 6–2: From *The 13 Keys to the Presidency* by Allan Lichtman and Ken DeCell. (Lanham, MD: Madison Books, 1990), p. 7.

Box 6–3: From *A Brief History of Money in Politics: Campaign Finance and Campaign Finance Reform in the United States* by the Center for Responsive Politics. Copyright © 1995.

Box 6–5: From *Time,* August 14, 1995, p. 20 and *The Price of Admission: Campaign Spending in the 1994 Elections* by Larry Makinum, The Center for Responsive Politics, 1995, p. 17. Copyright © 1995 Time, Inc. Reprinted by permission.

Box 6–7: From "Voter Anxiety Dividing GOP: Energized Dems Backing Clinton" from the Times Mirror Center for the People and the Press News Release, November 14, 1995, p. 22.

Box 6–8: From CNN/Time AllPolitics and Voter News Service, November 5, 1996.

Box 7–1: Adapted from "Congress: The First and the 100th." From the *New York Times,* January 5, 1987, p. A14. Copyright © 1987 by The New York Times Company. Reprinted by permission.

Box 7–3: From *Thickening Government* by Paul Light. (Washington, DC: Brookings Institution/Governance Institute, 1995), p. 157.

Box 7–5: From *Congress A to Z.* (Washington, DC: CQ Press, 1993), p. 233.

Box 8–2: From *Presidential Leadership: Politics and Policy Making* by George Edwards III and Stephen Wayne. (New York: St. Martin's Press, 1994), p. 176.

Box 8–3: From the *Washington Post,* February 5, 1993, p. A23. Copyright © 1993 by The Washington Post Writers Group. Reprinted with permission.

Box 8–5: From "Presidential Support and the Military Option" by Anne Cronin. From the *New York Times,* September 18, 1994, pp. 4–5E. Copyright © 1994 by The New York Times Company. Reprinted by permission.

Box 9–3: From *The Federal Machine: Beginnings of Bureaucracy in Jacksonian America* by Matthew Crenson. (Baltimore, MD: The Johns Hopkins University Press, 1976), pp. 77–78.

Box 9–4: From *Thickening Government* by Paul Light. (Washington, DC: Brookings Institution/Governance Institute, 1995), p. 12.

Box 9–7: From "Takin' on the Bacon" by Kirk Victor from the *National Journal,* May 16, 1995, p. 1084. Copyright © 1995 by the National Journal, Inc. All rights reserved. Reprinted by permission.

Box 9–8: From *Stupid Government Tricks* by John Kohut. Copyright © 1995 by John Kohut. Used by permission of Plume Books, a division of Penguin USA, Inc.

Box 10–1: From "Clinton's Legal Policy and the Courts: Rising from Disarray or Turning Around and Around" by

David O'Brien, as it appeared in *The Clinton Presidency: First Appraisals* ed. by Colin Campbell and Bert A. Rockman. (Chatham, NJ: Chatham House, 1996), p. 137. This material originally appeared in "Bush's Judicial Legacy: The Final Imprint" by Sheldon Goldman, in *JUDICATURE* 282 (1993).

Box 10–3: From *Vital Statistics on American Politics,* 5th edition, by Harold W. Stanley and Richard G. Niemi. (Washington, DC: CQ Press, 1995), p. 284.

Box 10–4: From *Justices and Presidents* by Henry Abraham, p. 68. Copyright © 1992 by Henry Abraham. Used by permission of Oxford University Press, Inc.

Box 10–6: From *Storm Center: The Supreme Court in American Politics,* 3rd edition, by David M. O'Brien, p. 209. Copyright © 1993, 1990, 1986 by David O'Brien. Reprinted by permission of W.W. Norton & Company, Inc.

Box 10–7: From *Storm Center: The Supreme Court in American Politics,* 3rd edition, by David M. O'Brien, p. 209. Copyright © 1993, 1990, 1986 by David O'Brien. Reprinted by permission of W.W. Norton & Company, Inc.

Box 10–8: From "Has the Court Lost Its Appeal?" by Joan Biskupic. From the *Washington Post,* October 12, 1995, p. A23. Copyright © 1995 Washington Post Writers Group. Reprinted with permission.

Box 11–2: From *Constitutional Law and Politics: Civil Rights and Civil Liberties,* vol. II, by David M. O'Brien, pp. 280–81. Copyright © 1991 by David M. O'Brien. Reprinted by permission of W.W. Norton & Company, Inc.

Box 11–5: From *Vital Statistics on American Politics,* 5th edition, by Harold W. Stanley and Richard G. Niemi. (Washington, DC: CQ Press, 1995), p. 367.

Box 11–6: From Time/CNN Poll conducted by Yankelovich Clancy Shulman, April 24–29, 1991. Reprinted by permission.

Box 12–5: "The Issue-Attention Cycle" by Anthony Downs. Reprinted with permission of the author and *The Public Interest,* (Summer 1972) vol. XX, no. 28, pp. 38–50. Copyright © 1991 by National Affairs, Inc.

Box 12–6: From *Rulemaking: How Government Agencies Write Law and Make Policy* by Cornelius Kerwin. (Washington, DC: CQ Press, 1994), pp. 39–42.

Photo Credits

Title page: Courtesy, The National Archives.

Chapter 1: Chapter opener and interior feature photo: Smithsonian Institution; 5: AP/Wide World; 10: (top photo) Culver Pictures; (bottom photo) Reuters/Corbis-Bettmann; 13: Copyright © 1996, Dan Lamont.

Chapter 2: Chapter opener and interior feature photo: Courtesy, Parks and History Association; 27: Culver Pictures; 35:

(left photo) AP/Wide World; (center photo) Corbis-Bettmann; (right photo) Corbis-Bettmann; 41: Janice Jacobs/Texas Alcalde; 47: Mike Okoniewski/Gamma Liaison.

Chapter 3: Chapter opener and interior feature photo: Paul S. Conklin/Monkmeyer; 57: (top left photo) AP/Wide World; (top right photo) AP/Wide World; (bottom photo) Corbis-Bettmann; 73: AP/Wide World; 77: Ira Wyman/Sygma; 81: (left photo) Corbis-Bettmann; (right photo) AP/Wide World.

Chapter 4: Chapter opener and interior feature photo: Courtesy, Democratic National Committee and Republican National Committee; 94: (left photo) Porter Gifford/Gamma Liaison; (right photo) AP/Wide World; 102: AP/Wide World; 116: Reuters/Bettmann; 120: Halstead/Gamma Liaison.

Chapter 5: Chapter opener and interior feature photo: AP/Wide World; 139: (left photo) UPI/Bettmann; (right photo) David Woo/Sygma; 143: UPI/Corbis-Bettmann; 158: AP/Wide World; 162: Rod Rolle/Gamma Liaison.

Chapter 6: Chapter opener and interior feature photo: AP/Wide World; 174: Corbis-Bettmann; 175: AP/Wide World; 184: Reuters/Corbis-Bettmann; 192: AP/Wide World; 198: UPI/Corbis-Bettmann

Chapter 7: Chapter opener and interior feature photo: Architect of the Capitol; 222: (top photo) Corbis-Bettmann; (bottom photo) AP/Wide World; 228: Reuters/Corbis-Bettmann; 231: AP/Wide World.

Chapter 8: Chapter opener and interior feature photo: Copyright © 1996, Bill Westheimer; 264: AP/Wide World; 268: AP/Wide World; 269: Corbis-Bettmann; 273: Corbis-Bettmann; 274: AP/Wide World; 276: AP/Wide World; 282: (left photo) AP/Wide World; (right photo) Reuters/Bettmann; 289: UPI/Bettmann.

Chapter 9: Chapter opener and interior feature photo: U.S. Department of Agriculture; 304: Brooks Kraft/Sygma; 308: Patrick Aventurier/Gamma Liaison; 326: AP/Wide World; 332: Alan Singer.

Chapter 10: Chapter opener and interior feature photo: Lois Long/Collection of the Supreme Court of the United States; 348: AP/Wide World; 351: Archive News Photos/Consolidated News; 359: (left photo) Bill Swersey/Gamma Liaison; (right photo) AP/Wide World.

Chapter 11: Chapter opener and interior feature photo: Courtesy, the Statue of Liberty National Monument; 392: Reuters/Corbis-Bettmann; 402: AP/Wide World; 404: AP/Wide World; 407: UPI/Bettmann; 410: AP/Wide World; 414: AP/Wide World; 418: AP/Wide World; 419: AP/Wide World.

Chapter 12: Chapter opener and interior feature photo: UPI/Bettmann; 434: AP/Wide World; 440: Diana Walker/Gamma Liaison; 450: Paul S. Conklin/Monkmeyer; 460: Paul S. Conklin/Monkmeyer.

INDEX